MAPS

FIGURES

PREFACE

As a specialist on Latin America and the Caribbean for nearly fifty years, including six years as director of the Institute of Latin American Studies at London University, I have always been conscious that the United States was much more than a nation-state. The United States, after all, had built both a territorial and informal empire in the region. Yet, although I had written extensively on this topic, my research was not primarily about the country.

Starting in the 1990s, I began to work on the relationship between the Latin American and Caribbean region and other parts of the world. In this research, the United States was often the elephant in the room, playing a key role by virtue of its global reach. However, it was only when I became director of Chatham House, the Royal Institute of International Affairs, that I was fully able to understand how the US "semiglobal empire" operated. This came about through meetings with world leaders, many of whom spoke at Chatham House during my time as director, as well as through the research programs that were organized under my direction.

The final ingredient needed to write this book was to live and work in the United States, and this I did for part of each year from 2007 to 2010. Although I have visited the United States on numerous occasions since my first visit in 1966, there is no substitute for living in a country to understand the way its people think. Indeed, it was this more recent experience, together with subsequent visits, that convinced me not only that the US empire is in retreat but also that the retreat is primarily due to internal rather than external reasons.

Any project on the United States as an empire should not be undertaken lightly, in view of the controversial nature of the term. I have approached it in a positive frame of mind, however, since I believe that my conclusions contain a note of optimism for both the United States and the world as a whole. Empires may have been normal in the past, but they are anachronistic in today's world. They carry huge costs not only for the subjects but also for the citizens of the imperial state. Retreat from empire is therefore something to celebrate, provided that it is managed in an orderly fashion. That, of course, requires leadership, but it is a very different kind of leadership to that which was previously needed to maintain control of the empire.

All states are sensitive to criticism by outsiders, and I am conscious of the perils of writing about a foreign country. This, however, is a problem I have had to address throughout my adult life since almost all my research has been concerned with other parts of the world. In my experience, as a matter of fact, it is in many ways easier to write about foreign countries objectively than it is about one's own country. Yet, in a way, that misses the point. To understand the United States at this moment in history, one needs a truly global perspective and no one has a monopoly on that.

ACKNOWLEDGMENTS

I started writing this book in 2012, as the first administration of President Barack Obama was coming to an end. However, the research for the book goes back much further and can be said to have started when I did my doctoral research on Central America in the 1970s. I have therefore accumulated a huge debt to a very large number of individuals and institutions over the years.

St. Antony's College at Oxford University, with its staff and students drawn from all over the world, gave me a deep understanding about the global role of the United States. Many visitors came from the United States itself, and their participation in the college's seminars provided a constant reminder of the complexities of the internal and external workings of their country.

The Institute of Latin American Studies at London University was also very helpful in shaping the ideas on which this book is based, especially as one of its sister institutes was the Institute of United States Studies. Its chairperson in those years, Margaret Thatcher, had very strong views on the global role of the United States that she was always happy to share with fellow board members such as myself.

As a member for many years of the Regional Advisory Program for Latin America of the Social Science Research Council (SSRC) in New York, I learned a great deal about the workings of US philanthropic foundations. I also benefited greatly from conversations with the network of scholars assembled by the SSRC. I worked during this period of my career as a consultant to a number of international financial institutions and multinational enterprises that proved to be an invaluable experience for understanding how the US empire operates.

At Chatham House I benefited greatly from lengthy discussions on the global role of the United States with specialists from the different regions of the world. I would like to thank in particular Roy Allison, Duncan Brack, Paul Cornish, Stephen Green, Rosemary Hollis, Gareth Price, Alex Vines, Richard Whitman, and Elizabeth Wilmshurst. At a more superficial level, my meetings with world leaders from Angola, Brazil, China, France, Germany, India, Iran, Mexico, Russia, South Africa, the United Kingdom, the United Nations, the United States, and many other countries were also very instructive.

Chatham House is part of a network of think tanks around the world and is the sister institute of the Council on Foreign Relations in the United States. Through this network, which also included the RAND Corporation and the Brookings Institution, I learned about the interaction between state and non-state actors. In particular, I discovered what a central role think tanks play in providing the intellectual foundations for the US empire.

Many people have commented on chapters of this book before final revisions, but I would like to thank in particular Jonathan Bell, John Coatsworth, Michael Cox, James Dunkerley, Eric Hershberg, Iwan Morgan, and John Welch. Last, but certainly not least, I would like to give a special vote of thanks to Barbara Bulmer-Thomas for the way in which she has challenged my ideas for half a century and helped me to avoid easy solutions or shallow conclusions.

ABBREVIATIONS

ABC	American Broadcasting Company
ABCFM	American Board of Commissioners for Foreign Missions
ABM	Anti-Ballistic Missile
ACHR	American Convention on Human Rights
ACS	American Colonial Society
AFL-CIO	American Federation of Labor and Congress of Industrial Organizations
AFP	Agence France-Presse
AGOA	Africa Growth and Opportunity Act
AIIB	Asian Infrastructure Investment Bank
AIL	Anti-Imperialist League
AIM	American Indian Movement
AIPAC	American Israel Public Affairs Committee
ALBA	Alianza Bolivariana de los Pueblos de Nuestra América
ALPRO	Alliance for Progress
AMAG	American Mission for Aid to Greece
ANSWER	Act Now to Stop War and End Racism
AP	Associated Press
APEC	Asia-Pacific Economic Cooperation
ARPA	Advanced Research Projects Agency
ASCE	American Society of Civil Engineers
ASEAN	Association of Southeast Asian Nations
AT&T	American Telephone & Telegraph Company
AUMF	Authorization for Use of Military Force
B&R	Belt and Road

BEA	Bureau of Economic Analysis
BEPS	base erosion and profit shifting
BIS	Bank for International Settlements
BIT	bilateral investment treaty
BLS	Bureau of Labor Statistics
BRICS	Brazil, Russia, India, China, and South Africa
BVI	British Virgin Islands
CBO	Congressional Budget Office
CBS	Columbia Broadcasting System
CCF	Congress for Cultural Freedom
CEDAW	Convention on the Elimination of All Forms of Discrimination against Women
CELAC	Community of Latin American and Caribbean States
CENTO	Central Treaty Organization
CEO	chief executive officer
CERN	Conseil Européen pour la Recherche Nucléaire
CFR	Council on Foreign Relations
CIA	Central Intelligence Agency
CISPES	Committee in Solidarity with the People of El Salvador
CPLCC	Central Polynesian Land and Commercial Company
CRC	Convention on the Rights of the Child
CRPD	Convention on the Rights of Persons with Disabilities
CRS	Common Reporting Standard
CUFTA	Canada-US Free Trade Agreement
DARPA	Defense Advanced Research Projects Agency
DEA	Drug Enforcement Agency
DoC	Department of Commerce
EAI	Enterprise for the Americas Initiative
EBRD	European Bank for Reconstruction and Development
EC	European Community
ECSC	European Coal and Steel Community
EEC	European Economic Community
EU	European Union
FARC	Fuerzas Armadas Revolucionarias de Colombia
FATCA	Foreign Account Tax Compliance Act
FBI	Federal Bureau of Investigation
FCC	Federal Communications Commission
FDI	foreign direct investment
FDR	Franklin Delano Roosevelt

FECA	Federal Electoral Commission Act
FFI	foreign financial institution
FINCEN	Financial Crimes Enforcement Network
FISA	Foreign Intelligence Surveillance Act
FISC	Foreign Intelligence Surveillance Court
FRED	Federal Reserve Bank of St. Louis
FSLN	Frente Sandinista de Liberación Nacional
FSU	former Soviet Union
FTA	free trade agreement
FTAA	Free Trade Area of the Americas
G2	Group of Two
G20	Group of Twenty
GATT	General Agreement on Tariffs and Trade
GDP	gross domestic product
HIID	Harvard Institute for International Development
HTML	Hypertext Markup Language
HTTP	Hypertext Transfer Protocol
IADB	Inter-American Development Bank
IBRD	International Bank for Reconstruction and Development
ICANN	Internet Corporation for Assigned Names and Numbers
ICC	International Criminal Court
ICJ	International Court of Justice
ICT	information and communications technology
IDA	International Development Association
IFC	International Finance Corporation
IGE	intergenerational income elasticity
IGM	international grant making
IIA	international investment agreement
IMF	International Monetary Fund
IP	intellectual property
IPC	Iraq Petroleum Company
IPRs	intellectual property rights
IS	Islamic State of Iraq and Syria
ISDS	investor-state dispute settlement
ITO	International Trade Organization
ITT	International Telephone & Telegraph
JCPOA	Joint Comprehensive Plan of Action
JSOC	Joint Special Operations Command
LAC	Latin America and the Caribbean

LDP	Liberal Democratic Party [Japan]
MCC	Millennium Challenge Corporation
MENA	Middle East and North Africa
MERCOSUR	Mercado Común del Sur
METO	Middle East Treaty Organization
MINUSTAH	United Nations Stabilization Mission in Haiti
MNE	multinational enterprise
MPAA	Motion Picture Association of America
MPLA	Movimento Popular de Libertação de Angola
NAACP	National Association for the Advancement of Colored People
NAE	National Association of Evangelicals
NAFTA	North American Free Trade Agreement
NASA	National Aeronautics and Space Administration
NATO	North Atlantic Treaty Organization
NBC	National Broadcasting Company
NCAI	National Congress of American Indians
NDC	Nationally Determined Contribution
NGO	nongovernmental organization
NIYC	National Indian Youth Council
NPR	Nuclear Posture Review
NPT	Non-Proliferation Treaty
NSA	nonstate actor
NSAg	National Security Agency
NSC	National Security Council
NSS	National Security Strategy
OAS	Organization of American States
OECD	Organisation for Economic Co-operation and Development
OPEC	Organization of the Petroleum Exporting Countries
P5	the five permanent members of the UNSC
PAC	political action committee
PCA	Permanent Court of Arbitration
PGT	Partido Guatemalteco de Trabajo
PISA	Programme for International Student Assessment
PKI	Partai Komunis Indonesia
PLA	People's Liberation Army
PLO	Palestine Liberation Organization
PNAC	Project for the New American Century

PPD	Partido Popular Democrático
PPP	purchasing power parity
PRC	People's Republic of China
PTA	preferential trade agreement
PVO	private voluntary organization
QDDR	*Quadrennial Diplomacy and Development Review*
R&D	research and development
R2P	Responsibility to Protect
RAC	Russian American Company
RCA	Radio Corporation of America
RCEP	Regional Comprehensive Economic Partnership
RMA	Revolution in Military Affairs
ROC	Republic of China
RTAA	Reciprocal Trade Agreement Act
SBC	Southern Baptist Convention
SCAP	Supreme Commander for the Allied Powers
SDS	Students for a Democratic Society
SEATO	Southeast Asia Treaty Organization
SEO	search engine optimization
SOCOM	Special Operations Command
SORT	Strategic Offensive Reductions Treaty
START	Strategic Arms Reduction Treaty
STEM	science, technology, engineering, and mathematics
TFP	total factor productivity
TIFA	Trade and Investment Framework Agreement
TISA	Trade in Services Agreement
TPA	Trade Promotion Authority
TPP	Trans-Pacific Partnership
TRIPS	trade-related aspects of intellectual property
TTIP	Transatlantic Trade and Investment Partnership
TTPI	Trust Territory of the Pacific Islands
UFCO	United Fruit Company
UFPJ	United for Peace and Justice
UK	United Kingdom
UN	United Nations
UNCLOS	UN Convention on the Law of the Sea
UNCTAD	United Nations Conference on Trade and Development
UNESCO	United Nations Educational, Scientific and Cultural Organization

UNFCCC	United Nations Framework Convention on Climate Change
UNHCR	United Nations High Commissioner for Refugees
UNITAF	Unified Task Force
UNSC	United Nations Security Council
UNSCR	United Nations Security Council Resolution
UPI	United Press International
URL	uniform resource locator
US	United States
USAFRICOM	United States Africa Command
USAID	United States Agency for International Development
USCYBERCOM	United States Cyber Command
USIA	United States Information Agency
USNORTHCOM	United States Northern Command
USSR	Union of Soviet Socialist Republics
USSTRATCOM	United States Strategic Command
USTR	United States trade representative
USVI	United States Virgin Islands
WIPO	World Intellectual Property Organization
WTO	World Trade Organization

INTRODUCTION

This is a book about the United States as an empire:[1] its territorial origins shortly after its birth as a nation-state (Part I), its consolidation as a semiglobal project after the Second World War (Part II), and its current retreat (Part III). Since the book argues that the main reasons for this change are internal rather than external, the implications can be seen as positive: the United States will not be as important in and to the world as before, but its new role will be more consistent with a majority of its citizens' aspirations. Retreat from empire does not necessarily imply the decline of the nation-state. Indeed, it can even strengthen the nation-state if the retreat is due mainly to internal factors.

The book is not—at least not primarily—about domestic affairs, although these do impinge on international relations in all sorts of ways. It is not a social or economic history, although both are intimately related to the operations of American empire.[2] It is therefore more like an imperial history, although it is not a conventional one, as it does not have an end date.

An imperial history cannot be written unless the country in question is an empire, and there are still, in America, plenty of empire deniers. The United States was born in opposition to empire, it was said, and therefore was anti-imperialist from birth. Its republican status precluded an empire with its implications of an emperor or constitutional monarch. A nation committed to freedom, it was argued, could never accept the subordinate status assigned to subjects in imperial systems.

Yet there have been three moments since the War of Independence when the country's imperial status has been widely accepted. The first relates to the generation of the Founding Fathers, for whom the terms "republic" and "empire" were not contradictory, and who used "empire" freely, if loosely. The second corresponds to the period after 1898 when the United States took possession of numerous former Spanish colonies. The third coincides with the "unipolar" moment after the Cold War when the United States no longer faced what it claimed had been an existential threat.

In between these three moments, there were long periods when the idea of the United States as an empire seemed alien to most Americans. And yet, in truth, the nation has been an empire ever since 1783, when it signed the Treaty of Paris, acquiring in the process a vast tract of territory over which none of the former thirteen colonies had exercised sovereignty and which was already inhabited by other peoples. Indeed, the arrangements adopted for this newly acquired land fit very well into even the narrowest definition of "empire" employed in the *Oxford English Dictionary*: "An extensive territory under the control of a supreme ruler . . . , often consisting of an aggregate of many separate states or territories. In later use also: an extensive group of subject territories ultimately under the rule of a single sovereign state."

As the territories gradually became states (many having to wait more than fifty years to do so), the territorial dimension of US empire became less important, although it has not entirely disappeared even today. In its place came an empire that was not geographically constrained and which I call a semiglobal empire.[3] This empire is different from its territorial predecessor. It relies much more on institutional control and the influence of nonstate actors (NSAs); however, it must be able to back this up with military force to be credible. In the worlds of Charles Maier, perhaps the foremost scholar of American empire,

> Empire does not mean just the accumulation of lands abroad by conquest. And it does not mean just the imposition of authoritarian regimes on overseas territories. Empire is a form of political organization in which the social elements that rule in the dominant state—the "mother country" or the "metropole"—create a network of allied elites in regions abroad who accept subordination in international affairs in return for the security of their position in their own administrative unit (the "colony" or, in spatial terms, the "periphery"). . . . They intertwine their economic resources with the dominant power, and they accept and even celebrate a set of values and tastes that privilege or defer to the culture of the metropole.[4]

Maier's definition draws attention to an important point that is often forgotten in debates about the American empire: the role of foreign elites. Even if all US citizens denied their country was an empire, unlikely though that might be, its status would still be a moot point if elites in other parts of the world continued to treat it as if it were. In other words, there are two sides to American empire, and both must be taken into account.

Of course, no definition on its own can ever persuade all skeptics that the United States has been, and still is, an empire. Secretary of Defense Donald Rumsfeld, for example, responded to a foreign reporter in 2003, "We don't seek empires. We're not imperialistic. We never have been. I can't imagine why you'd even ask the question."[5]

Since US troops were beginning their long occupation of Iraq at the time he uttered these words, Rumsfeld clearly had in mind a very narrow definition of empire involving permanent and direct political control of the "periphery" without the cooperation of foreign elites. This, however, is a definition that most scholars today find too restrictive, since it ignores the flexibility with which empires have always operated.

Americans are prepared to concede that the United States occupies a hegemonic position in the world, but many are still not willing to call this empire. Arthur Schlesinger Jr., for example, claimed in 2005, "Of course we enjoy an informal empire—military bases, status-of-forces agreements, trade concessions, multinational corporations, cultural penetrations, and other favors. But these are marginal to the subject of direct control. . . . In their days of imperial glory, Rome, London, Paris, despite slow and awkward lines of communication, really ruled their empires. Today communication is instantaneous. But despite the immediacy of contact, Washington, far from ruling an empire in the old sense, has become the virtual prisoner of its client states."[6]

Leaving aside the ambiguity of Schlesinger's accepting that the United States has "client states" while denying its imperial status, it is clear he also has in mind a narrow definition of empire that involves political control of states exercised through metropolitan officials rather than foreign elites. Yet the empires to which he refers—Roman, British, and French—also used indirect forms of control over other territories where it suited them and still did not hesitate to intervene where necessary.

The quotes from Rumsfeld and Schlesinger are representative of the empire deniers in the United States that wish to fight back against those legions of authors who claim that America after the Cold War, and especially after the terrorist attacks of 9/11, had become the new Rome and needed to accept its imperial burden with good grace. These "imperial enthusiasts," as they have been called, include subjects as well as citizens of the empire, demonstrating once again the importance of foreign elites.[7]

The imperial enthusiasts have tried to strip "empire" of its pejorative connotations, but they still give it a normative content. So do their opponents, the imperial critics, for whom empire leads to the corruption of democratic values and is ultimately self-defeating. Thus, all the participants in the modern empire debate have tended to define it as a good or bad thing rather than approaching it objectively.

That was not always the case. In his book *The Tragedy of American Diplo-macy*, first published in 1959, William Appleman Williams employed a notion of empire that—he argued—reflected more accurately the path of US history since independence. Williams's thesis was subject to attack and counterattack by countless specialists, but the concept of empire survived and even led to the foundation of a school of diplomatic history at the University of Wisconsin–Madison—a rare privilege for a scholar.

Thanks to the pioneering work of Williams, imperial history now has a place in the mainstream of academic life in the United States. Indeed, there is even an American Empire Project that produces a wide range of publications on con-temporary US affairs.[8] And "empire" has penetrated the daily lexicon not just of cultural studies and esoteric journals but also of business and the media. Mean-while, in the rest of the world "American empire" has never gone out of fashion.

Why did the United States become an empire so soon after its birth as an independent state? It was not forced to do so. America was not dragged reluc-tantly into an imperial role by land-hungry settlers, although some have tried to argue this was the case. It did not acquire an empire in a fit of absentminded-ness, as has been claimed for Great Britain. And it did not at first need an empire to support its model of capitalism.

The United States was born in an imperial age. Independent countries aspir-ing to greatness therefore needed to define themselves as empires. The Found-ing Fathers, never doubting the new state's potential grandeur, spoke with one voice on the country's imperial destiny, as did their counterparts in Brazil and Mexico following independence.[9] Powerful European states were the same, with Germany and Italy seeking empires soon after unification, toward the end of the nineteenth century.

Empires were supposed to confer commercial advantage, provide political in-fluence, and shape international dynamics. The British, Dutch, French, and Russian empires largely achieved this and provided useful models for other as-pirants. Yet imperial success could not be secured without military prowess, dip-lomatic skill, and economic growth. That the project succeeded in the United States, while failing in many other aspiring empires, was a consequence of the ruthlessness of the American model in the first century after independence. The details of how it did this, however, would need to be the subject of another book, as it takes us into the realm of domestic and military affairs.

Empires based mainly on territory have now largely disappeared. Why did the same not happen to the United States? The answer is that America's territorial empire would be replaced by something much more ambitious: an empire based on institutions that would allow the United States to set the international rules of the game that others would then follow. Powerful countries have always aspired to achieve this—the gold standard of imperial rule—but only the United States has been in a position fully to carry it out. It would have required a forbearance of biblical proportions for America not to have pursued this opportunity at the end of the Second World War.

Empires, of which there have been many in world history, can take many forms. The first is territorial, where land is acquired and where the occupants do not receive the same rights as the metropole's citizens. The United States has been an empire in this sense since 1783, when it acquired vast territories through the Treaty of Paris that were administered in a different fashion to the states of the union. Although most territories subsequently became states, there was often a long lag, and some territories under US control have never become states.

The second version of empire is informal. This is when the imperial state exerts such an influence on other countries that their sovereignty is severely compromised. The countries concerned can be protectorates or client states. In the case of protectorates, the imperial state exercises formal control over some aspects of state policy, while in the case of client states there is no need; client states are happy to follow the lead of the imperial power without the need for formal limitations on their sovereignty.

Most empires have had an informal component. The ancient ones did so, as have the more modern European ones. The United States is no exception, and there are plenty of countries that can easily be defined as American protectorates or client states. An informal empire can be imposed by force, but more often it comes about through attraction. Weaker countries instinctively gravitate toward those with more power—in all the senses of that word.

The third form of empire is institutional, and is much rarer. This is where a single nation-state exerts such an influence on the rules under which all nations interact with each other that it can be said to exercise a global empire. The key to this dimension of empire is world leadership, since the imperial power must not only set the rules but also enforce them. No country has ever truly achieved global domination, so the height of imperial ambition has been a semiglobal empire. The United Kingdom achieved this briefly after the Napoleonic Wars, and the United States after the Second World War.

The United States is therefore an empire in all three forms. Why, then, can it be said to be in retreat? It is not primarily the territorial dimension. The retreat from territorial empire took place a long time ago, both through the incorporation of territories as states (e.g., Hawaii) and through decolonization (e.g., the Philippines). The territorial empire is now very small in relation to the size of the United States and is not expected to change significantly in the future. Indeed, the only change that might happen in the next twenty years is the conversion of the territory of Puerto Rico into a state. Thus, the territorial empire will remain of limited importance.

The informal empire, on the other hand, is currently shrinking and will continue to do so. This is partly because of the rise of nationalism in many parts of the informal empire, but also because of US reluctance to accept the costs (in all senses) of keeping these countries in line. Techniques of control, from muscular diplomacy to military force, that were widely used during the Cold War are now employed more sparingly. The informal empire is still important, but it is much less extensive than it was twenty years ago.

The shrinking of the informal empire is not especially controversial in the United States and can easily be explained as a consequence of the end of the Cold War. It is the retreat from institutional empire that causes the greatest anxiety among some sections of the populace. Yet it is inevitable. Other countries are now reluctant to let America establish and enforce the rules of the game, while the United States itself is increasingly unable to exercise the global leadership that once came so naturally.

The world is therefore in transition, and America will occupy a less important role in the future. This does imply a decline in the geopolitical importance of the United States, and there will inevitably be a relative decline as well in its economic and financial strength. Yet this need not be an absolute decline and will not be unless the transition is very badly managed indeed. That, of course, depends not only on the United States itself but also on some of the external actors.

The United States became a territorial empire immediately after the War of Independence, and in the following years acquired an imperial mindset (inherited in part from its former British rulers). The expansion across the North American continent was made possible by the acquisition of territories in which Native Americans ("Indians") and non-Anglo settlers were living in significant numbers. These territories were governed—until they joined the Union—in a manner similar to that in some colonies in contemporary European empires.

When territories joined the Union, a process that could take many decades, they ceased to be colonies and became part of the nation-state. However, the territorial empire continued to expand, going "offshore" after the Mexican-American War (1846–48). By the end of the Spanish-American War (1898), the

United States had acquired several territories in the Asia-Pacific region and in the Caribbean, and would soon exercise control over part of Central America. In addition, Liberia in West Africa was a US colony until independence was declared in 1847, after which it became an American protectorate.

The process of land acquisition ended in the twentieth century and the territorial empire slowly shrank to its current modest proportions. However, the imperial mentality remained unaffected. The First World War and its aftermath provided the United States with a significant opportunity to expand its informal empire, especially in the Americas and the Middle East, while the end of the Second World War marked the beginning of a serious attempt at global hegemony. This ambition was never fully achieved as a result of resistance from the Soviet Union, China, and some of the nonaligned states, but America did become a semiglobal empire underpinned by international institutions, military bases, and NSAs.

This empire is now in retreat. With the benefit of hindsight we can identify intimations of its mortality even before the collapse of the Soviet Union. The scale of retreat was temporarily concealed by the unipolar moment the United States enjoyed in the decade before the second invasion of Iraq (2003), when it appeared to face no major competitor. However, subsequent events have confirmed that the retreat of the empire has continued. This process will not be reversed.

Empires can retreat for internal or external reasons. Although external factors may become more important in the future, particularly in relation to competition with China, the root causes of US retreat from empire are internal. The imperial mindset is slowly withering, and in the process the United States may succeed eventually in becoming "merely" a nation-state. This is not guaranteed, however, and the risks of violent conflict associated with a long retreat from empire are considerable.

To avoid the use of the word "empire" Americans have developed an enormous lexicon of synonyms. The best known is "exceptionalism," which is still in vogue today. Indeed, "American exceptionalism" has been a constant in US political discourse since the War of Independence, even if it has been defined in many different ways.[10] It surfaced dramatically in the 2016 presidential campaign when Hillary Clinton, the candidate of the Democratic Party, gave a speech to the American Legion in which she attacked her opponent, Republican Donald Trump, for his alleged lack of commitment to American exceptionalism and at the same time made clear the link between the concept and US empire:

The United States is an exceptional nation. . . . And part of what makes America an exceptional nation, is that we are also an indispensable nation. In fact, we are the indispensable nation. People all over the world look to us and follow our lead. . . . When we say America is exceptional . . . it means that we recognize America's unique and unparalleled ability to be a force for peace and progress, a champion for freedom and opportunity. Our power comes with a responsibility to lead. . . . Because, when America fails to lead, we leave a vacuum that either causes chaos or other countries or networks rush in to fill the void. So no matter how hard it gets, no matter how great the challenge, America must lead. . . . American leadership means standing with our allies because our network of allies is part of what makes us exceptional.[11]

"Leadership," as Clinton's speech made clear, is also a synonym for empire and is often embedded in the phrase "leadership of the free world"—or, these days, "leadership of the democratic world." "Force for good" is a phrase that is still heard frequently (Clinton referred to "force for peace and progress," which is the same thing) and is used to distinguish US interventions from those of other empires allegedly motivated only by narrow self-interest. And although "manifest destiny" is no longer employed, its abbreviated form "destiny" is still used by foreign elites, as in the speech by British prime minister Tony Blair to the US Congress in 2003: "I know it's hard on America, and in some small corner of this vast country, out in Nevada or Idaho or these places I've never been to, but always wanted to go. I know out there there's a guy getting on with his life, perfectly happily, minding his own business, saying to you, the political leaders of this country, 'Why me? And why us? And why America?' And the only answer is, 'Because destiny put you in this place in history, in this moment in time, and the task is yours to do.'"[12]

Some of the synonyms, such as "hegemony," sound so much like "empire" that they tend not to be used by those in public office. Other phrases are more subtle—especially "soft power"; Joseph Nye Jr. explains, "A country may obtain the outcomes it wants in world politics because other countries—admiring its values, emulating its example, aspiring to its level of prosperity and openness—want to follow it. In this sense, it is also important to set the agenda and attract others in world politics, and not only to force them to change by threatening military force or economic sanctions. This soft power—getting others to want the outcomes that you want—co-opts people rather than coerces them."[13]

Soft power has often been portrayed as an alternative to empire, but in truth it is a complement. Indeed, as the quote from Nye makes clear, it simply charts a more consensual route to the semiglobal empire that America has constructed rather than one based on force alone. Yet "soft power" without "hard power" would never be sufficient to sustain an empire, so soft power can only play a complementary role.

The American empire was built by the US state. As in all empires, however, NSAs have played an important part in this process. Their presence abroad has given America a strong justification for building and defending the empire, while their own actions have spread imperial values and helped to create the conditions in which the empire could flourish.

The most important NSA has been the US multinational enterprise (MNE) that operates in so many different locations. The United States did not invent this institution, but it was taken to a new level in the twentieth century as a result of the huge size of the US economy, the opportunities for profitable investment overseas, and the strong support the MNE has usually received from the US state.

After the Second World War, US MNEs exploded in number and size. Part of this was the close relation between public spending on defense and private companies that led President Dwight D. Eisenhower (1953–61) at the end of his term in office to warn of the dangers of the "military-industrial complex." Successive US governments promoted the expansion of MNEs, and political parties were rewarded with generous funding from the companies and their senior executives.

The brands of US MNEs have come to symbolize the semiglobal empire in many parts of the world and have become expressions of the US state—not just of its culture. Even in countries outside the empire, these brands are often esteemed by the population at large as symbols of liberty, making their governments reluctant to ban access to them for fear of popular resistance.

Other NSAs, however, have also been important in the process of empire building. These include the media, philanthropic foundations, think tanks, educational institutions, and religious organizations. Universities, for example, have established a strong presence in many countries through business schools, foreign campuses, and summer courses. Their scholarship programs attract the brightest students to the United States—albeit sometimes with unintended and unexpected consequences.

The culture needed for empires to flourish is complex. The educational system needs to support a national vision that justifies foreign interventions. The citizens of other countries, subjects of the empire, must be seen as less important than those of the metropole. The belief system must be widely supported. The media must be on board, and national history needs to be underpinned by a series of myths that convey a sense of cultural and racial superiority.

Until recently, American culture met these requirements with ease. Yet the consensus is now breaking down. Younger Americans no longer see their country as "exceptional" nor its actions abroad as necessarily motivated by a desire to act as "a force for good." Racism, it can be argued, is in decline despite the hostility still displayed by many whites toward nonwhite peoples. This has reduced the willingness of the citizens to pay the "blood price" so often associated with empire. In turn, this has severely restricted the degrees of freedom enjoyed by the executive in the past.

Nor is the relationship between MNEs and the US state as close as it once was. Many US MNEs are now truly global and irked by the restrictions of a semiglobal empire. They must also pay careful attention to their operations outside the semiglobal empire (especially in China), which can put them in conflict with the US state. And the fiscal needs of the American government increasingly generate friction with US MNEs.

As the empire retreats, the question often asked about the United States is, what next? The answer must be in two parts. The first concerns what happens to the nation-state and the second what happens to global governance. The two, of course, are related, but they are conceptually separate.

When states lose their empires they can be destroyed. This happened to the Roman empire, or at least the western part of it, following the foreign invasions of the fifth century. It also happened to the Ottoman and Austro-Hungarian empires after the First World War since the nation-states that came afterward bore little relation to their predecessors. In all of these cases, external aggression proved decisive in dismantling not just the empire but the imperial state as well.

However, the opposite can happen. When Belgium, France, Holland, Portugal, and the United Kingdom lost their empires after the Second World War, it had an exhilarating effect—after a short period of disruption—on the nation-state. All these countries had fought to retain parts of their empires, but it was resistance at home that proved crucial. The nation-state was now more comfortable in its postimperial skin, even if it would take many decades to finally shed the imperial mentality.

What will happen to America? The Vietnam War provides an illuminating experience. The United States did not withdraw from the war because of external pressure, however heroic Vietnamese resistance may have been. It withdrew because of opposition at home, and the nation-state eventually became reconciled to imperial retreat. Similarly, the semiglobal empire is retreating long before any other country, or group of countries, is ready to replace it because an increasing number of Americans are no longer comfortable with the burden it implies.

Whether America will come to regret this depends on what happens to global governance. In their magisterial book on empire, Michael Hardt and Antonio Negri claim,

> The concept of Empire is characterized fundamentally by a lack of boundaries: Empire's rule has no limits. First and foremost, then, the concept of Empire posits a regime that effectively encompasses the spatial totality, or really that rules over the entire "civilized" world. No territorial boundaries limit its reign. Second, the concept of Empire presents itself not as a historical regime originating in conquest, but rather as an order that effectively suspends history and thereby fixes the existing state of affairs for eternity. . . . Third, the rule of Empire operates on all registers of the social order extending down to the depths of the social world.[14]

The United States fulfilled this role for many decades, but now a vacuum is appearing that must be filled. Candidates for the role range from the utopian to the dystopian, with the United Nations family of independent nations at one end of the spectrum and a cabal of rogue states at the other. In between are more realistic options, including a cadre of regional hegemons and a duumvirate or triumvirate involving the United States and other powers.

Of all these options, it is the prospect of a duumvirate (G2) with China that has excited the most interest: the empire in retreat joining force with the rising power to arrange the affairs of the world in an orderly fashion. At first the Chinese rejected the idea on the grounds that it conflicted with their strongly held views on national sovereignty. Premier Wen Jiabao, speaking in 2009, could not have been clearer: "Some say that world affairs will be managed solely by China and the United States. I think that view is baseless and wrong. . . . It is impossible for a couple of countries or a group of big powers to resolve all global issues. Multipolarization and multilateralism represent the larger trend and the will of people."[15]

As the American imperial retreat continued, however, and China's rise continued unabated, Chinese leaders struck a different tone. Speaking in 2012, President Xi Jinping stated, "Both sides should, from the fundamental interest of the people of the two countries and of the world, join the efforts to build up China-U.S. cooperative partnership, trying to find a completely new way for the new type of great power relations, which would be unprecedented in history and open up the future."[16]

It is too early to be sure what will happen.[17] Both US imperial retreat and Chinese ascent still have some distance to go, and during this time other options will surely emerge. In addition, American citizens are not comfortable with the idea of sharing global power with China even if in some areas (e.g., the threat from North Korea) they already have no choice. However, the longer it takes, the more certain we can be that other countries will wish to stake a claim. The final outcome could be very messy indeed.

Just how messy was hinted at by the US presidential campaign in 2016. In the primaries for the Democratic nomination, a paleo, or traditional, imperialist (Hillary Clinton) fought a bitter, and ultimately successful, campaign against an anti-imperialist (Bernie Sanders) who—despite his advanced age—captured the enthusiasm of American youth. Meanwhile, on the Republican side, seventeen candidates competed for the nomination, with fifteen that could be characterized as paleo-imperialists, one as a neo-isolationist (Rand Paul), and one—the eventual winner—as a neo-imperialist (Donald Trump).

Given Trump's campaign rhetoric—Make America Great Again—some assumed he was just another paleo-imperialist. Others even argued he was a neo-isolationist in view of his negative comments on free trade agreements. Yet, although an imperialist, Trump offered a vision of empire that differed significantly from all previous administrations—one that emphasized the limitations of what America could do as a world leader and the inevitability of working with other states even if they did not share American interests, let alone values. For this reason he can be labeled a neo-imperialist.[18]

The 2016 presidential contest was therefore between a paleo-imperialist and a neo-imperialist, with neither candidate able to inspire a nation that is turning against empire. In the end, the neo-imperialist won, suggesting that imperial retreat will accelerate. Indeed, President Trump (2017–) soon found that his ability to shape the world in the American image was highly restricted, with other countries ever more determined to influence global proceedings.

The retreat from empire will therefore continue even as America still awaits its first "postimperial" president.[19] That will happen one day, and it could be a very liberating experience for many Americans. However, the imperial mindset will take longer to shed, just as has happened in many parts of Europe. "Do unto others as you would have them do unto you" is the hardest lesson for erstwhile imperialists to learn.

Part One

THE TERRITORIAL EMPIRE

1

CONTINENTAL EXPANSION

"Empire" today is a loaded and largely pejorative term. Yet it was not always so. Before the War of Independence began in 1775, the Founding Fathers had no quarrel with the concept of imperialism itself. George Washington fought against the French Empire to protect and expand the British one, while Benjamin Franklin campaigned for colonial union to advance imperial ambitions on both sides of the Atlantic.

It might be assumed that the war changed everything, but it did not. As soon as the ink was dry on the peace treaty in 1783 that ended hostilities, a new imperial project started—this time controlled by the United States rather than the British. Washington spoke warmly of "a rising empire," while Thomas Jefferson coined the phrase "empire for liberty." Alexander Hamilton described his country as "the embryo of a great empire." John Adams, father and son, as well as James Madison, were all equally enthusiastic.

European empires had been based on territorial expansion, and the British one was no exception. The thirteen colonies in what would become the United States had spread westward from the coast by displacing the indigenous[1] peoples through purchase, treaty, and war. As the flow of new immigrants accelerated, the need for further territory increased. Land speculation by the colonial elites became the surest and quickest way to build a fortune.

All the Founding Fathers participated in the process, and several were major shareholders in the land companies set up under colonialism to expand the frontiers. George Washington inherited from his brother Lawrence a substantial share of the Ohio Company that had been founded in 1747 to speculate in land south and north of the Ohio River. Benjamin Franklin was convinced that the "Ohio Country" was absolutely essential for the future prosperity of the colonies on the grounds that "our people . . . cannot much more increase in number" east of the Allegheny Mountains.[2]

The Treaty of Paris in 1763, which ended hostilities between Britain and France, seemed to meet the needs of British imperial expansion. France ceded her claims on the mainland of North America to Spain and Great Britain, including in the latter case the land east of the Mississippi River, and a vast area west of the Appalachian Mountains now appeared to be open to British settlers. However, the French had not consulted their Native American allies, who had no intention of vacating land they owned and occupied.

The result was Pontiac's War, which dragged Great Britain into a serious conflict that it was in no position to fight after so many years of hostilities. This was one of the reasons for the famous Royal Proclamation of 1763 drawing a line from Canada to Florida along the ridge of the Appalachian Mountains west of which no white settlers were permitted. It brought peace of a kind, but at a stroke of the pen George III had rendered worthless the assets of the land companies between the Mississippi River and the mountains.

This was an intolerable affront to the colonial elites, for whom territorial expansion now formed part of their DNA. All forms of pressure, including subterfuge, were adopted to undermine the impact of the Proclamation Line. The Illinois Company, with Franklin as a shareholder, pleaded with the colonial authorities for a grant of sixty-three million acres between the Illinois and Mississippi Rivers. A new company—variously called the Grand Ohio, the Walpole, or the Vandalia—was formed to petition the British government in London for an even bigger grant.

These efforts were only partially successful. By the Treaty of Fort Stanwix in 1768 Virginia was able to (re)claim some of the land south of the Ohio River; a few settlers "leased" land from Native American tribes, and this appeared not to breach the ban on white ownership. However, the land to the north of the river remained firmly out of bounds, and George III added insult to injury in 1774 by allocating this land (between the Ohio and Mississippi Rivers) to the Canadian province of Quebec.

Thus, on the eve of the War of Independence, settler expansion had been blocked north of the Ohio River and restricted to the south. Reversing this situation was one of the undeclared aims of the rebels. Not surprisingly, therefore, most of the Native American tribes eventually sided with the British since it was their land that was at stake.

Many of the battles were fought west of the Proclamation Line, and the Native American tribes—unlike the British—were not defeated. They remained in possession of most of the lands they owned before the war, but they were not present at the peace negotiations that led to the Treaty of Paris in 1783. Thus, it came as a complete shock to them to discover that the British had ceded the land east of the Mississippi River to the US commissioners.

This was not the first or the last time that the British would betray their Native American allies, but it was still a shocking act of perfidy. Many of the tribes had at first been reluctant to join with the British in the war and some had even sided with the rebels. Yet the majority had eventually been induced to take part on the assumption that this was the surest way to keep their lands.

The conclusion of the War of Independence was therefore a potential disaster for the Native American tribes. At the same time it was not at all clear what "rights" the United States had acquired from the departing British in the territory to the east of the Mississippi since the Native Americans had not signed the treaty. What was clear, however, was the commitment to territorial expansion by the new nation even if that meant armed confrontation.

The stage was therefore set for the first chapter in the formation of the American empire: continental expansion. Within seventy years of independence, the federal government had consolidated its hold on all the acreage east of the Mississippi, and the white subjects of the territories carved out of the newly acquired lands were gradually learning how to become citizens of the Union. West of the river, the federal government had acquired title to vast swaths of land previously claimed by the empires of France, Great Britain, Russia, and Spain, forming these into territories. Their inhabitants in most cases, however, would have to spend decades as colonial subjects of the new US empire before becoming citizens.

1.1. THE OLD NORTHWESTERN TERRITORIES

When the War of Independence ended, the vast majority of the US population were living on the eastern side of the mountains. Indeed, most were living within fifty miles of the coast. The first census in 1790 enumerated a free population of 3,231,533. This number, of course, excluded the slaves (nearly 700,000), but it also excluded the Native Americans.

No serious attempt was made to estimate their number, but recent scholarship suggests a figure in 1800 between 600,000 and 1,000,000 for North America as a whole.[3] Few of these lived east of the mountains, where the white population was concentrated. Thus, despite the spread of European diseases and decades of conflict, there was still a significant Indian population in the territories of interest to the federal government.

The Native Americans lived in villages and small towns where, in general, farming was carried out by the women and hunting by the men. We cannot be sure how many lived in the land between the Mississippi and Ohio Rivers (the old Northwestern territories), but in the late eighteenth century it was certainly more than the white settlers. Indeed, the 1790 census could not give a figure for the settlers in this region, and even in 1800 the number was tiny.[4]

The new republic knew that a claim to these lands based on cession by Great Britain amounted to little, but the government did believe that it had acquired title by conquest. By defeating the British, with whom so many of the tribes had been allied, it claimed all the Indian land (Box 1.1). However, before anything could be done about it, the federal government had to extinguish the land claims of the individual states. This was no simple matter, but the agreement of Virginia in 1784 to relinquish its claims to the land north of the Ohio River paved the way for the famous Northwest Ordinance of 1787.

This act marked the formal birth of the US empire and set a precedent for territorial expansion across the continent. It created a vast region (the Northwest Territory—see Map 1) in lands where the majority of the population were Native Americans and where the entry of slaves would not be permitted. The president was empowered to appoint a governor, a secretary, and three judges with sovereign powers subject only to presidential veto. Once the white male settler population exceeded five thousand, provision was made for elections to a House of Representatives, while a Legislative Council would be made up of those chosen by the president from a list presented by the House. The territory would then be entitled to send a nonvoting delegate to the US Congress.

This was a system of colonial rule that would have been very familiar to the British, Dutch, or French. The indigenous people had no rights, the white population had limited representation, and the colonial agents exercised enormous powers.[5] There was, however, one difference in the United States, and that was the assumption that a territory would eventually become a state of the Union. Yet this could take decades to achieve, and in the meantime the territory was ruled as a *de facto* colony.

That the federal government had colonies in North America may sound strange to modern ears, but it did not seem strange to contemporaries. Arthur St. Clair, the first governor of the Northwest Territory, wrote in 1795 that the land he ruled was a "dependent colony" whose settlers "ceased to be citizens of the United States and became their subjects." Nor did this colonial condition either surprise or worry many of the white inhabitants. In Wisconsin, for example, which was carved out of the Northwest Territory many years later, "large majorities were actively hostile to statehood long after the territory passed the

Map 1. Northwest Territory

sixty thousand population threshold that qualified it for admission under the Ordinance."[6]

The American government, believing it had acquired the land by conquest, summoned tribal leaders after the War of Independence ended and imposed treaties that obliged the signatories to relinquish territory. The majority of Native American tribal leaders in the Northwest Territory, however, did not accept that they had lost the right to their lands as a result of the British defeat. The victory the government claimed by virtue of conquest was, therefore, fraught with problems. A shift in policy—from entitlement by conquest to ownership by purchase—was therefore needed and was signaled by the Northwest Ordinance itself. This stated, "The utmost good faith shall always be observed towards the Indians, their lands and property shall never be taken from them without their

BOX 1.1

ABEL BUELL (1742–1822)

Cartography and empire building have always gone together, and the American empire is no exception. The first map of the United States to be done by a US citizen was published in 1784, by a Connecticut engraver named Abel Buell. A skilled draftsman, Buell had been convicted before the War of Independence of forging paper currency and was punished by branding ("C" for "counterfeiter" on his forehead), the loss of an ear, and a jail sentence. He then turned his talents to more respectable pursuits.

His map, only seven copies of which survive, was drawn when most of the former colonies had yet to cede their land claims west of the Proclamation Line to the federal government. It therefore shows the western boundaries of Connecticut, Virginia, North Carolina, South Carolina, and Georgia as the Mississippi River.

Buell's map also shows the location of many of the Native American tribes, including some west of the Mississippi River. The western portion of Georgia, for example, is marked as "Chactaw [sic] Land," while the territory west of Lake Michigan is shown as "Winnebago Land."

Most interesting of all is the physical description Buell gives to the land east of the Mississippi River. The land south of Lake Michigan and north of the Wabash River, for example, is described as "level rich and well watered. The road between these forts [St. Joseph and Miami] runs through many fine meadows. There are several small lakes and plenty of fish fowls and wild beasts."

Buell's map, done in four parts, was controversial because it presented the boundaries of each state west of the Allegheny Mountains as if they were agreed (they were not). It also gave the impression that most of this land was unoccupied by Native Americans, which was not true. And its description of the land, aimed at settlers and land companies, was worthy of a real estate developer.

consent, and in their property, rights and liberty, they shall never be invaded or disturbed, unless in just and lawful wars authorized by Congress."[7]

What, however, would happen if the Indians did not want to sell or, even worse, wanted to sell to some agency other than the federal government? This was a possibility the executive was not prepared to contemplate since the US government could not function without the land. It was needed to pay off the veterans, to meet the demands of settlers, and as a source of revenue (only the federal government was empowered to acquire land from the Native Americans, which could then be sold at a profit). Thus, it was no surprise that Congress was soon authorizing "just and lawful" wars against the Native Americans.

At first, these wars did not go well for the new republic. US forces lost a major battle in 1790 against a combination of Native American tribes. The following year St. Clair himself suffered a major defeat when his army was cut to pieces and 940 of his 1,400 soldiers were killed or wounded. However, the tide began to turn in 1794 when US forces under General Anthony Wayne somewhat fortuitously won the Battle of Fallen Timbers.[8]

US losses were in fact greater than those of the Native Americans at Fallen Timbers. However, some tribal leaders now believed it was impossible to hold the boundary between themselves and the United States at the Ohio River. In the Treaty of Greenville, signed in 1795, they therefore agreed on a new line of separation. This still left most of the Northwest Territory in the hands of Native American tribes, but it was the "foot in the door" that the federal government needed, and the new boundary—straight lines on a map north of the river—was easy for unscrupulous settlers to cross illegally.

It was not long after this that the first administrative hurdle of five thousand white male settlers had been met and the Northwest Territory moved to the second stage of territorial government in 1799. The following year the territory was divided with the creation of Indiana Territory. Despite being far larger than modern Indiana, its white settler population in 1800 was a mere 5,641, and most of these were of French descent. However, the rest of the Northwest Territory was rapidly filling up and by 1802 was in a position to petition for statehood. Ohio State, whose boundaries included some land not included in the Treaty of Greenville, then came into being in 1803 (Map 1).

Ohio State, now being in the Union, was no longer a colony. However, the remainder of the Northwest Territory (Indiana Territory) was and would remain so for some time. Indeed, its first governor (William Henry Harrison) was a classic example of a colonial ruler with a strong interest in land speculation as well. One of his biographers wrote, "Not a shadow of representative institutions existed in the territory, for all the offices were appointive and the laws were made by the governor and the judges."[9]

Harrison ruled the territory from Vincennes on the Wabash River, but it was too vast even for a man of his imperial ambitions. By 1805 Michigan Territory had been carved out of Indiana, and Illinois Territory would follow in 1809. Each had governors in the same mold as Harrison, and all would follow the new policy of trying to persuade the Native Americans to sell their land and move elsewhere.

This required "inducements," and no one understood this better than Thomas Jefferson, who became president in 1801. Writing to Harrison in 1803, he stated,

> When they [Indians] withdraw themselves to the culture of a small piece of land, they will perceive how useless to them are their extensive forests, and will be willing to pare them off from time to time in exchange for necessaries for their farms and families. . . . To promote this . . . we shall push our trading houses, and be glad to see the good and influential individuals among them run into debt, because we observe that when these debts get beyond what the individuals can pay, they become willing to lop them off by a cession of lands.[10]

Jefferson was promoting an extreme interpretation of the "civilization" policy, adopted a decade earlier by President George Washington (1789–97) and his secretary of war, Henry Knox. If implemented strictly, it would have at least created the possibility of a society in which whites and Native Americans lived side by side as agriculturalists. It was, however, undermined by Jefferson himself as a consequence of the Louisiana Purchase in 1803 (see Section 1.3).

Suddenly, with the Louisiana Purchase, the federal government found itself responsible for vast tracts of territory to the west of the Mississippi River. Native American lands to the east of the river could now be exchanged for land on the other side. The policy of "civilization," slow and expensive to implement, could be replaced by "removal"—a much quicker and cheaper alternative.

Harrison and the other governors experimented with all these policies. However, the one Harrison found most effective was to sign treaties with those tribal leaders that could be bribed. At the Treaty of Fort Wayne in 1809 he obtained the signatures of a handful of leaders to a swath of territory that encompassed land belonging to, among others, the Shawnees. One of their leaders, Tecumseh, denounced those that had signed, and he traveled to Vincennes to demand that Harrison reject the treaty.

Harrison would not back down and Tecumseh, whose brother Tenskwatawa ("the Prophet") was already raising pan-Indian consciousness across the old Northwest, started to recruit a mobile force that transcended tribal barriers. War was inevitable, but victory for the federal government was not. Indeed, were it not for the poor decision making of the Prophet, Tecumseh might well have won. Harrison's forces were small and the technological superiority of his army relatively minor. As it was, the Battle of Tippecanoe in 1811 cemented Harrison's military reputation and provided the rallying cry for his presidential campaign three decades later.[11]

Tecumseh was not present at Tippecanoe, and the following year the United States launched an ill-advised war against Great Britain to conquer the Canadian provinces and add them to the US empire. This gave the pan-Indian forces under Tecumseh another chance to push back US territorial expansion in the old Northwestern territories. Supported by the British under General Isaac Brock, Tecumseh's warriors won several battles. However, Brock was killed and his successor, General Henry Proctor, abandoned Tecumseh before the Battle of the Thames, where the great Shawnee leader was killed in 1813.

When the war ended in 1814, Native American resistance in the Northwest Territory was almost over. Betrayed (again) by the British, and without their charismatic leader, Native American rivalries and disputes returned. Territorial governors took full advantage to push for land cessions through treaty, while some Native American leaders exchanged their land for territory west of the Mississippi. There was now nothing to stop Indiana and Illinois entering the Union as states in 1816 and 1818, respectively (Map 1).

That left Michigan Territory, whose governor from 1813 to 1831 was Lewis Cass. Like Harrison, Cass was sympathetic to the idea of reversing the ban on slavery included in the Northwest Ordinance and ruled his territory like an old-fashioned colonial governor in the British Empire. During his period in office, the white settler population rapidly increased (it had been a mere 4,762 in 1810) and part of the territory joined the Union in 1837 as Michigan State (Map 1).

What now remained was Wisconsin Territory, carved out of Michigan in 1836. It would remain outside the Union until 1848, by which time it had effectively been ruled as a colony for sixty-one years, starting with the appointment of St. Clair in 1787. Even this period of long colonial rule was surpassed by the eastern part of modern Minnesota (Map 1), which lay within the old Northwest Territory and which finally achieved statehood in 1858, after seventy-one years.[12]

The old Northwestern territories gave the federal government its first experience of colonial rule. And it was a long one, starting in 1787 and ending in 1858. It had all the ingredients we have come to expect from colonies: subject peoples (in the form of both Native Americans and whites); recalcitrant and sometimes rebellious settlers; a colonial superstructure based on governors, secretaries, and judges; limited representative government; and imperial veto powers. All it lacked was a slave labor force, which was only to be found south of the Ohio River. It is to this area that we now turn.

1.2. THE OLD SOUTHWESTERN TERRITORIES

The claim of the young republic on the territory south of the Ohio River (the old Southwestern territories) was based on the 1783 Treaty of Paris. A few years later the United States government, relying on a "right of conquest" claim, signed the Treaties of Hopewell.[13] This attempted to establish a new boundary between the Native American tribes and the settlers. And southern states, whose claims ran all the way to the Mississippi River, also signed treaties designed to extend their authority over land occupied by the Indians.[14]

These preliminary efforts to extend the empire into the old Southwestern territories were unsuccessful. The Indians did not consider that they had been defeated, had not signed the Treaty of Paris, and were much more numerous south of the Ohio River than north of it. It is true that the Proclamation Line had been breached by the Treaty of Fort Stanwix in 1768,[15] giving the settlers access to lands in western Virginia beyond the Appalachian Mountains, and whites were to be found in significant numbers in western North Carolina. However, this still left most of the region in the possession of Native Americans.

When the federal government took office under the new US Constitution in 1789, it faced three major obstacles that prevented it extending the empire west to the lower Mississippi River and south to the Gulf of Mexico. First, Spain—the colonial power in both Louisiana and Florida—claimed the land between the Chattahoochee and Mississippi Rivers up to latitude 32° 28′ north, whereas the United States claimed the same land as far south as 31° north (Map 2).[16] Second, the southern states—especially Georgia—proved unwilling to cede their land claims west of the mountains. Third, the Indians were larger in number, better organized, and more diplomatically astute in the old Southwestern territories than in the Northwest Territory.

It would take the federal government half a century to overcome all these obstacles. Limited progress toward removing the first obstacle, however, was made fairly quickly. As a result of the Treaty of San Lorenzo in 1795, also known as Pinckney's Treaty, Spain recognized the border between western Florida and the United States as latitude 31° north (Map 2). Although Spain also gave the United States freedom to trade on the Mississippi and the right of deposit at New Orleans, this still left her in control of all of the Gulf of Mexico, and it would take many years before she was finally dislodged (see Section 1.4).

The second obstacle—states' western land claims—was particularly difficult to overcome. Yet it was essential for the success of the imperial exercise, since the Constitution made clear that only the federal government could negotiate and sign treaties with the Native Americans. Thus, breaking the power of the Indians and forcing land cessions required establishing federal authority over the states.

The federal government had no need to persuade Virginia to relinquish its land claims to the south of the Ohio River in Kentucky. This area had filled rapidly with settlers and their slaves after the Treaty of Fort Stanwix, the Indians had been driven out, and there was a sufficiently large white population to meet the requirements for statehood. Kentucky, after a brief period in the Southwest Territory (see below), therefore became a state in 1792.

South of Kentucky, the land was claimed by North Carolina. The state first ceded its claim in 1784, but this had led to the bizarre incident of the Franklinites, when a group of settlers unsuccessfully petitioned Congress to recognize "Franklin State" in eastern Tennessee. North Carolina then rescinded its land cession, only to cede it again in 1789. This paved the way for the federal government to create the Southwest Territory in 1790, although its southern boundary only extended to the 35th parallel where the Georgian land claims began.[17]

The Southwest Territory soon met the conditions for statehood and joined the Union as the State of Tennessee in 1796, although it still had a large Indian population in the center (they would be driven out in the next few years). The federal government then turned its attention to the area further south. The concessions by Spain in 1795 allowed the United States to proceed toward the first stage of territorial government by creating Mississippi Territory in 1798. This, however, only filled the space ceded by Spain and did not extend north to the southern border of Tennessee, as this land—as far south as 32° 28′—was still claimed by Georgia (Map 2).

Georgia not only claimed the land but also the right to sign treaties with the Indians. This was in open defiance of the Constitution, but the federal government failed to take action. However, the Georgians overreached themselves when selling land in what would become federal territory. The Yazoo scandals (there were two of them) were so outrageous that the Georgian government eventually agreed to cede the western lands to the federal government in 1802.[18] Two years later Mississippi Territory was extended north to the borders of Tennessee (Map 2).

The white population of the new territory was very small, despite the fact that it incorporated Alabama, and included French, Spanish, and British settlers as well as Americans. The loyalty of these imperial subjects concerned the governors. One of the first was William Claiborne (1801–3), who wrote to the secretary of state,

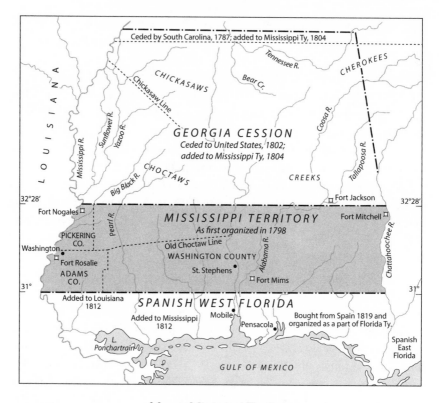

Map 2. Mississippi Territory

That a decided Majority of the People of this Territory, are Americans in
principles and attachments, I do verily believe. But (to my great Mortification)
there are persons here, on whose Judgments and hearts, former habits have
made unfortunate Impressions; favorable to Monarchy, and inimical to every
Government that recognizes the Rights of Man.—Several families from Kentucky, Tennessee and this Territory, have lately emigrated to the Province of
Louisiana, (and it is feared that this example may be followed by others); The
facility with which lands may be acquired under the Spanish authority, and
the prevalence of an opinion that the subjects of Spain are exempt from taxation, are probably the principal Inducements to this abandonment of their
Country.[19]

The principal obstacle facing all governors, however, was the opposition of the
Indians to further land cessions. The Native Americans of the old Southwestern territories had in the main sided with the British in the War of Independence, but they had not been defeated. They knew, however, that their survival

depended on tribal cohesion and accommodation wherever possible with the settlers.

The federal government considered the Indian tribes as sovereign and referred to them as "nations." In the case of the tribes in the Northwest Territory this was a convenient legal fiction serving the interests of both sides.[20] However, some of the tribes in the old Southwestern territories did succeed in constructing nations. This process was taken furthest by the Cherokees, who were the closest to the main centers of settler populations and whose institutions would come to mirror those in the federal government itself.

The US administration, despite the opposition of the states (especially Georgia), at first favored a policy of "civilization" with respect to these nations. This policy was in fact well received by many Indians, as the traditional economy of the tribes was being wiped out by the loss of hunting grounds and the reduction in the population of deer and other wild animals. Indian men not only took up plows and other farming instruments but some also acquired slaves and moved into cash crops such as tobacco and cotton. As early as 1802, Governor Claiborne could write optimistically to the secretary of war, "The progress of civilization among the Cherokees, Chickasaws, and upper Creeks, authorize a hope that the Indians within our Limits may ultimately be rescued from a State of Barbarism, & to contribute to the attainment of an object so interesting to humanity, would be to me a source of great gratification.—The Choctaws are indeed, generally involved in Savage life, but even among them, a Spirit of Industry has recently appeared; and the cultivation of the Soil is becoming the principal employment of several families."[21]

The pressure from the settlers was relentless, however, and they received the full support of the southern states. Inevitably, this led to new treaties with the federal government, in which the Native Americans were forced to cede land in the hope of protecting at least part of their domains. The Choctaws, for example, ceded 2.6 million acres in the 1801 Treaty of Fort Adams, 3.85 million in the 1803 Treaty of Hoe Buckintoopa, and 4.1 million in the 1805 Treaty of Mount Dexter. It was the same for the other tribes.

Resentment steadily increased, and Tecumseh's efforts to build a Pan-Indian alliance against the United States were welcomed by many in the south. When the War of 1812 against Great Britain was launched, it provided the excuse to mount attacks. A faction of the Creeks, the Red Sticks,[22] captured Fort Mims near the mouth of the Alabama River the following year and inflicted major casualties on US forces.

Not all Creeks were in favor of war, and neither were the Cherokees. General Andrew Jackson was therefore able to include some Native Americans in his

BOX 1.2
WAS "REMOVAL" GENOCIDE?

No reasonable person can deny that the forced removal of the Native Americans from the east to the west of the Mississippi River was ethnic cleansing, which today is a crime under international law. More controversially, was forced removal also genocide? This is an even more serious crime under international law today.

The Convention on Genocide was adopted by the United Nations in 1948, and Article 2 defines genocide to include

> any of the following acts committed with intent to destroy, in whole or in part, a national, ethnical, racial or religious group, as such:
> (a) Killing members of the group;
> (b) Causing serious bodily or mental harm to members of the group;
> (c) Deliberately inflicting on the group conditions of life calculated to bring about its physical destruction in whole or in part;
> (d) Imposing measures intended to prevent births within the group;
> (e) Forcibly transferring children of the group to another group.

Indian removal would seem to be covered by at least part of Article 2, especially 2(b). Indeed, the US government—clearly worried about the implications of Article 2—felt obliged to enter an "understanding" to the convention stating: "(1) That the term 'intent to destroy, in whole or in part, a national, ethnical, racial, or religious group as such' appearing in article II means the specific intent to destroy, in whole or in substantial part, a national, ethnical, racial or religious group as such by the acts specified in article II. (2) That the term 'mental harm' in article II (b) means permanent impairment of mental faculties through drugs, torture or similar techniques."

If Indian removal was genocide, then its principal architect was Andrew Jackson. During his presidency (1829–37), 100 million acres of Indian land were added to the public domain and hardly any Indians remained east of the Mississippi River. Jackson also defied the Supreme Court, the only US president to do so, when he refused to act after Georgia had been found in breach of federal law.

volunteer force that crushed the Red Sticks at the Battle of Horseshoe Bend in 1814. A few months later, at the Treaty of Fort Jackson, the Creek nation was forced to cede twenty-two million acres (one-third of their territory). This land included some of the richest agricultural land in the south, and those who had fought with Jackson suffered just as much as those who fought against.

The end of the war coincided with a big increase in cotton prices and a huge influx of new settlers. This allowed the federal government in 1817 to split Mississippi Territory, creating Alabama Territory in the east and admitting Mississippi as a state. Following Spain's decision in 1819 to transfer her remaining possessions in Florida to the United States (see Section 1.4 in this chapter), Alabama itself became a state. All of the old Southwestern territories were now in the Union.

This might have been an opportunity for a display of magnanimity by the federal government toward the Indians, many of whom were still on the east of the Mississippi River. The tribes had all signed land treaties with the United States, giving them ownership and occupation of a much reduced area and within which commercial agriculture was increasingly being practiced. A significant number had been converted to Christianity by the missionaries living among them, and literacy was gaining ground.[23] The Cherokees, where a system of writing in their own language had been developed, even adopted a constitution in 1827 modeled on that of the United States.

Far from welcoming these changes, the southern states and their settlers were appalled. They did not want to live side by side with Indians, however civilized. What they wanted was the rich agricultural land, the timber in the forests, and, following the discovery of gold in Cherokee territory in 1828, access to the minerals. And if the Indians would not move, they made it clear that the consequences would be severe. This was emphasized by the Alabama Legislature in 1829, where it was said, "It is believed that when they shall discover that the state of Alabama is determined upon her sovereign rights, and when they see and feel some palpable act of legislation under the authority of the state, then their veneration for their own law and customs will induce them speedily to remove."[24]

Under pressure from the southern states, therefore, the policy of the federal government in the old Southwestern territories shifted from "civilization" to removal (Box 1.2). Indeed, it went further since the ambition now was to crush the pretensions to statehood of the Indian nations. The aggression was led by Andrew Jackson long before he became president, but even James Monroe—once a firm believer in "civilization"—argued in his last presidential address in 1824 that the Indians must be induced to move west. And the campaign received a

boost from the Supreme Court in 1823 when Chief Justice John Marshall referred to the status of Native Americans as "dependent domestic nations" rather
than as sovereign states.[25]

When Andrew Jackson became president in 1829, he wasted no time in putting the new policy in place. The Indian Removal Act was passed by Congress
in 1830 and in the same year the Treaty of Dancing Rabbit Creek deprived the
Choctaws of their remaining land in the east. The Creeks, one of whose leaders
(William McIntosh) had already signed a fraudulent treaty in 1825 giving away
much of their land, were the next to go. In 1832 the Treaty of Pontotoc would
lead to the removal of the Chickasaws.[26]

The Cherokees were the last to be forced out, naively trusting US federal
law to protect them both against states and settlers as well as from fraudulent
treaties. It was all in vain. Some, led by the Ridge family, moved voluntarily, but
the majority under John Ross stayed until they were evicted by force. The hor-
rific tale of the resulting Trail of Tears in 1838–39 has been told many times, but
it becomes no less tragic through repetition.[27]

1.3. THE FRENCH TERRITORIES

Napoleon's ascent to power in France after 1798 coincided with the military
failure of French and British forces in Haiti. Determined to put down the successful slave revolt led by Toussaint L'Ouverture, he dispatched a major force
under his brother-in-law to the Caribbean. As a complement to anticipated success in Haiti, Napoleon planned to rebuild the French Empire in North America and persuaded Spain in a secret treaty to transfer its Louisiana colony back
to France (it had been French until 1763). This gave France once again a presence all the way from the Gulf of Mexico to the Canadian border.[28]

The Treaty of San Ildefonso, as it was called, was signed in 1800. When news
of it leaked out the following year, Jefferson had become president and he was
deeply concerned. The United States faced the prospect of a powerful and
imperially ambitious neighbor across the whole western side of the Mississippi
River. Even more worrying was French control of New Orleans at the mouth of
the river, through which so much of US trade was bound to pass.[29]

Jefferson neither wanted, nor expected, to acquire the whole of Louisiana.[30]
Instead, he authorized his ambassador in Paris, together with James Monroe, to
explore the possibility of a much more modest territorial cession including New
Orleans and a small part of the lower Mississippi on the western bank. This
would have been sufficient to secure US strategic interests. The budget was set
at $10 million.

By one of the ironies of history, negotiations began in Paris not long after the French army had been crushed in Haiti, laying waste to Napoleon's dream of reviving the French Empire in North America. Napoleon now had no need of Louisiana and offered to sell the whole of it, including New Orleans, for $15 million. The offer was accepted without waiting for Jefferson's approval.

Jefferson was not the sort of man to pass up an opportunity to expand his "empire for liberty," and the Louisiana Purchase, which doubled the size of territory controlled by the federal government, is usually portrayed as the greatest land cession in history (Map 3).[31] Yet it is not at all clear that this was so. The only secure title in the cession was to New Orleans and a small area in the lower Mississippi. It would take the United States over a century to secure title to the rest, by which time twenty thousand Americans and countless Indians had been killed, with at least $750 million spent on military campaigns (not to mention the millions of dollars for land cessions from, and annuities to, the Native Americans themselves).

Jefferson was so uncertain of what he had bought that he posed a set of questions to William Claiborne, the first governor of the new territories. His answers are illuminating:

> There are I believe, [no maps] extant that can be depended upon. . . . I am also informed, that a number of partial but accurate Geographical Sketches of that Country, have been taken by different Spanish officers; but that it has been the policy of their Gov [to] prevent the publication of them. . . . On this question [regarding boundaries], I have not been able to obtain any satisfactory information. . . . The information [on white settlers] I have as yet been able to collect concerning the population, position &c of the several divisions, is not sufficiently authentic, to justify my hazarding an Answer in detail to this question. . . . [On Indian population] I am unable to make an estimate with the accuracy required.[32]

Undeterred by this and other potential obstacles,[33] Jefferson proceeded to organize the French territories along now traditional lines. This, however, was no simple matter. The cession included land that would in time become the whole of Arkansas, Kansas, Iowa, Missouri, Nebraska, and Oklahoma and parts of Colorado, Louisiana, Minnesota, Montana, New Mexico, North Dakota, South Dakota, Texas, and Wyoming (Map 3).[34]

After a brief period of military rule, the Territory of Orleans was formed in 1804 in what would become (approximately) the State of Louisiana, and the rest of the French territories were designated the District of Louisiana (it would be called the Territory of Louisiana from 1805 onward). The white settlers of

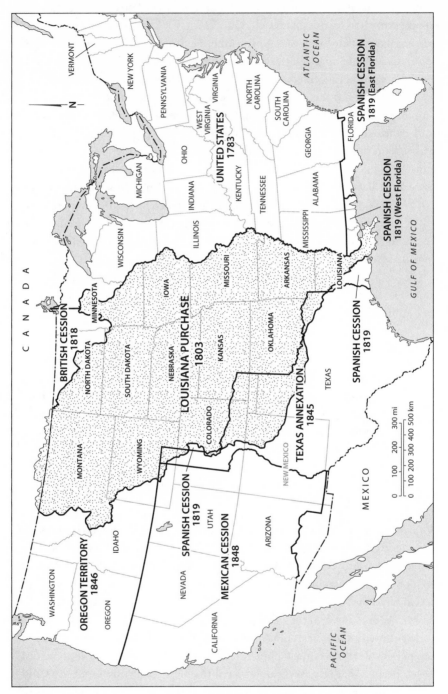

Map 3. French and Spanish territories

Orleans Territory were a mixture of French, British, Spanish, American, and German (there were also many "free people of color"). Far from being delighted with their new status, however, there were many complaints from these colonial subjects—especially the French—whose objections were very similar to those in European colonies:

> [The general causes of discontent are] the sudden introduction of the English language, which hardly anybody understands, into the daily exercise of public authority and in the most important acts of private life; the affrays and tumults resulting from the struggle for pre-eminence, and the preference shown for American over French dances at public balls; the invasion of bayonets into the halls of amusement and the closing of halls; the active participation of the American general and governor in those quarrels; the revolting partiality exhibited in favor of Americans or Englishmen, both in the audiences granted by the authorities and in the judgments rendered; the marked substitution of American for Creole majorities in all administrative and judicial bodies; the arbitrary mixture of old usages with new ones, under pretext of change of domination; the intemperate speeches; the scandalous orgies; the savage manners and habits; the wretched appointments to office.[35]

It is doubtful if the president was much troubled by any of this. Of more concern to Jefferson was the use to which the new territories would be put. His preferred solution was a constitutional amendment under which the new territories would have become a vast Indian reserve allowing not only for the removal to the west of those Indians on the east of the Mississippi River but also for the removal to the east of those whites on the west. However, Congress defeated his proposal, not wishing to put any constraints on white settlement.

The stage was therefore set for a great human tragedy, the first act of which had already taken place without Jefferson even knowing.[36] This was the death through disease of perhaps one-third of all Indians in the new territories and further west starting in the 1780s as a result of smallpox, cholera, bubonic plague, streptococcal infections, influenza, measles, and whooping cough. Indeed, a smallpox epidemic in 1837 on the northern plains cut in half the Indian population in one year.[37]

The Indians in the area ceded to the United States by France had adapted to their environment in two very different ways that would have profound implications for the form that empire building took. Along the Missouri and its tributaries, as well as the other rivers that flowed east into the lower Mississippi, the Indians lived in riverine horticultural villages where farming was the principal activity. In the uplands west, southwest, and northwest of the Missouri as far as the Rocky Mountains, they formed nomadic hunting bands.

The village dwellers had a lifestyle with which the federal government was familiar. Treaties were signed almost immediately providing for land cessions, removal further west, and the payment of gifts and annuities. Of course, the lands to which these Indians were removed were not empty, and this necessitated further treaties with those most affected. Nonetheless, by 1812 Orleans Territory was ready to enter the Union as the slave-owning State of Louisiana. The Territory of Louisiana was then renamed Missouri Territory. In 1819 it was split, with the southern part becoming Arkansaw [*sic*] Territory.[38]

This division was designed to prepare the way for a small part of Missouri Territory, where cotton farming was rapidly expanding, to enter the Union as the State of Missouri. However, this proved to be highly controversial because of the use of slave labor in the territory. It took two years before the (in)famous Missouri Compromise was thrashed out, banning slavery above latitude 36° 30′ north except in the case of Missouri itself.

At this point the federal government and Congress gave serious thought to a "permanent" settlement of the Indian population through the creation of a territory for Indians bounded on the east by Arkansas Territory[39] and Missouri State, on the south by the Red River, on the west by Mexico,[40] and on the northern boundary by the Platte River. In this way, claimed Secretary of War John C. Calhoun, the United States would reach a satisfactory solution to competition for land between whites and Indians: "One of the greatest evils to which they [Indians] are subject is that incessant pressure of our population, which forces them from seat to seat. . . . To guard against this evil . . . there ought to be the strongest and the most solemn assurance that the country given them should be theirs, as a permanent home for themselves and their posterity."[41]

This land was formally declared to be Indian Territory in 1830, and four years later Congress debated a bill for it to become "organized" with a confederated government formed by the tribes, a nonvoting delegate sent to Washington, DC, and eventual admission to the Union as a state. Unfortunately, the bill did not pass and Indian Territory remained "unorganized." It therefore lacked any legal protections and became instead a dumping ground for Indians from the east under the removal policy.

After the admission of Missouri as a state in 1821, the rest of Missouri Territory—stretching all the way to the Canadian border—became known at first as "unorganized territory," meaning that Congress had not yet passed organic acts to divide it into different administrative units. In this vast area, whites had a growing presence through trade, forts, trails, and missions. However, the pressure on the nomadic Native Americans was not yet severe. Indeed, it is doubtful if the settlers outnumbered the Indians in the whole of the Louisiana Purchase—let alone on the northern plains—when Arkansas became a state in 1836.

By midcentury, however, everything suddenly changed. Oregon had been acquired, Texas was annexed, Mexico lost half its territory, and the United States found itself with a new coastline stretching all the way from Baja California to British Columbia.[42] The gold mines of California, the fertile valleys of the West Coast, and the fur trade on the Pacific inevitably attracted a steady stream of settlers.

The Native Americans of the old French territories were now no longer at the western extremities of the United States. Instead, they were in the middle and, from the point of view of the settlers and the federal government, in the way. Trails needed to be prepared, and roads built, and in a few years railways and telegraphs would need to be laid down. To support this, an enhanced network of military forts and trading posts had to be established. The increased flow of settlers disrupted the wildlife on which nomadic life depended and, to make matters worse, industrialization in the east was creating a new type of demand for buffalo hides that no longer required skilled Indian labor to meet it.

At the Treaty of Fort Laramie in 1851, the federal government signaled the change that was coming. Many of the Plains tribes, including the Mandan, Crow, Blackfeet, Cheyenne, and Arapahoe, were obliged not only to accept reduced hunting ranges that would in due course become reservations but also to permit safe passage across their land by migrants on the Oregon Trail and to allow the construction of roads and forts on their territories. In return, the federal government promised to keep out settlers—a promise that was broken within a few years following the discovery of gold near Pike's Peak.

In 1854 the "unorganized" land west of Arkansas, Missouri, and Iowa States[43] and Minnesota Territory was formed into Kansas and Nebraska Territory, cutting deep into hunting grounds that the Indians had assumed was theirs to use indefinitely. The Kansas-Nebraska Act was the prelude to the Civil War, as every student of US history is aware, since it effectively repealed the Missouri Compromise on slavery. However, the Civil War also had major implications for the Native Americans since, once again, the majority of the tribes backed the losing side.[44]

By the end of the war, whatever goodwill toward the Indians that might have existed in Washington, DC, had evaporated (Box 1.3). Native Americans were subjected to a sustained attack that almost completely destroyed what remained of their societies. The assault had numerous dimensions—economic, cultural,

BOX 1.3

ELY SAMUEL PARKER (1828–95)

The expansion of the US empire across the continent relied on agents acting for or on behalf of the federal government. Among these agents were governors, judges, military officers, missionaries, and superintendents of trade. Some of the most important, however, were appointed to deal exclusively with Indian affairs.

President Washington had given the War Department responsibility for Indian matters, including supervision of the various Trade and Intercourse Acts, and Congress had approved in 1824 a Bureau of Indian Affairs within the War Department. When in 1849 responsibility for Indian affairs was handed to the Department of the Interior, the bureau moved with it.

The most important agent in the bureau was the commissioner for Indian affairs, and the appointment was always a white man until 1869, when President Ulysses S. Grant (1869–77) appointed Ely Samuel Parker to the post. Parker was the son of a Seneca chief who had been born on the Tonawanda reservation in New York and given the name Donehogawa at birth. He had been formally educated at a missionary school. His efforts to study law were rebuffed because he was an Indian and therefore not a US citizen, but he was able to train as an engineer. This brought him to the attention of President Grant before the Civil War.

The appointment was a bold one, but the timing was terrible for Parker. The Bureau of Indian Affairs was extremely corrupt, its board composed only of whites, and US action—despite Grant's proclaimed "peace policy"—deeply hostile to Indians. Indeed, one of Parker's first tasks at the start of his tenure was to investigate the massacre of the Piegan Blackfeet by the US military.

Parker secured some successes, but his efforts to reduce corruption in the bureau and blocking of illegal mining in Wyoming made him many enemies. He was charged in Congress on thirteen counts, including misappropriation of funds. Although eventually cleared of all charges, he was so disgusted at his treatment that he resigned his post in the summer of 1871.

legal, political, and religious—and involved armed force, including massacres. It was a genocide that had reduced the Native American population to its lowest point in history by 1900.[45]

The federal government signaled the change by ending the treaty system. Henceforth, Indians would not be treated as "sovereign nations" but as dependent tribes with whom one-sided negotiations would take place. One of the last treaties to be signed, however, was also one of the most important. In the 1868 Treaty of Fort Laramie, the federal government guaranteed to the Lakota Indians ownership of the Black Hills in South Dakota and closed the Powder River Country to whites. Both "guarantees" would be withdrawn, leading to some of the bloodiest incidents in the Indian Wars before the final massacre at Wounded Knee in 1890.

As the genocide was drawing to a close, Congress prepared the legislation to draw the remaining territories in the north of the Louisiana Purchase—Dakota, Montana, and Wyoming—into the Union. It had been a long process, during which Congress had been unable to resist the temptation to meddle in territorial affairs. Indeed, by the 1880s the restrictions on what territorial legislatures could do had expanded enormously:

> Among the more important of these limitations now in force are those prohibiting the passage of acts interfering with the primary disposal of the soil, imposing a tax on property of the United States, taxing the property of non-residents higher than that of residents, having a special or local character in respect to any of a large number of enumerated cases, such as divorce, regulating county or township affairs, the assessment and collection of taxes, the punishment of crimes, the granting to any corporation, association or individual of any special or exclusive privilege, immunity or franchise, etc., or generally in any other case where a general law could be made applicable. No special or special charter to any private corporation can be granted, but a general incorporation law may be enacted. Other limitations upon the power of Territories are those prohibiting the Territories from contracting any debt except for certain purposes, and even then only to the total amount not exceeding a certain percentum of the assessed value of property in the Territory for purposes of taxation.[46]

Under these circumstances, it is not surprising that many white settlers in the territories chafed at their colonial status. One had the audacity to compare an unpopular governor with George III, while another described the territories as "mere colonies, occupying much the same relation to the General Government as the colonies did to the British government prior to the Revolution."[47]

Delegate Martin Maginnis of Montana Territory went even further, telling the House of Representatives in 1884: "The present Territorial system . . . is the most infamous system of colonial government that was ever seen on the face of the globe. . . . [The territories] are the colonies of your Republic, situated three thousand miles away from Washington by land, as the thirteen colonies were situated three thousand miles away from London by water. And it is a strange thing that the fathers of our Republic . . . established a colonial government as much worse than that which they revolted against as one form of such government can be worse than another."[48]

The colonial status of these northern territories ended in 1889–90 when they joined the Union. At that moment, Congress also created the Territory of Oklahoma from the western portion of Indian Territory, and the long process of attrition of Indian land rights was almost at an end. The Dawes Act of 1887, suppressing communal land ownership, was gradually extended to Indian Territory and land cessions accelerated. The two territories were then admitted to the Union as the State of Oklahoma in 1907, the last state wholly within the Louisiana Purchase of 1803 to do so.[49]

1.4. THE SPANISH TERRITORIES

The United States, following the Louisiana Purchase in 1803, continued to share a boundary with Spain in the south (the Floridas), but the exact border between the two empires was again in dispute as the United States insisted West Florida was included in the sale. Spain's colony of Nueva España (soon to become Mexico) was now the neighbor in the west, although where the boundary ran was even more contentious than in West Florida.

In the north, the boundary was still with Great Britain, but no final agreement had as yet been reached on where the frontier lay west of the Great Lakes. And in the Pacific Northwest, boundary disputes involved not just the United States, the United Kingdom, and Spain but also Russia, whose territorial empire had spread across the Pacific to the Americas. Thus, the scene was set for a territorial struggle between old and new empires that would take several decades to resolve (Map 3).

During its brief period of British colonial rule (1763–83), Florida had been divided into West and East at the Apalachicola River, with separate capitals at Pensacola and St. Augustine, and this was how Spain had administered the colony on its retrocession. West Florida included Baton Rouge on the east side of the Mississippi River, although a majority of the population was American by 1803. By the 1795 Treaty of San Lorenzo, Spain had given up its claim to the area north of the 31st parallel, but it had never relinquished its claim on West Florida, and France always understood that to be the case.

The US claim that Louisiana included West Florida was therefore very weak and indeed contradicted by the 1795 Treaty of San Lorenzo.[50] Undaunted, however, Congress passed the Mobile Act in 1804, annexing most of West Florida to Mississippi Territory. Spain protested and was strong enough to prevent the upstart empire from enforcing its claim by defeating a filibuster expedition that same year. President Jefferson did not respond and contented himself with opening a customs post on the Mobile River just north of the Spanish border.

Spanish ability to resist further US encroachment was fatally weakened by Napoleon's invasion of the Iberian Peninsula in 1808. Royalist troops in the Americas were left to fend for themselves, with little or no hope of reinforcement. US insurgents seized Baton Rouge in 1810, giving President Madison the excuse he needed to annex West Florida as far as the Pearl River and include it in Orleans Territory.

This time Spanish protests could not be backed up by force, and worse was to come. When the War of 1812 erupted, Great Britain saw an opportunity to encircle the United States by invading from the south, seizing New Orleans and controlling the Mississippi. Andrew Jackson was dispatched to deal with this threat and, without declaring war on Spain, defeated the British and secured the remainder of West Florida with the exception of Pensacola (occupied but returned to Spain in 1815).

The defeat of Napoleon in 1814 brought Fernando VII back to power in Spain. This should have marked a reassertion of Spanish authority in the Floridas, but the opportunity was undermined by the wars of independence in Latin America. The Floridas were too marginal in Spanish imperial thinking and the royalist garrison was left to fend for itself. When Jackson invaded East Florida in 1818, ostensibly in hot pursuit of the Seminoles fleeing from Georgia,[51] Spain was unable to respond. By the middle of the year, Spanish authority was reduced to St. Augustine.

Jackson's campaign, although never officially authorized by President Monroe, gave the secretary of state (John Quincy Adams) a huge advantage in the negotiations with his Spanish counterpart (Don Luis de Onís y González) that had been going on for some years. When the Adams-Onís Treaty was signed in 1819, it gave all of Florida to the United States. Ratification was delayed by two years, but—following a brief period of US military rule—the Territory of Florida came into being in 1822.

Since most of the Spaniards left for Cuba, the white population was now very small. However, the Indian population was still substantial. The federal government therefore pressured the Seminole chiefs to sign the Treaty of Moultrie Creek in 1823, which established a reservation in the middle of Florida with an annuity guaranteed for twenty years. Settlers and their slaves now moved into Florida to plant cotton and raise other cash crops.

Florida was big enough to accommodate the needs of planters and Seminoles, as well as the requirements of the numerous free blacks who resided in the territory. However, any chance of accommodation was destroyed by Jackson's Indian Removal Act. The Seminole chiefs were summoned to a new meeting in 1832 and tricked into signing the Treaty of Fort Payne requiring them to move west of the Mississippi. Many Seminoles, including Osceola, resisted removal, and the Second Seminole War began in 1835.

It was one of the bloodiest wars in US imperial history and included the massacre of Major Francis L. Dade and his two companies.[52] The Seminoles never fully surrendered, but the survivors were driven further south into the Everglades (Box 1.4). At the end of the war in 1842, Congress passed the Armed Occupation Act giving 160 acres of land to any settlers willing to improve the land in the south of the territory and defend themselves from Indians. Florida was now ready for statehood and joined the Union in 1845. The southern boundary of the United States was now the Caribbean sea and the Gulf of Mexico.

The Adams-Onís Treaty did not limit itself to the transfer of Florida. It also set the Spanish-American boundary throughout the continent. Texas remained part of Nueva España, whose northern border was now set at 42° north. Beyond that—up to British-controlled Canada and Russian-controlled Alaska—was still undefined, but a door to the Pacific through what would now be called Oregon Country had been opened for the United States.

Sovereignty over Oregon Country would now be disputed between three imperial powers: Great Britain, Russia, and the United States. Yet it was already the home of several tribes, some of whom lived from fishing or agriculture and had no desire to leave. White sailors, trappers, and explorers from the 1770s onward had brought with them a series of diseases that had reduced the Indians' numbers, but there were still estimated to be 110,000 as late as 1835.[53] At that time, there were less than one thousand white settlers in the region.

None of the imperial powers had a strong claim on Oregon Country. The Russians had been on the northwest Pacific for the longest, following the epic voyage of Vitus Bering in 1741 down the coast of Alaska. The British had gained a foothold after the Nootka Sound Conventions with Spain[54] and the overland journey to the Pacific of Alexander Mackenzie in the 1790s. The United States pointed to the voyage of Robert Gray in 1792 to the mouth of the Columbia

BOX 1.4
ETHAN ALLEN HITCHCOCK (1798–1870)

US territories would eventually be filled by settlers, but they first had to be secured by the military. This meant that army officers played a crucial role in extending the US empire across the continent. Some of these men would go on to play a prominent part in politics, even occupying the presidency in a few cases. Most were unreservedly committed to the imperialist project, but there was a handful who were able to see the exercise more objectively while remaining loyal.

One such officer was Ethan Allen Hitchcock, the grandson of a revolutionary war hero. Graduating from the US Military Academy in 1817, he volunteered to serve with Andrew Jackson in the First Seminole War but was turned down. By the time the second war broke out in 1835, however, he was a captain and saw service.

Hitchcock kept a detailed diary, an edited version of which was published posthumously in 1909. His observations on the Second Seminole War were remarkable, documenting the folly and dishonesty of his military superiors: "I confess to a very considerable disgust in this service. I remember the cause of the war, and that annoys me. I think of the folly and stupidity with which it has been conducted, particularly of the puerile character of the present commanding general, and I am quite out of patience" (Hitchcock, *Fifty Years in Camp and Field*, 123).

After the war, by this time a major, Hitchcock was sent to Indian Territory to investigate the allegations of fraud raised against the contractors paid by the federal government to carry out removal of the Five Civilized Tribes. His diary entries were not only full of insight (see Foreman, *A Traveler in Indian Territory*) but also provided the basis for his searing report to President John Tyler in 1842.

Hitchcock, by now a lieutenant colonel, saw service in the Mexican-American War where his diary once again was very revealing: "Our people ought to be damned for their impudent arrogance and domineering presumption" (192). He would eventually rise to the rank of major general and commanded the Pacific Division, during which time he visited Oregon Territory.

River and the explorations of Meriwether Lewis and William Clark, who reached Oregon Country in 1805.[55]

Undaunted by the weakness of their claims, the three powers had proceeded to establish a presence. Oregon Country was desired not just for its furs, fishing, timber, and agricultural land (minerals would come later) but also for its coastline, providing magnificent harbors from which the Pacific could be crossed. And, as always in imperial rivalry, there was the constant worry of other powers arriving first and blocking access to the others.

The competition between the United States and the United Kingdom focused at first on the fur trade. John Jacob Astor opened a trading post (modestly named Astoria) at the mouth of the Columbia River in 1811, which was unceremoniously seized by the Hudson's Bay Company in 1817.[56] The following year the two countries reached agreement that the boundary between Canada and the United States from the Great Lakes to the Rockies should follow the 49th parallel while sovereignty would be shared west of the continental divide.

Russia, well established in Alaska and with a military presence in California, was more ambitious. The czar issued a *ukase* in 1821 claiming sovereignty on the coast as far south as the 51st parallel and an exclusive maritime zone to the west. A second *ukase* granted a Russian company a twenty-year monopoly on trading in this area.[57]

John Quincy Adams, as secretary of state, responded with a wildly ambitious US claim of sovereignty up to 61° north. More significantly for hemispheric history, however, was the response of President Monroe. In December 1823, during his seventh annual message to Congress, the president outlined what would become known as the Monroe Doctrine:

> At the proposal of the Russian Imperial Government, made through the minister of the Emperor residing here, a full power and instructions have been transmitted to the minister of the United States at St. Petersburg to arrange by amicable negotiation the respective rights and interests of the two nations on the northwest coast of this continent. . . . In the discussions to which this interest has given rise and in the arrangements by which they may terminate the occasion has been judged proper for asserting, as a principle in which the rights and interests of the United States are involved, that the American continents, by the free and independent condition which they have assumed and maintain, are henceforth not to be considered as subjects for future colonization by any European powers.[58]

The following year the three rivals—Russia, the United Kingdom, and the United States—agreed that 54° 40′ north would be the southern limit of the

Russian claim and also the border between Russia and British Columbia. It did not, of course, mean that the US claim would extend so far north, although some hotheads assumed that it would ("Fifty-four forty or fight" was their rallying cry). It did mean, however, that imperial control of Oregon Country between the new northern border and the 42nd parallel was now a simple imperialist rivalry between the United Kingdom and the United States.

At this point the United States unleashed its not-so-secret weapon: settlers. The British, or at least the Hudson's Bay Company, preferred to see Oregon Country free of settlers because of the damage they did to the fur trade. US settlers (including missionaries), however, started following in the footsteps of Lewis and Clark in the 1830s. By the mid-1840s British interest in Oregon Country had diminished, while US interest was growing. After some saber rattling by both sides, the boundary was settled at the 49th parallel in 1846.

The United States had therefore acquired a Pacific coastline even before the start of the Mexican-American War (see Chapter 2). However, the task of colonization would take many years to complete. Oregon Territory was formed in 1848 and Washington Territory was split from it in 1853. Ten years later Idaho Territory was formed from part of Washington Territory (the other parts coming from Dakota and Nebraska Territories). The western portion of Oregon Territory became a state in 1859, but it was not until thirty years later that Washington and Idaho joined the Union.[59]

Why did statehood take so long? When the first census of Oregon Territory was taken in 1850, there were still only 13,294 settlers (far less than the Native Americans). However, inward migration accelerated after the federal government took control and the settlers wanted to take the land occupied by the Indians (the fur trade was now in steep decline). This inevitably meant confrontation, condemning the region to decades of warfare.

Congress appointed three commissioners in 1850 to secure the land, with instructions that were none too subtle ("to free the land west of the Cascades entirely of Indian title and to move all the Indians to some spot to the east").[60] These orders were then carried out through a series of treaties that aimed to push the Indians away from the lush valleys in the south of the territory where the bulk of the settlers sought to make their homes.

Among the numerous Indian tribes were the Niimíipu, who had been called Nez Perce[61] by French trappers. Members of the tribe, which at the time numbered around twelve thousand, had helped Lewis and Clark when the expedition's food supplies ran low after crossing the Continental Divide, but this act of kindness had been long forgotten when the Walla Walla Council met in 1855. The resulting treaties required the Nez Perce to cede 7.5 million acres and live on a reservation, where—unfortunately for them—gold would soon be discovered. Inevitably, this led to a flood of illegal settlers.

Another treaty would now be drawn up (in 1863), requiring the Nez Perce to relinquish 90 percent of their reservation.[62] This time, however, many chiefs refused to sign, and the stage was set for the Nez Perce War that erupted in 1877. The story of this legendary conflict, in which nearly three thousand members of the tribe were pursued by the US military over more than one thousand miles, has been told repeatedly, but it had deadly consequences for the Nez Perce. By 1900, squeezed into a small reservation in Idaho, the population of the tribe had dwindled to nineteen hundred.

2

MEXICO AND CENTRAL AMERICA

With the acquisition of Oregon, the United States should have had enough land to satisfy all but the most ardent imperialists. However, the non-Indian population was expanding fast and increased by one-third between 1830 and 1840, by which time it had reached seventeen million. The expansionists were therefore able to argue for continued territorial growth on the grounds that land would still be needed for future as well as current settlers.

The argument in favor of more land, however, was no longer as widely supported as it had been at the time of independence. The quasi-consensus in favor of the creation of the Northwest and Southwest Territories, the Louisiana Purchase, the acquisition of the Floridas, and the establishment of the Oregon Territory would now break down. This did not mean that the imperial project was over, but it did mean that it would become more contested.

The main problem was, of course, slavery. The southern states favored continued expansion partly because of the desire for more land, but above all to bring new states into the Union to protect the "peculiar institution." Not surprisingly, many of the citizens of the northern states opposed expansion for exactly the same reason.

Since the south could not outvote the north under normal circumstances— still less muster the two-thirds majority needed for certain legislative purposes— it might be assumed that the north would block expansion if the only reason for it was to bolster slavery. However, elites in the northern states often favored continued expansion for reasons that had nothing to do with slavery and which went beyond the traditional argument based on additional land.

One of these was the rise of the United States as an industrial power. Although still behind the United Kingdom, America was catching up quickly as a producer and even exporter of manufactured goods. Its gross domestic product (GDP) was growing rapidly, and US trade—at least in the first half of the nineteenth century—was growing even faster than GDP. This meant that the United States now had a stronger interest in trade and foreign markets than at the time of independence.

World trade in the first half of the nineteenth century was heavily influenced by systems of imperial preference, under which empires not only discriminated against imports into the metropolitan states but also into their colonies if they originated from outside the empire. The United States was therefore at a disadvantage when trading with European powers and their colonies. Ending discrimination against US exports, or even shifting it in favor of the United States, was becoming an important strategic priority, and this meant an America big and powerful enough to rival other empires.

In the context of the 1840s, US territorial expansion could realistically only take place northward or southward. The dream of acquiring British-controlled Canada had not died with the War of 1812, and friction would remain with Great Britain for many years to come.[1] However, with the adjustment of the Maine border in 1842 and the settlement of the dispute over Oregon Country a few years later, the prospects of northern expansion did not look promising.

That left expansion toward the south, where Mexican rebels had defeated Spain and created an independent state in 1821. Although the US border with the Spanish colony had been agreed on in 1819, Mexico discovered soon after its independence what Native American tribes had known for decades: US settlers did not regard border treaties as sacrosanct, were prepared to challenge them by force if necessary, and could usually expect a sympathetic response from the federal government.

The result was the Texan War of Independence (1835–36), strongly supported by the southern states, who assumed a Texas where slavery was legal would soon join the Union. That did indeed happen a decade later, by which time a further argument for imperial expansion had come to prominence in the United States. This was Manifest Destiny, a rationale for expansion that had been implicit since independence but which was now rendered explicit.

Manifest Destiny was an ideological, racist, and quasi-religious doctrine that underpinned a US claim to all lands in North America from the Atlantic to the Pacific. It was always controversial, but in the hands of a skilled politician could become a powerful tool in favor of territorial aggrandizement. Such a man was President James K. Polk (1845–49), who used the argument to great effect to launch a war against Mexico and strip her of half her territory. This not only vastly expanded the size of the United States but also gave her a long Pacific coastline.

The United States was now truly a transcontinental power, and this brought new challenges at a time when the two coasts were still only connected by sea travel (except for those prepared to undertake the long and dangerous overland route). Most trade in goods between the coasts was required to go by sea around Cape Horn in South America—a slow and expensive journey. The United States now also needed two navies to patrol its shores. Only a canal at some point across the Americas could alleviate this situation. The search for a transit route therefore became a US priority.

Many routes were considered, but a canal through Nicaragua quickly established itself as the favorite. However, other imperial powers—especially Great Britain and France—had come to the same conclusion. Thus, a small Central American state became the focus not just of close US attention but also of intense imperial rivalries that would endure for decades. It also attracted the interest of an American filibuster and supporter of slavery—William Walker.

Nicaragua came close to annexation by the United States in the 1850s, but imperial ambition was thwarted first through the defeat of Walker by the Central Americans and second by the Civil War. US interest in Nicaragua did not, however, disappear, and the country would become a US protectorate at the beginning of the twentieth century.

The Nicaraguan route was the preferred one for most of the nineteenth century. Although longer by distance than the route through Panama (a province of Colombia until 1903), the latter was thought to be more costly and more difficult. Indeed, this had been borne out by the failure of Ferdinand de Lesseps's canal project in the 1880s. The United States, however, decided to hedge its bets in the 1890s and signed an agreement with Colombia for exclusive control of any canal that might be built.

The story of how the refusal of the Colombian Congress to ratify the treaty led to Panamanian "independence" and the construction of the canal is well known. Yet it is also an illustration of the different forms that US imperialism could take. Panama would—like Nicaragua a few years later—become a US protectorate, while the Panama Canal Zone became a full-blown American territory. The sovereignty of the rest of Central America was severely compromised as a result.

The advance of the American empire southward represented a key shift in the imperial project. While muscular diplomacy had been used to secure territory in North America from European empires, military force was used to do the same with Mexico, Colombia, and Nicaragua. This was naked imperial aggression that could not be disguised by the use of slogans such as Manifest Destiny, and it could no longer be claimed that American empire was based only on western expansion and settler colonialism. In addition, this was now an empire that aspired to geopolitical leadership with access to two oceans and prospects for hegemony in Latin America and the Pacific.

2.1. TEXAS

The location of the border between French and Spanish territories in North America had not been definitively settled when Louisiana was purchased in 1803. This allowed Presidents Thomas Jefferson, James Madison, and James Monroe to claim that Louisiana included at least part of what is now Texas. The claim was very flimsy, but John Quincy Adams cited it repeatedly in his protracted negotiations with his Spanish counterpart for a border treaty.

Although the claim was weak, it was asserted with such authority that many Americans came to believe it. At the same time, revolutionaries in Nueva España were struggling to break free from Spanish control. The result was a series of filibusters into Spanish-controlled Texas by Mexican rebels and US settlers. Indeed, the first filibuster in 1811 was a joint venture between the two although it quickly fell apart when the different goals of the US and Mexican leaders became apparent. Filibusters continued for a decade, the final one being led by James Long in 1821.

Long, unlike his filibustering predecessors, did not receive overt or covert support from the federal government. The reason was simple. The Adams-Onís Treaty, signed in 1819, had recognized that Texas was a province of the Spanish colony of Nueva España (Adams and President Monroe had accepted this because Spain had agreed to transfer the Floridas to the United States). It would therefore have been an act of extreme bad faith to support Long's filibuster so soon after the boundary had been settled.

Ratification of the Adams-Onís Treaty was delayed so long that Mexico had become independent (in 1821) before it could be enforced. However, the boundary between Mexico and the United States was later reaffirmed by both sides as being the same as agreed to in the treaty (Map 4). The Sabine River therefore marked where Louisiana ended and Texas started. Mexico, briefly an empire under Agustín Iturbide until the establishment of a republic in 1823, then organized its territory into states with Texas joined to Coahuila as one province.

The transition from part of the Spanish Empire to Mexican republic did not alter the facts on the ground as far as Texas was concerned. This was a fertile

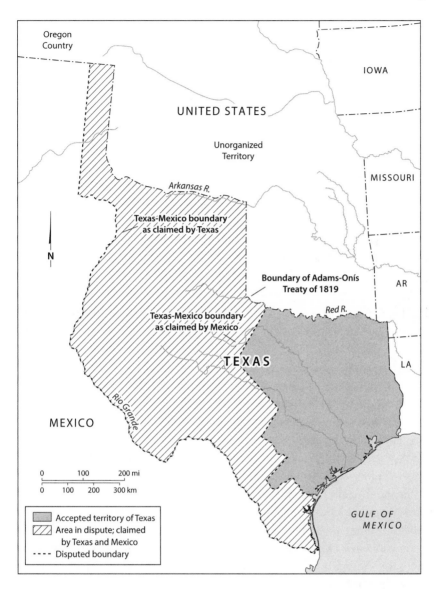

Map 4. Texas, 1836–45

area, suitable for growing cotton, tobacco, sugar, and other cash crops, where the Indian population far outnumbered Spanish settlers. Furthermore, the Indians—mainly Cherokees in the east, Wichitas in the center, and Comanches in the west—were not inclined to let their land be taken from them without a fight.

Texas was also an area that the Spanish had struggled to control militarily because of the semiarid and depopulated regions that separated it from the rest of Mexico and through which royalist armies had to pass. Indeed, such was the difficulty of protecting settlers against Indians that the Spanish abandoned Texas for long periods. The Comanches in particular had been very successful at extending their own area of control, known as Comanchería, as their skill on horseback had given them an advantage in mobile warfare.[2]

At the time that Spanish rule was coming to an end, there were only a small number of settlers in Texas, and the royalist forces could not guarantee their safety against Indian attacks. It was the Indian threat, rather than the filibusters, which persuaded the authorities in 1819 to create a system of land grants designed to encourage American immigration. Even so, the Spanish were careful to put many restrictions on the immigrants in order to ensure that they did not become a Trojan horse. These included an oath of allegiance to the Spanish crown and the adoption of Roman Catholicism.

Moses Austin, the first beneficiary of this *empresario* system, seemed an ideal candidate from the royalist perspective as he had lived as a Spanish subject in Louisiana before the Treaty of Ildefonso. However, Moses Austin died before he could fulfill the contract. It was left to his son, Stephen, to renegotiate the details with the Mexican government after independence.

Stephen Austin was at first a loyal Mexican subject and helped to put down the so-called Fredonia Republic set up by one of the US colonists in 1826. However, there was one subject that gave him perpetual difficulty with the authorities, and that was slavery. The Spanish grant to his father had not mentioned slaves, meaning that the colonists felt free to import them. Yet Mexico after independence gradually phased out the practice.

Stephen Austin worked hard to ensure that Texas was exempt from all the slavery legislation passed by Mexico. In 1825 he wrote, "If slavery should be prohibited immigration would be stopped, or if any came, they would be of the lower economic class, able only to eke out a bare existence and unable to promote the prosperity of the country; for in the cultivation of corn, cotton, and sugar, the principal products of the province, the use of many laborers, of slaves who are accustomed to the type of work, is indispensable."[3]

In these efforts he had some success, but the decision of the Mexican government in 1829 to ban slavery altogether put a serious doubt over the whole scheme of colonization. Although Austin achieved a temporary reprieve from this nationwide ban, his efforts were undermined the following year by the government's decision to stop foreign immigration. This was clearly aimed at

US colonists, who already outnumbered Mexicans in Texas and whose allegiance to the state—let alone adoption of Catholicism—was now suspect.

By this time Andrew Jackson had assumed the presidency. For years he had lambasted John Quincy Adams for not including Texas in the treaty that bears his name (although Adams had tried to make amends during his own presidency by offering to buy Texas from the Mexicans, he had been rebuffed). Jackson was therefore susceptible to the charms of an unscrupulous entrepreneur, Anthony Butler, who convinced him that Texas could be bought for $5 million.

Jackson's overtures were also rebuffed, but by now the Mexican authorities were becoming justifiably paranoid about the possibility of losing Texas. Don Manuel Mier y Terán, the Mexican boundary commissioner, wrote to his superiors, "The wealthy Americans of Louisiana and other Western states are anxious to secure land in Texas for speculation but they are restrained by the laws prohibiting slavery. . . . The repeal of these laws is a point toward which the colonists are directing their efforts. . . . Therefore, I now warn you to take timely measures. Texas could throw the whole nation into revolution."[4] Steps were then taken to occupy the province militarily and to establish colonies of Mexicans whose loyalty could be trusted. In addition, the tax holiday on customs duties enjoyed by the colonists was phased out and, finally, US immigration itself was stopped.

None of this went down well with the US colonists, whose attachment to Mexico—except for Austin—had always been skin-deep. Yet as late as 1832 in the Convention of Texas their representatives were still saying that "a decided declaration should be made by the people of Texas . . . of our firm and unshaken adherence to the Mexican Confederation and Constitution and our readiness to do our duty as Mexican Citizens."[5] However, the decision of President Antonio López de Santa Anna in 1834 to suppress Congress and establish a dictatorship, as well as his decision to refuse Austin's request for a separation of Texas from Coahuila, provoked the American colonists into rebellion.

When the war started, events moved fast and independence, followed by annexation to the United States, quickly became the colonists' priority. The defeat of the Mexican Army and the capture of Santa Anna at San Jacinto in April 1836 did indeed lead to Texan independence and a unanimous request for annexation. However, there was initially a deafening silence on the US side despite the fact that Jackson was still president.

This was not due to a change of heart by the president on the need for annexation (he would later write "we must regain Texas, peaceably if we can, forcibly if we must"). He had, for example, dispatched General Edmund P. Gaines during the war to the area between the Sabine and Nueces Rivers.[6] Yet Jackson proceeded with uncharacteristic caution for several reasons. First, he did not want the issue of slavery to undermine the chances of his protégé Martin Van Buren in the upcoming presidential election and, second, he did not want to start a war with Mexico. It was not until his final hours in office that Jackson even recognized Texas as an independent state.

By this time the Texans had drawn up their own constitution that not only legalized slavery but also the importation of slaves from the United States: "All persons of color who were slaves for life previous to their emigration to Texas, and who are now held in bondage, shall remain in the like state of servitude. . . . Congress shall pass no laws to prohibit emigrants from bringing their slaves into the republic with them . . . nor shall any slaveholder be allowed to emancipate his or her slave or slaves without the consent of congress. . . . No free person of African descent, either in whole or in part, shall be permitted to reside permanently in the republic."[7]

Annexation now became such a contentious issue that President Van Buren (1837–41) felt unable to put it to a vote in Congress. Instead, Texas was left to its own devices as an independent state under its first president (Sam Houston) and recognized only by the United States. Enthusiasm for annexation began to wane even in Texas itself, and the second president (Mirabeau Buonaparte Lamar—Box 2.1) rejected it outright.

President Lamar (1838–41) was a failure in most respects and plunged Texas into financial crisis. However, he did succeed in securing recognition from several European countries. One of these was Great Britain, which saw an opportunity both to phase out slavery in Texas (it had been abolished in British colonies in 1834) as well as gain trading and other privileges. In return, Great Britain—or so it was hoped by Lamar—would guarantee Texan independence against a Mexican *revanche*.

The prospect of a Texas under British tutelage was not one to appeal to US lawmakers. When the Anglo-Texan treaty was ratified in 1842, therefore, the issue of annexation rapidly moved up the US agenda. By this time Sam Houston, a supporter of annexation, was once again president of Texas. However, President John Tyler (1841–45) still had some work to do in Washington, DC, to overcome the opposition of abolitionists.

This proved more difficult than expected and, just before the end of his presidential term, he had to resort to the highly dubious mechanism of a joint resolution of Congress, requiring only a simple majority of both houses, to secure

BOX 2.1

MIRABEAU BUONAPARTE LAMAR (1798–1859)

Mirabeau Buonaparte Lamar was born in Georgia in 1798. A firm believer in slavery, he arrived in Texas just before the War of Independence, in which he acquitted himself bravely at the battle of San Jacinto. This brought him to the attention of Sam Houston and subsequent high office. At the time he shared Houston's enthusiasm for annexation.

Houston was not eligible to run in the 1838 Texan presidential elections, when Lamar was one of four candidates. Bizarrely, however, he would soon become the only serious candidate, as his two main rivals died suddenly (one shot himself and the other drowned in the Bay of Galveston). Lamar then received 6,995 votes, while the one remaining candidate received 252.

In his inaugural address he made it clear that he would reverse Houston's policy of negotiation with the Indians and advocated "the prosecution of an exterminating war upon the warriors which will admit of no compromise and have no termination except in their total extinction and total expulsion." This was no idle rhetoric, as his forces then destroyed the Cherokees and Caddos in the east, although they failed to defeat the Comanches in the west.

President Lamar also denounced annexation, arguing instead for an independent Texas that would stretch from coast to coast. He failed to win congressional support for a military campaign to achieve this, but at his own expense recruited volunteers to try and seize Santa Fe as a prelude to taking California. The plan was an abject failure, but it helped to shape US territorial ambitions in the Mexican-American War (1846–48).

Lamar's stewardship of the public finances was a disaster (he was forced to issue "redbacks" with little value) and the republic was saddled with an unsustainable debt at the end of his term. Not surprisingly, therefore, he became once again a supporter of annexation after his term finished. His final reward was a posting to Nicaragua as US ambassador after the fall of William Walker.

what he wanted. The offer of annexation was then dispatched to Texas, where it was unanimously accepted in September 1845.

Texas would now become part of the Union as a slaveholding state. It was never a territory of the United States, and it was unusual in other respects as well. While other states had largely crushed Native American resistance before joining the Union with the help of the federal army, Texas would spend its first three decades as a state engaged in a bloody war that was genocidal in both intent and outcome. The main resistance came from the Comanches, and the instruments of their destruction were the federal troops under Colonel Ranald S. MacKenzie and the Texas Rangers.[8]

2.2. MEXICO

The loss of Texas was a blow to Mexico, but it should not be exaggerated. Although the Republic of Texas may have had vast territorial ambitions, its effective borders were much smaller than the State of Texas today (Map 4). Its southern border stopped at the Nueces River, south of which lay the Mexican states of Tamaulipas and Coahuila. In the west, the borders were disputed but did not yet stretch—as the Texan government claimed—to the Río Bravo del Norte (Río Grande).[9]

Mexico was in fact almost as large in size as the United States, even after the loss of Texas in 1836 (Map 5), although its population was much smaller. However, the Mexican economy was still not increasing as a result of damage to the mines during the war of independence and the subsequent political upheavals. Thus, Mexico had to deal with the threat from the north with a shrunken economy that did not generate sufficient resources for defense expenditure on troops and equipment.

Mexico was also stretched militarily. Spain had tried to retake its former colony in 1829, the province of Yucatán had declared independence in the same year that the Republic of Texas was formed, and two years later (in 1838) the French had invaded Vera Cruz. Although Mexico had some successes (the Spanish and French threats were neutralized, and Spain recognized Mexican independence in 1836), all this left Mexico very vulnerable to any hostile American action.

The biggest concern for Mexico was California.[10] Although the Adams-Onís Treaty in 1819 had opened a route to the Pacific for the United States through Oregon, by general consent the best harbors were further south and the best of all was San Francisco in California. Adams himself during his presidency (1825–29) had claimed to be the first statesman to raise the question of US

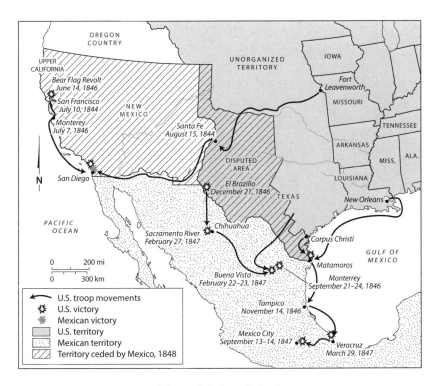

Map 5. Mexico, 1846–48

ownership of California, but he had in mind acquisition through purchase rather than war.

Those that followed John Quincy Adams were not so circumspect. Secretary of State Daniel Webster had raised the question with Lord Ashburton in 1842 and had been told that the United Kingdom would have no objection. It was Andrew Jackson, however, who was most explicit. When trying to explain to a puzzled Texan government why the US president was reluctant to proceed with annexation, William Wharton, minister of Texas to the United States, summarized Jackson's view: "General Jackson says that Texas must claim the Californias on the Pacific, in order to paralyze the opposition of the North and East to annexation. . . . He is very earnest and anxious on this point of claiming the Californias, and says we must not consent to less."[11]

Similar sentiments were expressed by many others, including Sir George Simpson in 1842, who—when visiting the Swiss adventurer Captain John Sutter—stated that "if he [Sutter] had the talent and courage to make the most of his position, he is not unlikely to render California a second Texas."[12] Sutter, of course, made his mark in another way by confirming the existence of gold in the Sacramento Valley at the end of the Mexican-American War.

Texas had not consolidated a hold over California by the time of annexation despite the best efforts of President Lamar (Box 2.1). It was therefore left to President Polk (1845–49), agitated by an unfounded rumor of British pretensions to California, to put the case more forcibly. Writing to Senator Thomas Hart Benton in October 1845, he cited the Monroe Doctrine and claimed that in his diplomatic policy "I had California and the fine bay of San Francisco as much in view as Oregon."[13]

All that Polk—a firm believer in Manifest Destiny (Box 2.2)—needed was a *casus belli*, and it was not long in coming. The annexation of Texas, confirmed by the Senate in January 1846, could not fail to elicit a response from Mexico. Although the odds were stacked against her, she essentially faced a choice of defeat with honor or capitulation with dishonor and chose the former. When Polk ordered General Zachary Taylor to place his troops south of the Nueces River, it was inevitable that Mexican forces would respond.[14]

Polk now claimed that the United States had been attacked on American soil, which assumed that the area between the Nueces and the Río Grande was US territory. It was an outrageous claim, but patriotic fervor was enough to secure congressional support for war. A few brave souls, including John Quincy Adams, voted against it, and Abraham Lincoln (who took his seat only after the vote) would make a name for himself with his eight "spot" resolutions calling on Polk to explain exactly where on US soil American forces had been attacked.

US forces advanced on several fronts (Map 5). California, where the Bear Flag Republic had been created in 1846,[15] was swiftly occupied with little resistance. Fighting in northern Mexico was fiercer, however, so the Americans allowed Santa Anna to return from exile in the hope that he would quickly sue for peace. When he did not, General Winfield Scott was dispatched to seize the port of Vera Cruz, from which Mexico derived so much of its customs revenue. Scott then proceeded inland and occupied Mexico City.

Mexican casualties were high. However, losses on the US side were also substantial, although most of these were due to illness and poor sanitation. And there were plenty of critics of the war even among the officers themselves. Colonel Ethan Allen Hitchcock, writing in his diary in 1846, claimed, "I have said from the first that the United States are the aggressors. We have outraged the Mexican government and people by an arrogance and presumption that deserve to be punished. For ten years we have been encroaching on Mexico and insulting her. . . . But now, I see, the United States of America, as a people, are under-

BOX 2.2

MANIFEST DESTINY

Although the phrase "Manifest Destiny" was believed to have been coined first by John O'Sullivan in 1845, it was perhaps best expressed much earlier in the words of the great Spanish diplomat Luis de Onís himself: "They consider themselves superior to the rest of mankind and look upon their Republic as the only establishment upon earth, founded upon a grand and solid basis, embellished by wisdom, and destined one day to become the most sublime colossus of human power, and the wonder of the universe" (Lowrie, *Culture Conflict*, 96, quoting Onís's memoirs).

Onís drew attention to two facets of "Manifest Destiny": American exceptionalism and the inevitably of expansion. However, he did not mention a third (a belief in racial superiority) that was perhaps best expressed by O'Sullivan himself. In the same article in which he first used the phrase "Manifest Destiny," he justified taking California from Mexico in the following terms: "The Anglo-Saxon foot is already [1845] on its borders. Already the advance guard of the irresistible army of Anglo-Saxon emigration has begun to pour down upon it, armed with the plough and rifle, and marking its trail with schools and colleges, courts and representative halls, mills and meeting-houses."

Manifest Destiny was not universally supported nor could it be used to justify empire where the nonwhite population was too large to be "removed." John Calhoun, for example, denounced Mexican annexation in the Senate in 1848 precisely because it risked diluting the racial "purity" of the United States:

> We have never dreamt of incorporating into our Union any but the Caucasian race—the free white race. To incorporate Mexico, would be the very first instance of the kind, of incorporating an Indian race; for more than half of the Mexicans are Indians, and the other is composed chiefly of mixed tribes. I protest against such a union as that! Ours, sir, is the Government of a white race. . . . We are anxious to force free government on all; and I see that it has been urged . . . that it is the mission of this country to spread civil and religious liberty over all the world, and especially over this continent. It is a great mistake.

going changes in character, and the real status and principles for which our forefathers fought are fast being lost sight of."[16]

By late 1847 Mexico was desperate for peace at almost any price. Polk and his secretary of state, James Buchanan, sent a draft treaty to Nicholas Trist, the presidential envoy in Mexico. It called for the cession of all Mexican territory north and east of the Río Grande as well as New Mexico and the two Californias. Anticipating the need for an isthmian route that these cessions would entail, it also called for rights of passage through the Isthmus of Tehuantepec and a payment of $15 million to Mexico.

The United States could easily have forced Mexico to agree, but by a strange twist of fate it did not turn out that way. Trist was recalled by Polk in October 1847 on the grounds that he was untrustworthy, but he chose to ignore the order. He then negotiated a separate treaty, which left out Baja California and the rights of passage through the Isthmus of Tehuantepec. Polk was furious, but chose to accept it anyway with only one change (he removed the clause guaranteeing Mexican land titles in the ceded areas). The Treaty of Guadalupe-Hidalgo, as it was called, was then passed by the Senate in March 1848.

When Polk left office the following year, he might have assumed that the United States had taken all it needed from Mexico. However, territorial cession surfaced again a few years later, when James Gadsden, a railway entrepreneur and US minister to Mexico, persuaded Jefferson Davis, secretary of war in the government of President Franklin Pierce (1853–57), that the best route for a railroad between Charleston and California lay south of the border. By then Santa Anna was back in power and in desperate need of funds. The Gadsden Purchase, as it became known, was duly carried out in December 1853 in return for $10 million.

The prospect of acquiring additional territory from Mexico had raised questions about slavery as soon as the war started. In August 1846 David Wilmot, a Democrat, added a clause to an appropriations bill to the effect that slavery would not be permitted in any of the land taken from the southern neighbor. The Wilmot "proviso" did not pass, but it left on the table an unanswered question: Would slavery be permitted in the new territories?

The answer came four years later in the Compromise of 1850. Drafted by Henry Clay, this consisted of eight resolutions. It excluded slavery from California, but any other territories formed out of the Mexican acquisitions would be free to decide what to do. It ended the slave trade from neighboring states into the District of Columbia, but introduced a much tougher fugitive slave law for the restitution of "persons bound to service or labor, in any State, who may escape into any other State or Territory of this Union."[17]

Slavery was excluded from California because it was impossible to delay a decision (events had moved so fast), and allowing slavery there would have been politically difficult. The Russians had dismantled the last of their forts in 1842, when the non-Indian population of Alta California was around 5,000 and that of US settlers as few as 360. The discovery of gold in January 1848 then led to mass immigration, and the non-Indian population had jumped to 107,000 by January 1850.[18]

This was large enough for California to jump to statehood without first becoming a US territory, and it duly entered the Union in September 1850. Subjugation of the Indian population was therefore conducted after statehood rather than before, with a leading role played by the white settlers themselves rather than federal troops.[19] This also happened in Texas, and in both cases the consequences were especially tragic for the Native Americans.

The Spanish had only settled Alta California in the late eighteenth century. As a result, it still had a large Indian population. This was soon reduced by disease as a result of contact with the Europeans, but as late as 1849 it was still estimated at 100,000. By 1860, however, it had collapsed to 35,000, and by 1890 it had fallen to 18,000. This time disease was not the main factor.

The rapid immigration of settlers to California after the Mexican-American War led to competition for resources leading to starvation in many cases. The state legislature passed an antivagrancy law for the indenture of "loitering and orphaned" Indians that was little better than slavery (boys and girls as young as twelve were taken). Settlers took matters into their own hands and carried out numerous massacres. It is difficult to disagree with Russell Thornton's assessment that "California is the one place in the United States where few would dispute that a genocide of Native Americans occurred."[20]

The Compromise of 1850 not only admitted California to the Union as a state but also established two new territories: New Mexico and Utah (with boundaries much bigger than these states today).[21] Expectations were high that the territories would soon enter the Union as states. New Mexico in particular, with its capital at Santa Fe, had a relatively large non-Indian population, although Utah's population—where the Mormons under Brigham Young had established themselves—was smaller.

These expectations had to be rapidly changed. Even before the territory of New Mexico was formed, the governor (appointed by the US military) had been murdered by an alliance of Mexicans and Indians. There then followed a series of wars against the Apaches in particular that started in 1849 and did not end until the surrender of Geronimo in 1886. Even then, sporadic fighting continued until Indian resistance was finally broken in 1906.[22]

Statehood therefore took decades to achieve for some parts of the territories acquired from Mexico. After California, Nevada was the first to become a state. It was separated from Utah Territory in 1861, following the discovery of silver, and joined the Union after a mere three years, as silver was such a vital commodity in the Civil War. Utah, whose first governor had been Brigham Young himself, was the second although it had to wait until 1896 in view of the controversies surrounding the Mormon religion.[23]

New Mexico took even longer as a result, above all, of the Indian Wars. The Confederacy in 1861 established Arizona Territory in the south, to which the Union responded in 1863 by creating its own Arizona Territory and splitting off the western half of New Mexico. There was then a long hiatus until Arizona and New Mexico joined the Union in 1912. By this time they had spent sixty-two years under territorial government, during which they were effectively US colonies. Indeed, when Arizonan Barry Goldwater declared his presidential candidacy, his opponents ruled that he was not eligible to run as he had been born outside the United States.[24]

2.3. PANAMA

The Gadsden Purchase had given the US government the rights of passage across the Isthmus of Tehuantepec denied by the Treaty of Guadalupe-Hidalgo. However, the new treaty left the proposed railroad under the control of Mexico. Much more promising for US ambitions to have exclusive control of an isthmian route, therefore, was the Bidlack-Mallarino Treaty between the United States and New Granada (today Colombia)[25] signed in 1846 and ratified two years later.

This treaty not only gave guarantees "that the right of way or transit across the *Isthmus of Panama,* upon any modes of communication that now exist or that may be hereafter constructed, shall be open and free to the government and citizens of the United States," but also committed the United States to maintain the "perfect neutrality" of the isthmus and to guarantee "the rights of sovereignty and property which New Granada has and possesses over the said territory."[26]

The prospects for building a canal across the isthmus did not look good at the time in view of the engineering obstacles, but a railway was another matter. A private US company was established for this purpose, work began in 1852, and it was completed in 1855. This was too late to take advantage of those seeking to reach California in time for the gold rush, but it was still a very profitable operation from the start.

The US government was now responsible under the terms of the 1846 treaty for protecting the route in the event of any local disturbance. This was not uncommon in nineteenth-century Colombia and the United States would find itself embroiled in numerous political disputes before the century ended.

The first year in which US troops were landed in Panama was 1856. This was followed by military interventions in 1860, 1865, 1868, 1873, 1885, and 1895. And these interventions could have major implications. In 1885, for example, US troops put down a rebellion by members of the Liberal Party that restored the Conservatives to power and led to the harsh dictatorship of Rafael Núñez.

The 1846 treaty had therefore converted the province of Panama into a US protectorate. This suited the purposes of President Polk and his immediate successors, but it was President Lincoln (1861–65) who came closest to creating a US colony in Panama in the nineteenth century. In his address to leaders of the free blacks at the White House in August 1862, he said, "But for your race among us there could not be war, although many men engaged on either side do not care for you one way or the other. . . . It is better for us both, therefore, to be separated. . . . The place I am thinking about having for a colony is in Central America. . . . The particular place I have in view is to be a great highway from the Atlantic or Caribbean Sea to the Pacific Ocean, and this particular place has all the advantages for a colony."[27]

Lincoln did not mention the isthmus by name, but the "particular place" he had in mind was western Panama, where the Chiriqui Improvement Company had been established. He had already instructed his secretary of the interior to purchase two million acres from the US-controlled company established there, and he had secured $600,000 from Congress for his colonization scheme.

It is perhaps fortunate for Lincoln's future reputation that the scheme never took off. Most black leaders, including Frederick Douglass, opposed it as racist. In addition, Lincoln had failed to take into account that he would need a treaty with Colombia if the scheme were to go ahead. In the end, therefore, the idea was dropped, although Lincoln did finance a colonization scheme for free blacks in Haiti that was a miserable failure.[28]

The 1846 treaty required the United States to guarantee the "perfect neutrality" of the isthmus, but it had not explicitly authorized the use of force. To resolve this uncertainty, successive administrations from President Pierce onward negotiated a series of treaties with the Colombian authorities. Yet none of these were ratified, as a result of reservations either by the Colombian or US senates (the former argued that the treaty in question gave away too much, while the latter claimed that it ceded too little).

The first of these treaties set the tone. Following a riot in Panama in 1856 that caused much loss of life and property, the US negotiators were able to persuade the Colombian executive to sign a treaty which

> provided that the United States government should buy, for cash, all New Granada's reserved rights in the railroad, and also secure control of strategic islands in the harbors at either terminus, for naval stations. Then, in order to provide for the neutralization of the route, in fact as well as in theory, [the negotiators] also proposed that a belt of land twenty miles broad, lying on both sides of the railway line, and extending from sea to sea, be carved out of the territory of New Granada and handed over to the jurisdiction of two free municipalities to be established in Aspinwall [modern Colón] and Panama [City].[29]

This treaty, if implemented, would have undoubtedly created a US colony on the isthmus, so it is not surprising that the Colombian Senate baulked at the idea. Yet the next treaty in 1869 went even further, as it would have given the United States "the sole right of constructing a canal" and allowed the nation "to employ their military forces if the occasion should arise." When in another treaty the following year the Colombian negotiators stripped out a reference to the use of force, it was the US Congress that refused to ratify. The last of these treaties was in 1902, which was unanimously rejected by the Colombian Senate on the grounds that the hundred years proposed for US control of the proposed canal was too long.

Frustrated by its inability to conclude a deal with the United States that would have led to the construction of a canal, the Colombian government was very receptive to a French proposal put forward in 1876 by Ferdinand de Lesseps. Flushed with his success in building the Suez Canal, Lesseps expected to have no trouble in raising the initial funds. However, he needed to avoid outright opposition from the United States if the scheme was to have a reasonable chance of success.

In this he was to be disappointed. In a meeting at the White House with Lesseps, President Rutherford B. Hayes (1877–81) was very candid:

> I deem it proper to state briefly my opinion as to the policy of the United States with respect to the construction of an inter-oceanic canal by any route across the American Isthmus. The policy of this country is a canal under American control. The United States cannot consent to the surrender of this control to any European powers. If existing treaties between the United States and other nations, or if the rights of sovereignty or property of other nations stand in the way of this policy—a contingency which is not apprehended—suitable steps

should be taken by just and liberal negotiations to promote and establish the American policy on this subject, consistently with the rights of the nations to be affected by it.[30]

Despite this, the project went ahead in 1882 with the subsequent participation of Philippe Bunau-Varilla (Box 2.3). Fortunately for the American government, however, Lesseps misjudged the engineering complexities of building the canal, exhausted the funds in inflated expenses, and was soon unable to secure additional loans. The French canal scheme then collapsed in 1888 after the death of thousands of workers (only twenty miles of the route was completed).

The collapse of the French scheme confirmed the view of those in the United States who had always regarded the Nicaraguan route as superior on financial and engineering grounds. However, progress toward the construction of a canal through Nicaragua was blocked in the 1890s (see below). Thus, when Theodore Roosevelt became president in September 1901,[31] US attention was once again focused on Panama. When a "revolution" took place on the isthmus on November 3, 1903, the leaders proclaimed Panama's independence and asked for US recognition. This was given three days later, US warships were dispatched to both sides of the isthmus, and Colombian troops were prevented from reaching Panama City.[32]

Converting "independent" Panama into a US protectorate was now a simple matter since the leaders of the 1903 revolt owed their victory to US support. Two weeks after independence, a treaty was signed giving America sovereignty in perpetuity over a new Canal Zone (ten miles wide across the center of the country) and the right to intervene in Panama City and Colón (both outside the zone) to maintain public order.[33] Subsequently, Panama placed the United States in charge of collecting customs duties (the largest source of government revenue), with the US dollar as the country's currency.

Despite these extraordinary powers, the United States often had difficulty in mediating disputes between local politicians. America at first favored the Conservative faction and one of their leaders, Manuel Amador, was installed as president in 1904. The Liberals were then dissatisfied and sought US support for a change of government. These sometimes violent struggles among the political elites continued for nearly three decades. However, there was never any threat to US strategic interests, as all participants understood very clearly the rules of the imperial game.

Following a coup in 1931, Panamanian politics changed abruptly. The revolt brought to power Harmodio Arias, who—with his brother Arnulfo—would

BOX 2.3
PHILIPPE BUNAU-VARILLA ("MR. CANAL")

President Theodore Roosevelt (1901–9) would have built an isthmian canal during his tenure under almost any circumstances. However, his choice of Panama over Nicaragua was greatly influenced by Philippe Bunau-Varilla, a Frenchman born in Paris in 1859. Bunau-Varilla went to Panama in 1884 to work for Ferdinand de Lesseps in the Panama Canal Company. The company collapsed in 1888, but another firm—the New Panama Canal Company—was established in 1894 with Bunau-Varilla as an investor.

As late as 1901 the US government still favored Nicaragua as the route for a canal. Bunau-Varilla, however, was determined that the US government should choose Panama. He campaigned tirelessly through many states and even sent to all US senators postage stamps of Mount Momotombo in Nicaragua erupting. He hoped in this way to demonstrate the riskiness of the Nicaraguan route.

These efforts paid off, as the Senate in June 1902 passed the Spooner Act under which the New Panama Canal Company would be purchased for $40 million if Colombia would agree to a treaty allowing for a canal to be built under exclusive US control. This treaty was signed, but Colombia did not ratify it. Bunau-Varilla therefore provided funds to dissidents in Panama and persuaded them that they could count on US recognition if they led an uprising against Colombia. He even brought them to Washington, DC, and presented them with a draft constitution (his flag design, however, was later rejected). The revolt then took place on November 3, 1903.

As soon as the Roosevelt administration recognized the independence of Panama, Bunau-Varilla had himself declared ambassador of Panama to the United States. He then negotiated in a few days the infamous treaty that bears his name (the Hay–Bunau-Varilla Treaty). This gave the United States everything that it desired. No Panamanian signed this treaty, but the leaders of the revolt felt they had no choice but to ratify it on December 2, 1903. Bunau-Varilla later returned to France, where he fought in the First World War and lost a leg at the Battle of Verdun. He died in 1940, having campaigned to the end to convert the canal from a system of locks to a sea-level waterway.

dominate the political scene for decades. Indeed, the last time one of the brothers occupied the presidency was as late as 1968. The family would also achieve notoriety outside Panama, while one of Harmodio's sons (Roberto) married the brilliant British ballerina Margot Fonteyn in 1955.[34]

The Arias brothers were no anti-imperialist radicals, but they were nationalists and sought to build a Panamanian identity. This inevitably involved many clashes with the United States. Their main target was the one-sided 1903 treaty. Their efforts, helped by the launch of the Good Neighbor policy of President Franklin Delano Roosevelt (1933–45),[35] eventually bore fruit in 1936 with a renegotiation of the treaty in which the United States gave up the right to intervene unilaterally in Panamanian affairs and to pay a larger annual subvention for use of the canal.[36]

The treaty revisions did not end Panama's status as a protectorate, as the United States did not give up its military bases or its fiscal and monetary control of the country. And, of course, it also kept the Panama Canal Zone as a US territory. Nor did it cease to intervene in local affairs since the treaty said nothing about favoring one faction over another. And without US support, no Panamanian leader could survive for long.

This was made abundantly clear a few years after the new treaty was ratified when Arnulfo Arias became president in October 1940. Since he was convinced Germany would win the Second World War (he had been Panama's ambassador to both Adolf Hitler's Germany and Benito Mussolini's Italy, and had fascist sympathies), he became increasingly suspect in US eyes. His unauthorized departure as president from the country in 1941 became the opportunity for him to be replaced with a more pliant ruler.

No US troops were used, and no articles of the new American-Panamanian treaty had been broken. Instead, the next president had consulted with the chief of civil intelligence in the Canal Zone who confirmed that the United States would be happy to see Arnulfo Arias removed from office. This information was all that was needed for the plotters and, indeed, for those who had supported Arias up to that moment.

Despite the treaty revisions, the United States intervened in Panama and the Canal Zone on numerous occasions—the last time being the military invasion in 1989. By then, however, the US Senate had ratified the 1977 Canal Treaties under which the Canal Zone would cease to exist on October 1, 1979, making it no longer a US territory, and a Panama Canal Commission would gradually take control of the operation of the canal by December 31, 1999.[37] At that point the Panamanian protectorate that had begun 150 years before finally came to an end.

2.4. NICARAGUA

Although the isthmian canal was eventually built in Panama, there had been an international consensus throughout almost all the nineteenth century that a canal through Nicaragua offered the best prospects. As soon as the Spanish empire ended, therefore, there was competition among the imperial powers to establish control over what would become the Republic of Nicaragua.[38] The US government was the first of these powers to recognize the United Provinces of Central America[39] after the new country declared its independence from Mexico and a US canal company was formed in 1826.[40]

Unfortunately for the United States, the British were already firmly ensconced in the region. The Belize Settlement was being transformed into a British colony, the Bay Islands off the northern coast of Honduras were occupied in 1842, and Great Britain was rebuilding its protectorate over Mosquitia—the eastern portion of Nicaragua and Honduras.[41] The British government was even laying claim to the coast of Costa Rica and an island off Panama, potentially giving it control over all Caribbean points of entry to an isthmian canal.

What followed was therefore an intense rivalry between the old (UK) and new (US) imperial powers for hegemony over Nicaragua, in which two diplomats in Central America played a leading part: Ephraim Squier for the United States and Frederick Chatfield for Great Britain. However, the struggle was orchestrated from London and Washington, DC, becoming increasingly bitter and dangerous.

All surveys had agreed that the best route for the Nicaraguan canal starting on the Caribbean side involved navigation up the Río San Juan to the Lago de Nicaragua. This river, which marks the border between Costa Rica and Nicaragua for most of its length, reaches the sea at the port of San Juan. Since the town lay within the territory claimed by Great Britain as part of the Mosquitia protectorate, the British government seized it in January 1848, expelled the Nicaraguan commandant, and changed the name to Greytown.[42]

The Nicaraguan government protested in vain. However, a year later—under the stimulus of the Californian gold rush—it signed an agreement with Cornelius Vanderbilt establishing a Companía de Tránsito de Nicaragua (known in English as the Accessory Transit Company) to ferry people and goods across the isthmus. Since the route taken passed through San Juan, the US government now had even more reason to challenge what was seen as a breach by the United Kingdom of the Monroe Doctrine.

Ephraim Squier acted swiftly. First, he secured a treaty with the Nicaraguan government for construction of a canal by Vanderbilt's company under exclusive US control. This provided land for US colonization across the isthmus and a monopoly for the company of steam navigation on Nicaragua's lakes and rivers. Second, he signed a treaty with the Honduran government that ceded Tigre Island in the Gulf of Fonseca, where the canal was expected to enter the Pacific, as well as land for fortifications on the Honduran coast.[43]

Squier's actions were designed to create US protectorates in both Honduras and Nicaragua, and they threatened to stymie British plans for building a canal since the United States would have been left in control of the waters guarding the entrance to a canal on the Pacific side. The British Navy therefore seized Tigre Island before the United States could occupy it and refused to back down when the United States threatened war.

It was time for cooler heads, and the result was the Clayton-Bulwer Treaty of 1850. This treaty recognized that neither the United Kingdom nor the United States was strong enough to impose its will on the other in Central America and that neither would seek to establish exclusive control over a ship canal "which may be constructed between the Atlantic and Pacific Oceans by way of the river San Juan de Nicaragua and either or both of the lakes of Nicaragua or Managua."[44]

The Clayton-Bulwer Treaty was seen at the time as a triumph for US diplomacy and a defeat for the British. However, the wording was highly ambiguous and would soon cause a great deal of friction. Furthermore, as the US government became increasingly committed to a canal through Nicaragua under its exclusive control, it looked for ways to abrogate or revise the treaty. The British stubbornly refused to comply on the grounds that the treaty had been signed and ratified in good faith by both parties.

The US government therefore turned its attention to Nicaragua itself. However, the embarrassing Walker episode in the 1850s (Box 2.4) created a poisonous legacy for the United States that has still not entirely drained. The best that US diplomacy could manage, therefore, was the 1868 Dickinson-Ayon Treaty.[45]

The treaty gave the United States much that it desired, but it could make no mention of "exclusive" control in view of the wording of the Clayton-Bulwer Treaty. The sense of frustration deepened with the publication in 1890 of Alfred Thayer Mahan's *The Influence of Sea Power upon History*, which was widely interpreted as presenting an overwhelming case for an interoceanic canal to enhance US naval power. And, of course, that canal had to be controlled exclusively by the United States itself.

It was not until 1901 that America was finally able to persuade the British to abrogate the 1850 treaty and sign a new one giving the United States exclusive control over any isthmian canal. This was the Hay-Pauncefote Treaty. The British

BOX 2.4
WILLIAM WALKER ("THE GREY-EYED MAN OF DESTINY")

William Walker was born in Tennessee and had a distinguished education. A strong believer in Manifest Destiny, he was convinced that the decision not to push the US boundaries further south after the war with Mexico was a mistake. He therefore led a filibuster to Baja California in 1853, had himself declared president of the Republic of Sonora (in which he included Baja California), and legalized slavery.

After he was expelled by the Mexican Army, he accepted an invitation from the Liberals in Nicaragua to help them in their civil war with the Conservatives. He arrived in 1855 and the Liberals took power the following year. Walker was at first content with the role of commander in chief, but by July 1856 he had made himself president of Nicaragua through a fraudulent election.

His government legalized slavery, made English the official language, and planned to take over all Central America. These actions ensured the opposition not only of many in Nicaragua but also the governments of other Central American countries. In addition, he foolishly made an enemy of Cornelius Vanderbilt, whose Accessory Transit Company was a major power in Nicaragua. The combination of all these forces was sufficient to defeat Walker militarily in May 1857.

All this could have been dismissed as *opera buffa* were it not for the ambiguous relationship Walker enjoyed with the United States. President Franklin Pierce (1804–69) gave diplomatic recognition to Walker's Nicaragua in 1856. When he surrendered to the US Navy in 1857, he was not handed back to the Nicaraguan authorities. When he was charged in New Orleans in 1858 with breaking US neutrality laws, he was acquitted. When he returned to Nicaragua in 1859, he was arrested by the US Navy and then released on the orders of the administration of President James Buchanan (1857–61).

Walker made a third attempt to reach Nicaragua. This time he landed at Trujillo in Honduras, where locals turned him over to the British Navy. They in turn handed him to the Honduran government, who ordered him to be shot in September 1860.

resisted as long as possible, but eventually accepted the inevitable and ratified the treaty.

By this time President José Santos Zelaya (1893–1909) was in power in Nicaragua and he had every reason to assume that the canal would now be built in his country. Not only were all the US engineering studies, interoceanic commissions, and congressional reports pointing in that direction, but Zelaya himself in 1894 had also incorporated Mosquitia into Nicaragua and ended the threat of British intervention.[46]

The news that the canal would be built through Panama was, therefore, not well received by President Zelaya. Not surprisingly, he tried to keep his options open and turned to Germany and Japan to initiate negotiations on financing an interoceanic canal through Nicaragua that would have posed a considerable threat to the commercial success of the Panama Canal if it had been built. It would also have given a potential enemy a big stake in the region.

When news of these arrangements reached Washington, DC, it meant that a red line had been crossed. Plans were made to remove Zelaya, and a local "revolution" would provide the perfect excuse. At the end of 1909, US troops briefly landed on the Caribbean coast and a familiar pattern was repeated. A customs receivership was established in 1911, which continued until 1947. Loans to European creditors were replaced with loans to US bankers. A "loyal" politician was maneuvered into the presidency. A US protectorate over Nicaragua, which had been threatening since the 1840s, had finally become a reality.[47]

This exercise in US imperialism had not, however, taken account of the deep divisions in Nicaraguan society between Conservatives and Liberals. With Zelaya (a Liberal) in exile, the leaders of both parties understood perfectly the unwritten bargain between the United States and a protectorate. However, they could not work with each other. Thus, political instability reached a high level, and the US Marines returned in 1912. This time, it would be a long stay.[48]

One of the first acts of the US occupation was to prepare the ground for a treaty that would settle the canal question once and for all. This was the Bryan-Chamorro Treaty of 1916, which gave the United States rights to any canal built in Nicaragua in perpetuity and a renewable ninety-nine-year option to establish a naval base in the Gulf of Fonseca. The United States, of course, now had no intention of building such a canal, but the treaty ensured that no other country could do so.[49]

A series of pliant Conservative leaders lulled the occupying force into a sense of complacency. Indeed, one—Adolfo Díaz—had even proposed annexation by the United States in 1924. When the marines left in 1925, however, it led to a period of deep political instability and the troops returned the following year.

Henry Stimson, US secretary of state, would then negotiate a pact with both Nicaraguan parties that bore a striking similarity to those in Haiti and the Dominican Republic (see Chapter 4). In particular, it led to the formation of an allegedly nonpartisan national guard.[50]

Resistance to the US-brokered pact was led by Augusto César Sandino, an army officer and a nationalist. The guerrilla forces had inferior weapons, but they could not be defeated. Sandino and his followers survived in the mountains until the last US troops had left in 1933. By this time, the United States had chosen as the head of the national guard a young officer called Anastasio Somoza, who would trick Sandino into accepting negotiations in February 1934 and then assassinate him. Despite this, or perhaps because of this, Somoza remained a firm favorite of US officials in the country.[51]

His "reward" was to be the presidency of Nicaragua, which he held directly and indirectly until his own assassination in 1956. Somoza was a consummate player of the imperial game and knew exactly what he needed to do to retain US support. Indeed, on one of his official visits to Washington, DC, he allegedly provoked the comment from President Franklin Roosevelt that "he may be a son of a bitch, but he's our son of a bitch."[52]

Anastasio Somoza was followed by his two sons, the first of whom died in 1963. The second son ruled until 1979 as head of a regime that became increasingly brutal and eventually lost US support. He was overthrown by the Sandinistas in a revolution that subsequently disappointed many of its supporters, although it did end the country's status as a US client state.[53]

Control of Nicaragua and Panama for most of the twentieth century met US security needs in Central America. However, imperialist countries are always sensitive to the need to neutralize any threat that might arise to their colonies, protectorates, or client states from neighboring countries. In particular, the United States was anxious to avoid any government coming to power that could threaten its vital strategic interests in the region. Additional strategies were therefore needed for the rest of Central America.

Following a peace conference hosted in Washington, DC, by the United States, the Central American states established in 1907 a Central American Court of Justice, with its headquarters in Costa Rica. The expectation was that the court would uphold the rule of law and therefore protect US interests. It started well, but the United States lost interest when the Court ruled that Nicaragua was acting illegally when it granted America a ninety-nine-year lease on the Corn Islands in the Caribbean.[54]

The United States then called another conference, which led in 1923 to the Central American International Tribunal, with its headquarters in Washington,

DC, and fifteen judges appointed by the US government. The tribunal, which operated for nearly a decade, was an early example of US imperial power relying on control of institutions.[55]

US imperial control in Central America was more complete than in any other part of the world. Yet, apart from the Panama Canal Zone, it did not depend on colonies. Control was exercised through protectorates in Nicaragua and Panama and client states elsewhere (Costa Rica, El Salvador, Guatemala, and Honduras). In 1920, for example, Franklin Roosevelt—at the time a vice presidential nominee—could boast that the United States controlled the votes of all six Central American countries in the proposed League of Nations.[56]

3

Africa and the Pacific

One of the more commonly held myths about the US empire is that it did not go "offshore" until after the Spanish-American War in 1898. Long before then, however, American imperialism had penetrated different parts of the world outside the western hemisphere. This chapter looks at the process by which American empire was extended to Africa and the Pacific.

There was no uniform pattern by which US influence spread and imperial acquisitions ranged from territories (i.e., colonies) to protectorates and—in the case of China—treaty port concessions. Yet this was no different from what happened in European empires. British India, for example, was ruled by a private company (the East India Company) until 1858 and yet only a pedant would argue that it was not part of the British Empire before then.

US interest in the Pacific was awakened by the Meriwether Lewis and William Clark expedition at the start of the nineteenth century, but it was not until the Adams-Onís Treaty of 1819 gave the country a foothold on the Pacific shore that anything significant could be done about it. From that point onward, the United States was determined to dislodge as far as possible other imperial powers along the coast. When Mexico in 1821 replaced imperial Spain as the sovereign power south of Oregon Country, the same applied to her.

Spain's trade with China, routed through Acapulco in Mexico and Manila in the Philippines, had long excited the interest of other empires. It was no different with the United States. A Pacific coastline gave America its chance to gain access to the fabled Chinese market, with its millions of consumers, as long as it was not excluded either by China itself or by other imperial powers. China and the surrounding countries were also a magnet for US missionaries seeking to spread the message of Christianity.

Even before Commodore Matthew Perry in 1854 sailed into Edo (Tokyo) Harbor, the United States had demonstrated its commercial and diplomatic prowess in the region. It had also shown the skill of its navy. Yet the opening of the Japanese market as well as footholds in China required a more strategic approach to the Pacific. Using the Guano Islands Act in 1856 as a first step, a string of islands was secured across the Pacific that could be used by US ships.

The territorial presence included bigger islands as well. Hawaii was brought into the US sphere of influence as a protectorate long before annexation in 1898, while the United States almost went to war with Great Britain and Germany in order to gain control of part of Samoa. And Alaska, of course, was purchased from Russia in 1867, leaving the United States in control of the whole North American Pacific coastline except for British Columbia in Canada.

The US empire was therefore well established in the region before the Spanish-American War. However, success in that war brought new imperial possessions in the Pacific—notably the Philippines and Guam (one of the Mariana Islands). The other (northern) Mariana Islands, on the other hand, were sold by Spain to Germany in 1899, as the United States had no use for them at the time.

When Germany was defeated in the First World War, it might have been expected that the Northern Marianas and other German-controlled islands would be claimed by the United States. However, the islands were taken by Japan as part of the spoils of war. It was not until the end of the Second World War that the Japanese-controlled islands were formed into the Trust Territory of the Pacific Islands (TTPI) and placed under US control by the United Nations (the organization that replaced the League of Nations).

With the occupation of Japan and part of the Korean Peninsula, the United States then extended its formidable imperial presence in the Pacific even further. At the same time, although the Philippines may have been formally decolonized in 1946, the independence treaty—together with huge naval and air bases—ensured that the country would remain inside the US sphere of influence as a protectorate. And when the TTPI ended in the 1980s, some islands simply became US protectorates, while the Northern Mariana Islands chose to remain a US colony with a similar status to Puerto Rico.

The empire that the United States built in the Pacific in the nineteenth century demonstrated that America could even then match the imperial ambitions of any other country. And as soon as the Spanish-American War concluded, the European powers began to recognize the United States as "first among equals" in the regional struggle for power and influence. The two world wars then left the United States in a hegemonic position, untroubled by the remaining European presence and yet to face serious competition from China.

Africa never excited the same imperial interest in the United States as the Pacific, but it would be wrong to say there was none. The Barbary Wars, it is true, were fought by the United States in self-defense and were therefore not imperial conflicts. However, the end of the legal slave trade in 1808 and the growing numbers of free blacks in the United States drove interest in African colonization. This culminated in the establishment of the American Colonization Society (ACS) at the end of 1816.

The ACS, a private organization, is best known for the foundation of a series of colonies in West Africa that eventually came together to form the Commonwealth of Liberia. However, these efforts would never have prospered without the support of the US federal government. Thus, right from the start Liberia can be considered an American colony. Indeed, it was a form of settler colonialism very similar to what was happening in the US mainland territories, though with the settlers (Libero Americans) being black rather than white.

Liberia declared "independence" in 1847. However, a treaty of recognition, delayed until 1862 because of southern opposition, gave the United States the right to intervene under certain circumstances. By 1912 Liberia had formally become a US protectorate with a customs receivership and various other restrictions on national sovereignty. Even when the receivership ended, Liberia remained in the US sphere of influence as a client state, with the US dollar as its currency and one of the most pro-American foreign policy regimes in the world.

The United States did not participate in the "scramble for Africa" after the Berlin Conference (1884–85) organized by Chancellor Otto von Bismarck of Germany. Yet it was invited to the conference and sent a strong delegation to sit alongside the other imperial powers (Box 3.1). The delegates, including Henry Morton Stanley, then backed the plans of King Leopold of Belgium for a Congo Free State in the belief that this—rather than formal colonies—would secure US interests on the subcontinent. It was not until after the Second World War that the United States would raise its voice against European imperialism in Africa, and even then it would be highly selective.

3.1. LIBERIA

When the first US census was held in 1790, the category "all other free persons" contained around fifty thousand people (just over 1 percent of the population). These free blacks were not regarded as the social or political equals of their white counterparts in the nonslave states and were treated with deep suspicion in the slave ones. As their numbers increased, both black and white opinion divided between those who favored integration and those who championed the establishments of colonies to which the free blacks would be encouraged to move.

Thomas Jefferson was among the most vocal who favored colonies. Indeed, he had promoted the idea as early as 1777 when drafting a new constitution for Virginia.[1] Later, as president, he tried to persuade the British government to allow freed slaves to move to the colony of Sierra Leone in West Africa (the request was rejected). After the abolition of the slave trade in 1808, however, the matter became more urgent for the US government as slaves intercepted on the high seas needed to be sent somewhere other than the US mainland.

The response was the ACS, founded in December 1816. Its members included white abolitionists, Christian missionaries, and some free blacks. However, its most powerful members were slaveholders and those who supported the "peculiar institution." Indeed, Henry Clay (chairman of the meeting that established the ACS) made clear that no attempt was being made "to touch or agitate in the slightest degree, a delicate question, connected with another portion of the colored population of this country. It was not proposed to deliberate upon or consider at all, any question of emancipation, or that which was connected with the abolition of slavery. It was upon that condition alone he was sure, that many gentlemen from the South and West, whom he saw present, had attended, or could be expected to cooperate. It was upon that condition alone that he himself had attended."[2]

Subject to these conditions, the ACS was formally established in 1817 with Bushrod Washington[3] as president and held its first meeting in the halls of Congress. Although it was always a private organization, it enjoyed government support at the highest levels. Indeed, US naval officers accompanied a small group of colonists in 1821 and secured the first land cessions from the local chiefs in return for "Six muskets, one box Beads, two hogsheads Tobacco, one cask Gunpowder, six bars Iron, ten iron Pots, one dozen Knives and Forks, one dozen Spoons, six pieces blue Baft, four Hats, three Coats, three pair Shoes, one box Pipes, one keg Nails, twenty Looking-glasses, three pieces Handkerchiefs, three pieces Calico, three Canes, four Umbrellas, one box Soap, one barrel Rum."[4]

The US naval officers, acting on behalf of the ACS, had used the same techniques as the British settlers in North America two centuries earlier to secure territory, and their methods would be just as dubious. The tribes people never accepted this, nor subsequent land cessions, and there would be conflict between the Libero Americans, as they came to be called, and the indigenous population for more than a century.

Still, the United States now had its African foothold (Map 6). Indeed, individual states would go on to found colonization societies and their own

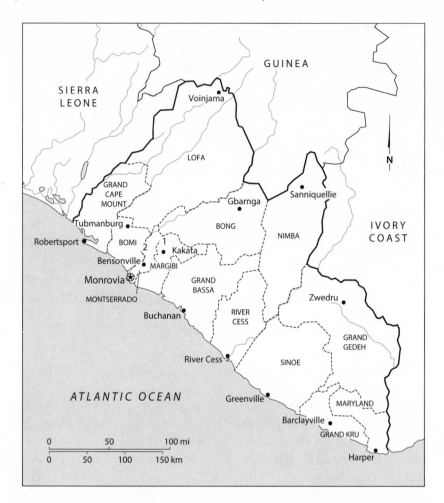

Map 6. Liberia

colonies in West Africa.[5] Gradually, the population of these colonies increased and the question of governance had to be addressed. As the US government would not officially take responsibility, it was left to the ACS to appoint agents and in 1838 their status was raised to governor. Their choice in that year was Thomas Buchanan, cousin of a future American president (James Buchanan, 1857–61).

The patrician Buchanan arrived at Monrovia,[6] the capital of the Commonwealth of Liberia (as it had become known), armed with a new constitution drafted by the ACS. Liberia now looked to all intents and purposes like a US colony and set about funding itself through customs duties on imports. These, however, fell on goods exported by other imperial countries (not just the United States).

The countries most affected were Great Britain and France, whose colonies shared (undefined) borders with Liberia. As the principal trading country, the United Kingdom wanted to know what was the legal basis on which Liberia applied taxes on British goods, and the British minister in Washington, DC, wrote in 1843 to Secretary of State Abel P. Upshur for clarification. Upshur confirmed that Liberia was not a formal US colony, but that the US government "would be very unwilling to see [Liberia] despoiled of its territory rightfully acquired, or improperly restrained in the exercise of its necessary rights and powers as an independent settlement."[7]

The British government was unconvinced by this argument and encouraged its traders not to pay customs duties. Without such taxes, Liberia was not viable and Joseph Jenkins Roberts, who had replaced Thomas Buchanan as governor in 1841, decided that the only option was to cut the link with the ACS and become an independent republic.

Liberia declared its independence on July 26, 1847. The declaration began with a list of complaints against the United States: "In some parts of that country, we were debarred by law from all rights and privileges of men—in other parts, public sentiment, more powerful than law, frowned us down. We were excluded from all participation in government. We were taxed without our consent. We were compelled to contribute to the resources of a country, which gave us no protection."[8]

Despite this, the Libero Americans—a tiny band of less than fifteen thousand—chose a flag modeled on the Stars and Stripes, adopted a constitution drafted by a white jurist from Massachusetts, and included clauses that reproduced the same injustices in Liberia that they objected to in their former home. The most offensive of these were Article 1, Section 11, and Article 5, Sections 12 and 13, effectively excluding the indigenous population from participation in civic life and restricting citizenship and property ownership to the Libero Americans themselves.[9]

Great Britain was the first to recognize Liberia's independence and now accepted the right of the government to impose customs duties. However, it was a Pyrrhic victory since Great Britain and France proceeded to challenge the new state's borders and force territorial concessions. This should have been the moment for the United States to rattle its imperial saber, but the federal government failed to recognize the independence of Liberia until 1862.[10]

The treaty of recognition gave the United States the right to intervene in Liberia's internal affairs under certain circumstances.[11] The federal government therefore gave support to Liberia in its efforts both to resist territorial encroachments by France and Great Britain and to suppress internal revolts by the indigenous population. These undertakings put a huge strain on Liberia's public revenue, and in 1871 the government contracted a debt with British creditors for £100,000 (nearly $500,000).

This loan was a textbook example of British imperialism at its most rapacious. After commissions and advance payment of all interest due over the next twenty years, it is estimated that the Liberian government received only £30,000. Fiscal weakness, with the threat of British intervention to ensure debt payments, continued unabated. Finally, in 1908 the Liberian government appealed to the US government for a guarantee of territorial and political integrity.

An earlier appeal might have fallen on stony ground, but this was soon to be the era of dollar diplomacy. President Theodore Roosevelt accepted that "the relations of the United States to Liberia are such as to make it an imperative duty for us to do all in our power to help the little republic which is struggling under such adverse conditions."[12] A commission was then appointed by the secretary of state and dispatched to Liberia.

By the time the commission reported, President Roosevelt had been replaced by President William Howard Taft (1909–13). Taft fully supported the commission's recommendations, however, of which the most important was for the establishment of a US customs receivership. The Liberian government accepted this, a loan was provided by a US syndicate to pay off the European creditors, and it was agreed that the US customs receiver would also be financial adviser to the Liberian government.

Liberia was now formally a US protectorate, and the financial adviser, in one of his first acts, recommended reimposition of the unpopular hut tax (see note 9). This increased the opposition Libero Americans faced from the indigenous population and led to a series of revolts. Coupled with the loss of customs duties following the outbreak of the First World War, the Liberian government could not service its debt and the US customs receiver accepted the need for default.

Liberia remained a protectorate because of its financial difficulties, but—as had happened in parts of Central America—it would now also come under the sway of a single US company (Firestone). The circumstances under which this happened are worth repeating for the light it sheds on imperialism more generally.

The British government, although victorious, came out of the First World War severely weakened in financial terms. It therefore looked to means by which it could raise money to service its debts to its creditors (principally the United States). Since American imports of rubber were rising rapidly in response to the

BOX 3.1

HENRY SHELTON SANFORD (1823–91)

The US government did not initiate the Berlin Conference (1884–85) and did not participate in the subsequent "scramble for Africa." Yet it did send a high-powered delegation to Berlin that not only endorsed King Leopold II's scheme for a Congo Free State but also established the ground rules for future colonization of Africa.

The key member of the US delegation was Henry Sanford. Best known for his Florida ventures (the town of Sanford in Seminole County is named after him), he served as a US diplomat in Belgium in the 1860s, where he first met King Leopold II. This friendship led him to support Leopold's sinister plan in 1876 to establish an International African Association that appeared at first to have philanthropic purposes.

Sanford was drawn to this scheme partly by naïveté (he was dazzled by aristocratic Europe), partly by commercial interest (his business ventures kept failing and he was always looking to rebuild his fortune), and partly by his southern connections (he hoped that the Congo would rival Liberia as "the ground to draw the gathering electricity from the black cloud spreading over the Southern states which . . . [is] growing big with destructive elements").

Sanford's greatest success was persuading the US government to recognize the association before the Berlin Conference began. In this he was helped by Senator John Morgan of Alabama, chairman of the Foreign Relations Committee, and a firm believer in African colonization schemes for African Americans. Without this recognition, it is by no means certain that the powers at Berlin would have accepted Leopold's plans to turn the association into the Congo Free State.

Sanford persuaded the king to allow him to establish the Sanford Exploring Expedition as the first trading company on the Upper Congo. Leopold II's officials, however, did not give the company the promised support and, like Sanford's other business ventures, it soon failed. Sanford lived just long enough to realize that he had been duped by Leopold II, whose real interest in the Congo was venal in the extreme.

growth of the motor vehicle industry and UK colonies in Asia controlled a large part of the world's exports, the British government adopted the Stevenson Plan. This restricted export supply and helped to push up rubber prices.

The big loser from this price increase was the United States, which accounted for about 70 percent of world rubber imports. Three American capitalists— Thomas Edison, Henry Ford, and Harvey Firestone—now swung into action. Edison concentrated on increasing rubber production in the United States, but died before his plans could come into full effect. Ford developed rubber planta- tions in Brazil (Box 6.1), but these were crippled by disease and labor shortages. That left only Firestone, whose focus was Liberia.

Following intense discussion with US officials, Firestone reached an agree- ment with the Liberian government in 1926 to lease up to one million acres for ninety-nine years at six cents an acre.[13] It also acquired rights "to construct, maintain, and operate roads and highways, waterways, railroads, telephone and power lines, hydroelectric plants, and a radio station powerful enough for di- rect communications with the United States." A subsidiary of the Firestone Company then lent the Liberian government $5 million, the servicing of which was guaranteed by various government revenues. For its part, the Liberian gov- ernment agreed to several actions:

> [It] would appoint and pay the salary of: (a) a Financial Adviser, designated by the President of the United States and approved by the President of Libe- ria; (b) five other officials to organise the customs and the internal revenue administration of Liberia, approved by the United States Department of State; and (c) four American army officers to lead the Liberian Frontier Force, to be recommended by the President of the United States. The Liberian [govern- ment] would install the pre-audit system, which gave the auditor the right to monitor Government expenditures [and] would prepare the Government budget in consultation with the American Financial Adviser.[14]

Liberia was now an extreme version of a US protectorate in which a single com- pany (Firestone) exercised enormous influence alongside the Customs Receiver. Yet Liberia had all the trappings of an independent country, including member- ship of the new League of Nations. The US Senate, however, refused to ratify the founding treaty, leaving the United States outside the organization. When the League of Nations therefore chose in 1930 to investigate well-founded accusations of forced labor and slavery against the Liberian government, the US government struggled to prevent Liberia becoming a protectorate of the League as well.

US interests were too strongly entrenched in Liberia and the League failed to impose its authority. When the customs receivership and the American protectorate ended, Liberia did not cease to be a part of the US empire. Instead, it allowed the United States to establish military bases in the country at the start of the Second World War and adopted the US dollar as its currency in 1943. With the election to the presidency the following year of William Tubman, Liberia would complete its transition from US protectorate to client state.[15]

3.2. CHINA AND JAPAN

Before the War of Independence, there was no direct British trade with Japan and only a limited one with China. Since Great Britain also prevented its colonies from trading directly with China, no ships from the thirteen colonies had ever gone there. Instead, imports from China (mainly tea) reached the thirteen colonies via Great Britain itself.

Independence therefore brought the prospect of direct trade ties with China, and there was much anticipation of huge profits. China's population of nearly four hundred million was one hundred times larger than the United States, and it was easy to be carried away by the potential for exports. The first ship, *Empress of China*, sailed from New York in 1784. As was customary in those days, it sailed eastward around the Cape of Good Hope and returned the following year by the same route.

The owners made a profit, but it was not enormous. Instead, they discovered what the British already knew: China had little need for imports and was not much interested in foreign trade. Thus, an intensive search began for products that might be of value to China. These included the skins of seals and sea otters that could keep the Chinese elite warm in winter, ginseng that was alleged to cure sexual impotency, sandalwood for burning in temples, and even sea cucumbers that were a gourmet's delight.

As a result of these endeavors, US traders learned a great deal about the Pacific—both its eastern and western coastlines as well as its network of small islands. Soon American merchant ships could be found in the Dutch East Indies, the Philippines (despite Spanish restrictions on trade), Malaya, and Siam (modern Thailand). Indeed, Edmund Roberts (a New England merchant) signed trade treaties with Siam and Muscat in 1835 on behalf of the US government. Three years later Lieutenant Charles Wilkes was dispatched on an epic four-year journey that produced charts of most of the Pacific for the US government and traders.

However, even Yankee ingenuity could not disguise the fact that the value of commodity exports was never enough to cover the cost of imports of tea, silk, and cotton textiles from China. This meant that the balance had to be paid through the shipment of scarce silver coins, and this drained *specie* from the US economy, creating the risk of deflation.[16]

US traders therefore adopted the practice that the British East India Company had been engaged in for some time: selling opium to the Chinese. The East India Company had a monopoly on Indian supplies of opium (until 1831), so the US traders had to buy it elsewhere (their favorite source was Smyrna, on the Black Sea). Regardless of the source, however, the Chinese were determined to suppress the trade in opium because of the social problems it caused. The trade was therefore largely illegal even through Canton (the only port permitted by the Chinese emperor to engage in foreign trade).

When China in 1839 cracked down even harder on the illegal opium trade in an effort finally to stamp it out, the British and American traders involved were furious. The US Navy, small and chiefly confined to the Atlantic, was in no position to respond. The British Navy, however, was only too happy to do so and launched what became known as the First Opium War (1839–42). Thus began what the Chinese today call the century of humiliation.

It is fair to say that many ordinary Americans were appalled by this display of British imperialism. That was not, however, the majority view among elites for whom opening China to trade had become an article of faith. Congressman John Quincy Adams, for example, was delighted: "The justice of the cause between the two parties—which has the righteous cause? I answer, Britain has the righteous cause. The opium question is not the cause of war, but the arrogant and insupportable pretensions of China, that she will hold commercial intercourse with the rest of mankind, not upon terms of equal reciprocity, but upon the insulting and degrading forms of the relation between lord and vassal."[17]

The British emerged victorious, and the Treaty of Nanjing in 1842 gave them what they wanted: a resumption of opium sales, the island of Hong Kong, and greater freedoms for British merchants in Canton. However, the treaty also opened five other ports to British traders and this sent alarm bells ringing in Washington, DC (Map 7). To counter the threat of Great Britain acquiring trading advantages over the United States, President John Tyler quickly sent Caleb Cushing to negotiate a treaty on similar terms to those now enjoyed by the British.

The result was the 1844 Treaty of Wanghia. It was a triumph of US diplomacy, but also the moment that America became an imperialist power in Asia instead of just another trading nation. The treaty not only gave the United States the same rights of privileged access as the United Kingdom to the five ports (Kwangchow, Amoy, Fuchow, Ningpo, and Shanghai) but also for the first time enshrined the concept of extraterritoriality. From now on, US citizens found guilty of crimes against Chinese citizens would not be charged under Chinese law and instead would only have to answer to the US consul in the port concerned. The Chinese government also gave Americans the right to build hospitals, churches, and cemeteries in the open ports.

China included a most favored nation clause in the treaty, meaning that the United States could claim any future concessions granted subsequently to other treaty powers. And, to demonstrate the unequal nature of the treaty, China in Article 2 agreed not to change customs duties without the consent of the United States: "Citizens of the United States resorting to China for the purposes of commerce will pay the duties of import and export prescribed in the Tariff, which is fixed by and made a part of this Treaty. . . . If the Chinese Government desire to modify, in any respect, the said Tariff, such modifications shall be made only in consultation with consuls or other functionaries thereto duly authorized in behalf of the United States, and with consent thereof."[18]

The Treaty of Wanghia meant that the Chinese government had partially relinquished its sovereignty, and the implications were soon apparent. In Shanghai, the most important of the five new ports, the United Kingdom and the United States established a system of municipal government, which eventually became known as the Shanghai International Settlement. Its mayor, on one occasion a US citizen, wielded enormous power over a city with more than one million inhabitants. It would survive for almost a century until the middle of the Second World War.

Following the annexation of California and the growing possibility of an interoceanic canal, the federal government became convinced that the Pacific could become a zone of special US influence. However, many obstacles still had to be overcome. Other imperialist powers—notably Great Britain, France, and Russia—had similar ambitions, and they would be joined by Germany toward the end of the century and Japan soon after. Furthermore, the Monroe Doctrine, designed for the Americas, could not be extended to the Pacific with any credibility. Thus, acquiring large swaths of territory in the Pacific was always going to be difficult for the United States.

A small step was taken in the decade after the Treaty of Wanghia when Congress passed the Guano Islands Act in 1856. This controversial piece of legislation gave private citizens the right to claim as US territory any island with guano that was unoccupied and not claimed by other states.[19] Within a few years, the United States—helped by the magnificent charts compiled by Lieutenant Wilkes—had accumulated claims to more than sixty islands in the Pacific.[20]

The status of these islands was at first unclear under federal law, but gradually the idea developed of making some of them "unincorporated territories" (a

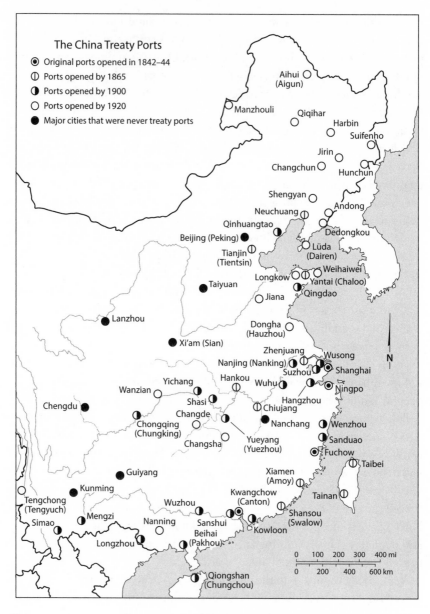

Map 7. China treaty ports

phrase that would only be formally adopted later). This meant that they had no right to join the Union, but it did mean that no other imperial power could occupy them. Most of the guano islands lost utility once the bird droppings had been removed, but some became permanent US territories. The best known is Midway Island, first claimed in 1859.[21]

US trade in the Pacific region expanded steadily, if not spectacularly, and most of it was accounted for by China. As sail gave way to steam, it became increasingly important to establish coaling stations where the ships could refuel. Rumors began to circulate of vast coal deposits in Japan, where trade was restricted to the Dutch and Chinese at one port.

Early efforts by the British and the Americans to open Japan to foreign commerce had been unsuccessful, but the rumors of large coal deposits persuaded the United States to try again. Commodore Matthew Perry was the chosen instrument. Although urged not to use force against Japan except in self-defense, Perry was under no illusions about what he was attempting to do. He had considered the opening of the Chinese ports by war as "one of the most humane and useful acts"[22] which Great Britain had ever undertaken and he had every intention of doing the same to Japan.

Perry departed for Japan in 1853. On the way he staked a claim to Okinawa in the Ryukyu Islands and purchased one of the Bonin Islands for the United States.[23] After a show of force in Edo (Tokyo) Harbor, he left a letter for the Japanese emperor and returned the following year to learn that the Japanese government was willing to grant limited access to US traders at two minor ports. The British—whose foreign secretary had said of Perry's mission, "better to leave it to the Government of the United States to make that experiment; and if the experiment is successful, Her Majesty's Government can take advantage of its success"—were quick to follow suit.

Perry is usually credited with opening Japan to foreign trade. However, the real breakthrough came three years later when Townshend Harris negotiated the Shimoda Convention. Japan agreed to open additional ports and conceded extraterritoriality to the United States. This paved the way for a series of treaties, each more unequal than the last, which deprived Japan of the power to set customs duties, opened more ports, and granted religious freedom to foreigners.

These unequal treaties led inevitably to friction, and a series of incidents in 1863 resulted in war between Japan and the imperial powers. The United States was in the middle of its Civil War, so the British navy took the lead. However, it was keen to participate and—despite having only one sailing ship in the area of conflict—was able to join in "when the Americans rented a small, unarmed steamer and transferred a gun and crew from the sailing ship to carry the United States flag into battle."[24]

Japan would draw the inevitable conclusions from this and other humiliations at the hands of the imperialist powers: the need to modernize and establish a strong navy. With the restoration of the executive powers of the emperor in 1868, change came rapidly. Japan would now be transformed, and the first real test of its military prowess came in 1894–95 when it defeated China in a dispute over Korea.

So absolute was Japan's victory (due mainly to sea power) that the treaty powers had to intercede to prevent Japan from carving out too many concessions from China for itself. In return, Japan was able to renegotiate the unequal treaties signed with the treaty powers. It entered the twentieth century with its sovereignty fully restored and was now on course to becoming an imperialist country itself.[25]

In China, meanwhile, the humiliations at the hands of foreigners continued, with the United States prominent among the treaty powers responsible. The long-running Taiping Rebellion (1850–64) could only be suppressed with the help of foreign forces, which led to further concessions to the United States and other imperial countries through treaties. The Chinese government, for example, lost the right to set its own tariffs, and the United States won the right to establish a court in its Shanghai consulate to try any of its citizens accused of a crime.

Although the United States did not take part in the Second Opium War (1856–60) and the destruction of the Summer Palace, it took a leading role in bombarding Formosa (Taiwan) a few years later in response to acts of piracy. It also passed the China Exclusion Act in 1882, restricting Chinese immigration to the United States. And in 1888 it passed a further piece of legislation, which caused even deeper offense in China, making it impossible for any Chinese in the United States to return after visiting China.

Most serious of all was the response of the treaty powers to the Boxer Rebellion (1898–1900).[26] The China Relief Expedition, comprising eight nations including the United States, invaded China in 1900 and penetrated as far as Beijing to protect their nationals and put down the uprising.[27] Looting and other outrages by all foreign troops were commonplace, while the Chinese government was forced by the Boxer Protocol in 1901 to pay an enormous indemnity to their governments. Cartoons captured the mood.[28]

Such was China's weakness that it now risked being dismembered by the imperialist countries. Yet this was a danger for the imperialists as well. Not only would it increase the chance of an interimperial war, but it would also lead to the disintegration of the fabled Chinese market. Although it had often disappointed, Chinese imports could still be enormous provided that its territory was preserved.

It was at this point that US Secretary of State John Hay published his two "Open Door" notes and none of the other treaty powers objected.[29] China would not be carved up, there would be equal access (at least for the treaty powers), and there would be no war. However, China was still subject to unequal treaties, and even more restrictions were placed on the Chinese in America (Chinese merchants responded with a half-hearted boycott of US goods). President Taft also deployed dollar diplomacy to put together an international consortium to keep China open for investment and stabilize its currency.

The United States was by no means the worst offender among the imperial powers in China. However, that misses the point. It *was* one of the powers that heaped humiliation on China and restricted its sovereignty. Thus, for the Chinese there was no reason to distinguish between the United States and other countries unless they saw some opportunity to play one off against the other. And America was content to work with the other imperial powers where necessary in order to secure its interests.

3.3. HAWAII, SAMOA, AND ALASKA

By virtue of its location in the middle of the Pacific (see Map 8), Hawaii was always going to excite the interest of imperialists. Great Britain was the first, based on the voyage of Captain James Cook in 1778 and the "cession" of the islands to Captain George Vancouver in 1794, but the claim was never seriously pursued. France and Russia would also claim Hawaii based on even more tenuous justifications.

The country that established the most powerful presence in Hawaii was in fact the United States. First to come were the traders loaded with skins and furs from the Pacific Northwest, using Hawaii as a base on their way to Canton in China and purchasing sandalwood. Then the whaling ships arrived, using Hawaii not only as a place to obtain provisions but also to rest between seasons.

Even more significant was the arrival of American missionaries in 1820. In an effort to resolve doctrinal disputes in New England, an American Board of Commissioners for Foreign Missions (ABCFM) had been set up in 1810. US missionaries had then fanned out across the Pacific, reaching Burma, British India, and China. The reception was not welcoming, and the missionaries sent to Hawaii probably expected something similar.

Fortunately for the missionaries, King Kamehameha I had died the year before they arrived. His successor, Liholiho (Kamehameha II), was a modernizer who was prepared to break many of the old traditions. He allowed the missionaries to settle among his 100,000 subjects, and soon they had established schools, a printing press, and a written language.

When Liholiho died in 1824 during a state visit to Great Britain, he was succeeded by Kauikeaouli, his son of twelve years. Although King Kamehameha III (as he was now called) had regents, the missionaries soon acquired a position of importance as advisers and mentors. Indeed, the first treaty between the United States and Hawaii was signed in 1826, although it was never ratified by Congress.

Kauikeaouli attended a Christian school and learned to read and write. However, what he desired above all was recognition of Hawaii by the imperial powers in order to put its independence on a more secure footing. He therefore sent a two-person delegation to Washington, DC, in 1842. One was Timoteo Haalilio, a Hawaiian noble, while the other was William Richards, a former American missionary.[30]

The negotiators met Secretary of State Daniel Webster and President Tyler. Both procrastinated over recognition until the Hawaiian delegation hinted at the possibility of becoming a protectorate of another power. This did the trick, and Tyler gave the following endorsement:

> Considering, therefore, that the United States possesses so very large a share of the intercourse with those islands, it is deemed not unfit to make the declaration that their Government seeks nevertheless no peculiar advantages, no exclusive control over the Hawaiian Government, but is content with its independent existence, and anxiously wishes for its security and prosperity. . . . Its forbearance in this respect, under the circumstances of the very large intercourse of their citizens with the islands, would justify the Government, should events hereafter arise, to require it, in making a decided remonstrance against the adoption of an opposite policy by any other power.[31]

The Tyler Doctrine, as it would become known, was therefore much more than recognition of Hawaiian independence. It effectively turned Hawaii into a US protectorate, since its government was no longer free to conduct relations with other foreign powers without taking into consideration US interests and could not now contemplate becoming a dependency of any European country.

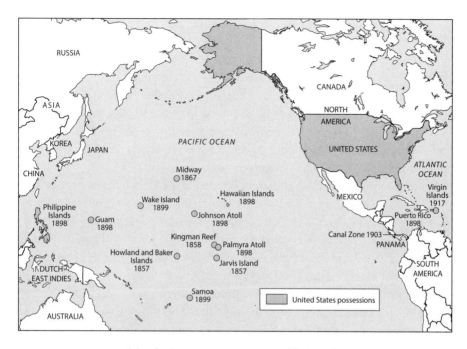

Map 8. American possessions in the Pacific

Hawaii was now inside the US sphere of influence, but commercial developments would take it even further. Sugar had first been exported in 1839, and the
industry grew modestly until two things happened. First, the United States acquired Oregon and California at the end of the 1840s, giving Hawaii a new market for sugar. Second, the whaling industry went into decline at the end of the
1850s, leading to a search for alternative exports.

Sugar development brought US capital to Hawaii in vast quantities. It forced
an end to feudalism and allowed for foreign ownership of land. It also created a
demand for labor that could not be met locally, leading to mass immigration of
Chinese and Japanese workers. However, Hawaiian sugar had to compete in the
US market with other foreign sugars as well as domestic cane and (later) beet
sugar. This led to calls either for annexation or for "reciprocity," under which
Hawaii would have duty-free access to the US market in return for zero tariffs
on US imports.

Negotiations nearly reached a successful conclusion in the 1850s, but were
then interrupted by the Civil War. When talks on reciprocity restarted, they
were complicated by the death of King Kamehameha V in 1872. His successor
died in February 1874 and US troops landed to put down a rebellion against the

new king (David Kalakaua). From then onward negotiations proceeded rapidly, and the Reciprocity Treaty was concluded in 1875.

Such treaties were and are commonplace and need not be imperialist in character. This was no ordinary treaty, however, as Article 4 made clear: "It is agreed on the part of His Hawaiian Majesty, that, so long as this treaty shall remain in force, he will not lease or otherwise dispose of or create any lien upon any port, harbor, or other territory in his dominion, or grant any special privilege or rights of use therein, to any other power, state, or government, nor make any treaty by which any other nation shall obtain the same privileges, relative to the admission of any articles free of duty, hereby secured to the United States."[32] Article 4 not only further restricted the sovereignty of the Hawaiian government but was also included as a result of the refusal of the Hawaiian negotiators to lease Pearl Harbor to the United States under the treaty. By 1887, however, Hawaiian resistance had ended and Pearl Harbor came into US possession as part of the renegotiation of the 1875 Treaty of Reciprocity.

Reciprocity and Pearl Harbor were more than sufficient to secure US interests, but Hawaii was still nominally sovereign. This did not matter as long as the monarch was pliant, but in 1891 Queen Liliuokalani (Box 3.2) ascended the throne. She had been born in 1838 and she had seen the sovereignty and independence of the kingdom steadily compromised. The native population was in decline and was now in a minority, while US settlers and their descendants dominated commerce and politics. To make matters worse, the McKinley Tariff in 1890 had wiped out the advantages of the Reciprocity Treaty.[33] It was time, she decided, to take a stand.

The queen miscalculated, and those in favor of annexation gained the upper hand. Domestic considerations in the United States delayed passage of an annexation treaty until 1898 and Hawaii then became a US territory in 1900. Its transition to statehood was held up first by southern resistance to a nonwhite population and then by the Japanese attack on Pearl Harbor in December 1941. It would eventually join the Union as the fiftieth state in 1959.

While Hawaii gave the United States a foothold in the northern Pacific, eastern Samoa would do the same in the southern part of the ocean. The Samoan Islands occupy a strategic position between the Americas and Oceania and are directly on the trading routes from Hawaii to Australia. The neighboring islands—Fiji, Tahiti, Tonga, and the Cooks—had excited the interest of European imperial powers since the late eighteenth century, and it was therefore to be expected that the United States would seek to establish a presence in the region.

BOX 3.2

QUEEN LILIUOKALANI (1838–1917)

Liliuokalani was the daughter of a close adviser of King Kamehameha III. She attended a missionary school and married John Owen Dominis, the son of a US sea captain. She was groomed for many years to ascend to the throne and traveled to London in 1887 for the Golden Jubilee of Queen Victoria. It was the same year that King Kalakaua was forced by US interests on the island to accept the so-called Bayonet Constitution that weakened the powers of the monarchy.

On ascending to the throne in 1891, Queen Liliuokalani was determined to adopt a new constitution that would have restored the monarch's powers. Unable to do so through parliament, she attempted to do so by decree. She was then overthrown in January 1893 by annexationists led by Sanford Dole, who was backed up by US troops on board the USS *Boston*. A treaty of annexation was then hastily prepared by President Benjamin Harrison (1889–93), but he left office before it could be adopted by Congress.

His successor, President Grover Cleveland (1893–97), dispatched James Blount to investigate the circumstances surrounding the coup, and Blount's report condemned US interference. Before the queen could be restored to power, however, the Senate commissioned its own report chaired by John T. Morgan. This document, dismissed by the *Philadelphia Record* as "a mere incoherent yawp of jingoism," was enough to preserve the *status quo*.

Cleveland, despite his reputation as an anti-imperialist, then recognized Sanford Dole as president of the Republic of Hawaii. Dole imprisoned Liliuokalani in 1895 and she was not released until November 1896. She immediately traveled to Washington, DC, but her cause was now hopeless. She returned to Hawaii, where she lived until her death in 1917. She continued to write songs, her best known one being "Aloha Oe," and remained an accomplished musician (she played the piano, ukulele, guitar, zither, and organ).

US troops landed in Samoa as early as 1841 to burn villages in retaliation for the murder of a US sailor by natives. However, the British already had a strong position on the islands and it was not until 1873 that a coherent US imperial plan took shape. In that year Albert Steinberger was dispatched by President Ulysses S. Grant to Samoa as a special envoy to explore the possibility of securing a US protectorate.

At the time Samoa was recovering from a civil war between the two leading families (Malietoa and Tupua). Steinberger was therefore invited to draft a constitution which was adopted with himself as premier. This gave him supreme executive power and should have marked the moment all Samoa became a US colony. However, Steinberger's actions earned the enmity not only of Great Britain and Germany but also the US consul.

Steinberger was deposed in 1875 before American control could be consolidated, but three years later the Samoan government agreed to a treaty in Washington, DC, that gave the US government what it really wanted: a coaling and naval station at Pago Pago Harbor on Tutuila Island in eastern Samoa. However, the treaty also committed the United States to mediate between Samoa and other powers.

Disputes escalated rapidly and centered on many issues, including land ownership. Samoan tradition required that land be held communally and—unlike in Hawaii—the law had not been changed. This meant that bribery and corruption by foreigners were common in an effort to gain *de facto* control of land, and one of the principal offenders was the US Central Polynesian Land and Commercial Company (CPLCC).[34]

An effort was made in 1887 by the three principal powers—Germany, the United Kingdom, and the United States—to resolve their differences, but to no avail. Two years later it would have come to war in Samoan waters if it were not for the eruption of a powerful storm. Chancellor Bismarck then summoned the powers to Berlin, where a joint protectorate was established over the islands by Germany (in the west), Great Britain (undefined), and the United States (in the east). This left America in control of the harbor at Pago Pago, its most important strategic objective.

The Samoan government was still nominally sovereign and so the opportunities for misunderstanding and meddling by the foreign powers were legion. In 1899, therefore, the three powers agreed to a formal division of labor. Western Samoa became a German colony (it would be given to New Zealand by the League of Nations after the First World War) and the rest became the US colony of American Samoa. Great Britain dropped its territorial claims.

The act of annexation was signed by President William McKinley (1897–1901), who—in recognition of the importance of the harbor at Pago Pago—promptly passed American Samoa to the US Navy. Congress played no role in this imperial episode until 1929, when the cession to the United States was formally approved.[35] American Samoa would remain a responsibility of the US Navy until

1951, when civilian rule under the Department of the Interior was established. American Samoa remains a US colony today.

Alaska, the Russian colony in the Pacific Northwest, had been administered by the Russian American Company (RAC) since its foundation in 1799, with the state as a minority shareholder. The company at first was highly profitable, but the decline in the number of skins and furs as a result of overfishing by American, British, and Russian sailors soon changed this. The Russian government did not wish to subsidize the RAC and, following a gloomy report on the company's prospects in 1862, resolved to sell the territory.

Russia could conceivably have offered Alaska to Great Britain, but relations were much better with the United States. Since the borders of Alaska (including the Aleutian Islands and other islands) had been largely defined in the Anglo-Russian Convention of 1825, negotiations were straightforward. A price of $7.2 million was agreed to in 1867, and the sale was approved by the US Senate after a mammoth three-hour speech in support by Senator Charles Sumner.

Neither Senator Sumner nor the United States and Russian governments paid the slightest attention to the indigenous population, whose numbers were estimated at 26,000 (or 27,500 if the mixed population is included). Since the white population was only 483, of which 150 were Americans, the US government decided that Alaska could not become a territory. The new colony was therefore placed under military rule.

Military rule was not uncommon in building the US empire, but it lasted for longer in Alaska than anywhere else. The absence of any representative institutions meant that the more unscrupulous elements of US society were able to operate without much accountability. In particular, Alaska came to the attention of the Guggenheim company, which established an Alaskan syndicate to create a series of monopolies in natural resource extraction, transport, and power.

The population grew slowly until the discovery of gold in the Klondike River in 1896. This produced the inevitable gold rush and a jump in the number of white settlers from around six thousand in 1890 to thirty-four thousand in 1900. This was more than enough for Alaska to proceed to the first stage of territorial government, but there were still further delays. Indeed, it was not until 1912 that Alaska became a US territory.

Territorial government in Alaska was even more "colonial" than in other US territories. The act establishing a territory limited the powers of the legislature: "It may not pass any law interfering with the primary disposal of the soil; it may not levy taxes that are not uniform upon the same class of subjects; it may not grant any exclusive or special privileges without the affirmative approval of Congress . . . it may not authorize . . . any debt by the Territory . . . it may not appropriate any public money for the benefit of any sectarian or denominational school . . . it may not alter, amend, modify or repeal the game and fish laws passed by Congress and in force in Alaska."[36] The last point was particularly resented by the population—settler and indigenous—as it suggested that Alaska had become an early experiment in conservation by Congress.[37] The native population, however, had no way of protesting until 1915 when they were granted citizenship—albeit under highly restrictive conditions.

By the end of the Second World War, the population was large enough for statehood to be considered. A referendum was therefore held in 1946, with a majority in favor. However, more than 40 percent voted against, so it was some years before the territory could join the Union.[38] This finally happened in January 1959, bringing to an end nearly a century of US colonial rule in Alaska.

3.4. THE SPOILS OF WAR

The Philippines were added to the Spanish empire in 1565. For the next three centuries Spanish authority went largely uncontested not only in the archipelago but also in the surrounding islands of Micronesia. These included the Mariana, Carolina, and Marshall Islands, which Spain claimed but—with the exception of Guam—had not occupied or fortified in any meaningful way. Nor had Spain resisted the arrival in the second half of the nineteenth century of Protestant missionaries and foreign traders as permanent residents.

Inevitably, these small island groups began to attract the attention of the other imperial powers. Of these, Germany was the most assertive and in 1885 she occupied a number of islands in both the Carolinas and the Marshalls. Spain protested and war was only avoided when both sides agreed to a German proposal to seek arbitration by Pope Leo XIII.

The Protocol of Rome, drawn up by the pope at the end of 1885, acknowledged Spanish sovereignty over the Carolinas. However, it was a Pyrrhic victory. Germany was left in control of the Marshall Islands with the right to establish coaling and naval stations in the Carolinas. Furthermore, Spain's subsequent attempts to conquer the Carolina Islands provoked considerable resistance from the indigenous population and demonstrated to other powers how militarily frail she was.[39]

These events did not go unnoticed in the United States, whose missionaries had long been established in many of the islands. Spanish weakness also drew US attention to the Philippines, where resistance to imperial rule had been building up since the 1860s. The archipelago, so close to the Chinese mainland, occupied a strategic position and made its control a tempting proposition for any power interested in increasing trade with Asia.

The Filipinos, as the indigenous people were called by foreigners, had no desire to replace Spanish rule with that of another imperial power. By the 1890s they had formed a powerful nationalist movement led by Emilio Aguinaldo with the goal of independence or, at least, autonomy. By April 1898 the rebels were largely in control, and the Spanish forces were pinned down in Manila. Spain was unable to provide adequate reinforcements due to the Second War of Independence in Cuba (1895–98), and the Filipino insurgents looked forward to victory.

It was at this point that the United States declared war on Spain. Although the principal motivation was to end Spanish rule in Cuba and Puerto Rico, President McKinley had, even before the declaration, taken the precaution of moving the US Asiatic Fleet under Commodore Dewey to Hong Kong in preparation for an assault on the Spanish fleet in Manila Bay.[40] As soon as war was declared, the Spanish fleet in the harbor was utterly destroyed.[41]

Dewey, soon to be made an admiral, lacked the land forces to take Manila. The Filipino rebels could have taken it, but this would have left them in control of the Philippines. American reinforcements were therefore quickly dispatched from the mainland, stopping briefly at Guam in the Marianas to annex the island.[42] The rebels were told firmly to stay away, and Manila was surrendered by Spain with scarcely a shot being fired.[43]

Whatever doubts President McKinley may have had about advancing US imperial ambitions had been resolved by the time of the Paris peace conference in December 1898.[44] Both Guam and the Philippines were ceded by Spain to the United States, and the indigenous peoples were not consulted. The United States did not, however, take the Northern Marianas or Carolina Islands although she could undoubtedly have done so if she wished.[45] As Spain was now in no position to hold them, she sold them in 1899 to Germany.

Guam was put under the control of the US Navy, which proceeded to govern the island with very little oversight from Congress or any other institution.[46] The 7,100 islands making up the Philippine archipelago could not be controlled so easily since the forces under Aguinaldo's command had no intention of laying down their arms. The United States therefore engaged in a ferocious colonial war in which torture was common and the civilian population was herded into concentration camps.[47]

Aguinaldo was captured in 1901 and the worst of the fighting was over by the following year. The number of Filipino deaths will never be known for certain,

BOX 3.3
"THE WHITE MAN'S BURDEN"

Rudyard Kipling (1865–1936) was an Anglo-Indian writer famous for his poems and children's stories. He was also a staunch defender of British imperialism. Yet his most famous imperialist poem is addressed to the people of the United States and concerns the Philippines.

Kipling's wife was American, and they honeymooned in the United States. They then set up home in Connecticut, where he wrote many of the works for which he is most famous. Although not living in the United States at the time of the Spanish-American War, he sent a copy of his paean to imperialism, "The White Man's Burden: The United States and the Philippine Islands," to Theodore Roosevelt in November 1898 urging him to support colonization.

Roosevelt sent the poem to Senator Henry Cabot Lodge with a note extolling its imperialist message but deploring its literary merit. Lodge, who received it shortly before the Senate voted on annexation of the Philippines, replied that he liked both the message and the poetry. The poem was published in *McClure's* magazine in the same month as the Senate vote (February 1899).

The poem has been much admired by imperialists through the ages, and some of its words were used by Max Boot in 2002 in the title of his book (*The Savage Wars of Peace*) in defense of US empire. It also provoked a series of hostile responses from anti-imperialists and satirists. In April 1899, for example, H. T. Johnson—an African American clergyman—published a poem that included the following lines: "Pile on the Black Man's Burden / His wail with laughter drown / You've sealed the Red Man's problem, / and will take up the Brown."

In the same year, Henry Labouchère published in *Truth* magazine perhaps the best-known riposte to Kipling, with the immortal lines, "Pile on the brown man's burden, / compel him to be free; / Let all your manifestoes / Reek with philanthropy."

but it has been estimated as high as 250,000 when disease and starvation are taken into account.[48] US imperialists, however, never doubted the virtue of their cause. In October 1900 the secretary of war, Elihu Root, stated, "Nothing can be more preposterous than the proposition that these men [the Filipino forces under Aguinaldo] were entitled to receive from us sovereignty over the entire country which we were invading. As well the friendly Indians, who have helped us in our

Indian wars, might have claimed the sovereignty of the West. They knew that we were incurring no such obligation and they expected no such reward."[49]

Guam and the Philippines were now US territories, but their legal status was still ambiguous. Hawaii had been annexed in 1898 and was on the long path to statehood. Eastern Samoa, on the other hand, had become a US colony the following year with no prospect of joining the Union. The same was true of all those possessions, such as Midway Island, acquired by the United States under the Guano Islands Act. What should happen to Guam and the Philippines?

There was little support in the United States for statehood to be given to the new territories. Guam was too small, and the nonwhite population of the Philippines too large (about 10 percent of the US population). The Supreme Court was therefore asked to rule on the status of the new possessions in a series of decisions that became known as the Insular Cases.[50]

The Supreme Court proved to be a very malleable tool in the service of US imperialism. The judges, albeit by a narrow majority, established that Guam and the Philippines were "unincorporated" territories and therefore not entitled to statehood.[51] Indeed, in a ruling that left most people puzzled, the court ruled that the inhabitants of unincorporated territories were only entitled to "fundamental" rights under the US Constitution, but not "formal" or "procedural" rights.[52]

The path was now cleared for the US administration and Congress to do whatever it wanted. Guam was left under the control of the US Navy and would remain there until 1951, when civilian rule was finally established. An Organic Act for the Philippines was passed in 1902 that gave some concessions to exporters, but still left the country outside the US tariff wall (it would only come inside after 1909).[53] And to ensure that a lobby was not formed pushing for statehood, Congress imposed various restrictions on US inward investment into the Philippines.[54]

Once inside the tariff wall, Philippine exports of sugar, hemp, tobacco, and coconut oil expanded rapidly and began to challenge domestic producers in the United States. Filipino workers, taking advantage of one of their "fundamental" rights under the US Constitution, also started moving to the mainland in significant numbers.[55] Opposition to the Philippines' unincorporated status became more and more vocal both from those demanding restrictions on Philippine exports and from those calling for an end to immigration.

Congress was powerless to act unless the Philippines ceased to be a US colony. The Great Depression, however, finally tipped the balance. Domestic producers were now more determined than ever to block Philippine exports, while mainland unemployment rendered unrestricted Filipino migration even more controversial. With the passage of the Tydings-McDuffie Act in 1934, a schedule was set for eventual independence. Filipino immigration and unrestricted trade ended immediately.[56]

Plans for independence were interrupted by the outbreak of the Second World War and the Japanese invasion of the Philippines in 1941. When independence finally came in 1946, it was hedged around with so many restrictions that it would be more accurate to describe the Philippines as becoming a US protectorate. Thus, the end of colonialism in the Philippines did not mean the end of US imperial control.

The United States retained its gigantic naval and air bases and would not relinquish them until 1992.[57] Under the Bell Trade Act, which the Philippine government signed two days before independence, the United States set out the tariff schedule and export quotas to be applied for the next three decades, pegged the currency to the US dollar, and awarded parity to American individuals and corporations in the exploitation of the country's natural resources.[58] Since this last provision conflicted with the Philippine Constitution, the US legislators took the precaution of adding, "The Government of the Philippines will promptly take such steps as are necessary to secure the amendment of the Constitution of the Philippines so as to permit the taking effect as laws of the Philippines of such part of the provisions of Paragraph 1 of this Article as is in conflict with such Constitution before such an amendment."[59]

By the beginning of the twentieth century, the US empire in the Pacific was well established and in geopolitical competition with the empires of France, Great Britain, and Germany. Japan had also become an imperial power, especially after its military victories against China in 1895 and Russia in 1905, but it did not yet control any islands close to US possessions.[60]

All this would change with the outbreak of the First World War in August 1914. Japan immediately occupied the German islands in the Marianas, Carolinas, and Marshalls with little resistance from either Germany itself or the local population. The methods, however, were frequently brutal. The United States, neutral until April 1917, could do nothing and looked on with some concern.[61]

When the war ended, Japan looked for diplomatic support to keep the islands it had occupied. It found a willing ally in Great Britain, with whom it had been in alliance since 1902 and who had also seized a number of German territories in the Pacific.[62] The United States, however, resisted and President Woodrow Wilson (1913–21) argued at the peace conference in Paris that all the German territories should be governed as League of Nations' mandates without the administering nation exercising full sovereignty.

The US proposal carried the day, but not before the British had emasculated it by proposing a threefold categorization of mandates. The Japanese-held islands were put in Class C, meaning that Japan could now do what she wanted, and she proceeded to turn them into traditional colonies.[63] When Congress rejected the 1920 Treaty of Paris, Wilson tried again in his last months to "internationalize" the Japanese islands. His successor, President Warren G. Harding (1921–25), won a few minor concessions, but not enough to change the fact that Japan had gained colonies close to the American ones.[64]

The United States now faced a formidable competitor, and the more astute American strategists began to anticipate trouble.[65] The bombing of Pearl Harbor in December 1941 proved them right. The war against Japan lasted nearly four years but, when it ended, the United States was left in control of all the Japanese islands in the Pacific and the question immediately arose of what to do with them.

The solution was very much the same as that found for Japan after the First World War.[66] The new imperial acquisitions, covering a sea area of three million square miles, were renamed the United Nations Trust Territory of the Pacific Islands (TTPI).[67] They included the Carolinas, the Marshalls, and the Northern Marianas.[68] All the islands were now US colonies, but their colonial status had become something of an embarrassment by the 1970s. The United States, in consultation with the local peoples, was therefore obliged to come up with new constitutional arrangements.

The answer was found in most cases through "independence" in "free association with the United States." Three new states were born—Palau, the Federated State of Micronesia,[69] and the Marshall Islands—and joined the United Nations, although the United States controls their defense and foreign affairs (the three states invariably vote with the United States).[70] The Northern Marianas, however, chose to remain a colony under the name Commonwealth of the Northern Mariana Islands.[71]

The US territorial empire in the Pacific has therefore not ended, although it is much smaller than when it included the Philippines. Alaska and Hawaii have become states, but Guam, Samoa, Palau, the Marshall Islands, the Federated State of Micronesia, the Commonwealth of the Northern Mariana Islands, Midway Island, Wake Island, Johnson Atoll, Kingman Reef, Palmyra Atoll, Jarvis Island, Baker Island, and Howland Island are all imperial responsibilities. It is quite an impressive list for a country that officially does not have an empire!

4

THE CARIBBEAN

Despite geographic proximity, the American empire was slow to reach the Caribbean. This was not for lack of interest. The republic had early on acquired a geopolitical stake in the region as a result first of the Louisiana Purchase (1803) and, second, the acquisition of Florida (1819). The United States now had a Caribbean shoreline and all parties shared a desire both to promote commerce with the new neighbors and to protect America from possible attack by European powers.

Slave-owning Cuba was the largest island in the Caribbean, with by far the most dynamic economy until the 1870s. The interest in annexing Cuba before the US Civil War was therefore immense among the southern states, but—as the jewel in their crown—the Spanish had no desire to sell it. After the Civil War, slave-owning Cuba was no longer a target for US acquisition. It was only after the final emancipation of the slaves in 1886 that control of Cuba once again became a US priority.

If US interest in Cuba initially declined after the Civil War, the opposite was true in the case of the rest of the Caribbean. By 1870 one-third of all US imports came from the Americas, and much of it passed through the Caribbean. This meant there was a pressing need for naval bases and coaling stations to defend the sea lanes. At the same time, US interest in an interoceanic canal was stronger than ever after the Civil War, and this would also require naval bases in the Caribbean whichever route was chosen.

Yet the expansion of the US empire into the rest of the Caribbean faced the same obstacles as with Cuba. Almost all islands were colonies of European powers, so that a transfer of sovereignty was only possible if either a sale could be agreed or a successful military campaign undertaken. However, the United

States was not prepared for military action so soon after the Civil War, and an attempt to purchase the Danish West Indies in 1867 failed.

There were, nevertheless, two Caribbean countries that were not ruled by European powers. The first was Haiti, which had thrown off the shackles of France after a successful slave revolt and declared its independence in 1804 (the Haitians had defeated an invading British force as well). The second was Santo Domingo, later renamed the Dominican Republic,[1] which had revolted against Haitian rule and become independent in 1844. Both nations had splendid natural harbors that would have provided coaling stations and appropriate bases for the US Navy if terms could be agreed.

The two countries, which share the island of Hispaniola, came under enormous pressure from the US administration to make territorial concessions. Yet the Haitian government, which was only recognized diplomatically by the US government in 1862, refused to budge. For this it would pay a heavy price.

The Dominicans, on the other hand, were very receptive. A treaty of annexation was signed in 1869, and the country would have become a US territory the following year if President Ulysses S. Grant (1869–77) had been able to muster the necessary two-thirds majority in the US Senate. He failed, and his subsequent effort to secure annexation through a joint resolution of both houses of Congress (as happened with Texas) was also unsuccessful.

An American empire in the Caribbean could not therefore begin in earnest until after the Spanish-American War (1898) despite the fact that it had been a dream of some of the Founding Fathers more than a century before. Yet in the next five decades, it would eclipse the European powers and turn the Caribbean into an American lake (Map 9). Hundreds of young men and women would work in the region in civilian roles and thousands of troops would be stationed there. There was an enormous attention to detail in social and economic planning.

Two territories (Puerto Rico and the Virgin Islands[2]) became US colonies. Three others—Cuba, the Dominican Republic, and Haiti—were controlled through a series of devices that would have been familiar to European imperialists. These included military occupation, customs receiverships, naval bases, asymmetrical bilateral treaties, and US foreign investment. The widespread use of the US dollar was also an effective form of control (the British, Dutch, and French used the same technique in many of their dependencies beyond the Caribbean where the pound, guilder, and franc circulated freely).

Above all, the US authorities knew that no government in the "independent" countries of the Caribbean could survive for long in the face of nonrecognition. This weapon in the imperial armory was extremely powerful. It meant that

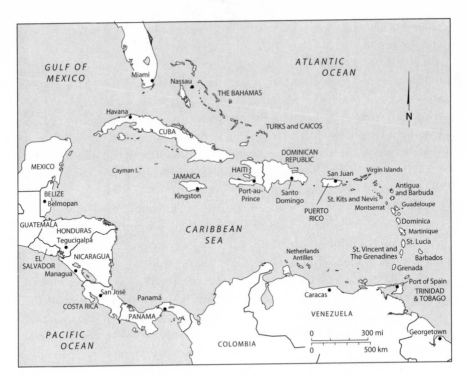

Map 9. The Caribbean and Central America

aspiring politicians needed to win the support of the United States before taking power (those that failed to do so were very vulnerable). And this tactic was
effective not just in the Caribbean but also elsewhere in Latin America.

Despite such a degree of imperial control, this was not always how it seemed
to US officials. Those "on the ground" constantly complained of the difficulties of securing US interests, of disloyalty by favored politicians, of duplicity by
governments. This was a constant complaint by imperial officials around the
world: the "native" could never be trusted, and no good deed ever went unpun-
ished. The British, Dutch, and French would say much the same.

Once started, the American empire in the Caribbean was constructed swiftly.
Opposition to it outside the United States was slower to emerge—except in the
countries directly affected. However, imperial possessions sat uneasily with US
rhetoric about itself and its place in the world. Indeed, the negotiations at Paris
conducted by President Woodrow Wilson in 1919, in which he called for a League
of Nations and self-determination for national peoples, were greatly complicated by the US occupations at the time of Haiti, the Dominican Republic, and
Nicaragua.

This conflict between rhetoric and reality became worse in the 1920s and reached a climax at the Sixth Pan-American Conference in Havana in 1928. An Argentine diplomat, Honorio Pueyrredón, even had the audacity to introduce an open declaration against US military intervention in which he stated, "Diplomatic or armed intervention, whether permanent or temporary, is an attack against the independence of states and is not justified by the duty of protecting nations, as weak nations are, in their turn, unable to exercise such right."[3]

US policy emerged from Havana battered and bruised. It was clear therefore that a new approach to hemispheric affairs was required. This would be announced by President Franklin Delano Roosevelt (FDR) in his inaugural address in March 1933 where he outlined the Good Neighbor policy. Later that year he confirmed that "the definite policy of the United States from now on is one opposed to armed intervention."[4]

In US mythology this was the moment when the imperial project, initiated after the Spanish-American War, came to an end. Troops were withdrawn from Haiti and Nicaragua and the Platt Amendment[5] was revoked, leaving Cuba in theory as a sovereign independent nation. By the end of the 1930s even intervention in Panama had been foresworn. Yet, as we will see, imperial retreat was far from being the case. The empire survived, but the methods to sustain it changed.

American empire always secured what it wanted in the Caribbean on matters of national importance even after the adoption of the Good Neighbor policy (at least until the Cuban Revolution), only losing out on relatively trivial issues. As an exercise in imperialism, the US empire in the Caribbean up to the end of the Second World War and even beyond was as complete as any in history. It even brought about the subordination of the colonies of other empires— something that Belgian, British, Dutch, French, or Italian officials could only dream about as they competed with each other in Africa, Asia, and the Middle East.

4.1. THE DOMINICAN REPUBLIC

If Haiti was off-limits to US colonization in the nineteenth century, the Dominican Republic was a different story. A weak and fragile state on independence, it feared being recolonized by Haiti and sought a foreign protector. All the major European powers were approached and the country even became a Spanish colony for a few years (1861–65), a violation of the Monroe Doctrine made possible by the distractions of the US Civil War. However, Spanish rule proved unpopular and was ended by a successful revolt.

President Grant now seized his opportunity. Not only did the Dominican Republic at Samaná Bay have one of the finest natural harbors in the Caribbean, but its political and economic elites were also keen for the country to join the United States. A treaty was drawn up with President Buenaventura Báez of the Dominican Republic and presented to the US Senate in 1869.

The treaty provided for annexation of the whole country with the promise of eventual Dominican statehood and a payment of $1.5 million (an alternative treaty was also drafted that would have given the United States a lease on Samaná Bay only). The US Navy stood offshore to reinforce the message, and Haiti, which still claimed the eastern half of the island, was warned to expect repercussions if she tried to block annexation.[6]

This would have been the first US territory in the Caribbean, but the treaty of annexation was defeated by the US Senate (the vote was 28–28, a two-thirds majority being required). The opposition was led by Senator Charles Sumner (Box 4.1), without whose intervention the proposal might have passed. The senator continued his attacks on the imperialist plans of the Grant administration even after the vote. A year later, in 1871, he addressed the Senate once again on the matter of annexation: "Over all is that other question whether we will begin a system, which, first fastening upon Dominica [the Dominican Republic], must . . . next take Hayti, and then in succession the whole tropical groupe [*sic*] of the Caribbean sea, so that we are now to determine if all the Islands of the West Indies shall be a component part of our Republic, helping to govern us, while the African race is dispossessed of its natural home in this hemisphere. No question, equal in magnitude, unless it be that of Slavery, has arisen since the days of Washington."[7]

US interest in acquiring the Dominican Republic did not disappear after the failure of the annexation treaty. Indeed, US influence steadily advanced through the operations of the San Domingo Improvement Company controlled by American capitalists. This business acquired the financial interests of European investors in the 1890s, which in turn gave it the right to collect customs duties. As these accounted for the bulk of government revenue, it was a powerful lever—albeit in the hands at first of a private company rather than the US government.[8]

The Dominican Republic also signed a bilateral trade treaty in 1892, providing for tariff reductions on imports from the United States.[9] Since America was the main source of imports, and since customs duties accounted for nearly 100 percent of government revenue, this contributed to the fiscal weakness of the state and its inability to service its foreign debt. In return, the Dominican

BOX 4.1
CHARLES SUMNER (1811–74)

Charles Sumner was born in Boston, Massachusetts, and became a strong supporter of abolition in the 1830s. A founder member of the Free Soil Party, he was elected to the US Senate in 1851. His speech "The Crime against Kansas" in 1856 so outraged his southern opponents that one of them physically attacked him on the floor of the Senate two days later. Sumner nearly died and it was several years before he could return to his duties. He then became chairman of the powerful Senate Foreign Relations Committee.

Sumner had opposed the annexation of Texas, but he was not an anti-imperialist. He supported the purchase of Alaska in 1867 (but not the Danish West Indies) and sought the cession of Canada as retribution for Great Britain's assistance to the Confederacy in the Civil War. When President Ulysses S. Grant (1869–77) came to his house unexpectedly on January 2, 1870, to seek his support for the treaty of annexation of the Dominican Republic, he did not register any opposition.

Yet he proved to be Grant's most formidable opponent, and it is quite possible that annexation might have gone ahead without his intervention. Grant never forgave Sumner for what he saw as an act of betrayal and ensured that he was removed from his post as chairman of the Senate Foreign Relations Committee after the vote on the treaty failed to give the president what he wanted.

Sumner's opposition to annexation was motivated by many considerations. One was the unsavory nature of those pushing for it in the Dominican Republic itself. These included two American entrepreneurs (General William Cazneau and Joseph Fabens), who had the support of General Orville Babcock in the White House. In his famous speech of March 27, 1871, Sumner referred to Babcock as "[a] young officer, inexperienced in life, ignorant of the world, untaught in the Spanish language [Sumner was fluent], unversed in 'international law,' knowing absolutely nothing of the intercourse between nations, and unconscious of the Constitution of his country."

Republic received a small preference in the US market for its main exports (especially sugar).[10]

Despite these concessions to the United States, the harbor at Samaná Bay could still not be used by the US Navy. After the failure of the annexation treaty, a New York company (assumed to be a front for the US government) had leased the facilities, but the contract was canceled in 1874 due to nonpayment. Successive US administrations then watched with some concern the entry of the German Navy into the Caribbean (the Haitian capital had been bombarded by German frigates in 1872), knowing that the US Navy was not yet in a position to respond.

Since 1823 the United States had relied on the Monroe Doctrine to guide its interests in the Americas. It had served the republic well despite the occasional breach (as when Spain had recolonized Santo Domingo during the Civil War). However, it lacked the force of international law, and there was no guarantee that the European powers would respect it. A US imperial presence in the Caribbean Basin therefore required a more muscular approach.

As the main bondholders for the independent states of the Caribbean, there was always the danger that the European powers might respond to financial turbulence by intervention. This had happened to Venezuela in 1902, when an Anglo-German-Italian fleet blockaded the main port. President Theodore Roosevelt (1901–9) had even been forced to send the US Navy to prevent German troops landing in 1903. The following year in his State of the Union address he therefore enunciated his own interpretation of the Monroe Doctrine:

> If a nation shows that it knows how to act with reasonable efficiency and decency in social and political matters, if it keeps order and pays its obligations, it need fear no interference from the United States. Chronic wrongdoing, or an impotence which results in a general loosening of the ties of civilized society, may in America, as elsewhere, ultimately require intervention by some civilized nation, and in the Western Hemisphere the adherence of the United States to the Monroe Doctrine may force the United States, however reluctantly, in flagrant cases of such wrongdoing or impotence, to the exercise of an international police power.[11]

The Roosevelt Corollary, as it would come to be known, had far-reaching implications for the US empire in the Caribbean. Whereas the Monroe Doctrine had warned European powers against attempts at (re)colonization in the Americas, the Roosevelt Corollary spelled out the likely response to those independent states that threatened US interests in any way. In particular, countries that ran into financial difficulties could expect special attention in order to obviate the need for European intervention.

This, of course, meant dollar diplomacy.[12] Debts owed by independent states to European powers would be replaced wherever possible with loans from US sources. To ensure prompt payment of debt service, the collection of customs duties would be handed to US officials. The use of the US dollar in domestic transactions would be encouraged. In extreme cases, countries would be occupied militarily by US troops. Imperial control would be exercised without the need for the formal colonial apparatus of European powers, but the US empire would nonetheless be significantly expanded.

The first country to feel the full force of the Roosevelt Corollary was the Dominican Republic. The country in 1900 had already adopted the US dollar as its medium of exchange, but had still failed to control its finances and service its debts. A US customs receivership was therefore established in 1905 without waiting for congressional approval, giving American officials control over the duties that accounted for 99 percent of government revenue. The first call on the receipts was prompt payment of debt servicing costs, ensuring that no foreign power had any reason to intervene. The balance of income was then handed to the Dominican government.[13]

This arrangement was formally approved by Congress in 1907 and would be renewed in 1924. It would not end until 1940, by which time the United States had been in control of Dominican customs receipts—the largest source of government revenue—for thirty-five years. The agreement even allowed up to 5 percent of the receipts to be spent to cover the costs of the US receivership itself, including the housing needs of officials.

Such an arrangement was nothing less than a protectorate. The Dominican Republic was never officially a US colony, but it had no independence in foreign affairs. Dominican politicians were left fighting for scraps, and "revolutions" were common. These sordid contests were at first of little concern to the United States. In 1913–14, for example, there were two "revolutions" that inevitably reduced the amount of revenue collected by the receivership, but debt service payments continued to receive priority, and all that changed was the amount (much smaller) handed over to the Dominican authorities.

The First World War brought an even greater involvement by the US administration in the affairs of the Dominican Republic. Although the United States was at first neutral, it could not rule out the possibility of a German invasion of the Dominican Republic. A Dominican revolution in May 1916 was therefore used as the excuse for US military occupation and the Dominican Republic now became *de facto* a US colony. The Dominican presidency was replaced with a military government led by a US naval officer. All this happened during the presidency of Woodrow Wilson (1913–21), who would present himself at the Versailles Peace Conference in 1919 as an anti-imperialist.

Although the Dominican political elite at first put up little resistance, this was not true of all sections of society, and armed opposition to the occupation was soon under way—especially in the east of the country. The US military therefore became involved in a brutal colonial war—no different from those fought by European powers in Africa and Asia. The guerrilla forces (known as *gavilleros*) were eventually crushed, but not without considerable loss of life. The counterinsurgency techniques used by US forces included scorched-earth tactics and aerial bombing.[14]

By 1922 resistance had been crushed, and President Warren Harding (1921–25), who opposed the occupation before becoming president, was ready to look for an exit. In what would become a familiar pattern, a supposedly nonpartisan National Guard was established and Dominicans were sent for training. In 1924 the occupation ended and a Dominican assumed the presidency, but not before the second American-Dominican Convention had been ratified. This renewed the customs receivership for a further eighteen years.[15] Thus, the Dominican Republic remained firmly inside the US empire—this time as a protectorate rather than a *de facto* colony.

The next task for the US authorities was to choose the head of the Dominican National Guard. Their choice—Rafael Leónidas Trujillo—was to have devastating consequences. Trujillo, a fluent English speaker, understood perfectly the unwritten bargain that rulers of American protectorates were expected to make. In return for unwavering support of the foreign and defense policies of the imperial power, he would be allowed a free hand in internal affairs.[16]

After engineering his way into the presidency in 1930 with US connivance, Trujillo ruled the Dominican Republic as a ruthless dictator while always respecting US strategic interests. His most heinous act was the slaughter of up to thirty thousand Haitians in the west of the country in 1937. In the following year he was persuaded by the US authorities to pay $750,000 to the Haitian government in reparations (a sum reduced a year later to $525,000).[17] Yet he was always warmly received in Washington, DC, and was among the first to declare war on Japan after the bombing of Pearl Harbor.

Trujillo survived the end of the Second World War and soon established his anticommunist credentials during the Cold War. For the sake of appearances, he would allow puppets to hold the presidency while maintaining full control himself. This farce satisfied US sensitivities, but eventually he overreached and became a liability. Although he was an outspoken critic of Fidel Castro, he earned the ire of President John F. Kennedy (1961–63) for trying to overthrow the democratic government in Venezuela. Trujillo's opponents, sensing that he was losing US support, seized their chance and assassinated him in 1961.

That should have been the moment for the Dominican Republic to establish a postimperial relationship with the United States, but it was not yet to be. In 1965 the US Marines invaded in order to prevent Juan Bosch, a left-of-center politician, returning to the presidency. President Lyndon Johnson (1963–69) then helped to engineer the rise to power of Joaquín Balaguer after the marines left in 1966.[18] This loyal supporter of Trujillo for more than thirty years had been the puppet president at the time of the dictator's assassination. Balaguer, despite going blind, would be in and out of office until 1996, when he turned ninety.[19]

4.2. HAITI

Haiti was the second country in the Americas to win its independence. It was therefore the only country for a number of years where the United States could sell its exports without facing discriminatory tariffs.[20] America took full advantage of this and very quickly became the main supplier to Haiti. By 1820, when total US exports were $70 million, Haitian imports from the United States were valued at $2.25 million, so Haiti accounted for roughly 3 percent of US exports at that time.

It would have been natural, therefore, for the United States to have been among the first to give diplomatic recognition to Haiti. Yet this did not take into account the visceral opposition of the southern states, who viewed recognition as tantamount to treason in view of the success of the slave revolt in Haiti. As Senator Robert Hayne of South Carolina explained in 1825, "Our policy with regard to Hayti is plain. We never can acknowledge her independence . . . which the peace and safety of a large portion of our Union forbids us even to discuss."[21]

The opposition of the southern states to recognition was also the reason why the United States failed to take part in the Congress of Panama in 1826, when Simón Bolívar invited all the independent countries of the Americas to debate issues of hemispheric importance.[22] By this time, France and Great Britain had recognized the independence of Haiti, which then showed its displeasure at the United States by imposing an additional tariff on imports from America for a number of years.[23] The southern states, however, would not be moved.

Relations between the United States and Haiti were therefore strained for many years. Agitation in the northern states for recognition was matched by southern contempt for the idea that commercial considerations should be given precedence over all others. Senator McPherson Berrien of Georgia stated,

"These merely *commercial* considerations sink into insignificance—they are swallowed up in the magnitude of the danger with which we are menaced. . . . Do our brethren [northern mercantile interests] differ from us as to the danger of this intercourse? . . . *Ours* is the *post of danger. They* are in comparative *safety.* Who, then, should decide the question?"[24] The US government then made the situation even worse by allowing a private company to seize Navassa Island off the coast of Haiti in 1857, using as pretext the Guano Islands Act of the previous year.

A change in the relationship had to wait for the outbreak of the Civil War. No longer constrained by the opposition of the southern states, President Abraham Lincoln—encouraged by Senator Sumner—was able to grant diplomatic recognition to Haiti in 1862. A commercial treaty soon followed. However, the end of the Civil War marked the beginning of a new, more aggressive, phase in US policy toward Haiti.

Haiti guarded its national sovereignty fiercely, although it failed to recover Navassa Island (it remains a US territory today).[25] Having defeated the French and British in their war of independence, Haitian leaders had no intention of submitting to any foreign power. Haiti therefore resisted American efforts in the late 1880s to secure a naval base at Môle St. Nicholas, a process described by one US historian as "one of the more unsavory episodes in the history of American diplomacy."[26]

Haiti incurred further US displeasure when she rejected the offer of a bilateral trade treaty in 1892. This would have given the US duty-free access to the Haitian market in return for tariff preferences on Haitian exports. However, 99 percent of Haitian government revenue came from customs duties, the United States was the main supplier, and Haitian exports (dominated by coffee) went overwhelmingly to Europe. The treaty therefore had little attraction for Haiti, but its rejection brought a harsh response when the United States imposed retaliatory duties on the main exports.

Haiti, scrupulously servicing its foreign obligations if not its domestic ones, at first escaped the full rigor of the Roosevelt Corollary when it was announced in 1904. However, the external debt was owed to French banks. In addition, some of the domestic loans were provided by German merchants living in Haiti. This raised the possibility in US eyes of foreign intervention by France and/or Germany—in defense of the creditors, but in defiance of the Monroe Doctrine. This was not a risk that US presidents would now be willing to take.

When the Banque Nationale d'Haiti[27] was restructured in 1910 as the Banque Nationale de la Republique d'Haiti, the US administration therefore insisted it was done with the participation of the National City Bank of New York. This

BOX 4.2

FREDERICK DOUGLASS (1818–95)

Frederick Douglass was born in Maryland in 1818 to a slave mother and an unidentified white father. He escaped from slavery in 1838 and lived the risky life of a fugitive in the northern states until the Civil War, when he came to the attention of President Abraham Lincoln (1861–65).

After the war Douglass was in favor of the annexation of the Dominican Republic on paternalistic grounds. He wrote in his autobiography, "To Mr. Sumner, annexation was a measure to extinguish a coloured nation, and to do so by dishonourable means and for selfish motives. To me it meant the alliance of a weak and defenseless people, having few or none of the attributes of a nation, torn and rent by internal feuds and unable to maintain order at home or command respect abroad, to a government which would give it peace, stability, prosperity and civilization."

It was no great surprise, therefore, that President Benjamin Harrison (1889–93) appointed him as minister [today ambassador] to Haiti. Unfortunately for Douglass, his arrival in October 1889 coincided with the start of the bullying campaign by the United States to acquire Môle St. Nicholas as a naval base. This put him in an unenviable position, which was made worse when Admiral Bancroft Gherardi arrived in January 1890 with instructions from Secretary of State James Blaine to secure a lease.

Douglass did his best to mediate, and warned Blaine that Gherardi's aggressive tactics would backfire: "[Seven US men-of-war in the port] made a most unfortunate impression on the entire country. . . . Haiti could not enter negotiations without appearing to yield to foreign pressure and to compromise, *de facto,* [her] existence as an independent people." When the Haitian government in April 1891 refused to give the United States what it wanted, Douglass was made to take the blame. He then resigned in July.

gave the United States a stake in Haitian public finance, since under the restructuring the bank collected customs duties as they were paid and passed them to the Haitian government at the end of the fiscal year (September 30).

On October 1, 1914, the first day of the new fiscal year, the bank abruptly announced it was withdrawing from this arrangement and would not provide short-term loans to tide the government over until September 30 (as had been traditional since 1910). To ensure that the Haitian government did not seize the bank's funds, US Marines were landed to escort $500,000 on board the USS *Machias* for transfer to the National City Bank of New York. The Haitian state was therefore insolvent, and political turmoil soon resulted. US troops, which had been preparing for this eventuality for some time, occupied the country on July 28, 1915.

Haiti was occupied militarily before the Dominican Republic, but the troops stayed much longer. Indeed, they would not be withdrawn until August 1934. This was in large part because of the opposition of the Haitians themselves. Although only one soldier had resisted the landing of the US Marines, there was a fierce nationalist tradition in Haiti and it was not long before resentment at the occupation was stirred up. Guerrilla forces (known as *cacos*) were soon in operation and their defeat was a long and bloody affair. In the first five years alone, 2,250 Haitians were killed.

The responsibility for crushing the rebels lay both with the US Marines and the Gendarmerie d'Haiti, established in 1915 by the occupying force. Rumors of human rights abuse by both soon circulated widely, so much so that the US brigade commander issued a confidential order in October 1919: "The brigade commander has had brought to his attention an alleged charge against marines and gendarmes in Haiti to the effect that in the past prisoners and wounded bandits have been summarily shot without trial. Furthermore, the troops in the field have declared and carried on what is commonly known as 'open season,' where care is not taken to determine whether or not the natives encountered are bandits or 'good citizens' and where houses have been ruthlessly burned merely because they were unoccupied and native property otherwise destroyed."[28]

During the twenty years of occupation, the US authorities were responsible for most internal as well as all external affairs. It was therefore as complete an example of colonial rule as could be found anywhere in Africa or Asia, although a puppet presidency was allowed to operate alongside it.[29] It even included for the first few years a system of forced labor, known as the *corvée*, in which peasants were obliged to work on local roads in lieu of paying a road tax.[30]

The Haitian-American Convention of 1915 was the key to this arrangement, as it gave the US control of public finances, security, and foreign affairs. It provided for the appointment by the United States of a general receiver and all the customs service personnel, who "should collect the revenues and apply them, first, to the expense of the receivership; second, to the service of the debt; third, to the maintenance of a constabulary; and, finally, to the ordinary expenses of the Haitian government."[31] Haiti was also forbidden to increase the debt or reduce the customs revenue without US consent.

Yet even this degree of imperial oversight was considered insufficient. The Haitian Constitution, despite various revisions, still prevented foreigners from owning land. A new constitution was therefore introduced in 1918 (Franklin Roosevelt would claim that as a young naval officer he had drafted it[32]) that abolished this restriction. The path was then cleared for the entry of US capital into agro-industries such as sugar, bananas, and sisal.

The Convention of 1915 was renewed for a further ten years in 1925. A series of violent strikes in 1929 then led the administration of President Herbert Hoover (1929–33) to dispatch a commission to Haiti to explore ways in which the US presence could be ended earlier than planned. These plans were well advanced when President Roosevelt took office and announced the Good Neighbor policy. The marines then left in 1934.

As in the Dominican Republic, the local constabulary took over security duties from the US Marines. However, the customs receivership continued, thereby maintaining a US protectorate in Haiti, since customs duties accounted for the bulk of government revenue. It was not until 1947, after all inherited debt obligations had been met, that the customs receivership was ended.

This long period of *de facto* colonial rule had a very damaging impact on Haiti, and it was exacerbated by the decision of the authorities to send southern officers to command the US forces during the occupation. The inability of these officers to make a distinction between "black" and "mulatto" among the Haitian elite—a distinction that for better or worse had played a key role in Haitian history since independence—was one of the factors behind the *négritude* movement in Haiti.[33]

Championed by Haitian intellectuals, *négritude* was also espoused by Dr. François "Papa Doc" Duvalier. It was one of the reasons why he was able to win the presidential elections in 1957 and provided the ideological basis for his long period of dictatorial government (he died in office in 1971). Although his brutal methods of rule were anathema to President Kennedy, he survived a half-hearted US attempt to dislodge him through skillful use of the anticommunist card.[34]

Haiti under Papa Doc was not a US protectorate, but it was a client state. His brutal domestic rule was tolerated on condition that he recognized and respected US hemispheric priorities. Generally he played the game. Much the same could be said about his son, Jean Claude "Baby Doc" Duvalier, who succeeded to the presidency in 1971. Lacking his father's domestic political skills, however, he was forced into exile by the military in 1986.

The United States now found itself on the back foot. A coup was no longer considered acceptable in Latin America and pressure was put on the military government to allow free elections. These were eventually held in 1990 and brought to power a radical Catholic priest, Jean-Bertrand Aristide. Not surprisingly, relations between Aristide and the military soon broke down and he was driven from office. A United Nations embargo was imposed in 1993 and President Bill Clinton (1993–2001) ordered the US Navy to Haitian waters to enforce it.[35]

These efforts were successful, the military fled into exile, and US troops re-entered Haiti in September 1994 after an absence of sixty years. Haiti had once again become a US protectorate. This time, however, the occupation only lasted a few years while the ground was prepared for the restoration of democracy. Aristide was allowed to serve out the remainder of his term, which ended in 1996. When elections were held in 2000, Aristide then returned to power.

Any hopes that Haiti would once again become a sovereign, independent state—free from US interference—were soon dashed. Aristide's agenda—both domestic and foreign—was considered dangerously radical by both his political opponents and the administration of President George W. Bush (2001–9). In 2004 he was forced under pressure from the United States to "resign" and fled into exile.[36] This time, it was a UN Mission (MINUSTAH) rather than the US Marines that occupied the country, but it was still the United States that was in effective control.

More than a century after the 1915 invasion by the US Marines, Haiti still cannot be described as a sovereign independent state. Its problems are legion and cannot all be laid at the door of the United States. They include a degenerate political class, corruption, and widespread poverty. There have also been terrible natural disasters (especially the earthquake in January 2010). However, the United States cannot escape its own responsibility for failing to establish some semblance of normality in Haiti after such a long period of American tutelage.

4.3. CUBA

Cuba early on attracted especial attention from the United States as a result of its geographic closeness, its expanding foreign trade, and—for the southern states at least—its large slave population. As early as 1823 Secretary of State John Quincy Adams had written, "There are laws of political as well as physical gravitation; and if an apple severed by the tempest from its native tree cannot choose but fall to the ground, Cuba, forcibly disjoined from its own unnatural connection with Spain, and incapable of self-support, can gravitate only towards the North American Union which by the same law of nature, cannot cast her off its bosom."[37] More prosaically, and probably more accurately, Thomas Jefferson in the same year had written to President James Monroe, saying, "I candidly confess, that I have ever looked on Cuba as the most interesting addition which could ever be made to our system of States. The control which, with Florida Point, this island would give us over the Gulf of Mexico, and the countries and isthmus bordering on it, as well as all those whose waters flow into it, would fill up the measure of our political well-being."[38]

Acquiring Cuba, however, was not a simple matter. Spain, having lost all its mainland colonies by the 1820s, not surprisingly rebuffed US attempts to buy the "ever-faithful" island.[39] Yet a military invasion was not realistic before the Civil War given the small size of the US Navy. Furthermore, other European powers were not willing to let Cuba fall into US hands despite their traditional rivalry with Spain. Thus, the use of force by the United States risked a war not just with Spain but with other European powers as well.

Spanish rule was increasingly unpopular on the island. Cuba's economic expansion was used by a stagnant Spain to extract large surpluses for employment elsewhere. A resistance movement was therefore established with the aim of driving out the Spanish authorities. However, this was not at first a movement for independence—as had happened on the mainland. This was a campaign for American annexation. One of its leaders, Narciso López, even adopted a national flag that bore a striking resemblance to the Stars and Stripes.[40] Ironically, it is still in use today.

US opinion was sharply divided on the wisdom of acquiring a territory with a large number of slaves. The southern states were strongly in favor, hoping that the acquisition of Cuba would eventually lead to a new slave state in the Union. The northern states, of course, were implacably opposed. The stalemate continued until the Civil War, after which the abolition of slavery in the United States made acquiring slave-owning Cuba impossible. It was not until slavery ended in Cuba in 1886 that the issue became live again.[41] By then the US private sector had acquired strong interests in sugar, railroads, and mining and was pushing for a more proactive US policy.

By the mid-1890s the US administration still had little to show for all its imperial efforts in the Caribbean. A few unoccupied islands had been acquired under the Guano Islands Act;[42] the McKinley Tariff Act of 1890 had been used to sign bilateral trade treaties with Spain and the United Kingdom (on behalf of their Caribbean colonies) and with the Dominican Republic that gave privileges to US exporters.[43] US capital was invested in the larger islands, but only in the Dominican Republic could it be said to be dominant.

All this would change soon after the outbreak of Cuba's Second War of Independence (1895–98).[44] Spain, the colonial power, was struggling to crush a revolt which rapidly spread to Puerto Rico (its other Caribbean colony) and which this time was aimed at independence (not annexation). The temptation in Washington, DC, to intervene was strong, and the "mood music" in the country had changed. Imperial ambitions were now openly on display and much of the press was clamoring for war. All that was lacking was the *casus belli*.

That came with the sinking of the battleship USS *Maine* in February 1898.[45] The United States declared war on Spain and victory swiftly followed. Cuba and Puerto Rico were occupied militarily. At the peace negotiations in Paris, the nationalists were excluded despite their heroic sacrifices. The United States secured the cession of Puerto Rico, which then became a US colony (its first in the Caribbean) with a governor and all the other apparatus of imperial rule (its name was even changed to Porto Rico to ease pronunciation by the new colonial masters).[46]

Many predicted that Cuba would follow the same path. This, after all, is what Jefferson and Adams had called for almost a century earlier, and the imperial logic had not changed. Indeed, it was what many inside and outside Congress demanded. However, there was an insuperable obstacle in the form of the Teller Amendment. This had been passed by the US Congress in April 1898 at the time war was declared on Spain, and it ensured that Cuba would become nominally independent rather than a formal US colony.

Henry Teller, a Republican senator from Colorado, was no anti-imperialist. However, among other motives, he recognized the danger that a Cuba inside the US tariff wall would represent to the domestic sugar industry (by this time present in almost half the continental states). Coping with competition from Puerto Rico or Hawaii was one thing, but Cuban sugar was a whole different story. One of the lowest cost producers in the world, Cuba could have wiped out not just cane sugar in Florida, Louisiana, and Texas, but also beet sugar in other states (beet sugar is a perfect substitute for cane sugar, and Teller was from a beet-producing state).

Thus, Cuba would become "independent" after four years of military occupation that brought huge advances in health, sanitation, public works, and education. Indeed, it was in many respects a colonial interlude of which any European imperial country would have been proud. Havana Harbor was cleaned up, mortality rates dramatically reduced, and public finances put on a more sustainable keel. Yet it was an independence that was subject to such onerous conditions that Cuba in reality became a US protectorate, the model for many others in the future.

These conditions were laid out in the Platt Amendment, introduced to Congress by Senator Orville Platt (Box 4.3) in 1901 and passed by a vote of 43–20 (it

BOX 4.3
ORVILLE PLATT (1827–1905)

Orville Hitchcock Platt was born to a farming family in Connecticut in 1827. His parents were abolitionists, and the son inherited their views. He cast his first vote for the Free Soilers before joining the Know Nothing Party in the 1850s. Later he joined the Republican Party and played an important part in Connecticut state politics during and after the Civil War.

He first entered the US Senate in 1879 and was a strong supporter of tariff protection for domestic manufacturing. More significantly, he was a member of the Senate Committee on Territories from 1883 to 1895 and chaired it for six years, from 1887 to 1893.

These were the years when the expansion of the US empire into the Caribbean was very much on the agenda. Platt was a strong supporter of the Spanish-American War in 1898 and favored the annexation of Hawaii, the Philippines, and Puerto Rico. He also welcomed the idea of absorbing Cuba, but the Teller Amendment required an alternative to formal annexation.

Platt's solution, although he did not draft it, was the amendment that bears his name. Its eight articles systematically robbed Cuba of any possibility of becoming a sovereign independent country. When the Cuban Congress was forced to absorb the amendment into its 1902 constitution, it made it very difficult to change.

Article 7 allowed the United States to choose Guantánamo Bay for one of its naval bases in Cuba. Although some of the articles of the Platt Amendment were repealed in 1934, the United States negotiated a new treaty with Cuba allowing it to keep Guantánamo Bay provided that it was used only for its original purpose.

had in fact been drafted by Secretary of War Elihu Root). It established eight conditions that Cuba had to accept before the US military would be withdrawn and independence declared. Article 3, for example, stated: "The Government of Cuba consents that the United States may exercise the right to intervene for the preservation of Cuban independence, the maintenance of a government adequate for the protection of life, property, and individual liberty, and for discharging the obligations with respect to Cuba imposed by the Treaty of Paris

on the United States, now to be assumed and undertaken by the Government
of Cuba."

If Article 3 gave the United States a blank check to intervene at will, Article
7 paved the way for the all-important naval bases that had eluded the United
States for so long. It stated that "to enable the United States to maintain the independence of Cuba, and to protect the people thereof, as well as for its own
defense, the Government of Cuba will sell or lease to the United States lands
necessary for coaling or naval stations, at certain specified points, to be agreed
upon with the President of the United States."[47]

The Cuban Assembly, despite being a largely supine body during the military occupation, was so offended by the Platt Amendment that it initially voted
against the conditions. When it became clear that US forces would not withdraw, the assembly changed its mind and the amendment was incorporated into
the new Cuban Constitution without a word being altered. Within a year, the
United States had selected its preferred sites for coaling and naval stations. They
would include Guantánamo Bay.[48]

US forces left in 1902, independence was declared the same year, and Cuba
became the first Caribbean country since the Dominican Republic in 1844 to
escape formal colonial control. However, its sovereignty was heavily restricted.
This was demonstrated not only by the Platt Amendment but also by the Cuban-
American Treaty of 1903, which gave the United States a wide range of tariff
preferences in the Cuban market in exchange for duty reductions for raw sugar
and tobacco imports. This paved the way for the massive entry of US capital,
and a new sugar boom was soon under way on the island.

As a protectorate, Cuba was now firmly in the US orbit. However, as many
European powers had found in their own informal empires, protectorates could
still be very troublesome. US troops were back in Cuba in 1906 when election
results were disputed, and they did not leave until 1909. Three years later they
were back again to help put down an insurrection sparked by the suppression of
the Partido Independiente de Color, a movement started by black veterans
of the Second War of Independence in protest against discrimination. The tradition in which the US authorities would become the arbiter of domestic political disputes in Cuba was now well established.

After FDR outlined the Good Neighbor policy, optimists could argue that
Cuba was no longer a US protectorate. However, this was not true, as the United
States retained Guantánamo Bay and a revised Cuban-American Treaty in
1934 still gave America special privileges.[49] In addition, US sugar policy toward
Cuba had changed, and this crucial export was now subject to quotas that
could be raised or lowered according to US whim.[50] In any case, the dominant

position of the United States in domestic politics was very quickly demonstrated.

The US ambassador to Cuba (Sumner Welles) found himself in 1933 in conflict with President Gerardo Machado, whose term of office was due to expire in May 1935. Machado had been favored by US officials in the 1920s, and this had helped him to retain the presidency under dubious circumstances. However, he had now outlived his usefulness and had become increasingly discredited.

Welles negotiated with the Cuban army for intervention against Machado, and he was duly ousted from office in August 1933. His successor (Carlos Manuel de Céspedes), however, was too weak to deal with the numerous social conflicts that arose in the wake of the Great Depression. This had hit Cuba very hard, and the result was a series of strikes and protests that became increasingly radical.

The protests included sections of the armed forces themselves. A barracks revolt, led by Sergeant Fulgencio Batista, unleashed a series of events that resulted in the fall of the government. A provisional government was then formed, led by Ramón Grau San Martín, an intellectual and a respected figure in Cuban political life. He promised to establish a modern democracy and launched a number of social reforms.

This was too radical for Sumner Welles, and US recognition of the government was withheld. This guaranteed that Grau San Martín's presidency would be short-lived. Welles then encouraged the Cuban Army—now led by Batista—to intervene. Batista instantly became the "strong man" of Cuban politics, ruling either through a series of puppets, albeit elected, or as president himself until his flight from Cuba on January 1, 1959.[51]

His reward for overthrowing the Cuban government in 1934 and installing a new president was US recognition of his regime. Cuba was still a protectorate and Batista, like the other dictators in the Caribbean, understood that in order to retain power he had to protect US interests. The US protectorate over Cuba only ended with the Cuban Revolution, which helps to explain the ferocity with which Fidel Castro's government was greeted by the administration of President Dwight D. Eisenhower and subsequent administrations.

4.4. AMERICAN COLONIES

Puerto Rico was annexed in 1898, but it was a few years before its constitutional status would be clarified. The American military authorities on the island, unsure of the final status, began by lowering (but not eliminating) the tariff on imports from Puerto Rico into the United States. The Organic Act of 1900, sponsored by Senator Joseph Foraker, was then passed; it was similar to that for the Philippines. This left Puerto Rico as "unincorporated," meaning it had no right to statehood. The Foraker Act provided for a locally elected House of Delegates, but a US-appointed upper chamber and governor.[52]

Puerto Rico came fully inside the US tariff wall in 1902 (this was a decade before the Philippines). No duties or quotas would now be applied to goods exported from the island to the United States. This gave export industries an advantage over competitors in the Caribbean. An export boom then commenced and within a few years virtually all trade was with the United States.

Puerto Rico was now a US colony. Federal taxes were not applied to the island, but customs duties raised very little (almost all trade was with the mainland) and budget subsidies from the mainland were nonexistent. The island therefore suffered from the problems common to many colonies. However, under the 1917 Jones Act Puerto Ricans became US citizens (this never happened in the Philippines). This did not give them the right to vote in US elections, but it did give them unrestricted entry to the United States.[53] The Jones Act also provided for a locally elected upper chamber.

The colonial government, anxious to avoid the emergence of a strong US lobby in favor of statehood, at first restricted the size of landholdings to five hundred hectares.[54] However, this was quietly ignored when it became clear that it was an obstacle to the expansion of sugar exports. Duty-free access to the US market for sugar had a spectacular impact and US capital poured into the island.

Unfortunately for Puerto Rico, it was too successful. When the crisis of the world's sugar industry reached a climax in the Great Depression, the island was obliged to make a major sacrifice. Under the 1934 US Sugar Act, the island kept its duty-free access but lost its quota-free position. The sugar industry therefore lost its dynamism, unemployment soared, and migration to the United States—especially New York City—accelerated.

This was the moment when Puerto Rico's colonial status nearly ended. Senator Millard Tydings, who had sponsored the bill in 1934 that provided for the eventual independence of the Philippines, tried to do the same for Puerto Rico in 1936. Many Puerto Ricans supported the bill, although none had a vote, but the political class on the island was divided. Senator Tydings then withdrew his bill. The main opponent of independence was Luis Muñoz Marín, who would go on to form the Partido Popular Democrático (PPD) and become the first elected governor in 1948.[55]

The decision of the US government in the Second World War to return to Puerto Rico the federal excise duties collected on rum exports gave a big boost to the island, as it coincided with the wartime switch on the mainland from whisky to rum consumption.[56] It also provided the resources for a colonial experiment in state-owned enterprises (the Puerto Rican Development Company and Development Bank). Although implemented by the local Puerto Rican government, the experiment was the brainchild of the colonial governor.

Encouraged by the results, Puerto Rico adopted Operation Bootstrap after the Second World War with spectacular results. Boosted by local fiscal incentives and the absence of federal taxes, manufacturing on the island soared and Puerto Rico became for many a model of development. Sir Arthur Lewis, whose work on development economics earned him a Nobel Prize, was particularly enthusiastic.

As had happened with sugar, the experiment was too successful. The impact of fiscal concessions on the US federal budget became too large, and they started to be withdrawn in the 1990s (Box 4.4). The result was a decline in manufacturing on the island and a big increase in unemployment and net outward migration. Those who previously looked to Puerto Rico as an inspiration for the Caribbean started to look elsewhere.

Puerto Rico is now in limbo and bankrupt. A majority says it wants a change in the island's constitutional status. Yet only a small minority favor independence, as it would mean losing both federal welfare benefits and unrestricted access to the United States. There is for the first time a majority in favor of statehood, but no certainty that it can be achieved, as the decision can only be taken by Congress.[57]

Puerto Rico became a US colony as a result of war. The US Virgin Islands, on the other hand, became a dependency by a very different route. Secretary of State William Seward had returned from a tour of the Caribbean after the Civil War enthused by the idea of acquiring the magnificent harbor at St. Thomas in the Danish West Indies.[58] An attempt was made by the US government to purchase the three islands from Denmark in 1867. It looked as if it would meet with success (the Danish Parliament had voted in favor), but the treaty was rejected by the US Senate in 1870.[59]

Embarrassing though it was, this would not be a major blow to the US government. By the end of the century Cuba had been turned into a protectorate and Puerto Rico had become a colony. The occupation of Haiti (1915) and the Dominican Republic (1916) then left the United States in a dominant position in the Caribbean.

BOX 4.4
CARIBBEAN COLONIES AND US FISCAL POLICY

By the beginning of the twentieth century, the US economy had become so large in relation to all Caribbean colonies that any change in US fiscal policy was bound to have a major impact. This was true not just for the US colonies/protectorates but also for the European colonies.

When the United States eliminated its sugar tariff for Puerto Rico in 1901 and lowered it for Cuba in 1903, it led to a sugar boom on the two islands. It also led to trade diversion away from the British colonies that had previously supplied the United States with much of its needs. These colonies then shifted exports to Canada, taking advantage of the recent introduction of imperial preference there.

The 1919 Prohibition Act in the United States effectively imposed an infinite tariff on rum imports. Suddenly, St. Pierre and Miquelon—two tiny French islands at the mouth of the St. Lawrence River—became major destinations for exports from numerous Caribbean islands. From there alcoholic drinks entered Canada legally before being imported as contraband into the United States. The Virgin Islands, on the other hand, turned the alcohol into bay rum in order to stay within the law.

The decision by the United States to return the excise duty on rum consumption to the US colonies (1954 for the Virgin Islands, earlier for Puerto Rico) not only boosted the industry but also damaged exports from other Caribbean countries. When the Virgin Islands started to use the funds in 2010 to subsidize the operations of multinational enterprises manufacturing spirits, the other Caribbean countries launched a claim against the United States at the World Trade Organization.

When federal tax exemption became available for the operations of US companies in Puerto Rico after the Second World War, manufacturing boomed and reached 50 percent of GDP (twice the US ratio). However, when the tax breaks were phased out during the administration of President Bill Clinton (1993–2001) it had a crippling effect. Only the pharmaceutical companies, still allowed to write off their research and development expenditure on the mainland against their profits on the island, were able to survive.

France and Great Britain controlled most of the other islands, and the United States had little to fear from them. When the First World War broke out in August 1914, America remained neutral. The security of the Panama Canal, opened to international traffic in the same month as the war started, therefore appeared assured to the strategists in Washington, DC.

There was still, however, one weak link: the colonies of the neutral European powers. Neither Denmark nor Holland had gone to war in 1914, and both controlled islands that were either close to the US mainland or to the Panama Canal.[60] If Germany should invade Denmark or Holland, these islands could fall into the hands of a potential enemy. In particular, the United States was conscious of the risk that the Danish harbor of St. Thomas—perhaps the finest in the Caribbean for naval purposes—might become a base for German submarines.

Thus, President Wilson was persuaded to return again to the vexed question of the transfer of sovereignty of the Danish West Indies. This time, however, the matter was urgent and negotiations were concluded quickly. The price ($25 million) was much higher than suggested before, but that was now immaterial. By the end of March 1917, just before US entry into the First World War, the Stars and Stripes had replaced the Danish flag on the territory that would be known as the US Virgin Islands.

The United States now had two Caribbean colonies, but their administration was very different.[61] The navy was put in charge of the Virgin Islands until 1931 in recognition of its maritime importance. This led, however, to some strange decisions such as the navy chaplain in 1924 being put in charge of the newly established Department of Agriculture. And colonial governance was not helped by Prohibition (1919–33), since it crippled one of the main industries on the island.[62]

Duty-free access to the US market for the islands' sugar from 1917 onward did not have the anticipated effect, so the authorities conducted an unusual colonial experiment.[63] This was the creation in 1934 of the state-owned Virgin Islands Corporation with the power to control all aspects of the sugar, rum, and molasses industries and later branching out into banking, tourism, and public utilities. It was an experiment that the British would later copy in some of their African colonies, although state control was never taken as far.

By the end of the 1930s the United States had consolidated its empire through its two colonies and its three protectorates over the "independent" states of the Caribbean. However, that still left the European colonies. Great Britain, France, and Holland between them controlled all the smaller islands (except the US

Virgin Islands) as well as the littoral territories of Belize (British Honduras) and the three Guianas.

All three European powers adopted commercial policies that favored the exports of their own companies to their colonies.[64] This was standard among imperial powers. Indeed, the United States did the same with its Caribbean colonies, with Cuba (through the reciprocity treaty), and with Haiti and the Dominican Republic through the customs receiverships (tariff revisions invariably favored US exporters). However, the State Department under Cordell Hull became increasingly irritated with the imperial preference of the European powers, as it ran counter to US efforts to liberalize trade in the 1930s.[65]

This irritation led to a bilateral treaty with the United Kingdom in 1937 to ensure that US firms had the same access to Caribbean colonies as British companies. It also meant that US firms could export from these colonies to the United Kingdom without fear of discrimination. At the same time, the Dutch colonies were becoming increasingly important for US strategic needs as a result of the oil refineries on Aruba and Curaçao and the bauxite deposits in Suriname. US investments therefore started pouring into the British and Dutch colonies (the French ones would remain impenetrable).

The new *modus vivendi* between the European and American empires in the Caribbean was disrupted by the outbreak of the Second World War in September 1939. No longer could the United States assume that the European powers would take care of security in their colonies. In particular, the Panama Canal could be under threat if hostile forces acquired any of the territories in the region.

The invasion of France and Holland by Germany in June 1940 dramatically raised the stakes. The Dutch Caribbean territories remained loyal to the government in exile, but had no means of defending themselves in the case of attack. The French Caribbean colonies declared their allegiance to the Vichy government and were therefore vulnerable to German pressure. The United Kingdom survived the Battle of Britain, but was increasingly desperate for *materiel* with which to conduct the war.

The result was an enormous expansion of the US imperial presence in the region even before American entry into the Second World War. Troops were dispatched to the Dutch colonies to protect the oil refineries and bauxite mines, while no trade was permitted with German-occupied Holland. Naval vessels patrolled the seas off the French colonies to ensure there was no trade with Vichy France or Germany. For the first time ever, the United States became the main trade partner for these territories.

Military bases were leased for ninety-nine years from Great Britain on several of its Caribbean colonies in return for US destroyers. The local population was not consulted, and the arrival of US armed forces was to prove controversial. In Trinidad & Tobago, the base inspired a famous calypso song ("Rum and Coca Cola") whose second and third verses left little to the imagination.

When the United States entered the war in December 1941, it therefore had all it needed in the Caribbean to protect its interests. An Anglo-American Caribbean Commission was established in 1942 to deal with wartime issues. France and Holland joined in 1946 to participate in postwar planning. This was a conscious effort by the empires to establish the framework for continuing imperial control of the Caribbean. Not much attention was paid to local aspirations, much to the disgust of Eric Williams (the first prime minister of Trinidad & Tobago) who worked for the commission during the war.[66]

Until the end of the 1950s, the United States had every reason therefore to assume its empire in the Caribbean was secure. However, the Cuban Revolution was a major challenge to US authority. Cuba was by far the most important country in the region and its "loss" harmed the prestige of the United States in many ways. Just as damaging, however, were the policies adopted by America against Cuba even after the threat to national security had passed.[67]

The US territorial empire in the Caribbean has not ended (there are, after all, two colonies) and the United States has continued to intervene occasionally by force.[68] However, American imperialism takes a different form—not just in the Caribbean but in other parts of the world as well—and the territorial empire is no longer so important. How this transformation in the American empire took place is the subject of Part II.

Part Two

THE SEMIGLOBAL EMPIRE

5

INSTITUTIONS

At the beginning of the twentieth century, the US territorial empire was still extensive. It included five enormous territories on the mainland of North America (Alaska, Arizona, Indian Territory, New Mexico, and Oklahoma); several colonies in the Caribbean, the Pacific, and Central America; a number of protectorates in West Africa, Central America, and the Caribbean; territorial concessions in China; and numerous small "unincorporated" islands.

A few additions would shortly be made to the territorial empire. These included one new colony (the former Danish West Indies), new protectorates in the Caribbean (the Dominican Republic and Haiti), and customs receiverships in South America (Bolivia and Peru).[1] However, the North American territories (except Alaska) would soon enter the Union, and the Philippines from 1934 onward would be on the path to independence, while the protectorates and customs receiverships would eventually come to an end.

The territorial empire had therefore shrunk significantly by the end of the Second World War and subsequently there would be little expansion.[2] However, this did not mean the end of American empire as new forms of imperial control had already started to come into play. Some of these echoed the looser forms of imperial control popular among European states, but the United States went much further in pursuit of its empire.

The reasons for this are not hard to find. The United States that emerged from the Civil War would soon become an industrial power of the first rank and was on course to become the world's largest economy. It therefore needed foreign markets for its surplus production. An empire based only on US dependencies would never be sufficient for this purpose. However, the imperial preference exercised by European powers in their territories was an obstacle to

US manufactured exports. These barriers therefore needed to be dismantled, but ideally without the use of force.

By the end of the First World War another important change had taken place in the US economy. It had gone from being a net debtor, importing capital, to a net creditor. US capital would now flow abroad in ever-growing quantities, either as portfolio capital or as foreign direct investment. This meant the US government needed to secure as much influence as possible over the countries to which its capital would now be exported in order to protect the property rights of US investors. And this meant hegemony over large swaths of the world—not just American territories.

The final change was the emergence of the United States from the Second World War as the unrivaled economic and financial global powerhouse. Relatively unscarred by the war itself, US agricultural and industrial output reached levels that were previously unimaginable. At the same time, its financial system was the envy of the world and the United States was virtually the only source of external credit for a vast array of countries. This meant America was in a position to pursue a much more ambitious type of empire than one based only on territories.

From the late nineteenth century onward, therefore, the United States was in transition from being *a* world industrial power to becoming *the* global economic and financial force. The evolution of its empire matched this transformation. It began to outgrow the limits of a territorial empire on the European model. Indeed, the Philippines was to show the obvious pitfalls of such a model to a country so concerned with race and the protection of domestic economic interests.

Instead, the United States built an empire based primarily on institutional rather than territorial control. This was a relatively novel concept in a world where regional, let alone global, institutions were rare and in which treaties were assumed to impose equal duties and obligations on the signatories. Yet in this institutional empire that the United States built, ways would be found of ensuring that American interests would receive priority and be given more weight than those of other partners.

The first attempt at building an empire based primarily on institutions was in the western hemisphere, in accordance with the theory that rising powers seek first to dominate their own region.[3] The inter-American system constructed by the United States from the late nineteenth century onward has survived to this day and, until very recently, was underpinned by the Monroe Doctrine—the principle that guided US foreign policy for almost two centuries.

The inter-American system also provided the model for the global architecture—the League of Nations—that President Woodrow Wilson (1913–21) tried to construct at the end of the First World War. It was a bold attempt at global leadership, but American power was not yet commensurate with the country's ambitions and the experiment failed. Yet it provided the template for the much more successful United Nations (UN) system built by the United States at the end of the Second World War.

The UN system started well, but its ability to promote US national security interests was weakened by the Cold War. The United States therefore needed to build a separate set of institutions that would look after its security needs. This, together with hundreds of military bases around the world, was swiftly done. In these institutions other countries understood the subordinate *de facto* role they played while being treated *de jure* as equals. It could not be otherwise given the imbalance in defense spending between the United States and its allies.

Finally, the United States after the Second World War built a system of trade and financial institutions that did not even attempt to preserve the fiction of state equality under the law. In the most important of these institutions, such as the International Monetary Fund (IMF) and the World Bank, the United States acquired a dominant position by treaty so that its authority could not easily be challenged. Indeed, America is the only country that enjoys a veto over changes in these institutions, meaning that reform cannot be undertaken without US approval.

The postwar system built by the United States was, and still is, an empire. Arguably, no other country in history has enjoyed such a dominant world position, and certainly none has done so to such effect through the control of institutions. Yet, although often described as such, it was never a truly global empire since the United States confronted a Soviet Union that was its equal in terms of military power. America therefore faced a Soviet empire that it could only "contain" until its eventual collapse in 1989. Thus, the postwar American empire is best described as a semiglobal one.

5.1. THE INTER-AMERICAN SYSTEM

The Monroe Doctrine was never an international treaty or convention, nor was it ever part of customary international law. Yet it is impossible to understand the empire the United States built in the Americas without a reference to it. Indeed, the Monroe Doctrine was the foundation stone of the US-inspired inter-American system. It also guided US policy in the western hemisphere, and in some cases other regions, for nearly two hundred years.[4]

John Quincy Adams, as secretary of state, was concerned about Russian expansion on the Pacific coastline of North America (see Chapter 1). Although the threat had passed by the time President James Monroe delivered his seventh annual message to Congress on December 2, 1823, Adams drafted these prescient words for the president:

> We . . . declare that we should consider any attempt on their [European] part to extend their system to any portion of this hemisphere, as dangerous to our peace and safety. . . . With the existing colonies or dependencies of any European power we have not interfered, and shall not interfere. But with the governments who have declared their independence, and maintained it, and whose independence we have, on great consideration, and on just principles, acknowledged, we could not view any interposition for the purpose of oppressing them, or controlling, in any other manner, their destiny, by any European power in any other light than as the manifestation of an unfriendly disposition towards the United States.[5]

The significance of these words was not fully appreciated at the time, either in the United States or elsewhere. The federal government, after all, was in no position to stop European powers that wanted to act in an imperial fashion in the region,[6] and those European governments that did pay attention to the president's words were unimpressed. The Russian czar responded that the message deserved "only the most profound contempt." The French minister of foreign affairs said that it "should be resisted by all the powers having commercial or territorial interests in that hemisphere." Prince Metternich of Austria referred to the president's words as "indecent declarations."

Despite this unpromising start, Monroe's message gradually caught hold of the US imagination. It was not until President James K. Polk (1845–49) that the famous words would become widely known as the Monroe "principle" (it would not be called the Monroe Doctrine before 1853). Yet Polk's dealings with European powers, especially Great Britain, demonstrated some of the internal contradictions of the Monroe Doctrine. It was ineffective in the face of European intransigence, and it could do little at first to block an American state that chose to have close relations with an outside power.

The Monroe Doctrine, therefore, required recognition by European powers and American states alike that the United States was hegemonic in the western hemisphere and was prepared to use force to protect its interests. This was no simple matter, since the United States before 1860 did not have the moral authority or the military capability to do this. However, the Civil War changed everything, and it was not long before the United States started to flex its muscles.

The first attempt to build an inter-American system was by James Blaine, secretary of state in the short-lived administration of President James A. Garfield

(1881), who issued invitations to Latin American governments to attend a conference in Washington, DC.[7] Blaine was motivated primarily by two considerations: conflict among American states or within a single state that could lead to European intervention,[8] and the desire to increase US exports to Latin America at the expense of European powers; in his own words: "first, to bring about peace . . . ; second, to cultivate such friendly commercial relations with all American countries as would lead to a large increase in the export trade of the United States. To obtain the second object the first must be accomplished."[9]

When President Garfield was assassinated, Blaine lost his post and his successor withdrew the invitations. However, Congress passed an act in 1888 calling for an inter-American conference. When Blaine was appointed secretary of state in the administration of President Benjamin Harrison (1889–93), it fell to him once again to issue the invitations. This time, however, his position had hardened: "I think it will be demonstrated in the very near future that the United States will have to assume a much more decided tone in South America than the one which I took and which was rescinded, or else it will have to back out of it, and say that it is a domain that does not belong to us, and we surrender it to Europe."[10]

Needless to say, Blaine had no intention of "surrendering to Europe," and the first inter-American conference duly took place in Washington, DC, in 1889–90. Blaine's agenda, however, was too ambitious, and the Latin American republics did not accept his proposal for a customs union or compulsory arbitration of inter-American conflicts. Nonetheless, US hegemony in the region was implicitly accepted and the groundwork was laid for what would become the US-dominated Pan-American Union.

US hemispheric ambitions were soon laid bare in a dispute involving Great Britain and Venezuela over the border between the latter and the colony of British Guiana. Ostensibly, this dispute had nothing to do with the United States, since President Monroe had said that his government would not interfere with existing European colonies. However, the administration of President Grover Cleveland (1893–97) was determined to use this dispute to demonstrate that the United States was indispensible to the resolution of hemispheric conflicts. Secretary of State Richard Olney therefore wrote these (in)famous words to the British foreign secretary, Lord Salisbury, in 1895:

Today the United States is practically sovereign on this continent, and its fiat is law upon the subjects to which it confines its interposition. Why? It is not because of the pure friendship or good will felt for it. It is not simply by reason of its high character as a civilized state, nor because wisdom and justice and equity are the invariable characteristics of the dealings of the United States. It is because, in addition to all other grounds, its infinite resources combined with its isolated position render it master of the situation and practically invulnerable as against any or all other powers.[11]

Lord Salisbury responded in equally arrogant terms, but it was not long before the British government had capitulated. Arbitration was agreed, a board was established to include two American citizens, and Venezuela was not consulted.[12] It was a turning point in Anglo-American relations, Great Britain now accepting US hegemony in Latin America, but it also proved to be a crucial moment in hemispheric relations.

The inter-American system under US tutelage now evolved rapidly. The Spanish-American War (1898), in which the United States clearly *did* interfere with the "existing colonies of a European power," marked one turning point. The Roosevelt Corollary (1904), in which President Theodore Roosevelt (1901–9) gave a distinctly aggressive interpretation to the Monroe Doctrine, marked another. Dollar diplomacy under President William Howard Taft (1909–13) took the process a stage further and the "anti-imperialist" president Wilson would intervene repeatedly in Mexico, Central America, and the Caribbean.

These imperialist interventions generated considerable resentment throughout Latin America. Although Brazil in 1910 had introduced a motion at the fourth inter-American conference praising the Monroe Doctrine, it won no support and had to be withdrawn. By the time of the sixth conference in 1928, opposition had risen. US hegemony survived thanks to diplomacy by former secretary of state Charles Evan Hughes, but influential Republicans and Democrats recognized that a more nuanced approach to US empire in the hemisphere was required.

The key to this change was not to renounce the Monroe Doctrine but to secure "buy-in" from the Latin American states themselves. Indeed, as early as 1916 "Colonel" Edward M. House (adviser to President Wilson) had said the president's purpose was "to broaden the Monroe Doctrine so that it may be upheld by all the American Republics instead of by the United States alone as of now."[13] Secretary of State William Jennings Bryan repeated this to the Chilean ambassador.

It was left to Franklin Delano Roosevelt (FDR, 1933–45), however, to explain more clearly what was required. Writing in *Foreign Affairs* in 1928, nearly five years before he became president, FDR stated,

It is possible that in the days to come one of our sister nations may fall upon evil days; disorder and bad government may require that a helping hand be given her citizens as a matter of temporary necessity to bring back order and stability. In that event it is not the right or the duty of the United States to intervene alone. It is rather the duty of the United States to associate with itself other American Republics, to give intelligent joint study to the problem, and, if the conditions warrant, to offer the helping hand or hands in the name of the Americas. Single-handed intervention by us in the internal affairs of other nations must end; with the cooperation of others we shall have more order in this hemisphere and less dislike.[14]

This was the outline of the Good Neighbor policy that FDR would announce as soon as he became president in 1933. It was swiftly welcomed by the Latin American republics at the seventh inter-American conference in December 1933, but they were too quick to assume it marked the end of US imperialism. The Good Neighbor policy was instead an abrogation of unilateral military intervention in return for broad Latin American support for US hegemony in the western hemisphere.

No one understood this more clearly than Sumner Welles, President Roosevelt's undersecretary of state from 1937 to 1943, who had vast experience of hemispheric diplomacy. Just before the Second World War he explained,

It would not be correct to say that the Monroe Doctrine had been replaced or superseded by the group of inter-American agreements that has grown up in recent years. . . . The Monroe Doctrine was promulgated, in the first place, as a unilateral declaration on the part of the United States. It still stands as such a declaration. It could still be invoked, if there were occasion, unilaterally, by the United States. . . . But what has happened is this. The purposes that it sought to accomplish have become the recognized concern of all the American nations and they have declared, multilaterally, their support of its objectives. . . . Thus we may naturally expect in the future the unilateral character of the Doctrine will be pushed more and more into the background and its multilateral character emphasized. . . . What has taken place is not a change in policy but a change in emphasis. The emphasis is now on joint action rather than on single action.[15]

This new approach would pay a handsome dividend. Within days of the United States entering the Second World War in December 1941, almost all Latin American states had declared war on the Axis powers despite the sympathy many of their governments had previously expressed for fascism. Foreign trade in the hemisphere was quickly reorientated to serve the needs of the US war effort and an Inter-American Defense Board was established to provide Latin American support for US security objectives.

The economic and financial schemes put in place for the hemisphere during the war lapsed as soon as hostilities ended, much to the frustration of the Latin American republics. The same might have happened to the security arrangements were it not for the eruption of the Cold War, which the United States deemed required an immediate regional response. A meeting was called, and the Inter-American Conference for the Maintenance of Continental Peace and Security was held in August 1947.

The result was the Inter-American Treaty of Reciprocal Assistance, commonly known as the Rio Treaty. Article 3 established the principle that an armed attack on any American state was an attack on all of them, thus laying down the principle of collective self-defense. This was relatively uncontroversial, as Article 51 of the United Nations Charter had already recognized the right of a country or group of countries to use force in self-defense. Clearly, however, Article 3 could be used by the United States in case of a communist attack on any part of the Americas.[16]

The Rio Treaty proved much more controversial when it also spelled out in Article 6 what would happen "if the inviolability or the integrity of the territory or the sovereignty or political independence of any American State should be affected by an aggression which is not an armed attack or by an extra-continental or intra-continental conflict, or by any other fact or situation that might endanger the peace of America."[17] This was a very broad definition and, in the context of the Cold War, it would clearly rest with the US government to define whether a breach of the peace had taken place. In such a case, "the Organ of Consultation of the Inter-American System" would establish what response to take, including the use of armed force.[18]

The Rio Treaty would be ratified by all American states. It provided for collective security in the event of aggression and was the culmination of the long effort to find an institutional expression for the Monroe Doctrine that would avoid the need for unilateral US action. Flushed with success, the United States then turned its attention to the rest of the inter-American system.

The Ninth International Conference of American States, as it was now known, was held in Colombia in 1948. The most important outcome was the Charter of the Organization of American States (OAS). Article 5(d) called for all members to be organized "on the basis of the effective exercise of representative democracy." This was certainly not a reflection of reality at the time, but it could of course be used at a later date by the United States in the event of a military coup or unconstitutional change of government.[19]

BOX 5.1
THE UNITED STATES AND HUMAN RIGHTS IN THE AMERICAS

At the Ninth International Conference of American States in 1948, all twenty-one republics adopted the American Declaration of the Rights and Duties of Man (this was several months before the UN Declaration of Human Rights). In 1959 an Inter-American Commission on Human Rights was established in Washington, DC. A decade later an American Convention on Human Rights was signed and an Inter-American Court of Human Rights was established in Costa Rica.

Although the convention was not yet operating, the human rights architecture of the inter-American system was almost fully in place when President Jimmy Carter (1977–81) was elected. With Carter's emphasis on human rights as a key feature of US foreign policy, it was expected that the administration would then put all its weight behind the protection of human rights within the inter-American system.

Yet the US Senate never ratified the convention, and it went into force in 1978 without US participation. This has made it difficult for the United States to push a human rights agenda in the Americas despite the fact that it has the right to be represented on the Inter-American Commission on Human Rights and the Inter-American Court of Human Rights (the two bodies that oversee compliance with the convention).

The United States therefore lost an opportunity to use its influence in support of human rights in the hemisphere and has had to rely instead on the annual report on human rights of the State Department. This unilateral approach, however, is somewhat discredited by the US practice of using a country's alleged noncompliance with human rights in order to secure US interests in other areas.

The convention placed severe restrictions on the use of the death penalty, which is one reason why it was not ratified by the United States. When a protocol was added to the convention in 1990 outlawing the death penalty altogether, it ensured that the United States would probably never ratify. Thus, the United States will remain partially outside the inter-American human rights system for the foreseeable future.

The OAS would now replace its predecessor, the Union of American Republics, but its headquarters were still in Washington, DC, and its budget largely came from the federal government. Despite a number of grievances, Latin American states were not prepared to stand in the way of a United States determined to use the OAS for its own ends. When Secretary of State John Foster Dulles therefore proposed at the OAS meeting in 1954 that "the domination or control of the political institutions of any American state by the international communist movement . . . would constitute a threat" to the entire hemisphere and would require "appropriate action in accordance with existing treaties,"[20] they acquiesced.

Their agreement, given in some cases reluctantly, would convert the OAS into a crude instrument of American empire. An institution that had hitherto seemed rather bland would now be in the front line of US efforts to confront and overthrow left-wing political movements in the hemisphere. And following the Cuban Revolution, the OAS was supplemented both by an Inter-American Development Bank (IADB) providing loans and an Alliance for Progress (ALPRO) offering grants. Both were designed and controlled by US administrations to channel resources to sympathetic hemispheric governments and win the battle for "hearts and minds."

The United States was able to suspend Cuba's membership of the OAS in 1962 and secure the organization's approval for the US invasion of the Dominican Republic a few years later. These efforts, however, steadily discredited the OAS in the eyes of Latin American societies and eventually many of their governments as well. And ALPRO, never properly funded, soon withered once the Cuban threat had passed.

The OAS at least survived, but by the 1970s it had ceased to be a major focus of US attention. More important for the preservation of US hemispheric hegemony were some of the bodies created within the inter-American system that were nominally under OAS auspices (Box 5.1). Furthermore, with the end of the Cold War, the United States no longer felt an obligation to support anticommunist military and authoritarian governments and was able to throw its weight behind the regional movement in favor of democracy.

One result was the Inter-American Democratic Charter, adopted on September 11, 2001, which laid down what democracy entailed and what would happen in the case of "an unconstitutional interruption of the democratic order." It was clearly intended by the United States to ensure that communist Cuba could not reenter the inter-American system without a change of government. However, the expectation was that it could also be used to apply pressure on any hemispheric regime that departed from the liberal, democratic order favored by the United States.

5.2. FROM LEAGUE OF NATIONS TO UNITED NATIONS

Unlike what happened in the rest of the Americas, the United States was not the first to take the lead in trying to establish global institutions in support of peace and security. Instead, it was Czar Nicholas II of Russia who convoked the international peace conference that led to the first Hague Convention in 1899 and a Permanent Court of Arbitration. The aims of the conference were to promote disarmament, establish procedures for the rules of war, and identify war crimes.

The United States was present, but played a supporting rather than leading role. Within a few years, however, this had changed. It was President Theodore Roosevelt who proposed the next international peace conference leading to the second Hague Convention in 1907. The subject matter was similar to the first conference, and plans were made for a third in 1914, but the outbreak of the First World War destroyed any chance of holding it.

The war started soon after President Woodrow Wilson came to power. By the time the United States entered in April 1917, it was clear that it would be heavily involved in whatever global institutional arrangements might emerge after peace was restored. No one understood this more than Wilson, whose Fourteen Points speech to Congress in January 1918 provided the framework for the peace conference in Paris at the end of the war.[21]

Wilson came to Paris with a highly ambitious agenda that would—if implemented—have put the United States at the center of world affairs and global institutions. His main interest was in the establishment of a League of Nations that would allow both for the peaceful resolution of disputes between states through arbitration and for the use of force in certain circumstances. Although unenthusiastic, the other victorious powers (France, Italy, Japan, and the United Kingdom) were willing to go along with this in order to secure US support for their own agendas.

One of the most important concerns of these powers was the preservation, or even expansion, of their empires. Wilson's fifth point stated, "A free, open-minded, and absolutely impartial adjustment of all colonial claims, based upon a strict observance of the principle that in determining all such questions of sovereignty the interests of the populations concerned must have equal weight with the equitable claims of the government whose title is to be determined."[22]

This was at first interpreted to mean that Wilson favored self-determination for all peoples, but it soon became clear at the peace conference that the allied European powers had nothing to fear. Instead, Wilson introduced the notion of League of Nations "mandates" under which the territories of the defeated nations would be governed as virtual colonies by imperial states. Indeed, the United States itself came very close to taking mandates in the collapsing Ottoman Empire.[23]

At the peace conference, the United States faced a dilemma with which it has struggled ever since: how to establish global institutions that can be used to promote US interests effectively without those same institutions being used against the United States itself. Wilson thought he had found the answer in a League of Nations Council made up of the victorious powers (including, of course, the United States) as permanent members and four rotating members with decisions taken by unanimity. He also took the precaution of inserting Article 21 into the League of Nations Covenant that states: "Nothing in this Covenant shall be deemed to affect the validity of international engagements, such as treaties of arbitration or regional understandings like the Monroe doctrine, for securing the maintenance of peace."[24]

The League of Nations Covenant became part of the peace treaty, and participants in the Paris conference duly ratified it. However, the protection it gave US interests was considered insufficient by Wilson's opponents in the Senate, who added a series of "reservations" as conditions for their support. These reservations, tabled by Senator Henry Cabot Lodge, were designed to exempt the United States from any collective action by the League, to uphold the primacy of the Monroe Doctrine, and to allow the United States to define unilaterally "what constituted a question within its exclusive domestic jurisdiction."[25]

Lodge was an opponent of both Wilson and the League. He and his supporters have therefore been portrayed as "isolationists." However, this is misleading, as they were almost all imperialists who simply wanted no restrictions on US freedom of action. Indeed, the peace treaty with the Lodge reservations almost secured the necessary two-thirds majority in the US Senate.[26] It was in fact Wilson's refusal to compromise that prevented passage of the peace treaty in the Senate, since the allies had reluctantly agreed to go along with the reservations in order to secure support for US ratification.

Without US participation, the League of Nations was doomed to failure and that is what duly happened. During the interwar years the United States made a few attempts to provide global leadership outside the framework of the League of Nations. The most important was the Washington Conference (1921–22), which ended the Anglo-Japanese Alliance and in which Great Britain conceded naval parity with the United States. There was also the Kellogg-Briand Pact of 1928 in which participating countries agreed not to go to war to resolve "disputes or conflicts of whatever nature or of whatever origin they may be, which may arise among them." None of these US initiatives, however, could prevent the relentless march toward war in the 1930s.

When the Second World War started, President Franklin Roosevelt was determined to ensure that the United States was at the heart of any new postwar institutional arrangement that might emerge. The first clue to his thinking came even before the United States entered the war with the Anglo-American Atlantic Charter in August 1941 and its commitment to a postwar policing role for the United States.

At the time, FDR was not an enthusiast for a revived League of Nations. He preferred a system that became known as the "four policemen" in which four powers (China, the Soviet Union, the United Kingdom, and the United States) would exercise hegemony in their own spheres of influence while cooperating among themselves on global issues. Soon after the United States entered the war, however, FDR embraced the concept of a United Nations that would become the basis for the new postwar global order.[27]

It was not until the Dumbarton Oaks Conference in 1944 that flesh could be put on the UN bones. Participants, independent countries on the Allied side, took it for granted that the meeting would be held in the United States. It was also clear from the nature of the participants, nearly half of which came from Latin America, that the United States would have a dominant position in the new organization. It was for this reason that the Union of Soviet Socialist Republics (USSR) called for separate representation by each of its sixteen parts.

FDR's vision of "four policemen" was reflected in the structure of the proposed UN Security Council (UNSC), since each "policeman" would be a permanent member (at British insistence, France was added to this select group, making it five in all). Still fearful of being outvoted, the USSR called for a veto over UN decisions by the permanent members. No resolution of these sensitive matters was possible at Dumbarton Oaks, but at Yalta in February 1945 the United States persuaded the Soviet Union to accept only two additional seats (Ukraine and Byelorussia). FDR also informed Stalin that the conference to draw up a UN Charter would be held in San Francisco in April.

Invitations to attend the San Francisco conference were supposed to be issued only to those states that had declared war on the Axis powers before March. Despite this, the United States invited Argentina so that all twenty Latin American republics were present.[28] Together with close allies from outside the Americas, the United States could count on the support of the overwhelming majority among the fifty countries present.[29] The conference was then very much a US affair.

The Soviet Union, vastly outnumbered at San Francisco, still insisted on a veto to protect its interests. The United States had no choice but to grant this if it wanted Soviet participation in the new organization (Box 5.2). However, the veto was limited to the permanent members of the Security Council,[30] was reserved for "substantive" rather than "procedural" matters, and did not apply to resolutions in the General Assembly where the United States at first could count on a large majority.

The UN Charter included the creation of an International Court of Justice (ICJ). As the successor to the Permanent Court of International Justice established by the League of Nations in Holland, the ICJ was set up in the Hague under UN auspices with compulsory powers in the case of arbitration between states. However, rulings of the ICJ could only be enforced by the Security Council where the veto operated. Thus, the United States as a permanent member could block the ICJ *in extremis*.

Three years later, in 1948, the UN General Assembly approved two landmark documents. The first was the Universal Declaration of Human Rights, in the passage of which Eleanor Roosevelt (FDR's widow) played a leading role. The second was the Convention on the Prevention and Punishment of the Crime of Genocide. Numerous UN agencies were also established, such as those dealing with refugees (the UNHCR) and education, science, and culture (UNESCO).

By the end of the 1940s, therefore, the United States had presided over the establishment of a set of global institutions and conventions under UN auspices designed to further her national interests. Yet it is often assumed that the outbreak of the Cold War and the veto for permanent members crippled the UN system and prevented it from serving American purposes. This is incorrect, as we shall now see, as the United States was able for many years to make the UN system work to its advantage.

There were in fact areas of convergence between the United States and the USSR even after the start of the Cold War. A good example is the vote in the General Assembly in 1947 on the partition of Palestine, the territory awarded to Great Britain under a League of Nations mandate after the First World War.[31] Both the United States and the Soviet Union favored partition with opposition coming mainly from the Arab states. The vote in favor of partition was duly passed,[32] the State of Israel came into being the following year, and Israel was admitted to the UN when none of the permanent members used their veto to block it.[33]

BOX 5.2

THE UN SECURITY COUNCIL AND THE VETO

The veto has always been one of the most controversial features of the UN system, and yet nowhere in the UN Charter does the word "veto" appear. Instead, Article 27 states:

1. Each member of the Security Council shall have one vote.
2. Decisions of the Security Council on procedural matters shall be made by an affirmative vote of nine members.
3. Decisions of the Security Council on all other matters shall be made by an affirmative vote of nine members including the concurring votes of the permanent members.

Article 27 is therefore the basis of the veto given to the United States and the other permanent members. It was only supposed to be used when vital national interests were at stake, but its first use (by the Soviet Union in February 1946) was over a relatively minor matter involving the withdrawal of French troops from Lebanon and Syria.

The United States refrained from using its veto until March 1970. This involved a Security Council proposal to refer the southern Rhodesian (Zimbabwean) question to the General Assembly, which the United Kingdom would have vetoed in any case. Thus, the first US veto was unnecessary. The second was in 1972 and blocked a resolution on Israel.

Before 1970 most vetoes were cast by the USSR and very few by China (Taiwan), France, and the United Kingdom. Since 1970 over half of all vetoes have been cast by the United States, with most of these related to the conflict between Israel and Palestine. The People's Republic of China has used its veto very sparingly since joining the Security Council in 1971, preferring to abstain when in disagreement. The United Kingdom, following the independence of Zimbabwe in 1980, and France have hardly used the veto at all. Russia, which took the place of the Soviet Union in 1992, has used its veto much more sparingly than did the USSR.

The United States also found ways of circumventing the Soviet veto by using procedural rules to ensure that the matter under consideration was dealt with by the General Assembly rather than the Security Council. Thus, in November 1947 the General Assembly, under US pressure and in the face of Soviet opposition, established an Interim Committee that had the authority to meet when the General Assembly was not in session. The Interim Committee, where the veto could not be applied, was then used by the United States to secure its desired outcome in Greece, where a right-wing monarchist government was facing a left-wing insurgency.

These tactics worked because the United States could count on a majority in both the General Assembly and the Interim Committee. Thus, the United States had a strong interest in preventing any new state from joining the UN that might be too closely allied with the Soviet Union. Indeed Albania, the first applicant, was just such a country, and it was blocked for many years by the United States.[34] The same would happen when the People's Republic of China (PRC) applied to join after defeating the nationalists in 1949.[35] This had the scandalous result that Taiwan would keep a seat on the Security Council as a permanent member until the thaw between the United States and PRC in 1971.[36]

Because of the majority support it enjoyed in both the General Assembly and the Security Council, the United States did not need to use its own veto.[37] Indeed America, unlike the Soviet Union, never cast a veto until 1970. Yet it was prepared to use the threat of veto on a number of occasions in order to protect its interests. One such occasion was in 1954, when the United States was anxious to avoid discussion of Guatemala in the UN.[38] Instead, it wanted to refer the matter to the OAS, where it was assured of a more sympathetic audience. President Dwight D. Eisenhower (1953–61) authorized his ambassador to cast a veto in the Security Council if necessary. This was sufficient to secure US interests and the veto was not applied.

Sometimes US tactics to secure its way in the UN were not very subtle. After the ratification of the Convention on the Prevention and Punishment of the Crime of Genocide, the first application was made by a US organization itself on behalf of African Americans. The Civil Rights Congress, which included Paul Robeson among its members, drafted a document accusing the United States of genocide against "the negro people" and sought to petition the General Assembly at its Paris meeting in 1951.[39] However, copies of the petition mailed to Paris never arrived, Paul Robeson was prevented from travel, and the main organizer, William Patterson, was stripped of his passport.[40]

The United States, of course, did not always get its way. For example, its delegation in 1946 failed to prevent General Assembly condemnation of the treatment by South Africa of its Indian minority.[41] These were relatively minor setbacks. However, the growth of membership in the 1950s and 1960s, including a number of countries allied to the Soviet Union, made it much harder for the United States to control the UN agenda. America could now no longer rely on a built-in majority and started to use its veto more than any other country from 1970 onward. In this way it could at least be certain that the UN would not work *against* it even if it could no longer ensure that the UN would work *for* it.

5.3. COLD WAR INSTITUTIONS

Shortly after the German invasion of Russia in June 1941, the British Foreign Secretary Anthony Eden flew to Moscow to ask Joseph Stalin what help the Soviet Union needed. The Soviet leader expressed interest in a political alliance and a territorial settlement involving Russia's borders. Exactly what he had in mind was then explained to Eden six months later, after the Japanese attack on Pearl Harbor; he passed the information on to US officials. In their words,

> At his conference with Eden, following Pearl Harbour, Stalin indicated that he wanted a Soviet-Polish boundary based on the Curzon Line, parts of Finland and Hungary were to be incorporated into the Soviet Union, while the Baltic States were to be absorbed. In addition Stalin also proposed the restoration of Austria as an independent state; the detachment of the Rhineland from Germany as an independent state or protectorate; possibly the constitution of an independent state of Bavaria; the transfer of East Prussia to Poland; the return of the Sudetenland to Czechoslovakia; Yugoslavia should be restored and receive certain additional territory from Italy; Albania should be reconstituted as an independent state; Turkey should receive the Dodecanese Islands, with possible readjustments of Aegean islands in favour of Greece; Turkey might also receive some territory from Bulgaria and in northern Syria; Germany should pay reparations in kind, particularly in machine tools, but not reparations in money.[42]

Three years later, after the Soviet Union had suffered extraordinary losses in the war against Nazi Germany,[43] Stalin's position on territorial adjustments had not changed. The British government had always recognized that the Soviet Union would demand a "sphere of influence" on its western border after the war, and Prime Minister Winston Churchill therefore flew to Moscow in October 1944 to negotiate a deal. The result was the "percentages agreement" under which the Soviet Union was awarded 90 percent dominance in Romania, 80 percent in Bulgaria and Hungary, and 50 percent in Yugoslavia. Greece, on the other hand, would be 90 percent British.[44]

The US government also knew that the Soviet Union would demand a sphere of influence at the end of the war. In a letter to a friend, George Kennan (Box 5.3) wrote in January 1945, "I recognize that Russia's war effort has been masterful

BOX 5.3
GEORGE FROST KENNAN (1904–2005)

George Kennan, who died at the age of 101, is often described as the father of "containment." His Long Telegram from Moscow in February 1946 and his article in *Foreign Affairs* the following year, signed "X," are cited as evidence of this. Yet he came to oppose many of the policies adopted in the name of containment.

Kennan was born in 1904. He had a gift for foreign languages and chose a career in the US Foreign Service. He arrived in Moscow just after President Franklin Delano Roosevelt (1933–45) recognized the Soviet Union in 1933. He left in 1937, but returned to the US embassy in 1944. His knowledge of the Soviet Union was much greater than that of the US ambassador, which is why he was asked to respond to a question from the Treasury Department about the unwillingness of the USSR to join the IMF and World Bank. The result was the Long Telegram.

Kennan did not make it sufficiently clear in either the Long Telegram or the "X" article that what he meant by "containment" was economic and political rather than military. He also wished to confine it to Europe. He was therefore strongly opposed to the much more aggressive postures adopted by the US government in the Truman Doctrine and NSC-68. In his own words, "My thoughts about containment were of course distorted by the people who understood it and pursued it exclusively as a military concept; and I think that that, as much as any other cause, led to [the] 40 years of unnecessary, fearfully expensive and disorientated process of the Cold War."

During his long life, Kennan was highly consistent in his objection to a militarized US foreign policy. He opposed the building of the hydrogen bomb and the rearmament of (West) Germany, US involvement in Vietnam in the 1960s, the arms race in the 1970s and first half of the 1980s, the widening of NATO after the Cold War, and the second Iraq War in 2003. Yet, paradoxically, it was the success of his own earlier writings that led inexorably to this broad US military engagement that he so strongly opposed.

and effective and must, to a certain extent, find its reward at the expense of other peoples in eastern and central Europe."[45]

This was not, however, the official position of the US government during the war, and FDR had not given his blessing to the percentages agreement (although he had not openly opposed it). Thus, the three leaders—Churchill, Roosevelt, and Stalin—went into the Yalta Conference in February 1945 with different ambitions. Stalin was determined to secure a sphere of influence on the Russian border. FDR, on the other hand, was keen to secure an agreement consistent with the Atlantic Charter, whose third article stated that "they [Churchill and FDR] respect the right of all peoples to choose the form of government under which they will live; and they wish to see sovereign rights and self government restored to those who have been forcibly deprived of them."[46]

Yalta papered over the cracks between these different positions, calling for liberated countries "to create democratic institutions of their own choice."[47] All those present knew what this meant, and Stalin duly went ahead to create the sphere of Soviet influence to which he had aspired since Russia's entry into the war and which he had outlined to Anthony Eden in December 1941. Indeed, by the time the three powers met again (at Potsdam in July 1945), Poland, Bulgaria, Romania, and the Baltic States had all been added to the Soviet sphere of influence.[48]

President Harry S. Truman (1945–53) had succeeded to the US presidency in April 1945 on the death of FDR.[49] He had almost no experience in international affairs, and had only once traveled abroad before being chosen as FDR's vice presidential candidate in 1944. He therefore relied heavily on his foreign policy advisers, who were much influenced by the famous Long Telegram sent by George Kennan from Moscow in February 1946, in which he wrote, "Soviet power . . . is neither schematic nor adventuristic. It does not work by fixed plans. It does not take unnecessary risks. Impervious to logic of reason . . . it is highly sensitive to logic of force. For this reason it can easily withdraw—and usually does—when strong resistance is encountered at any point. Thus, if the adversary has sufficient force and makes clear his readiness to use it, he rarely has to do so."[50]

With these prophetic words, Kennan outlined a policy of "containment" that would guide US actions toward the Soviet Union for several decades. Yet it was not clear in 1946 where the USSR would or could be "contained" given its dominant position in central and eastern Europe. The answer would come the following year, when the United Kingdom informed the United States that it could no longer support the Greek government militarily or financially and would also have to end economic assistance to Turkey.

Greece, it will be remembered, was a country where Churchill and Stalin had agreed that Great Britain would have 90 percent influence. True to his word, Stalin had therefore not assisted the partisans fighting against the royalist government restored to power by the British government. Despite this, the partisans—aided by Yugoslavia—were gaining ground and threatening to establish a communist-led government in Greece.

Warned by his advisers that the withdrawal of British assistance to Greece and Turkey could generate a "domino" effect in the Mediterranean, the US president rushed to Congress in March 1947 to outline what would immediately become known as the Truman Doctrine. In addition to seeking financial and military assistance for Greece and Turkey, Truman stated,

> At the present moment in world history nearly every nation must choose between alternative ways of life. The choice is too often not a free one. One way of life is based upon the will of the majority, and is distinguished by free institutions, representative government, free elections, guarantees of individual liberty, freedom of speech and religion, and freedom from political oppression. The second way of life is based upon the will of a minority forcibly imposed upon the majority. It relies upon terror and oppression, a controlled press and radio, fixed elections, and the suppression of personal freedoms. I believe that it must be the policy of the United States to support free peoples who are resisting attempted subjugation by armed minorities or by outside pressures. . . . The free peoples of the world look to us for support in maintaining their freedoms.[51]

Although most US officials were reluctant to describe the Truman Doctrine as a global version of the Monroe Doctrine,[52] that is exactly what it was. In two years the US government had gone from ambivalence toward a Soviet sphere of influence limited to central and eastern Europe to an apparently open-ended obligation to defeat left-wing insurgencies in every part of the world. No other government in the history of the world had taken on such a broad commitment.

Truman's speech, although broadly supported in the country at large, failed to specify how this new imperial policy would be implemented. In July 1947, however, the National Security Act established a single Department of Defense, a Joint Chiefs of Staff, a National Security Council (NSC), and a Central Intelligence Agency. The institutionalization of the Truman Doctrine was now well under way.

Three years later, by which time the Soviet Union had acquired an atomic bomb and the Communist Party had taken power in China, a paper written for the NSC and adopted by the executive took the Truman Doctrine a stage further.[53] It outlined the steps that the United States needed to take not only to contain the Soviet Union but also to roll it back. It concluded that the United States "must lead in building a successfully functioning political and economic system in the free world" if it was to achieve its strategic aim: "To reduce the power and influence of the USSR to limits which no longer constitute a threat to the peace, national independence, and stability of the world family of nations [and] to bring about a basic change in the conduct of international relations by the government in power in Russia, to conform with the purposes and principles set forth in the UN Charter."[54] The enemy now was not just left-wing insurgencies but also those governments anywhere in the world that exhibited sympathy with communism in general and the Soviet Union in particular.

The Truman Doctrine, like the Monroe Doctrine, needed to be supported by multilateral institutions if it was to be effective. The priority area for the United States was western Europe, especially West Germany, because it bordered Soviet-controlled eastern Europe. At the same time, postwar recovery in western Europe had been so anemic that the countries, traditionally major markets for US exports, were in no position to import high volumes of goods and services from the United States on a commercial basis.

The solution was found in the Marshall Plan, named after the secretary of state.[55] Outlined by George Marshall in 1947, it was approved by Congress in March 1948 as "An Act to promote world peace and the general welfare, national interest, and foreign policy of the United States through economic, financial, and other measures necessary to the maintenance of conditions abroad in which free institutions may survive and consistent with the maintenance of the strength and stability of the United States."[56]

The Soviet Union and its European allies were invited to participate in the Marshall Plan, but it was designed in such a way that the offer would be declined.[57] The aid was then disbursed to sixteen European countries (including Turkey) through a new multilateral agency, the Organisation for European Economic Co-operation.[58] It was highly successful, and rapid economic recovery, especially in West Germany, made it possible in a few years for participating countries to pay for imports of goods and services from the United States on normal terms.

The Marshall Plan was described by Churchill as "the most unselfish act by any great power in history." Yet Dean Acheson, one of its architects and US undersecretary of state at the time, was probably closer to the mark when he said, "These measures of relief and reconstruction have been only in part suggested by humanitarianism. Your Congress has authorized and your Government is carrying out a policy of relief and reconstruction today chiefly as a matter of national self-interest. For it is generally agreed that until the various countries of the world get on their feet and become self-supporting there can be no political or economic stability in the world and no lasting peace or prosperity for any of us."[59]

The Marshall Plan addressed the economic and financial needs of western Europe, but not its security requirements. A number of western European countries had signed the Treaty of Brussels in March 1948 to pool military resources, but the Soviet blockade of Berlin later that year demonstrated how inadequate these resources were unless supported by the United States. This then led to the North Atlantic Treaty, signed in Washington, DC, in April 1949, and the creation of the North Atlantic Treaty Organization (NATO).

Although NATO was based in Brussels, with a European secretary-general, it was (and still is) a US-dominated institution. The United States provided most of the budget and—crucially—the hardware that would make collective defense credible. In addition, its supreme commander was, and is, always a US citizen and the first was none other than General Dwight Eisenhower. Indeed, US domination of NATO was so strong that France under President Charles de Gaulle engineered a partial withdrawal from the organization in order to protect its national sovereignty.

In words reminiscent of the 1947 Rio Treaty (see above), Article 5 of the North Atlantic Treaty states:

> The Parties agree that an armed attack against one or more of [the countries] in Europe or North America shall be considered an attack against them all and consequently they agree that, if such an armed attack occurs, each of them, in exercise of the right of individual or collective self-defence recognised by Article 51 of the Charter of the United Nations, will assist the Party or Parties so attacked by taking forthwith, individually and in concert with the other Parties, such action as it deems necessary, including the use of armed force, to restore and maintain the security of the North Atlantic area.[60]

This seemed to put all the states on an equal footing. However, only the United States had the military capability to resist a Soviet advance. Thus, Article 5 committed the United States to an open-ended defense of western Europe without the European members being able to contribute much by way of conventional forces in the case of a Soviet attack on North America. In return, the United States expected—and generally received—broad support from the other members for its foreign policy stance in other parts of the world.

Article 5 never needed to be invoked during the Cold War.[61] This was a measure of its success, and NATO would become the template for other similar organizations in different parts of the world. The first was the Southeast Asia Treaty Organization (SEATO), signed by the United States and other countries in 1954 following the collapse of France's colonial empire in Indochina.[62] The second was the Central Treaty Organization (CENTO), signed in 1955 by a number of Middle Eastern countries, including Iran.[63]

Although neither SEATO nor CENTO worked in the two regions as the United States intended,[64] the goals of the Truman Doctrine were much better served by the network of bilateral security agreements signed by the United States with a large number of countries in Asia, Oceania, the Middle East and, of course, Europe and the Americas. These agreements allowed for the establishment of US military bases around the world and gave the United States significant leverage in and over the many countries involved. At the height of the Cold War there were nearly 800 military bases and even today there are US military installations in over 150 countries with a deployment of 160,000 active-duty personnel (Map 10).

For a few years (1945–49) the United States had a monopoly on nuclear weapons. This gave America a preeminent position in the world, but it was undermined by the testing of such weapons in the Soviet Union (1949) and China (1964).[65] A new approach was required, one that recognized the semiglobal nature of the empire over which the United States presided. The result was the Treaty on the Non-Proliferation of Nuclear Weapons, commonly called the Non-Proliferation Treaty (NPT) that came into force in 1970.

The NPT, ratified eventually by all countries except Israel, India, and Pakistan,[66] divided the world into nuclear and nonnuclear weapon states. The latter agreed never to acquire nuclear weapons under any circumstances, while the former (the United States plus China, France, the United Kingdom, and the USSR) merely committed to eventual nuclear disarmament, without any firm date. This asymmetry went largely unchallenged by member states during the Cold War, so that the NPT was a key institution in reinforcing US hegemony outside China and the USSR.

5.4. ECONOMIC INSTITUTIONS

Long before the Second World War the United States had taken a leading role in global economic organization. The International Institute of Agriculture had been founded on the initiative of a US citizen as early as 1905. Charles Dawes, US vice president from 1925 to 1929, had given his name to the conference in 1924 to reorder the arrangements for German reparations, while the

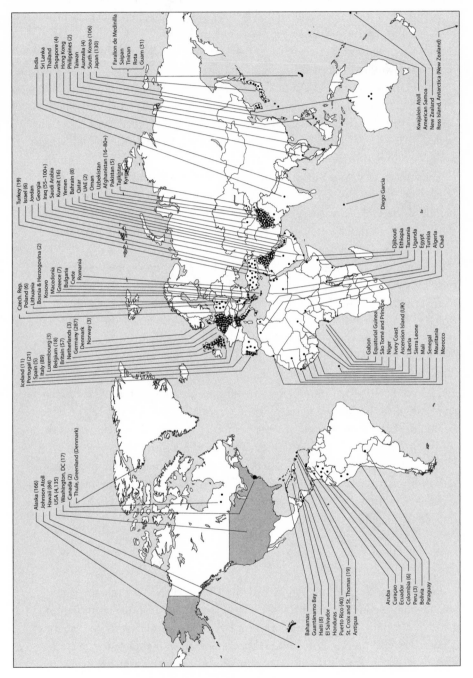

Map 10. US military bases

Alaska (166)
Johnson Atoll
Hawaii (84)
USA (4,135)
Washington, DC (17)
Canada (2)
Thule, Greenland (Denmark)

Bahamas
Guantánamo Bay
Haiti (8)
El Salvador
Honduras
Puerto Rico (40)
St. Croix and St. Thomas (19)
Antigua

Aruba
Curaçao
Ecuador
Colombia (6)
Peru (3)
Bolivia
Paraguay

Iceland (11)
Portugal (21)
Italy (89)
Spain (5)
Luxembourg (3)
Belgium (18)
Britain (57)
Netherlands (3)
Germany (287)
Denmark
Norway (3)

Czech. Rep.
Poland (6)
Lithuania
Bosnia & Herzegovina (2)
Kosovo
Macedonia
Greece (7)
Bulgaria
Crete
Romania

Turkey (19)
Israel (6)
Jordan
Georgia
Iraq (55–100+)
Saudi Arabia
Kuwait (16)
Yemen
Bahrain (8)
Qatar
UAE (2)
Oman
Uzbekistan
Afghanistan (16–80+)
Tajikistan
Pakistan (5)
Kyrgyzstan

India
Sri Lanka
Thailand
Singapore (4)
Hong Kong
Philippines (2)
Taiwan
Australia (4)
South Korea (106)
Japan (130)

Faralion de Medinilla
Saipan
Tinmian
Rota
Guam (31)

Kwajalein Atoll
American Samoa
New Zealand
Ross Island, Antarctica (New Zealand)

Diego Garcia

Djibouti
Ethiopia
Tanzania
Uganda
Egypt
Tunisia
Algeria
Chad

Gabon
Equatorial Guinea
São Tomé and Príncipe
Ivory Coast
Ascension Island (UK)
Liberia
Sierra Leone
Mali
Senegal
Mauritania
Morocco

Bank for International Settlements (BIS) had been established in 1930 on the suggestion of Owen Young, a US industrialist.

None of this had prevented the Great Depression and economic collapse in the interwar years. Thus, the United States entered the Second World War determined to build a set of global economic institutions in which it would not merely play a leading role but would also be dominant. Indeed, within a week of the Japanese attack on Pearl Harbor, Henry Morgenthau, the US Treasury secretary, had instructed his director of monetary research, Harry Dexter White, to provide a blueprint for postwar global economic organization.

White's ideas evolved in the months leading up to the Bretton Woods Conference in July 1944. However, the main ideas remained constant and, indeed, had been outlined by White as early as 1934.[67] The United States demanded international monetary stabilization, since business needed to expand overseas and this was only possible with a system of fixed exchange rates. The US dollar would have to be at the center of this system and gold would still play a role, even if a return to the pre–World War I gold standard was not feasible.

The final details of this scheme were settled at the conference and led to the establishment of the International Monetary Fund (IMF). Often presented as an Anglo-American initiative with other countries ignored or unrepresented, the IMF as finally agreed on was in fact a US creation. Despite the intellectual brilliance of the chief British negotiator, John Maynard Keynes, he was no match for the raw power of the US team led by Harry Dexter White (Box 5.4). On virtually all major matters, and most of the minor ones as well, it was the American view that prevailed.

At the heart of American control of the IMF was the system of quotas allocated to each country according to a complex formula that gave the United States by far the largest share. Indeed, the quotas agreed on at Bretton Woods gave the United States over one-third of the total. Since voting in the IMF was to be primarily on the basis of quotas, the United States had a dominant position. America also had an effective veto on decision making as changes to the Articles of Agreement, and some other decisions as well, required a majority of 80 percent of the votes.[68] In addition, the United States insisted the IMF be located in Washington, DC.[69]

Although final authority was vested in a board of governors, the vast majority of decisions were to be taken by the executive directors. The five largest quota holders each had their own executive director, while all other countries initially had to share seven directors among themselves. Given the voting structure, this would have been more than enough for the US director (representing the

BOX 5.4
HARRY DEXTER WHITE (1892–1948)

The IMF and the World Bank, born at Bretton Woods in 1944, were US creations. They would become key institutions in the semiglobal empire built by the United States after the Second World War. The man who was most responsible for their birth was Harry Dexter White. Yet, ironically, he was publicly accused of being a Soviet agent shortly before his death.

White was born in modest circumstances in Boston of Lithuanian parents. He studied economics and completed his PhD at Harvard University in 1930 on "The International Payments of France, 1880–1913." He taught at Harvard for a number of years on an annual contract as an instructor in economics but left when it was clear he would not receive tenure. He would later join the US Treasury.

His interest in money and banking persisted, and in Washington, DC, he wrote in 1934 a paper entitled "Selection of a Monetary Standard for the United States." Thus, he was well placed to address postwar questions when he was invited by Henry Morgenthau in 1941 to look at the whole question of global monetary stabilization.

White's duel with John Maynard Keynes at Bretton Woods has been well documented. Keynes may have had the intellectual edge, but he was no match for White's tactical brilliance. Knowing Keynes's lack of interest in the World Bank, White put him in charge of the negotiations, leaving him unable to give the time needed to the numerous drafts of the Articles of Agreement for the IMF.

White was denounced to the Federal Bureau of Investigation (FBI) in 1941 as a Soviet agent by Elizabeth Bentley. She went public with her accusations in mid-1948 before the House Committee on Un-American Activities. White defended himself on August 13 but died three days later. His exact relationship with the Soviet Union is still not entirely clear, but he served the interests of the American empire well at Bretton Woods.

US Treasury) to control proceedings, but as a further precaution the United States was able to include in the original Articles of Agreement that two of the seven directorships should be reserved for Latin American republics.

The system of fixed exchange rates established by the IMF served the United States well for the first twenty-five years. Countries fixed their currencies to the US dollar, while the United States fixed the dollar to gold at thirty-five dollars per fine ounce. This was a gold exchange standard rather than a gold standard, as only central banks were free to exchange their dollars for gold held by the United States at the fixed price. However, US balance of payments deficits during the Vietnam War created a surplus of dollar holdings outside the United States, and the fixed exchange rate system crumbled in August 1971 when President Richard M. Nixon (1969–74) broke the link between gold and the US dollar.

The IMF, still controlled by the United States, might easily have passed into oblivion at that point. Indeed, the 1970s were difficult years for the Fund. However, the fortunes of the IMF were transformed by the Latin American debt crisis that erupted in August 1982. The US Treasury was keen to see the Fund play a leading role in resolving the crisis, and the conditions attached to IMF lending ensured that the US vision for global economic management prevailed.

The US invitation to forty-four countries to attend the Bretton Woods Conference "for formulating definite proposals for an International Monetary Fund" had also stated "and possibly a Bank for Reconstruction and Development." As the invitation implied, an International Bank for Reconstruction and Development (IBRD) was not the highest priority for the United States, and the proposal was initially opposed by the British delegation.

Despite this, the IBRD (commonly known today as the World Bank) was established at Bretton Woods with the same weighted voting structure as the IMF. This, together with the Bank's location in Washington, DC, gave the US government, through the State Department, a dominant role in the new organization.[70] It was also agreed that no country could join the IBRD without being a member of the US-controlled IMF. Finally, the United States insisted that the president of the World Bank should be a US citizen.

The World Bank, reflecting US interests, at first gave priority to reconstruction. For the US government this meant loans to western Europe, but these were insufficient and were soon replaced by Marshall Plan assistance. At this point the World Bank might easily have ceased to have much relevance, were it not for President Truman's inaugural address delivered in January 1949. In his fourth point, he stated, "We must embark on a bold new program for making the benefits of our scientific advances and industrial progress available for the improvement and growth of underdeveloped areas. More than half the people of the world are living in conditions approaching misery. Their food is inadequate. They are victims of disease. Their economic life is primitive and stagnant. Their poverty is a handicap and a threat both to them and to more prosperous areas."[71]

The Point Four Program, as it became known, provided a US rationale for lending by the World Bank to developing countries in the context of the Cold

War. These loans came with many conditions attached, reflecting contemporary US thinking on development strategies, and were paid to governments or state-owned enterprises. In order to make loans to the private sector, the International Finance Corporation (IFC) was established within the World Bank in 1956, while lending on more concessional terms was made possible in 1960 through another subsidiary (the International Development Association—IDA).

The operations of the IDA required periodic infusions of capital by the World Bank. For most members this was unproblematic, but for the United States it required congressional approval. This gave Congress a regular opportunity to tighten its grip on the World Bank and ensure that it reflected US interests more closely. A much quoted example was the ban on World Bank lending to Vietnam in the 1970s in order to secure US support for IDA replenishment.[72] Robert McNamara, former US secretary of defense and a key architect of Vietnam War policy, was president of the World Bank at the time.

The US government had chosen not to push for a world trade organization at Bretton Woods, as the agenda was already very full and participants mainly came from central banks and finance ministries. However, it had already developed a clear vision of what it wanted and took the first steps the following year. This was the publication in November 1945 of a document entitled *Proposals for Expansion of World Trade and Employment*.[73]

The US proposals, which provided a detailed blueprint for the organization of world trade, had in fact been in gestation for several years. Starting with the 1934 Reciprocal Trade Agreement Act (RTAA), the United States had signed bilateral trade treaties with a large number of countries before the war, and Congress had extended the RTAA for a further three years in 1945. However, the first commitment to *multilateral* trade liberalization was contained in Article 7 of the Lend-Lease agreement with the United Kingdom in February 1942, in which the two governments committed themselves "to the elimination of all forms of discriminatory treatment in international commerce, and to the reduction of tariffs and other trade barriers."[74] The State Department had then started detailed work on the proposals in 1943.

The proposals, negotiated first in London and then Geneva, were ready for submission by late 1947. This was done in Cuba, where fifty-four countries in March 1948 signed the Havana Charter establishing an International Trade Organization (ITO).[75] It contained almost all of what had been included in the original US proposals, but also allowed for many exceptions to trade liberalization. In addition, as the US government had proposed in London in 1946, it gave each country one vote.[76] This proposal, quite unlike the weighted voting systems in the IMF and IBRD, was justified by the State Department as follows: "We have felt that where the interests of the United States are directly at stake, in actions of the Organization, we might ask for special majorities rather than weighted voting, but since most of the acts of the Conference . . . are in the nature of recommendations to governments for action, which has to be implemented by governments, the importance of the recommendation is not merely determined by the weights of the votes that you can collect on an issue, but on the numbers of countries that are willing to accept the obligations."[77]

The other signatories then waited for US ratification of the Havana Charter, but this never came. The Truman administration delayed until 1950 before submitting it to Congress and withdrew it before putting it to a vote. As a result, no other country ratified and the ITO was stillborn. A combination of a lukewarm (at least after 1948) administration, a skeptical business community, and the usual protectionist lobbies in Congress killed it.[78]

This might have destroyed US efforts to oversee the multilateral liberalization of foreign trade were it not for the fact that the Truman administration, almost without realizing it, had been pursuing a two-track approach. While negotiations on the charter were under way in London in 1946, the US secretary of state announced that it wished to negotiate on tariffs with the participating countries.[79] These negotiations were then held the following year in Geneva and produced a General Agreement on Tariffs and Trade (GATT). The tariff reductions then went into force in 1948, as the United States did not need to seek legislative approval.[80]

It was always assumed that GATT was subordinate to the Havana Charter and the ITO, into which it would be subsumed at some point. It therefore had a perilous existence when the charter was not ratified. In addition, when extending the RTAA for a further period, Congress had included in the act the following less than enthusiastic words: "The enactment of this Act shall not be construed to determine or indicate the approval or disapproval of the Executive Agreement known as the General Agreement on Tariffs and Trade."[81]

Yet GATT not only survived but also became the primary instrument for US control over world trade liberalization. Tariffs tumbled among member states over a series of trade "rounds" that had started in Geneva in 1947, and the number of states involved steadily expanded. Although some important countries were not represented, tariff reductions agreed on through GATT covered most world trade and a very high proportion of US imports and exports.

Given GATT's humble origins, all this was most encouraging for successive US administrations. However, GATT still suffered from a number of weaknesses. First, with the advance of the US economy, GATT did not cover the new areas of concern to US companies such as trade in services, intellectual

property, labor and environmental standards, and protection of foreign investments. Second, US legislators had a habit of excluding from GATT various sectors of interest to their constituents. They also introduced various protectionist
measures that made it more difficult for the US administration to persuade other
countries to abandon theirs.

For all these reasons, the US government was persuaded after the seventh
round of GATT negotiations in the 1970s to adopt a new and much more ambitious approach. This led to the launch of the Uruguay Round in 1986, the
agenda for which included all the new areas of interest to the US administration.
When finally approved nearly a decade later, it led to the birth of the World
Trade Organization (WTO) in 1995 (see Chapter 8). Thus, nearly fifty years
after the Havana Charter, the US government had finally secured the international trade organization that had eluded it in 1948.

6

NONSTATE ACTORS

No empire can operate without a metropolitan state at its heart, but states still need broad public support if they are to sustain an imperial project. This support comes from a range of nonstate actors (NSAs) that varies from empire to empire. In the case of the US semiglobal empire, the most important NSAs have been multinational enterprises (MNEs), nongovernmental organizations (NGOs), the media, and religious groups. This chapter looks at each of these in turn.

MNEs have a long history in the United States, although it is only since the Second World War that they have received much attention. That is because their postwar growth has been spectacular in both quantitative and qualitative terms. Present throughout the world, American MNEs are noted for their enormous size, efficiency, and technological sophistication. They are global in reach, but rooted in the United States in a legal, cultural, and historical sense.

Even if the United States did not produce the first international businesses, it can take a large part of the credit for inventing the modern MNE. Nowadays many states—developed and developing—have their own MNEs, and yet most of these countries are not empires. The United States, however, was an empire *before* the rise of its MNEs. Thus, the state had imperial, not just national, interests to which the MNEs had to adapt from the start. These companies, therefore, have engaged with the state on a very different basis to those in, say, Brazil or South Korea.

MNEs have global interests and are sometimes seen as more powerful than states. That may be true in certain countries, but it is not true of the United States. Instead, there has been a symbiotic relationship in America between the state and the MNE in which both need and use each other. This is helped by the close relationship in the United States between government and business more generally. Thus, as we shall see, the state has used MNEs in pursuit of its semiglobal empire while the companies have lobbied hard to ensure that the state's agenda is consistent with their own needs.

Some NGOs are also long established in the United States. However, the vast majority have been created since the Second World War and it is in this more recent period that many of them have become important political actors. Not all, by any means, are at the service of the imperial project, but some of the most important ones play a crucial role in supporting, defending, and defining the state's global ambitions. These include large foundations started by MNEs themselves, "think tanks" in the main cities, and NGOs focused on single issues.

Empires have ideological underpinnings, which are given broad popular appeal through the media. It was a journalist who coined the phrase "Manifest Destiny" that captured the imperial mood of the mid-nineteenth century in the United States, while it was film that did so much to perpetuate the thinking underlying American government action in the Cold War. Meanwhile, television helped to reinforce many of the ideas on which the semiglobal empire has been based.

Last but not least has been the role of religion. This includes the churches, many of which are active outside the United States in those countries that constitute part of the semiglobal empire, and whose missionaries have played such an important part in spreading knowledge not only about the gospel but also the United States itself. It also includes many private voluntary organizations (PVOs) that operate either under the auspices of different churches or in their own name.

There are, of course, some "anti-imperialist" NSAs in the United States, while within NSAs that are broadly supportive of the forms that American global engagement takes there are plenty of individuals who play a subaltern role. Yet this misses the point. What is striking about the US semiglobal empire is the broad support it has commanded among a large part of society for so much of the time despite occasional moments of conflict, such as during the Vietnam War.

NSAs are part of the "soft power" that is often considered an important part of modern diplomacy. Normally associated with the state itself, soft power can be exercised by NSAs as well since they also have the ability to "attract and co-opt rather than coerce" even if money—despite the claims of soft power theory—is often involved. However, soft power can never replace hard power, over which the state continues to have a monopoly. At its best, soft power is merely a complement to hard power and can never be a substitute. Thus, American NSAs have been extremely useful in supporting the semiglobal empire, but could never have created it on their own.

6.1. MULTINATIONAL ENTERPRISES (MNEs)

A few intrepid American traders had established themselves abroad even before 1776. Others followed after independence as US capitalists spread across the globe to Africa, Asia, Europe, and the rest of the Americas. Indeed, as we saw in Part I, businessmen were present in some countries of the Asia-Pacific region and the Caribbean even before they became part of the US territorial empire.

These businesses, however, were not multinational enterprises (MNEs) in the usual sense of a company headquartered in the United States with branches overseas.[1] That development had to wait until after the Civil War, when the US mainland was integrated physically by means of the transcontinental railway and the telegraph. Competition, restricted by high tariffs, then gave way to oligopoly as a wave of mergers and acquisitions produced the giant companies for which the United States is still famous.

Writing at the end of the nineteenth century, J. A. Hobson described the process as follows:

> There are four principal reasons why the Trust or close combination, with monopoly, assumes greater prominence in the United States than in England and elsewhere. First: the railroad as an economic factor is more important than elsewhere. . . . Secondly: the tariff . . . renders profitable combinations more feasible than in a country of free imports. Moreover, in none of the protective countries of Europe have the great manufacturing interests obtained so exclusive a control over the tariff policy as in the United States. Thirdly: the corrupt domination of politics by business interests, stronger in the United States than in any great industrial nation of Europe, enables the great railroad and business corporations to procure municipal and state charters and other profitable privileges, to override many laws with impunity, and to avoid their fair share of contribution to the public purse. Fourthly: the greater absorption of the national energy in business operations . . . the sanguine and audacious temperament of the American business man, coupled with freedom from many of the legal or customary restraints which hamper the "logical" evolution of capitalistic enterprise in Europe, have evolved a type of industrial and financial "hustler" with bigger ideas and more rapid and unscrupulous modes of realising them than is found in Europe.[2]

The companies to which Hobson referred had such enormous power that the federal government in 1890 passed the Sherman Antitrust Act designed to outlaw actions in restraint of trade. However, the act said nothing about mergers, so the result—coupled with the mid-1890s recession—was a further wave of consolidation in industries subject to economies of scale. This led many firms to open branches outside the US mainland, and the MNE soon became an established feature of the business landscape.

Mira Wilkins, who studied this process in great depth, concluded, "The extension of business abroad before 1893 was dwarfed by what followed. The 1890s saw a steady growth of U.S. enterprise in foreign lands. . . . At the turn of the century there was a veritable 'wave' of new U.S. corporations introducing operations beyond the American boundaries; United States direct investment flowed into Canada as never before. Between 1897 and 1902, Europeans pointed to 'the American invasion of Europe'—an invasion of American-manufactured goods."[3] Indeed, no fewer than three publications appeared in London in 1901–2 with the following sensational titles: *The American Invasion, The American Invaders,* and *The Americanization of the World.*

Although some of the trusts would be broken up in the decade before the First World War,[4] the federal government was generally supportive of big business operating abroad. President William Howard Taft (1909–13) declared his government was "lending all proper support to legitimate and beneficial American enterprises in foreign countries" and that the Department of State was being reorganized to "make it a thoroughly efficient instrument in the furtherance of foreign trade and of American interest abroad."[5] His successor, President Woodrow Wilson (1913–21), removed the ban on overseas branches by US banks and paved the way for the global expansion of US finance.

US MNEs continued to expand between the two world wars and could be found in many parts of the globe. However, they made few investments in the colonies of European empires as they faced formal and informal obstacles from British, Dutch, and French imperial officials. Their expansion, therefore, was most rapid in the Americas where their operations included mining, agriculture, real estate, transport, manufacturing, banking, and insurance (Box 6.1).

Although the foreign operations of US MNEs before the Second World War were extensive, they were eclipsed by what happened after 1945. As the undisputed world economic power at a time of global dollar shortage and a US balance of payments current account surplus, American MNEs were extraordinarily well placed to expand their operations overseas through mergers, acquisitions, and new investments.

BOX 6.1

THE FORD MOTOR COMPANY AND FORDLANDIA

Henry Ford launched the Ford Motor Company in 1903 and the fourth car it manufactured was exported. Right from the start, therefore, Ford was an international company and it came to operate on six continents with production facilities in many different countries.

Ford introduced new production and management techniques to vehicle production, leading to the use of the word "Fordism" to describe these innovations. However, Ford did not believe in outsourcing, preferring instead vertical integration. This meant establishing facilities to produce the raw materials from which vehicles are made.

One of these raw materials is rubber, used primarily for tires. When world rubber prices rose in the 1920s as a result of a cartel established by the United Kingdom throughout the British Empire, the main US importers of rubber planned their response. Henry Ford, throwing caution to the wind, chose to purchase an area of land in the Brazilian Amazon almost as large as Connecticut to grow rubber trees and produce latex (see Grandin, *Fordlandia*).

By the time the contract with the Brazilian authorities had been signed in 1927, the world price of rubber had collapsed. However, Ford persisted with the project. To house the workers he built a town that would not have looked out of place in the United States. Indeed, Walt Disney himself came to visit it.

Right from the start Fordlandia, as it was called, was an utter failure and Ford was forced to ask the administration of President Herbert Hoover (1929–33) to intervene with the Brazilian government. This resolved most of the man-made issues, but not those caused by nature and the Brazilian jungle.

Fordlandia continued to flounder until it was effectively nationalized by the US government during the Second World War. After the war it was sold to the government of the State of Pará in Brazil for a fraction of what Ford had spent on it. By that time, synthetic rubber was becoming commonplace and the Ford Motor Company no longer needed its own rubber plantations.

The numbers speak for themselves. Between 1946 and 1969, the book value of US foreign direct investment (FDI) rose tenfold, from $7.2 billion to $70.8 billion.[6] This was roughly two-thirds of the world's total at the time. Thirty years later, it had reached $1,100 billion.[7] This, however, was a smaller share of global FDI stocks (about one quarter) as a result of the rapid expansion of outward FDI flows from many other countries.

If the federal government had been broadly supportive of MNE expansion abroad before the Second World War, it was now even more engaged, as the outflow was seen as crucial not only for the health of the US economy but also to underpin the strategic aims of the semiglobal empire. The main US companies now became heavily dependent on overseas markets.

American companies were encouraged in every way, including through the tax regime, to invest in Western Europe to promote its reconstruction. Research and development funds flowed from government agencies to "sensitive" sectors such as defense, the aerospace industry, computers, and even pharmaceuticals. US oil companies were persuaded to invest in extraction in countries where commercial considerations alone might have led to a different outcome. Barriers to US inward investment in Japan were gradually broken down by the federal government.

There were, of course, occasional points of friction between the imperial state and US MNEs. The administration's *penchant* for legislation with extraterritorial reach sometimes created problems.[8] As Joseph Nye and Seymour Rubin observed many years ago, "The United States has attempted through extraterritorial control of the trading relations of affiliates of US-based corporations to extend its foreign policy embargoes into the jurisdiction of other states. Similarly, in the 1960s, the United States used guidelines on capital transfers by multinationals to strengthen its international monetary position. It has also been alleged that the United States government has on occasion been able to use, wittingly and unwittingly, the information-gathering capacities of global corporations domiciled in America for intelligence purposes."[9] Yet these points of friction should not be exaggerated. The relationship between MNEs and the federal government was generally close after the war with both sides needing and depending on each other.

Once western European recovery was consolidated and the European integration project launched with the Treaty of Rome in 1957,[10] the administration paid more attention to promoting FDI in the developing countries. A US government guarantee program for new investments, originally established for Europe, was extended to other parts of the world. By 1967, US guarantees were available for seventy-eight developing countries, and by 1970 the government had provided cover for thirty-five hundred new private investments.[11]

Congress at first was equally supportive. The Hickenlooper Amendment in 1962, for example, was designed to protect US MNEs against expropriation abroad.[12] However, in the same year, Congress passed the Revenue Act that withdrew some of the tax concessions on the foreign operations of US MNEs in the light of balance of payments difficulties. Of even more concern was the threat later in the decade of legislation imposing costs on big business to deal with environmental problems. And when Congress in 1971 debated the Burke-Hartke bill that—if passed—would have removed the tax breaks for companies that invested overseas, US MNEs recognized that the relatively passive approach of big business to government and Congress needed to change.[13]

Despite—or perhaps because of—their enormous size, US MNEs had not developed an effective lobby before the 1970s. Bodies such as the US Chamber of Commerce, the National Foreign Trade Council, or the National Association of Manufacturers may have been long established, but they were not good at speaking authoritatively with one voice. Part of the problem was the unwillingness of chief executive officers (CEOs) to attend meetings in person. The early 1970s, however, suggested a more proactive approach was needed, and the result was the Business Roundtable established in 1972 with representation only by CEOs.

The Business Roundtable soon discovered that the most effective way for corporate interests to be heard was through lobbying. By 1998 it had overtaken most other lobbying organizations in terms of total spending. In that year the only organizations to outspend it were a handful of individual MNEs themselves, the US Chamber of Commerce, and the American Medical Association.[14]

At the same time big business became more actively involved in the funding of candidates of the two main political parties at all levels, from the presidential downward. Although direct funding by corporations and national banks of federal campaigns had been declared illegal in 1907, the Federal Electoral Commission Act (FECA) of 1971 authorized political action committees (PACs), by means of which companies could legitimately funnel resources to candidates.[15] When limits on funding were lifted by the Supreme Court in 2010, it opened the way for even greater funding of politics by MNEs.

From the 1970s onward, therefore, big business had a powerful voice and used it to influence public policy in its favor. This was also the moment when globalization—the liberalization of trade and capital flows—was taking a qualitative leap forward. MNEs now had a strong interest in adding new themes to the agenda of international negotiations. These included trade in intellectual property, trade-related investment measures, and strengthening protection against nationalization.

The new agenda was of interest to companies and governments outside the United States—especially in Europe and Japan. However, it had a special meaning for the federal government, since the survival of the semiglobal empire depended on the success of US business abroad. Thus, the MNEs through their lobbying organizations found a sympathetic hearing in Washington, DC. And since both the Democratic and Republican Parties can be broadly defined as "pro-business," there was no danger of policy reversal if one party should lose power.

The first battleground for the new agenda was the Uruguay Round of trade negotiations. Launched in 1985, the US team faced a formidable set of obstacles in achieving the consensus needed to bring about a successful conclusion. It took nearly a decade, but at the end the US government and its MNEs had achieved almost all of what they wanted with the added bonus of a new organization (the World Trade Organization—WTO) with responsibility to implement the new agenda.

A good illustration of the close working relationship between US MNEs and the imperial state was provided by the agreement on trade-related aspects of intellectual property (TRIPS). Prior to the Uruguay Round, the negotiation and oversight of intellectual property agreements had been the responsibility of the World Intellectual Property Organization (WIPO), a toothless body under UN auspices. The growing importance of intellectual property for US MNEs persuaded Pfizer, an American pharmaceutical firm, to take the initiative in seeking a different solution.

The strategy adopted by Pfizer has been summarized as follows:

Firstly, Pfizer sought to infiltrate its high-level managers into policy-making bodies worldwide. This involved chairing fora and advisory groups as well as supporting the protection of IPRs [intellectual property rights] in other associations with which they were affiliated. Secondly, Pfizer deployed considerable time and resources on building and managing coalitions between corporations to ensure that the "line" taken with governments was consistent and could therefore be used to lead policy makers in the direction that Pfizer and its allies desired. Thirdly, and perhaps more specifically, Pfizer and their associates were able to utilize the strong position of the US in trade negotiations to further their ends—which of course also encouraged non-US corporations to seek ways of influencing the Pfizer-led alliance, thereby further strengthening the alliance's ability to mobilize private sector resources elsewhere. Finally . . . the Pfizer-led group was instrumental in arguing for a shift in fora, from the WIPO to the WTO.[16]

Pfizer and the US trade negotiators were successful, and the intellectual property rights of US MNEs were significantly strengthened by TRIPS. Pfizer could not have done this alone, but nor could the US trade negotiators.[17] As Ravi Ramamurti explained,

> Only US pharmaceutical firms had a home government powerful enough to lead the fight to change global IP [intellectual property] rules. None of the European nations—Switzerland, Germany, or even the United Kingdom—had sufficient leverage over trading partners to force them to reform IP laws, and getting the European Community to act in unison on any issue, including IP, would have been difficult. It might also be argued that by the 1980s the US government was much more receptive to policy advice from the private sector than was the European Commission to similar advice from firms in member countries. The importance of US leverage in trade negotiations becomes apparent when one examines the process by which the TRIPS agreement came to be negotiated.[18]

Although US MNEs have a global reach, there was never any doubt in the twentieth century that they were American companies with their headquarters in one of the fifty states. As firms have become more global, however, the allegiance of some to the United States has been questioned. The issue has been exacerbated by the (non)payment of tax in the home country as well as the need for MNEs to show loyalty to the countries hosting their investments. Thus, the symbiotic relationship between the federal government and US MNEs is no longer so secure. The implications of this will be explored in Chapter 11.

6.2. NONGOVERNMENTAL ORGANIZATIONS (NGOs)

NGOs are often seen as part of the counterculture in the United States. Images of people with placards supporting specific NGOs in protests, marches, and clashes with law-enforcement agencies are commonplace in the US media. Among the estimated 1.5 million US NGOs there are indeed plenty that fit this description. In general, however, NGOs have supported the value system that underpins the semiglobal empire. This is especially true of the larger, more influential ones engaged in international affairs.

The link between the imperial state and those NGOs focused on foreign policy goes back a century. It was "Colonel" Edward M. House, adviser to President Wilson, who brought together in 1917 a group of young men to advise on what the world should look like after the Great War ended. The Inquiry, as it was known, was in effect an early foreign affairs think tank that would go on to form the nucleus of the Council on Foreign Relations (CFR) in 1921 (Box 6.2).

The membership of the CFR was imbued with the idea that the United States would become the world's greatest power and needed to shape the postwar order to that effect. Its outlook was imperialist in all but name. A journal, *Foreign Affairs*, was launched in 1922 that the historian of the CFR described as follows: "While the editors saw themselves as the models of impartiality, no reader could be fooled into thinking that the journal was anything other than a plea for a forward United States foreign policy, interested in exploiting the world's natural resources and putting affairs in Washington in the hands of serene, dispassionate experts who, unlike the public at large, knew what they were doing."[19]

During the interwar years the federal government found the experience of working with NGOs concerned with world affairs so positive that US Secretary of State Edward Stettinius suggested to his UN partners in 1945 a mechanism through which "national and international organizations of a nongovernmental character, having interest in international problems falling within the competence of the Economic and Social Council, could bring their views to the attention of the Organization."[20]

It is fair to say that most other countries, including the Soviet Union, were horrified by this potential challenge to government authority. Such was the hegemony of the United States, however, that an article was included in the UN Charter giving the United States what it wanted with only Egypt and Iran voting against.

The experience proved positive from the US point of view. Indeed, the federal government was sufficiently confident of the support it would receive from NGOs in the pursuit of its foreign policy goals that it pushed for them to be given a voice in the Bretton Woods institutions. This was formalized in the 1980s with such bodies as the NGO–World Bank Committee.[21]

In theory, providing access to the IMF and the World Bank in this way benefits NGOs all over the world. In practice, however, it favors those in Washington, DC, so much so that two scholars concluded at the end of the millennium, "Activism by United States NGOs has probably expanded the already disproportionate role of the United States in the international financial institutions, especially the World Bank."[22]

BOX 6.2

THE COUNCIL ON FOREIGN RELATIONS

The Council on Foreign Relations (CFR), founded in 1921, can lay claim to being the ultimate "establishment" think tank. With a narrow membership drawn from the highest echelons of American business, academic, and political circles, it sought influence on public opinion and government policy above all else. The liberal internationalist ideology of most of the membership fitted in well with the state project to construct a semiglobal empire with the United States at its heart.

Influence is hard to prove, but the CFR claimed with some justification that the London Naval Treaty signed in 1930, which pursued disarmament while ensuring a leading position for the US Navy, was due to the earlier work of a CFR study group. The War and Peace Studies groups would also claim to have "set the boundaries of debate within the government on [the Second World] war."

The Vietnam War offered special challenges for the CFR as its membership, like US society as a whole, was deeply divided. Henry Kissinger was invited in 1969 to present a scenario for how the war might end, and a group was then put together to influence the administration of President Richard M. Nixon (1969–74) as soon as Kissinger became national security adviser, but it was rebuffed. CFR influence then steadily declined and led Kenneth Galbraith to pen these cruel words in his letter of resignation: "[CFR] is serviceable in one respect. If you want to know what the current cliché is, there is no better place to find out."

The connection with Kissinger, a director of the CFR from 1977 to 1981, would come back to haunt the council. A mildly critical piece in *Foreign Affairs* in 2004 by CFR staff member Kenneth Maxwell on Kissinger's role in Chile led to a heavy-handed intervention by Kissinger's allies to censor the journal. It demonstrated that in the perennial think tank trade-off between influence and independence, the council has always given preference to the former.

Since the end of the Second World War there has been exponential growth in the number of US NGOs. Most of these are small and focused on domestic rather than foreign policy. They therefore need not concern us here. Of those concerned with international affairs, there are two sorts of special interest to a study of the US semiglobal empire.[23] The first are the big philanthropic foundations engaged in international grant making (IGM), while the second are those think tanks with an interest in the outside world.[24]

The big philanthropic organizations almost invariably were founded by business using the fortunes established by their principal owners. The first was the Carnegie Corporation,[25] which was set up by Andrew Carnegie in 1911 for the purpose of "the advancement and diffusion of knowledge and understanding among the peoples of the United States and the British Dominions and Colonies."[26] This was a plea for leadership of the world to be shared between the United States and the British Empire and therefore struck a chord in the federal government. It was certainly not a challenge to US hegemony.

The second was the Rockefeller Foundation, although it was nearly the first, as John D. Rockefeller Sr. had earmarked, as early as 1909, $50 million in shares for establishing a philanthropic trust. However, he instructed the trustees to apply to the US Senate for a charter that would be "subject to alteration, amendment, or repeal at the pleasure of the Congress." While this demonstrated the close expected relationship between government and the charity, the timing was most unfortunate, as Congress was investigating Standard Oil, Rockefeller's flagship company, for market abuse at the time.[27] The Rockefeller Foundation was finally established in 1913 after receiving a charter from the New York State Legislature.[28]

Many other philanthropic foundations would then be established before the Ford Foundation was launched in 1936. Always close to government, except briefly in the 1980s, the Ford Foundation only became a major presence after the Second World War when it went even further than the others in providing implicit, and in some cases, explicit support for government foreign policy. Trustees of the Ford Foundation included former national security advisers and National Security Council members, presidents of the World Bank, chairmen of MNEs, and one who had been secretary of defense.

These three—Carnegie, Ford, and Rockefeller—were known for years as the Big Three of philanthropic foundations. However, they were joined in 2000 by the Gates Foundation, the endowment for which came at first from the founder of Microsoft (Bill Gates).[29] Although the origins of this charity are therefore similar to the Big Three, the Gates Foundation stands out for the size of its assets and the volume of its annual giving.[30] As a result, in its priority area (global health) the foundation's grants are comparable in size to those of the federal government.

The number of philanthropic foundations has now soared to over fifty thousand. Most of these, however, are still focused on domestic issues. Among those engaged in IGM, the top fifteen accounted for nearly two-thirds of the total in

2010. In addition to what is now the Big Four, the list includes such famous names as the Walton Family Foundation, the Hewlett Foundation, the Packard Foundation, the MacArthur Foundation, the Bloomberg Family Foundation and the Mellon Foundation.

Numerous mechanisms, formal and informal, operate to ensure that these foundations either support US foreign policy agendas or at least do not undermine them. First, the tax system is very generous to the foundations and their donors, with individuals qualifying for income tax deductions on charitable gifts if donating to foundations that operate or make grants to organizations abroad. Under the US tax code, the organization abroad must be "under the complete control of the US charity" and "funds are to be used in a foreign country by a US organization as opposed to being used by a foreign organization."[31]

Second, the trustees of the foundations are drawn from the networks of US elites that have served in government, big business, university administration, and the media.[32] While the occasional radical may slip through the net, the vast majority of trustees have been supportive of the federal government's broad foreign policy agenda. Thus, during the Cold War the international agendas of the leading foundations not only helped to build social science systems in developing countries that endorsed US values of liberal internationalism but also ensured that no money would go to those governments or nonstate actors that opposed US policy.

Finally, for a government not noted for its generosity in terms of official development assistance (foreign aid),[33] the IGM of the foundations provides a very useful supplement. The most extreme example is illustrated by the enormous grants to global health from the Gates Foundation. These complement the work of the federal government and provide a strong incentive for the latter to channel funds through the foundations in order to increase leverage.

Think tanks in the United States have a similar history to philanthropic foundations, although their endowments have been much smaller. One of the first was the Carnegie Endowment for International Peace established in 1910. Then came the Institute for Government Research in 1916 (renamed the Brookings Institution in 1927); the Hoover Institution on War, Revolution, and Peace in 1919; and the CFR in 1921. During and immediately after the Second World War came names that are familiar today, such as the American Enterprise Institute, the RAND Corporation, the Heritage Foundation, and the Cato Institute.

Before the Second World War the small number of foreign affairs think tanks operated very much as part of a US establishment. Nominally independent, in practice they saw their role as providing the ideas and policies that would help to guide the United States toward its new role as global leader.[34] As a result, they were uniformly opposed to "isolationism," which was seen—correctly—as ruling out a hegemonic role for the United States in world affairs.

After the war there was an explosion in the number of think tanks. Indeed, 91 percent of those in existence at the beginning of the twenty-first century were founded after 1951, and the number more than doubled after 1980.[35] Many of the newer ones have *not* been supportive of government policy, but invariably these are concerned with domestic rather than foreign policy. By contrast, the foreign policy think tanks generally share the values that underpin the semiglobal empire, including US exceptionalism, America as the "indispensable" nation in foreign affairs, and the need for the United States to provide global leadership.

Think tanks are not usually ranked by endowments but by influence (as judged by peers). There is now a Think Tank Index in which the top fifteen are separated into "the policymakers," "the scholars," "the activists," and "the partisans."[36] The first group includes the RAND Corporation, which played a key role throughout the Cold War in advising government on the technology of warfare as well as military tactics and strategy.[37] The second group includes the CFR, which suffered a loss of influence as a result of the divisions among US elites during and after the Vietnam War.[38]

The third and fourth groups have been more problematic for government. The activists, who include organizations such as Human Rights Watch, often reinforce government policy by focusing on abuse in countries subject to US sanctions. However, they sometimes shine an embarrassing spotlight on abuses by states that America is keen to support for imperial reasons. By contrast, the partisans are the think tanks with an explicit political agenda such as the left-leaning Center for American Progress and the right-wing Heritage Foundation. This creates a potential for conflict with the federal government, since it cannot please all the partisans, but the most serious problems have been over domestic rather than foreign affairs.

In general, the leading think tanks have been supportive of the semiglobal empire. In addition to the relevance in this context of those arguments advanced above to explain the support given to government by foundations, think tanks cannot afford to be too distant from US administrations if they are to preserve their all-important "influence." Potential members will be driven away by a think tank that is ignored by government, while officials from foreign states are attracted to those institutions thought to be close to the administration. In the words of Thomas Medvetz, one of the leading scholars of contemporary US think tanks, "[T]hink tanks have collectively developed their own social forms, including their own conventions, norms, and hierarchies, built on a common need for political recognition, funding and media attention. These needs powerfully limit the think tank's capacity to challenge the unspoken premises of policy debate, to ask original questions, and to offer policy prescriptions that run counter to the interests of financial donors, politicians or media institutions."[39]

Philanthropic foundations and think tanks worked closely with the US government to build and consolidate the semiglobal empire during and after the Cold War. Occasionally, as in the case of the second Iraq War (2003), the ideas originated in NGOs.[40] More commonly, the foreign policies originated on the government side and were then taken up and refined by NGOs. In a few cases the policies originated in Congress, which funds its own think tank (the United States Institute for Peace).

Many years ago Samuel Huntington, despite his discomfort in using the word "empire," correctly recognized the role of NGOs together with government in spreading US influence globally: "American expansion has been characterized not by the acquisition of new territories but by their *penetration*. In the past, the penetration of one society by the economic, religious, or military representatives of another society was usually the prelude to political acquisition. This has not been the case with the American empire, and there is nothing to suggest that it will be the case. . . . US expansion has been pluralistic expansion in which a variety of organizations, governmental and non-governmental, have attempted to pursue the objectives important to them within the territories of other societies."[41]

6.3. MEDIA

Protected by the first amendment, US media have never been subject to formal government control except during war or national emergencies. "Free speech" has always been a quintessential American value, and this was noted by Alexis de Tocqueville in his travels through the country. Writing in 1835, he said, "Among the twelve million people living in the territory of the United States, there is not one single man who has dared to suggest restricting the freedom of the press. . . . In the United States printers need no licenses, and newspapers no stamps or registration . . . so the number of periodical and semi-periodical productions surpasses all belief. . . . There is hardly a hamlet in America without its newspaper."[42]

Tocqueville was writing as the first "penny newspapers" were launched for mass circulation and New York City was quick to take advantage with the launch of the *New York Sun* (1833), *New York Morning Herald* (1835), *New York Tribune* (1841), and *New York Times* (1851). However, other cities were not far behind and

San Francisco boasted no fewer than twelve dailies soon after California joined the Union.[43]

With so many newspapers in circulation, it was not to be expected that the press would share a common view on anything. And yet, when it came to imperial expansion and the building of the territorial empire, there was a high degree of unanimity by the 1840s. Several years before John O'Sullivan coined the phrase "Manifest Destiny," for example, *Sailor's Magazine and Naval Journal* carried an article on California (still part of Mexico), stating in 1840, "It appears as if it was designed by the Creator to be the medium of connecting commercially Asia with America."[44] A few years later press support for the federal government in the Mexican-American War (1846–48) was universal.

With mass communications subject to economies of scale, and with the advent of new technology after the Civil War, it was inevitable that there would be consolidation of the press. This led to the establishment of the first "media empires" and included those created by William Randolph Hearst, Joseph Pulitzer, Edward Willis Scripps, and Adolph Simon Ochs. After the First World War these entrepreneurs would be joined by others such as Henry R. Luce, Robert Rutherford McCormick, and Joseph Medill Patterson.

The newspapers purchased or established by these media barons covered foreign as well as domestic news. This was notoriously expensive and gave rise to the phenomenon of the press agency. Indeed, the first (the Associated Press—AP) had been formed in 1846 by the New York papers to help cover the Mexican-American War (Box 6.3). It was followed by the United Press Associations (created by Scripps in 1907) and the International News Service (founded by Hearst in 1909).

The news flow to the US public was now very much in the hands of a small number of media tycoons. At the same time, the growth of the US press agencies meant that many people in the rest of the world, especially in Latin America, were dependent on US news-gathering techniques as well.

The media barons were all men of strong opinions, and on domestic politics they disagreed strongly with each other. However, there was much less disagreement when it came to the need for American empire—both the territorial one and later the semiglobal one. A United States expanding in terms of both territory and global influence was a shared strategic goal among the press owners, even if they might disagree on tactics. And, in general, the readers supported them.

William Randolph Hearst was the most notorious when it came to the territorial empire because of his outspoken support for a war against Spain in 1898. An accidental explosion on the battleship USS *Maine* in Havana Harbor was

BOX 6.3
THE ASSOCIATED PRESS

When the New York Associated Press (AP) was formed in 1846, the world news flow was dominated by Reuters (United Kingdom) and Havas (France). In 1870 these European press agencies then carved up the world, giving Great Britain, Holland, and their colonies to Reuters; France, Italy, Spain, Portugal, and the Levant went to Havas; and the two agreed to operate jointly in the Ottoman Empire, the Balkans, Egypt, and Belgium. They also exchanged news with the AP so that European news reached America mainly through Reuters.

This was resented in the United States, and in 1913 the president of the AP, Frank Noyes, felt compelled to write, "The objection to this method was that the news as received in London was alleged to be impressed with an English bias—in any event it was concededly not collected from an American viewpoint."

Noyes was also distressed by the fact that Latin America received its news about the United States mainly from the European agencies: "These countries [Central and South American nations] secure their news of the United States by way of Europe, and it consists mainly of murders, lynchings and embezzlements. The antipathy to the United States by the people of these countries is undoubtedly largely due to the false perspective given by their newspapers."

Noyes was president of the AP for thirty-eight years (1900–38) and succeeded in building the AP into a quasi-monopoly in the United States until it fell foul of the Anti-Trust Act in 1945. This did not stop its global expansion, however, and after the Second World War the AP replaced the European agencies as the principal source of information about the United States in most parts of the world.

By the start of the new century, the AP was operating in 120 countries and its news was published in seventeen hundred newspapers and carried by more than five thousand television and radio broadcasters. However, it faced a big challenge from the rise of new media outlets across the world. This reduced its global dominance and required cutbacks as gross revenues started to decline after 2010.

all that was needed to accuse Spain of an act of aggression, and war soon followed.[45] His newspapers then threw their weight enthusiastically behind the campaign once the Spanish-American War had started.

By the time Henry R. Luce established *Time* magazine in 1923,[46] the debate over the territorial empire had largely ended. Instead, Luce worked in an age when the extent of US global influence was becoming the key issue. Writing in February 1941, before the US entry into World War II, Luce outlined the global empire to which the United States could aspire after the Second World War. It would prove to be a very influential article.

Luce was careful never to use the word "empire." Instead, he spoke of the "American Century" in words that made clear this would be an empire in all but name:

> We are in a war to defend and even to promote, encourage and incite so-called democratic principles throughout the world. . . . America cannot be responsible for the good behavior of the entire world, but America is responsible to herself as well as to history for the world environment in which she lives . . . and now in this moment of testing there may come clear at last the vision which will guide us to the authentic creation of the 20th Century—our Century. . . . It is for America and for America alone to determine whether a system of free economic enterprise—an economic order compatible with freedom and progress—shall or shall not prevail in this century. We know perfectly well that there is not the slightest chance of anything faintly resembling a free economic system prevailing in this country if it prevails nowhere else.[47]

The press in the United States was "born free," but its young rival, radio—coming of age as Luce penned his prophetic words—was largely a government creation. As soon as the United States entered the First World War in 1917, the administration of President Wilson took over the patents of the main companies manufacturing radio equipment and established a federal monopoly on all uses of radio technology. At the end of the war the government then promised General Electric a monopoly of long-distance radio communications if it set up a US-owned radio company.[48]

The result was the Radio Corporation of America (RCA), alongside which would later emerge the great national networks: the National Broadcasting Company (NBC), the Columbia Broadcasting System (CBS), and the American Broadcasting Company (ABC). Thus, right from the start, radio was tightly controlled by a small group of companies and subject to regulation from 1927 by the Federal Radio Commission. This became in 1934 the Federal Communications Commission (FCC), which in due course would take over the regulation of television as soon as commercial operations began a few years later.[49]

The FCC did not censor radio and television (except in war time), but it did introduce a Fairness Doctrine requiring broadcasters to "editorialize with fairness." This led to many controversies in the coverage of domestic politics, but none in the field of foreign affairs where US global leadership was taken for granted by the small number of owners that dominated the media industry. And the US government now had its own vehicle, Voice of America, to ensure that the administration's interpretation of world events was heard around the globe.[50]

The Second World War demonstrated how tight control of the news flow could be used to influence public opinion across the world, and Latin America provided a good example. Appointed as coordinator of inter-American affairs, Nelson Rockefeller "provided not only 'canned' editorials, photographs, exclusives, feature stories and other such news material, but manufactured its own mass circulation magazines, supplements, pamphlets and newsreels. To ensure understanding of the 'issues' being advanced in Latin America, [Rockefeller's] Office sent 13,000 carefully selected 'opinion leaders' a weekly newsletter which was to help them 'clarify' the issues of the day."[51]

When the war ended, so did this kind of crude manipulation of the news flow. However, the start of the Cold War in 1946 and the anticommunist campaign of Senator Joseph McCarthy a few years later gave a decidedly "conformist" character to media coverage of US foreign policy and to the vast amount of information the rest of the world was receiving about America from its news agencies and major networks. The notion of the US government as "leader of the free world" battling the forces of darkness in the rest of the world was soon deeply embedded.

No part of the media played a more important role in this transformation than the film industry. Dominated by Hollywood, the industry established the Motion Picture Association of America (MPAA) in 1922 and regulated itself so successfully that the fear of government intervention was never realized.[52]

Hollywood then shaped US historical imagination through a series of films that have paid more attention to imagination than history. Yet, because of the popularity of film, these movies have been the primary vehicle of historical communication for many people. As early as 1935, a Chicago academic had felt compelled to write to the president of Metro-Goldwyn-Mayer to complain: "If the cinema art is going to draw its subjects so generously from history, it owes it to its patrons and its own higher ideals to achieve greater accuracy. No picture of a historical nature ought to be offered to the public until a reputable historian has had a chance to criticize and revise it."[53]

Needless to say, this advice was not taken, and Hollywood played a key role in spreading the message after the Second World War that the United States was engaged in an existential struggle against communism in which the means justified the ends. This view was shared so widely across the media that it was not until the 1970s that a few brave voices were raised in the press against errors and excesses in foreign policy.

The catalyst for these acts of courage was the Vietnam War—so much so that sections of the US "establishment" would accuse the media of being responsible for America's first major defeat in war. Yet, as more serious analysis has shown, "Research over the past few years has indicated that such a belief is misplaced. Content analyses of newspaper and television coverage show that, more often than not, the press reported official information, statements, and views with relatively little dissent."[54]

Part of the reason for this was the growing dependence of the media on the supply of news from the press agencies or even government sources, as cost pressures led to a remorseless decline in the number of correspondents that newspapers, radio, and television could support themselves. And cost pressures had affected the agencies as well, leading first to the merger of the United Press with the International News Service in 1958 to form United Press International (UPI), and then later the decline of UPI itself.

This left the AP as the dominant agency not just for America but also for the rest of the world. It was concern outside the United States at this dominance that led to the UNESCO-sponsored New World Information and Communication Order. This was a serious attempt, starting in the 1970s, to free the media in the developing countries from their dependence on information provided by US sources.[55] It led to the publication in 1980 of the MacBride Report, which stated, "Transformations in the structures of international communications, as a factor inherent in the conceptual foundations of international relations and of development, are frequently called for. It is argued that a world built on mutual understanding, acceptance of diversity, promotion of détente and coexistence, encouragement of trends towards real independence, not only needs but makes room for new, different patterns in international communication."[56]

This was a direct challenge to US dominance of international communication and it would lead to the departure of the United States from UNESCO in 1984. And yet, ironically, this was the moment when the federal government itself set about overhauling and tackling the quasi-monopolistic character of mass communications in the United States with the breakup of the American Telephone & Telegraph Company (AT&T) in telephony and cable,[57] the abandonment of the Fairness Doctrine, and finally, in 1996, with the passage of the Telecommunications Act.

The Telecommunications Act was intended to foster competition, but its relaxation on rules restricting ownership of radio and television stations instead set off a wave of mergers in which seven gigantic multimedia companies came to dominate communications in the United States.[58] These companies own newspapers and magazines, movie production studios, television networks, cable channels (including news, political, and business channels), publishing houses, and Internet services. They are controlled by individuals and boards who are strongly in favor of global US leadership and who share with the federal government a commitment to a US-dominated semiglobal empire.

The Telecommunications Act therefore did little to change the oligopolistic structure of the US media industry and it left the dominant position of the AP unaffected. At the same time, it coincided with a dramatic reduction in international news coverage in the United States. The time devoted to foreign news on network television, for example, declined from 45 percent in the 1970s to 13.5 percent in 1995.[59] Meanwhile, international news in the press declined from 10.2 percent in 1971 to 6 percent in 1988 and 2 percent in 1998.[60]

The combination of a high degree of concentration in the media coupled with low coverage of foreign affairs left the federal government relatively free to pursue its imperial project during the Cold War and, indeed, afterward (see Chapter 8). Criticism from the media tended to focus on tactics rather than strategy (this was true even during the Vietnam War). Meanwhile, the noncommunist world received a flow of information about the United States and its foreign policies from a range of US sources that was generally pro-American.

As long as the rest of the noncommunist world had access to few other sources of information to form a view of American foreign policy, US imperial interests were usually—if not always—protected. However, the growth of the Internet, the rise of Islamic extremism, and the spread of nationalism have dramatically changed the situation, leaving the United States in a much more vulnerable global position (see Chapter 11).

6.4. RELIGIOUS GROUPS

The US imperial project has been underpinned by a series of ideas that are widely shared by the country's citizens. The oldest of these, and the most deeply embedded, is the belief in US "exceptionalism": the sense that America is different from other countries, that it is blessed with a "special providence,"[61] and that this gives it a unique place in world affairs. In the words of James Skillen,

"The people who . . . organized themselves into . . . [a] republic believed that their project as a whole, including both its limited government and its free individuals, represented a unique, providential blessing and appointment of God in history. Consequently, the nation came to see itself as a chosen people called to serve as a light to the world."[62]

The idea has its roots in the history of American Protestantism. However, it is a view now widely shared by adherents of other faiths as well. Thus, there is a close relationship between religion and empire, since American exceptionalism inevitably led to an imperial destiny. This has been true during both the territorial as well as the semiglobal empire.

The missionaries sent out by the American Board of Commissioners for Foreign Missions[63] after its establishment in 1810 went primarily to non-Christian countries with high illiteracy rates. Education was therefore emphasized in missionary work, and this helped to spread knowledge of the United States. Some of these countries, such as Hawaii and Samoa, would in due course become part of the territorial empire.[64]

By the end of the nineteenth century there were more than five thousand US missionaries working abroad. Since they were either the only US citizens in a country or were closely associated with other US expatriates, they were usually considered by the indigenous population to be representing the US government. Thus, when local uprisings targeted foreign imperialists, as during the 1900 Boxer Rebellion in China, US missionaries were often the first to be attacked.

After the Spanish-American War, when imperialism became an explicit US government policy, there was a rapid rise in missionary work overseas, so much so that the number of US missionaries had reached fifteen thousand by 1915.[65] All of them could be considered "evangelicals" in the sense that they considered it their duty to spread the word of God to the less fortunate or to the heathen.

This brand of evangelicalism was then threatened at home by the rise of liberal Protestantism, which had been influenced by secularism and modern science. As this version of Protestantism became mainline, evangelicals reacted in two very different ways. The first was toward fundamentalism, which was dedicated to a return to biblical orthodoxy. The second was toward neo-evangelicalism that Harold Ockenga, one of its founders, defined as follows: "The new evangelicalism embraces the full orthodoxy of fundamentalism, but manifests a social consciousness and responsibility which was strangely absent from fundamentalism. The new evangelicalism concerns itself not only with personal salvation, doctrinal truth and an eternal point of reference, but also with the problems of race, of war, of class struggle, of liquor control, of juvenile delinquency, of immorality, and of *national imperialism*. . . . The new evangelicalism believes that orthodox Christians cannot abdicate their responsibility in the social scene."[66]

Ockenga, who helped to establish the National Association of Evangelicals (NAE) in 1942, clearly thought that the new evangelicalism would be antiimperialist.[67] Yet, ironically, it became one of the most powerful forces in support of the US semiglobal empire after the Second World War and the reasons are not hard to find. The first was the eruption of the Cold War, the second was the birth of Israel, and the third was the rise of Islamic extremism.

The Cold War pitted the US government against the Soviet Union, an atheistic state in which religious freedom was not permitted. This was anathema to the vast majority of American citizens, especially the evangelicals, and the situation was made worse in 1949 when the nationalists led by Chiang Kai-shek were defeated by the communists in China.[68] Anticommunism propelled evangelicalism, while at the same time it provided strong support for US foreign policy during the Cold War. Indeed, "There is solid evidence that evangelical affiliation, orthodox doctrine, and high religious commitment fostered antiCommunist attitudes and support for higher defense spending—the makings of the dimensions of militarism or militant internationalism discovered by foreign policy opinion analysts."[69]

The creation of the State of Israel and its subsequent struggle for survival was also a key factor in the spread of US evangelicalism. Identification of evangelicals with Israel has many causes and has been widely studied, but it was perhaps best summarized by Walter Russell Mead when he stated, "The return of the Jews to the Holy Land, their extraordinary victories over larger Arab armies, and even the rising tide of hatred that threatens Jews in Israel and abroad strengthen not only the evangelical commitment to Israel but also the position of evangelical life in American life."[70]

Last but not least, the rise of Islamic extremism and the targeting of Christians as well as numerous symbols of US power in some Muslim-majority countries provided a further stimulus for the growth of US evangelicalism long before the atrocities of September 11, 2001. Thus, three key areas of foreign policy concern in the semiglobal empire—containment of communism, support for Israel, and resistance to Islamic extremism—enjoyed massive support among evangelicals and, indeed, most other Christian churches as well.

The growth of the NAE after the Second World War was spectacular, with a membership of around thirty million at the turn of the century and forty-five thousand churches from forty-eight denominations. This does not even include the Southern Baptist Convention (SBC), the largest church in the United States, which chose to stay outside the NAE, nor the millions of evangelicals associated with independent churches, including megachurches, and parachurches unaffiliated with any established church. Altogether, it is estimated that by the end of the twentieth century nearly 30 percent of the US population—around 100 million people—could be classified as evangelical.[71]

Unlike their nineteenth-century counterparts, the US evangelical missionaries going abroad since the Second World War have not given preference to non-Christian countries. Thus, US evangelical missionaries are present in virtually every country where they are permitted. And other faiths, notably Catholicism, have continued to dispatch missionaries from the United States to many countries around the world as well.

At the beginning of the new century the United States was sending out more than 100,000 missionaries of all Christian faiths, roughly one quarter of all missionaries sent abroad in the world.[72]And this large number does not include the missionaries recruited locally that have been such an important part of the growth of Pentecostal and Charismatic Christianity outside the United States.

The main focus of the US missionaries sent abroad is the low-income countries of Africa, the Asia-Pacific, and the Latin American and Caribbean region. For the evangelicals, however, this is relatively recent. When Billy Graham, perhaps the greatest of all US evangelists, began his foreign "crusades" in 1954, he chose to go to western Europe.[73] In 1960, however, he went to Africa, the Middle East, and Latin America, setting a trend for the future.

Most US missionaries would no doubt agree with Graham's claim that "when I go to preach the gospel, I go as an ambassador for the Kingdom of God—not America."[74] However, for the faithful in the recipient countries it is different. US missions bring not only a spiritual message but also a wide array of material benefits funded by US donors. These can include education, scholarships, reading materials, health clinics, hospitals, and radio and television stations. In many places the mission has either replaced the state as the main provider of social services or is the only one to provide these services in the first place.

US missionaries, especially the evangelical ones, have therefore helped to create a constituency abroad that is very aware of what the United States has to offer and in some cases is sympathetic to US foreign policy goals.[75] In addition, missionaries were regularly debriefed by the CIA about local conditions on their return to the United States. And as parts of the Catholic Church moved toward liberation theology with its progressive and anti-imperialist message, the evangelical churches with their socially conservative and anticommunist views began to be viewed more favorably by right-wing governments across the globe.

The semiglobal empire therefore benefited in numerous ways from the growth of US evangelical churches. At the same time, those same churches became more effective in influencing foreign policy in the United States itself. Starting with the attendance of President Dwight D. Eisenhower (1953–61) at the first National Prayer Breakfast in 1953,[76] there has been a growing acceptance of the need for foreign policy to take into account this new and important constituency.

In addition to the ties of friendship between various evangelists and US presidents, more formal links have developed over the years between the evangelical churches and the federal government.[77] The churches have also become very skilled at lobbying Congress. As a result, they can point to numerous examples of foreign policy or legislation that were changed as a result of their efforts after the Second World War.

These efforts started in 1949 with the determination of evangelicals to prevent the US government from recognizing Communist China, a decision with far-reaching implications for the semiglobal empire.[78] They continued throughout the Cold War, culminating in the close cooperation between the administration of President Ronald Reagan (1981–89) and the evangelical movement in the counterrevolution in Central America.[79]

After the Cold War, the evangelical movement played a key role in the passage of the 1998 International Religious Freedom Act that makes the promotion of religious freedom part of the foreign policy of the United States and provides for sanctions against governments supporting religious persecution. The movement also played an important part in the Sudan Peace Act of 2002 that contributed in no small way to the establishment of South Sudan as an independent state in 2011.

Evangelicals also played a big part in persuading President George W. Bush (2001–9) to increase humanitarian assistance—especially to Africa. At the end of the Bush presidency, US churches (not just evangelical but also Catholic and mainline Protestant) were spending $13 billion on overseas relief and development—a massive figure in its own right. However, the federal government spent $29 billion, a big increase on previous years.[80]

The proportion of the US population now calling itself Christian is in decline.[81] However, this decline is concentrated among mainline Protestants and Catholics. Between 2007 and 2014, according to the Pew Research Center's Religious Landscape Survey, the share self-identifying as evangelical hardly fell at all (from 26.3 percent to 25.4 percent). This suggests that the important role played by evangelical churches in the construction of the semiglobal empire since the Second World War is not about to end.

BOX 6.4

WORLD VISION

World Vision was started in 1950 by Bob Pierce, a Youth for Christ evangelist. Pierce, a fervent anticommunist, had spent many years in Asia and was a strong supporter of the nationalists in China. The trigger for World Vision was the attack by communist North Korea against South Korea, leading to a desperate need for emergency supplies in hospitals, schools, and orphanages.

Three years later, concerned at the number of children fathered by US soldiers in South Korea, Pierce introduced the concept of child sponsorship for which World Vision is still famous. A strong link was thereby established between sponsors in the United States and children in the rest of the world (later on, World Vision would permit sponsorship by non-US citizens).

The impact of World Vision was relatively modest until the International Congress on World Evangelization in 1974 in Lausanne. As one World Vision executive explained, "The emphasis on social action ministries hand in hand with evangelistic outreach put World Vision in a unique catalytic and leadership position in Evangelical Christianity" (King, "The New Internationalists," 932).

Soon after Lausanne, World Vision appointed Senator Mark Hatfield to the board and close ties quickly developed with Congress and the administration. World Vision started to receive large grants in cash and kind from the federal government. Today it is present in nearly one hundred countries and is the largest evangelical relief and development organization in the world.

World Vision has often been surrounded by political controversy, notably in Central America in the 1980s when it worked closely with the administration of President Ronald Reagan (1981–89) and right-wing governments in the region. It has never wavered in its anticommunism and was quick to move into eastern Europe following the collapse of the Soviet Union.

It may, however, become more limited. First, the missions in the developing world are increasingly run by locals with US missionaries confined to less important roles. The priorities of these leaders are not necessarily the same as the US-based churches to which they are affiliated (the most striking example is the Pentecostal Church in Brazil, which—despite owing its origins to US evangelists—is now completely autonomous).[82]

Second, a very large number of countries are now closed or partially closed to receiving foreign missionaries. These include countries such as Peru, Venezuela, Kenya, Indonesia, and Tanzania that have traditionally formed part of the semiglobal empire. This reduces the role that US religious organizations can play in it. Indeed, it is no accident that many of the countries that have the highest ratio of missionaries per million of the population are today either tiny islands or are in the US territorial empire itself.[83]

Third, the socially conservative agenda of most evangelical churches can now cause problems for the US government. On issues such as homosexuality, gay marriage, and abortion most evangelical churches stand far to the right of the federal government regardless of which party is in power. And in many parts of the semiglobal empire aggressive support for socially conservative policies by US missionaries causes friction with the local government.

Finally, a series of scandals involving key US evangelists and some evangelical organizations has reduced the ability of churches to influence US decision making. The impact of these scandals will eventually fade, but it is hard to imagine religious organizations—let alone evangelical churches—exercising the influence over foreign policy that they did during the Cold War and in its immediate aftermath.

7

THE EMPIRE IN ACTION

The empire built by the United States after the Second World War was based on rules fashioned in Washington, DC, and underpinned by US-controlled institutions. The values on which it was based were then carried abroad by a series of state and nonstate actors (NSAs). It did not depend on territorial acquisition and therefore, in an ideal world, there would have been no need for US intervention in the affairs of foreign states. The institutions would ensure that other countries followed the rules and the moral force of NSAs would encourage them to do so.

In practice, of course, the world did not always operate in this way, and the US government felt obliged to intervene on numerous occasions. These interventions became increasingly frequent after the start of the Cold War, as the competition first with the Soviet Union and later with the People's Republic of China (PRC) not only challenged the rules and institutions established by the United States but also held out to other countries the prospect of a very different world order.

US intervention took many forms. Sometimes it was direct and involved the US military; on other occasions it made use of proxy forces; often, although not widely realized at the time, the intervention was covert and not always legal even under US law. This intervention took place in all the regions—Western Europe, the Asia-Pacific, the Middle East, Africa, and the Americas—where the empire operated.

Most of these interventions succeeded in their short-term objectives, although there were a number of minor and major setbacks. Yet even the major defeats—in Angola, Cuba, Iran, and Vietnam—did not mean the empire had gone into reverse. On the contrary, the semiglobal empire (it never included the USSR and PRC) was still strong as the Cold War came to an end.

The scale of intervention was not only unprecedented in terms of the national story but almost certainly in respect of world history as well. No other country has ever undertaken such a vast commitment over such a large area of the world, and it would not have been possible without control of institutions at the global and regional level. That it needed massive military resources goes without saying, but it also required the support of the majority of the population. To secure that support, the American state depended heavily on the NSAs examined in Chapter 6.

7.1. WESTERN EUROPE

Incorporating western Europe into the empire after the Second World War was a big challenge for the United States. Several states were empires themselves, and the United States needed these to be dismantled without alienating their governments and citizens in the process. Western Europe also needed to recover economically if it was to have any chance of remaining in the capitalist camp. And democracy needed to be promoted without risking a communist victory in any of the countries concerned.

At the heart of Europe lay Germany. Long before its unconditional surrender in May 1945, the United States had developed plans for what to do during the inevitable military occupation that would follow Germany's defeat. As agreed at Teheran in 1943, and confirmed at Yalta and Potsdam in 1945, Germany would be divided into zones in which each of the occupying powers would have almost unlimited powers.[1]

The American zone (Map 11) was in the south, with the Soviet Union to the east, the British to the north,[2] and a small French zone in the west[3] (Berlin in east Germany was also divided among the four powers). By 1947 the US government had persuaded the British to merge their two zones and the French could be left, if necessary, to their own devices. Thus, two years after the collapse of Nazi Germany the United States was in a position to shape what would become West Germany into a protectorate in the knowledge that neither the German people nor the British government were in any position to resist US demands.

In this imperial exercise the US government was supremely successful, and West Germany was the most faithful European ally of the United States during the Cold War. US-inspired currency reform in the non-Soviet zones in 1948 put West Germany on the path to economic recovery, and the country was allowed to participate in the Marshall Plan the following year.

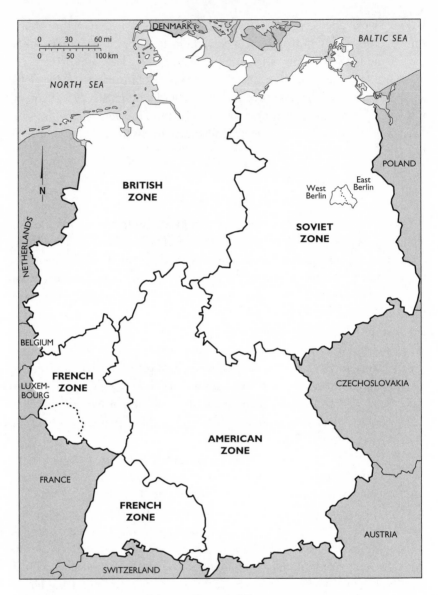

Map 11. Occupied Germany

Soviet resistance to the *de facto* partition of Germany implied by the new currency proved futile,[4] and the Federal Republic of Germany was born in 1949 with a Basic Law shaped by US officials.[5] By 1955 the US government had overcome the resistance of its allies and allowed West Germany to rearm and join NATO. The West German economic and political structures were now considered so stable that the United States and its allies ended the military occupation of the country everywhere except West Berlin.[6]

West German governments were always staunchly anticommunist, and the Basic Law made it almost impossible for communists to gain even a foothold in parliament. This was not the case elsewhere in western Europe, where communists were often popular as a result in part of the leading role they had played in the fight against fascism. Nowhere was this more true than in Greece, where communist military success had led to the launch of the Truman Doctrine in March 1947.

With the end of the German occupation in sight, a coalition government had been formed in Greece as early as May 1944 with the participation of communists. This soon crumbled, and a civil war broke out before the end of the year. The British intervened massively on the side of the anticommunists, but by early 1947—despite the death of fifty thousand Greeks—they had failed to defeat them.

It was at this point that the administration of President Harry S. Truman (1945–53) intervened and converted Greece into a US protectorate. The communists, who were supported by Albania, Bulgaria, and Yugoslavia but not the Soviet Union, were defeated militarily and excluded from political life. An American Mission for Aid to Greece (AMAG) was established with extraordinary powers. A State Department directive to Dwight Griswold, head of AMAG, set the tone:

> A question involving a high policy decision affecting the operations of AMAG . . . shall be . . . brought to the attention of the Department before any action is taken. . . . By "high policy" decision is meant one which involves major political repercussions. . . . Among the matters on which such high policy decisions would be required are:
>
> a) any action by United States representatives in connection with a change in the Greek Cabinet;
> b) any action by the United States representatives to bring about or to prevent a change in the high command of the Greek armed forces;
> c) any substantial increase or decrease in the size of the Greek armed forces;
> d) any disagreement arising with the Greek or British authorities which, regardless of its source, may impair co-operation between American officials in Greece and Greek and British officials;
> e) any major question involving the relations of Greece with the United Nations or any foreign nation other than the United States;
> f) any major question involving the policies of the Greek Government toward Greek political parties, trade unions, subversive elements, rebel

armed forces, etc., including questions of punishment, amnesties and the like;

g) any question involving the holding of elections in Greece.

The foregoing list is not intended to be inclusive but rather to give examples.[7]

This tight American control left the politicians fighting for scraps as in other US protectorates.[8] Prime ministers needed to demonstrate their loyalty to Washington, DC, before they could be elected. One such was George Papandreou, but his son (Andreas) was more independent minded. When elections in 1967 looked as if they would return the elderly father to power with an important role for the son, the military intervened to establish a dictatorship. US officials were well aware of the plans but chose not to intervene.[9]

Subsequent support for the brutal military regime (1967–74) led to serious reputational damage for the US government,[10] but it was considered at the time as a price worth paying in return for Greek loyalty during the Cold War. However, the regime overreached itself in 1974 when it overthrew the government in Cyprus and provoked an invasion by Turkey (another NATO ally).[11] The junta had become a major liability, and the US government was content to see the restoration of civilian rule provided the new leaders remained loyal to the United States.

The end of the Second World War led to the formation of coalition governments in a number of western European countries in which communists took part. The most important was France, where the Communist Party had derived considerable prestige from its opposition to Nazi Germany with a big increase in membership.[12] Furthermore, in the elections for the Legislative Assembly in November 1946 the Communist Party secured more votes than any other party.

Ousting the communists from the French government therefore became a top US priority after the announcement of the Truman Doctrine. One of the chosen instruments was the World Bank, which made France the first country to receive a loan subject to various conditions. In his biography of John McCloy, the American president of the World Bank, Kai Bird explained what then happened while negotiations over the conditions took place: "Simultaneously, the State Department bluntly informed the French that they would have to 'correct the present situation' by removing any communist representatives in the Cabinet. The Communist Party was pushed out of the coalition government in early May 1947 and within hours, as if to underscore the linkage, McCloy announced that the [World Bank] loan would go ahead."[13]

Ousting the Communist Party from government in Italy would prove more difficult as a result of its enormous size.[14] Although communists had been pushed out of government in May 1947,[15] at the same time as in France (and Belgium), the party was well placed to win the April 1948 legislative elections. Indeed, its coalition with the Socialist Party made it almost certain that it would do so.

This prospect galvanized the US government into action using all the tools at its disposal. In addition to conventional methods (e.g., funding for noncommunist parties, increased broadcasts by the Voice of America, and mass circulation of US documentary and feature films), the campaign made use of a new technique in which Americans of Italian origin were encouraged to write to their relatives and friends in Italy warning of the dire consequences of a communist victory. To facilitate this, the US government arranged for publication of sample letters in newspapers.

The campaign worked spectacularly well, and support for the left-wing coalition collapsed in the weeks before the election. The Christian Democrats were returned to power and governed Italy for nearly fifty years. The communists were permanently excluded from power. The Christian Democrat leadership proved to be a loyal ally of the US government and Italy was effectively a protectorate throughout the Cold War with dozens of American military bases providing security.

Marginalizing communist parties was necessary, but not sufficient, if the US semiglobal empire was to be consolidated in western Europe. Communist parties garnered electoral support more for their domestic than their foreign policies. Thus, it was also necessary to encourage a noncommunist political culture that was, as far as possible, pro-American.

This work had begun in Germany as soon as the war ended, with the sponsorship of newspapers, including the highly successful *Neue Zeitung*. When William Benton was appointed assistant secretary of state for public and cultural relations in August 1945, he wasted no time in securing Hollywood's agreement to "a voluntary system of consultation with the State Department in their representation of international matters."[16] This laid the basis for a long-lasting association between the US government and the film industry in the promotion of propaganda.

Not everyone was happy with these new initiatives. In April 1947 Secretary of State George Marshall wrote to Benton, "The use of propaganda as such is contrary to our generally accepted precepts of democracy and to the public statements I have made. Another consideration is that we could be playing directly into the hands of the Soviets who are masters in the use of such techniques. Our sole aim in our overseas information program must be to present nothing but the truth, in a completely factual and unbiased manner. Only by this means can we justify the procedure and establish a reputation before the world for integrity of action."[17]

Marshall's scruples and those of others were soon overcome, however, and the propaganda program (albeit not in the crude form practiced by the USSR) was put on a more secure footing in 1948 with the passage of the Smith-Mundt Act to spread "information about the United States, its peoples, and policies." This paved the way for the establishment in 1953 of the United States Information Agency (USIA) that was then given broad global responsibility to promote US interests abroad including through the Voice of America.

The operations of USIA were in the public domain, but there was also a covert program operated by the CIA. This led in Europe in 1950 to the creation of Radio Free Europe and to the establishment of the Congress for Cultural Freedom (CCF). The latter in turn used CIA finances to establish a series of publications in western European countries that were highly influential (and pro-American) until their funding sources were revealed in 1966.[18]

When the United States started its program of "cultural diplomacy" for Europe after the war, the western states faced a grim economic future. Recovery was slow and hesitant until foreign aid under the Marshall Plan put it on a more sustainable basis. This economic assistance, however, could never be more than temporary and, indeed, ended in 1952. Under these circumstances, the administrations of Harry S. Truman and Dwight D. Eisenhower (1953–61) were strongly in favor of any policies likely to promote western European economic growth.

The proposal in 1950 for a European Coal and Steel Community (ECSC) was therefore greeted enthusiastically by the US government. Designed by Jean Monnet, a Frenchman who had spent the war years in Washington, DC, and had become a special adviser to President Franklin Delano Roosevelt (1933–45), the ECSC was always seen as a prelude to a wider and more ambitious scheme for European integration. This duly occurred when the European Economic Community (EEC) was formed by six states (Belgium, France, Germany, Holland, Italy, and Luxembourg) following the Treaty of Rome in 1957.

Although the Treaty of Rome anticipated a customs union that would lead to some trade diversion at the expense of the United States, it was still supported by the Eisenhower administration on the grounds that it would promote economic growth, reduce the need for US assistance, and provide resources for national defense. In addition, the United States applied pressure to ensure there was no discrimination against inward investment by US companies, making it more acceptable to the private sector.

Integration was so successful that western Europe would in due course achieve parity with the United States on many economic indicators.[19] The region might therefore have been expected to shed completely the American imperial mantle spread across it immediately after the Second World War. However, western Europe remained militarily dependent on the United States throughout the Cold War despite its growing economic strength. National security was therefore the Achilles heel of the European integration project.

The reasons for this are to be found in the perceived threat of a Soviet invasion. Always exaggerated, it was nonetheless seen as sufficiently menacing to persuade the main European countries outside the Soviet bloc (including Turkey) to join forces with the United States in NATO. Yet the only credible defense against the threat of a Soviet attack was the possession of nuclear weapons. Since these were under American control, NATO countries were ultimately dependent on the United States for their own defense and were therefore not fully sovereign.[20] As David Calleo, a distinguished US scholar of transatlantic relations, explained, "The strategic defense of America and Europe may be indivisible, and NATO may be a collective umbrella, but only the American president can decide when to put it up. In short, the decisive weapons for NATO's defense are not subject to integration, but are under direct American control."[21]

NATO, despite its outward appearance, has always been dominated by the United States. During the Cold War the main commands and most of the subordinate ones were held by US military officers and member states played host to a vast array of US army, naval, and air bases.[22] However, the US armed forces also built bases in some European countries considered ineligible for NATO membership. The most important was Spain, which was considered so strategically important that the Eisenhower administration was prepared to overlook its dictatorial system of government under the staunchly anticommunist general Francisco Franco.

Western Europe was transformed economically, politically, and socially during the Cold War, but it remained militarily dependent on the United States. It was, therefore, part of the semiglobal empire. This struck many Europeans as an acceptable compromise, but it could only work if the USSR was perceived as a serious threat and if US taxpayers were prepared to contribute to European defense. That is why cultural diplomacy, including propaganda, was so important for the success of the US imperial project.

BOX 7.1
THE UK-US "SPECIAL RELATIONSHIP"

British prime minister Winston Churchill, desperate to bring the United States into the Second World War, often used language designed to flatter his American audiences. This included the phrase "special relationship" to describe the historical links between the two countries, although for most of American history before the twentieth century the United Kingdom and United States had been strategic rivals.

When the United States finally entered the war after the Japanese attack on Pearl Harbor in December 1941, the two allies did indeed work closely together. Yet even before the war had ended, the subordinate position of the United Kingdom was clear for all to see and the United States gave no special favors to its wartime ally in the immediate postwar years.

Just how "unspecial" the relationship had become was laid bare by the US response to the British invasion (together with France and Israel) of Egypt in 1956 (see Chapter 7.3). The Eisenhower administration condemned the aggression, applied sanctions, and only reversed its position when the British withdrew their troops.

After the formation in 1958 of the European Economic Community, without British participation, the United States increasingly looked to West Germany as its key ally in Europe. Despite this, British prime ministers have continued to use the phrase "special relationship" and US presidents have generally been happy to let them do so.

The reasons for this are not hard to find even if there is little substance in the claim. For US administrations Great Britain has become a client state whose armed forces work well with the American military. Secrets are shared through an intelligence alliance (known as the "five eyes" because it also includes Australia, Canada, and New Zealand) and the United Kingdom rarely votes against the United States in the UN Security Council. For British prime ministers it is a harmless conceit that exaggerates British influence in the world and helps to assuage the loss of empire.

In reality, imperial powers—especially one with a semiglobal empire—cannot afford to have special relationships with any single country. Instead, the United States is happy to let many countries claim a special relationship as long as they do not expect special favors in return.

7.2. THE ASIA-PACIFIC REGION

The United States was already a major imperial power in the Asia-Pacific region even before the Second World War started. Following the unconditional surrender of Japan in August 1945, she would acquire additional territories (see Chapter 3).[23] Yet the most important acquisition was Japan itself, occupied militarily by the United States immediately after the surrender of the Japanese armed forces.

Unlike what happened in West Germany, the US government chose not to share responsibility with any other power during the Japanese occupation. To assuage Allied sensitivities, a Far Eastern Commission composed of eleven nations was set up in Washington, DC, and an Allied Council with four members (China, the United Kingdom, the United States, and the USSR) in Tokyo. However, these bodies had no executive powers and were largely ignored by US authorities.

US policy, implemented by General Douglas MacArthur, Supreme Commander for the Allied Powers (SCAP), was at first driven by the doctrine of "punishment and reform." War crimes trials were held, some 200,000 Japanese citizens were barred from public life, and a constitution was written for Japan that banned the creation of armed forces or the right of the state to conduct war.[24] All this was done on the assumption that China would be the key ally of the United States in the Asia-Pacific region, relegating Japan to a relatively minor role in international affairs.

The victory of Mao Tse-tung in China in 1949 and the outbreak of the Korean War the following year forced the Truman administration swiftly to modify its plans for Japan. The country would now become nominally independent, albeit as a protectorate, following ratification of a peace treaty signed at San Francisco in 1951 by forty-eight countries,[25] while simultaneously a bilateral security treaty gave the United States extraordinary powers to intervene in Japanese domestic affairs and maintain military bases throughout the country.

The security treaty was revised in 1960, but it still left the United States in a dominant position in Japan. Okinawa, where the United States had built its largest military base in the Asia-Pacific region, remained a US colony, and Japanese jurisdiction over military personnel stationed there was very limited.[26] The US government also imposed restrictions on Japanese trade with Communist China until the United States itself recognized the PRC in 1971.

The dominant US position was unpopular with much of the Japanese electorate, especially the Socialist Party, but the CIA provided generous funding for the conservative Liberal Democrat Party (LDP). This helped the LDP to retain power throughout the Cold War, which provided successive US administrations with staunchly pro-American governments in Japan.

Just how unequal the relationship between Japan and the United States remained even after revision of the security treaty was revealed during the visit of President Richard M. Nixon (1969–74) and Henry Kissinger to China in February 1972. Mao and his foreign minister, Chou En-lai, used the opportunity to protest the US military presence in Japan. In the words of Michael Schaller, drawing on the memoranda of conversations between the leaders, "Nixon answered that without the security treaty and US bases the 'wild horse of Japan could not be controlled.' Kissinger added that the security pact restrained the Japanese from developing their own nuclear weapons . . . or from 'reaching out into Korea or Taiwan or China.' The US alliance provided 'leverage over Japan' without which, Nixon said, our 'remonstrations would be like an empty cannon' and the 'wild horse would not be tamed.'"[27]

After making due allowance for the rhetoric associated with summit meetings, these conversations revealed how the wheel had almost come full circle since the Second World War when the United States had expected China at the end of hostilities to become its principal ally in the Asia-Pacific region and its partner in preventing Japan from ever again posing a threat to peace. Indeed, as early as 1943 the administration of Franklin Delano Roosevelt (1933–45) had not only committed itself to the restoration of China's territorial integrity but was also pushing for China to become one of the permanent members of a future United Nations Security Council.

The US government did what it could to try and prevent civil war between the communists and nationalists in China starting again as soon as Japan was defeated. However, it was an impossible task and Mao's victory in October 1949 obliged the United States to rethink its whole Asia-Pacific strategy. Even as it did so, however, the Truman administration was rapidly overtaken by events. In particular, as early as February 1950, China and the Soviet Union signed a far-reaching agreement, including a mutual defense pact in the case of aggression by Japan or "any state allied with her" (a clear reference to the United States).[28]

Many countries, not just in the Soviet bloc, subsequently took the opportunity to recognize the PRC as the sole representative of China. Yet the Truman administration, under enormous pressure from many quarters, refused to do so.[29] Instead, the United States chose to recognize the Republic of China (ROC), Chiang Kai-shek's administration in Taiwan, as the only legitimate Chinese government.

This momentous decision meant that Taiwan, a small island with only seven million people, would represent the whole of China in the UN and have a permanent seat on the Security Council. However, it also meant that Taiwan would become a US protectorate as the ROC had no other way of ensuring its own survival in the event of a Chinese attack. This subordinate status became clear in June 1950 when President Truman declared,

> The occupation of Formosa [Taiwan] by Communist forces would be a direct threat to the security of the Pacific area and to United States forces performing their lawful and necessary functions in that area. Accordingly, I have ordered the 7th Fleet to prevent any attack on Formosa. As a corollary of this action, I am calling upon the Chinese Government on Formosa to cease all air and sea operations against the mainland. The 7th Fleet will see that this is done. The determination of the future status of Formosa must await the restoration of security in the Pacific, a peace settlement with Japan, or consideration by the United Nations.[30]

A Mutual Defense Treaty was then agreed on between the Eisenhower administration and Taiwan in 1954, committing the United States to defend the island in the case of attack.[31] Article 7 of the treaty also gave the United States the right to establish military bases on Taiwan (there would be many). The treaty remained in force even after the PRC replaced the ROC in the UN in October 1971 and was only terminated in 1980, a year after the United States switched its diplomatic allegiance away from the Taiwanese administration to the government in Beijing.[32]

In the years before the Second World War, the United States had paid little attention to Korea. Following Japanese intervention in 1905, the main concern of the administration of Theodore Roosevelt (1901–9) was not to condemn Japan but to secure from her assurances that this aggressive act did not threaten the US colony in the Philippines. However, the policy changed completely with the US occupation of Japan at the end of the war. Korea—less than one hundred miles from Japan at the closest point—would now acquire strategic importance.

Korea had in fact been part of US postwar planning since at least 1943. Allied leaders had committed themselves to the independence of Korea, but then added the worrying phrase "in due course." At Yalta, Winston Churchill, Franklin Delano Roosevelt (FDR), and Joseph Stalin had agreed to establish a four-power trusteeship for the peninsula.[33] By September 1945, however, only two powers were involved, with the USSR accepting the surrender of Japanese troops north of the 38th parallel while US forces did the same in the south.[34]

Both powers, unable to agree on how unification might be achieved, then moved swiftly to establish protectorates. In the south, the US occupation forces found in the aged and authoritarian Syngman Rhee a leader they could trust.[35] Elections were held in 1948, Rhee was declared president of the Republic of Korea, and US forces then left. Rhee, however, remained committed to unification and a series of incidents of increasing violence culminated in invasion from the north in June 1950.

The Truman administration rushed to the defense of its protectorate, and the Korean War entered a new and more deadly phase. Helped by the temporary absence of the Soviet Union from the Security Council, the United States was able to secure UN diplomatic support and put together a coalition of sixteen countries.[36] Yet a swift victory for the allies was ruled out when Chinese forces entered the war at the end of 1950.

The war ended in mid-1953 with virtually the same territorial division of Korea as when it had started. The Republic of Korea (i.e., South Korea) would now become a key part of the American empire in the Asia-Pacific region. A mutual defense agreement was quickly signed giving the United States the right to station its armed forces all over the country.[37] US foreign aid and investment then poured into the country, helping to turn South Korea into a poster child for economic development. The same would happen in Taiwan.

Since North Korea had not been defeated, there were many Americans who regarded the end of the war as marking a failure of imperial policy due to US unwillingness to use overwhelming military force. The Eisenhower administration was therefore under enormous pressure to ensure the same thing did not happen again elsewhere, and it would be put to the test early on in Indochina.

Colonized by France in the nineteenth century and comprising modern Cambodia, Laos, and Vietnam (Map 12), Indochina had become a Japanese possession in the Second World War. FDR at first opposed France's plans to recover its Asian empire, but at Yalta softened his position. After the Japanese surrender in August 1945, fighting soon broke out in Indochina between Vietnamese nationalists, led by Ho Chi Minh (Box 7.2), and French forces. Although Stalin had no interest in Southeast Asia and refused to recognize Ho's Democratic Republic of Vietnam, the Truman administration gave its support to France.[38]

This assistance did not prevent the defeat of French forces, and in 1954 at Geneva a peace agreement was signed (the United Kingdom and the USSR were cosponsors). The outcome in Cambodia and Laos was the formation of governments acceptable to the Eisenhower administration (not itself a signatory to the agreement). Vietnam, however, was to be temporarily partitioned pending elections to be held in July 1956 with Ho Chi Minh in command in the north.

Map 12. Indochina

The Eisenhower administration now moved swiftly to impose its imperial will on the region. The Southeast Asia Treaty Organization (SEATO) was formed on September 8, 1954, with eight members. Three countries (France, the United Kingdom, and the United States) were imperial powers in the region; two (Australia and New Zealand), anticipating a decline in British naval power, were looking to the United States for future protection;[39] and one (Pakistan) hoped for US assistance in its struggle with India.

Only two members were from the region, and one of these was a US protectorate and former colony (the Philippines).[40] However, Article 4, Paragraph 1, of the treaty establishing SEATO stated, "Each Party recognizes that aggression by means of armed attack in the treaty area against any of the Parties *or against any State or territory which the Parties by unanimous agreement may hereafter designate*, would endanger its own peace and safety, and agrees that it will in that event act to meet the common danger in accordance with its constitutional processes."[41] What this meant was revealed the same day the treaty was signed by the addition of a protocol that identified Cambodia, Laos, and "the free territory under the jurisdiction of the State of Vietnam" (i.e., the area not controlled by Ho Chi Minh) as the territories to be designated for protection against aggression.

The Eisenhower administration now had legal cover that could be used to intervene in the south of Vietnam as the French withdrew. Ngo Dinh Diem, a Vietnamese who had held office under both the French and Japanese colonial governments, was identified as a reliable future leader and engineered into the presidency of the State of Vietnam in 1955. Diem, with US blessing, then refused to hold the promised elections in July 1956 on the grounds that his government had not signed the Geneva Accords. The real reason, of course, was that Ho Chi Minh would probably have won.

Two decades later, after the death and displacement of millions of Vietnamese, the United States and its allies had been defeated in Indochina.[42] Yet defeat, despite all the domestic and international repercussions, did not mark the end of American empire in the Asia-Pacific region—let alone elsewhere. The domino theory, outlined by President Eisenhower, had predicted widespread consequences if South Vietnam collapsed, but the only dominoes to fall were Cambodia and Laos. Not even Thailand, Malaysia, or Burma, all neighboring countries with left-wing insurgencies, succumbed.

Indeed, even while experiencing one setback after another in Indochina, the US government secured a much bigger and more important prize when Indonesia, the world's fifth largest country in terms of population, committed itself to the American fold. From the late 1960s onward, it began to follow an economic development model that promoted foreign investment, trade liberalization, and regional integration from which US companies benefited enormously.

Indonesia (Dutch East Indies) had been a colony of Holland until the Second World War, when it was occupied by Japan. The Truman administration looked favorably on the Netherlands recovering its former possession for the same reasons it had done so in the case of France and Indochina (see above). However, a Dutch failure in 1948 to observe the terms of a US-brokered settlement led to a change of policy, and Indonesian independence in 1949 received US support.[43]

The undisputed leader of the independence struggle was Sukarno, who had no intention of replacing Dutch colonialism with a US protectorate. He mani-

BOX 7.2

HO CHI MINH (1890–1969)

As European empires crumbled after the Second World War, there emerged a series of nationalist leaders who had been in the vanguard of the anticolonial struggle. Although in many cases they were communists, they were not necessarily anti-American unless circumstances forced them to be so.

Ho Chi Minh was typical of this kind of leader. Born in 1890 in a Vietnamese village, he chose to travel the world after his father was demoted from his position as a French imperial magistrate. He worked in a series of relatively menial jobs in the United States and United Kingdom before settling in France in 1919.

He joined forces with other Vietnamese activists to lobby the negotiators at the Versailles Conference to recognize an independent Vietnam. When this failed he joined the French Communist Party as a founder member before moving first to the Soviet Union and then to China.

He returned permanently to Vietnam in 1941 after the Japanese occupation and helped to form the Viet Minh as a resistance force. After the Japanese surrender, he proclaimed the birth of the Democratic Republic of Vietnam with the opening words taken directly from the US Declaration of Independence. However, neither the United States nor the USSR recognized his government (the USSR would only do so in 1950).

He tried to reach an accommodation with the newly established French government in Paris but failed, and war broke out again in 1946. It ended with the spectacular defeat of the French forces at Dien Bien Phu in 1954. In Geneva, however, he reluctantly agreed to a temporary partition of Vietnam at the 17th parallel. When the administration of President Dwight D. Eisenhower (1953–61) threw its support behind the anticommunist State of Vietnam, war was again inevitable.

Ho Chi Minh did not live to see the final defeat of the United States, but he did live long enough to witness the Tet Offensive in 1968 that demonstrated the capacity of a mobile guerrilla force to defeat a superior enemy. From then on, negotiations between Vietnam and the US government only had one possible outcome.

fested Indonesian autonomy not only in economic policy but also in hosting the Bandung Conference in 1955 that became the forerunner of the Non-Aligned Movement. He also cooperated with the Partai Komunis Indonesia (PKI), by then the largest communist party in the world outside China and the USSR.

The overthrow of Sukarno in 1965 and the crushing of the PKI by Suharto, a pro-American general, was an extremely violent process leading to an estimated 1.5 million deaths. The details are still not fully known, especially the role of the CIA, but it was a textbook intervention involving US state and nonstate actors that would be repeated in other countries.[44] Indonesia under Suharto, who ruled until his overthrow in 1998, acknowledged US strategic and economic hegemony in the region in return for a free hand in suppressing domestic opponents.

The empire built by the United States in the Asia-Pacific region was therefore extensive. It did not embrace China or the Soviet Union nor, after 1975, any part of Indochina, but it was still impressive. The biggest gap was India, which stayed resolutely neutral after independence and close to the Soviet Union. Yet the semiglobal empire during the Cold War was not about territory as such and much more about influence and penetration. Even in India, US penetration was not negligible and would increase substantially once the Cold War ended.

7.3. THE MIDDLE EAST AND SUB-SAHARAN AFRICA

In the Middle East and sub-Saharan Africa (see Map 13), unlike in the Asia-Pacific region, the United States had no territorial possessions before the Second World War. Indeed, US formal responsibilities were limited to its protectorate over Liberia in Africa. Instead, countries in these two regions were almost all controlled by different European powers as colonies or protectorates while the US presence—apart from its diplomats—was essentially limited to the investments of a small number of American firms and the activities of numerous missionaries and philanthropic foundations.

All this would change dramatically after the Second World War when US administrations set themselves a series of ambitious goals. In the Middle East[45] (sub-Saharan Africa will be considered below), the first objective was to end exclusive control by European imperialists; the second was to obtain reliable supplies of energy; the third was to ensure the security of Israel; and the fourth was to prevent the USSR from gaining a major foothold in the region. These objectives required the incorporation of the Middle East into the American empire, and this is exactly what happened. However, the objectives sometimes conflicted with each other so that the US empire was never as secure in the Middle East as in other parts of the world.

By the end of the Second World War, the Italian Empire in the Middle East had collapsed so that France and Great Britain were the only imperial powers.[46] French attempts to reestablish authority over Lebanon and Syria under the League of Nations mandate were thwarted by the combined efforts of the United Kingdom and the United States,[47] leaving France with only Algeria, Morocco, and Tunisia. The last two became independent in 1956, while Algeria—legally a department of France and not a colony—became independent in 1962 after a bitter war.

That left Great Britain as the one remaining European imperial power in the Middle East. US administrations did not wish her to stay, but at the same time they were reluctant to see her depart too swiftly. Thus, British withdrawal was a long, drawn-out affair that began in 1945 and ended in 1971. As the British withdrew, the United States either stepped in to play a similar "protective" role, used proxies to do the same thing, or relied on the network of institutions and NSAs (outlined in Chapters 5 and 6) to secure compliance with US goals.

The first transfer took place in Saudi Arabia in 1945, when the Saudi and US governments signed an agreement leading to the construction of an air base close to the oil fields controlled by an American company.[48] The second was in Palestine in 1948, where the United States took the lead in ending the British mandate and helping to secure the creation of the State of Israel. The third was in Iran in 1953, where a joint UK-US covert operation led to the overthrow of Prime Minister Mohammad Mosaddeq and was followed by a rapid reduction in British influence.[49] The fourth was in Egypt in 1956, where a Franco-British-Israeli attempt to reverse nationalization of the Suez Canal was thwarted by President Eisenhower.[50]

In all these cases the decline of British power was balanced in due course by a rise in US influence. A nationalist rebellion in Iraq in 1958 then ended the British protectorate, and Kuwait became independent from Britain in 1961, limiting British responsibilities to Jordan and the small states in the Persian Gulf. The United States then replaced the United Kingdom as the hegemonic power in Iraq, Jordan, and Kuwait,[51] while using Iran as its proxy in the Persian Gulf after the British withdrew in 1971. Following the Iranian Revolution in 1979, however, the United States itself took on an imperial role in the gulf.

The collapse of the Ottoman Empire after World War I was seen by American oil companies as a great opportunity despite the fact that the US economy was still largely self-sufficient in energy.[52] Great Britain and France tried to keep the oil in the hands of their own companies, but American pressure forced them to allow US participation in the gigantic Iraq Petroleum Company (IPC) in 1922.[53] The participants in the IPC—British, French, and US oil firms, together with Calouste Gulbenkian[54]—then agreed not to compete with each other in the former Ottoman Empire.[55]

The State Department colluded in this restraint of trade, which left excluded US companies at a disadvantage. Undeterred, Standard Oil of California secured a long-term contract in Saudi Arabia in 1933 and then sold part of its share to Texaco to defray costs. By 1938 the partnership, soon to be renamed Aramco, struck oil just outside Dhahran.

Aramco's discovery was the most important ever made in oil history and transformed US relations with Saudi Arabia. In 1943 the kingdom was made a beneficiary of Lend-Lease assistance despite the fact it was a nonbelligerent in the Second World War. When Aramco invited two other US firms (Jersey Standard and Mobil) to participate in building the Trans-Arabian Pipeline to the Mediterranean, the Truman administration first overruled the antitrust objections of the Justice Department on national security grounds and then allowed the CIA to plot the overthrow of the Syrian government that was blocking the project.[56] And when the Saudi king in 1950 insisted on a fifty-fifty profit share, the State and Treasury Departments agreed on the "golden gimmick" under which Aramco could receive a foreign tax credit to offset increased royalty payments.

By the end of the Second World War, US oil consumption was rising much faster than domestic oil reserves. This meant that the US economy, not just those of western Europe, risked becoming dependent on Middle East oil. The State Department therefore looked for new sources of oil. Outside Saudi Arabia, the largest reserves were in Iran and the covert operation against the government in 1953 provided the perfect opportunity. The Anglo-Iranian Oil Company, previously controlled by British interests, was reconstituted to provide for the participation of US firms.

The US government now had the energy security it desired. In addition, friendly governments in Libya,[57] Kuwait, and the small states in the Persian Gulf region provided a warm welcome for US investments. However, the companies demanded too much, and the US government was too slow to address the problem. The Organization of the Petroleum Exporting Countries (OPEC) was founded in Iraq in 1960 and was able to push up oil prices dramatically in the 1970s. Governments, even those friendly to the United States, then nationalized foreign oil companies. And anti-Americanism played a key role in the Iranian Revolution that brought to power in 1979 a radical Islamist government that was determined to reduce US influence in the region. From then onward, the United States increasingly looked elsewhere for its energy security.

When FDR met Ibn Saud in February 1945, the Saudi monarch made clear his vitriolic opposition to Zionism and to the creation of a Jewish state in Palestine. Mindful of this, the Truman administration at first acted cautiously on the issue. Indeed, after the UN vote in November 1947 in favor of partition, the prospect of war persuaded the US ambassador to the UN to declare partition impracticable and to back a UN trusteeship for Palestine instead.[58] And when Israel declared its independence on May 14, 1948, many high-ranking US officials, including Secretary of State George Marshall, were against recognition.

Despite this, President Truman did recognize the new state within eleven minutes of its declaration of independence.[59] Yet he and his successor were always careful to try and appear even-handed in the dispute between Israel and its Arab neighbors. It was not until the presidencies of John F. Kennedy (1961–63) and Lyndon Johnson (1963–69) that US policies toward Israel—on nuclear weapons, borders, settlements, and (lack of) support for a Palestinian state[60]— became so one-sided.[61] And these policies continued almost without interruption throughout the Cold War.

The partisan nature of US policy toward Israel has often been attributed to the power of the Jewish lobby, especially the American Israel Public Affairs Committee (AIPAC).[62] No one can deny that electoral considerations have always been very important in support for Israel (and may have been crucial in the case of Truman's recognition of the Jewish state), but no imperial power has ever allowed a special interest group to impose a policy that conflicts with broader state interests. Thus, support for Israel has always been consistent with other strategic objectives.

Although Israel often irritated the United States with its domestic policies, it was a strong ally during the Cold War. Indeed, inside and outside the Middle East, Israel could be counted on to support the United States in its global competition with the Soviet Union.[63] It played a crucial role in 1970 in preventing the overthrow by Arab nationalists of the Jordanian king, a key US ally. Later it would serve US interests in Africa, Central America, and South America. As the Cold War drew to a close, it was among the first countries to be awarded the title by the United States of "major non-NATO ally."

Unlike the United States, Russia had been an imperial power in the Middle East before the First World War. Geography, especially the Black Sea, guaranteed that the Soviet Union would try to maintain a presence. Indeed, the USSR (together with the United Kingdom) occupied Iran in 1941 and tried unsuccessfully to annex northern Iran to (Soviet) Azerbaijan after the war.[64] Yet the switch in the Middle East after the Second World War from British, French, and Italian hegemony to that of the United States was so swift that the Soviet Union found itself frozen out even before the Cold War started.

The overthrow of King Farouk in Egypt in 1952 by radical nationalist army officers led by Gamal Abdel Nasser gave the Soviet Union its first chance to establish a meaningful presence in the Middle East. Nasser was not anti-American, but he soon realized he would never receive from President Eisenhower the weapons he wanted to confront Israel, while his ambitious plans to construct a dam on the Nile were blocked by the World Bank acting on US instructions. The Soviet Union was then happy to fill both the military and the funding gap and signed a pact with the nationalist government in Syria as well.

Eisenhower's swift response to the Suez Crisis, effectively siding with Nasser, gave the United States a chance to rebuild its relationship with Egypt in particular and pan-Arab nationalism in general. However, the opportunity was wasted and instead Congress passed a joint resolution in March 1957, later known as the Eisenhower Doctrine, stating that "the United States regards as vital to the national interest and world peace the preservation of the independence and integrity of the nations of the Middle East."[65] This was a green light to intervene in the Middle East wherever there was a perceived threat to US hegemony.

The first application of the Eisenhower Doctrine came the following year. Soviet influence in the Middle East took a big step forward when radical pan-Arab nationalist regimes in Egypt and Syria announced their union as the United Arab Republic in February 1958.[66] When civil unrest in Lebanon then threatened the position of the pro-American government, Eisenhower dispatched troops, naval vessels, and aircraft. The spread of pan-Arab nationalism was halted, but Nasser concluded that he needed to strengthen ties with the Soviet Union.

Lebanon was the first US invasion of a Middle Eastern country, and it prompted the Eisenhower administration to seek a more multilateral approach to restrict the Soviet presence in the region. The solution found was the Central Treaty Organization (CENTO), modeled on NATO, whose Middle Eastern members were Turkey, Iran, and Pakistan.[67] These countries constituted a buffer between the Soviet Union and the rest of the Middle East. CENTO was then complemented by a vast array of American military bases across the region designed to help the United States to secure its objectives in the Middle East.

Despite this, US goals in the Middle East were only partly achieved. European empires did come to an end, the United States established itself as the leading foreign power, and Israel's survival was guaranteed. However, the United

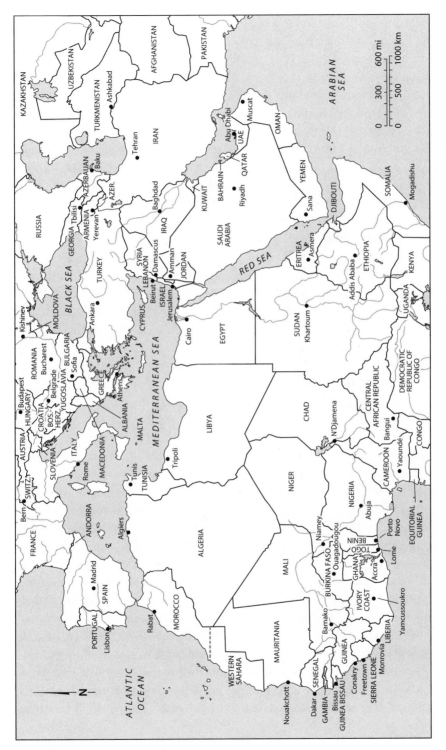

Map 13. North Africa and the Middle East

States was only able to broker peace treaties with two of Israel's neighbors (Egypt and Jordan), and energy security proved to be elusive as a result both of oil nationalizations and OPEC. Pan-Arab nationalism and the Soviet presence in the region went into reverse after the death of Nasser in 1970, but radical Islam—especially in Iran—would prove to be a much greater challenge.

Of all the regions in the world where the United States would build its semiglobal empire, sub-Saharan Africa had the lowest priority at the end of the Second World War. The United States did retain a number of military bases and the one in Ethiopia, later named Kagnew Air Base, was expanded after 1953 providing valuable support to Emperor Haile Selassie until his overthrow in 1974. Kagnew, however, was close to the Red Sea, guarding the shipping lanes in and out of the Suez Canal, and the base was therefore closely tied to US interests in the Middle East rather than sub-Saharan Africa.[68]

It was not until 1949 that the post of assistant secretary for African affairs was created in the State Department, and even then it was combined with Near Eastern and South Asian affairs. The first official to be appointed was George McGhee, and in 1950 he outlined four US objectives for Africa: progressive development of African peoples toward self-government or independence; development of mutually advantageous economic relations between the colonial powers and their African colonies; preservation of the rights to equal economic treatment for all businesses in Africa; and creation of an environment in which Africans would want to be associated with the United States and its allies.[69]

These objectives led the United States to take a relaxed approach to decolonization by the remaining imperial powers[70] (all US allies), since the US government wanted to be sure that independence would not create a political opening for the Soviet Union and a decline in economic access for American companies. And since decolonization would eventually add over fifty seats to the United Nations (roughly the same number as the founding members), it was considered imperative to limit Soviet influence to ensure that the new African states were either pro-American or at least not pro-Soviet.

By and large, these objectives were met. Decolonization started in 1956 and was completed in 1990.[71] It created only a few opportunities for the Soviet Union, and even where it did—as, for example, in Guinea or Ghana—these proved not to be permanent.[72] However, the reputational damage to the United States as a result of its efforts could be severe (for the case of the Congo, see Box 7.3).

The US-controlled institutions built after the Second World War proved very efficacious in keeping African countries inside the semiglobal empire. The UN generally worked as the United States had planned, with the USSR unwilling

BOX 7.3
THE REPUBLIC OF CONGO (1960–65)

The Belgian colony of the Congo represented all that was worst about European imperialism in Africa. Thus, the decision by the colonial power to grant independence on June 30, 1960, after multiparty elections, should have marked an opportunity for the country's advancement. This did not happen, and the United States must take much of the blame.

Within days of independence, the mineral-rich province of Katanga seceded under the leadership of Moise Tshombe. The Congolese prime minister Patrice Lumumba, a radical nationalist, pleaded for outside assistance. Belgian troops were dispatched but did nothing to put down the rebellion, as Tshombe promised to protect foreign mining interests. The Eisenhower administration responded by securing UN support for a multilateral force that also did nothing to end the secession. Lumumba then turned to the Soviet Union for support. He was soon deposed by Colonel Joseph Mobutu, a CIA asset, and murdered.

President John F. Kennedy (1961–63) inherited the problem and helped to secure the election of the malleable Cyrille Adoula as prime minister. The Katanga secession was quickly ended and Tshombe sent into exile. However, rebel factions loyal to the memory of Lumumba fought on and had gained the upper hand by 1964. President Lyndon Johnson (1963–69) then permitted the CIA to recruit white mercenaries, mainly from Rhodesia and South Africa, who committed appalling atrocities in confronting the rebels. Tshombe was then brought back from exile and installed as prime minister.

Under pressure from its allies in Africa and elsewhere, the Soviet Union finally responded with military and financial aid for the rebels. Cuba also helped, sending a small contingent of troops under the command of Che Guevara. All this assistance arrived too late, however, and the rebels were crushed.

Congo's nightmare, grim though it had been, was still far from over. In November 1965, Joseph Mobutu overthrew Prime Minister Tshombe and imposed a kleptocracy upon the country, whose name he changed to Zaire in 1971 (it would be renamed the Democratic Republic of the Congo after his overthrow in 1997). He remained on good terms with the United States throughout his long period of rule.

to use its veto when dealing with African affairs. International Monetary Fund and World Bank programs ensured that US companies had access to almost all African markets throughout the Cold War on a nondiscriminatory basis, and the continent was a useful source of raw materials for the US economy.[73] In addition, American multinational enterprises invested heavily in mining, including strategically important mineral extraction in South Africa, and enjoyed strong support from US governments.

Yet there was one country whose independence represented a major setback for the United States, and that was Angola. Nationalists had launched in 1961 a guerrilla war against Portugal, the colonial power ruled dictatorially by António Salazar from 1932 to 1968. Portugal, however, was a key American ally as a result of allowing the United States to operate an air base in the Azores, and the United States was therefore reluctant to support any of the guerrilla factions.[74] When Salazar's successor was overthrown in 1974, the Angolan faction that had Soviet support, the Movimento Popular de Libertação de Angola (MPLA), then defeated its rivals in a civil war and Angola declared its independence in 1975.

The United States, anxious to avoid a Soviet "victory," then gave its backing to the defeated factions that also had the support of the apartheid regime in South Africa.[75] As the Angolan government came under attack from South African troops, Cuba—without informing the USSR—responded to a request for military assistance.[76] Its troops helped to secure a series of stunning victories that should have brought the civil war to an end. However, the United States and apartheid South Africa continued to support the anti-MPLA factions, which plunged Angola into a further ten years of conflict.[77] This put the United States firmly on the wrong side of history in Angola, since it had both failed to support decolonization and also cooperated with apartheid South Africa.[78]

7.4. THE AMERICAS

By the end of the Second World War, the US government exercised such enormous leverage over the other states in the Americas that they were assigned a low priority in peacetime planning. However, the start of the Cold War drew US attention to those countries where left-wing parties and trade unions had gained influence as a result of the wartime US-Soviet alliance. Policy then changed very quickly and governments in the region came under pressure to change course.

The impact of the change in policy was swift. Communist parties were declared illegal in most countries. Brazil and Chile severed relations with the Soviet Union in 1947. In the same year US pressure undermined the coalition in Bolivia that governed with the support of a Marxist party and contributed in the following year to the military coup in Venezuela that overthrew a progressive government. A major offensive was launched by the US labor federation AFL-CIO against left-wing trade unions and new anticommunist confederations were established. The British government also played its part, sacking in 1953 the left-wing administration of Cheddi Jagan in the colony of British Guiana.[79]

From the US perspective these measures were so successful that communist influence had been virtually eliminated in the Americas by 1954. There was, however, one important exception: Guatemala. The Central American republic, whose long-serving dictator had been overthrown in a popular revolt in 1944, had held its first free presidential elections the following year. The winner was Juan José Arévalo, who cautiously began to tackle Guatemala's legacy of social backwardness and capitalist privilege.

Inevitably this brought him into conflict with US-owned companies, including the United Fruit Company (UFCO), which owned vast areas of land and enjoyed a virtual monopoly over railways, telegraphs, and ports.[80] The Truman administration then applied intense pressure to try and force Arévalo to change course. This included an embargo on arms sales, no Point Four foreign aid, and the threat of a veto against any loans from the World Bank.[81]

President Arévalo, to the surprise of many, survived this US onslaught. His successor, also elected in free elections, was not so fortunate. Colonel Jacobo Arbenz was not a communist, but he did legalize the Partido Guatemalteco de Trabajo (PGT), purchased arms secretly from Czechoslovakia, and passed legislation (Decree 900) to expropriate the largest farms, including those owned by UFCO. These actions earned him the fury of the US establishment. The Council on Foreign Relations, in a confidential report, captured the mood: "The Guatemalan situation is quite simply the penetration of Central America by a frankly Russian-dominated Communist group. . . . There should be no hesitation . . . in quite overtly working with the forces opposed to Communism, and eventually backing a political tide which will force the Guatemalan government either to exclude its Communists or to change."[82]

Arbenz was driven from office in 1954 by an invasion force from Honduras organized by the CIA, and Carlos Castillo Armas was installed as a puppet president.[83] Guatemala was then condemned to three decades of civil war and the loss of more than 100,000 lives. At the time, however, the covert operation was hailed as a great success. The Eisenhower administration was then free to concentrate on other regions of the world, confident that international communism had been purged from the Americas.

This confidence proved to be premature. Herbert Matthews's articles in the *New York Times* in February 1957 had drawn attention to the guerrilla movement in eastern Cuba led by Fidel Castro, and events thereafter moved swiftly. President Eisenhower, who had supported Fulgencio Batista as a bulwark against communism, took exception to the increasingly brutal methods employed by the Cuban dictator to defeat his opponents and suspended arms sales in mid-1958. However, US diplomatic efforts to find a suitable replacement for Batista failed and Castro entered Havana triumphantly on January 3, 1959.

Castro then implemented a government program very similar to that adopted by Arévalo and Arbenz in Guatemala, with land reform as its centerpiece. Eisenhower responded exactly as he had done a few years earlier and authorized the CIA to organize an exile force to invade Cuba. Castro, however, had learned the lessons of history and was well prepared. The exiles were defeated at the Bay of Pigs in April 1961, by which time President Kennedy was in power, and later that year Castro announced that the Cuban Revolution was Marxist-Leninist and allied to the Soviet Union.

This was a huge blow to US prestige, and it was only partially reversed by the resolution of the Cuban Missile Crisis in October 1962 when the Soviet Union agreed to withdraw its nuclear missiles from the island in return for a US promise not to invade Cuba. Kennedy recognized early on in his administration that US policy in the Americas needed to change and to pay more attention to the economic and social grievances that underpinned revolutionary upheaval. As a result, the Inter-American Development Bank (IADB) began operations, the US Agency for International Development (USAID) was started, and the Alliance for Progress (ALPRO) was launched.[84]

Castro's survival, albeit subject to a trade embargo and many other restrictions, meant that US administrations were now much more sensitive to any leftward shift in the region and would react quickly in the event that it happened. The first test, however, came not in Latin America but in the Caribbean colony of British Guiana where Cheddi Jagan, returned to "office but not power" in 1957, had been reelected in 1961.[85]

Jagan was determined to take the British colony to independence as soon as possible. Frustrated by the lack of cooperation from the British government, he secured an interview with President Kennedy in October 1961. The Kennedy administration, however, concluded that Jagan was dangerously left-wing and set out to destabilize his government with the connivance of the British authorities. All state and nonstate instruments were employed including the CIA, the AFL-CIO, the US Information Service and the Christian Anti-Communist Crusade.[86]

The key to promoting instability was a general strike that was then used by the British government as an excuse to rewrite the Constitution of British Guiana and impose a new electoral law based on proportional representation. Fresh elections were then held in 1964. Although Jagan's party won the largest number of seats, it no longer commanded a majority. The governor then invited Forbes Burnham, leader of a rival party, to form a government and independence was granted two years later. Guyana (as it was now called) accepted US hegemony but suffered two decades of economic incompetence, human rights abuse, and mass emigration.

The defeat of Jagan in 1964 appeared to the Johnson administration to remove the last challenge to US hegemony in the Caribbean outside of Cuba. Most of the islands were still either US colonies or territories of European powers that were members of NATO.[87] Among the numerous British colonies, only Jamaica and Trinidad & Tobago had become independent, and both wanted good relations with the United States.[88] François "Papa Doc" Duvalier, Haitian president for life, had survived a half-hearted US attempt to unseat him and was happy to play the anticommunist card in return for US tolerance of his dictatorial regime.

That left only the Dominican Republic, where the United States had intervened in 1961 by authorizing the assassination of President Rafael Trujillo and again in 1963 by supporting the overthrow of President Juan Bosch.[89] A triumvirate was then established that met all US requirements. However, when the new regime was itself overthrown in April 1965 by young officers and rebels allied to Bosch, President Johnson ordered an immediate invasion by US troops. The intervention was in due course supported by the OAS and Joaquín Balaguer, a close ally of Trujillo, was installed as president the following year.

One of the few Latin American countries to send troops to the Dominican Republic in support of US intervention was Brazil. This was in return for the support the army had received from the Johnson administration the previous year in the military coup against President João Goulart. It was not the first time the US administration supported the military in removing a democratically elected head of state, nor would it be the last. However, it was a rare intervention in Brazil, a country that from its independence in 1822 had been a staunch supporter of US policy and even of the Monroe Doctrine.

Goulart had made many enemies among the Brazilian elites. He had adopted progressive social policies, including land reform, and had nationalized a number of foreign-owned companies. He also favored junior officers in the armed forces over their more conservative senior colleagues. None of this was sufficient to justify US support for a military coup, but those close to President Johnson convinced him that Brazil was moving closer to Cuba and could even fall under the influence of the PRC. The United States then employed the usual array of covert instruments, including funding for civil society groups opposed to the government, but even more important was the signal to the rebellious officers that a coup would enjoy US support.

This signal would be employed again in Chile nearly a decade later when President Salvador Allende, elected by popular vote in September 1970 and endorsed by Congress the following month, was overthrown in a military coup on September 11, 1973.[90] The plotters, including General Augusto Pinochet, had kept US authorities informed of their plans and knew they would not suffer sanctions if they were successful.

The fall of Allende was the culmination of a ten-year campaign by US agencies to undermine him and isolate him politically. Allende, a member of the Chilean Socialist Party, had come close to winning the 1958 presidential election. He vociferously opposed the Bay of Pigs invasion of Cuba in 1961 and US authorities became concerned he might win the presidency in 1964. A major program of covert action against him was unleashed. In the words of a US Senate select committee, "Covert American activity was a factor in almost every major election in Chile in the decade between 1963 and 1973. In several instances the United States intervention was massive. . . . The 1964 presidential election was the most prominent example of a large-scale election project. The Central Intelligence Agency spent more than $2.6 million in support of the election of the Christian Democratic Candidate [Eduardo Frei]. . . . More than half of the Christian Democratic candidate's campaign was financed by the United States, although he was not informed of this assistance."[91]

The campaign was very successful and Allende was easily defeated in 1964, but similar efforts failed to avert his victory in 1970. There then began a campaign to discredit Allende and destabilize the Chilean economy that was orchestrated by the 40 Committee, an interagency body chaired by Henry Kissinger to oversee covert CIA activities. It included a veto on new loans from US or US-controlled institutions as well as funding of opposition political parties and local media.[92]

The message from the fall of Allende in 1973 was clear. The US government would not stand in the way of military intervention if its strategic interests could conceivably be threatened. Military coups then followed in Argentina and Uruguay, leaving most of South America in the hands of authoritarian figures sure to protect US interests. This was similar to the situation in Central America, where the fall of Arbenz in 1954 had appeared to remove any threat to US concerns.

The overthrow of Anastasio Somoza by the Sandinistas in Nicaragua in July 1979 therefore took US authorities by surprise.[93] President Jimmy Carter

BOX 7.4

THE US INVASION OF PANAMA (1989)

There were seven US invasions of Panama in the twentieth century, and the last occurred in December 1989. At the time there was a civilian president, but power was in the hands of General Manuel Noriega, commander of the Panamanian Defense Forces.

Noriega had been of great assistance to numerous US agencies and was considered a CIA asset. However, he had overstepped the mark by providing sensitive US intelligence information to Cuba and Libya. Details of his drug-dealing and money-laundering activities were then revealed to Seymour Hersch and published in a series of articles in the *New York Times* in July 1986. He was indicted by a US court in February 1988.

When Noriega refused to step down from his position as Panama's *de facto* ruler, his days were numbered. He survived two unsuccessful coup attempts but could do nothing in the face of the US invasion in which the number of fatalities may have reached several thousand.

The invasion was authorized by President George H. W. Bush (1989–93), who as director of the CIA (1976–77) had worked closely with Noriega. The invasion was justified in the following terms:

Safeguarding the lives of U.S. citizens in Panama.
Defending democracy and human rights in Panama.
Combating drug trafficking.
Protecting the integrity of the Torrijos–Carter Treaties.

The fourth justification was probably the most important, as it reflected the long-standing US strategic interest in the Panama Canal. However, the second and third were harbingers of things to come (the first can be ignored, as there were already eleven thousand US troops in the Canal Zone). US interventions did not end with the Cold War, but they could no longer be justified in terms of an alleged Soviet threat.

(1977–81) was not unaware of the opposition to Somoza, whose family had ruled Nicaragua with US support since 1936, but he had assumed that a moderate alternative to both Somoza and the Sandinistas could be found. Carter tried to protect US interests without destabilizing the new government but his successor, President Ronald Reagan (1981–89), had very different ideas.

Reagan's campaign against the Sandinistas, although ultimately successful, took the United States into some very dark places that seriously undermined public confidence in the American imperialist system. It involved covert support for the anti-Sandinista contras that broke congressional laws and involved US agencies in major human rights abuses.[94] It also included the mining of ports and the destruction of shipping in a sovereign state with which the United States was not at war.[95]

US operations (overt and covert) helped to wreck the Nicaraguan economy, and the Sandinistas were easily defeated in the 1990 presidential elections. By this time the US government had also ensured there would be no military victory by left-wing guerrillas in Nicaragua's neighboring countries,[96] had dispatched the US Marines to Grenada in 1983,[97] and had invaded Panama in 1989 (Box 7.4). Central America and the Caribbean, other than Cuba, were once again firmly under US control as the Cold War came to an end.

8

THE UNIPOLAR MOMENT

The disintegration of the Soviet Union at the end of 1991 removed the main obstacle that had prevented the United States from building a fully global empire after 1945. For a brief moment it even looked as if the forces that had swept away communism in Russia might do the same to the ruling Communist Party in China. Thus, US governments after President Ronald Reagan (1981–89) found themselves in a unique position of global power about which their predecessors could only dream.

Very few expected this unipolar moment to be permanent. Other powers, it was widely assumed, would eventually rise to the point where they could challenge American dominance, but that was expected to be some way in the future. In the meantime, there was a window of opportunity to strengthen the global rules and institutions in such a way that US interests would be securely protected while using the nation's military dominance to punish those governments or nonstate actors (NSAs) that stepped out of line.

The first challenge was to build a truly global system of free market capitalism that would sweep away the last remaining barriers to the penetration of American investment. The Cold War had ended not just with the collapse of the Soviet Union but also with an ideological victory for free markets over state control of production. Translating this victory into a global framework that provides a secure position for private enterprise has been a constant theme of all recent US presidential administrations.

This new wave of globalization has coincided with trends in capitalism that privilege information and communications technology (ICT). Ensuring that American companies occupy a dominant position in these new ICT markets has been a high priority for all US governments since the end of the Cold War. The results have been spectacularly successful, with American firms establishing a hegemonic position by the start of the new millennium across all the subsectors that make up ICT.

Those hoping for a peace dividend after the end of the Cold War were swiftly disappointed. The technological gap between the US military and the rest of the world grew wider, so that the decline in the quantity of those in the armed forces was offset by an increase in the quality of equipment used. US military bases mushroomed around the world now that Cold War restrictions were removed. And space became a new area in which the United States sought dominance.

US military invasions—with or without UN approval—have been frequent since the end of the Cold War, but other forms of intervention (such as the use of drones to target individuals) have also become common. In particular, sanctions have become a weapon of choice for all presidents in the projection of US power. And forcing individuals and companies to pay taxes owed to the federal government has led to even greater use of extraterritorial powers by American administrations.

Much has been made of the differences among post–Cold War administrations in relation to foreign policy. Yet these can be exaggerated. It is true that President Barack Obama (2019–17)—unlike President George W. Bush (2001–9)—would not have invaded Iraq in 2003 if he had been in power at the time. However, Presidents Bill Clinton (1993–2001), George H. W. Bush (1989–93), and Donald Trump (2017–) probably would have. And on the principle of the use of force against America's enemies without the backing of international law, there has been no divergence among the five heads of state. All administrations have been committed to the preservation of American empire, although they may have differed over tactics in relation to particular issues.

The unipolar moment provided the United States with an opportunity to exert imperial power in an unprecedented fashion. America moved almost seamlessly from a Cold War world in which it faced certain limits to one in which it was virtually unconstrained. Many Americans concluded that the projection of their empire was the best way to secure world order and that belief was reinforced rather than undermined by the horrors of 9/11. It was now America's "destiny," as many members of the foreign elite were quick to point out, to impose order on a chaotic world, and many Americans were only too happy to accept this new imperial burden.

8.1. GLOBALIZATION

Globalization in the modern era was well under way even before the end of the Cold War. However, there were many barriers to the liberalization of trade in goods and services while international capital flows were also restricted in numerous ways. With the launch of the Uruguay Round in 1986, US negotiators pushed a new agenda designed to remove these obstacles, but they faced considerable resistance from the governments of many other countries.

The end of the Cold War broke this resistance. The American ideological victory was captured in a seminal, if hubristic, article by Francis Fukuyama: "The triumph of the West, of the Western idea, is evident first of all in the total exhaustion of viable systematic alternatives to Western liberalism. . . . What we may be witnessing is not just the end of the Cold War, or the passing of a particular period of post-war history, but the end of history as such: that is, the end point of mankind's ideological evolution and the universalization of Western liberal democracy as the final form of human government."[1]

The Uruguay Round was completed in 1994, and the World Trade Organization (WTO) replaced GATT the following year. The United States now had a truly global institution that met its requirements for promoting free market capitalism. All trade in goods and services was covered (with only minor exceptions), most obstacles to foreign investment were removed, and intellectual property was heavily protected. Disputes could now be settled through the WTO without countries being able to block arbitration panels, and the US government would no longer need to rely so heavily on domestic legislation to secure its global interests.

Just as important, the United States now had an institution which almost all countries outside the WTO aspired to join.[2] The most important excluded countries included the Russian Federation (successor state to the USSR) and the People's Republic of China (PRC), but there were many others. Since WTO decisions on new members are by consensus, the United States was able to impose the conditions under which these countries could participate.[3] As Joseph Stiglitz explained in the case of developing countries:

> The U.S. has bargained with dozens of countries. It knows what are likely to be sensitive clauses, provisions that can have large effects, either in terms of benefits or costs. It has large staffs which can write, review, and analyze such agreements, clause by clause.
>
> Because of the size of its economy, it has virtually every industry that might be affected by the agreement, and they are, in effect, at the table . . . trade negotiators from several developing countries engaged in "negotiations" with

the U.S. have repeatedly said these are not negotiations in any meaningful sense. There can be some negotiations around the edges . . . but on any core issue, there is no give.[4]

The results were impressive, with the WTO presiding over a huge increase in world trade and cross-border investments in its first two decades despite occasional financial crises.[5] By 2017 membership had grown to 164 countries, with Iran as the largest economy still outside the WTO. China secured membership in 2001 after fifteen years of negotiations (it originally applied to join GATT) but was forced to sit alongside Taiwan.[6] Russia took even longer to gain entry but was finally admitted in 2012.[7]

The dispute settlement process under the WTO was a source of particular satisfaction for the United States. Frustrated by what happened (or more often did not happen) under GATT rules, Congress in 1974 passed Section 301 of the Trade Act that threatened unilateral sanctions against "unreasonable and unjustifiable" barriers to US exports. The threat was usually sufficient to secure what the US government wanted, but the outcome could leave a sour taste.

The WTO dispute settlement procedures are different from those of GATT, as the process is nonvoluntary and binding. This might be seen as a threat to US sovereignty, but the opposite has been the case. WTO panels can rule that US practice is illegal, but only the US legislature can change the law. If the United States refuses to comply, a foreign government can retaliate against American exports. However, the asymmetry in size between the United States and other economies means that this is a very risky strategy and has only rarely been carried out. In the words of Robert Lawrence, an expert on trade policy,

> Far from limiting U.S. sovereignty, this form of retaliation actually favors the United States. The United States has a very large market and its ability to grant concessions makes it unusually influential in a system in which agreements are based on reciprocity. The ability to retaliate also provides the United States . . . the greatest ability, first, to bargain in the shadow of the law, i.e., use the implicit threat of bringing cases to induce compliance from other countries; second, to enforce rulings against other countries in the event of noncompliance; and third, to withstand retaliation in the event that others are authorized to take action against it. While all WTO members are formally equal, the system's design gives some countries more power than others.[8]

Success in establishing the WTO, however, came at a price. Civil society in member states (including the United States) became increasingly dissatisfied with the way the WTO operated and in particular for the disdain with which

BOX 8.1
THE US DOLLAR: EMPIRE'S GREATEST ASSET?

National currencies play a key part in imperial expansion, and the role of the US dollar in expanding the American empire is no exception. The dollar emerged from the Second World War as the world's main reserve currency. This gave an enormous advantage to the US economy, but it could not at first be fully exploited by US governments as there was an obligation under the Bretton Woods system to sell gold at a fixed dollar price. This placed restraints on US fiscal and monetary policy.

These restraints disappeared with the collapse of the Bretton Woods system in 1971. From then onward, the US economy could increase both balance of payments and fiscal deficits almost without limit in the knowledge that the deficits would be financed by issuing debt in US dollars. Countries with surpluses would be obliged to recycle these back to US capital markets as long as the dollar remained the international reserve currency of choice. As a result, the total debt surged to nearly $20 trillion at the end of fiscal year 2017, with a third of it held outside the United States.

Globalization deepened US capital markets and removed restrictions on the free movement of capital around the world. American financial institutions facilitated the movement of funds, earning huge profits in the process. Quantitative easing after the financial crisis in 2008 then led to such low rates of interest that borrowing in US dollars became almost costless.

Access to cheap finance from the rest of the world in US dollars has allowed the US government to have both more "guns and butter" rather than choosing between them, as happens in other countries. Military spending has expanded without a commensurate reduction in consumer spending. As one observer has commented, "[T]oday's international economic architecture ensures that the normal operation of world market forces . . . tends to yield disproportionate benefits to Americans, and confers autonomy on US policymakers while curbing the autonomy of others. . . . The economic benefits that accrue to the United States as a consequence of the normal working of market forces within this particular framework provide the financial basis of American military supremacy" (Wade, "The Invisible Hand of the American Empire," 64).

its decisions appeared to treat environmental and labor concerns. Protestors followed WTO negotiators around the world,[9] but US administrations ignored them and called for a deepening of the WTO process with the launch of the Doha Round in 2001.[10] This was too ambitious, however, and it soon ran into difficulties that made its completion impossible.[11]

It was fortunate, therefore, for the United States that it had been pursuing a twin-track strategy toward globalization for many years. Initially suspicious of a regional approach to globalization,[12] America had taken its first steps in this direction in 1985 with the signing of the Israel-US Free Trade Agreement. This was seen at the time as justified on strategic rather than economic grounds, but it paved the way for the Canada-US Free Trade Agreement (CUFTA) that came into force in January 1989.

Canada and the United States were each other's largest trade partners at the time. However, the US market was far more important to the Canadian economy than the other way around. When Congress started preparing the ground for an even tougher version of Section 301 in the form of the Super 301 provisions of the Omnibus Trade and Competitiveness Act (finally passed in 1988), the Canadian government looked for ways to avoid unilateral threats from the US government to its exports and proposed a bilateral agreement.

The result was CUFTA, which went way beyond what was being discussed in the Uruguay Round and gave Canada the assurances it needed that its exports would not be subject to unilateral measures. Canada, of course, secured access to the US market in almost all goods and services. In return, however, Canada had to accept much more liberal measures on cross-border investments and strict rules on expropriation of US-controlled firms.[13]

CUFTA would now become the template for numerous free trade agreements (FTAs) signed by the United States with other countries or regions. Each was more ambitious than the last, with a particular focus by US negotiators on protection of intellectual property, public procurement, protection of foreign investments against "unfair" expropriation, and regular reviews of trading partners' labor and environmental practices. Overall this network of FTAs, with the United States at the center, secured for the US government a framework for free market capitalism that is at the heart of its vision of globalization.

CUFTA was succeeded by NAFTA—the North American Free Trade Agreement—that was signed in 1992 by Canada, Mexico, and the United States. It was the first FTA between developed and developing countries and gave Mexico almost unrestricted access to its most important markets. However, it gave the US government something that was much more important: a guarantee that Mexico would commit to free market capitalism as long as NAFTA survived. The implications of this for the rest of Latin America, and indeed the rest of the developing world, were huge.

NAFTA also included strict rules for investor-state dispute settlement (ISDS) under Chapter 11 of the treaty, which would become the model for other FTAs. These procedures would also be written into bilateral investment treaties (BITs) and international investment agreements (IIAs). American companies have made frequent (and often successful) use of these provisions, but foreign companies have been much less successful in the United States itself. Indeed, the US trade representative (USTR) could proudly claim in 2015, "ISDS in U.S. trade agreements is significantly better defined and restricted than in other countries' agreements. . . . Because of the safeguards in U.S. agreements and because of the high standards of our legal system, foreign investors rarely pursue arbitration against the United States and have never been successful when they have done so. . . . Over the past 25 years, under the 50 agreements the U.S. has which include ISDS, the United States has faced only 17 ISDS cases, 13 of which were brought to conclusion. . . . *Though the U.S. government regularly loses cases in domestic court, we have never once lost an ISDS case.*"[14]

Officials working for the US government negotiated the network of agreements that underpinned free market capitalism in a globalized world. However, they did not work alone and were supported at every stage by a plethora of US multinational enterprises (MNEs). These companies, as was shown in Chapter 6, had organized themselves though institutions such as the Business Roundtable to push for public policies more favorable to corporate interests. Globalization, and in particular the liberalization of financial markets, was at the top of the agenda.

Their efforts were very successful and even succeeded in sweeping away domestic restrictions imposed during the New Deal to avoid future financial crises.[15] As a result, the financial sector became increasingly dominant, with its share of domestic corporate profits rising from 16 percent to 1985 to over 40 percent three decades later. Not surprisingly, donations from financial institutions to political candidates far outstripped those of other corporate sectors.[16]

A revolving door began to operate between Wall Street and Washington, DC, giving finance even greater influence over key policy decisions. Ultimately this would lead inexorably to the US financial crisis that began in 2008 and spread to other parts of the world. The precrisis atmosphere was captured by Simon Johnson, chief economist (2007–8) at the IMF, when he stated,

The American financial industry gained political power by amassing a kind of cultural capital—a belief system. Once, perhaps, what was good for General Motors was good for the country. Over the past decade, the attitude took hold that what was good for Wall Street was good for the country. The banking-and-securities industry has become one of the top contributors to political campaigns, but at the peak of its influence, it did not have to buy favors the way, for example, the tobacco companies or military contractors might have to. Instead, it benefited from the fact that Washington insiders already believed that large financial institutions and free-flowing capital markets were crucial to America's position in the world.[17]

The lobbying efforts by American MNEs paid off and helped to bring about a globalized world that privileged cross-border capital flows. The stock of US foreign direct investment (FDI) abroad rose from $0.7 trillion in 1990 to $6.3 trillion in 2014. Although the US share of world FDI has fallen (hardly surprising in view of the rapid growth of MNEs outside the United States), the share in 2014 was still nearly one quarter. And the total stock was four times greater than that of the country ranked second (Germany).[18]

It was not only MNEs that helped to spread the US version of free market capitalism across the world. The US-controlled institutions and NSAs outlined in Chapters 5 and 6 also played a key role. Indeed, even before the end of the Cold War the IMF and the World Bank had promoted a package of reforms that came to be known as the Washington Consensus. This was then applied to all those countries in need of assistance from the Washington-based institutions.

At first, the package was relatively uncontroversial and concentrated mainly on macroeconomic stabilization. By the end of the Cold War, however, the reforms embraced deregulation, privatization, and the liberalization of financial markets. These reforms were then promoted in the countries of the former Soviet Union, where the IMF and World Bank were assisted by a new institution (the European Bank for Reconstruction and Development—EBRD) that had been created with US support specifically for this purpose.[19]

The impact of this enlarged package—dubbed by its critics "stabilize, liberalize, and privatize"[20]—was dramatic. It affected not only those countries in Latin America, Africa, and Asia already inside the US sphere of influence but also the countries of the former Soviet Union and its allies such as Vietnam. In Russia itself the reforms, encouraged by the Harvard Institute for International Development (HIID), with funds from USAID, led to a fire sale of state-owned assets for a fraction of their value and the rapid privatization of the economy.[21]

Inevitably, there was a backlash against the Washington Consensus and the neoliberal agenda promoted by the US government. Indeed, the backlash constitutes part of the retreat from empire analyzed in Part III of this book. However, it is important to emphasize how successful the US government had been in seizing the opportunity provided by the unipolar moment to spread its vision of free market capitalism across the world. Many countries embraced the vision with enthusiasm and sought closer ties with the United States through trade and investment. And even in those countries that experienced the most hostile reaction, the reforms promoted by the United States and its institutional allies were not totally eclipsed.

8.2. INFORMATION AND COMMUNICATIONS TECHNOLOGY

The United States enjoyed a commanding lead over all other countries in communications during most of the Cold War. The launch by the Soviet Union in 1957 of Sputnik 1—the world's first artificial satellite—may have come as a huge shock to most Americans, but the response of the administrations of Presidents Dwight D. Eisenhower (1953–61) and John F. Kennedy (1961–63) was swift and ultimately successful. The National Aeronautics and Space Administration (NASA) was established in 1958 and the United States quickly caught up, and then overtook, the Soviet Union in terms of prowess in space.

With the collapse of the Soviet Union, the Russian Federation was unable to sustain its expensive space program at the same level as before and US governments looked to a future in which US leadership in space would be unchallenged, its commercial interests assured, and its right to police space unquestioned. It was the very model of an imperial policy for the post–Cold War period. In its statement of national space policy in 2010, the US government affirmed all these assumptions: "The United States is committed to encouraging and facilitating the growth of a U.S. commercial space sector that supports U.S. needs, is globally competitive, and advances U.S. leadership in the generation of new markets and innovation-driven entrepreneurship. . . . The United States will employ a variety of measures to help assure the use of space for all responsible parties, and, consistent with the inherent right of self-defense, deter others from interference and attack, defend our space systems and contribute to the defense of allied space systems, and, if deterrence fails, defeat efforts to attack them."[22]

Broadly speaking, US administrations achieved their goals for space during the unipolar moment. In 2015, according to the Union of Concerned Scientists, the United States had nearly half of all operating satellites in space and four times more than both Russia and China. Out of 549 US satellites in operation, 250 were commercial (the rest were government, military or civilian), so that space became an important arena for US business. And when US domination of space became increasingly contested, the US government responded with the establishment of US Cyber Command (see Section 8.3) to protect the nation's interests against cyberwarfare while refining its capability to carry out such attacks itself.

The launch of Sputnik 1 had other far-reaching implications for US hegemonic pretensions. President Eisenhower had responded immediately to Sputnik by establishing in 1958 the Defense Advanced Research Projects Agency (DARPA) as a branch of the Department of Defense.[23] DARPA focused on space until its expertise in this area was transferred to NASA, at which point it started to invest in technologies that would transform the US economy and lead to the creation of the giant technology companies that are so dominant globally today.

DARPA has always seen its role as giving the US global leadership in the technologies that matter to national security. With a large budget and a small staff, that meant working with researchers in universities, companies, and government departments. The results, it is fair to say, have been extraordinary and have given the US leadership in many fields that have commercial as well as military benefits. In the agency's own words, "Working with innovators inside and outside of government, DARPA has repeatedly delivered on [its] mission, transforming revolutionary concepts and even seeming impossibilities into practical capabilities such as precision weapons and stealth technology, but also such icons of modern civilian society such as the Internet, automated voice recognition and language translation, and Global Positioning System receivers small enough to embed in myriad consumer devices."[24]

DARPA invested heavily in computers and funded computer science departments across the country. Its activities in this area were overseen by its Information Processing Techniques Office, established in 1962, which contributed to the fabrication of computer chips in the 1970s. At the same time US authorities were increasingly concerned about the risk to communications from a nuclear attack. This led DARPA to invest heavily in a decentralized network of communication stations that would become known as ARPANET.

Controlled at first by the US military, ARPANET was gradually opened up to nonmilitary users in the 1980s to become the Internet. With the invention of the World Wide Web by Tim Berners-Lee in 1989, the Internet was poised to take off.[25] At first its management was assigned to a single researcher based in California under the watchful eye of the US Department of Commerce (DoC), but the Internet's growth was so rapid that this soon had to change. In 1998 therefore a private not-for profit organization was registered in California operating under a memorandum of understanding with the DoC.

The Internet Corporation for Assigned Names and Numbers (ICANN), as the organization is called, has always been based in Los Angeles. It operated under the benevolent tutelage of the DoC until the US government was confident that its mode of working was consistent with US strategic interests. Although the contract with the DoC has now ended, the US government has been able to resist calls for ICANN to be replaced with an interstate body operating under the auspices of the UN or the International Telecommunications Union.

American entrepreneurs, helped by the twin advantages of a huge domestic market and a very supportive government, have been quick to exploit the enormous commercial possibilities opened up both by personal computing and the Internet. And, unlike their multinational predecessors a century ago, there has been virtually no time lag between the launch of their operations in the domestic and foreign markets. The Internet has in fact made their services accessible to foreigners often at the same time as Americans.

These companies therefore enjoyed a dominant global position almost from the beginning. A few companies not based in the United States eventually caught up, but as late as 2015 six out of the top ten information technology companies ranked by revenue were American (including Apple, HP, and Microsoft).[26] And in the case of those companies where most business is done over the Internet, the dominance of US companies in 2015 was even more remarkable. No fewer than thirteen out of the top twenty ranked by revenue were US companies, and the list includes some of the most famous corporate names in the world such as Amazon, Google, eBay, Facebook, and Twitter.[27]

Internet companies are responsible for almost all communications today.[28] This means the United States enjoys a dominant role in global communications by virtue of the size of its large Internet companies. Yet US corporate dominance is even greater than these figures imply. Of the seven Internet companies in the top twenty that are not American, five are Chinese.[29] These Chinese companies are enormous, but their services are accessible mainly to those who understand Chinese characters. Thus, consumers outside China are almost entirely dependent on US companies.

This is a degree of global dominance about which earlier generations of US MNEs could only dream. Even consumers in Russia have come to rely heavily on American Internet giants. Not surprisingly, it has brought accusations of excessive power, and the European Union in particular has used its legislative authority to try and curb the quasi-monopolistic position of some of these companies. Yet, despite this, the companies have remained strong and have not had to alter their behavior in significant ways.

The rapid growth of global electronic communications, much of which passed through servers located in the United States, created extraordinary temptations

BOX 8.2

GOOGLE SEARCH

When Google became a subsidiary of Alphabet in 2015, it signaled how much the company had diversified since its humble origins in 1998 when Larry Page and Sergey Brin incorporated Google in a garage in California. However, Google Search with its famous PageRank algorithm remains the jewel in the crown.

The majority of searches in virtually every country are done on Google (the main exceptions are China, Japan, Russia, and South Korea). Indeed, Google has more than 90 percent market share in many countries and a deal on search cooperation with Yahoo makes the effective share even greater. Thus, Google Search has a huge impact on global perceptions of just about everything including history, current affairs, and the United States itself.

Google has been accused of many things, including bias toward its own content, monopoly power, and collaborating with state censorship in China. And when small companies successfully use search engine optimization (SEO) to build up a presence on the Web, they can find their footprint disappear overnight when Google modifies its PageRank algorithm.

As a gigantic MNE with a Russian-born president (of Alphabet) and an Indian-born CEO (of Google), the company might seem to epitomize an international spirit that rises above nationalism. However, Google is very much a US company and its search results are anything but neutral. Frequently, the user is directed to other large US companies or influential US think tanks who seem to have mastered SEO more successfully than those from other countries.

The top of the search results is often Wikipedia, a US company that invariably adds editorial comment challenging the veracity of articles highly critical of US policy. An article on cyberwarfare by the United States, for example, carries a health warning. An article on free markets, on the other hand, merely encourages the reader to add more references.

Search can never be entirely neutral, so it is no surprise that Google often reveals an American bias. Its market dominance, however, makes it a prized asset for US governments and a useful tool in the preservation of American empire.

for the US intelligence services. After rampant illegality during the Vietnam War, the FBI, the CIA, and army intelligence had been the subject of a Senate investigation known as the Church Committee Report.[30] This had led to the Foreign Intelligence Surveillance Act (FISA) in 1978, which sought to end the previous abuses while giving the intelligence services a great deal of flexibility in dealing with non-US persons[31] and external threats.

This might have left it unclear what to do about electronic surveillance *inside* the United States for foreign intelligence purposes. FISA, however, established a Foreign Intelligence Surveillance Court (FISC) and required government agencies to seek a warrant from the court for such activities. In addition, Executive Order 12333 had been passed in 1981 setting out guidelines "requiring each element of the Intelligence Community to have in place procedures prescribing how it can collect, retain, and disseminate intelligence about US persons."[32]

It is fair to say, therefore, that the intelligence services were sufficiently well placed to exploit the opportunities provided by the growth of global electronic communications after the birth of the Internet in a perfectly legal fashion. However, the failure of the intelligence agencies to prevent the terrorist attacks of September 11, 2001, led to a wave of national panic that swept away many of the remaining constraints on their activities.

The new powers were contained in the Patriot Act. Among other things, it amended FISA by adding Section 215 that authorizes the FISC to force private companies to turn over to the government "any tangible things including books, records, papers, documents, and other items." This could include financial information about a US citizen or telephone calling data, but it was assumed by the American public at large that it did not include access to all their traffic across the Internet.

This assumption proved to be false. The firewall that FISA had tried to build between the communications of US and non-US persons was almost impossible to maintain in the age of the Internet. Indeed, President George W. Bush immediately after 9/11 had secretly authorized the National Security Agency (NSAg) "to conduct foreign intelligence surveillance of individuals who were *inside* the United States without complying with FISA."[33]

When this came to light in 2005, Congress tried to reimpose the firewall by passing the Protect America Act in 2007 and the FISA Amendments Act of 2008. The latter included Section 702, which authorized the FISC to approve annual certifications on surveillance while leaving it to the NSAg to decide which individuals to target. These laws gave the intelligence services unrestrained freedom to intercept the communications of non-US persons. However, they failed to protect US persons, as was made clear by the revelations starting in 2013 of Edward Snowden, an employee of a private firm subcontracted by the NSAg.

Snowden, through a number of journalists he trusted, revealed the existence of a clandestine surveillance program run by the NSAg called PRISM. The program collected data from all the main US Internet companies under Section 702 of the amended FISA. According to Snowden, Microsoft was the first to come on board (in 2007), followed by Yahoo (2008); Google, Facebook, and Paltalk (2009); YouTube (2010); AOL and Skype (2011); and Apple (2012). This was a broad range of companies, but Snowden also revealed that 98 percent of PRISM production came from just three companies (Microsoft, Yahoo, and Google).

PRISM gave the intelligence services access to information across the globe on US and non-US persons that their predecessors in the Cold War could barely have imagined was possible. Once revealed, it caused outrage around the world and led to a number of judicial challenges in the US courts themselves. President Obama reacted by establishing a Review Group on Intelligence and Communications Technologies that made a number of recommendations.[34] However, the Obama administration consistently defended the legality of PRISM, and Congress had little appetite to make anything other than minor changes to existing laws. The result was the USA Freedom Act, passed in June 2015, which still leaves the NSAg with enormous powers of surveillance against both US and non-US persons.[35]

The imperial state had created the conditions under which US companies would come to dominate global communications, and now those same companies were helping the state to protect its empire by allowing it to spy on domestic and foreign targets. It seemed a match made in heaven. Technology, however, is a double-edged sword, and the US government as well as some US companies soon discovered that they were vulnerable to the clandestine surveillance of other states and NSAs.

Most of these cyberattacks came from outside the United States. However, one of the most damaging came from inside when a member of the US armed forces passed classified information to WikiLeaks, a website specializing in the release of government and corporate secrets. Cablegate, as it came to be called, was made up of 251,287 cables sent from 274 US embassies and consulates around the world, covering the years 2003–10.[36]

Although clearly a threat to national security, there is no doubt that Cablegate offered a unique perspective on the nature of American empire and its mode of operation after the end of the Cold War. While the cables revealed an empire in robust shape, able and willing to intervene against governments not acting in

US interests, it also showed a diplomatic corps that was knowledgeable—at least in the larger countries—about local conditions and sending reasonably accurate information back to Washington, DC, where the key decisions would then be made.

The US government was embarrassed by both Cablegate and Edward Snowden's revelations but did not significantly change its behavior. As an empire in an age of global communications, it had little choice in the matter. Julian Assange, the founder of WikiLeaks, was only slightly exaggerating when he wrote, "Carved into stone or inked into parchment, empires from Babylon to the Ming dynasty left records of the organizational center communicating with its peripheries. However, by the 1950s students of historical empires realized that somehow the communications medium *was* the empire. Its methods for organizing the inscription, transportation, indexing and storage of its communications, and for designating who was authorized to read and write them, in a real sense *constituted* the empire. When the methods an empire used to communicate changed, the empire also changed."[37]

8.3. SECURITY

The collapse of the Soviet Union and the dissolution of the Warsaw Pact[38] left the United States in a very privileged position. Yet so sudden was the collapse that it took US authorities some time to adjust to the new realities. Consequently, the administration of President George H. W. Bush, whose key figures were steeped in the legacy of the Cold War, struggled to develop a strategy that matched the moment.

President Bill Clinton came to office under very different circumstances from those of his predecessor. Not only had the USSR imploded but the successor state (the Russian Federation) had seen its economy shrink dramatically as a result of the painful shift from a planned to a market economy. With the deepening of economic reforms in China, the United States now had an opportunity to spread its vision of a free market global economy more widely than ever before. In the words of President Clinton's first National Security Strategy (NSS) in 1995,

[W]e have unparalleled opportunities to make our nation safer and more prosperous. Our military might is unparalleled. We now have a truly global economy linked by an instantaneous communications network, which offers growing scope for American jobs and American investment. . . .

Never has American leadership been more essential—to navigate the shoals of the world's new dangers and to capitalize on its opportunities. American assets are unique: our military strength, our dynamic economy, our powerful ideals and, above all, our people.

The establishment of a world free market was a long-standing ambition of American empire. So was the need for a military with global reach. What was new this time was the growing belief that US empire would best be served by the promotion of democracy abroad—or at least an American version of democracy— on the grounds that US security, free market economies and democracies are mutually reinforcing. As the NSS stated, "Secure nations are much more likely to support free trade and maintain democratic structures. Nations with growing economies and strong trade ties are more likely to feel secure and to work toward freedom. And democratic states are less likely to threaten our interests and more likely to cooperate with the U.S. to meet security threats and promote sustainable development."[39]

The promotion of free market capitalism and democracy around the globe placed a huge burden on the US military, which had seen its budget and manpower cut since the mid-1980s. However, the end of the Cold War coincided with the so-called Revolution in Military Affairs (RMA) that put more emphasis on information superiority and precision-guided weaponry. The RMA played to US strengths and contributed to the formation of a new military-industrial complex in which US companies would provide the technologies that would leave the nation's forces with no serious rival. In *Joint Vision 2020*, a document compiled in 2000 by all branches of the military, it was said: "The overarching focus of this vision is full spectrum dominance—achieved through the interdependent application of dominant maneuver, precision engagement, focused logistics, and full dimensional protection. Attaining that goal requires the steady infusion of new technology and modernization and replacement of equipment. However, material superiority alone is not sufficient. Of greater importance is the development of doctrine, organizations, training and education, leaders, and people that effectively take advantage of the technology."[40]

"Full spectrum dominance" included a role for nuclear weapons as outlined by the first Nuclear Posture Review (NPR) in 1994. This role was expected to be less important than in the past, but the following year the Clinton administration successfully pushed for an indefinite extension of the nuclear Non-Proliferation Treaty (NPT). This held out the prospect of a permanent monopoly of nuclear weapons by the officially recognized nuclear states (China, France, Russia, the United Kingdom, and the United States). With France and the United Kingdom as NATO allies, Russia in steep decline, and China focused on a "peaceful rise" through rapid economic growth, the United States was able to concentrate its efforts on ensuring that other states did not acquire nuclear weapons.[41]

Full spectrum dominance would not have been possible in the age of the Soviet Union. To ensure that its successor would never be able to match the military prowess of the USSR, the US authorities had engaged in a series of negotiations that had proceeded very smoothly as a result of the asymmetry in power between the two states. The Cooperative Threat Reduction Program, sponsored by Senators Sam Nunn and Richard Lugar, provided funds and expertise to decommission nuclear, biological, and chemical weapon in the states of the former Soviet Union (FSU).[42] And President George H. W. Bush himself had, in the last days of his presidency, signed the second Strategic Arms Reduction Treaty (START II) with President Boris Yeltsin in January 1993.[43]

NATO, the military alliance established in 1949, now had no clear purpose. Logically, it should have been dissolved. Yet this ignored the key role that NATO played in US imperial designs, and the exact opposite happened. In 1994 the Clinton administration had succeeded in securing a commitment in favor of expansion at the NATO Summit. By 2009 twelve new states in Central and Eastern Europe had joined,[44] pushing the boundaries of NATO right up to the Russian Federation in defiance of what had previously been promised.[45]

The risks of NATO expansion were recognized at the time and were articulated in an open letter to President Clinton by fifty former senators, cabinet secretaries, and ambassadors.[46] Others had written privately, warning that expansion "risked endangering the long-term viability of NATO, significantly exacerbating the instability that now exists in the zone that lies between Germany and Russia, and convincing most Russians that the United States and the West [were] attempting to isolate, encircle, and subordinate them, rather than integrating them into a new European system of collective security."[47] All such concerns, however, were swept aside by the Clinton administration as it sought to assert US hegemony across the globe.

Although President Clinton made extensive use of the opportunities for expanding the US empire after the end of the Cold War, intervening abroad on frequent occasions (see Section 8.4), there were some influential Americans for whom his administration's imperial efforts were insufficient. A warning signal was fired by an article in 1996 in *Foreign Affairs*, the flagship journal of the Council on Foreign Relations, in which William Kristol and Robert Kagan outlined a US role for the long-term: "What should that role be? Benevolent global hegemony. Having defeated the 'evil empire,' the United States enjoys strategic and ideological predominance. . . . The aspiration to benevolent hegemony might strike some as either hubristic or morally suspect. But a hegemon is nothing more or less than a leader with a preponderant influence and authority over all others in its domain. This is America's position in the world today."[48]

These prophetic words then launched the Project for the New American Century (PNAC), a Washington-based think tank that outlined its neoconservative vision for the next administration in September 2000. Among other ambitions, it established four core missions for US military forces: "Defend the US homeland; fight and decisively win multiple, simultaneous major theater wars; perform the 'constabulary' duties associated with shaping the security environment in critical regions; and transform US forces to exploit the 'revolution in military affairs.'"[49]

It also advocated the maintenance of nuclear strategic superiority, the restoration of military strength, the repositioning of US forces around the globe, the development and deployment of global missile defenses, the control of the new "international commons" of space and cyberspace, and a sharp increase in defense spending as a share of GDP.

These ideas proved so influential that many of the leading figures in the administration of President George W. Bush were drawn from the ranks of the PNAC, including Vice President Richard Cheney, Defense Secretary Donald Rumsfeld, Defense Policy Board chairman Richard Perle, and Deputy Defense Secretary Paul Wolfowitz. Other members of the PNAC who joined the administration in less prominent capacities included John Bolton, Elliott Abrahams, and Robert Zoellick.

There can be little doubt that the Bush administration, with the PNAC and other neoconservative groups behind it, would have enhanced the American imperial project in numerous ways even without the terrorist attacks of 9/11. Those atrocities, however, accelerated the process and provided a much greater level of public support than would otherwise have been the case. A new strategy rapidly took shape that was outlined in the 2002 NSS. In that document, the Bush administration laid out the framework for US empire with a special emphasis on the use of "preemption" to forestall the possibility of future attacks and the need for an expansion of the US military presence across the globe: "The United States has long maintained the option of preemptive actions to counter a sufficient threat to our national security. . . . To forestall or prevent such hostile acts by our adversaries, the United States will, if necessary, act preemptively. . . . To contend with uncertainty and to meet the many security challenges we face, the United States will require bases and stations within and beyond Western Europe and Northeast Asia, as well as temporary access arrangements for the long-distance deployment of U.S. forces."[50]

President Bush was correct to remind readers of NSS 2002 that preemption has a long history in the United States. From the Indian Wars of the eighteenth century onward, the US government had often fought preemptive "wars of choice" as part of its imperial expansion. Preemption, of course, is more difficult if the state is constrained by international treaties, which is why US history has been replete with interstate agreements that failed to secure ratification. Yet this did not sit easily after the Second World War with a semi-global empire that depended so heavily on international arrangements to constrain other states' behavior.

The Bush administration resolved this dilemma after 9/11 through unilateral action. As early as December 2001, it withdrew from the Anti-Ballistic Missile Treaty (this had major implications for arms control as Russia then withdrew from START II).[51] It then "unsigned" the Rome Statute of the International Criminal Court (ICC) in 2002 and instead signed bilateral agreements with dozens of states to exempt US military and government personnel from the ICC's jurisdiction.[52] In the same year it refused to ratify the Optional Protocol to the Convention against Torture, and in 2008 did the same with the Convention on Cluster Munitions.

NSS 2002 had also referred to the need to expand the geographical scope of US military bases. This duly happened, and by the end of the Bush presidency the United States was operating 909 military facilities in countries and territories outside the fifty states with 190,000 troops and 115,000 civilian employees.[53] The bases now spread deep into the FSU and its allies with facilities in the Czech Republic, Poland, Bosnia & Herzogovina, Kosovo, Macedonia, Bulgaria, Romania, Georgia, Uzbekistan, Tajikistan, and Kyrgyzstan. There was also a new emphasis on Africa, with facilities in some twenty different countries.

Even this did not tell the full story, as some of the overseas expansion took place in small bases known colloquially as lily pads that did not always show up in the official figures. These facilities have few if any US troops and sometimes rely on private contractors, which operate drones and surveillance aircraft.[54] There have also been "access agreements," giving the US forces the right to use foreign airfields, ports, and military bases without the need to establish a US facility. In the first fifteen years after the Cold War, "the number of agreements permitting the presence of U.S. troops on foreign soil more than doubled, from forty-five to more than ninety."[55]

The expansion of the US military presence abroad required a reorganization of the command structure (there are now nine commands in total, six being geographical and three thematic). Every independent state in the world is assigned to one of the six geographical commands, and two new ones were created

BOX 8.3
GUANTÁNAMO BAY

The US government had set its sights on Guantánamo Bay in Cuba as a suitable base for its navy long before the Spanish-American War in 1898. It was not until Spain's surrender, however, that plans could be put into action.

Under two agreements in 1903, the second of which was replaced by a new one in 1934, the United States leased indefinitely an area on the south coast of Cuba "for the purposes of coaling and naval stations" with the proviso that "no corporation shall be permitted to establish or maintain a commercial, industrial or other enterprise."

The rent was set at $2,000 per year, but Cuba was required to purchase all private lands and real property in the area. The United States agreed to advance Cuba the money to do so on condition that the funds be deducted from future rents. Thus, it is very unlikely that Cuba received any rental income for many years.

The rent was subsequently doubled, and at the time of the Cuban Revolution the United States was paying $4,085 per year. The first check in 1959 was cashed (due to "confusion," according to Fidel Castro), but none were afterward. Thus, the US Navy has had free use of Guantánamo Bay since 1960, although the Department of Defense in its *Base Structure Report* for 2015 estimated the value of the facilities at $3.65 billion.

The base has had many uses since the Cuban Revolution, including as a temporary home for Haitian refugees, as a prison for many captured in the "global war on terror," and as a place where suspects can be tortured without breaching US law (Guantánamo Bay is sovereign Cuban territory and therefore not subject to US Supreme Court rulings).

Cuba regularly calls for the restoration of the base but can do nothing as that requires the agreement of both sides. If the case were to go to an international tribunal, however, Cuba would certainly win, as the base is no longer used exclusively for its original purposes while commercial activities (McDonald's, Burger King, etc.) take place there. In any case, normalization of the bilateral relationship—a publicly stated goal of both sides following the restoration of diplomatic relations in 2015—will require the return of the base to Cuba at some point.

after 9/11. The first was United States Northern Command (USNORTHCOM) with responsibility for air, land and sea approaches to North America out to five hundred nautical miles. The second was United States Africa Command (USAFRICOM), with responsibility for all fifty-four independent African states.

The three thematic commands were created before 9/11, but their responsibilities changed afterward. In particular, United States Strategic Command (USSTRATCOM) created in 2009 a subcommand for cyberspace called United States Cyber Command (USCYBERCOM), with a mission to carry forward US imperial ambitions for the control of cyberspace. The importance of USCYBERCOM cannot be underestimated, and it has been tasked with preemptive strikes if needed. In its second strategy paper in 2015, it was stated: "If directed by the President or the Secretary of Defense, the U.S. military may conduct cyber operations to counter an imminent or on-going attack against the U.S. homeland or U.S. interests in cyberspace. The purpose of such a defensive measure is to blunt an attack and prevent the destruction of property or the loss of life. [The Department of Defense] seeks to synchronize its capabilities with other government agencies to develop a range of options and methods for disrupting cyberattacks of significant consequence before they can have an impact, to include law enforcement, intelligence, and diplomatic tools."[56]

Throughout the period of the semiglobal empire, US military spending was enormous both in absolute and relative terms. Although spending as a share of GDP fell after the Cold War, the downward trend was reversed after 9/11. At its peak in 2011, spending on the military reached $711 billion, which was 4.6 percent of GDP and represented nearly 40 percent of global defense expenditure. And this high figure excluded many items, such as veterans' benefits and services, which might be considered part of national defense. No other country comes even close to these levels of defense spending and in only a very few cases is military expenditure higher as a share of GDP.[57]

The largest part of the military budget is consumed by personnel pay and the operation of bases (inside and outside the United States). However, a large part ($166 billion in 2014–15) is spent each year on procurement and research and development. Nearly all this money goes to thousands of defense contractors in the United States that make up the new military-industrial complex. Yet most of it goes to a small number of firms, including Lockheed Martin, Boeing, Raytheon, Northrop Grumman, and General Dynamics, that all contribute generously to candidates on both sides of the political divide.

The military-industrial complex also includes the private military contractors to whom defense is increasingly outsourced. These companies played an especially important role in Iraq, where the numbers employed are estimated to have reached nearly 100,000. As a result of controversies surrounding their lack of accountability, some have changed their name, while others have adopted different corporate structures.[58] However, they still play a key role in US security planning even if the issue of accountability is far from being resolved.

8.4. THE EMPIRE UNLEASHED

The end of the Cold War removed many of the constraints that had previously held back the United States from intervening abroad. As a result, interventions have been frequent under all presidential administrations since 1990. All five presidents (Bush Sr., Clinton, Bush Jr., Obama, and Trump) have used both multilateral and unilateral forms of intervention, and none of them has been unduly concerned whether their actions were consistent with international law. While there have undoubtedly been differences in the approach taken to intervention by each president, none has questioned the imperial project and the conviction that the United States is the world's leader.

The "gold standard" for US intervention has been multilaterally through the UN and therefore with the blessing of international law. The two states (China and Russia) most likely to block US initiatives in the United Nations Security Council (UNSC) during the Cold War were now much less likely to do so—albeit for very different reasons.[59] This gave the UN a new *raison d'être* for American administrations, as UNSC resolutions could now be drafted by US diplomats with much less risk of a veto being applied by one of the permanent members.

In the first forty-five years of UN operations, roughly 650 UNSC resolutions were passed—an average of fewer than 15 per year. In the next twenty-five years there would be roughly 1,600—an average of 64 per year. Furthermore, many of the resolutions passed after the Cold War ended were adopted under Chapter 7 of the UN Charter, which allows for coercion by member states—especially under Article 41 (sanctions) and Article 42 (military intervention).

UN-supported sanctions were only used twice during the Cold War. Since then, they have been adopted some twenty-five times. Not all of these resolutions were initiated by the United States, but most of them were. The first was passed against Iraq following its invasion of Kuwait in August 1990. There then followed numerous UN sanctions designed to deal with conflicts in the former Yugoslavia (1991–96), Haiti (1993–94), Somalia (1992 onward), Liberia (1992–2001), Angola (1993–2002), Rwanda (1994–2008), Sierra Leone (1997–2010), and Kosovo (1998–2001).

American administrations also pushed successfully for UN-sponsored sanctions to deal with two issues of special US concern. The first, nuclear proliferation, was of long standing, and UN sanctions were duly adopted against North Korea and Iran. The second, international terrorism, became a top priority in the 1990s after a series of bombings and assassinations threatened US interests and after the formation of al-Qaeda by Osama bin Laden. UN sanctions were adopted even before 9/11 against Libya (under President Muammar al-Gaddhafi), Sudan (under President Omar al-Bashir), Afghanistan (under the Taliban), and al-Qaeda itself.[60]

Sanctions could do terrible damage to the civilian population at large. US administrations, with others, therefore pushed for targeted sanctions designed to punish the culpable while protecting the innocent. These "smart" sanctions were much more efficacious, but even so they did not always work. Thus, US administrations needed to consider alternatives to sanctions, and their preferred option was usually a UNSC resolution under Article 42 since this complied with international law.

All US presidents since the end of the Cold War have adopted this strategy.[61] Following the failure of sanctions to persuade Saddam Hussein to withdraw his forces from Kuwait, the administration of President George H. W. Bush in November 1990 was able to secure a resolution (UNSCR 678) authorizing the use of military force against Iraq.[62] A coalition of twenty-eight countries was then put together led by the US military, which supplied nearly 75 percent of all troops. The Iraqi Army was crushed and Kuwait regained its independence, but the sanctions remained in place against Iraq until Saddam Hussein was overthrown in 2003.

UNSCR 678 contained the crucial phrase "all necessary means" that was effectively code for the use of military force. This was the same form of words used in UNSCR 794 in November 1992 authorizing action in Somalia. This time, however, the resolution explicitly recognized that the US military would take the lead. A Unified Task Force (UNITAF) was then dispatched to Mogadishu under US leadership to tackle the warlords and distribute humanitarian assistance. It handed back authority to the UN in May 1993.

US intervention in Somalia was always controversial domestically in view of the lack of clarity in the mission and numerous setbacks.[63] By contrast, there was little opposition to US intervention in Haiti in 1994 following adoption of UNSCR 940 with the stated purpose of deposing the military leaders who had overthrown President Jean-Bertrand Aristide in 1991. The same was even more true of UNSCR 1368, adopted on September 12, 2001, that authorized the United

States to use "all necessary means" in response to the terrorist attacks the day before.[64] This was followed by the US-led invasion of Afghanistan the following month.

President Obama came to power promising a different kind of foreign policy. However, it was not long before he, too, turned to the UN to seek approval for "all necessary means" to protect civilians in Libya. UNSCR 1973 was duly passed in March 2011, but with five abstentions (Brazil, China, Germany, India, and Russia). The high level of abstentions was due to the (justified) fear that the United States and its allies would use the resolution to remove Colonel Gaddhafi from power.[65]

All administrations after the end of the Cold War had therefore succeeded in gaining the support of the UN for US military action. Sometimes, however, that support was ambiguous or even nonexistent. This issue came to the fore in the former Yugoslavia as it broke apart into a series of separate states. Determined to prevent this, Serbia had committed war crimes (especially in Bosnia & Herzegovina) to which the UNSC had responded with sanctions, the authorization of peacekeepers, and the application of a no-fly zone.

How to enforce these UN resolutions in the face of Serbian intransigence exercised US administrations in the 1990s. Gradually, NATO emerged as the preferred instrument and the US-controlled organization carried out a series of bombings that played a crucial role in bringing President Slobodan Milosevic to the negotiating table in 1995.[66] NATO bombings were so effective that the UN secretary-general eventually gave the UN military commander the authority to request NATO air strikes, thus putting beyond doubt the legality of NATO actions.

When Kosovo sought its independence from Serbia a few years later, it looked at first as if history would repeat itself. However, China and Russia made it clear they would use their veto in the UNSC to block the use of force against the Serbian military. NATO, at the request of the Clinton administration, then carried out a series of bombing raids that were *not* authorized by the UN. This meant the NATO action was illegal, although its defenders would still claim it was "legitimate."[67] NATO, led as always by US forces, would then go on to play a key role in counterinsurgency operations in Afghanistan after the fall of the Taliban, in suppressing piracy off the coast of East Africa, and in the overthrow of Colonel Gaddhafi in Libya.

The Clinton administration was unconcerned by accusations of illegality, as US governments have never felt constrained by international law. This was made abundantly clear in early 2003, when President George W. Bush failed to secure a resolution in the UNSC authorizing "all necessary means" to over-

BOX 8.4

US EXTRATERRITORIALITY

Extraterritoriality—defined both as the application of national laws outside the nation's territory and as immunity from foreign laws by the nation's citizens—has always been practiced by imperial powers, including the United States. However, there was a big increase in extraterritoriality during the unipolar moment.

The first examples come from legislation aimed at Cuba. The 1992 Cuban Democracy ("Torricelli") Act prohibited foreign subsidiaries of US companies from trading with Cuba. The 1996 Helms-Burton Act went further and penalized all foreign companies "trafficking" in properties formerly owned by US citizens or Cubans who later became US citizens. Directors of such companies were unable to visit the United States, and many "establishment" figures were affected (including a deputy director of the Bank of England).

The spread of US bases, private security companies, and US Special Forces around the world also led to a big increase in extraterritoriality as US administrations used their imperial authority to ensure that their citizens were not subject to local laws while operating in these countries. In particular, the administration of President George W. Bush (2001–9) put enormous pressure on countries to sign "Article 98" agreements to prevent US forces from coming under the scope of the International Criminal Court when in action abroad.

The "war on drugs" became another area for the growth of extraterritoriality. Non-US citizens have frequently been arrested by American agents on foreign soil, and countries have been pressured into signing shiprider agreements. US law also forces foreign companies to disassociate themselves from named kingpins or face sanctions of various forms.

The pursuit of America's own citizens for tax evasion has also led to a huge extension of extraterritoriality by US governments. The 2010 Foreign Account Tax Compliance Act (FATCA), for example, requires non-US financial institutions all over the world to provide information to the Internal Revenue Service or be subject to sanctions on their US operations.

throw Saddam Hussein in Iraq. Since NATO was also divided, the Bush administration went ahead with a "coalition of the willing" in defiance of international law after securing overwhelming support from Congress.

US administrations now had a new multilateral instrument to intervene abroad when UN and/or NATO approval was not forthcoming. A "coalition of the willing" was next employed by President Bush in 2004 when Canada and France joined forces with the United States in Haiti to force President Aristide into exile. A peacekeeping mission (MINUSTAH), was subsequently authorized by the UNSC, but this could not disguise the illegal nature of the overthrow of Aristide himself.

"Coalitions of the willing" proved popular during the Obama administration as well. They have been used in the Middle East, where UN- or NATO-sponsored actions have not been an option.[68] In particular, US intervention in Syria after 2011 (training and arming rebels opposed to President Bashar al-Assad) has been part of an informal coalition. President Obama also used a "coalition of the willing" to bomb Islamic State of Iraq and Syria (IS) targets in Iraq and Syria after IS made big territorial gains in 2014.[69]

When multilateral intervention—with or without UN approval—is not possible, US governments have never hesitated to employ unilateral action. This was true during the Cold War and it continued afterward. Indeed, the list of unilateral interventions is a very long one, and still expanding, although there are almost certainly some episodes of which we are still unaware as a result of the relevant information not yet having been declassified.

Some of the unilateral interventions are well known. They include sanctions against individual states, of which the most enduring have been against Cuba despite the fact that the US government is almost completely isolated in the United Nations on the issue.[70] Examples of other unilateral sanctions applied during the unipolar moment include those against Belarus, Burma, Iran, Russia, and Venezuela.[71] Unlike the Cuban ones, these sanctions were aimed at key individuals or strategic sectors of the economy rather than applied across the board.

The opposition of US governments to the trade in illegal narcotics has also produced a swath of unilateral interventions. Although the "war on drugs" goes back to 1971, there has been a huge increase in unilateralism since the end of the Cold War as a result of changes in legislation. This includes an annual survey by the US State Department that can lead to "decertification" of a country that is deemed not to be cooperating with US antidrug agencies.[72] It also includes the 1999 Foreign Narcotics Kingpin Designation Act that has been used not only to target individuals but also businesses.

US presidents may have complained bitterly about cyberwarfare against some of the nation's agencies and companies, but this form of unilateral intervention has almost certainly been carried out by the US government itself. Indeed, as the National Commission for the Review of the Research and Development Programs of the United States Intelligence Community stated in 2013, "Failure to properly resource and use our own R&D to appraise, exploit, and counter the scientific and technical developments of our adversaries—including both state and non-state actors—may have more immediate and catastrophic consequences than failure in any other field of intelligence."[73]

It is therefore no surprise to learn that US agencies have hacked into Chinese servers on numerous occasions. More controversially, US programmers are likely to have been behind the Stuxnet cyberworm that attacked Iran's nuclear facilities at Natanz in 2010 and which may have set back Iranian nuclear ambitions by several years.

Unilateral intervention in the Cold War had been mainly about destabilizing the governments of foreign states. In the aftermath of the Cold War, however, it was a range of NSAs that led to a huge expansion in US intervention. International terrorist groups figured prominently among these NSAs, and the Clinton administration in particular had taken unilateral action against the best known (al-Qaeda) even before 9/11.

Following 9/11, legislation was swiftly passed giving future US governments almost unrestricted freedom of action in the "war on global terrorism." The 2001 Authorization for Use of Military Force (AUMF) stated, "The President is authorized to use all necessary and appropriate force against those nations, organizations, or persons he determines planned, authorized, committed, or aided the terrorist attacks that occurred on September 11, 2001, or harbored such organizations or persons, in order to prevent any future acts of international terrorism against the United States by such nations, organizations or persons."[74]

This domestic law has been used extensively by Presidents Bush, Obama, and Trump to intervene unilaterally in different parts of the world in ways that were largely unavailable to previous commanders in chief. These interventions have included the use of unmanned aerial vehicles, usually called drones, which can be used for targeted assassinations including of US citizens.[75] The main countries affected have been Afghanistan, Pakistan, Somalia, Syria, and Yemen, and the numbers killed, including civilians, have been extensive. This practice (almost certainly illegal under international law) had been outlawed in 1976 by President Gerald R. Ford (1974–77) but returned with a vengeance after 9/11.

There has also been a significant expansion in US Special Forces since 2001, of which the most important is Joint Special Operations Command (JSOC). US

Special Operations Command (SOCOM) operates in dozens of countries (between 70 and 90 on any given day, according to its own version of events) and has operated in nearly 150 since 9/11. Unlike the "covert" operations practiced by the CIA, the "clandestine" operations of US Special Forces do not require presidential approval or regular reports to Congress, as they are covered by a blanket executive order.[76]

This use of "hard" power stirred up anti-Americanism not only in the countries where it was carried out, but in many of those that were not directly affected as well. At the same time "soft" power, defined as the ability to attract and co-opt rather than coerce, use force, or give money as a means of persuasion, was clearly not working. Gradually, the idea of "smart" power began to take shape in which the "hard" and "soft" forms would be combined to secure US interests without provoking so much hostility.[77] As a result, the State Department produced the first *Quadrennial Diplomacy and Development Review* (QDDR) in 2010.

It was clear from the first QDDR that cooperation among different agencies was still going to lead to an imperial agenda in which smart power would very often be exercised unilaterally:

> When the work of these agencies is aligned, it protects America's interests and projects our leadership. We help prevent fragile states from descending into chaos, spur economic growth abroad, secure investments for American business, open new markets for American goods, promote trade overseas, and create jobs here at home. . . . We support civil society groups in countries around the world in their work to choose their governments and hold those governments accountable. . . . This is an affirmative American agenda—a global agenda—that is uncompromising in its defense of our security but equally committed to advancing our prosperity and standing up for our values.[78]

Smart power therefore changed nothing. It was essentially a more sophisticated way of promoting US imperial interests without, it was hoped, attracting as much hostility as through the use of hard power alone. Intervention, both unilateral and multilateral, therefore continued very much as before and to many—including most anti-imperialists—it seemed as if the empire was expanding. And yet the opposite was in fact the case. The empire was already in full retreat, and had been for some years. This is the subject of Part III.

Part Three

THE EMPIRE IN RETREAT

9

ANTI-IMPERIALISM IN THE UNITED STATES

The American empire is now in retreat as a result of internal and external pressures. These will be examined in the next three chapters, but first it is necessary to acknowledge the role that anti-imperialism in the United States itself has played since the formation of the republic. This anti-imperialist tradition, going back nearly 250 years, provides a rich seam that modern opponents of American empire mine with increasing frequency.

It is now widely accepted that the War of Independence was fought against the British Empire but not generally against the idea of empire itself.[1] Yet the citizens of the new nation were keen to avoid a situation where the republic would reproduce those features that had led Great Britain to act in a supposedly tyrannical fashion toward its former colonies. And some of them saw in the US Constitution, adopted in 1787, a dangerous trend toward a tyrannical empire that they were quick to denounce.

These citizens recognized the flaws in the Articles of Confederation but considered the new Constitution a step too far. They never called themselves anti-imperialists, but those who followed in their footsteps were often opposed to territorial expansion for a variety of reasons. They can therefore be described as anti-expansionists. As a result, they represent the first strand in American anti-imperialism—that is, those who opposed the construction and consolidation of the territorial empire.

After the First World War, anti-expansionism became less relevant, as the imperial project was no longer about the acquisition of territory. By then, however, anti-imperialism was increasingly associated with isolationism, which—like anti-expansionism—has also had a long tradition in US history. Indeed, it can trace its origins to George Washington's Farewell Address in 1796, if not before, and to the subsequent pronouncements of many of the Founding Fathers.

Not all isolationists were anti-imperialists, since isolationism can easily be used as a cover for unilateralism. And, just like anti-expansionists, not all isolationists have been consistent in either their words or deeds. Yet some *were* anti-imperialists, and the tradition has lived on, so that neo-isolationism is still an important strand in US politics. Indeed, in the primary season for presidential elections it is very rare indeed not to find at least one neo-isolationist and anti-imperialist candidate.

Currently in the United States the armed forces are granted a degree of respect that often puzzles visitors. However, appearances can be deceptive, and antimilitarism has a long history in America that has survived to this day. Even during the War of Independence many citizens were fearful of the implications of a large standing army, and the Federal Constitution tried to put strict limits on the republic's military ambitions.

These limits were gradually swept away by the executive in the pursuit first of territorial expansion and later of a semiglobal empire, but the antimilitarist tradition lived on among members of Congress, the churches, and civil society. Resistance to conscription was always strong and reached a peak during the Vietnam War when antimilitarism was especially virulent.

Antimilitarism was seen as a grave threat to the semiglobal empire after Vietnam, and enormous efforts were expended in overcoming it. These efforts were largely successful, and antimilitarism almost disappeared after 9/11. However, the tradition soon revived, and it remains an important contributor to US anti-imperialism today.

Anti-expansionists, isolationists, and antimilitarists do not necessarily reject American "exceptionalism"—the doctrine on which US empire ultimately is founded. Indeed, it is fair to say that most of them see no inconsistency between their own views and an acceptance of US exceptionalism. This means, however, that their anti-imperialist credentials are inevitably suspect, since they have not rejected the core imperial tenet.

That cannot be said of the anti-exceptionalists, the fourth and final category of US anti-imperialists, who reject American exceptionalism as a myth and who deny that US history is fundamentally different from that of other nations that have practiced settler colonialism.[2] Starting with those Native Americans who had to confront the reality of an expanding empire after independence, anti-exceptionalism has spread to other groups and individuals in society. Indeed, over 80 percent of young people ("millennials") now deny that the United States is exceptional.

The American empire is now in retreat, and much of this has to do with internal forces. The four strands of anti-imperialism have played a large part in this transformation, and their importance is growing. The imperialist tradition and belief system is still strong, however, implying major conflicts over the next decade or so between the two forces. Yet the direction of travel is clear even if the ride will be bumpy. And the internal pressures are increasingly being joined by external forces, which make it inevitable that the empire will continue to retreat.

9.1. ANTI-EXPANSIONISTS

The Federal Constitution of 1787 is today considered almost a sacred text, but plenty of Americans opposed its adoption at the time. Not all of these men and women can be considered anti-imperialists, since some of their objections were either parochial, sectional, or had to do with process.[3] However, for many of the opponents the great fear was a United States of America whose sheer size would require restrictions on the liberty of its citizens in a manner that undermined the lofty sentiments in the Declaration of Independence.

For these early opponents of territorial expansion, or anti-Federalists as they were known at the time, the writings of the French political philosopher Montesquieu had become an article of faith. Montesquieu had argued in the eighteenth century that a democratic republic needed to be small if it was to remain democratic, for otherwise it would be forced to adopt increasingly tyrannical measures as it became large.

The anti-Federalists were as eloquent as the Federalists they opposed and their *oeuvres* have been brought together in the *Anti-Federalist Papers*.[4] Writing under pseudonyms such as Cato, Brutus, and Centinel, they campaigned long and hard against what they saw as the imperialist tendencies of an expanding federal state. Centinel, for example, wrote as early as October 1787,

> [I]f the united states are to be melted down into one empire, it becomes you to consider, whether such a government, however constructed, would be eligible in so extended a territory; and whether it would be practicable, consistent with freedom? It is the opinion of the greatest writers, that a very extensive country cannot be governed on democratical principles, on any other plan, than a confederation of a number of small republics, possessing all the powers of internal government, but united in the management of their foreign and general concerns. It would not be difficult to prove, that any thing short of despotism, could not bind so great a country under one government; and that whatever plan you might, at the first setting out, establish, it would issue in a despotism.[5]

Not to be outdone, Cato wrote on the same theme later in the same month and pointedly referred to ancient Greek history in which the generation that had fought the War of Independence was so thoroughly steeped:

> [I]n a large [republic], there are men of large fortunes, and consequently of less moderation; there are too great deposits to trust in the hands of a single subject, an ambitious person soon becomes sensible that he may be happy, great, and glorious by oppressing his fellow citizens, and that he might raise himself to grandeur, on the ruins of his country. In large republics, the public good is sacrificed to a thousand views, in a small one, the interest of the public is easily perceived, better understood, and more within the reach of every citizen; abuses have a less extent, and of course are less protected. He also shows you, that the duration of the republic of Sparta was owing to its having continued with the same extent of territory after all its wars; and that the ambition of Athens and Lacedemon to command and direct the union, lost them their liberties, and gave them a monarchy.[6]

With the ratification of the Constitution and the inauguration of George Washington as president in 1789, the anti-Federalists were defeated. However, their cause was not dead, and they would soon be confronted with a new opportunity to oppose US imperial expansion. This was the Louisiana Purchase in 1803, which threatened to double the territory of the United States and render even more relevant Montesquieu's warnings about the relationship between a republic's size and its capacity for democracy.

President Thomas Jefferson (1801–9), in theory a strict constitutionalist, had grave doubts about the legality of the Louisiana Purchase.[7] However, he had no doubts at all about the wisdom of imperial expansion and was therefore able to overcome the concerns of his conscience relatively easily. Most of the Senate supported the treaty of cession in 1803 that secured the Louisiana Purchase for the United States, but a significant minority opposed it. They included Roger Griswold from Connecticut, who said, "It is not consistent with the spirit of a republican government that its territory should be exceedingly large, for as you extend your limits you increase the difficulties arising from a want of that similarity of customs, habits, and manners so essential for its support."[8]

The opposition in the Senate failed in part because they so clearly represented the sectional interests of New England. Nevertheless, in predicting that territorial expansion on this scale could lead to civil war they made some telling points. These have been summarized by Kevin Gannon as follows, using in many cases the senators' own words:

A consolidated republic would persevere over time; but rapid and reckless expansion would only endanger the nation. The Louisiana Purchase was the epitome of recklessness. "Now, by adding an unmeasured world beyond that river [the Mississippi], we rush like a comet into infinite space," worried Fisher Ames. "In our wild career, we may jostle some other world out of its orbit, but we shall, in every event, quench the light of our own." The "security of our government" would be threatened by such rapid expansion, argued William Plumer. "An extension of the body politic will enfeeble the circulation of its powers & energies in the extreme parts."[9]

The Louisiana Purchase was a major setback for the anti-expansionists, but they were far from defeated, as they showed in the War of 1812. Ostensibly fought as a war of self-defense against the British, the War of 1812 was as much— if not more so—about the conquest of Canada and, in the minds of the southern states, Florida as well. Anti-expansionists in Congress were therefore alerted to the danger, and when President James Madison (1809–17) asked for authority to declare war, they were prepared.

Congress approved the war, but not by a large margin. It was 79–49 in the House of Representatives and 19–13 in the Senate. The opposition included almost all Federalists, whose stronghold was New England, where mercantile trade was concentrated, but no less than 25 percent of Madison's own party (Democratic-Republicans) abstained and some voted against. Nor could the Federalists be dismissed this time as defending purely sectional interests. As Congressman Morris Miller of New York told the governing party, "Let it not be said that we refuse you the means of defense. For that we have always been & we still are ready to pen the treasure of the nation. We will give you millions for defense; but not a cent for the conquest of Canada & not the ninety-ninth part of a cent for the extermination of its inhabitants."[10]

The War of 1812 appeared at first to have popular support, which convinced President Madison that he could fight it with a volunteer army. However, the War Department could only secure ten thousand one-year volunteers instead of the fifty thousand authorized by Congress. Madison's attempts to introduce conscription were then defeated by Congress, forcing the president to draft militia from the individual states.

The anti-expansionists also had some of the press on their side. The leading antiwar newspaper was the *Federal Republican and Commercial Gazette*, founded in Baltimore by Alexander Contee Hanson, although he had to move the paper to Georgetown, DC, after nearly being beaten to death by a mob in July 1812 for his opposition to the war.

Public opinion would become even more important in the next battle fought by the anti-expansionists: the proposed annexation of Texas. Although the former Mexican state had declared independence in 1836, its citizens had made clear their preference for annexation by the United States. The matter was then debated in Congress, where the petitions of more than 100,000 people—most of them against annexation—were laid on the table. The former president John Quincy Adams, now in the House of Representatives, would lead the charge against annexation, speaking all morning, every morning, from June 16 to July 7, 1838.

Adams carried the day and the proposal to annex Texas was dropped. However, it was only a temporary victory for the anti-expansionists, as the war against Mexico a few years later put annexation (not only of Texas this time) firmly back on the agenda. This time a jingoistic press, driven by talk of "Manifest Destiny," had a massive influence on public opinion and opposition to expansion was at first largely confined to a small number of brave individuals. They did, however, occupy the high moral ground, and their words have echoed down the years since the war itself.

Abraham Lincoln, first elected to the House of Representatives in late 1846 when opposition to the war was on the rise, is the best known of the anti-expansionists with his "spot" resolutions. Yet Lincoln did not vote against material support for the US troops. It was left to some of his colleagues to capture the increasingly radical mood among the anti-expansionists. Robert Toombs of Georgia, for example, urged Americans to "put a check upon this lust of dominion. We had territory enough, Heaven knew,"[11] while Thomas Corwin of Ohio went further telling the Senate "If I were a Mexican, I would tell you, 'Have you not room in your own country to bury your dead men? If you come into mine we will greet you with bloody hands, and welcome you to hospitable graves.'"[12]

Nor were all sections of the press silenced by the jingoism of Manifest Destiny. The *Liberator*, edited by the abolitionist William Lloyd Garrison, expressed its "hope that, if blood has had to flow, that it has been that of the Americans."[13] And correspondents of the *Religious Recorder* declaimed that "War is unmoral and depraved . . . the army is an unnatural and corrupt organization. . . . Every gazette brings us new lessons on the vanity, vice, and misery of war. . . . if one lives through a battle it is to assist in throwing his companions into a hole—and be—forgot."[14]

The Mexican-American War was followed by the Gadsden Purchase in 1853, completing the acquisition of territory that would become known as the Lower Forty-Eight. Yet expansionist tendencies did not end, and would be renewed with vigor as soon as the Civil War was over. This time, however, the target was territory that was either offshore or not contiguous with the continental United States.

The first acquisition was Alaska, purchased from Russia in 1867. It passed without much opposition in the Senate but faced a stiffer test in the House of Representatives that had to vote on the money. Indeed, the purchase became known as Seward's Folly after Secretary of State William Seward, who had pushed for it. The anti-expansionists in the House of Representatives were led by Cadwalader Washburn, who argued,

> First, that at the time the treaty for Alaska was negotiated, not a soul in the whole United States asked for it; second, that it was secretly negotiated, and in a manner to prevent the representatives of the people from being heard; third, that by existing treaties we possess every right that is of any value to us, without the responsibility and never-ending expense of governing a nation of savages; fourth, that the country ceded is absolutely without value; fifth, that it is the right and duty of the House to inquire into the treaty, and to vote or not vote the money, according to its best judgment.[15]

Seward presented Congress with a *fait accompli,* and the purchase went ahead with the support of Senator Charles Sumner. However, Sumner was able to establish his anti-expansionist credentials soon afterward by helping to block the purchase of the Danish West Indies from Denmark and by swaying the Senate against the annexation of Santo Domingo (Dominican Republic). His speeches against Dominican annexation made him justifiably famous.[16]

Sumner was not alone among anti-expansionists in struggling to achieve consistency. Indeed, the widespread acceptance among the nineteenth-century public of US exceptionalism, the Monroe Doctrine, and Manifest Destiny made it almost inevitable that inconsistencies would occur even among the most determined of anti-expansionists.[17] At the same time, anti-expansionists needed to justify themselves in different ways, since the *antebellum* arguments based on the threat to democracy from a large republic no longer had as much salience.

The outbreak of the Spanish-American War in April 1898 gave them the cause they needed. The possibility that the United States would acquire a swath of overseas territories in the Caribbean and the Pacific provided the perfect opportunity for anti-expansionists of all stripes to unite in protest and within months an Anti-Imperialist League (AIL) had been formed with branches all over the country.[18] The membership was broadly based and had the support of many newspapers, while women also figured prominently in AIL activities.[19] It also included leading figures from the US establishment, one of whom (Carl Schurz) defined his position as follows:

BOX 9.1
JANE ADDAMS (1860–1935)

Jane Addams was the daughter of a Civil War veteran and Illinois state senator who was a friend of Abraham Lincoln. After being educated at Rockford Female Seminary, she developed a passion for social reform. Addams established a home in Chicago (Hull House) "to provide a center for a higher civic and social life; to institute and maintain educational and philanthropic enterprises and to investigate and improve the conditions in the industrial districts of Chicago." She also supported the international peace movement throughout her life, being awarded the Nobel Prize for Peace in 1931.

The Nobel Committee made reference in its citation to Addams's numerous struggles for international peace, which included opposition to US entry into the First World War (for which she was expelled from the Daughters of the American Revolution). However, the committee made no mention of her earlier campaign against US imperialism after the Spanish-American War.

Addams joined the Anti-Imperialist League soon after its formation in 1898 and was one of its leading members. In a speech on April 30, 1899, to the Chicago Liberty Meeting, where she was the only woman among eight plenary speakers, she emphasized the threat to democracy from imperialism: "There is a growing conviction among workingmen of all countries that, whatever may be accomplished by a national war . . . , there is one inevitable result—an increased standing army. . . . The men in these armies spend their muscular force in drilling, their mental force in thoughts of warfare. The mere hours of idleness conduce mental and moral deterioration."

Like many US anti-imperialists, Jane Addams struggled to find an approach that was consistent with her other beliefs. Her passion for social reform, for example, led her to nominate Theodore Roosevelt for the presidency in 1912 as the candidate of the Progressive Party despite the fact that he had been, and remained, a committed imperialist. The search for international peace, however, was her main interest throughout her life. She saw US territorial expansion through this lens and opposed it as a threat to democracy and the American way of life.

I believe that this Republic . . . can endure so long as it remains true to the principles upon which it was founded, but that it will morally decay if it abandons them. I believe that this democracy, the government of, by, and for the people, is not fitted for a colonial policy, which means conquest by force . . . and arbitrary rule over subject populations. I believe that, if it attempts such a policy on a large scale, its inevitable degeneracy will hurt the progress of civilization more than it can possibly further that progress by planting its flag upon foreign soil on which its fundamental principles of government cannot live.[20]

The AIL failed to block the Treaty of Paris at the end of 1898, which transferred Guam, the Philippines, and Puerto Rico to the United States, nor were they able to block the annexation of Hawaii in the same year.[21] This did not mark the end of the anti-expansionist campaign. However, the movement increasingly focused only on the Philippines, where the threat of unrestricted entry to the United States by ten million nonwhite people brought out the less principled side of American anti-imperialism.[22]

The AIL backed the presidential candidacy of William Jennings Bryan in 1900 "on a platform that contained a thoroughly satisfactory anti-imperialist plank dictated by Bryan himself."[23] Bryan's defeat to William McKinley was therefore a big setback for anti-expansionists. However, the tide soon turned against formal colonial rule and US imperialism began to take a different form. When the national AIL ended in the 1920s, US imperial ambitions were set on global leadership rather than the acquisition of territory. Anti-imperialism therefore had to take a different form.

Anti-expansionism did not entirely die with the shift from a territorial to a semiglobal empire. In order to secure the latter, the US expanded its military bases around the world (to nearly eight hundred as of today), creating an "empire of bases." The bases are operated under different rules, but all imply some diminution of the sovereignty of the countries where they are located. US opposition to this network of foreign bases, captured in books such as *Bases of Empire* and *Base Nation*, has been vocal and enjoys some popular support.[24]

9.2. ISOLATIONISTS

If the Declaration of Independence became the sacred text of anti-expansionists, the isolationists drew their inspiration from George Washington's Farewell Address in 1796: "The great rule of conduct for us in regard to foreign nations is, in extending our commercial relations, to have with them as little political connection as possible. . . . It is our true policy to steer clear of permanent alliances with any portion of the foreign world. . . . Harmony, liberal intercourse with all nations, are recommended by policy, humanity, and interest. But even our commercial policy should hold an equal and impartial hand; neither seeking nor granting exclusive favors or preferences."[25]

Washington never used the phrase "avoid entangling alliances," but others were quick to interpret his speech as meaning just that. Indeed, even before Washington's address the anti-Federalist Elbridge Gerry had feared that sending diplomatic agents abroad could lead to the "inconveniences of being entangled with European politics, of being the puppets of European Statesmen, of being gradually divested of our virtuous republican principles, of being a divided, influenced and dissipated people."[26] Thomas Jefferson then used his inaugural address in 1801 to assert "peace, commerce, and honest friendship with all nations, entangling alliances with none."[27]

The avoidance of entangling alliances has been a constant theme among isolationists. Yet its meaning was, and is, highly ambiguous. For Washington, Jefferson, and the other Founding Fathers it did not rule out unilateralism and empire building across the continent. For them, and many of those that followed in their footsteps, there was no contradiction between isolationism and imperialism.

However, among some anti-imperialists in the United States, isolationism—especially in recent years—has been an important theme. If we define it as "the voluntary abstention by a state from taking part in security-related politics in an area of the international system over which it is capable of exerting control,"[28] it becomes easier to understand its relevance. For isolationism in this sense is quintessentially a response to the building of a semiglobal empire rather than a response to territorial expansion across the continent after the War of Independence.

After an initial flurry of interest in the late eighteenth century, therefore, isolationism ceased to be of much relevance until American global leadership became a real possibility. And the first real test was provided by the First World War (1914–18) when the possibility of US entry worried both those concerned about entangling alliances and also those fearful of the introduction of conscription.

In 1916, the same year that Woodrow Wilson based his presidential campaign on the slogan "He kept us out of the war," one million people signed a petition in favor of an arms embargo against all belligerents in the conflict.[29] Wilson's appeal in April 1917 to a joint session of Congress for a declaration of war was, therefore, something of a shock. No fewer than six senators and fifty representatives voted against, with many others abstaining.

The senators who voted against, together with a few others who joined them later, would become known as the "irreconcilables" in their opposition to the League of Nations when it came up for debate in 1920. Not all senators who voted against the League were anti-imperialists, since many of them simply wanted a League that put no restrictions on US actions abroad. However, the irreconcilables were different. Their isolationist stance was by and large an anti-imperialist one reflecting their fears that the United States would be obliged to police the world or, as Senator Hiram Johnson put it, "pledging our country in various directions, which will require us to keep troops possibly in Togo Land, the Samerian [*sic*], and even in the Dardanelles."[30]

The irreconcilables, or Peace Progressives as they have been called, joined forces with the unilateralists in the Senate to defeat the League of Nations Covenant, but they soon parted company with their imperialist colleagues as the United States staked a claim to global leadership and extended its empire in the Americas. In 1928, for example, Senator John Blaine—an irreconcilable and anti-imperialist—protested in a speech summarized by Robert Johnson that President Calvin Coolidge (1923–29) had warped the Monroe Doctrine, a "doctrine of inherent fairness and justice that the strong must not ride down the weak," into a dictum that "exalted greed," which in turn weakened American moral power. Americans, as the "monsters of imperialism," could no longer denounce French atrocities in North Africa, British policies in India and other colonies, or even Japanese excesses in East Asia (because of "our indefensible extraterritorial policy" in China).[31]

Despite the best efforts of the irreconcilables, America was not isolationist in the interwar period and established itself as *primus inter pares* among the world's global leaders.[32] Yet the isolationists could point to some successes in their efforts to avoid entangling alliances. The United States stayed out of the World Court as a result of clever maneuvering by the anti-imperialist group of senators.[33] At the same time, isolationists secured the passage of the three Neutrality Acts passed between 1935 and 1937 that were "the very epitome of American isolationism, embracing every conceivable device to protect the country from the dangers to which it had been exposed in 1914–1917."[34]

The outbreak of the Second World War in September 1939 led President Franklin Delano Roosevelt (1933–45) to campaign against the Neutrality Acts. He succeeded and the arms embargo was lifted by the end of the year. Yet far from marking the end of isolationism, this was the catalyst for the launch of a mass movement known as the America First Committee that was designed to keep the United States out of the war. Although it is best known for its elite members and supporters, including future presidents John F. Kennedy (1961–63) and Gerald R. Ford (1974–77), it enjoyed a large membership of 800,000 in 450 chapters.[35]

The America First Committee could not survive Pearl Harbor in December 1941, since isolationism now appeared unpatriotic. The committee was therefore dissolved soon afterward. Isolationism then appeared to have ended following US entry into the Second World War, and many commentators inside and outside America were ready to write it off. However, it was merely slumbering and it reemerged again soon after the Second World War.

The empire that the United States built after the war was based in large part on US-controlled organizations. Thus, it was natural that isolationists came to focus on those very same institutions. Only seven senators voted against the United Nations Participation Act in December 1945, but sixteen supported a subsequent amendment by Robert Taft that would have banned the use of atomic weapons. Given that none of them had spoken out against dropping the atomic bomb on Japan, this was a significant change.

The announcement of the Truman Doctrine in March 1947 increased the fears of isolationists from both the left and the right that the United States was embarked on an imperial project unlike anything that had gone before. However, the left was soon emasculated by the rise of the Cold War and played little part in the anti-imperialist struggle until the Vietnam War. Its demise was captured by the humiliation of Henry Wallace in the presidential election of 1948, when he won the support of only 2.4 percent of the vote as the candidate of the Progressive Party.[36]

It therefore fell to the right to carry the isolationist and anti-imperialist torch for a while. A chance to demonstrate their credentials came with the Senate debate in 1949 on NATO, an organization that would clearly involve the United States in entangling alliances with Europe. They failed, but thirteen senators led by Robert Taft voted against the treaty.[37] Outside Congress, their views were echoed by the businessman Sterling Morton, who said, "Should our country cross this Rubicon [joining NATO], we will . . . have taken the decisive step toward a complete change in our national way of life . . . and shall have embarked upon a path which can lead only to eventual bankruptcy, eventual dictatorship, and the end of that system of life known as 'the American Way.'"[38]

The Cold War presented isolationists, or neo-isolationists, as they would now be called, with both opportunities and obstacles. On the one hand, increasing US involvement in overt and covert conflicts allowed them to warn about the dangers of military overreach and imperial hubris. At the same time, the patriotic fervor associated with the conflict against the Soviet Union rendered them liable to the charge at best of being naive and at worst of undermining the state at a moment of existential crisis.

For those on the left neo-isolationism was particularly dangerous, as they ran the risk of being branded as fellow travelers (i.e., sympathetic to communism and the USSR). Even those on the right were reluctant to use the "i" word, which meant that they were increasingly defined by their political opponents who lost no opportunity to pour scorn on them. As the Vietnam War drew toward its end, for example, the historian Walter Laqueur wrote, "Neo-isolationism as a mood, an expression of boredom or revulsion with world politics, is psychologically understandable. But the neo-isolationist creed breaks down once its spokesmen attempt to provide a more or less coherent and ideologically respectable justification. There is no reason to assume that neo-isolationism will make for a more peaceful world or that it will solve any problems at all. If neo-isolationism has a claim to moral superiority, it is roughly speaking that of Pontius Pilate."[39]

It was not until the end of the Cold War that neo-isolationists could find an effective voice. As US elites debated the choice of foreign policy strategy for a world in which the Soviet Union no longer existed, neo-isolationism was able to portray itself as a respectable option—and the only anti-imperialist one—among other "grand strategies."[40]

To do so, neo-isolationists had to define their creed rather than allow others to do it for them. One of the first after the Cold War was Eric Nordlinger, whose influential book *Isolationism Reconfigured* was first published a year after he died: "The strategic vision of historical and contemporary isolationism is one of quiet strength and national autonomy. Its advocates have confidently opted for a strong, self-denying strategy, a purposefully considered choice not to go abroad politically and militarily. . . . In fact, going abroad for these reasons can be depicted as weakness, conceptualized as a loss of autonomy. For we have indeed been much constrained by others, opponents, allies, and clients alike, in bearing sizable costs and risks—from expensive military forces, through support for ethically unpalatable regimes, unto intermittent interventions and wars."[41]

Isolationists had therefore found their voice again, but that did not mean they were popular. Indeed, as late as 2002 only 30 percent were willing to answer in the affirmative when asked if the United States "should mind its own business internationally and let other countries get along the best they can on their own." Yet in one poll in 2013—only a decade later—52 percent agreed with the question, putting neo-isolationists in a majority for the first time since the question was originally asked in 1964.[42]

This change in social attitudes toward isolationism, and therefore toward US imperialism, has had many causes and is therefore a complex phenomenon. Perhaps that is why neo-isolationism is no longer a view mainly associated with the right and the elderly in US politics. Today it affects the left and the young just as much. Indeed, neo-isolationism today cannot be dismissed as exclusively a right-wing phenomenon in the way that it was for many years (Box 9.2).

The new mood was captured in the 2016 presidential election, where the Democratic and Republican Party each fielded a strong candidate in the primaries that were widely perceived as neo-isolationists. Bernie Sanders (Democrat) and Donald Trump (Republican) may have differed on almost everything else, but they both agreed that the imperial burden carried by the US government and its people had become too great for the country to bear alone. However, while Sanders *was* a neo-isolationist and therefore an anti-imperialist, Trump— it turned out—was not.[43] This became abundantly clear after the Trump administration was formed and he took office as the forty-fifth president.

It might be assumed that the growing popularity of neo-isolationism in the United States had much to do with the rise of the antiglobalization movement. Neo-isolationism, however, is primarily a doctrine of national security, while antiglobalization is about economic policy. Thus, it is possible for the same person to take a different view toward both. Indeed, until recently Americans remained positive about US involvement in the global economy, including participation in free trade agreements, even as they expressed growing skepticism about the projection of US military power overseas.

Today, however, the mood has changed. The antiglobalization movement in the United States, which first came to public notice in the violent protests against the WTO in Seattle in 1999, has become much more mainstream. Only 20 percent of Americans now believe that trade with other countries leads to an increase in jobs, and an even smaller percentage believe that it increases wages.[44] Indeed, the leading candidates in the 2016 primary elections all felt obliged—with different degrees of sincerity—to distance themselves from the Trans-Pacific Partnership (TPP), the flagship trade agreement signed by the administration of President Barack Obama (2009–17).[45]

The foundations of the US semiglobal empire rested on open foreign markets for US goods and services, freedom of movement for US capital, and the projection of US power around the world in support of these goals. As the Obama presidency came to an end, it had become abundantly clear that the imperial project was losing support among precisely the people who were supposed to benefit from it. Neo-isolationism and antiglobalization had become symptoms of an empire in retreat.

BOX 9.2
PATRICK BUCHANAN (1938–)

Patrick Buchanan is a conservative who is opposed to free trade agreements and is not afraid to call himself a neo-isolationist. Buchanan worked as a speechwriter for President Richard M. Nixon (1969–74), where he coined the phrase "the silent majority." Later he became communications director under President Ronald Reagan (1981–89). On leaving the White House, he was free to develop his own ideas in print and wrote an article in 1990 entitled "America First—and Second, and Third" in which he argued for neo-isolationism but was not yet brave enough to use the word (he called it "disengagement").

Buchanan challenged George H. W. Bush for the Republican presidential nomination in 1992 and lost, although his level of support in the early primaries was respectable. He ran again in 1996 on an explicitly neo-isolationist and antiglobalization program. He performed well as the "antiestablishment" figure in the first Republican primary contests but ultimately was defeated by the "establishment" candidate Robert Dole. His third attempt at the presidency in 2000, however, was a complete failure.

In 1999 he published a book entitled *A Republic, Not an Empire* in which he spelled out his neo-isolationist views: "Present U.S. foreign policy, which commits America to go to war for scores of nations in regions where we have never fought before, is unsustainable. As we pile commitment upon commitment in Eastern Europe, the Balkans, the Middle East, and the Persian Gulf, American power continues to contract—a sure formula for foreign policy disaster."

The book was controversial on many counts, but especially for espousing the view that the United States should not have entered the Second World War. However, it was the end of the Cold War more than anything else that strengthened Buchanan's neo-isolationist convictions, and in 2013 he wrote, "The roots of the new isolationism are not difficult to discern. There is, first, the end of the Cold War, the liberation of the captive nations of Europe, the dissolution of our great adversary, the Soviet Empire, and the breakup of the Soviet Union. The Cold War, our war, was over. Time to come home."

9.3. ANTIMILITARISTS

The former colonists knew what the British had been able to do with a standing army and most of them were in no mood to replicate the experience. The Founding Fathers were united by rhetoric in their opposition to the republic controlling a large military force, Jefferson as always exceeding all of them with the exuberance of his flowery language: "I am for relying, for internal defence, on our militia solely, till actual invasion, and for such naval force only as may protect our coasts and harbors from such depredations as we have experienced; and not for a standing army in time of peace, which may overawe the public sentiment; nor for a navy, which, by its own expenses and the eternal wars in which it will implicate us, will grind us with public burthens, & sink us under them."[46] The demands of high office, however, soon imposed splits in this rhetorical unity. The result was a compromise, with the 1787 Constitution giving the executive the right to raise an army, but placing it under civilian control with appropriations authorized by Congress and limited to two years at a time.

These restrictions were not enough for some of the new republic's leaders. In 1798 Benjamin Rush wanted the War Department to carry the caption "An office for butchering the human species."[47] When Secretary of War Henry Knox in 1790 asked the Senate for a sixfold increase in the size of the army, William Maclay predicted, "Give Knox his army, and he will soon have a war on his hands." And when warned about alleged Spanish intrigues among the Southwest Indians, he noted, "New phantoms for the day must be created."[48]

Antimilitarism was so strong that the United States entered the War of 1812 with a small army and navy that was woefully unprepared for the fight with Great Britain. Not surprisingly, therefore, those calling for greater professionalism in the US armed forces gained the upper hand. The United States Military Academy at West Point, first established by President Jefferson in 1802, was overhauled under Colonel Sylvanus Thayer and trained an elite officer corps including future generals Ulysses S. Grant and Robert E. Lee.

Yet antimilitarism survived, leading to the establishment of the first of many peace societies in 1812 in New York and their merger into the American Peace Society in 1828. It also played a prominent role in the Mexican-American War (1846–48) despite the jingoism of the popular press. Henry David Thoreau, author of *Resistance to Civil Government*, received lasting fame with his refusal to pay tax in opposition to the war.[49] John Hale from New Hampshire caused a sensation in the Senate when he was the only member to oppose a resolution of thanks to Generals Zachary Taylor and Winfield Scott.[50] And his colleague, Thomas Corwin, denounced the war in the following words: "I trust we shall abandon the idea, the heathen, barbarian notion, that our true national glory is to be won, or retained, by military prowess or skill, in the art of destroying life."[51]

Antimilitarists failed to stop either the War of 1812 or the Mexican-American War. However, they did enjoy much greater success in their opposition to conscription. When Secretary of War James Monroe presented a bill in 1814 to authorize the federal government to draft eighty thousand men, it was mauled in the Senate and defeated in the House of Representatives, where Daniel Webster made one of his most famous speeches: "[W]here is it written in the Constitution. . . . That you may take children from their parents, and parents from their children, and compel them to fight the battles of any war in which the folly or the wickedness of government may engage it?"[52]

Two decades later, when Secretary of War Joel Poinsett tried to introduce conscription, the proposal was also defeated in Congress. The House of Representatives even went so far as to adopt a resolution drafted by Daniel Webster that claimed that the administration's conscription project "has been so scorched by public rebuke and reprobation, that no man raises his hand or opens his mouth in its favor."[53]

Conscription was used by both sides in the Civil War, but it was only militarily important to the South and was not seen as setting a precedent for future wars.[54] However, any hopes President Wilson may have had for relying on a volunteer army in the First World War were soon dashed when his administration's plans for an army of one million men produced only seventy-three thousand volunteers.[55]

Conscription soon followed but was deeply unpopular on both the left and right of American politics. The left, represented by the Socialist Party of America and the Industrial Workers of the World (the "Wobblies"), were particularly active in opposition to the draft. Indeed, Eugene Debs—the leader of the Socialist Party—was jailed in 1918 for a speech he made in opposition to the draft and had to fight his fifth and final presidential election in 1920 from jail.[56]

No sooner was the war ended than a stream of pamphlets, articles, and books began to be published alleging profiteering by American munitions companies. The accusations may have been unfair in some cases, but the perception took hold among many members of the US public that their government had been in league with arms manufacturers to push the country into war. And the stories became more lurid with the passage of time, including titles such as *Merchants of Death* in 1934 and *War Is a Racket* the following year.[57]

The Roosevelt administration felt compelled to respond and gave its support for what it hoped would be a limited investigation. However, the chairmanship of the Senate Committee on Investigations of the Munitions Committee was given to Gerald Nye, an antimilitarist from North Dakota, who oversaw a dev-astating critique of the arms industry. The committee, for example, found that "almost without exception, the American munitions companies investigated have at times resorted to such unusual approaches, questionable favors and com-missions, and methods of 'doing the needful' as to constitute, in effect, a form of bribery of foreign government officials or of their close friends in order to secure business. . . . The Committee finds such practices on the part of any munitions company, domestic or foreign, to be highly unethical, a discredit to American business, and an unavoidable reflection upon those American governmental agencies which have unwittingly aided in the transactions so contaminated."[58]

Antiwar sentiment quickly subsided after Pearl Harbor, when antimilitarist Americans were confronted with a choice between antifascism and anti-imperialism. And this time, unlike in the First World War, there would be little opposition to the reintroduction of conscription. Furthermore, the Cold War made it relatively easy for President Harry S. Truman (1945–53) to extend the draft after the Second World War had ended. As a result, it was in place when the Korean War started in June 1950.

Public support for the war was initially high. Even Henry Wallace supported it, arguing in favor of the use of atomic weapons if necessary.[59] However, sup-port soon declined. By January 1951, two-thirds of Americans wanted the United States to pull out of Korea altogether, and by the end of the following year a majority had concluded that the war was not worth fighting.[60] Indeed, opposi-tion to the war is often cited as one of the reasons for Dwight D. Eisenhower's victory in the 1952 presidential election, when he promised "to bring the Ko-rean War to an early and honorable end."

President Eisenhower (1953–61) did end the war, but he did not end conscrip-tion. Only a handful of young men had been convicted of "delinquency" in the war years,[61] but the continuation of the draft after the war and the inequitable way in which it operated caused deep resentment. As a result, staying on at col-lege became a popular route to deferment, although it was not always success-ful, as one witty rhyme made clear:

"Today in college
To gain more knowledge
More and more I strive.

A student deferment
Is my preferment
'Til I reach thirty-five.

But Selective Service
Has me nervous
They grant but one degree.

Despite my plea
For a Ph.D.
They offer me a P.F.C."[62]

President Kennedy was no more successful than Eisenhower in ending the draft, so that it was still in operation as the United States committed ground troops to Vietnam under President Lyndon Johnson (1963–69) starting in 1965. Conscription was not the only reason for the public displays of antimilitarism in the United States during the Vietnam War, but it was certainly a major factor and it was used by the antiwar organization Students for a Democratic Society (SDS) to mobilize unprecedented numbers of Americans.

Starting with a demonstration at the Washington Monument in April 1965 with twenty-five thousand participants,[63] the antiwar movement was attracting crowds in excess of one million by the end of the decade.[64] Nor could this level of participation be explained purely by self-preservation, since many of those involved were not eligible to be drafted anyway.[65] Even the soldiers themselves were involved in these displays of antimilitarism through desertion, demonstrations by veterans, and "fragging."[66] And one soldier, Keith Franklin, left a letter on the battlefield to be opened only in the event of his death:

Dear Mom and Dad: If you are reading this letter, you will never see me again, the reason being that if you are reading this I have died. The question is whether or not my death has been in vain. The answer is yes. The war that has taken my life and many thousands before me is immoral, unlawful and an atrocity unlike any misfit of good judgement known to man. I had no choice as to my fate. It was predetermined by the war-mongering hypocrites in Washington. As I lie dead, please grant my last request. Help me inform the American people, the silent majority who have not yet voiced their opinions.[67]

The last US combat troops left Vietnam in August 1972 and President Richard M. Nixon (1969–74) ended conscription the following year. This was seen as a victory for antimilitarism, made all the sweeter by the recommendations of the Church Committee in 1976 to end the illegal operations of the intelligence agencies. However, the antimilitarist movement could not rest on its laurels for long and was soon back in action.

BOX 9.3
J. WILLIAM FULBRIGHT (1905–95)

J. William Fulbright was born in 1905 in Missouri. At the tender age of thirty-four he became president of the University of Arkansas, and he was elected to the House of Representatives in 1942. He was then elected to the Senate in 1944, where he served as chairman of the Foreign Affairs Committee from 1959 until he lost his seat in 1974.

Nothing in the first part of Fulbright's long life suggested that he would be anything other than a loyal supporter of the semiglobal empire. A committed southerner who backed segregation, he was a strong believer in US-dominated institutions such as the United Nations and NATO, backed the Marshall Plan, and gave his name to the "soft power" instrument of scholarships known as the Fulbright Exchange Program. He even supported the Gulf of Tonkin Resolution in 1964 that paved the way for US entry into the Vietnam War. Yet he ended his life as a staunch antimilitarist and opponent of American empire.

The first indication of his future role came in 1954 when he was the only senator to vote against appropriations for Joseph McCarthy's Permanent Subcommittee on Investigations. He then made clear to President John F. Kennedy (1961–63) his opposition to the Bay of Pigs invasion of Cuba in 1961 and publicly denounced the 1965 invasion of the Dominican Republic as orchestrated by the administration of President Lyndon Johnson (1963–69).

It was Fulbright's opposition to the Vietnam War, however, that would establish his anti-imperialist credentials. Speaking to the American Bar Association in 1967 he said, "We are well on our way to becoming a traditional great power, an imperial nation if you will—engaged in the exercise of power for its own sake, exercising it to the limit of our capacity and beyond, filling every vacuum and extending the American 'presence' to the farthest reaches of the earth. And, as with the great empires of the past, as the power grows, it is becoming an end itself . . . governed, it would seem, by its own mystique, power without philosophy or purpose."

The televised hearings of the Foreign Relations Committee under his chairmanship did much to undermine support for the Vietnam War among the American public. The same could be said for some of his books, published with provocative titles, such as *Arrogance of Power, The Pentagon Propaganda Machine,* and *The Crippled Giant.*

The reason was the cycle of civil wars that broke out in Central America at the end of the 1970s and which were seen as a direct threat to the semiglobal empire by US administrations. President Jimmy Carter (1977–81) had focused on supporting the military in El Salvador against a guerrilla insurgency, but President Ronald Reagan (1981–89) widened the battlefront to include support for the military in Guatemala as well and to undermine the Sandinistas in Nicaragua.

These actions led to the formation of a Central America Peace and Solidarity Movement in the United States that mobilized a mass movement against the proxy wars being fought by the administration. In the case of El Salvador, the lead was taken by the Committee in Solidarity with the People of El Salvador (CISPES), and their efforts secured a limitation on the amount of military support the administration could give.[68]

In the case of Nicaragua, the Reagan administration supported the contras, based in Honduras, in their efforts to topple the Sandinistas. Their gruesome human rights record, however, led to a wave of protests and the passage of three amendments through the Senate prohibiting the use of US funds to overthrow the Nicaraguan government. And when the Reagan administration was condemned in the International Court of Justice for mining Nicaragua's main port, eighty thousand Americans signed a Pledge of Resistance committing themselves to civil disobedience if the United States invaded.[69]

The antimilitarist movement took other forms as well. A new organization, Veterans for Peace, was formed in 1985 and called for the closure of the School of the Americas at Fort Benning, Georgia, where many Central American military officers were trained.[70] A sanctuary movement was set up to help thousands of refugees from Central America enter the United States illegally. Witness for Peace, founded in 1983, sent US citizens to war zones in Nicaragua who reported on human rights abuses by the contras.

The mobilization against US proxy wars in Central America always had public opinion on its side. In a sense, antimilitarism was pushing on an open door in the 1980s. It was much harder when the public favored military intervention abroad. It was also difficult to shore up public support for antimilitarism once US troops had been committed, as happened after the start of the first Gulf War in 1991.

Antimilitarism therefore looked like a lost cause after 9/11 as the American public overwhelmingly seemed in favor of armed intervention wherever al-Qaeda was located. And yet the opposite turned out to be the case. Act Now to Stop War and End Racism (ANSWER) was formed three days after the terrorist attacks, while United for Peace and Justice (UFPJ) was created a year later. Both organizations, formed by broad coalitions, held major demonstrations against the second Gulf War not only before the invasion of Iraq in March 2003 but also afterward.[71]

As the invasions of Afghanistan and Iraq turned into quagmires, the American people became more disillusioned than ever with military interventions abroad. Large majorities opposed US troops being sent to Libya, Syria, and Ukraine—all countries where US security interests were heavily engaged after 2010. Even previous military interventions were reevaluated, with a mere 12 percent in 2014 taking pride in US participation against Serbia in the Bosnian War of the 1990s.[72]

A majority of Americans still regard it as "very important" that the United States "maintain superior military power worldwide," but the proportion of the population doing so has dropped sharply (from 68 percent in 2002 to 52 in 2014). Furthermore, this objective is now ranked sixth (out of ten) among foreign policy objectives in the eyes of the public (the most important is considered to be "protecting the jobs of American workers"). Antimilitarism has therefore been gaining ground, as is demonstrated by the large majorities that now think the wars in Afghanistan and Iraq were "not worthwhile."[73]

9.4. ANTI-EXCEPTIONALISTS

The belief that America is "exceptional" and therefore destined to play a hegemonic role in world affairs is deeply rooted in American society and goes back to the days of the first colonizers. Until very recently no serious presidential candidate would survive for long if they denied US exceptionalism and presidents often feel compelled to demonstrate their credentials by emphasizing their belief in it.

Even President Obama, whose "exceptionalist" credentials were at first challenged by his political opponents, was not afraid to use the word on numerous occasions. In 2013, for example, he stated in relation to Syria, "[W]hen, with modest effort and risk, we can stop children from being gassed to death, and thereby make our own children safer over the long run, I believe we should act. That's what makes America different. That's what makes us exceptional."[74] And the following year, at the US Military Academy, he proclaimed: "I believe in American exceptionalism with every fiber of my being."[75]

If the notion of exceptionalism is the foundation of American empire, then those who deny that the United States is exceptional are anti-imperialists. The first anti-exceptionalists were, not surprisingly, to be found among the Native Americans who resisted the expansion of the United States after the War of

Independence. For the leaders of these nations, the incursions of the Americans—as they were now called—were no different to those of the Spanish, French, or British who had preceded them.

Among the leaders was Handsome Lake, a member of the Seneca tribe, whose apocalyptic vision around 1799 would eventually be recorded. In "How America was Discovered," Handsome Lake challenges the foundation myth that provides the basis of US exceptionalism. The story relates how the devil welcomes a young man to his home:

> "Listen to me, young man, and you will be rich. . . . Across the ocean there is a great country of which you have never heard. The people there are virtuous; they have no evil habits or appetites but are honest and single-minded. A great reward is yours if you enter into my plans and carry them out. Here are five things. Carry them over to the people across the ocean and never shall you want for wealth, position or power. Take these cards, this money, this fiddle, this whiskey and this blood corruption and give them all to the people across the water. . . ." The young man thought this a good bargain and promised to do as the man had commanded him. Soon a great flock of ships came over the ocean and white men came swarming into the country bringing with them cards, money, fiddles, whiskey and blood corruption. . . . Now the man who had appeared in the gold palace was the devil and when afterward he saw what his words had done, he said that he had made a great mistake and even he lamented that his evil had been so enormous.[76]

Not all Native Americans were anti-exceptionalists and some, such as the Cherokee Elias Boudinot, argued that only through assimilation with the Indians could the white population achieve their vision of the "city upon the hill."[77] Boudinot, however, was murdered in 1839 and it became increasingly difficult to argue that there was a place for Native Americans in US society. They had no automatic right of citizenship until 1924 and official discourse openly referred to their eventual disappearance.

Native Americans, however, did not disappear, and their numbers started to increase in the twentieth century. From a low point of 266,732 in 1900, the figure had reached 377,273 in 1950. In 1960, however, for the first time the Census Bureau allowed respondents to choose their ethnic category, and the number jumped to 551,636. Since then the Native American population has grown exponentially and in 2010 reached 5,220,579 (1.7 percent of the total population). Furthermore, the jump between 2000 and 2010 (26.7 percent) was the fastest increase of all categories in the census.[78]

The growth in numbers is impressive, and it has gone hand in hand with an increase in political organization. The National Congress of American Indians (NCAI) was formed in 1944, the National Indian Youth Council (NIYC) in 1961, and the American Indian Movement (AIM) in 1968. AIM was heavily involved in the seventy-one–day occupation of the town of Wounded Knee in 1973, an incident that received extensive national coverage thanks in part to the extraordinary success of the book *Bury My Heart at Wounded Knee* published three years earlier.[79]

Ideological disputes over what direction Native Americans should take have weakened the movement's political impact and have led to organizational splits. These should not, however, obscure the pioneering role that American Indians have played in promoting anti-exceptionalism in the United States. And disputes over insensitive references to Native Americans in sport and education demonstrate that a growing proportion of Americans of all ethnicities are no longer comfortable with the conventional, and exceptionalist, interpretations of an imperial past.[80]

The first anti-exceptionalists were found among the Native Americans, but they were soon joined by many African Americans. The experience of slavery was utterly inconsistent with the rhetoric of exceptionalism, and the British had tried to exploit this in the War of Independence through Lord Dunmore's proclamation offering those slaves held by rebels their freedom if they fought on the other side.[81]

The same tactic was used, this time with more success, by the British in the War of 1812. Admiral Sir George Cockburn recruited a Corps of Colonial Marines from "people of colour" and wrote to his superiors in London that large numbers of escaped slaves could be recruited. He asserted that their participation on the British side was motivated by their desire "to obtain settlements in the British colonies in North America where they will be most useful subjects from their hatred to the citizens of the United States."[82]

As more and more blacks won their freedom, African Americans became heavily involved in the campaign to end slavery. The abolitionists—white as well as black—never used the word "anti-exceptionalism," but their emphasis on the injustice and unfairness of the "peculiar institution" laid bare the contrast between the myth of exceptionalism and the reality of life for the vast majority of African Americans.

This contrast did not end with the Thirteenth Amendment. Nearly twenty-five years after the end of slavery, Frederick Douglass reminded his audience of the unexceptional nature of American history when he declared, "I deny and utterly scout the idea, that there is now, properly speaking, any such thing as a negro problem before the American people. It is not the negro, educated or illiterate, intelligent or ignorant, who is on trial, or whose qualities are giving trouble to the nation. . . . The real question, the all-commanding question, is whether American justice, American liberty, American civilization, American law, and American Christianity can be made to include and protect, alike and forever, all American citizens."[83]

Douglass died three years before the start of the Spanish-American War. African Americans mostly opposed this venture into formal colonialism and it might have been natural for them to join the Anti-Imperialist League (AIL) in large numbers. However, AIL was a very white organization and, in addition, some of its members were racists who had only joined because they did not want nonwhite Filipinos to become US citizens.

As a result, African Americans joined other organizations such as the Colored National Anti-Imperialist League or the even more explicitly named National Negro Anti-Expansion, Anti-Imperialist, Anti-Trust and Anti-Lynching League. W. E. B. Du Bois, who would later cofound the National Association for the Advancement of Colored People (NAACP), made the connection between overseas expansion and Jim Crow laws when he asked, "Where in the world may we go and be safe from lying and brute force?"[84] Kelly Miller, a mathematics and sociology professor at Howard University, emphasized the parallels between discrimination at home and abroad when he wrote, "Acquiescence on the part of the negro in the political rape upon the Filipino would give ground of justification to the assaults upon his rights at home. The Filipino is at least his equal in capacity for self-government. The negro would show himself unworthy of the rights which he claims should he deny the same to a struggling people under another sky."[85]

The anti-exceptionalist discourse in African American struggles continued throughout the twentieth century and beyond. When the Civil Rights Congress (founded in 1946) charged the US government with genocide against African Americans at the United Nations, it was explicitly rejecting American exceptionalism.[86] And when Muhammad Ali refused to serve in the US Army during the Vietnam War, he spoke for many when he said,

> Why should they ask me to put on a uniform and go 10,000 miles from home and drop bombs and bullets on Brown people in Vietnam while so-called Negro people in Louisville are treated like dogs and denied simple human rights? No I'm not going 10,000 miles from home to help murder and burn another poor nation simply to continue the domination of white slave masters of the darker people the world over. This is the day when such evils must come

to an end. I have been warned that to take such a stand would cost me millions of dollars. But I have said it once and I will say it again. The real enemy of my people is here.[87]

African American protests against the Vietnam War were closely allied with the civil rights movement in the 1960s. All civil rights leaders were opposed to the war, but the war made it possible to link the protest movement to the domestic struggle for human rights through the language of anti-exceptionalism. Martin Luther King Jr. spoke of "the greatest purveyor of violence in the world today—my own government,"[88] while Malcolm X (Box 9.4) linked the black liberation struggle to that of national liberation movements around the world. And Stokely Carmichael argued against conscription on the grounds that it involved "white people sending black people to make war on yellow people in order to defend the land they stole from red people."[89]

Anti-exceptionalism among African Americans did not end with desegregation and massive expansion of the black middle class, but it continued to cause controversy among those Americans who believed in the exceptionalist myth. When Jeremiah Wright (pastor to Barack Obama before he became president) gave a sermon in 2003 on God and government, he used anti-exceptionalist language that would not have seemed particularly shocking to his African American audience, but the revelation in 2008 that the future US president had regularly attended the church where the words were uttered made huge waves in the mainstream media.[90]

The belief in American exceptionalism among the white population was until recently so deep-rooted that previous generations of anti-imperialists would have objected to being labeled anti-exceptionalists. Perhaps a few staunch abolitionists such as John Brown, Harriet Beecher Stowe, and William Lloyd Garrison might have been willing to wear the label, but Jane Addams (Box 9.1), Patrick Buchanan (Box 9.2), and William Fulbright (Box 9.3) all embraced American exceptionalism despite their anti-imperialism and, indeed, used it as the standard by which to judge US behavior in foreign affairs.

This has now changed. In a 2014 Pew Research Center survey that surprised many, only 15 percent of "millennials" (those born in the early 1980s and later) claimed that the United States was "the greatest country in the world." For the nation as a whole the figure was higher, but was still at only 28 percent. Indeed, not a single category of those polled voted in a majority in answer to the question.[91] Since exceptionalists have always believed that America *is* the greatest country in the world, the survey indicated by how much support for exceptionalism has fallen in recent years.

BOX 9.4

MALCOLM X (1925–65)

There was nothing in the early life of Malcolm Little to suggest any-thing remarkable. Born in Omaha, Nebraska, in 1925, he dropped out of high school, engaged in petty crime, and was sentenced to jail in 1946. There, however, he was radicalized, joined Elijah Muhammad's Nation of Islam, and changed his name to Malcolm X.

He worked for the Nation of Islam on leaving prison in 1952 and was very successful in building up its membership. His oratorical powers brought him a large following inside the United States and recognition outside. He came to the attention of a number of foreign leaders, mainly from Africa, who helped him to make the connection between their na-tional liberation movements and what he saw as the anticolonial struggles of African Americans themselves.

This made him an anti-exceptionalist, but he was suspicious at first of the civil rights movement led by Martin Luther King Jr. and its emphasis on nonviolence. It was not until he broke with the Nation of Islam in 1964 and founded the Organization of Afro-American Unity that he became— with some qualifications—reconciled to the movement's goals.

Malcolm X was murdered in 1965 and was buried as Al Hajj Malik al-Shabazz. At the time of his death he was still a divisive figure in the black community and reviled by white society. Martin Luther King Jr., on the other hand, had been awarded the Nobel Peace Prize in 1964, and his as-sassination in 1968 united the nation in grief.

The passage of time has dramatically softened the perception of Mal-colm X. Helped by his autobiography (published shortly after his death) and by Spike Lee's 1992 biopic, the public was able to see that Malcolm X by the end of his life sought to heal the wounds in American society rather than deepen them.

Today he has become a respected figure, with schools, roads, and hospi-tals named after him. It is a classic story of redemption, but the transfor-mation in his perception can also be seen as a metaphor for rejection of the exceptionalist myth by so many Americans.

The cornerstone on which US imperialism has been constructed—American exceptionalism—is therefore crumbling and the edifice is being challenged from within the empire. That is why it is possible to say with some confidence that the US empire is in retreat. Why this is so, and how it has come about, is the subject of the next three chapters.

10

THE US ECONOMY

The fortunes of imperial powers have always been highly correlated with the size and performance of their economies. A large economy provides the resources that empires need to match their ambitions, while a growing economy normally ensures that most of the citizens of the imperial power share in the benefits. Without these attributes, an imperial economy becomes vulnerable to attack from outside militarily or to being undermined from inside politically.

The United States was far from being the largest economy in the world after the War of Independence, but it grew rapidly by the standards of the time as a result of productivity increases and net inward migration. By the 1870s it had become the biggest in the world as measured by gross domestic product (GDP). However, its share of the global economy is now shrinking and on some measures of GDP it is no longer the largest.

The *relative* decline of the US economy is therefore not in dispute. Indeed, the same is happening to other advanced capitalist countries, but it matters more for the United States as its semiglobal empire was only made possible by virtue of the size of its economy relative to others. With the US share now shrinking, its ability to protect—let alone extend—its imperial interests is being called into question.

Empires normally export capital to other parts of the world, using surpluses in the current account of the balance of payments as means of payment. Control of foreign assets then provides influence for the imperial power even outside its formal empire. Imperial powers in western Europe followed this path, as did the Soviet Union, and now China is doing the same.

This was also the model followed by the American semiglobal empire after the Second World War. However, the outflow of capital is no longer financed by surpluses in the current account, as the United States has gone from being a creditor to a debtor. Outflows of capital are therefore financed by even larger inflows—in the form either of foreign direct investment (FDI) or portfolio capital. America is now heavily dependent on these capital inflows from abroad, imposing constraints on what the nation can or cannot do and undermining its imperial position.

The US economy was for generations noted for its innovation and high levels of capital accumulation. Everyone, including the country's greatest critics, such as Vladimir Lenin, marveled at American "know-how" and the technological changes in its industrial and agricultural systems. These helped to sustain imperial expansion, since investment and innovation are prerequisites for a successful empire. Without them imperial economies stagnate and become dangerously dependent on foreign technology.

US innovation and capital accumulation have not come to an end, but they have diminished in importance. Net of capital consumption, domestic investment is in decline as a share of GDP, and one of the most serious consequences has been underinvestment in US infrastructure. Investment in "human capital" (i.e., the quality of the future labor force), has also lagged behind many competitor nations, and the United States has fallen down the ranking of countries on many educational indices despite the high quality of its top universities. Last but not least, the pace of technological change has dropped significantly in the last twenty years.

All this puts pressure on the ability of the American empire to maintain its global hegemony. However, what is really forcing a reexamination of America's place in the world is the rise in inequality in the last forty years. Once noted for its relatively egalitarian distribution of income, if not wealth, the United States has now become the most unequal among industrialized countries with a startling shift of income from the bottom 90 percent to the top 10 percent.

This shift, resulting in the stagnation of real wages and salaries for more than a generation and a fall in social mobility, has left many Americans wondering about their future and questioning the American dream. It also raises uncomfortable questions about an imperial system that can no longer assure a rising standard of living for so many of its citizens. Why, some are asking, should the state exercise such enormous external commitments in pursuit of a semiglobal empire when it cannot deliver basic services to its own people? It is a question that is becoming increasingly difficult to answer.

There are, of course, the optimists who believe that the rate of growth of the US economy can be doubled through massive infrastructure spending and the "onshoring" of high-paid manufacturing jobs. This, it is argued, would slow down the outflow of capital and therefore make the United States less dependent on capital inflows from the rest of the world. Indeed, this is the thinking behind the economic nationalism of President Donald Trump's administration (2017–), and it has proved popular with many voters.

Some of this may come to pass, but a doubling of long-term economic growth on a sustainable basis requires a massive increase in productivity. Given what is happening in other advanced capitalist countries, this is highly improbable. And faster growth would almost certainly require an increase in net immigration, for which there is no political support. Thus, the relative decline of the US economy is set to continue, driving America toward a further retreat from empire.

10.1. RELATIVE DECLINE

There are many ways in which the relative decline of the US economy can be demonstrated. However, not all of these are relevant to the issue of imperial power. In an age of globalization it does not matter very much for the health of the American empire that it makes a declining share of the world's steel, for example, nor that most of its automobiles are no longer considered state of the art.

There are even areas in which a relative decline is a sign of imperial strength, rather than the opposite. A good example is that the US share of global carbon emissions is now falling—albeit from a very high level—as a result of both structural change and efficiency gains in many sectors. This makes it easier for the United States to claim a leadership role in international negotiations, should it wish to do so, not only on climate change but in other areas as well.

So which are the metrics that do matter when measuring relative decline? There are three areas of special importance for American imperial power in the age of the semiglobal empire. The first is economic size, for which some measure of GDP is usually taken as a proxy. The second is foreign trade, normally measured by the gross value of exports and imports of goods and services. The third is the value of net capital outflows, especially FDI by US multinational enterprises (MNEs). Each of these will be considered in turn.

The overall size of the American economy relative to the rest of the world is very important, since the willingness of other countries to allow the United States to shape the global "rules of the game" was predicated on its hegemonic economic position at the end of the Second World War. Military power on its own would have been insufficient, and any settlement imposed by force would have broken down before long. It would also have been unsustainable without a large and growing economy.

Of course, the United States could not possibly have expected to maintain forever the dominant position it enjoyed in 1945. The subsequent recovery of the rest of the world—especially Europe, Japan, and the Soviet Union—was bound to produce a relative decline in the size of the US economy. Yet what is striking is how *modest* this change in share was for the first four decades. Indeed, the United States was still responsible for between 20 and 30 percent of world GDP in the mid-1980s depending on which measure is used.[1]

No other country came close to this share, which is why other countries in the semiglobal empire accepted US leadership in global economic affairs with only minor reservations. It was, for example, the United States that led all global trade negotiations after the war. In particular, it launched the crucial Uruguay Round in 1985 that finished in 1994 and established the World Trade Organization. Without American leadership, none of this would have happened.

Since the mid-1980s, however, the relative decline of the US economy has been rapid and has proceeded with almost no interruptions. This can be demonstrated most clearly by using the measure of GDP that converts national currencies to US dollars at their purchasing power parity (PPP) exchange rate.[2] The results are shown in Figure 10.1, which uses not only historical data from 1980 up to the present but also forecasts for the next few years provided by the IMF.

Figure 10.1 shows that by 2021 the global share of the US economy is expected to have fallen to just over 14 percent. Furthermore, IMF forecasts assume a relatively robust performance by the US economy, albeit at a lower rate than the world economy as a whole.[3] Thus, this projection is if anything on the optimistic side and the US economy could represent an even smaller share by then.

Figure 10.1 can also be used to predict the fall in the share of the US economy in the years *beyond* 2021. If the annual decline is the same as between 2000 and 2021, then the US share of the world economy will have fallen to 12.2 percent by 2030, to 9.1 percent by 2040, and to 6 percent by 2050. Not even the most convinced imperialist would expect the United States to be able to maintain its current semiglobal empire under such circumstances.

It is easy to assume that the decline in the US share is simply a reflection of the spectacular growth of the Chinese economy in the last few decades. China has indeed grown rapidly and overtook the United States as the largest economy in the world on a PPP basis in 2014. However, this is by no means the only reason for the fall in the US share. Among the twenty largest economies in the world (the G20), the United States since 2000 has had a slower rate of growth of GDP (measured at constant prices) than all of them except five.[4]

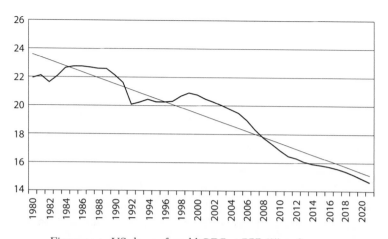

Figure 10.1. US share of world GDP at PPP (%), 1980–2021.
Source: Derived by the author from World Bank, *World Development Indicators*, and IMF, *World Economic Outlook.*

The US falling share of global GDP is an important signal that imperial retreat is under way, but it is not the only one. The second is the US share of world trade—not just in goods but services as well. The semiglobal empire was based on a dominant position for the United States in global commerce as a result of its ability to shape the institutional architecture for globalization and establish until recently a privileged position for itself.

Trade performance was critical for the fortunes of many European empires, especially Denmark, France, Holland, Portugal, Spain, Sweden, and the United Kingdom. Trade played a less important part in the early US territorial empire, however, as economic policy concentrated heavily on import-substitution in the nineteenth century. This began to change in the first half of the twentieth century when a serious effort was made to open up foreign markets to American goods, but it was only after the Second World War that trade liberalization became a strategic priority.

The US share of world trade in goods and services never reached the same level as its share of global GDP, but it had come close by the end of the twentieth century. Trade liberalization was working to America's advantage, and its share of the world total peaked at 16.2 percent in the year 2000 (see Figure 10.2).[5] And because imports of goods and services were much larger than exports of goods and services, their share of the global total reached 18.6 percent at that time.[6]

BOX 10.1

OIL DEPENDENCE AND AMERICAN EMPIRE

Oil dependence (the share of consumption that is imported) has been a major determinant of modern empires. Soon after becoming First Lord of the Admiralty in 1911, Winston Churchill made the momentous decision to convert the British Navy from coal to oil. With no domestic oil production, his government then extended the British empire in the Middle East in the search for secure supplies.

When President Franklin Delano Roosevelt (1933–45) met King Abdul Aziz Ibn Saud in 1943, immediately after the Yalta Conference, he declared Saudi Arabian oil vital to American strategic interests. At a stroke, the US empire was thrust deep into the Middle East and has remained there ever since.

At the time of the meeting the United States was a net exporter of oil, but FDR knew that this was about to change. By 1950 net imports of oil had reached 8.4 percent of consumption and by 1978 they had reached 42.5 percent. Twenty years later the share exceeded 50 percent before peaking at 60.3 percent in 2005.

By then Canada had replaced Saudi Arabia as the principal source of imports (it was 40 percent in 2015). However, no American government could afford to retreat from its empire in the Middle East as long as the US economy was so dependent on supplies from the region.

Since then, two things have happened. The economy has become much more fuel-efficient through technological change, especially in transport, and there has been a shift to less energy-intensive sectors. At the same time, US production of oil started to increase through the use of biofuels and fracking. As a result, oil dependence had fallen sharply by 2015 to 24 percent, with only 16 percent of imports (equivalent to 3.8 percent of consumption) coming from the Middle East.

Oil dependence is therefore rapidly disappearing as an argument for American empire in the Middle East. Of course, the executive may wish to stay for other reasons, but they will no longer be able to justify it in terms of oil. Imperial retreat is therefore a real possibility.

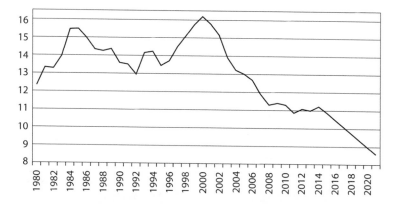

Figure 10.2. US share of world trade in goods and services (%), 1980–2021.
Source: For 1980–2014, derived by the author from World Bank, *World Development Indicators;* later years are forecasts assuming the same annual change in the US share as occurred between 2000 and 2014.

Since the start of the new millennium, however, the US share of global trade in goods and services has fallen steeply. Furthermore, the decline has been rapid for *both* exports and imports.[7] The United States is no longer the world's largest exporter of goods and services, having been replaced by China in 2014, although it is still the largest importer. And if the annual change in the US trade share between 2000 and 2014 is projected into the future, then it will have fallen to 8.6 percent by 2021.[8]

This helps to explain the failure of the United States to bring the Doha Round of trade negotiations, launched in 2001, to a successful conclusion. The United States, with its rapidly declining share of global trade, is no longer in a position to force negotiations to a successful conclusion. Instead, it prefers to concentrate on preferential trade agreements (PTAs) with a smaller number of countries where it can more easily impose its will.

The third indication of relative decline is provided by the US share of net outward FDI.[9] A typical feature of empires is a surplus on the trade account of the balance of payments matched by capital outflows. The United Kingdom was in this position for almost the whole of the nineteenth century, and its export of capital to different countries played a key part in sustaining the British Empire.

The United States moved into this position in the last quarter of the nineteenth century when merchandise exports overtook imports.[10] From then onward, American private capital flowed in increasing quantities to different parts of the world, including countries in both its territorial and also informal

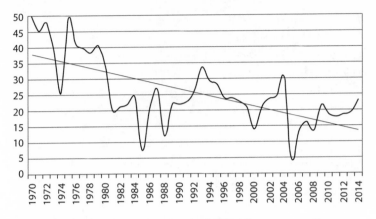

Figure 10.3. US share of net outward FDI (%), 1970–2014. *Source:*
Derived by the author from World Bank, *World Development Indicators.*

empire, such as Cuba and Mexico, respectively.[11] This outflow coincided with
the formation of the first American MNEs, which would come to dominate the
export of US capital.

Outward FDI by American companies did not stop in the interwar years, but
flows were disrupted by the Second World War. Opening foreign markets to
penetration by US capital was therefore a strategic priority after the war and the
policy was largely successful. In 1970, for example, US companies accounted for
half the net outflow of FDI (see Figure 10.3), and almost certainly as large a proportion of the global stock.[12]

FDI outflows are subject to marked volatility from one year to the next. Since
1970, however, there has been a clear downward trend in the US share (see Figure 10.3). Furthermore, the US share of the global *stock* of outward FDI, which
is much less volatile, has shown a similar trend. In 2014, for example, it had
fallen to just under 25 percent, having been nearly 40 percent as recently as
2000.[13]

One quarter of the world's stock of net outward FDI is still a very large share,
and the absolute value (US$6.3 trillion) is enormous. It is a tribute to the global
nature of many US firms and their massive investments around the world. However, the US share of both flows and stocks is clearly trending downward. And
the downward trend is likely to continue. The tax laws that encouraged such
large outflows in the past are no longer so favorable as they were and are likely
to become even less so in the future.[14] US hard power, regularly used in the past
in defense of US MNEs, is no longer so feasible as an option. The US government and the MNEs increasingly have to rely on the arbitration systems estab-

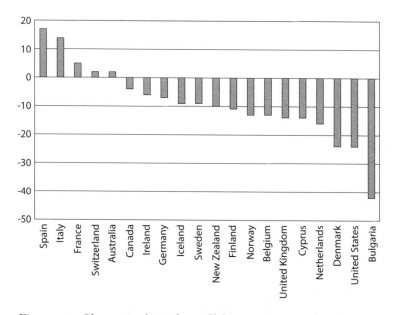

Figure 10.4. Changes in the ranking of life expectancy among top twenty countries, 1960 and 2014. *Source:* Derived by the author from World Bank, *World Development Indicators.*

lished under bilateral and multilateral investment treaties where the outcome cannot so easily be assured.

The three metrics chosen to demonstrate US relative economic decline are the most important for the issue of imperial power. However, there is one other measure that is worth reporting—life expectancy. This serves as a proxy for relative economic and social health and is often used to measure a country's progress. The United States has never had the highest life expectancy in the world, but in 1960 it was nearly seventy years (only four years lower than Norway, the highest-ranked country at that time).[15]

If we now rank life expectancy among the top twenty independent countries in 1960 and compare it with the same countries today, we can see how each country's ranking has changed over these years (see Figure 10.4). The United States has been the worst performer (apart from Bulgaria), since life expectancy has not improved by anything like as much as elsewhere. Furthermore, life expectancy in the United States is now lower than in Chile, Costa Rica, and Cuba, not to mention three US colonies (Guam, Puerto Rico, and the Virgin Islands).[16]

Figures 10.1–10.4 shown here demonstrate the extent of US relative economic decline in recent years. This does not mean the US economy is in absolute decline (it is clearly not), but several features of its performance have posed challenges for the maintenance of American empire. Coupled with the relative decline, they help to explain the imperial retreat that is now under way. It is to these that we now turn.

10.2. FROM CREDITOR TO DEBTOR

After the Second World War, the US economy swiftly moved back into a position of surplus both in terms of the government budget and even more so in terms of the current account of the balance of payments. And, despite the strains imposed by military spending during the Cold War, the economy continued on a relatively normal path until the beginning of the 1960s.

At that point, a "new normal" took hold. The Vietnam War massively increased public expenditure, federal government net savings turned negative and the budget deficit rose significantly.[17] Then in the 1970s surpluses in the current account of the balance of payments gave way to deficits, and by the end of the 1980s the United States had become a net debtor, with its holdings of international assets falling below the value of US assets held by foreigners.[18]

The capital outflows continued (indeed, they increased), but they now had to be financed by borrowing from abroad. Were it not for the privileged position given to the United States by its ability to issue debt exclusively in its own currency and the continued use of the dollar as the main international reserve currency, a crisis would undoubtedly have occurred forcing major structural changes in the American economy.

The "new normal" was therefore very far from being a healthy situation, and it has brought into question the very nature of the semiglobal empire. To understand this, it is necessary to engage in some simple accounting. The output (GDP) of a country can be expressed as the sum of private consumption and investment, public spending, and exports less imports. However, output is the same as income, which in turn is equal to the sum of spending and savings from all sources. A little arithmetic then yields the simple identity:

Private Investment plus Government Deficit
equals
Private Savings plus Current Account Deficit[19]

This equation is called an identity since it is true at all times for all countries. However, it is written in this form to account for the peculiarities of the American economy in the last few decades. If the government deficit increases, for example, without any change in private investment or private savings, then the current account deficit (imports less exports) must also increase (and vice versa). And if private savings are roughly equal to private investment, then the two deficits must be the same.[20]

Let us look first at private investment. The Bureau of Economic Analysis (BEA), the official source for the US national accounts, breaks this down into business investment in structures, equipment, and intellectual property products together with household residential investment. There is also a small component that represents changes in private inventories.

When expressed as a percentage of GDP, the main change in the last fifty years has been the increase in investment in intellectual property products by businesses. During this long period there have also been marked business cycles leading to rises and falls in the share of private investment in GDP. These included a rise in the 1970s, a fall in the 1980s, a rise in the 1990s, and a fall in the first decade of the twenty-first century, followed by a rise since the end of the Great Recession (2007–9).

However, what is striking about gross private investment—given all the other changes in the US economy—is the absence of a long-run trend in its overall share of GDP despite the rise in investment in intellectual property products. The share has fluctuated between 15 and 20 percent with only one exception— the collapse during the Great Recession (2007–9). Thus, we need to look elsewhere to understand why the United States has gone from being a (net) creditor to a (net) debtor.

We do not need to look too far. The next item in the identity above is the government deficit, and its size has been a matter of concern for many years. Yet the American government by tradition has been fiscally conservative, only running large deficits during national emergencies. Indeed, before the Second World War budget deficits in peacetime were the exception rather than the rule.

When the Second World War ended, the American public once again made clear its preference for balanced budgets: "In August 1946, in connection with the winding down of the war effort, respondents were asked 'Which do you think is more important to do in the coming year—balance the budget or cut income taxes?' Seventy-one percent thought it was more important to balance the budget, with only 20% giving priority to the tax cut."[21]

Given these attitudes, it is not surprising that the fiscal deficit was either small or nonexistent for many years after the Second World War, Congress even resisting a proposed tax cut by President John F. Kennedy (1961–63) in 1962 for fear of the budgetary consequences.

Imperial commitments, however, would soon trump fiscal rectitude. The Vietnam War led to a surge in government spending and the fiscal deficit

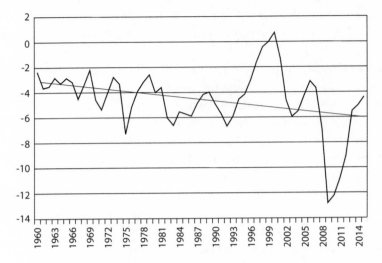

Figure 10.5. Government deficit as share of GDP (%), 1960–2015.
Source: Derived by the author from US Bureau of Economic Analysis
website, http://www.bea.gov.

increased significantly (see Figure 10.5). Numerous attempts were subsequently made to eliminate the deficit, but only one of them succeeded. This was during the second administration of President Bill Clinton (1997–2001), when a combination of tax changes and good fortune briefly restored the fiscal accounts to surplus.[22] The deficit soon returned, however, and the trend line in Figure 10.5 makes clear how it has widened in the last half century.

The government deficit aggregates federal and state fiscal accounts. Many states have encountered problems and continue to do so, but they are subject to much greater constraints when it comes to running deficits than the federal government. It is no surprise to learn, therefore, that the authorities in Washington, DC, have been responsible for most of the deficit, with the ratio varying since 1960 from 60 to 100 percent.

Figure 10.5 gives the deficit as a share of GDP with the trend moving strongly downward after 1960. Some other countries have occasionally had larger deficits as a share of GDP without even having the privilege of issuing debt in their own currency. That is why some Americans are relaxed about the deficit, arguing that this is yet another example of US exceptionalism.

What Figure 10.5 fails to capture, however, is the scale of the absolute numbers. Each year the government deficit is now on average close to $500 billion—a number larger than the GDP of every country in the world except the top fifteen. If this just happened in one year, it would be relatively easy to ignore. However, it reoccurs every year. As a result, from 2001 to 2015 the accumulated deficit was nearly $14 trillion. This is the same as the value of US GDP in 2006.

If private savings had increased significantly, then these large government deficits could have been funded without borrowing from the rest of the world. This would have required a reduction in consumption as a share of GDP and it would have had consequences for the distribution of income, but it would not have threatened the foundations of the semiglobal empire.

What actually happened, however, was the exact opposite. Private savings as a share of GDP *declined* rather than increased. This was not because business saved less but because households increased their consumption. Personal savings, which had been nearly 10 percent of GDP in the first half of the 1970s, had almost disappeared forty years later.[23]

The reasons for this decline in personal savings are well known. American households became addicted to debt, aided by a financial and marketing system that found ever more ingenious ways of encouraging an increase in consumption. As a result, consumer credit debt (excluding mortgages) as a share of GDP has risen almost without interruption and at the beginning of 2016 stood at a record 20 percent.[24]

The fall in private savings left the United States with no alternative other than to borrow from abroad (see the identity above). The current account of the balance of payments therefore moved into deficit. The balance between exports and imports of goods, which had been in surplus for roughly a century, turned negative in 1971 and then permanently from 1976 onward. The current account followed suit, becoming permanently in deficit from 1982 onward with the exception of just one year.

At first the deficits were modest. In 1982, for example, the United States borrowed a "mere" $11.6 billion. Within three years, however, the numbers were above $100 billion and by 2000 exceeded $400 billion. In one year (2006), they even exceeded $800 billion. And the average level of borrowing in the first fifteen years of the new century was above $500 billion.

Foreigners have been offered a vast array of US assets from which to choose including bonds, equities, companies, real estate, and even works of art. Generally they have responded positively, seeing the United States as a safe haven despite the low yield on many of the assets (especially government debt). Almost every year, in consequence, the value of the stock of assets owned by foreigners rose—not only in absolute terms but also as a percentage of GDP.

US administrations professed not to mind. At first it was not difficult to understand why. The foreigners buying companies were overwhelmingly private firms from western Europe or Japan whose governments were either members of NATO or tied to the United States by security alliances. Those buying government bonds were often governments or institutions from the same countries.

The borrowing requirement, however, has been so large that the purchase of US assets is no longer limited to those whose security interests are closely aligned with those of America. All foreign countries with large surpluses in the current account of their balance of payments have been recycling funds into the United States, as it is the home to the widest range of assets with the greatest liquidity. These countries include China and—until the collapse of oil prices in 2015—Russia, Saudi Arabia, and Venezuela.

The stock of external assets (i.e., those US assets owned by foreigners) is now much larger than the country's GDP. Best known are the US federal government debt obligations held by foreigners. At the end of the fiscal year 2016, these were valued at $6.3 trillion—roughly one-third of the total.[25] Then there are the debts of the financial system to foreigners together with the debts of the nonfinancial sector and intercompany loans to give a grand total of $19 trillion for the gross external debt position of the United States.[26]

Large though this figure is, it is by no means the end of the story. The stock of net inward FDI was valued at $5.4 trillion at the end of 2015 and includes some of the most iconic names in American business that are now under foreign ownership.[27] Then there are those assets controlled by foreigners, such as residential housing, on which it is difficult to place a value together with others whose ownership is obscured by complex trust arrangements. Altogether, the value of external assets owned by foreigners could be as much as $30 trillion.

The extent of these US external assets, and their continued growth as a result of US borrowing every year, has major implications for the semiglobal empire. As interest rates increase, the cost of issuing new debt and servicing the existing stock of external assets will rise. America eventually will be forced to live within its means, and that is bound to include a reduction in military spending, which in this century has been roughly the same every year as the United States borrows from abroad. Imperial retreat, already under way, will follow.

Yet many Americans remain in denial. The United States, it is said, can not only issue debt to foreigners at low rates of interest but can also make a much higher return on the foreign assets it currently holds and turn a profit in the process despite the country being a net debtor.[28] Another argument, reminiscent of one used by John Maynard Keynes, is that foreigners whose US assets are large in value acquire a strong stake in the maintenance of the *status quo*.[29] Others

BOX 10.2

US EXTERNAL ASSETS AND SAUDI ARABIA

When the US Senate unanimously passed a bill in May 2016 that would allow relatives of the victims of 9/11 to sue any Saudi officials implicated in the attacks, Saudi Arabia announced that it would be forced to sell its US external assets in order to protect itself from court action if the bill went into law.

The Saudi foreign minister put a figure of $750 billion on the value of the assets. This took everyone by surprise, as Saudi holdings of government bonds and other assets were not publicly known at the time, being buried in US Treasury statistics among the holdings of "Middle Eastern oil-exporting countries."

The US Treasury responded by revealing for the first time that Saudi Arabia held at the end of March 2016 nearly $120 billion of its bonds. The Saudi stock of foreign direct investment is also known by the US authorities, but is still not revealed to the public (the BEA claims that this is done "to avoid disclosure of data of individual companies"). However, even the most generous estimates put it no higher than $30 billion.

That left a gap of at least $600 billion between what the Saudi government claimed in assets and what the US statistics revealed. Part of this gap will be due to the use of other jurisdictions, such as the Cayman Islands, for Saudi purchase of Treasury bonds. In addition, some Saudi foreign direct investment is not classified as FDI as it does not reach the level needed to establish "control." And assets owned by individuals may not be classified as Saudi Arabian if their beneficial owners have chosen to conceal their identity.

Even after making all these adjustments, it is hard to close the gap entirely, suggesting that the Saudi foreign minister may have been economical with the truth. In addition, questions were raised as to how the assets could be liquidated without doing serious damage to the Saudi economy.

The Senate bill duly passed Congress, despite having to overcome a presidential veto, but the resolution gave just enough discretion to the executive for Saudi Arabia not to carry out her threat. However, the episode temporarily damaged US relations with the kingdom and increased the chances that the imperial links will one day be severed.

have argued that the imbalances in the US economy will be self-correcting and that no remedial action need therefore be taken.[30]

History teaches us that net borrowers are normally at a serious disadvantage in international affairs. Greece and other heavily indebted countries discovered this to their cost in the eurozone crisis after 2008. When the United States was a net creditor, it was not afraid to use its bargaining power to devastating effect, even with its allies.[31] It is unrealistic to assume that other creditor countries will not behave in the same way as and when the opportunity arises (Box 10.2).

10.3. CAPITAL AND INNOVATION

Successful empires need to invest heavily for the future, relying as far as possible on a stream of innovations produced by their citizens if they are to maintain their dominant position. By contrast, an inability to promote technological change through domestic inventions is a sure sign that an empire is in trouble. By the end of the eighteenth century, for example, the Ottoman Empire had become heavily dependent on foreign missions to keep it competitive in naval warfare and its European rivals were quick to take advantage.[32]

For at least two centuries after independence, the US empire demonstrated enormous dynamism when it came to capital accumulation and innovation. Inventions flowed thick and fast—indeed, the process had begun even before independence—giving the United States a well-earned reputation for technological progress and entrepreneurial spirits.

Robert Gordon has studied this process in depth in the case of the United States:

> A useful organizing principle to understand the pace of growth since 1750 is the sequence of three industrial revolutions. The first (IR #1) with its main inventions between 1750 and 1830 created steam engines, cotton spinning, and railroads. The second (IR #2) was the most important, with its three central inventions of electricity, the internal combustion engine, and running water with indoor plumbing, in the relatively short interval of 1870 to 1900. Both the first two revolutions required about 100 years for their full effects to percolate through the economy. During the two decades 1950–70 the benefits of the IR #2 were still transforming the economy, including air conditioning, home appliances, and the interstate highway system. . . . The computer and Internet revolution (IR #3) began around 1960 and reached its climax in the dot.com era of the late 1990s.[33]

These three industrial revolutions have played a key part in the growth of US GDP since independence. The growth itself, however, can be attributed not just to the accumulation of capital but to other factors as well. This can be shown formally in an accounting framework known as the Cobb-Douglas production function that economists have used for generations. At its simplest, it states that GDP growth can be explained by the accumulation of capital and labor inputs as well as the efficiency with which these two inputs are combined (total factor productivity—TFP).

TFP is the X factor in growth and in many ways the most important. It clearly depends on advances in technology, but that is not a sufficient explanation. A study on TFP in the United States done by the IMF gives a good definition of what is involved: "In general, TFP captures the efficiency with which labor and capital are combined to generate output. This depends not only on businesses' ability to innovate but also on the extent to which they operate in an institutional, regulatory, and legal environment that fosters competition, removes unnecessary administrative burden, provides modern and efficient infrastructure, and allows easy access to finance."[34]

The three elements in the Cobb-Douglas model—capital, labor, and TFP—powered the US economy successfully for decades and helped it to achieve global dominance. All three elements, however, are now less effective in securing growth, and this has added to the pressures on the American empire. Why this is so requires an explanation. We will start with capital accumulation.

It was noted above (see Section 10.2) that gross private investment as a share of GDP has remained fairly stable in the United States for many years. However, what matters for economic growth is *net* investment (i.e., gross investment less the consumption of fixed capital). This depreciation, as it is often called, depends to some extent on the tax regime, and this became increasingly generous after 1980. In consequence, the consumption of fixed capital has gone from around 50 percent of gross private investment before 1980 to nearly 80 percent today.[35]

The result has been a decline in *net* private domestic investment as a share of GDP (see the top line in Figure 10.6). The share averaged around 8 percent before 1980, but then started to fall. It even turned negative during the Great Recession because the consumption of fixed capital was greater than gross investment. And the recovery since then has only raised the ratio to 4 percent (half of what it was before 1980).

If net *public* investment had increased to take up the slack, this might not have mattered so much. However, the pressure on federal spending has led to a

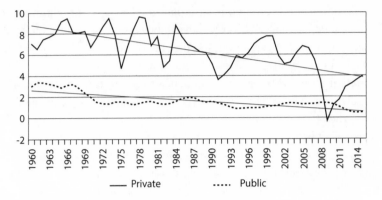

Figure 10.6. Net private and public domestic investment (% of GDP),
1960–2015. *Source:* Derived by the author from US Bureau of Economic
Analysis website, http://www.bea.gov.

cut in public investment and a fall in net public investment as a share of GDP
(see the bottom line in Figure 10.6). Net public investment, which came close
to 4 percent in the 1960s, is now below 1 percent of GDP. And it rose only modestly during the Great Recession, as so much of the fiscal stimulus consisted of
tax cuts and increases in current spending rather than fixed investment.[36]

The fall in the net investment ratio is a big problem for the United States,
because it undermines so much of what underpins its role as the global hegemon. For example, one of the main casualties from the decline in the net
investment ratio (public and private) has been spending on infrastructure,
which is crucial for enterprise competitiveness.[37] The United States, first in the
world as recently as 1990 on some measures, has been drifting down international league tables of countries ranked by the quantity and quality of their infrastructure. In many surveys, the United States is no longer in the top ten.[38]

Most citizens and many visitors have experienced the dire state of American
infrastructure that ranges from crumbling bridges to clogged roads and rusty
pipes. In the words of the American Society of Civil Engineers (ASCE), "For
the U.S. economy to be the most competitive in the world, we need a first class
infrastructure system—transport systems that move people and goods efficiently
and at reasonable cost by land, water, and air; transmission systems that deliver
reliable, low-cost power from a wide range of energy sources; and water systems
that drive industrial processes as well as the daily functions in our homes. Yet
today, our infrastructure systems are failing to keep pace with the current and
expanding needs, and investment in infrastructure is faltering."[39]

The ASCE, it might be argued, has a vested interest in exaggerating the woeful state of the nation's infrastructure in view of its association with civil engineering. Yet much the same argument has been put forward more prosaically, but no less effectively, by the President's Council of Economic Advisers:

> In 2014, the average age of public streets and highways, water supply facilities, sewer systems, power facilities, and transportation assets reached historic highs. . . . And the average age of public transit assets increased nearly 20 percent over the decade ended 2014. . . . Many U.S. roadways and bridges, in particular, are in poor condition . . . nearly 21 percent of U.S. roadways provided a substandard ride quality in 2013 . . . the number of bridges that were rated as structurally deficient was just above 61,000, while the number that were rated as functionally obsolete, or inadequate for performing the tasks for which the structures were originally designed, was slightly below 85,000.[40]

The second element in the Cobb-Douglas production function used to explain economic growth is labor. The US economy long ago ceased to depend mainly on unskilled workers, so that the relevant metric for many years has been the quantity of labor inputs adjusted for quality. And the quality of workers depends on investment in "human capital" (i.e., spending on such things as education and health).

Studies invariably show that the most important of these investments in human capital is education.[41] This was recognized early on in the United States where education—public and private—was seen as a priority and the country developed an enviable reputation as a world leader. As early as 1847 Domingo Sarmiento, a Latin American educationalist, came to study the nation's schools and public libraries and used the US system as the model when he became president of Argentina.[42]

US investment in education was spectacularly successful. It increased labor productivity, making possible the payment of high wages, and contributed handsomely to economic growth.[43] Indeed, it was so successful that for a time Americans worried that workers were becoming overeducated with the wage premium for skill steadily falling in the first decades of the twentieth century as the supply of graduates threatened to outstrip demand.[44]

It was therefore something of a shock when in April 1983 the Department of Education released a report entitled *A Nation at Risk: The Imperative for Educational Reform* with these stark words: "We report to the American people that while we can take justifiable pride in what our schools and colleges have historically accomplished and contributed to the United States and the well-being of its people, the educational foundations of our society are presently being eroded by a rising tide of mediocrity that threatens our very future as a Nation and a people. What was unimaginable a generation ago has begun to occur—others are matching and surpassing our educational attainments."[45]

The report turned out to be very prescient. Numerous reforms were undertaken, and much more attention was paid to the problem.[46] However, studies confirmed a *rise* in the wage premium for skilled workers as the supply of education failed to keep pace with the demand for graduates.[47] And the government struggled to close the gap on its competitors as they invested more heavily (and more wisely?) in education, leaving the United States in the latest survey of thirty-five OECD countries in thirty-first position in mathematics, nineteenth in science, and twentieth in reading.[48]

The third, and final element, in the Cobb-Douglas production function is TFP. It is also the most important, as studies of advanced capitalist economies invariably show TFP to play the largest part in the growth story. TFP captures technological progress and innovation, as well as general improvements in managerial systems and logistics, so its rate of change is a good indicator of the dynamism of the business sector.

The US economy was once noted for its fast rate of growth of TFP.[49] It would therefore be easy to assume that TFP growth has remained high given the nation's expenditure on research and development (R&D), its prestigious universities, and its globally renowned high-tech sector (especially in Silicon Valley—see Box 10.3). Yet, with one exception, the growth of TFP has fallen in every decade since the Second World War (see Figure 10.7).

The one exception is the decade 1996–2005, when the US economy reaped a handsome windfall from earlier investments in computers and information technology despite the bursting of the dot-com bubble in 2000–2001. That windfall could not be sustained, however, and TFP growth in the subsequent decade was lower than at any time in the postwar period.

The decline in the rate of change of TFP has been mirrored by a similar fall in the rate of increase of labor productivity.[50] Both trends have generated major debates in the United States as well as a huge amount of research.[51] The "techno-optimists," as they are sometimes called, point to ongoing American research in such areas as energy, biotechnology, the Internet of Things, and robotics. Yet work on these new technologies has been going on for years without any apparent impact on TFP at the national level.

The United States still leads the world in terms of spending on R&D, although China is catching up fast.[52] However, most R&D spending is now "applied" rather than "basic" and carried out by the private sector. This is a big change compared with fifty years ago, when two-thirds of the funding for total

BOX 10.3

SILICON VALLEY

Silicon Valley is in California and acquired its name from the number of technology-intensive companies that set up operations there to manufacture silicon chips for the booming computer market in the 1970s. It has continued to attract high-tech companies, now including such household names as Apple, Alphabet (the parent company of Google), Facebook, Cisco, Oracle, and Intel.

As a result of its origins, the name Silicon Valley has become synonymous with clusters of innovative, high-tech companies throughout the country (and not just in California). These clusters are seen as the best hope for innovation and growth in the United States since the high-tech firms located there have the highest proportions of science, technology, engineering, and mathematics (STEM) graduate employees.

For many years high-tech companies, which constitute just over 4 percent of US private sector firms, had a good record of creating more jobs than they destroyed. That ended in 2001 with the bursting of the dot-com bubble, after which job destruction has often exceeded job creation (see the US Census Bureau's Longitudinal Business Database at https://www.census .gov/ces/dataproducts/datasets/lbd.html).

High-tech companies are also aging rapidly. The number of young firms (defined as those five years or younger) peaked in 2001 and has declined steadily since then. Having constituted nearly 60 percent of all high-tech firms in 1982, the proportion of young firms is now not very different from the private sector as a whole (see Haltiwanger, Hathaway, and Miranda, *Declining Business Dynamism*, p. 8, Figure 4).

None of this might matter if high-tech companies were continuing to invest heavily in the United States in areas that stood a good chance of raising the rate of increase in productivity in the rest of the economy. However, high-tech companies are the most likely to accumulate cash outside the United States, preferring to hoard it or distribute it as dividends rather than risk being taxed. By the end of 2015, five high-tech companies alone (Apple, Microsoft, Alphabet, Cisco, and Oracle) held more than $500 billion offshore. This makes it much harder for high-tech companies to play the role expected by techno-optimists in spreading innovation throughout the United States.

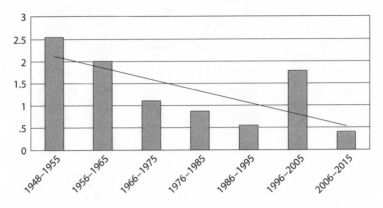

Figure 10.7. Annual growth (%) of TFP, 1948–2015. *Source:* Derived by
the author from Federal Reserve Bank of San Francisco, "Total Factor
Productivity," http://www.frbsf.org/economic-research/indicators-data
/total-factor-productivity-tfp/.

R&D came from the federal government and was largely dedicated to basic research.[53] And much of what the government today spends on basic research is
for new weapons systems that are not likely to have much effect—if any—on
TFP.

There is nothing wrong with applied research, but it is unlikely to have the
same transformative effects on the whole economy as basic research. That is
why developments in the high-tech sector in the United States, especially Silicon Valley (see Box 10.3), are not having the impact on TFP that were expected
by some. The new apps and gadgets that appear with such frequency are admi-
rable in many ways, but they tend to improve the consumer experience and enhance leisure time rather than transform the productive system itself.

Many leading US economists now talk of the economy being in "secular
stagnation."[54] This is not universally accepted, and there are plenty of other
explanations for the long-term decline in US growth. Whatever the cause,
however, it is clear that economic performance is now seriously out of line with
the imperial role that the United States set for itself in the semiglobal empire.

10.4. RISING INEQUALITY AND SOCIAL IMMOBILITY

All empires create myths about themselves and the United States is no exception. One of the most powerful myths involves the "land of opportunity" en-
capsulated in the phrase "the American dream," which brilliantly reflects the

idea that anyone by means of hard work and dedication can rise through society regardless of how humble their origins might have been.

Hollywood films have reinforced the myth, while the life stories of many prominent Americans—including Benjamin Franklin, Henry Ford, and Andrew Carnegie—gave it credence among the public. And opportunity in the United States has always been contrasted with lack of opportunity elsewhere. In the words of James Truslow Adams, who popularized the phrase in his book *The Epic of America,*

> [T]here [is] the *American dream*, that dream of a land in which life should be better and richer and fuller for every man, with opportunity for each according to his ability or achievement. It is a difficult dream for the European upper classes to interpret adequately, and too many of us ourselves have grown weary and mistrustful of it. It is not a dream of motor cars and high wages merely, but a dream of social order in which each man and each woman shall be able to attain to the fullest stature of which they are innately capable, and be recognized by others for what they are, regardless of the fortuitous circumstances of birth or position.[55]

The American dream was underpinned by the assumption that the United States, unlike Europe, was a relatively egalitarian society in which the gap between the richest and poorest was moderate. The rich were therefore assumed to be not too remote from the rest of society and access to the top remained feasible. However, no empirical data were available to test this until 1915, when a remarkable book by Willford Isbell King, entitled *The Wealth and Income of the People of the United States,* was published.

King's book provided estimates of income and wealth inequality from 1850 to 1910 and it demonstrated that inequalities were not only huge but also as extreme as anything in Europe. In particular, King showed that less than 2 percent of households received 20 percent of income and that the top quintile received 50 percent.[56] Furthermore, King was able to demonstrate that this was similar to autocratic Prussia in Europe, hardly a model of egalitarianism.

King's book initially caused a stir and was widely reviewed. However, his research results were largely ignored for three reasons. First, the empirical data, from which the results were drawn, were dismissed as too unreliable to draw any significant conclusions.[57] Second, for those who accepted the results at face value, income (and wealth) inequality was considered an acceptable price to pay as long as social mobility allowed Americans to move upward in accordance with their education and ability. And, third, King's proposed remedy—restricting immigration—was not considered either feasible or desirable at the time.

In any case, inequalities of income and wealth declined after US entry into the First World War. And, with the exception of a few years in the 1920s, the trend continued during the interwar years and throughout the Second World War.[58] The United States therefore came out of the global conflict with a relatively egalitarian distribution of income (less so in the case of wealth). This reinforced belief in the American dream, which was underpinned by an explosion in educational opportunities.[59]

This state of affairs continued for another thirty years, during which average household incomes rose rapidly without any increase in income and wealth inequality. In other words, almost all social groups participated in the growth of the economy without any major shifts from one group to another. The semiglobal empire was delivering benefits to the majority of its citizens through an economic model that provided a large degree of social inclusion.

Starting in the mid-1970s, however, there was a dramatic shift in the distribution of income toward the top 10 percent and—within this group—toward the top 1 percent. Furthermore, this shift has been so rapid that arguably nothing like it has occurred in US history or indeed in the history of other advanced capitalist countries. Indeed, we have to go to countries ravaged by hyperinflation to find anything comparable.

The exact measurement of the shift varies according to the definition of income used, whether it refers to households or individuals and whether it is analyzed at the national or state level.[60] Yet, regardless of the metric used, all research shows a big shift to the richest in society. For example, the share of market income received by the top decile has risen from just over 30 percent to nearly 50 percent, while the share going to the top percentile has gone from under 10 percent to just over 20 percent.[61]

Wealth (i.e., assets net of liabilities) is invariably more unequally distributed than income. In the mid-1970s, for example, when family income was distributed in a relatively egalitarian fashion, the top 10 percent already owned over 65 percent of wealth, and this share increased in the next four decades to nearly 80 percent.[62] However, the top 1 percent (1.6 million families) did even better. Their share doubled from just over 20 percent to 42 percent.[63]

It is, of course, true that many advanced capitalist countries have experienced a shift of income (and wealth) to the top decile over this period. This is largely a consequence of the rise of globalization and the emergence of the "supermanager" whose pay, including stock options, has risen extremely fast.[64] In the United Kingdom, for example, the income share of the top 10 percent rose from nearly 30 to over 40 percent in the four decades before 2015.

In international comparisons of rich countries, however, the United States stands out. Not only has the income shift in other countries been smaller than in the United States, but it has also been mitigated to a greater extent by the impact of the tax system. The "secondary" (posttax) distribution of income (i.e., taking into effect the impact of fiscal policy) is much less unequal than the "primary" pretax distribution. In the United States, by contrast, secondary income is almost as unequally distributed as primary income.[65]

A big shift in the income share of the top decile, coupled with a modest rate of GDP growth, means that the richest cohort inevitably captures most of the increase in national income. If income goes from 100 to 150, for example, while the share of the top decile goes from 30 to 50 percent, then the top 10 percent receives 90 percent of the increase in income over the period.

This simple example corresponds fairly closely to the actual experience in the United States after 1973. In the previous four decades (1933–73), income shares did not change by much and the top 10 percent received roughly 30 percent of the increase in income (see Figure 10.8).[66] In the next thirty-five years, however, when there was a big shift in income, the share of the increase in income going to the top decile was an extraordinary 98 percent. And the share going to the top 1 percent rose from nearly 7 percent in the first period to nearly 70 percent in the second.

During the Great Recession, when the income of all groups fell, the top 10 percent experienced the greatest loss. This was not only because their average income declined but also because their *share* of income also fell. However, the return to growth after 2009 restored the new order. The share of the top 10 percent rose above what it had been before while average income again increased. The result was that the top decile took nearly 90 percent of the increase in income from 2009 to 2014 (see Figure 10.8).

When the top 10 percent receives such a large share of any increase in income, there is not much left for anyone else. This is essentially what has happened in the United States since the mid-1970s. Demonstrating it, however, is not always straightforward because any metric that refers to "average" income includes the top 10 percent. Furthermore, household income includes government transfers that are not affected by the shift of market income to the top decile. That is why the American public has been bombarded with apparently contradictory statistics.

The easiest way to understand what has been happening is to look at wages and salaries adjusted for inflation because the income of the "bottom 90 percent" is so dependent on them. Furthermore, real wages take into account changes in

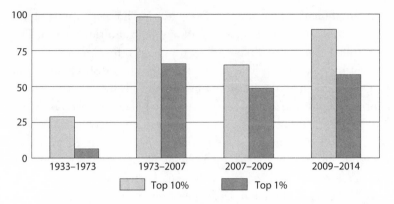

Figure 10.8. Share of change in income accruing to richest groups (%),
1933–2014. *Source*: "Table 1. Real Income Growth by Groups,"
http://elsa.berkeley.edu/~saez/TabFig2013prel.xls.

minimum wage rates at the state and federal levels. And last but not least, the
United States has an abundance of data on real wages and salaries provided by
the Bureau of Labor Statistics (BLS).

The BLS has a series starting in 1979 that shows "median usual weekly earnings" for all full-time employees aged sixteen and over.[67] It adjusts wages and
salaries to the price level in 1982–84 and shows that earnings were $332 in 1979
and $341 in 2015.[68] In other words, in nearly forty years there has been virtually
no change in average earnings despite the increase in real GDP, labor productivity, and average levels of education. And for men only, there was a drop over
these years, from $401 to $377.

When we look at household income, which takes into account government
transfers, the long-run trend at first sight appears slightly more encouraging. In
the three decades before 2014, for example, the real median household income
rose by 10.3 percent, although it should be remembered that this is only equivalent to an annual increase of 0.3 percent.[69]

This figure, however, is distorted by the large increases enjoyed by the richest
families. Over the four decades from 1975 to 2014, the bottom quintile of
households had virtually no increase in income since the value (at 2014 prices)
was $11,644 in 1975 and $11,676 in 2014.[70] And if we focus only on the period
since 2000, the four bottom quintiles all experienced a *drop* in average real
household incomes. This was also a period when inflation-adjusted wages and
salaries of the bottom 10 percent dropped by 3.7 percent with a fall of 3 percent
for the bottom 25 percent.[71]

Until recently, Americans were not unduly troubled either by income inequalities or stagnant earnings because they assumed that hard work and dedication could propel an individual and their family up the ladder of social mobility. Yet this is no longer the reality. In the words of one specialist in social mobility across the world,

> [T]here is a disconnect between the way Americans see themselves and the way the economy and society actually function. Many Americans may hold the belief that hard work is what it takes to get ahead, but in actual fact the playing field is a good deal stickier than it appears. Family background, not just individual effort and hard work, is importantly related to one's position in the economic and social hierarchy. This disconnect is brought into particular relief by placing the United States in an international context. In fact, children are much more likely as adults to end up in the same place on the income and status ladder as their parents in the United States than in most other countries.[72]

The deeper the inequalities, the harder it becomes to close the gap through merit alone. Empirical research has now demonstrated conclusively that social mobility has not only declined in the United States but the nation has also become one of the least socially mobile societies among advanced capitalist countries. One study, for example, ranks the United States eleventh out of thirteen OECD countries, with social mobility much lower even than in France, Germany, and Japan and only just ahead of class-ridden Great Britain.[73]

Most of the empirical research on social mobility focuses on intergenerational income elasticity (IGE), which measures the extent to which differences in income are passed from one generation to the next and varies from 0 (extreme mobility) to 1 (extreme immobility). If elasticity is low (0.2), as in Canada, it means that an individual earning $10,000 more than the average will pass on to their children only 20 percent of that difference. In other words, the child's income will be largely determined by his or her dedication and ability.

IGE in the United States, by contrast, is high and rising. The most careful research suggests it is close to 0.5 for all incomes and almost 0.7 for parental income in the upper income brackets.[74] The corollary of this is that families are increasingly likely to stay in the income quintile into which they were born. Specifically, nearly half of those born to families in the top and bottom quintiles will remain there as adults, and the chances of moving from the bottom to the top or vice versa are now very small indeed.[75]

Rising inequality and falling social mobility have left many Americans confused and angry. Their sense of alienation has taken many forms, from right-wing

BOX 10.4

HIGHER EDUCATION

For decades the United States led the world in the proportion of students going on to higher education. As a result, many young people from poor backgrounds gained opportunities that were unavailable to their parents. Higher education played a key role in promoting social mobility and by 2010, according to the National Center for Educational Statistics, some eighteen million undergraduates were enrolled in degree-granting post-secondary institutions.

Since 2010, however, the numbers enrolled have been falling. This is largely due to the explosion in the cost of going to a private university, which has outpaced the Consumer Price Index almost every year for the last forty years. As a result, according to a study by Cornell University, college tuition now takes up 56 percent of median family income, compared with 26 percent in 1980. Not surprisingly, therefore, student debt had risen to $1.2 trillion by 2016—higher even than credit card debt.

The children of rich families have been much less affected by rising fees than poor ones. Among the birth cohort born between 1979 and 1982, 80 percent of the top quartile by family income went to university compared with less than 30 percent for the bottom quartile. And only 9 percent of the bottom quartile completed their studies (see Duncan and Murnane, *Whither Opportunity?*, Figures 6.2 and 6.3).

And the children of the rich are much more likely to go to the top universities that invest so heavily in preserving their rankings and whose reputations provide such a crucial passport into high-income jobs in the labor market. The average annual income of the parents of children at Harvard University, for example, is estimated at $450,000 (see Piketty, *Capital in the Twenty-First Century*, 485). Lower-ranked universities, by contrast, find themselves in a vicious circle of modest fees, inadequate endowments, and poor reputations that make it hard for their students to start in well-paid jobs.

Higher education has therefore ceased to play the positive role in encouraging social mobility that it used to enjoy. The conventional ranking system for universities now promotes social *immobility* rather than the reverse.

populism to left-wing activism. If at first there appears to be nothing in common between the Tea Party on the one hand and Occupy Wall Street on the other, there is no doubt that both have been venting their fury at the established order. The 2016 presidential election demonstrated this clearly.

In this respect, what is happening in the United States is similar to what is happening in many other advanced capitalist countries. However, the United States is an empire, not merely a nation-state, and the implications are more far-reaching in America. Specifically, the unease of many Americans has come to focus on opposition to globalization, with over half claiming free trade agreements are "mostly harmful because they send jobs overseas and drive down wages." And if it is assumed that this high figure is due mainly to Democrats, the opposite turns out to be true with even higher numbers for Republicans.[76]

Free trade is the cornerstone of the American semiglobal empire. Remove it and the edifice starts to crumble. Thus, the opposition to globalization in the United States is a real challenge to those who seek to preserve the imperial project. Of course, much of the opposition is misplaced because stagnant real wages have many causes, of which free trade is only one (and probably less important than technological change). Yet perceptions are everything in domestic politics, and antiglobalization in the United States is gradually pushing the US empire into retreat.

11

THE DECLINE OF LEADERSHIP

The semiglobal empire was made possible by American leadership of the so-called free world. This leadership, as was shown in Part II, was underpinned by global and regional institutions created by the United States itself as well as the support of numerous nonstate actors (NSAs). It therefore did not depend exclusively on hard power, although military force was often used.

US hard power remains undiminished, but American global leadership has withered. There are numerous reasons for this, both internal and external. The first is that the institutions established by the United States at the height of its imperial powers are no longer so effective. The second is the failure of many American NSAs to support the imperial project as vigorously as before. The third is the obstructive role played by Congress in many areas of foreign policy. Finally, the executive has failed to articulate a post–Cold War imperial program that resonates with a majority of countries around the world.

The key global and regional institutions established by the United States after the Second World War have been outlined in Chapter 5. They are all still in existence, although one (GATT) has evolved into another (the WTO), and they remain under US control or subject to strong American influence. However, they are no longer as effective in promoting American power because the rest of the world has found ways of circumventing them. And faced with external pressure to reform these institutions, the United States has frequently placed itself on the wrong side of history, running the risk of being seen as a follower rather than leader.

NSAs played a key role in the Cold War as supporters of the semiglobal empire. The relationship between the main NSAs and the US state is still important, but it has broken down in several areas. In particular MNEs, many of whom operate on a truly global scale, now have strategies that are often in conflict with the imperial project.

The media, another important NSA, is now so fragmented that large parts of it undermine the state's efforts to articulate an imperial vision for the post–Cold War world, while the Internet has created unrivaled opportunities for America's opponents to discredit the US government in numerous ways. Even the nonprofit sector has failed to be as supportive of the semiglobal empire as in the past.

The Constitution gave Congress a special role in the conduct of foreign affairs, and this created the possibility of conflict with the executive. In general, these conflicts were resolved pragmatically—especially when the United States faced a perceived existential threat. Now, however, that threat has gone and Congress is gripped by extreme levels of political partisanship that make pragmatic solutions much more difficult.

The result has been a Congress that in recent years has become ever more obstructive and which has done little to help the executive formulate an imperial policy for the post–Cold War age. Furthermore, foreign affairs no longer command the attention of the best lawmakers in the way that they did in the past, so that congressional expertise is thinner and many of those who *are* interested in foreign policy appear stuck in the past.

All this makes it very difficult for the executive to display leadership in global matters. Presidents have bolstered the power of the White House and circumvented Congress in many ways, but this leaves US policy susceptible to a change in government and creates suspicions and doubts not just among America's enemies but also among its friends.

Just how serious these problems had become was made clear by the presidential transition in January 2017. President Donald Trump (2017–) promised a foreign policy based on "America first," including a withdrawal from numerous international commitments on trade and the environment, but at the same time calling for the maintenance of US global leadership especially on security matters. However, this simply emboldened America's enemies, encouraged its rivals, and confounded its allies. As America jettisoned its claim to global leadership in areas of special concern to its allies, it undermined its authority in other areas as well. As a result, imperial retreat accelerated.

11.1. INSTITUTIONS

At the epicenter of the global institutions established by the United States lies the United Nations Security Council (UNSC). It is the organ to which all countries, including the United States, turn when they seek to establish the legitimacy of their international actions. Failure to have the blessing of the UNSC risks rendering a state's action illegal under international law, while its support provides moral as well as legal cover.

At one level, the UNSC appears to work well from a US perspective. A quick glance at the resolutions passed in the last few years reveals that nearly all of them are passed unanimously and that they cover many different parts of the world where conflicts arise. Notably, there was consensus for the numerous US-sponsored resolutions aimed at Iran to ensure that its uranium enrichment program was compliant with its international obligations.[1]

However, all is not well with the UNSC despite the fact that two permanent members (France and the United Kingdom) have not used their veto since 1989. The United States, with one exception, has employed its veto to block even the mildest resolutions critical of Israel.[2] Russia followed suit, blocking all resolutions critical of its ally Syria or its behavior in Ukraine and Crimea. And China, until recently much more likely to abstain, has taken to using its veto on a number of occasions.

The result is that large numbers of conflicts around the world, including some of the most important for the United States, cannot be addressed by the UNSC. And just as worrying is the growing use of the "hidden" veto, where a permanent member makes it clear that it will use its veto if a vote is taken, thereby making it much more likely that no vote will be called.

Some will argue that these are old problems, and there is some truth in that. However, the end of the Cold War provided an opportunity for reform of the United Nations, including the UNSC, and the United States failed to provide the leadership both expected and required. The much-anticipated meeting held in 2005 in New York was noticeable more for the absence of concrete results than actual reforms.[3]

The overwhelming suspicion therefore is that the United States is no longer interested in substantive UN reform since it would dilute its historically privileged position.[4] The UNSC therefore remains unreformed and increasingly unreceptive to US pressure while some of those changes that have taken place in the UN system, including the establishment of the Human Rights Council, were greeted at first with sustained hostility by the US government.[5] And the United States also found itself increasingly marginalized on the question of Palestinian statehood, pursuing a course of action that left America isolated internationally and looking more like a follower than a leader.[6]

The International Monetary Fund (IMF) was one of the two key institutions established at the Bretton Woods Conference in 1944. It is an institution that has long been dominated by the United States as a result of the voting structure, US Treasury influence, and its location in Washington, DC. Legions of studies have demonstrated the imperial influence exercised by the United States over IMF lending policy, which remains highly orthodox in practice despite lip service being paid recently to more heterodox thinking.[7]

IMF reform, demanded for many years by developing countries, was finally achieved in 2016 after the US Congress accepted a change in the voting structure that would give more weight to China.[8] However, the American share hardly changed at all, leaving the United States as the only country with enough votes to block major reforms in the future.

US hegemony in the IMF was therefore maintained, but it was a Pyrrhic victory. Frustration among developing countries against the Fund had been building for years, and many had used the first decade of the twenty-first century to build up their foreign exchange reserves to avoid the need to go to the Fund in the future, while others paid off their debts to the organization in order to escape IMF conditions.

By the end of the administration of President Barack Obama (2009–17), therefore, IMF lending was no longer flowing in the usual directions. Instead, it was overwhelmingly going to highly indebted European countries as part of a bailout orchestrated by the European Commission and European Central Bank.[9] Apart from a few low-income countries with no alternatives, IMF (and therefore US) influence in developing countries was very modest.[10]

The other institution established at Bretton Woods was the International Bank for Reconstruction and Development (commonly known as the World Bank). Located in Washington, DC, with a president that has always been an American citizen, the US government has exercised a viselike grip on the World Bank from its inception and has never been afraid to use its leverage to secure support for US imperial interests, as many scholars have noted: "Our results provide support for . . . a particularly strong leverage of the United States on the World Bank. . . . [T]his [is] because the United States is the largest contributor to the IDA [International Development Association], the World Bank President is always American, the World Bank depends on U.S. capital markets to finance its operations, and the United States carries out detailed reviews of Bank loan proposals. This provides the United States with substantial influence as the Bank thereby pays closer attention to it than to any other major shareholder."[11]

Over the years, the US government through the Treasury Department has fought off numerous attempts to make the World Bank reflect more closely the view of all its members. It has forced the resignation of one of its chief economists (himself an American citizen) as a result of his criticisms of US influence.[12]

It has also watered down all draft reports that reflected an approach to development economics that ran counter to official US thinking.[13]

As with the IMF, however, this ideological purity has proved to be a Pyrrhic victory. Frustration among developing countries over US control of the World Bank
finally led to two initiatives that undermine the Bank's influence in developing
countries. The first is the New Development Bank, supported by the BRICS
countries.[14] The second is the Asian Infrastructure Investment Bank (AIIB).

China has been a leading proponent of the new banks, both of which are located in the country. However, the AIIB is likely to be the more important in
view of its larger size and broader membership. In particular, it offers Asian
countries a chance to escape from the conditions applied to World Bank lending. For that reason the US government was strongly opposed to the establishment of the AIIB but was unable to block it. The AIIB is therefore likely to
represent a major challenge to US leadership and is a significant milestone in
China's quest for regional hegemony.

The World Trade Organization (WTO), successor to GATT, is the third
global economic organization used by the United States to promote its interests.
Very much a product of US thinking, the WTO after its founding in 1995 was
at first highly successful in promoting free markets for goods, services, and capital while aggressively protecting intellectual property rights. And, although
located in Geneva, its secretary-general was until recently always handpicked
by the US government and could be relied on to promote an American vision
of free market capitalism.

Under these circumstances, the launch of the Doha Round of trade negotiations in 2001 was expected by the administration of President George W. Bush
(2001–9) to lead swiftly to a successful outcome. The United States, it was assumed, would build a coalition in support of its trade agenda (the WTO operates by consensus), as it had done in eight previous trade rounds. In the next
fifteen years, however, the talks had ended in acrimony, a new secretary-general
from Brazil was appointed without initial American support, and the member
states had to settle for a weak agreement in 2013 on "trade facilitation" that did
little more than save the blushes of the main participants.[15]

Kristen Hopewell, a scholar of the WTO, has explained clearly what went
wrong:

> For more than fifty years, the US has enjoyed the privileges of hegemony, act-
> ing and being treated as the exceptional state in the international system. . . .
> The US has long claimed the right to intervene in the affairs of other states,
> through its dominant position in multilateral institutions . . . and justified by

the discourse of neoliberal economics. Now, however, the rising developing country powers are behaving in the same way and demanding an equal right to intervene in the internal trade and economic policies of the US. . . . The new powers have sought to curtail the privileges of the US and insist that it be treated as a state like any other. . . . Yet, in that process, they have destabilized that very system of global economic governance.[16]

The United States, not yet being ready to be "treated as a state like any other," adjusted to the collapse of the Doha Round by embarking on a series of regional trade negotiations such as the Trans-Pacific Partnership (TPP) where it could more easily control the agenda and from which China could be excluded. Yet this was *de facto* recognition of the failure of US global leadership in trade negotiations. And, ironically, this more limited initiative was not certain to succeed in view of the growing opposition within the United States itself to *any* form of trade agreement.[17]

The global institutions have all survived and are still dominated by the United States, but their efficacy in projecting American power has diminished as other countries have successfully developed alternative strategies that undermine the reach of the global institutions themselves. In the trade-off between retaining American control of largely unreformed institutions and opening them up to far-reaching reform at the risk of diluting American power, the United States has invariably chosen the former.

The same happened to the regional institutions created by the United States after the Second World War, including in the Americas themselves. The Organization of American States (OAS) served US interests well during the Cold War and looked set to do the same afterward, when "democracy promotion" and "free trade" were added to its mission. Indeed, the OAS was the main institution involved in the launch of the Summit of the Americas in Miami in 1994 where the administration of President Bill Clinton (1993–2001) laid out a bold vision for the region under US leadership.

The US vision excluded Cuba, a policy opposed by all Latin American countries by the start of the new millennium. Anxious not to anger the United States, the main Latin American countries at first proceeded cautiously. A Rio Group, for example, was established during the 1980s by eight countries to find a peaceful solution to the Central American crisis, and this soon expanded to include other states, most of whom had no desire to antagonize the United States.[18]

US leadership of the OAS was at first not contested. Indeed, the tough OAS response to the failed coup in Venezuela in 2002 was seen as a demonstration of a welcome change of direction by the US government, as was the initial OAS response to the successful coup in Honduras in 2009.[19] However, the subsequent decision by the Obama administration to ignore OAS resolutions and accept the outcome of the coup precipitated a crisis between the United States and Latin America.[20]

The result was the formation of the Community of Latin American and Caribbean States (CELAC) that includes Cuba and excludes the United States and Canada. And in 2013 at the Sixth Summit of the Americas, which excluded Cuba, CELAC members made it clear that future Summits of the Americas would only take place if Cuba were invited. This unprecedented challenge to US authority then precipitated the restoration of diplomatic relations between the United States and Cuba, a process that was announced at the end of 2014 and completed in July 2015.

Cuba was therefore present at the Seventh Summit of the Americas in Panama in 2015 but chose not to accept the invitation to apply to rejoin the OAS (Box 11.1). The institution, located in Washington, DC, is still under heavy American influence, but it is an increasingly empty vessel. The CELAC states now have an alternative institution to discuss hemispheric affairs, even if some of their more ambitious plans have so far failed to come to fruition.[21]

The final US-dominated institution to be considered is the North Atlantic Treaty Organization (NATO). Established at the start of the Cold War, NATO appeared to have served its purpose by November 1989 when the Berlin Wall crumbled. The hope at the time—not only of Mikhail Gorbachev but of many European leaders as well—was that NATO could be folded into a pan-European security arrangement embracing the USSR as well as European states.[22]

US administrations had other ideas. NATO remained firmly in existence and its membership expanded rapidly to embrace the countries of eastern Europe and parts of the Balkans. By the end of 2009, NATO had twenty-eight members, several of whom shared a border with Russia, and was contemplating further expansion. US governments would then deploy NATO forces in numerous "out-of-area" operations from Afghanistan to Libya.

The transformation of NATO, it would seem, has made a mockery of any notion that the United States was retreating from empire or failing to act as a global leader. It is an institution that remains firmly under US control and whose members appear to have no desire to create an alternative. For better or worse, it is the most visible symbol of US hard power and imperial reach.

This US strategy, however, has been fraught with problems. None of the other NATO members—not even the United Kingdom—was prepared to pull its weight in terms of military spending as a share of GDP.[23] Yet these same coun-

BOX 11.1

THE OAS, CUBA, AND THE UNITED STATES

Although often described as an expulsion, Cuba's membership in the OAS was merely "suspended" in January 1962 when fourteen countries voted in favor of the resolution (Argentina, Bolivia, Brazil, Chile, Ecuador, and Mexico abstained). Despite numerous attempts by Latin American countries to have the suspension lifted, it was not until June 2009, when President Barack Obama (2009–17) was in office, that it was finally ended.

This was assumed to be the prelude to an application by Cuba to rejoin the organization, during which the US government would have tried to use the Inter-American Democratic Charter to commit President Raúl Castro to political reform. However, Cuba had other ideas and in effect said, "Thanks, but no thanks."

This left President Obama with no options other than to pursue normalization of US relations with Cuba outside the framework of the OAS. The secret negotiations, involving the Vatican as well as other intermediaries, finally led to the restoration of diplomatic relations in 2015 and the visit of President Obama to Cuba in March 2016.

The improved relations between Cuba and the United States, despite the cancellation of some measures by President Trump in 2017, have been widely welcomed. Travel restrictions have been eased, direct commercial flights have been restored, ferry links have been opened, and Americans can now bring back Cuban cigars and rum. However, all of this falls short of full normalization, as the trade embargo can only be lifted by Congress and the United States continues to occupy a part of Cuba (Guantánamo Bay).

This demonstrates the difficulties for the United States in exercising leadership when institutional control is no longer so effective. Lacking the leverage provided by the OAS, the US government was the one that had to make the most adjustment toward normalization of the bilateral relationship. The Cuban political system has not changed at all, and the OAS continues to be condemned by the Castro government as "an instrument of imperialist domination."

tries expected the United States to come to their aid if they were ever under attack or threatened, while US relations with one member (Turkey) became increasingly complicated as their national interests diverged over the Syrian crisis.

There could, of course, be only one major source of threat for NATO members, and that was Russia, which had become increasingly irritated by the alliance's enlargement. In the words of one Russian analyst, "NATO expansion is nothing more than the extension of its zone of influence—and in the most sensitive military and political spheres. And yet [American] unwillingness to abandon that effort is coupled with a repeated refusal to recognize Russia's right to have its own zone of interest. So NATO expansion has left the Cold War unfinished. The ideological and military confrontation that underlay it is gone, but the geopolitical rivalry that it entailed has returned to the fore."[24]

Russian irritation was at first expressed in words, but—as its economy stabilized—in deeds as well. A war with Georgia in 2008 sent a clear signal to the United States that Russia would not contemplate any further NATO expansion. When that message was not heeded, Russia annexed Crimea in 2014 and started a proxy war in eastern Ukraine. And since the United States has no intention to back down on NATO enlargement, it is unlikely to be the last example of Russian aggression.[25]

The survival of NATO is therefore a mixed blessing for the United States. On the one hand, it demonstrates continued US leadership of the so-called free world while, on the other, it has pushed the United States into commitments that are financially costly and geopolitically risky. Its allies refuse to share the burden while Russia can choose the time and place for future confrontations. In the absence of a Russian collapse, an eventual American retreat seems inevitable. Indeed, this was the message that Donald Trump conveyed on the campaign trail in 2016 even if, as president, he had to soften his position.

11.2. NONSTATE ACTORS

The relationship between NSAs and the state was explored in Chapter 6. Among the most important NSAs are American multinational enterprises (MNEs), who continue to work closely with government through extensive lobbying efforts and by participation in detailed trade negotiations. These MNEs also remain the most important funders for political parties and candidates of almost all persuasions.

This close relationship has not ended, but it has started to fray in a number of ways. As beneficiaries of the policies pursued by the US government throughout the years of the semiglobal empire, many of these companies are now truly global and, in many respects, operate on a more global basis than the state itself. Although headquartered in the United States, they need to plan and operate on a world scale—a strategy that can put them at odds with US administrations.

Corporate taxation provides an illuminating example.[26] The US marginal tax rate (35 percent) is the highest among OECD countries and one of the highest in the world.[27] The US government is also one of only six OECD countries to tax companies on the basis of their worldwide profits. However, numerous loopholes—skillfully preserved and enlarged by corporate lobbyists—make a mockery of the principle of worldwide taxation and have led to a decline in the effective tax rate to around 20 percent.

The most important loophole has been the privilege awarded to MNEs to defer additional US taxes on foreign affiliates' profits until they are repatriated. Since these companies can operate in almost any country, the temptation to establish operations in "tax havens" and use transfer pricing to shift profits to these places has been overwhelming. As a result, between $2 and $3 trillion was estimated to be held by American MNEs outside the United States by the end of 2016.[28]

Efforts by US governments to increase the effective corporate tax rate have therefore been thwarted by the operations of MNEs, and the situation has been made worse by the practice of "tax inversion." This involves a US MNE buying a foreign firm and adopting its tax domicile, allowing it not only to pay lower taxes in perpetuity but also to pay out accumulated profits without incurring additional tax.

In its last year in office, stung by a threatened tax inversion by a pharmaceutical company (Pfizer), the Obama administration felt compelled to act against this corporate practice.[29] By then, however, much damage had been done to the close relationship between the state and MNEs.[30] In the words of the *Economist* magazine, normally a strong supporter of US capitalism, "The spat makes everyone look bad. It reveals an administration that is capricious and a Republican Party establishment so out of touch that it thinks it should be the mouthpiece for firms that renounce their citizenship. It shows great companies, such as Pfizer, reduced to shifty deal-junkies that are obsessed with financial fixes. It exposes a tax system that is 30 years out of date and obsolete in an age of globalisation. And it highlights a hyper-partisan political system that is incapable of reform."[31]

The global nature of these companies has also caused friction with the US state in relation to China. Almost all of them now have a presence in the country, a position that was at first given strong official encouragement. US administrations calculated that China would not only prove to be highly profitable for American firms but that the presence of US companies would also accelerate reform and push China toward the kind of free market capitalism, and perhaps even representative democracy, favored by the United States.

The calculations proved to be very far off the mark. Slowly but surely, US policy on China has shifted toward something that more closely resembles containment (see Chapter 12) coupled with the threat of sanctions in response to cyberattacks and the blocking of certain Chinese investments in the United States on security grounds. This, however, runs counter to the interests of all those US companies for whom a Chinese presence is an essential part of their global strategies.

The conflict between the US state and a number of American technology companies over their links with China has been aggravated by revelations of the close ties some of these firms enjoy with the Chinese military. IBM in particular was singled out in a report commissioned by the Department of Defense in 2015: "IBM is endangering the national and economic security of the United States, risking the cybersecurity of their customers globally, and undermining decades of U.S. nonproliferation policies regarding high-performance computing."[32] Yet, despite these close ties, US companies operating in China are now more vulnerable than before. Acquisitions of major Chinese firms leading to control by US companies are increasingly rare, while Chinese companies are using the country's vast foreign exchange reserves to buy stakes in US companies already in China. American companies increasingly complain of being less welcome in China, as they have been subject to aggressive investigations involving health and safety as well as antibribery and antitrust accusations. Then, after the same companies sell part of their assets to Chinese partners, many of these investigations cease.

American technology companies are particularly at risk from the more aggressive stance taken by China. New cybersecurity laws, introduced after the revelations by Edward Snowden on the use of US tech firms by the National Security Agency to engage in spying around the world, require these companies to store their data in China and submit to security checks. Companies are also "encouraged" to deepen their ties with local partners and transfer sensitive intellectual property.

Despite this, very few US companies have given up on China, and most have decided to stay the course because of the long-run profitability of the market even if this means becoming a minority partner in a Chinese-controlled firm.[33]

BOX 11.2

APPLE, CHINA, AND THE UNITED STATES

With annual revenue of nearly $250 billion and a market capitalization above $500 billion in 2016, Apple is a high-technology behemoth with sales in almost all countries. It has long outgrown its home market in America and considers itself strong enough to resist pressure from the US government. It has also vigorously defended itself against the European Commission's efforts to force it to pay more tax.

When Apple was named by Edward Snowden as one of the companies cooperating with the National Security Agency in the secret PRISM program, the company issued a flat denial, saying, "We have never heard of PRISM." And when the administration of President Barack Obama (2009–17) demanded Apple release the source codes to hack into an iPhone implicated in a terrorist attack, it refused to do so (the FBI found a way to hack it independently).

Apple may have been willing to confront the US executive, but it has shown much less willingness to do so in the case of the Chinese government. Court rulings against the company, clearly influenced by the Chinese authorities, are accepted meekly. When the Chinese government calls for new investments by Apple in the country, the company responds, even putting the interests of other US MNEs at risk in the process (its investment of $1 billion in the Chinese app-based independent taxi service Didi Chuxing was the final straw that led Uber to abandon its own operations in China—see note 33).

So when China says "Jump," Apple asks "How high?" And when the US demands compliance, Apple resists. Yet this corporate strategy is perfectly logical and is an inevitable consequence of the discounted cash flow expected from the world's largest market over the next decades.

Apple's activities in China even became an electoral issue in 2016 when Donald Trump made much of the "export" of manufacturing jobs from the United States to China to produce high-tech products. This proved very appealing to many voters, but reversing it during the Trump administration will be very difficult without draconian controls on capital flows.

This means going along with Chinese state policy, but it also creates frictions with the US government for precisely that reason.

The damage to the reputation of US tech firms from Snowden's revelations affected the profitability of their businesses in many countries, not just in China, as a result of the erosion of trust. One study concluded, "The NSA programs, and public awareness of them, have had an immediate and detrimental impact on the U.S. economy. They have cost U.S. companies billions of dollars in lost sales, even as companies have seen their market shares decline. American multinational corporations have had to develop new products and programs to offset the revelations and to build consumer confidence. At the same time, foreign entities have seen revenues increase."[34] This caused further tensions between some US technology companies and the state, encouraging at least one (Apple) to resist when asked publicly to cooperate in sharing source codes and private keys after a terrorist attack.[35] It is safe to assume that there have been many other cases where the US government has unsuccessfully demanded access to secret codes controlled by high-tech companies since there is now an inherent conflict between the state's pursuit of national security and the firms' need to rebuild the public's trust.

The overwhelming support given by the media to the imperial policy of US administrations during the Cold War and the start of the unipolar moment has been well documented. Indeed, this support seemed set to continue after the terrorist attacks on 9/11, when the US media threw its collective weight behind the invasions of Afghanistan and Iraq.

Today the situation is very different. The media has become increasingly fragmented as a result of the rise of digital outlets, and this has contributed to the polarization of views in America. What should have been a welcome increase in competition among media outlets is now seen increasingly as a threat not just to social cohesion but also to any hope of a shared view of the outside world. As one journalist has noted,

> In the era of "big broadcast," prior to the Internet, scholars were concerned about the lack of media diversity and the fact that citizens were a "captive audience" potentially subject to mass manipulation. Thus, many hoped that the democratization of news media, particularly online, could have a positive impact on political participation, civic engagement and the production of information. However, in a digital era featuring media abundance, scholars now worry about what they call "selective exposure." A more fragmented media environment may prompt citizens to seek out more like-minded news sources, contributing to the reinforcement of prior beliefs and opinions and exacerbating polarization.[36]

This effect is sometimes known as the echo chamber and used to be associated with media outlets such as Fox News (on the right) and MSNBC (on the left). Today, however, these outlets seem positively sober compared with some of the other increasingly popular channels, the most extreme of which can all be found on the right of US politics and which have attracted large audiences.[37]

One of these outlets is Breitbart News, to which a large number of conservatives have been turning and which strongly supported Donald Trump's presidential campaign in 2016.[38] Yet Breitbart does not carry any of its own news, simply reposting articles published elsewhere that are consistent with its editorial policy. This reinforces the links between media fragmentation and political polarization, making it very difficult for any US administration to forge a consensus on foreign policy. In the words of one despairing journalist,

> Almost all of our news outlets now can be easily identified as having a particular, and often very narrow, political bent and they act like nothing more than TV sit-coms desperately searching for a sellable demographic which will keep them afloat. . . . This means that most "news" organizations are only interested in stories and truths that their audience will want to hear. Quite simply, nothing could be more antithetical to both the pursuit of truth (which is quite often very UN-popular) as well as the maintenance of a country which has enough "knowledge" in common so as to be able to function as a remotely unified society.[39]

There are still many NSAs that have a close and symbiotic relationship with the imperial project. The main philanthropic foundations remain broadly supportive, while the Gates Foundation in particular has become almost an arm of the state itself. And a new organization, the Clinton Foundation (established at the end of the Clinton presidency), functioned in much the same way during the Obama administration.

The same, it might be assumed, could be said about the leading think tanks. However, in a surprising twist President Obama revealed in an interview in 2016 his frustrations with much of the think tank establishment, where his views were summarized as follows: "By 2013, Obama's resentments were well developed. . . . He resented the foreign-policy think-tank complex. A widely held sentiment inside the White House is that many of the most prominent foreign-policy think tanks in Washington are doing the bidding of their Arab and pro-Israel funders. I've heard one administration official refer to Massachusetts Avenue, the home of many of these think tanks, as 'Arab-occupied territory.' "[40] This may simply reflect the frustrations of a president at the failure of others to grasp the significance of what he has tried to achieve. However, it may point to something more substantial and possibly more enduring: an attempt by the administration to define what kind of country the United States needs to be in a postimperial age at a time when the leading NSAs still adhere to a belief in the semiglobal empire.

This potential conflict between where the United States is heading and where many of the leading NSAs would like it to go has also expressed itself in relation to some of those religious organizations that worked closely with the US state during the Cold War and its immediate aftermath.

US administrations, both Democrat and Republican, now adopt social policies that can broadly be described as "progressive," at least up to the end of the Obama presidency, and promote these same policies in other countries.[41] Many religious organizations, especially the evangelical churches, find this abhorrent. These same churches also work closely with their counterparts abroad, where they can find themselves campaigning against the policies favored by the US government. This has led to many conflicts.

11.3. CONGRESS

The Founding Fathers were all too aware of the dangers of an unbridled executive conducting foreign policy in such a way as to endanger the security of the nation or bankrupt the state through costly foreign wars. Conscious therefore of the need for checks and balances on the executive, they allocated a special role to Congress in the conduct of foreign affairs. This role is defined—not always clearly—in the Constitution, and responsibility is allocated between the two houses, with both having significant powers. As one expert explains, "Congress shares significant authority with the executive branch to shape and make foreign and defense policy. The Constitution's framers established the president's explicit authorities in this realm as serving as commander in chief of the armed forces, negotiating treaties, and appointing ambassadors and senior officials. They gave Congress the powers to declare war, appropriate funds, raise and support armies, provide and maintain a navy, and regulate foreign commerce. To the Senate alone the framers bestowed the responsibility of providing advice and consent on treaties and presidential nominees."[42]

The Constitution therefore placed considerable responsibilities on Congress in the conduct of foreign affairs, and these have not been amended significantly by law in the last 250 years. However, Congress is made up of individuals who serve geographic rather than national constituencies. This can make it difficult for Congress to see the bigger picture where foreign affairs are concerned. As a result, the executive has always looked for ways to circumvent congressional involvement in foreign policy, creating considerable ambiguity now over who is responsible, for example, for declaring war and approving international agreements.

Despite this, Congress—at least until the end of the Cold War—only occasionally blocked the executive in its conduct of foreign affairs (the best known example is the failure of the Senate to approve the Versailles Treaty in 1920, which meant the United States was unable to participate in the League of Nations). As a result, relations between the executive and the legislature in the fields of foreign affairs and national security were generally productive without necessarily being harmonious.

There have been several reasons for this. First, the executive has the advantage of the "bully pulpit," allowing it to appeal to the broader population over the heads of Congress as well as engage in crude horse-trading to secure the necessary votes. Second, the executive has become ever more skilled in exploiting loopholes in the Constitution to work around Congress on controversial issues. Third, Congress has normally been very supportive of the presidency where the nation faced a perceived existential threat.

The final such perceived threat ended with the fall of the Berlin Wall in 1989. Efforts to replace the alleged existential challenge from the Soviet Union with that from international terrorism at first had some success, especially after the trauma of 9/11, and Americans regularly place it at the top of their perceived threats (along with the possibility of Iran acquiring nuclear weapons). However, al-Qaeda and its successors, although willing to use the most brutal tactics against US targets abroad, never posed a serious challenge to American homeland security after 2001 and terrorism was downgraded by the nation's defense establishment in its list of threats to national security.[43]

As a result, Congress has not been under any real pressure from perceived existential threats since the 1980s. This, however, is also the period when political partisanship has reached previously unknown levels as an unintended consequence of the redrawing of electoral boundaries. This has left most seats in the House of Representatives uncompetitive except during the primary contests, where the voice of moderates is easily drowned out. And the same lack of competition is now a feature of many seats in the Senate.

Congress is therefore increasingly made up of members whose greatest challenge is to keep their support during the primary season, and this makes them reluctant to support the kind of pragmatic compromises that worked in the past. It has also contributed to the decline in foreign policy expertise among congressional members, as foreign affairs (in the way usually defined) are not normally the issues that excite the primary voters.[44] This trend has been noted by many students of Congress:

The nation's political landscape has been realigning since the 1970s, usher-
ing in deep partisanship, severe polarization, a combative 24/7 media, and diminished civility. Over time, this environment has given lawmakers greater
incentive to advance personal and partisan agendas by any means, including
the manipulation of congressional rules and procedures. It has politicized the
national security arena that, while never immune to partisanship, more often
than not used to bring out the "country first" instincts in lawmakers. . . .
Congress has struggled for years to play a consistent and constructive role as
a partner to as well as a check and balance on the executive branch on international issues.[45]

Under the Constitution, the Senate has a special role in providing "advice
and consent" on international treaties. In the two centuries after the Declaration of Independence, the Senate ratified fifteen hundred treaties and rejected
only twenty-one, which suggests that the Senate generally played a very responsible role in the formulation of foreign policy. Apart from the Treaty of Versailles
(rejected twice by the Senate), the only major blow in these years to American
aspirations to be a global leader was the rejection of the Law of the Sea Convention in 1960 (Box 11.3).

In this long period, from 1776 to 1976, there were also four hundred treaties
submitted by the executive that were not put to a vote (these are described by
constitutional lawyers as "unperfected").[46] Such a large number (an average of
two per year) suggests that the relationship between the Senate and the presidency over international agreements may not have been so harmonious after all.
In some respects that is correct, but many of these unperfected treaties were
later withdrawn by the executive, and very few of them affected American global
leadership, where the Senate remained broadly supportive.

The situation since the bicentenary has been quite different. Many treaties
that would have helped to secure American global leadership have been rejected. Even more have been left "unperfected." And some treaties, essential to
the international reputation of the United States, were passed only after decades
of congressional scrutiny (the best known example is the Convention on the
Prevention and Punishment of the Crime of Genocide, which the United States
signed in 1948 and the Senate did not ratify until 1989).[47]

The treaties of relevance to American aspirations to global leadership that the
Senate has either rejected or not ratified fall into three categories. The first is
international human rights; the second is the global environment; and the third
is international security. In each case, the Senate has placed the executive in a
difficult position, raising allegations by other countries of hypocrisy or worse.

BOX 11.3

UNCLOS, THE SENATE, AND CHINA

The first United Nations Law of the Sea Convention was presented to the Senate on May 26, 1960, and passed with a vote of 77–4. The same day a motion to reconsider was filed and the treaty was rejected 49–30. It then remained on the calendar of the Committee on Foreign Relations until 2000, when it was returned to the president.

By this time a different treaty, the United Nations Convention on the Law of the Sea (UNCLOS), had entered into force although it has never been ratified by the US Senate. Yet for the administration of President George W. Bush (2001–9) UNCLOS was a high priority, with Secretary of State Condoleezza Rice claiming, "Joining the [Law of the Sea] Convention will advance the interests of the U.S. military. As the world's leading maritime power, the United States benefits more than any other nation from the navigation provisions of the Convention."

The Senate was unmoved, and the treaty remains "unperfected" to this day. Meanwhile, the US government was becoming increasingly concerned by the aggressive actions of the Chinese government in the South China Sea but was unable to use UNCLOS—not being a member—to protest.

It was therefore left to the government of the Republic of the Philippines to use the arbitration provisions of UNCLOS to take its case to the Permanent Court of Arbitration (PCA) in the Hague. In 2016 the PCA ruled that China's position on the South China Sea was inconsistent with UNCLOS, of which China is a member, and that its actions were inconsistent with international law. The ruling hugely embarrassed China and demonstrated the importance of international treaties.

Ironically, there was a change of government in the Philippines just before the ruling and the new administration of President Rodrigo Duterte (2016–) soon made clear its desire to end the American protectorate over the archipelago and establish close relations with China. Thus, it will be much more difficult for future US administrations to use the Philippines as a proxy in its battle against Chinese expansion in the South China Sea.

In its campaign in 2016 to win a seat on the UN Human Rights Council, the US government made the following pledge: "The deep commitment of the United States to championing the human rights enshrined in the Universal Declaration of Human Rights is driven by the founding values of our nation and the conviction that international peace, security, and prosperity are strengthened when human rights and fundamental freedoms are respected and protected. As the United States seeks to advance human rights and fundamental freedoms around the world, we do so cognizant of our own commitment to address challenges and to live up to our ideals at home and to meet our international human rights obligations."[48]

This pledge is difficult to reconcile with US practice by both the executive and Congress. In the field of international human rights, there are a number of treaties or conventions that the US executive itself has not signed.[49] The Senate, of course, cannot be blamed for the failure to ratify in these cases, although part of the reason why the treaties have not received presidential signature may have been the fear that the Senate would not give its approval. However, there are four human rights treaties that have been signed and sent to the Senate but have never been ratified:

- American Convention on Human Rights (ACHR). Signed in 1977.
- Convention on the Elimination of All Forms of Discrimination against Women (CEDAW). Signed in 1980.
- Convention on the Rights of the Child (CRC). Signed in 1995.
- Convention on the Rights of Persons with Disabilities (CRPD). Signed in 2009.

The ACHR has already been discussed (Box 5.1), and the failure to ratify has placed the US government in a difficult position in its own hemisphere. Similarly, the failure of the Senate to ratify CEDAW places the United States in the company of Iran, Somalia, South Sudan, and Sudan.[50] Its failure to do so is a reflection of domestic US disputes on abortion and other matters, but the rest of the world sees it as showing a lack of leadership. And the failure of the Senate to pass the CRC is even more embarrassing as the United States (following the ratification by Somalia in 2015) is now the only country in the world not to have done so.

US governments since the Second World War have all aspired to global leadership in human rights. That was not true in the case of combating man-made climate change, where the skepticism of the public was for many years matched by that of both Congress and the executive.

This began to change in 1992 when President George H. W. Bush (1989–93) signed and ratified the UN Framework Convention on Climate Change (UNFCCC).[51] When President Clinton the next year signed the Convention on Biological Diversity, however, its unambiguous treaty status obliged him to submit it to the Senate for ratification, where it was promptly rejected.[52] The Clinton administration, recognizing both the global nature of the climate change problem and the desirability of American leadership, then signed the Kyoto Protocol in 1997. This committed developed countries to reduce their carbon emissions substantially below their 1990 levels.

The US Senate had other ideas, and so the Kyoto Protocol was never submitted for ratification, but it went ahead in 2005 when a sufficiently large number of countries had approved it.[53] The Senate's failure to ratify therefore severely weakened the US claim to leadership, but the American government was at least able to participate in the UNFCCC.

That slender thread was nearly severed during the George W. Bush administration (2001–9), when combating climate change was not only viewed skeptically by Congress but also by the executive. The lead US negotiator cut a lonely figure in those years, a position that President Obama was determined to reverse by placing the United States "back in the game." This he succeeded in doing, although the Paris Agreement on climate change in December 2015 was the result of collective rather than American leadership involving principally the United States, China, and the European Union.

The Paris Agreement commits participating countries to reduce their emissions by means of Nationally Determined Contributions (NDCs).[54] Although the United States signed the agreement on the first day possible (April 22, 2016), it still needed to be ratified and the Senate made clear its unwillingness to do so. President Obama therefore ratified it by executive order, despite its clear status as a treaty, leaving the agreement vulnerable to subsequent rejection.[55] Thus, US leadership was once again called into question as a result of congressional (in)action.[56]

International security is the third area where the Senate's role is undermining American global leadership. While the Cold War was in effect, the executive could normally count on Senate support. This was especially true in the case of arms control agreements.[57] And this support continued after the end of the Cold War with the ratification of START I, START II, SORT, and New START.[58]

As soon as the Cold War ended, however, the Senate failed to ratify the UN Convention on the Law of the Sea (UNCLOS) that had been specifically amended in 1994 to meet the concerns of the George H. W. Bush and Clinton administrations.[59] As a result, the US government was not in a strong position twenty years later to confront Chinese aggression in the South China Sea (Box 11.3). The Senate also rejected (51–48) the Comprehensive Nuclear Test Ban Treaty in 1999.

The Clinton administration in 1998 signed the Rome Statute of the International Criminal Court (ICC). This was an important initiative to address a major gap in international security designed to ensure that political leaders would in the future be held responsible for genocide, crimes against humanity, and war crimes. However, it was never submitted to the Senate, despite being amended in various ways to meet US concerns, as it would never have passed.[60] The ICC was nonetheless established in 2002, leaving the United States unable to play any leadership role in this crucial global area.[61]

While the Senate has constrained the executive by rejecting or failing to pass international treaties, the House of Representatives has used the power of the purse strings for the same purpose. Even before the end of the Cold War, for example, Congress had damaged the attempt of President Jimmy Carter (1977–81) to reach out to the Sandinistas in Nicaragua by attaching humiliating conditions to an appropriations bill in 1979 providing the new government with a loan from USAID.

This practice was rare before the bicentenary but has become much more common—especially when the House of Representatives is controlled by a different party from the executive. When President Obama, for example, attempted by executive order to close the prison at Guantánamo Bay in Cuba (a pledge on which he had campaigned in 2008), the House attached a clause to a spending bill that banned the use of federal dollars for the transfer of inmates.[62] The prison therefore remained in operation at the end of Obama's presidency.

Even more worrying for the conduct of US foreign policy and the claim to global leadership has been the decline in interest in foreign affairs in Congress. The key committees in both houses (armed services and foreign affairs) are now usually chaired by individuals who lack the stature of their predecessors. The chair of the Senate Foreign Relations Committee, for example, had almost no experience with international relations before being elected to this key post.[63]

The one exception is Senator John McCain, elected to the chair of the Senate Armed Services Committee in 2015.[64] Although he had a distinguished congressional record and armed forces career, he often appeared hopelessly out of touch with an America whose empire is in retreat. He therefore reflects a more general problem with Congress, which is that of inertia.[65] On a whole range of issues (e.g., climate change, human rights, security, Cuba, and Iran), Congress has a built-in preference to defend long-established positions. This is a luxury that the executive cannot afford.

11.4. THE EXECUTIVE

Global leadership requires a leader, and that is the self-appointed role adopted by the US executive during the semiglobal empire, albeit with the acquiescence of many other countries. Congress, the judiciary, NSAs, and public opinion all play a part, but it is the presidency where policy is formulated and which has responsibility for implementing it.

It is therefore the executive that must be the first to respond to changes in the world and America's place in it. And this is no easy task. Reflecting on the unipolar moment after leaving office in 2001, President Clinton drew attention to the responsibilities as well as privileges that go with global leadership:

> If you believe that maintaining power and control and absolute freedom of movement and sovereignty is important to your country's future, there's nothing inconsistent in that. We're the biggest most powerful country in the world now we've got the juice and we're going to use it. . . . But if you believe that we should be trying to create a world with rules and partnerships and habits of behavior that we would like to live in when we're no longer the military political economic superpower in the world, then you wouldn't do that.[66]

Clinton, from the safety of retirement, was drawing attention to an important, if unpalatable, truth: the need to create an international framework that would place the same rights and duties on the United States as on other countries. That can only be done through executive action, but this can be heavily circumscribed. Thus, current and future presidents in an age of imperial retreat need to find ways to resolve this dilemma.

Presidents have always looked for ways to circumvent the restrictions placed by others on the executive's freedom of action in foreign policy. The answer at first seemed to be executive orders where the signature of the president is sufficient to achieve an international agreement without the need for a two-thirds majority of the Senate. From 1939 to 1989, for example, the United States entered into 11,698 executive agreements and only 702 treaties as defined by the Constitution.[67] And the proportions have remained roughly the same since the end of the Cold War.

The rest of the world considers executive agreements with a presidential signature to be the same as international treaties. However, under the US Constitution this is a gray area. When the Senate in 1999, for example, rejected the

Comprehensive Nuclear Test Ban Treaty, President Clinton declared, "I signed that treaty, it still binds us unless I go, in effect, and erase our name—unless the President does that and takes our name off, we are bound by it."[68] However, that is not how it was interpreted by Congress, and presidential signatures have been frequently challenged in the courts. As a result, there are now much stricter limits on what American presidents can achieve through what are called "sole executive agreements."[69]

One example is provided by the power to engage in military action. The Constitution gave Congress the sole power to "declare war," but it has used that power sparingly and never since 1942. Instead, Congress has authorized the use of force in other ways, such as the Gulf of Tonkin Resolution in 1964 that was used by President Lyndon Johnson (1963–69) to commit US troops to Vietnam.[70] Anxious to avoid the disaster of Vietnam in the future, Congress then passed in 1973 the War Powers Act designed to curtail sharply the ability of the executive to wage war without congressional consent.[71]

Most US military interventions since 1973 have been consistent with the War Powers Act, but not all, and the act has restricted executive action in many ways. In early 1999, for example, President Clinton planned a NATO bombing campaign against Serbia designed to protect Kosovo. Without a UNSC resolution it was clearly illegal under international law, but not necessarily under the US Constitution. Clinton therefore wrote to the Senate leadership on March 23 asking for "legislative support as we address the crisis in Kosovo . . . without regard to our differing views on the Constitution about the use of force."[72]

Clinton received the support of the Senate immediately and began the bombing campaign the next day. However, one month later the House invoked the War Powers Act and in a tied vote (213–213) failed to grant authorization for air strikes. The war was now illegal not just under international law but under domestic law as well. The campaign did not stop immediately, and Congress never cut off funding, but the Clinton administration was restricted in what it could do.

The executive would later claim that it secured what it wanted in the Kosovo campaign despite congressional opposition. That is debatable since President Slobodan Milosevic of Serbia did not resign until October 2000. However, a much more serious test came nearly fifteen years later, when President Obama judged that a "red line" had been crossed in Syria where the regime of Bashar al-Assad was deemed to have used chemical weapons. This justified in the executive's eyes the use of force and an opportunity to show global leadership, but government opinion was divided over whether it needed congressional support.

BOX 11.4
JCPOA, THE EXECUTIVE, AND CONGRESS

In 2015, after two years of intense negotiations, the five permanent members of the UNSC plus Germany (P5+1) reached a historic agreement with Iran on its nuclear program. Known as the Joint Comprehensive Plan of Action (JCPOA), it set strict limits for Iran to continue enriching uranium for civilian purposes, a huge reduction in Iran's existing stockpile, and a tough inspections regime. In return, Iran was promised the lifting of those sanctions related to its nuclear program and an end to all enrichment restrictions for civilian purposes after a maximum of fifteen years.

The US government played the leading role in P5+1, several of whose members had failed to reach agreement with Iran on numerous previous occasions. Without US leadership, the agreement would never have happened. Indeed, the JPCOA is in many ways a model for the kind of global leadership the United States claims it can deliver in an age of imperial retreat.

Despite this, the JPCOA was nearly derailed by a hostile Congress that adopted almost unanimously the Iran Nuclear Agreement Review Act in July 2015. This gave Congress sixty days to review whatever deal the executive achieved with Iran, at the end of which there would be a vote to approve or disapprove the JPCOA.

As the deadline approached, the House of Representatives, as expected, failed to approve the agreement. In the Senate, however, a Democratic filibuster could not be blocked as Republicans fell two votes short of the sixty needed. The JPCOA therefore survived and a presidential veto was not needed, but it failed to receive a single Republican vote in favor and even some Democrats voted against it.

President Trump (2017–) campaigned against JCPOA during the presidential campaign in 2016 and promised to "tear it up" if elected. As president, however, he faced considerable resistance even among Republicans. Even if the United States withdrew, it is very unlikely that the other members of the P5+1 would follow suit. Thus, JPCOA will probably survive regardless of what the United States does.

Many in the administration believed that there was no need to go to Congress, but the president thought differently.[73] Conscious that he would never secure a UNSC resolution authorizing the use of force, he was anxious to ensure that military action was at least legal under domestic law. The legislature was therefore asked to give approval. It soon became clear, however, that Congress was going to do no such thing.[74] Military action therefore never took place, and the president was only rescued from humiliation by an offer from Russia to force President Assad to give up his chemical weapons. The chance for America to show global leadership disappeared.[75]

International trade is another area where executive efforts to demonstrate global leadership are increasingly restrained by the behavior of other domestic actors (let alone foreign ones). The United States took the lead in the deepening of globalization in the 1970s and accepted the argument of its partners that reaching international agreements would be hampered if Congress could unpick trade deals after negotiations were complete. The result was Trade Promotion Authority (TPA), which was first passed by Congress in 1974.[76]

TPA gave the executive the authority to negotiate trade deals subject to a straight up-or-down vote at the end. It was extended at regular intervals and used to ratify not only the first preferential trade agreements (PTAs) by the United States but also the multilateral Uruguay Round. However, it was not renewed after 1994 as a result of partisan congressional politics.[77] It was only the election of a Republican to the presidency in 2000 that made it possible for Republicans in Congress to drop their opposition. TPA was then renewed in 2002.[78]

The new authority expired in 2007 but could still be used after that date for agreements signed beforehand. Thus, both President George W. Bush and President Obama were able to secure approval for a swath of bilateral PTAs, but by the end of 2011 there were none left outstanding.[79] Without a new TPA, the executive was powerless to conclude new trade deals.

Even before his second term, President Obama had pinned American leadership on securing a Trans-Pacific Partnership (TPP) agreement that would lay down new rules for trade and investment with eleven countries in the Asia-Pacific region while isolating China; a hugely ambitious agreement with the European Union called the Transatlantic Trade and Investment Partnership (TTIP); and a global Trade in Services Agreement (TISA).

If all came to fruition, the United States could justifiably claim still to be the world leader in trade and foreign investment, both arenas of central importance to the semiglobal empire. The executive had strong support from US MNEs from the beginning, but other domestic actors were increasingly disillusioned with globalization. It therefore took the executive three years to persuade a skeptical, and highly partisan, Congress before TPA was finally passed in 2015.

By this time, trade agreements had become so toxic for much of the American public that many of the presidential candidates had turned against new deals.[80] As a result, Congress was unable to pass the TPP before the Obama administration ended and President Trump withdrew it immediately after his inauguration (the same fate will surely await TTIP and TISA if they ever reach that far). Meanwhile, China was busy concluding its own version of the TPP in the Asia-Pacific region without US participation.[81] American efforts to lead the world in an area crucial to the semiglobal empire had been thwarted.

Where the United States did lead after the Second World War was on promoting the free movement of capital, a key component of globalization and perhaps even more important for American capitalism than free movement of goods and services. As capital flowed round the world in ever greater quantities, two questions arose: Who would receive it, and where would tax be paid?

Federal governments from President John F. Kennedy (1961–63) onward, facing balance of payments deficits, had pushed through measures to ensure that a large share of international capital flows ended up in the United States, while state governments (especially Delaware, Nevada, Wyoming and, more recently, South Dakota) were equally proactive in providing tax incentives and promises of secrecy that enticed capital into their jurisdictions. As a result, the United States acquired a well-earned reputation as a tax haven for offshore funds.[82]

Most of these funds were owned by foreigners. Since the US government operated a worldwide tax on American citizens, it could afford to ignore tax avoidance/evasion by nonresidents despite protestations by foreign governments. However, the financial crash that began in late 2007 changed everything. This crisis had "made in America" stamped all over it, but the free movement of capital caused it to spread very quickly to other countries. A new approach was needed if the United States was to retain leadership of global economic governance.

The US government turned first to those institutions such as the IMF that it controlled, but these were soon deemed insufficient. As a result, the G20—hitherto a largely toothless body designed to soothe the vanities of large economies underrepresented in the established organizations—was upgraded in 2009. The G20, although not under US control, was then given a crucial role in managing the financial crisis and coming up with proposals for reform.

The most important proposal to come out of the G20 has been its plan to ensure that MNEs pay their fair share of tax in all jurisdictions in which they operate. Its base erosion and profit shifting (BEPS) project was endorsed by G20 leaders in 2015 and supported by all OECD members.[83] It requires those states joining the project (eighty-five by mid-2016) to specify how they plan to legislate domestically to bring their tax laws in line with BEPS.

This was a chance for the US executive to show global leadership. However, many of the MNEs engaged in tax avoidance are American companies that have donated generously to political parties and candidates. Furthermore, their global tax avoidance strategies do not eliminate their obligation to pay US corporate tax if/when the profits are repatriated. Thus, payment of additional tax to foreign jurisdictions by these companies reduces potential future US tax revenues.

The United States has, therefore, not shown leadership on this issue, preferring to argue that its domestic laws are fully in line with BEPS and therefore no changes are required. In responding to the various actions needed, as specified by the G20, the US government stonewalled and argued in the case of each "action" that no new legislation was required. Even in the case of actions on transfer pricing, which MNEs frequently use to reduce profits, the Treasury Department claimed that the consistency of existing domestic transfer pricing principles with Actions 8–10 meant that harmonizing the two does not require "substantial" changes to the US transfer pricing regulations.[84]

In theory, it is possible that the US tax treatment of MNEs is so perfect that no changes are needed. A more likely explanation, however, is that a Republican-controlled Senate made it impossible for the executive to bring in new tax rules for MNEs under a Democratic president.[85] And the same has been true of efforts by the executive to shake off the "tax haven" label.

President Obama chose his first State of the Union address in 2009 to focus on the need to crack down on tax havens. The following year the Foreign Account Tax Compliance Act (FATCA) was passed, forcing US persons to report their non-US financial accounts to the Financial Crimes Enforcement Network (FINCEN). It also obliged foreign financial institutions (FFIs) to report all assets of US persons to the Treasury Department.

The lead taken by the US government was soon followed by other governments following the adoption of the OECD Common Reporting Standard (CRS). This, of course, requires the United States to report on non-US persons' financial assets in exactly the same way as FATCA does for US persons. Yet reciprocity has proven to be difficult for the executive to provide. Many states value their tax haven status, the Senate has refused to ratify the bilateral tax treaties that would allow the relevant information to be handed over to foreign governments, and financial institutions complain about the workload. As FINCEN itself reported, "Financial institutions noted that a requirement to 'look back' to obtain beneficial ownership information from existing customers would be a substantial burden. FINCEN proposes that the beneficial ownership requirement will apply only with respect to legal entity customers that open new accounts going forward from the date of implementation."[86] Once again, domestic constraints have made it difficult, if not impossible, for the executive to show global leadership even when it wants to do so. The "checks and balances" for which the US system is so famous have become more about checks and less about balances. As a result, the semiglobal empire that America created after the Second World War has become increasingly difficult to sustain.

12

HEGEMONY UNDER THREAT

The American empire is still functioning, but the extent of its retreat is clearly revealed by an examination of US influence in the different regions of the world. This chapter will look in turn at the Americas, Europe, Africa, the Middle East, and the Asia-Pacific region, outlining US policy toward each region and gauging the extent to which US goals are, or are not, being achieved. While there have been, and will continue to be, examples where policy has met with success, this has been more than outweighed by many cases of outright failure or even American irrelevance.

The US empire began in the Americas, and it might be expected that this is where it would last the longest. Indeed, despite paying lip service to "mutual partnership and coresponsibility," it is rare for speeches by officials not to draw attention to the need for US "leadership" in the hemisphere. Yet US policy toward the region has achieved only modest success and American leadership is increasingly challenged—even by countries that were once close allies.

Europe since the Cold War has been willing to play a largely supportive role in the American empire. This marks a rare example of continuity in the relations between the United States and the rest of the world and reflects the broadly similar view of the world that Europe and America hold. Yet Europe is very much the junior partner in this relationship as a consequence of its dependence on the United States for its security. And the readiness of US policy makers to exploit this asymmetry in power has given rise to major tensions with European civil societies and occasionally with governments as well.

Sub-Saharan Africa has posed a very different set of problems for US governments. The defense of apartheid in South Africa, support for anticommunist insurgents in Angola, and the close relationship with numerous African dictators had damaged perceptions of the United States as the Cold War came to an end. The administration of President Bill Clinton (1993–2001), however, was quick to seize the opportunity created by the collapse of the Soviet Union with a package of measures designed to entice all sub-Saharan African countries into the imperial fold.

Public opinion started to move in favor of the United States and barely changed course even after the invasion of Iraq. However, the United States was unable to capitalize on this. The relationship did not turn sour, but it was overshadowed by the rise of China in sub-Saharan Africa. Clinton's successors could do nothing to prevent China becoming the dominant commercial partner for the region, and this has affected political relations as well.

The Middle East has always been a challenging region for the United States. Competition with the USSR was intense during the Cold War, and the Iranian Revolution in 1978–79 complicated matters further. However, the collapse of the Soviet Union in 1991 coupled with victory in the first Iraq War suggested a brighter future for the American empire, especially as Iran was being seriously weakened by US sanctions as well.

The brighter future never transpired. The Taliban in Afghanistan, the Ba'athists in Iraq, and Muammar al-Gaddhafi in Libya were ousted from power, but the results were very far from what imperial America expected. Indeed, one of the main outcomes of the first two US invasions was the strengthening of Iran, since its most deadly regional competitors were removed. And America's client states in the region became increasingly reluctant to do the empire's bidding, adopting unilaterally policies that were a source of deep frustration to US governments.

The Asia-Pacific is a region into which American power has been projected for over two centuries, during which the United States has accumulated territories, protectorates, and client states. Its imperial status was reinforced at the end of the Second World War with the collapse of Japan. The communist victory in China and the projection of Soviet power into the region jolted America but at the same time reinforced alliances with nations dependent on US security.

The fall of the USSR and China's prioritization of economic growth left America in an exceptionally powerful position in the 1990s. It seemed the perfect opportunity for the US government to create a set of rules for the region that China would be obliged to respect. Yet it did not turn out that way, and US policy toward China moved from paternalism to containment without either word ever being used in official discourse.

Containing China is proving to be impossible. By virtue of its economic strength, its geography, and it cultural ties to the region, China is slowly replacing

America as the hegemonic power in the Asia-Pacific. It is an ancient pattern, one replicated by the United States itself in the Americas in the century after independence. Yet the process will probably not take so long for China, as geopolitical time has sped up.

In the five regions examined here, the US imperial presence has been waning. It will continue to do so, although the temptation to "make a stand" in at least one of them will be great. America still has allies, and they will not want to see the empire retreat too far or too fast. Yet even these allies can see the difficulties of relying on an America that is itself ambiguous about its imperial role and keen to withdraw from at least some of its commitments. Friendly nations are therefore preparing for the day when the US empire will no longer be their shield. Thus, internal and external pressures are combining to reduce America's imperial presence and hasten the day when it will become "just" a nation-state.

12.1. THE AMERICAS

After the Cold War ended, US policy toward the rest of the Americas changed. This was also the moment when Latin America and the Caribbean (LAC) was slowly emerging from the 1980s debt crisis, providing the US government—as the main source of credits—with strong leverage to push the region in the direction it wanted it to go.

At the top of the list was economics, with an emphasis on free trade, free movement of capital, protection of intellectual property, and guarantees for foreign investment. Collectively known as the Washington Consensus, this agenda was pushed aggressively at every level—bilateral and multilateral—and involved not just the imperial state but also many of its NSAs (especially MNEs).

American support for hemispheric dictatorships melted away in the warm glow afforded by the collapse of the Soviet Union. It was replaced by the promotion of representative democracy, provided that it was consistent with imperial priorities: periodic elections, political parties embracing private enterprise, and the subordination of national sovereignty to the demands of globalization.

Security concerns in the hemisphere were at first dominated by the "war on drugs," a throwback to 1971, when it was launched by President Richard M. Nixon (1969–74), and the goal of regime change in Cuba.[1] However, the terrorist atrocities of 9/11 sparked a new interest in possible hemispheric links with Islamic fundamentalism in view of the numerous Muslim minority populations in the region.

The US economics agenda for the hemisphere was initially dominated by free trade. The LAC countries had not waited for US pressure to dismantle the high levels of protection adopted in support of import-substituting industrialization. Instead, they had done so unilaterally in response to the debt crisis of the 1980s.[2] However, they had not sought special trade preferences from the United States nor given any to it.

This created an opportunity for the US government. Building on NAFTA, the Clinton administration launched in December 1994 an ambitious plan to create a Free Trade Area of the Americas (FTAA) by 2005.[3] This would not only have given the United States preferential access to all independent countries in the hemisphere (except Cuba) but would also have extended free trade to a broad range of services, strongly protected intellectual property, and provided for the settlement of disputes in special courts free of government interference.[4]

Formal negotiations commenced in 1998 but had collapsed before the deadline. The United States came up against a wall of opposition that it had never before encountered in the region. Opponents of the FTAA included civil society groups in all countries whose voices had often been drowned out under previous authoritarian regimes.[5] However, opposition also came from a range of governments that had traditionally been loyal supporters of US leadership in the region.

Some of these governments, all left of center, responded to the collapse of the FTAA by forming their own regional organization called Alianza Bolivariana de los Pueblos de Nuestra América (ALBA).[6] Always too dependent on Venezuelan energy wealth, and therefore vulnerable to the world oil price, ALBA offered a counternarrative to US imperialism in the Americas that encouraged subaltern behavior.

This revealed itself not just in the opposition to the FTAA but also in the neoliberal agenda advanced by the Washington Consensus. Specifically, ALBA supported the reversal of privatizations (many involving US companies) and the promotion of state companies during the administrations of Presidents George W. Bush (2001–9) and Barack Obama (2009–17).[7] Furthermore, this wave of nationalism affected not only ALBA countries but also others—such as Argentina and Brazil—where globalization was viewed with suspicion.

The collapse of the FTAA negotiations forced the US government to change tack. Instead of hemispheric free trade, the United States sought and secured a series of bilateral free trade agreements with Chile, Colombia, Panama, and Peru as well as one with Central America (including the Dominican Republic).[8] All these agreements gave the United States preferential access and helped to stave off the competition from China.

MNEs welcomed these agreements (US civil society was much more divided), but they fell far short of the hemispheric FTAA planned in 1994. In particular, they excluded MERCOSUR (Argentina, Brazil, Paraguay, Uruguay, and Venezuela), with almost half the LAC population.[9] American companies, lacking preferential access, struggled to compete with China, which had replaced the United States as the main source of imports for MERCOSUR by the end of the first Obama administration.[10]

The US political agenda for the region after the Cold War emphasized the promotion of democracy. Yet it soon became clear that "democracy" was a very fungible concept. In the words of the Bureau of Western Hemisphere Affairs (a branch of the State Department), the US political objective was an inter-American community formed by "Economic partners that are democratic, stable, and prosperous; friendly neighbors that help secure our region against terrorism and illegal drugs; nations that work together in the world to advance shared political and economic values."[11] Thus, hemispheric governments would be judged not only on their democratic credentials but also on their willingness to follow the US lead on a whole range of policies.

To achieve its goals, the US government in 2001 secured through the OAS the Inter-American Democratic Charter. However, the collapse in credibility of the OAS soon turned this into a blunt and ineffective instrument.[12] As a result, the State Department had to fall back on cruder methods. These included the pressure that could be exerted on hemispheric governments by means of annual reports covering human rights, narcotics, and trafficking in persons.[13]

The results could best be described as mixed. Representative democracy took root almost everywhere, but its quality deteriorated in many countries. Provided their governments were deemed "friendly," the US administration ignored these imperfections. And Haiti remained a stain on the US reputation, unable to adopt even the most minimal standards of representative democracy after more than two decades of American intervention.[14]

When governments were deemed "unfriendly," opposing American initiatives or decrying US policies, the government now found itself relatively powerless. This was a new experience in the Americas, where US military intervention had been used so frequently in the past. State Department pressure rarely worked, and unilateral intervention—albeit of the nonmilitary kind—was widely condemned. ALBA governments denounced US policy loudly but faced little retaliation.

Even non-ALBA countries found they could defy the United States without facing major consequences. When, for example, the Bush administration sought in early 2003 a second UN Security Council resolution authorizing the use of force against Iraq, no amount of arm-twisting was sufficient to persuade Chile and Mexico to support it.[15] And even Colombia, despite its dependence on US military and financial assistance, was vocal in its demand that Cuba be read-mitted to the hemispheric family.

The US security agenda in the hemisphere after the Cold War was at first dominated by the "war on drugs." With more emphasis put on reducing supply than demand, this placed many LAC countries in the front line either as source or transit countries. The Drug Enforcement Agency (DEA) became active throughout the region and countries came under huge pressure to conform. Shiprider and extradition agreements were reached with many LAC countries that substantially reduced their national sovereignty.[16]

Despite the enormous volume of resources devoted to supply reduction, the export of drugs continued, with tragic consequences for the most affected countries. Opposition to US policy expanded at all levels. ALBA countries adopted confrontational tactics, forcing the closure of military bases (in Ecuador), ex-pelling the DEA (in Bolivia) and even the US ambassador (in Venezuela). Non-ALBA countries promoted a new approach to narcotics that emphasized decriminalization (in Guatemala) or even legalization (in Uruguay).

By the end of the Obama administration, with several US states having legal-ized the consumption of marijuana, it was clear that US drug policy in the hemisphere had not only failed but had also alienated many LAC governments. A belated attempt to link the hemispheric drugs trade to the financing of terror-ism in the Middle East smacked of desperation and did little to alter the percep-tion that the US empire no longer commanded the respect in the region that it once enjoyed.[17]

Cuba had been designated a "state sponsor of terrorism" in 1982 and would remain on the US list even after the end of the Cold War. By then no LAC country shared this view of Cuba, which placed the US government in an in-vidious position. Despite this, Congress used Cuba's alleged links with interna-tional terrorism to pass legislation that deepened the embargo in the hope of achieving regime change, a policy that was widely condemned in Latin America.

The need to change course on Cuba forced the Obama administration to re-move the country from the list of state sponsors of terrorism in 2015 as part of the process of normalization between the two countries. Nothing had really changed in Cuba, but the US government had finally accepted the reality. Its long-running campaign to isolate the island's government had failed, and the empire was powerless to change it. It was a victory for common sense, but also a recognition that American hegemony in the western hemisphere was coming to an end.[18]

Imperial America continued to retain an attraction for many people, and sur-veys of public attitudes toward the United States regularly recorded a majority with favorable opinions—even in ALBA countries.[19] This allowed US officials a certain room for maneuver in the way policy was implemented. There were limits, however, as this perceptive quote from a member of the Latin American elites made clear: "One of the biggest gripes I have with the US is how they exert power and implement foreign policy without due diligence. As 'the only empire' in the world, exerting political influence is expected. The problem, however, is how they do it. In effect, America believes and promotes itself as the standard bearer of democratic values, which is hard to live up to. And the image they transmit to the rest of the world is tarnished due to the cavalier manner in which they implement their foreign policy."[20]

This "cavalier manner" showed up in many instances even after the end of the supposedly insensitive Bush administration. Relations with Argentina deteriorated dramatically after a relatively insignificant US judge was allowed to intervene on behalf of a small number of debt-owning "vulture" funds who wanted to be paid in full. The Brazilian government reacted angrily when Edward Snowden revealed that its president had been spied on by the NSAg.[21] Puerto Rico, a US colony and once a model for the rest of the Caribbean, collapsed into financial chaos after years of neglect.[22]

Yet the most compelling evidence pointing to the end of hegemony was the number of cases where the initiatives of the US imperial state proved largely irrelevant. The OAS, for decades a key institution for projecting US power in the region, declined in importance despite American efforts to revive it. The US government was unable to prevent a Chinese company from winning approval to build an interoceanic canal through Nicaragua.[23] It was also powerless to prevent Venezuela's descent into chaos after the death of President Hugo Chávez and the collapse of oil prices.

Above all, the United States played virtually no part in the peace agreement reached in Colombia in 2016 between the government and the largest rebel group (FARC), only appointing a special envoy for the peace process in its final stages. Indeed, by continuing to designate the FARC as a terrorist group, US policy showed itself to be badly out of touch. Given the extraordinary efforts to which the US government had gone in the 1990s to support the Colombian state in its struggle against drug traffickers and guerrillas, this was a remarkable change of circumstance.[24]

12.2. EUROPE

America's imperial relations with Europe by the end of the Cold War were focused on the European Community and its member states. In 1990 the two signed a Transatlantic Declaration setting out a series of "common goals" in-cluding a commitment to democracy promotion throughout the world, bring-ing central and eastern European states into the capitalist sphere and upholding the authority of US-controlled institutions.[25]

This was an American imperial agenda, albeit one that the European Union (EU) was happy to support.[26] At its heart, however, was the economic relation-ship between the two, which at the time—and arguably even today—was the most important in the world. Widening and deepening the relationship has been central to US thinking, as a result of which European integration has al-ways had the support of American administrations.

EU expansion creates huge opportunities for American firms, but it can also lead to trade diversion at the expense of some US companies. This might have led to only qualified American support for the European project. However, the American empire needed a Europe that was strong enough economically to share the burden of global security and that did not change with the end of the Cold War.

European integration plans were at first uncontroversial. The incorporation of most central and eastern European states into the EU proceeded relatively smoothly, with strong support from the United States. Although Russia shared a border with several of these countries, she raised no objections—in large part because she was in no condition to do so at the time. The Balkan States were also targeted for membership, with Slovenia joining in 2004, Croatia in 2013, and other countries on the path to join at a later date.

At this point the EU had expanded to twenty-eight members (it had been only twelve in 1990). However, when the EU with strong US support started serious negotiations with Georgia, Moldova, and Ukraine with a view to eventual mem-bership, it encountered strong resistance from Russia.[27] EU expansion was now seen as a hostile act, and Russia was determined to resist it.

The EU now lost its nerve—much to the disgust of officials in the Obama administration. A crisis developed in Ukraine, by far the largest and most impor-tant of the three countries, in which the United States brushed aside European reservations.[28] Russia, however, was no longer prepared to stand aside and an-nexed Crimea, a part of Ukraine, while also fomenting rebellion in the east of the country.[29] It was now clear that any further EU expansion in the vicinity of Rus-sia was going to be a long drawn out affair whatever the imperial designs of the United States.

Even as the EU was widening, the process of deepening was proceeding in tandem with the cautious blessing of the United States. The European Single Market had been launched in 1993, the monetary union (the eurozone) in 1999, and the new currency (the euro) started to circulate in 2002. A swath of new regulations were adopted to bring all this about, and the United States began to worry about possible discrimination against American companies.

President Obama therefore proposed in 2013 a Transatlantic Trade and Investment Partnership (TTIP) that would remove virtually all obstacles to trade and investment by US companies in the EU and harmonize regulations on both sides of the Atlantic. Negotiations were conducted in secret, but it soon became clear that what was proposed went far beyond what European public opinion was willing to accept. And, in response to mass demonstrations, some European governments publicly criticized the agreement in 2016, ensuring that it was unlikely to become law even if it received congressional approval.[30]

The American economic agenda for Europe had now run into difficulties, and tensions between the two sides were exacerbated by the determination of the European Commission to punish high-profile US companies for anticompetitive behavior and tax avoidance strategies. By the end of the Obama administration, the stirring words in the 1990 Transatlantic Declaration in favor of a global economic duumvirate (with the United States as the senior partner) seemed a distant memory.

The collapse of the Soviet empire in central and eastern Europe had led not only to the rapid expansion of the EU but also of NATO. The promises that had been made by US leaders not to expand NATO to the borders with Russia were ignored, and Russian protests were swept aside. The opportunity to expand the American imperial sphere was too tempting, and Russia under President Boris Yeltsin (1991–99) was too weak to resist.

Vladimir Putin, Yeltsin's successor as leader of the Russian Federation,[31] was in a much stronger position as a result of the stabilization of the Russian economy and the rise for many years in the price of its leading exports. He was determined to reverse Russian humiliations, concentrating in his first term on winning back from the oligarchs the political power that they had acquired through their business fortunes. He did not, however, antagonize the United States and was among the first to lend support to the American people after 9/11.

This contributed to the massive miscalculation by US leaders of Russian intentions, which manifested itself in imperial hubris. The continued expansion of NATO, the deployment of advanced weaponry on the Russian borders, and the operations of US NSAs provoked Russian fury. This time, however, Russia was in a position to do something about it.

The United States consequently found itself in a stalemate in Europe almost everywhere it turned. Plans to normalize Bosnia & Herzegovina's status as an independent country were blocked by Russian support for its Serbian enclave.[32]

All hopes of bringing Ukraine into the EU and NATO were stymied by Russian support for separatists in the east. The same happened in Georgia, after its president—promised a road map for NATO membership by the US government—engaged in an unwise attack on South Ossetia.[33] Kosovo, recognized by the United States the day after it declared independence in 2008, was unable to join the UN as a result of Russian opposition.[34]

Inevitably, cracks began to appear in American support for imperial expansion in Europe and even surfaced publicly during the 2016 presidential campaign.[35] NATO allies in Europe were largely passengers, unwilling to pay their share and unable to bring many military assets to the table. NATO operations "outside of area" were usually US operations with token participation by all other countries except France and the United Kingdom. At the same time, all these allies looked to the United States for their defense.

European allies compensated for their lack of military commitment by providing broad political support for US initiatives around the world. Divergences between America and Europe were wildly exaggerated.[36] The EU's Common Foreign and Security Policy, lacking a military dimension, never threatened to undermine US hegemony (and the European Security and Defence Policy even less so). And when the Obama administration committed to the fight against climate change, one of the main sources of friction disappeared.[37]

One of the issues on which the United States did diverge with a number of EU members was its decision to invade Iraq in 2003 without the backing of international law. Even here, however, many European states fell into line, fearing the consequences of opposing the imperial power on a matter of supposedly strategic national interest. And differences with the United States were soon patched up, as the Iraq crisis morphed into a more general struggle against international terrorism where the United States and EU shared common interests.

The imperial standing of the United States in Europe was also helped enormously by the election of Barack Obama as president in November 2008, replacing his unpopular predecessor George W. Bush in January 2009. At a stroke, public opinion in Europe toward America changed with large majorities in almost all countries recording a "favorable" or "very favorable" view. Even more remarkable was opinion of the US president himself, which jumped in one year from strongly negative to overwhelmingly positive.

Just as important was the renewed rhetoric by the US government about "partnership" in the transatlantic dialogue. In July 2016, for example, President Obama stated that "given our shared interests, Europe will remain a cornerstone of America's engagement with the world. European countries are and will remain among our closest allies and friends, and Europe is an indispensable partner around the globe. . . . [O]ur work today shows that we're going to continue to be focused on pressing global challenges."[38]

This sop to the vanities of Europeans made it easier for their governments to play a strongly supportive role in the American empire without running the risk of being seen by voters as servile. From mobilizing financial resources for Afghanistan to participation in the nuclear agreement with Iran and imposing sanctions on Russia, European states provided a useful adjunct to American power. And US officials became very skilled at playing this game, allowing EU states occasionally to take the lead in what were essentially US operations.[39]

As in the Americas, imperial policy was not without its successes in Europe. The reunification of Germany, once seen as a remote possibility, was achieved quickly after the fall of the Berlin Wall and the expanded country remained a member of NATO with Soviet (later Russian) acquiescence. Central and eastern European states became enthusiastic members of the western alliance, joining both the EU and NATO.[40] All looked to the United States for leadership on a whole host of issues, with public opinion strongly in support.[41]

NATO support for the United States was virtually guaranteed by virtue of its institutional structure and sources of finance. This was not necessarily true of the EU, which marketed itself as a new source of world power. However, the new members—together with a few "old" allies such as the United Kingdom—helped to ensure that the EU would never become a geostrategic rival even in the tense days after the US invasion of Iraq. Although American and European firms competed fiercely with each other in markets around the world, US governments knew that the EU and its member states would not harm American strategic interests and could usually be counted on to help promote them.

These successes could not disguise the fact that, as in the Americas, US policy suffered a number of setbacks. This time, however, it was more to do with imperial hubris than subaltern resistance. The ease with which Europeans allowed the United States to take the lead in the Balkans in the 1990s produced a false sense of confidence. More than twenty years after the Dayton Peace Agreement and the injection of millions of US dollars in foreign aid, Bosnia & Herzegovina was still very far from being able to join either NATO or the EU. Furthermore, public opinion registered strong disapproval of US leadership.[42]

Imperial setbacks in the Balkans could be dismissed as relatively minor in the broad scheme of things. Much more serious was the failure to develop a harmonious relationship with Russia after the rise to power of Vladimir Putin. In an age of imperial retreat, Russian collaboration was likely to be needed in many areas. US officials, however, made a series of misjudgments based on arrogance and ignorance. Although far from representing an existential threat, a hostile Russia was then able and willing to block American plans in numerous areas while exploiting any temporary differences between the United States and its European allies.

The United States, so central to western European development in the Cold War, also found itself largely irrelevant in some of the key events of the last decade. The financial crisis in the eurozone after 2008 put at risk the whole European project and therefore threatened the imperial interests of the United States. Yet the American government was largely a bystander in the unfolding drama, reduced to pressuring the IMF (without success) to persuade Germany to adopt a more flexible approach to sovereign debts.

Lack of influence during the eurozone crisis was frustrating, but even more galling was the American inability to influence the outcome of the British referendum on EU membership in 2016. A key US ally and one of only two countries in the EU with significant military capabilities, the United Kingdom was seen as so important to American imperial policy in Europe that President Obama was prepared to defy convention and tell British people how to vote. Yet his intervention had no effect on the outcome. The British electorate voted to leave the EU and, in so doing, seriously damaged the European project and therefore US interests in Europe.

US imperial interests in Europe then suffered a major setback with the election of President Trump in 2016. The new president immediately created a crisis in the relationship with his stance on global trade, international human rights, climate change mitigation, and NATO obligations. The region in the world that had previously been the most well disposed toward the continuation of American empire now had to reexamine its geopolitical assumptions. America was now seen by key countries in the EU, especially France and Germany, as an unreliable ally. Only a handful of countries, above all the United Kingdom, were now willing to support publicly the idea of continued US leadership in world affairs.

12.3. SUB-SAHARAN AFRICA

During the Cold War, America had found itself on the "wrong" side of history in many parts of Africa—especially the south. The end of apartheid in South Africa therefore provided the United States with an opportunity to start afresh. Indeed, as early as 1994 Congress had included Section 134 in the Uruguay Round Agreements Act mandating the Clinton administration to "develop and implement a comprehensive trade and development policy for the countries of Africa" and report annually to Congress on the progress made.[43]

The target for Congress was not just southern Africa but the grip exercised by European powers (especially France) over trade and investment with their former colonies in sub-Saharan Africa. Several of these countries were already energy exporters and others would soon follow, a matter of some strategic importance at a time when the US economy was still heavily dependent on oil imports.

The Clinton administration carried out its congressional mandate faithfully, while also exploring opportunities to promote US imperial interests more broadly in sub-Saharan Africa. And with the demise of the Soviet Union, the way now looked cleared to promote not just free markets, privatization, and globalization but also political pluralism and representative democracy.

The result was the Africa Growth and Opportunity Act (AGOA), which became law in 2000 and which offered sub-Saharan African countries privileged access to the US market for a wide range of exports. However, countries had to pass a test of eligibility, and the test was designed to ensure that those participating conformed to a strict definition of American imperial interests. In particular, the US president had to determine that each beneficiary country had established "a market-based economy that protects private property rights, incorporates an open rules-based trading system, and minimizes government interference in the economy. . . . [T]he rule of law, political pluralism, and the right to due process, a fair trial, and equal protection under the law; the elimination of barriers to United States trade and investment. . . . [and] does not engage in activities that undermine United States national security or foreign policy interests."[44]

AGOA was intended to be a powerful tool at the service of the American empire, and sub-Saharan African countries were at first keen to take advantage of its provisions, although not all succeeded. Indeed, countries were frequently added to or subtracted from the eligibility list in line with American strategic interests. And sometimes the mere threat of losing privileged access was sufficient.

AGOA was reinforced by the Millennium Challenge Corporation (MCC), established by Congress in 2004. Designed for low-income countries across the world, most of the beneficiary countries were in sub-Saharan Africa, where eligibility required each state to pass a test set by seventeen indicators—many of which were compiled by US think tanks.[45] Those that passed the test were then expected to draw up a "compact" with the MCC leading to the disbursement of funds.[46]

In a different age, AGOA and the MCC might have placed sub-Saharan African countries in an imperial grip from which there would be no escape. The benefits on offer were potentially enormous and poor countries were expected to jump through whatever hoops were placed in their way in order to qualify. The American empire in the region, without the need for the elaborate superstructure with which European powers had burdened themselves, would have been immeasurably strengthened without a single country being formally colonized.

It did not work out that way for several reasons. First, sub-Saharan African countries benefited from the commodity price boom at the start of the new millennium that gave many of them a huge increase in foreign exchange as well as new customers for their goods. As a result, very few of the 6,475 tariff preferences on offer under AGOA were taken up, and sub-Saharan nonoil exports to the United States were a modest $4.1 billion in 2015 (less than five dollars per head of population).

Second, US governments found it impossible to apply the criteria of eligibility either consistently or transparently. Thus, energy exporters were given virtually a free pass when it came to human rights violations.[47] When oil imports from Africa declined in importance, the same would happen to countries in the front line of the struggle against Islamic fundamentalism. And the money available under the MCC soon became so limited that it ceased to act as much of a lever.[48]

The main reason, however, was the emergence of China as the single most important country trading with and investing in sub-Saharan Africa. By 2011 China had overtaken the United States as the principal importer from sub-Saharan Africa and was soon responsible for a quarter of all purchases, compared with less than 10 percent for the United States.[49] And China, unlike the United States, applied no eligibility criteria for access to the Chinese market, undermining American leverage in many countries.

AGOA was extended in 2015 for a further ten years, but the US government had clearly concluded that it was no longer "fit for purpose" without being clear what would take its place. Many countries had started to reverse privatizations, discriminate against imports (including those from the United States), avoid political pluralism, and abuse human rights but were still being declared "eligible." The 2016 AGOA report for the Republic of Congo, by no means an atypical case, captured the mood: "Government officials make nearly all decisions related to foreign investment. . . . [E]stablished American businesses operating in ROC [the Republic of Congo] have encountered obstacles. . . . There is no political plurality in ROC. . . . Government policies on tax and land tenure have stymied job creation by private enterprises. . . . Human rights concerns persist in the form of infringement on privacy rights, restrictions on the right of citizens to change their government peacefully, and discrimination against women."[50] Yet the report concluded that "ROC is a strong supporter of anti-terrorism efforts, and military cooperation with the United States." In this, and in many other sub-Saharan countries, the US government therefore found itself reverting to a more traditional form of imperialism where security interests trumped all others. Indeed, the American military presence across Africa—coordinated by USAFRICOM— expanded rapidly in response to numerous threats.[51]

The most serious of these threats came from Islamic fundamentalism organized by groups either affiliated to, or inspired by, al-Qaeda. And the scale of the problem had become almost overwhelming by the end of the Obama administration. Addressing Congress in May 2016, the assistant secretary of state for Africa was forced to conclude, without being able to offer any solutions, that "instability and conflict persist in parts of the continent. This instability has a direct bearing on U.S. national interests and those of our closest allies. Conflict has been and remains a breeding ground for extremists that seek to do us harm. . . . We are also concerned about the presence of the Islamic State of Iraq and the Levant (ISIL) on the continent. As we have seen elsewhere in the world, ISIL seeks to co-opt local insurgencies and conflicts to advance its agenda and expand its networks."[52]

The American imperial presence in Africa, perhaps because it was very different from its European predecessors, was generally well received. It was to be expected that President Obama, with his African heritage, would be popular. However, the United States was held in high esteem even before Obama came to power, and Africa has consistently been the region of the world where the United States scores the highest in the Pew Research Center surveys.

Much of this has to do with the emphasis by recent US administrations and the large American foundations on assistance to the region in areas of special concern. President George W. Bush focused on the prevention of HIV/AIDS; President Obama targeted power;[53] the Gates and Clinton Foundations have given special attention to public health. In the countries surveyed by Pew in 2015, a majority in each case considered that US foreign aid was having a positive impact, and in the case of Kenya it was 78 percent.

All this was very welcome for a US administration that prided itself on being different from European imperialist powers, emphasizing instead a "partnership" with the region. President Obama visited sub-Saharan Africa four times, and in 2014 hosted the first ever US-Africa Leaders Summit in Washington, DC, where his formidable rhetorical powers were on full display.

Yet summitry could not disguise the fundamental weaknesses in the US position. China had been regularly holding such summits since 2000 and had used these occasions to bolster its commercial presence in the region. Thus, the US government found itself struggling to keep up with China, whose trade and investment with Africa now dwarfs that of the United States and which is also viewed favorably by public opinion despite the widespread belief that it acts in an imperialist fashion.

With sub-Saharan African countries accounting for almost fifty members of the United Nations, public opinion of the United States was a matter of some importance. Yet the Pew Research Center in 2015 was only able to survey nine of them.[54] As a sample, it was probably representative and included the most important countries. However, there were several countries where the US presence was highly problematic and ran counter to the official narrative that America was not imperialist.

One was South Sudan, which from the day of its birth in 2011 was effectively a US protectorate—albeit a very unsuccessful one despite its significant oil industry. Carved out of Sudan in a civil war, its Christian population had a special appeal for US evangelists, and their pressure, combined with energy interests, had engaged the American government from an early stage. The Bush administration played a key role in the 2005 Comprehensive Peace Agreement that paved the way for the independence of South Sudan six years later. Accordingly, US expectations for the new state ran high.

These hopes were soon dashed. By 2013 fighting had broken out among the different factions in South Sudan and the Obama administration found itself presiding over a crisis. In the words of the State Department itself, "The U.S. Government is the leading international donor to South Sudan, and provides significant humanitarian assistance to the hundreds of thousands of South Sudanese citizens displaced or otherwise affected since the start of the crisis. . . . The U.S. Government helps to provide basic services to citizens; to promote effective, inclusive, and accountable governance; to diversify the economy; and to combat poverty."[55]

The US government could not resolve the crisis, despite its prestige being on the line, and it risked looking foolish for assuming that the separation of South Sudan from Sudan would have enhanced stability. Africans for decades had warned of the risk of interfering with boundaries established by European colonial powers and they had been proved correct. Yet South Sudan was never going to rejoin the north, leaving it as a sickly ward in the US imperial court.

Somalia presented a different set of problems for US administrations. After humiliation in Mogadishu in 1993, US governments were powerless to impose stability on a country that had fractured badly, where warlords competed for power and which was used as a base for international terrorism (including piracy). It would be more than twenty years before Secretary of State John Kerry would finally be able to visit Mogadishu in 2015, where a fragile federal government had established itself with US support.

The United States had set itself ambitious goals in Africa after the Cold War, but they were very far from being fulfilled as the Obama administration came to an end. China was now the dominant commercial power, eclipsing the United States in terms of exports, imports, and inward investment. Only four countries signed bilateral investment treaties (BITs) with the United States, leaving American investors vulnerable to expropriation. And American political leverage was undermined by the United States not being a member of the International Criminal Court (ICC), forcing it to rely on its European allies when targeting gross violations of human rights by African leaders.

12.4. THE MIDDLE EAST AND NORTH AFRICA

The American empire in the Middle East and North Africa (MENA) had been constantly challenged by the Soviet Union and its allies during the Cold War.[56] And by the end of the 1970s, Iran had also joined the list of America's foes in the region. Yet by the time the presidency of George H. W. Bush (1989–93) ended, the US position appeared much stronger. The USSR had crumbled, weakening the position of its Syrian ally, while Saddam Hussein's occupation of Kuwait had ended with the first Iraq War in 1991. Last but not least, US sanctions were inflicting serious damage on Iran.

US policy toward the region could therefore be ambitious, and indeed it was. Barriers to US trade and investment in the region were to be scaled back and energy supplies rendered secure. Peace was to be achieved between Israel and Palestine, making it easier for Muslim states—not just Egypt and Jordan—to normalize relations with a key US ally. American foes, especially Iran and Libya, would be contained in the hope that the regimes in power would suffer the same fate as the Soviet Union.

Democracy promotion at first was timid. Strategic Cold War allies such as Egypt, Pakistan, Saudi Arabia, and Turkey would not be pressed too hard to reform, regardless of their human rights records, in order to preserve stability. However, the events of 9/11 convinced many in the US government that an even bolder approach was required. Democracy promotion was now on the agenda in a way it had never been before in the MENA region, starting in Afghanistan in 2001 and moving on to Iraq in 2003. The policy soon looked wildly optimistic, but democracy promotion was temporarily given a new lease of life by the Arab Spring that started at the end of 2010.

The key to American economic penetration was a network of free trade agreements (FTAs). Building on the one with Israel, the first ever signed by a US government, FTAs were reached with Jordan (2001), Bahrain (2006), Morocco (2006), and Oman (2009). Most countries reached Trade and Investment Framework Agreements (TIFAs) with the United States, and many signed BITs as well. Those countries that had not joined the WTO at birth were pushed to do so, with Oman joining in 2000, Saudi Arabia in 2005, Yemen in 2014, and even Afghanistan in 2016.[57]

The growth in US exports to the MENA region at first sight looked impressive—$9 billion in 1993 rising to $111 billion twenty years later.[58] Much of this was due to defense spending by MENA countries, especially Saudi Arabia, although other categories rose as well. However, China had replaced the United States as the region's principal source of imports by 2007 and was well on its way to selling twice as much as the United States a decade later. Indeed, the US share of MENA imports—15 percent in 1993—had almost halved by the time Donald Trump became president.

US economic ambitions were therefore thwarted, although the issue of energy dependence became less salient as American oil imports from the region declined in importance after 2005. Much the same happened to America's political goals. These had started well, with the Israeli and Palestinian leaders signing the Oslo Accords at the White House in 1993 and committing to negotiations on a final settlement.[59] Yet, despite the enormous effort expended by the Clinton administration, the talks collapsed in 2000.

The inability of subsequent presidents to bring about a diplomatic solution damaged US prestige in the region. America, it seemed, was either unwilling or unable to use its leverage to force an agreement in the way that it had done in the Balkans in the 1990s. Yet when the Obama administration did try to exercise leverage on Israel over settlement construction, it found itself unable to restrain its ally.

The stalemate between Israel and Palestine was one of the reasons for the sudden interest in democracy promotion by the George W. Bush administration after 9/11. If pluralism reigned in the region, it was argued, tensions between Israel and its neighbors would diminish, support for the United States would rise and the attraction of international terrorism diminish. Even Saudi Arabia would not be immune in the eyes of the more committed neoconservatives.

Afghanistan was the first candidate after the United States found itself in control of the country at the end of 2001.[60] Yet pluralism in Afghanistan, with its mixture of warlords and tribal politics, was always a stretch, and the United States in the end settled for a version of electoral politics that observed the form without the substance. Iraq, with its educated populace and large cities, was considered more promising, and the United States as the occupying force after the fall of Saddam Hussein set about its mission with zeal. However, electoral politics soon took a sectarian turn, leaving representatives of the majority Shia population in charge to the consternation of all other groups.

The Arab Spring that started in Tunisia in December 2010 offered a new opportunity for democracy promotion by the United States. In the next few months the Obama administration carried out regime change in Libya and did not block it in Egypt. Yet, soon after, it lost its nerve. Authoritarian regimes allied to the United States crushed protestors without any American resistance; the military returned to power in Egypt without the United States labeling it a coup;[61] Syria suppressed popular discontent by force without provoking direct US intervention; and Libya quickly became a magnate for jihadists and descended into civil war.

Frustrated in its economic and political ambitions, the American empire could still aspire to hegemony in the security field by wielding its formidable military arsenal. Yet even here it was thwarted. The Bush administration had invaded Afghanistan to defeat the Taliban and crush al-Qaeda. However, the former soon found refuge in neighboring Pakistan, despite its government being nominally allied to the United States, while the latter turned out to be hydra-headed and reappeared in different parts of the world.

One of those places was Iraq after the fall of Saddam Hussein, where the al-Qaeda franchise made common cause with the minority Sunni population to undermine American plans for state reconstruction.[62] Yet within ten years the al-Qaeda franchise had separated from its parent and morphed into something even more deadly—the Islamic State of Iraq and Syria (IS)—that reached into Syria and declared a caliphate in 2014. Even if it was no match militarily for the US Air Force and their allies on the ground, the mere existence of the caliphate attracted numerous supporters both inside and outside the region.

Oderint dum metuant was not the preferred *modus operandi* of the American semiglobal empire.[63] However, some of its allies in the region had no such scruples. Israel responded disproportionately to Palestinian attacks on its population, while the Bahraini government ruthlessly crushed all opposition during the Arab Spring. Saudi Arabia, normally the most cautious of all, behaved recklessly in Yemen after 2015 in support of one of the two factions claiming to be the government.[64] And the United Arab Emirates (UAE) joined forces with Bahrain, Egypt, and Saudi Arabia to boycott Qatar, another US ally, in 2017.[65]

Unable to control even its allies, US hegemony in the Middle East appeared doomed. However, the civil war in Syria appeared to the more hawkish elements in the US government to provide an opportunity to reassert American power. Wisely, since it almost certainly would not have worked as intended, President Obama declined to do so. Instead, Russia consolidated its position and extended its already very considerable strategic investment in the country.[66]

By the end of the Obama administration, public opinion of the United States in the MENA region was distinctly hostile. In all the majority Muslim countries polled by the Pew Center, those with a favorable opinion were in a minority and in two cases (Jordan and Pakistan) the proportion barely reached double figures. Only one country in the whole region (Israel) had a favorable opinion of the United States, but this did not transfer to the US president himself.[67] It was a painful legacy for a man whose Cairo speech in 2009 had been heralded with such acclaim.[68]

Although the retreat of the American empire in the Middle East and North Africa was clear to all, there were still some notable achievements along the way. It was the need for oil imports that had brought Franklin Delano Roosevelt (FDR) to the region in the first place and which remained a constant over the next decades. Yet by the time the Obama administration came to an end, US dependence on MENA energy was much reduced. Oil imports had fallen to about one-third of US consumption, and less than 20 percent of these imports came from the region.

Through a combination of lower consumption and higher domestic production, the United States had therefore put some distance between itself and the oil exporters of the MENA region. And among the regional countries providing imported oil, only Saudi Arabia figured in the top five sources.[69] The need to provide public support to authoritarian regimes was now diminished, although US officials were slow to take advantage of this.

The reduction in oil dependence allowed the United States greater room for maneuver. In particular, it facilitated a new approach to Iran, whose government had played a key role in the region to the detriment of US interests. The nuclear agreement reached in 2015 (see Box 11.4) did not pave the way for a reversal of imperial retreat, but it opened a path toward normalization of a bilateral relationship that was a necessary condition for progress in other areas.

Yet these two developments—reduction of oil dependence and the agreement with Iran—could not disguise the long list of US failures in the MENA region. At the top were the fractured states—Afghanistan, Iraq, and Libya—where American hard power had removed autocratic regimes without being able to reconstruct the state institutions they had destroyed. Although these disasters were commonly attributed to "mistakes" in planning, the reasons for failure were far more deep-rooted. The American empire was no longer willing or able to invest the time and resources in state building in the way that it had done in Germany and Japan after the Second World War.

Empires depend on loyalty from their client states. Yet the United States found it increasingly difficult to control its allies. Israel's behavior in the occupied territories has already been mentioned. Turkey, a member of NATO, switched sides in the Syrian Civil War when it found the US position inconsistent with its national interests.[70] Egypt, dependent on US military and financial support, backed a Russian peace plan in the UN Security Council that the United States wanted to block.[71] And Saudi Arabia and Qatar funded the very Islamist groups that US governments had condemned as terrorists.[72]

The Syrian Civil War that started in 2011 captured the dilemmas of an empire in full retreat. President Bashar al-Assad (2000–), like his father before him, meddled in Lebanon, refused to recognize Israel, and was supported by Iran. Removing him from power fitted well with US imperial interests. Yet congressional opposition, heavily influenced by public opinion, made it impossible for the Obama or Trump administrations to intervene with ground forces. Covert support for the "moderate" opposition, however, was undermined as soon as it came under the control of extreme Islamists allied to al-Qaeda. The United States was therefore marginalized, while the civil war dragged on.[73]

The MENA region had witnessed the destruction of many empires even before the rise of the Ottoman one. The collapse of the Ottoman Empire after the First World War was followed in due course by the end of British, French, Italian, and Soviet suzerainty. The American empire, never absolute in the region, is simply following the same path more than seventy years after the historic agreement between FDR and Ibn Saud. Even if the empire has not yet ended, the direction of travel is clear. At least in the MENA region, it cannot be restored and the American public has started to accept it.

12.5. THE ASIA-PACIFIC REGION

US governments since the Second World War have been tireless advocates of free markets and free movement of capital and nowhere have these efforts yielded more than in the Asia-Pacific region.[74] The fortunes of American MNEs are now inextricably linked with what happens in this region, which is home to nearly half the world's population and a growing share of world GDP, international trade, and global greenhouse gas emissions.

US governments have therefore given high priority in the Asia-Pacific to promoting globalization. However, the region is also home to some of the least democratic societies in the world. Balancing the need for free markets with the desire for open societies has proved challenging for American officials, who have found it difficult to pursue a consistent policy and have shifted position on numerous occasions.

Securing US strategic interests in the region has also proved tricky. Widely acknowledged as the regional hegemon at the end of the Cold War, America inherited an array of allies, some of whom now feel threatened by North Korea and anxious about China. Responding to the needs of these allies, without alienating China or provoking North Korea, has tested American empire to its limits and raised doubts about its ability in the long term to commit to the region.

When the Soviet Union collapsed, US imports from China were less than $20 billion. However, the value was growing fast as China became incorporated into commodity chains with American MNEs at their heart. The need to institutionalize the economic relationship with China was therefore a high priority for the Clinton administration. Thus, China was brought into the WTO in 2001 after lengthy negotiations, and the US government started in 1993 to construct an economic framework for the region called Asia-Pacific Economic Cooperation (APEC).

APEC and Chinese membership in the WTO, coupled with a plethora of free trade agreements among member states (several involving the United States), contributed to an extraordinary boom in trade. Within twenty years of APEC's formation, US trade in goods and services to and from the block reached $2.9 trillion—nearly 60 percent of the US total.[75] And US exports of goods and services to APEC were estimated by the Department of Commerce to support nearly six million jobs.

Within these totals, US imports of goods from China loomed large and had reached nearly $500 billion by 2015—much larger than US exports of goods to China.[76] A narrative gained ground in the United States that the Chinese surplus meant it did not play by the rules that the United States had written. In its last year, the George W. Bush administration therefore prepared the ground for a new set of rules—the TPP—from which China would be excluded. Only when these rules were consolidated, ran the argument, would China be invited to join.

The TPP was taken up enthusiastically by the Obama administration, but it was always a high-risk strategy—especially after the financial crisis in 2008–9. Although it was eventually signed by all states in February 2016, it was increasingly seen in the United States as a Trojan horse that would undermine jobs and living standards. It was therefore opposed by the main candidates in the presidential campaign that year and was never ratified. Meanwhile China, angered by its exclusion, was pressing ahead successfully with its own schemes: the

Regional Comprehensive Economic Partnership (RCEP) that excluded the United States and the Belt and Road (B&R) initiative that aimed to build in Eurasia a new Silk Road fit for the twenty-first century.[77]

China's exclusion from the TPP was part of a strategy of containment that became explicit under the Obama administration but which had been hinted at much earlier. The rise of China, described as "peaceful" by its leadership, was always going to be a problem for the existing hegemonic power in the Asia-Pacific region, and US officials had struggled to come up with a consistent approach. Those who favored a "strategic partnership" were matched by those who feared "unfair" competition and favored a more aggressive posture, leaving the US public confused.

It was President George W. Bush who pushed the United States toward a more consistent, if confrontational, policy. Having spoken of China as a "strategic competitor" during the 2000 presidential campaign, he engineered a *rapprochement* with India that reversed the US government's previous position on nuclear nonproliferation.[78] By legitimizing the nuclear ambitions of a state with which China had fought several wars, the United States sent a powerful signal that it intended to strengthen the position of those neighbors that feared Chinese aggression provided that they were willing to support the broad aims of American foreign policy.[79]

The Obama administration took the policy to its logical conclusion. In October 2011, Secretary of State Hillary Clinton published an article, provocatively entitled "America's Pacific Century" and which had been many months in preparation. In it she stated,

> As the war in Iraq winds down and America begins to withdraw its forces from Afghanistan, the United States stands at a pivot point. . . . At a time when [the Asia-Pacific region] is building a more mature security and economic architecture to promote stability and prosperity, U.S. commitment there is essential. It will help build that architecture and pay dividends for continued American leadership well into this century, just as our post–World War II commitment to building a comprehensive and lasting transatlantic network of institutions and relationships has paid off many times over—and continues to do so. The time has come for the United States to make similar investments as a Pacific power, a strategic course set by President Barack Obama from the outset of his administration and one that is already yielding benefits.[80]

The policy laid out in this article, officially described as a "rebalance" and unofficially as a "pivot," was in truth a strategy for containing China while not ruling out engagement on areas of specific mutual interest. Asia-Pacific countries, concerned about China's rise and wishing to avoid becoming overdependent, took note. China did its best in public to appear unconcerned by the rebalance but concluded that it would have to invest even more heavily in its own "security and economic architecture" for the region.

The rebalance initially focused on those countries in the region with which the United States already had a security alliance. A new arrangement, called Joint Defense Guidelines, was made with Japan in 2015 under which its government could now commit troops outside the territory, "mark[ing] the establishment," according to Secretary of State John Kerry, "of Japan's capacity to defend not just its own territory but also the U.S. and other partners as needed."[81] Plans were also put in place to allow South Korea to assume operational responsibility for its military alliance with the United States. Additional US troops were deployed to the American base in Darwin, in northern Australia, while military cooperation with New Zealand resumed after a hiatus of thirty years.[82]

These four countries, traditional US allies with concerns about the rise of China, were all democracies with a fair, if not unblemished, record on human rights. Many Asia-Pacific countries did not share that record. Yet US officials constantly stressed that the pivot was not just about security: "Promoting democracy and human rights, in Asia and around the world, is the right thing to do. It also strengthens our strategic presence and advances our strategic interests. . . . It supports our economic goals by promoting laws and institutions that secure property rights, enforce contracts, and fight corruption. . . . It aligns American leadership with the aspirations of everyday people in the region."[83]

This was always going to be a hard circle to square and the first country chosen, Myanmar, was one of the most difficult. Subject to US sanctions from 1997 onward as a result of its poor human rights record, the military rulers of the country were handsomely rewarded fifteen years later when they allowed a restricted form of democracy to prevail.[84] Ambassadors were exchanged in 2012, President Obama himself attended the ASEAN Summit in Myanmar in 2014, and all sanctions were lifted in 2016. This did not end Myanmar's close relationship with China, but it did reduce the country's dependence on its powerful neighbor—a primary purpose of the pivot.

Next up was Vietnam, a country with which the United States had fought a long and bitter war. Although diplomatic relations had been restored in 1995, this had not prevented Vietnam from becoming ever more entangled in the embrace of China (its wartime ally). However, concern over China's expansion in the South China Sea, including areas claimed by Vietnam, created an opportunity for the Obama administration. Despite Vietnam's poor record on human rights and democracy, a US-Vietnam Comprehensive Partnership was signed in 2013, a Joint Vision Statement was issued in 2015, and the ban on the sale of lethal weapons was lifted during President Obama's visit in 2016—all in the name of rebalancing.

The pivot boosted public opinion of the United States in the Asia-Pacific region. Already popular in many countries beforehand, the image of America improved markedly under President Obama. By 2015 the proportion expressing a favorable view of the United States in the Pew Research Center's survey of America's global image was 60 percent or above in the nine countries surveyed except China. Even more impressive were the majorities of young people, even in China, with a favorable view of the United States.

It is doubtful if much, if any, of this was due to the president having spent some of his formative years in the region.[85] And even a very favorable opinion among the public did not necessarily insulate the US government from difficulties. When Rodrigo Duterte, for example, was elected as president of the Philippines in 2016, the bilateral relationship rapidly deteriorated despite the fact that more than 90 percent of islanders had a positive opinion of the United States at the time.[86] What public opinion surveys did show, however, is that the American regional presence was generally welcome at a time when China was rapidly expanding its influence.

The pivot therefore seemed to have served America's interests well. However, it was essentially a holding strategy, buying the US government precious time while its hegemony in the Asia-Pacific region was slipping away. Although the pivot was welcomed in public, all US allies in the region have grave doubts about the ability of future American governments to "stay the course." Thus, they have to prepare for a time when China will replace the United States as the hegemonic power in the Asia-Pacific. Hillary Clinton's ringing phrase "America's Pacific Century" sounds hollow to their ears.

Rebalancing also changed the strategy adopted by China, leading to an acceleration of its own plans for a "security and economic architecture" for the Asia-Pacific region. The RCEP, B&R, AIIB, and all the other regional plans might have come to fruition anyway, but the pivot sped them up. China can now offer its neighbors a range of economic and financial benefits that America will struggle to match. Over time, these will prove irresistible.

Nor has China slowed down its military spending as a result of US efforts to strengthen security alliances in the region. On the contrary, China has pressed ahead more rapidly than ever with double-digit annual growth in spending. The People's Liberation Army (PLA) exceeds two million, and the Chinese government expects to achieve parity with the United States in air and sea power by

2030. Furthermore, this formidable military arsenal—unlike in the case of the United States—is concentrated almost exclusively in the Asia-Pacific region.

"The only lesson you can learn from history is that it repeats itself," it has been said.[87] America squeezed its European rivals out of its hemisphere without a major conflict, although it was prepared to fight one if necessary. China is doing the same in the Asia-Pacific region today. Neither side wants a conflict, but—if there is one—China will surely choose a moment when it is likely to win. For that and other reasons, the US retreat from hegemony—in the Asia-Pacific as elsewhere—is likely to be peaceful, and for that we can all be grateful.

EPILOGUE

The American empire reached its first centenary in the 1880s, just as the frontier was closing. At that point thirty-eight states had joined the Union. This still left a large territorial empire outside the Union, to which must be added many protectorates and client states whose number would grow significantly in the years ahead. Although not as large as the British or Russian empires in terms of territory, it was nonetheless very extensive and placed the United States in a strong position when it came to disputes with imperial rivals.

The American empire reached its second century in the 1980s, just as the Cold War was ending. No longer an empire based primarily on territory, this was a vast undertaking—labeled semiglobal in this book—that placed the US state in a privileged position in the world by virtue of its control over key global institutions and the support it received from a range of powerful nonstate actors (NSAs). And the impending collapse of the Soviet Union raised the prospect temporarily of an empire that would be truly global in scope.

Today the American empire looks very different. When it reaches its 250th anniversary in the 2030s, it will still be in operation. However, it will be a pale shadow of its former self. The retreat from empire will have continued, and the outlines of a new world order will have become clearer. The United States may still be at the center, but global power will be much more contested. The empire may even have the same foundations, but they will not be so solid and the empire will no longer be semiglobal.

As the empire retreats, the nation-state will loom larger. The line between the two will become less blurred. What is good for the preservation of the empire may not be so good for the nation-state, a theme that was heard repeatedly in the 2016 presidential election. Future presidents may be more reluctant than

Donald Trump openly to demand "America first," but they will express the same sentiments in different language. Failure to do so will render them unelectable.

The American empire is unlikely to reach its three hundredth anniversary. By then the United States will have become "just" a nation-state, one that may or may not be at peace with itself. Shedding the imperial skin acquired over decades, even centuries, is never painless, and America is experiencing that pain today. Yet it can eventually be a liberating experience, as the citizens of other erstwhile empires have discovered. And if the retreat from empire is mainly for internal reasons rather than due to external pressures, as is the case in America, it increases the chances of a successful transition.

If the three hundredth anniversary of American empire fails to materialize, it is already clear that the empire will have achieved a long life before it ends. Some two hundred fifty years, surely the minimum that the American empire will manage, is still a considerable length of time. Among nearly two hundred empires recorded in history, roughly two-thirds ended before they reached 250 years. And among the longer-lasting ones, most had been reduced to fairly feeble affairs before the end. The US empire by contrast still has some vigor even if its retreat has already begun. And it has outlived all the European empires with which it had to compete in its early years.

America's imperial destiny was a choice, but it was not especially controversial. The United States of America acquired by treaty, following skillful negotiations, a land mass that doubled the *de facto* size of the thirteen colonies. In theory, the Founding Fathers could have granted autonomy to the Native American and other populations in these territories or incorporated them immediately into the Union. However, no party or faction favored this, and it is therefore hardly surprising that the territories became effectively US colonies.

The last of the mainland colonies joined the Union in 1912 (or 1959, if we include Alaska), so that the continental empire survived a long time. The imperial mindset became deeply engrained and promoted ideas of expansion that took the empire offshore long before the Spanish-American War in 1898. This offshore expansion was more controversial than the continental one since—in addition to the question of slavery—it was complicated by issues of racism and protection of domestic interests. However, it was never reversed, and colonies simply became US protectorates after formal rule was ended in those rare cases where decolonization was permitted.

Offshore expansion of the empire was also a choice. The federal government could have survived without overseas colonies, treaty privileges in Chinese ports, unequal treaties with Pacific states, powers of intervention in Latin America, or commercial advantages in the Caribbean. Yet this was not how states that saw themselves as great powers operated. In an age of imperial preference, a great trading nation such as the United States needed an offshore empire to counteract what was seen as its commercial disadvantage and to counter the geopolitical ambitions of some European states.

Offshore imperial expansion could therefore be justified as the defense of national interests. The empire built after the Second World War, however, needed to be justified in a different way. This empire, based on global and regional institutions with the support of powerful NSAs, had taken shape even before the Cold War started, so it was not initially about defeating international communism. Only America, it was argued, could provide the global public goods that the world needed, since it was the only country in the world that could be trusted not to pursue a selfish agenda based on a narrow pursuit of self-interest.

This may have been self-deception of the highest order, but many countries— crippled by war—were only too happy for the United States to undertake this role. They may not have been fully convinced that US interventions were unlike those of other countries, motivated purely by acting as a "force for good," but they were willing to accept much of the ideology of American exceptionalism that has always underpinned the US imperial project. And in the United States itself belief in the country's exceptional nature was at its height as the Second World War came to an end.

The American empire is now in retreat. Indeed, it has been in retreat for some time. Yet this does not mean the nation-state is in decline. This point cannot be made strongly enough. Those who confuse imperial retreat with the decline of the nation-state have been able to deny the former in view of the strength of the latter. Yet imperial retreat is not the same as national decline, as many other countries can attest. Indeed, imperial retreat can strengthen the nation-state just as imperial expansion can weaken it. It all depends how and why imperial retreat has come about.

There is no single moment when the American empire can be said to have begun its retreat, nor is there a simple one-dimensional cause. It began long before external pressures became a consideration, even if they are now an important part of the story. Economic performance is part of the explanation but it is by no means the whole one. The increasing difficulty of using the international institutions built by the United States to promote an American agenda is another factor. The fracturing of the consensus in favor of empire among the leading NSAs has also been significant, as has been the increasingly dysfunctional nature of the political system. Above all, and reflecting all other considerations, has been the questioning of the myth of American exceptionalism. And, as a consequence of all these things, US governments have found it harder to exercise the kind of leadership that a semiglobal empire is expected to deliver.

For the first three decades after the Second World War, the performance of the American economy matched the imperial ambitions of the state. Resources expanded to meet not only the international requirements of the federal government but also the material dreams of the citizens. The US economy may not have been the fastest growing economy in the world, but it was growing fast enough to make any talk of relative decline—let alone absolute decline—seem absurd.

Since the mid-1970s all this has changed. The relative decline is apparent to all but the most blinkered. Absolute decline has never occurred, expect for very short periods, but the distribution of the national cake has changed dramatically. Many citizens, including members of the fabled middle-class, have struggled to adapt as their share of national income has fallen. And the poorest in society have faced real hardship. Imbalances in the US economy, including the trade and budget deficits, have not led to a big improvement in infrastructure, health care, or educational quality but instead have placed increasingly tight constraints on what policy makers can do.

America may still have the largest armed forces in the world, capable of deterring enemies and imposing enormous destruction on those in their path, but military intervention alone could never sustain a semiglobal empire based primarily on institutions and NSAs. Instead the nation's formidable hard power sits uneasily alongside a citizenry that is increasingly skeptical about foreign adventures and a world that is unwilling to unite behind US interventions. Coalitions of the willing are no substitute for military intervention based on domestic consensus and backed by the force of international law.

The global and regional institutions built by the United States after the Second World War are still in existence, but the federal government finds it ever more difficult to use these institutions to craft a world in its own image. To some extent, this is inevitable, as the organizations were constructed at a time when there were around fifty independent states rather than nearly two hundred, as is the case today. However, it is also due to ambivalence by the US state on the role played by international laws and treaties in global governance. Unwilling to commit fully to these institutions, especially the United Nations, the United States has been slow to permit the kinds of reforms that would allow them to function more effectively. As a result, the rest of the world has found ways of circumventing these very same institutions and is therefore more able to resist American pressure.

NSAs no longer play the same supportive role on behalf of the American empire as before. The media are much more fragmented, the philanthropic foundations are more independent, the think tanks are less subservient, and the churches have become more partisan. Above all, many multinational enterprises (MNEs) have become truly global and no longer feel committed to the American empire in the way that they did before.

Consider, for example, the "manifesto" published by Mark Zuckerberg (CEO of Facebook) in February 2017. Addressed to "our community," rather than citizens of the United States, he outlined a vision in which the federal government was never mentioned: "Our greatest opportunities are now global—like spreading prosperity and freedom, promoting peace and understanding, lifting people out of poverty, and accelerating science. Our greatest challenges also need global responses—like ending terrorism, fighting climate change, and preventing pandemics. Progress now requires humanity coming together not just as cities or nations, but also as a global community."[1] Even if these ambitious goals might chime with the interests of the American empire, it is clear that Zuckerberg imagines a world in which solutions will not depend on global leadership by the US state but rather on the actions of a "global community" that is pulled together by NSAs such as Facebook. Modern globalization may have been created by the American state, in this view, but it is now too important to be left to the United States alone to defend it.

All this has made it difficult for US governments to exercise global leadership, a problem exacerbated by the dysfunctional nature of the American political system. This problem, always acute, has become almost unbearable in the last twenty years as even the most skilled presidents have struggled to build bipartisan support for imperial policies. On trade, climate change, international security, and global human rights, American leadership has often been stymied by ideological divisions that have grown fiercer over time.

Part of the problem for US leaders has been the doubts expressed by a large part of the public with regard to American exceptionalism. If the United States is not exceptional, it can be argued, then there is less justification for the country exercising global leadership. And if economic resources are strained by current imperial commitments, then there is even less justification for extending them. Indeed, there is a strong case for cutting back.

These doubts could be overcome as long as most of the rest of the world was content to see America provide leadership on a global scale. That, however, is no longer the case. The pool of "loyal" allies is shrinking, with some countries once renowned for their deference to the United States now being willing to defy it. This is partly because these countries have become more self-confident, but also because they have come to doubt the ability of the American system to deliver the kind of leadership they desire.

Something similar has happened to US rivals outside the semiglobal empire. The Russian Federation, successor state to the Soviet Union, was too quickly dismissed as a geopolitical lightweight. Patronized at first by US governments, Russia never forgot the humiliations of the 1990s and reasserted itself on the international stage with some success. Although unable to match the super-power status of the Soviet Union, it has acquired the ability to thwart Ameri-can ambitions in numerous areas while building a network of like-minded states of its own.

The most important of these states is China, which now enjoys a close rela-tionship with Russia after centuries of intense rivalry. As China moved from an obsession with economic growth to becoming a major geopolitical force, it has clashed repeatedly with the United States. These disputes have so far been han-dled peacefully, but both sides are prepared for war. If force is used, however, the United States will no longer be able to count on a wide array of allies. China has been too successful at marketing itself as the rising power that other coun-tries will not wish to defy.

"American empire" was never mentioned in the 2016 primary and presiden-tial election campaigns, but it still loomed large. The visions for the United States outlined by the candidates all had different implications for the imperial project. One of the most ambitious was the one offered by Hillary Clinton, which insisted on American exceptionalism and called for a renewal of US lead-ership at the global level. Yet even this vision failed to articulate a trade strat-egy that would have perpetuated American hegemony, suggesting that retreat from empire would have still continued even if she had won the presidential election.

The alternative vision outlined by Donald Trump emphasized the limitations of American empire both in terms of what it had achieved for US citizens and also in terms of the obligations it imposed on the nation-state. This was recog-nition that imperial retreat was already under way and would continue in the future. While full of contradictions and inconsistencies, this vision still found favor with enough voters to secure Trump the support in the electoral college he needed to win.

President Donald Trump (2017–), soon after taking office, shifted foreign pol-icy in certain respects away from what had been outlined in his presidential campaign and moved closer to the mainstream. Yet in great swaths of interna-tional affairs, notably combating climate change and multilateral trade agreements, it was clear that the United States would not seek to lead. Instead, that role will be left to others, with predictable consequences for America's retreat from empire.

Allies, especially in Europe, have been stunned by this change in US policy. Having assumed that American empire would continue indefinitely, they had crafted their policies on the assumption that America would remain the global leader. Worse still for them has been the dismissive attitude shown by the Trump administration toward their most cherished achievements, in particular the European Union (EU) and their steadfast commitment to a two-state solution in the Middle East. These allies, it is fair to say, are now having to contemplate for the first time since 1945 a world in which the United States is not there to support them.

Retreat from empire is therefore becoming ever more apparent. Of course, no country is yet prepared or willing to take the place of the United States, and some have seen that as evidence that American empire can and must continue as before. However, that is wishful thinking. While we cannot be sure what will take its place as the American empire retreats, the space vacated cannot easily be reoccupied. Retreat chimes with a large part of the electorate, not just those that voted for President Trump, and they do not wish to see the United States accept the same imperial burden as in the past.

The imperial history of America has been a long one. Only now, however, as it enters its final phase, is it being fully recognized for what it is and has been. The number of books on American empire is expanding all the time and adding greatly to our understanding. This book hopefully will do the same. Most readers will probably agree with the premise even if not all of them accept the conclusions. Others will build on what is written here.

The American empire has not been unique, although it has had many unusual features. Imperial retreat will therefore find some parallels in what has gone before. Perhaps the biggest mistake the United States can make is to delay the retreat as long as possible, hoping that something will change in the meantime that might permit a restoration of hegemony. That rarely happens in history and would be highly unlikely this time around. It is better to embrace what is becoming inevitable. The hardest part will be shedding the imperial mindset, acquired over many generations. Yet, as other countries have shown, it can be done, and young people in the United States are leading the way.

NOTES

INTRODUCTION

1. I use "empire" rather than "Empire" to describe the United States because its imperial status is not officially acknowledged.

2. I use the terms "United States" and "America" interchangeably when referring to the United States of America.

3. I use the term "semiglobal" because the empire never covered the whole world.

4. Maier, *Among Empires*, 7.

5. Rumsfeld was responding to a question from a reporter for Al-Jazeera. Eric Schmitt, "Aftereffects: Military Presence; Rumsfeld Says U.S. Will Cut Forces in Gulf," *New York Times*, April 29, 2003, http://www.nytimes.com/2003/04/29/world/aftereffects-military -presence-rumsfeld-says-us-will-cut-forces-in-gulf.html.

6. Schlesinger, "The American Empire?," 45.

7. On "imperial enthusiasts," see MacDonald, "Those Who Forget," 48.

8. The American Empire Project was founded by Tom Engelhardt and Steve Fraser, leading to a stream of publications from Metropolitan Books, http://www.american empireproject.com.

9. Both Brazil and Mexico declared themselves to be empires on independence in 1821, although Mexico became a republic two years later.

10. On the different definitions of American exceptionalism, see Lipset, *American Excep- tionalism*; Bacevich, *The Limits of Power*; and Murray, *American Exceptionalism*.

11. Daniel White, "Read Hillary Clinton's Speech Touting 'American Exceptionalism,'" *Time*, August 31, 2016, http://time.com/4474619/read-hillary-clinton-american-legion -speech.

12. Blair's speech was delivered to a joint session of Congress. "Transcript of Blair's Speech to Congress," CNN, July 17, 2003, http://www.cnn.com/2003/US/07/17/blair.transcript/. On January 26, 2017, Prime Minister Theresa May used very similar words when she addressed a gathering of Republicans in Philadelphia; see Adam Bienkov, "Full Text: Theresa May's Speech to the Republican 'Congress of Tomorrow' Conference,"

Business Insider, January 26, 2017, http://www.businessinsider.com/full-text-theresa
-mays-speech-to-the-republican-congress-of-tomorrow-conference-2017-1.

13. Nye, *Soft Power*, 5.

14. Hardt and Negri, *Empire*, xiv–xv.

15. Wen Jiabao, quoted in Zeng and Breslin, "China's 'New Type of Great Power Relations,'" 774.

16. See a February 15, 2012, video presentation at a luncheon to celebrate the fiftieth anniversary of the National Committee on US-China relations, https://www.ncusr.org
/content/video-vice-president-xi-jinping-policy-address.

17. On possible options, see Womack, "Asymmetric Parity," 1463–80.

18. Trump even had the temerity to question "American exceptionalism," saying in
April 2015, before he declared his candidacy, "I don't think it is a very nice term." See
David Corn, "Donald Trump Says He Does Not Believe in 'American Exceptionalism,'" *Mother Jones*, June 7, 2016, http://www.motherjones.com/politics/2016/06/donald
-trump-american-exceptionalism.

19. Some have argued that Barack Obama (2009–17) was the first postimperial president.
Yet Obama was a true believer in American exceptionalism and cannot therefore
claim that role. See Chapter 9.4.

1. CONTINENTAL EXPANSION

1. The indigenous peoples would be called "Indians" following the arrival of Europeans, as a result of a geographical error by Christopher Columbus. The most commonly
used name today is "Native American," although "American Indian" or "Indian" is also
employed. I use all three variants in this book.

2. Benjamin Franklin, quoted in Weeks, *The New Cambridge History*, 9.

3. Thornton, "Population History of Native North Americans," 23.

4. The part of the Northwest Territory that would become Indiana, for example, had
only 2,632 white settlers of all ages in 1800.

5. For a comparison with the British Empire, see Go, *Patterns of Empire*.

6. Onuf, *Statehood and Union*, 87.

7. Banner, *How the Indians Lost Their Land*, 132.

8. The Indians thought they could count on their British allies, but the commanding
officer closed the gates of Fort Miami to the retreating Indians and their fate was
sealed. See Sugden, *Tecumseh*, 90.

9. Goebel, *William Henry Harrison*, 40–41.

10. Thomas Jefferson, quoted in Rockwell, *Indian Affairs*, 88.

11. The slogan for William Harrison, whose vice presidential nominee in the 1840 campaign was John Tyler, was "Tippecanoe and Tyler too."

12. Minnesota Territory had been formed in 1849, consisting of present-day Minnesota
and eastern portions of North and South Dakota.

13. Often referred to as one treaty, there were in fact three, with the Choctaws, Creeks, and
Cherokees, respectively. See Horsman, "United States Indian Policies, 1776–1815," 30.

14. Prucha, "United States Indian Policies, 1815–1860," 44.
15. On the Treaty of Fort Stanwix, see Wallace, *Jefferson and the Indians*, 61.
16. This conflict arose because the British had agreed to 31° north with the United States in the Treaty of Paris but implicitly had accepted the more northerly boundary in a separate treaty in the same year in which the Floridas were restored by Britain to Spain.
17. Linklater, *Measuring America*, 169–70.
18. The first Yazoo scandal was in 1789 when the Georgian legislature sold 25.4 million acres to three land companies in what was destined to become federal territory. Following the second (similar) Yazoo scandal, there was a backlash in Georgia itself when it was discovered that all but one of the legislators who had voted for the land sale stood to benefit personally.
19. William C. C. Claiborne to James Madison, February 16, 1802, Rowland, *Official Letter Books of W.C.C. Claiborne, 1801–16*, 1, 47.
20. Under the Constitution only the federal government could deal with "sovereign nations," so that designating the Indian tribes in this way conferred exclusive legitimacy on the US administration. This designation was not dropped until 1871, by which time the federal government had signed nearly four hundred treaties with Indians.
21. William C. C. Claiborne to Henry Dearborn, April 19, 1802, Mississippi Department of Archives and History, *Mississippi Territorial Archives, 1798–1803*, 419.
22. They were called Red Sticks because of the red clubs used to raise war parties.
23. See Conroy-Krutz, *Christian Imperialism*, Chapter 5.
24. Alabama Legislature, quoted in Green, "The Expansion of European Colonization," 517.
25. The Cherokee nation had brought suit against Georgia for violation of their sovereignty. The chief justice ruled that they could not do so in the federal courts as they were not a foreign nation.
26. Gibson, "Indian Land Transfers," 223.
27. Dunbar-Ortiz, *An Indigenous People's History*, 112–14.
28. Napoleon in return had promised to give to Spain various possessions in Italy.
29. In 1802, the last year of Spanish control, 170 of the 268 vessels that entered the Mississippi were American. See Thomas, *A History of Military Government*, 26.
30. As early as 1790, he had argued that it was better for Louisiana to be in Spanish possession, for the alternative was likely to be British control, with much more negative consequences for the United States. See Robertson, *Louisiana under the Rule*, 265–67, quoting Jefferson's memorandum.
31. Although the extent of the Louisiana Purchase was not known at the time, it is today calculated at 828,000 square miles (529,920,000 acres).
32. William C. C. Claiborne to Thomas Jefferson, in Carter, *The Territorial Papers*, 9:16.
33. The sale of the French territories by Napoleon was almost certainly illegal since he had not met the conditions laid down by Spain, including no sale to a third party, and he had not consulted the Chamber of Deputies. And Jefferson also had doubts about the legality of the purchase under the US Constitution.

34. At first it even included the southern portions of three Canadian provinces (this would be resolved by treaty with Great Britain in 1818).
35. Thomas, *A History of Military Government*, 40–41.
36. The second act in this tragedy was removal and the third, after the Civil War, was genocide.
37. Swagerty, "Indian Trade," 360.
38. It would be renamed as Arkansas a few years later.
39. The western portion of Arkansas Territory had been shrunk in 1824 in order to enlarge the proposed Indian Territory.
40. New Spain became Mexico in 1821, but the boundary had been agreed to in 1819 between Spain and the United States. See Section 1.4.
41. John C. Calhoun, quoted in Kvasnicka, "United States Indian Treaties," 221.
42. See Section 1.4 in this chapter for Oregon, Chapter 2.1 for Texas, and Chapter 2.2 for Mexico.
43. Iowa had become a state in 1846. It had been formed from the southeast portion of Iowa Territory, which had been split off from Wisconsin Territory in 1838. The rest of Iowa Territory had become "unorganized."
44. In addition, President Abraham Lincoln during the war passed the Homestead Act, the Morrill Act, and the Pacific Railroad Act. All three acts deprived Native Americans of vast amounts of territory granted to them in previous treaties. See Dunbar-Ortiz, *An Indigenous People's History*, 140–46.
45. It had fallen to its lowest point by 1900, after which it started to recover (accelerating since 1970—see Chapter 9.4). See Thornton, "Population History," 32, Table 2.7.
46. Willoughby, *Territories and Dependencies*, 57.
47. Pomeroy, *The Territories*, 104.
48. Pomeroy, *The Territories*, 103–4.
49. A small part of New Mexico was also inside the Louisiana Purchase, and this was not admitted to the Union until 1912.
50. This defined the boundary with Spain as the middle of the Mississippi.
51. This was the start of the First Seminole War. "Seminole" was the name given to those who had fled south across the border from Georgia. They included not just Indians but also slaves ("black Seminoles") who gained their freedom on arrival in Florida.
52. Dade County in southern Florida is named after him.
53. Nugent, *Habits of Empire*, 159.
54. In the third convention in 1794 the Spanish crown conceded the right of Great Britain to settle in areas claimed, but not occupied, by Spain.
55. The United States also inherited Spain's feeble claims on the region through the Adams-Onís Treaty.
56. It was restored to Astor in 1818 following a show of gunboat diplomacy by the United States.
57. See Landers, *Empires Apart*, Chapter 7. A *ukase* was a proclamation that had the force of law.

58. See Weeks, *John Quincy Adams*, 177.
59. It was 1889 in the case of Washington and 1890 in the case of Idaho.
60. US Congress, quoted in Nugent, *Habits of Empire*, 186.
61. The French had originally called them Nez Percé (pierced nose), but the accent was subsequently dropped by non-French speakers.
62. This treaty would be modified in 1868. It was the last the federal government ever signed with a Native American tribe.

2. MEXICO AND CENTRAL AMERICA

1. Great Britain is the name used for England, Scotland, and Wales. After the Act of Union with Ireland in 1802, the two islands were called the United Kingdom. Great Britain is used in this book as a synonym for the United Kingdom to avoid excessive repetition, although the two are not strictly the same (and since 1922 the United Kingdom has included only Northern Ireland).
2. See Hämäläinen, *The Comanche Empire*, 1–10.
3. Stephen Austin, quoted in Lowrie, *Culture Conflict in Texas*, 25.
4. Don Manuel Mier y Terán, quoted in Stephenson, *Texas and the Mexican War*, 24.
5. Proceedings of the General Convention of Delegates Representing the Citizens and Inhabitants of Texas, October 1832, http://landgrantpatent.org/law-texas/law01012.pdf, 7.
6. The Nueces River had been accepted as the southern boundary of Texas during the negotiations leading up to the Adams-Onís Treaty.
7. See General Provisions, Section 9, of the Constitution of the Republic of Texas, http://www.tamu.edu/faculty/ccbn/dewitt/adp/archives/documents/texascon.html.
8. See Gwynne, *Empire of the Summer Moon*, 363–70.
9. Since Mexico did not recognize the Republic of Texas, the western border was never defined. In reality, however, it was far to the east of where it now runs.
10. There were two Californias in Mexico—upper (Alta) and lower (Baja). The first corresponds to the modern State of California in the United States and the second to Baja California in Mexico today.
11. William Wharton, quoted in McElroy, *The Winning of the Far West*, 49. The Texan Congress duly obliged by passing a resolution soon after "extending her jurisdiction over the Californias to the Pacific."
12. Stephenson, *Texas and the Mexican War*, 182. Sutter was a Swiss who had been naturalized a Mexican and who later confirmed the discovery of gold on the American River in California in January 1848.
13. James Polk to Thomas Hart Benton, October 1845, quoted in Nugent, *Habits of Empire*, 193.
14. The Mexican Army did not respond to the presence of US troops until General Taylor was ordered to the Río Grande, where he built a fort and blockaded the river.
15. The Bear Flag Republic was launched by US settlers in northern California. The settlers were joined by John Frémont, who became their leader as the war started.

16. Hitchcock, *Fifty Years in Camp and Field*, 203, 212.

17. Clay's Fugitive Slave Law was widely denounced. Theodore Parker wrote, "I believe no one political act in America, since the treachery of Benedict Arnold, has excited so much moral indignation." Parker, quoted in McElroy, *The Winning of the Far West*, 342.

18. McElroy, *The Winning of the Far West*, 325.

19. By way of example, Trinity County in 1865 "was cleared of all Indians who lived in Rancherías. . . . The hostile tribes had been killed or captured, had been . . . driven by man, had been starved and beaten into absolute and final subjection." Bledsoe, *Indian Wars of the Northwest*, 260–61.

20. Thornton, "Population History of Native North Americans," 28. California was also one of the few states not to establish reservations, so the Indians were forced to survive as best they could on the margins of white society.

21. In addition, the Compromise of 1850 gave to New Mexico on the east much of the land that had been claimed by Texas.

22. See Dunbar-Ortiz, *An Indigenous People's History*, 149–51.

23. The biggest controversy had to do with the practice of polygamy by many Mormon men. Relations between the US government and the Mormons improved after 1890, when a "manifesto" was published by the Mormon leader ending the practice, and statehood soon followed.

24. The dispute went all the way to the Supreme Court, which ruled in Goldwater's favor. He ran unsuccessfully in the 1964 elections.

25. The name of the country was changed to Colombia in 1863.

26. Bevans, *Treaties*, 6:865–81.

27. Abraham Lincoln, quoted in Vorenberg, *The Emancipation Proclamation*, 15–16. The speech was reported the following day in the *New York Tribune*.

28. See Vorenberg, "Abraham Lincoln."

29. Keasbey, *The Nicaragua Canal*, 283.

30. Rutherford B. Hayes, quoted in Keasbey, *The Nicaragua Canal*, 374.

31. Roosevelt had stood as the vice presidential candidate when William McKinley was reelected in November 1900. He became president when McKinley was assassinated in September 1901.

32. See Conniff, "Panama since 1903," 606–7.

33. Some scholars argue that Panama did not grant the United States sovereignty over the Canal Zone on the grounds that Article 3 states the United States would be treated "as if" it were sovereign. There is no doubt, however, that both countries acted on the assumption that the United States *was* sovereign.

34. See Conniff, "Panama since 1903," 617–28.

35. Roosevelt announced the policy in his inaugural address in March 1933.

36. This rose from $250,000 to $430,000 per year, a fairly trivial sum even by the standards of the day.

37. The Canal Treaties are often known as the Carter-Torrijos Treaties after the presidents of the two countries at the time.

38. Central America, which included Chiapas at the time, declared its independence from Spain in September 1821. It then annexed itself to Mexico. It declared its independence from Mexico in 1823 but lost Chiapas in the process.

39. This was the name of the federation adopted by the five Central American countries (Costa Rica, El Salvador, Guatemala, Honduras, and Nicaragua) at the time of independence. The United Provinces of Central America was dissolved in 1838, after which the five countries became separate republics.

40. Its name was the Central American and United States Atlantic and Pacific Canal Company. Its directors included De Witt Clinton, governor of New York, and Monroe Robinson, president of the Bank of the United States.

41. Under a treaty in 1786 with Spain, Great Britain had agreed to abandon its protectorate in Mosquitia while retaining limited rights in Belize. The end of Spanish rule in the region provided the British with an opportunity to reestablish their control over the eastern coasts of Honduras and Nicaragua.

42. Greytown was named for Charles Edward Grey, the governor of the British colony of Jamaica at the time.

43. The treaty took no account of the fact that Tigre Island was also claimed by El Salvador and Nicaragua.

44. Since the treaty only mentioned a ship canal through Nicaragua, it left open the question of whether the United States could have exclusive control over a canal through Panama.

45. See Pletcher, *The Diplomacy of Trade and Investment,* 123.

46. Under the 1860 Treaty of Managua, the British had ended their protectorate in Mosquitia but left it "autonomous." There was always the risk, therefore, that they would return.

47. See Maurer, *The Empire Trap,* 113–17.

48. They would not finally leave until 1933, although there was a brief interregnum between 1925 and 1926. See Langley, *The Banana Wars,* Part 4.

49. Or so it thought. The abrogation of the Bryan-Chamorro Treaty in 1971, ending the US protectorate over Nicaragua, paved the way for other countries to express an interest. None did so until the twenty-first century, when a private Chinese company signed a contract with the Nicaraguan government to build a canal.

50. See Millett, *Guardians of the Dynasty,* 125–39.

51. See Diederich, *Somoza,* 18–19.

52. This remark, however, may be apocryphal. See Crawley, *Somoza and Roosevelt,* 153 n113.

53. The US protectorate over Nicaragua had ended in 1971 with the abrogation of the Bryan-Chamorro Treaty (see note 49). At that point Nicaragua became a client state.

54. The lease had been included in the 1916 Bryan-Chamorro Treaty. Other Central American states objected, and so the dispute went to the court.

55. It foundered in 1931 when Honduras refused to take its border dispute with Guatemala to the tribunal (an *ad hoc* court was then established with a US judge presiding).

56. See *New York Times,* August 19, 1920.

3. AFRICA AND THE PACIFIC

1. See Tyler-McGraw, *An African Republic*, 13.
2. Henry Clay, quoted in Sherwood, "The Formation of the American Colonization Society," 222.
3. Bushrod Washington was a nephew of George Washington.
4. See Anderson, *Liberia*, 68, quoting from the agreement of December 15, 1821.
5. The Maryland Colonization Society, for example, established the independent colony of Maryland in Liberia that only joined the rest of Liberia in 1856.
6. Monrovia was named after James Monroe, during whose presidency (1817–25) the first settlers had arrived.
7. Abel P. Upshur, quoted in Anderson, *Liberia*, 77.
8. The Declaration of Independence (Liberia), http://www.onliberia.org/Downloads /Liberia_Constitution_Declaration.doc.
9. Article 1, Section 11, limited restricted suffrage among the indigenous population to those that paid the hated hut tax. Article 5, Sections 12 and 13, limited real estate ownership to black citizens (i.e., the Libero Americans themselves).
10. The senators from southern states were able to block recognition of an independent black republic until the Civil War deprived them of their vote.
11. Article 8 allowed the US government to protect the Libero Americans against the indigenous population at the request of the Liberian government.
12. "Editorial Comment: Liberia," 963.
13. The lease was needed to circumvent the provision in the constitution that only black citizens could own real estate.
14. Chalk, "The Anatomy of an Investment," 30.
15. Tubman was president of Liberia from 1944 until his death in 1971.
16. Between 1821 (when figures were first published) and 1830, US imports from the Pacific were twice the value of exports. About 80% of this trade was with China. See Heffer, *The United States and the Pacific*, 367.
17. John Quincy Adams, quoted in Wells, *Romances*, 760.
18. "Treaty of Peace, Amity and Commerce between the United States and China Signed at Wang Hiya (Near Macao)," July 3, 1844, https://choices.edu/resources/documents/ch _1.pdf, Article 2.
19. Guano (bird droppings) is a natural fertilizer that before the Guano Islands Act was imported by the United States (mainly from Peru) at very high prices.
20. See Skaggs, *The Great Guano Rush*, Chapter 5.
21. The others are Baker Island, Howland Island, Jarvis Island, Johnston Atoll, and Kingman Reef. In addition, the United States subsequently claimed Wake Island (1899) and Palmyra Atoll (1912). All but the last are "unincorporated."
22. Neumann, *America Encounters Japan*, 2.
23. The US government did not endorse these actions by Perry, and both island chains would later be annexed by Japan.
24. See Neumann, *America Encounters Japan*, 60.

25. Japan had acquired Taiwan following the defeat of China in 1895 and would expand its overseas territories further following the defeat of Russia in 1905.

26. The Boxers, who were given their name by Christian missionaries, strongly opposed all foreign interference in China and targeted Christians in particular.

27. The others were Austria-Hungary, France, Germany, Italy, Japan, Russia, and the United Kingdom.

28. See, for example, the US literary magazine *Puck*, August 15, 1900, centerfold where the United States, represented by the bald eagle, joins the other imperial powers in dismembering the corpse of the Chinese dragon.

29. The first note had been published in 1899, and the second came out in the middle of the efforts to suppress the Boxer Rebellion.

30. Richards only resigned as a missionary after the King had asked him to be his official adviser.

31. John Tyler, quoted in Stevens, *American Expansion in Hawaii*, 4.

32. Treaty of Reciprocity between the United States of America and the Hawaiian Kingdom, 1875, Kingdom of Hawai'i, http://hrmakahinui.com/treaties-between-the-Hawai'i -Kingdom-and-United-States.php.

33. The McKinley Tariff eliminated duties on foreign sugar and gave a "bounty" (subsidy) to domestic sugar (cane and beet).

34. After a state department official raised the US flag at Pago Pago, he concluded, "This Treaty has been pushed and desired by these men [the CPLCC] in furtherance of [their] land schemes." See Rigby, "The Origins of American Expansion," 232n41.

35. By this time American Samoa included the Manu'a islands, ceded in 1904 by its chief, and Swain's Island, added in 1925 (it had been taken into US possession in 1856 under the Guano Islands Act).

36. Clark, *History of Alaska*, 133.

37. There is some truth in the accusation, but also plenty of justification for congressional action. Resources had indeed been pillaged by the Alaska syndicate and other corporate groups.

38. See Haycox, *Alaska: An American Colony*, 268–69. The main opposition came from the salmon industry, but the US military was also not in favor of statehood.

39. See Hezel, *The First Taint of Civilization*, 28–34.

40. As Hong Kong was a British colony, it may have seemed a strange place to base the US Asiatic Squadron. However, the British—having ruled out taking the islands themselves—favored US colonization of the Philippines, preferring it to the alternative (French, German, Japanese, or Russian control).

41. War was declared on April 25, 1898, and the naval battle was fought on May 1.

42. The US Navy on its way to the Philippines also claimed Wake Island.

43. Following token opposition, a deal was struck between Spain and the United States under which Manila would be surrendered. See Wolff, *Little Brown Brother*, 125–30.

44. There is a huge literature on this. See, for example, Blount, *The American Occupation*. What seems clear is that McKinley was determined from the start to expand the US empire in the Pacific one way or the other.

45. The US government considered its strategic goals in the Pacific could be met without these islands, although there were many who disagreed.
46. Only very occasionally did US officials intervene. One such occasion was in 1920, when Franklin Delano Roosevelt, as assistant secretary of the navy, overruled a ban on interracial marriage. See Rogers, *Destiny's Landfall*, 144–45.
47. See Kramer, *The Blood of Government*, 145–46.
48. See Kramer, *The Blood of Government*, Chapter 2. The population of the Philippines at the time was around eight million.
49. See Root, *The Military and Colonial Policy of the United States*, 39.
50. The number of such cases is disputed. There were between six and nine in 1901 alone and others later.
51. The rulings also applied to Puerto Rico.
52. See Wolff, *Little Brown Brother*, 338–40.
53. When the islands came inside the tariff wall in 1909, export quotas were still applied. These were lifted in 1912, after which the Philippines were fully inside.
54. See Maurer, *The Empire Trap*, 46–49.
55. Filipino immigration was particularly unpopular in California, where major riots took place in 1930.
56. A limit of fifty per year was put on Filipino migration to the United States.
57. These bases, Subic Bay for the navy, and Clark for the air force, were the largest outside the US mainland itself.
58. In some ways the Philippines were more vulnerable as a protectorate than as a colony, since there were now no restrictions on the size of US holdings.
59. See Article 7, Paragraph 2, of the Philippine Constitution, http://www.officialgazette .gov.ph/1946/07/04/a-proclamation-of-the-president-roxas-4-july-1946/.
60. Japan had annexed the Bonin Islands in 1868 and the Ryukyu Islands, including Okinawa, in 1879.
61. Some US strategists, including Alfred Thayer Mahan, argued that America should have taken all the Spanish islands in 1898 for precisely this reason.
62. These included New Guinea, Nauru, and western Samoa.
63. Class C mandates were defined as those that "can best be governed under the laws of the Mandatory as integral portions of its territory."
64. The United States gained the right of access to Yap in the western Carolinas, with its cable stations, and both Japan and the United States agreed not to fortify their islands west of Hawaii.
65. The most brilliant of these was Colonel Earl Hancock "Pete" Ellis, who anticipated with some accuracy the campaign the United States would have to fight against Japan in the Second World War.
66. The new acquisitions included the Bonin and Ryukyu Islands, which were US colonies until 1968 and 1972, respectively, when they were returned to Japan. The United States, however, kept its military, naval, and air bases on Okinawa.
67. The United Nations, established in 1945 under US leadership, decided that the former League of Nations mandates would be renamed UN Trusteeships. In theory, this gave other UN members some oversight. However, the United States insisted the

TTPI be designated a strategic area, which meant its status could only be changed by the UN Security Council, where the United States had a veto.

68. The Carolinas include Palau. The Marshalls include Bikini Island, where atomic tests were carried out. The Northern Marianas include all the islands in the group except Guam.

69. Palau had been part of the Carolinas, but chose not to join the other islands in a federation. The Federated States of Micronesia included all the other Carolinas.

70. The Marshall Islands and the Federated States of Micronesia joined the UN in 1986. Palau joined in 1994, at which point the TTPI was dissolved.

71. In practice there is not much difference among the former parts of the TTPI between being a "colony" and being "independent." All are US dependencies.

4. THE CARIBBEAN

1. The country was given other names as well. To avoid confusion, it is called the Dominican Republic throughout this chapter.

2. The US Virgin Islands (USVI), acquired from Denmark, should not be confused with the British Virgin Islands (BVI).

3. Honorio Pueyrredón, quoted in Sheinin, *Argentina and the United States*, 1.

4. Franklin Delano Roosevelt, Address before the Woodrow Wilson Foundation, December 28, 1933, American Presidency Project, http://www.presidency.ucsb.edu/ws/?pid=14593.

5. See Section 4.3.

6. See Montague, *Haiti and the United States*, 106.

7. Speech by Senator Charles Sumner to the US Senate, March 27, 1871, https://www.gutenberg.org/files/50386/50386-h/50386-h.htm#.

8. See Maurer, *The Empire Trap*, 61–62.

9. The McKinley Tariff Act in 1890 had threatened higher tariffs if the country exporting was deemed to be taxing imports from the United States "unfairly." Reciprocity treaties with a number of countries were then used to drive down tariffs on US imports.

10. The Dominican Republic only became a sugar exporter after the First Cuban War of Independence (1868–78), when Cuban exiles established a modern industry. By 1890 it had surpassed tobacco as the country's main export. Keeping access to the US market became crucial after Cuba was granted a sugar preference and this was the main reason for the Dominican government agreeing to the bilateral trade treaty.

11. Theodore Roosevelt, Fourth Annual Message, American Presidency Project, http://www.presidency.ucsb.edu/ws/?pid=29545.

12. This expression would not be widely used until the administration of President William Howard Taft (1909–13), but it was always implicit in the Roosevelt Corollary.

13. See Knight, *The Americans in Santo Domingo*, 26–39.

14. See Calder, *The Impact of Intervention*, 161–62.

15. The convention should have terminated in 1942, but it was ended two years earlier as the Dominican government was able to persuade the US administration that it had met all its debt service obligations.

16. How this worked is well described in Diederich, *Trujillo*, 20–26.

17. Even this reduced sum was not paid in full.

18. See Gleijeses, *The Dominican Crisis*, 280–81.

19. He nearly won the 2000 presidential election at the age of ninety-four.

20. In all other countries imperial preference favored the metropolitan country and therefore discriminated against the United States.

21. Robert Hayne, quoted in Schmidt, *The United States Occupation of Haiti*, 28.

22. Knowing that Haitian recognition would be on the agenda, the Senate engaged in such a prolonged debate that the US delegates to the Congress could not take part (one died on the way and the other arrived too late).

23. See Bulmer-Thomas, *The Economic History of the Caribbean*, Chapter 7.

24. McPherson Berrien, quoted in Montague, *Haiti and the United States*, 53; emphasis in the original.

25. It is known as a US Minor Outlying Island.

26. See Montague, *Haiti and the United States*, 162.

27. The Banque Nationale d'Haiti had been founded in 1880. Although it functioned like a central bank, it was a private institution owned by French interests.

28. Quoted in Schmidt, *The United States Occupation of Haiti*, 105.

29. This was therefore different from the situation in the Dominican Republic, which was under direct military rule throughout the US occupation.

30. The US authorities revived a long forgotten Haitian law of 1864 in order to introduce the *corvée*.

31. See Montague, *Haiti and the United States*, 215–16.

32. Roosevelt stated, "You know I have had something to do with the running of a couple of little republics. The facts are that I wrote Haiti's Constitution myself, and, if I do say it, I think it a pretty good Constitution." See *New York Times*, August 19, 1920.

33. See Nicholls, *Haiti in Caribbean Context*, Chapter 1.

34. US sanctions were applied temporarily against Haiti in 1962, but they were soon lifted.

35. See Hallward, *Damming the Flood*, Chapter 2.

36. Aristide never actually resigned, but he was forced to leave. See Dumas, *An Encounter with Haiti*, 51–53.

37. John Quincy Adams to Hugh Nelson, April 28, 1823, quoted in Gott, *Cuba: A New History*, 58.

38. Thomas Jefferson to James Monroe, October 24, 1823, in Jefferson, *The Life and Writings*, 185.

39. Because it had not rebelled, Cuba would be known by Spain as "la isla siempre fiel" (the ever-faithful island).

40. See Martínez-Fernández, *Torn between Empires*, 116–18.

41. Slavery was abolished in 1880, but the *patronato*—a system of apprenticeship similar to slavery—survived until 1886.

42. In addition to Navassa Island off the coast of Haiti, these included Serranilla Bank, Bajo Nuevo Bank, Quita Sueño Bank, Serrana Bank, Roncador Bank, the Corn Islands, and the Swan Islands.

43. Reciprocity treaties were scrapped in 1894 as a result of the Wilson Tariff Act, but the Dingley Act in 1897 reopened the possibility of negotiating them.

44. The First War of Independence spanned 1868–78. The rebels were eventually defeated.

45. Imperialists in the United States blamed Spain, but it is now thought that it was an accident.

46. Its name would not be changed back to Puerto Rico until 1932.

47. Articles 3 and 7, Treaty between the United States and Cuba, *American Journal of International Law* 4.2, supplement: "Official Documents" (1910), http://www.jstor.org/stable /2212059, 178.

48. The other base was at Bahía Honda on the northern coast.

49. These included tariff preferences for US firms not available to others.

50. The United States introduced quotas for sugar from Cuba and other countries in 1934. These were then revised annually.

51. He fled just before the Cuban rebels led by Fidel Castro entered Havana.

52. See Carr, *Puerto Rico*, 47–48.

53. There has always been a suspicion that part of the motive for this was to make Puerto Ricans available for the military draft (the United States entered World War I in April 1917).

54. See Dietz, *Economic History of Puerto Rico*, Chapter 2.

55. Four years later, in 1952, Puerto Rico would become known as an "Estado Libre Asociado." This is usually translated as "Commonwealth," a term that was used to suggest (incorrectly) that the country was not a colony.

56. The return of excise duty on rum had begun in 1917, but Prohibition soon rendered it irrelevant. The switch from whisky to rum consumption in the United States was a wartime measure designed to reduce transatlantic imports.

57. The last vote on the political status of Puerto Rico was in 2017.

58. The Danish West Indies comprised the three islands of St. Thomas, St. Croix, and St. John. St. Thomas was a major trading center in the Caribbean, while St. Croix was dedicated to sugar production.

59. Cost considerations, so soon after the purchase of Alaska, were the main reasons for rejection. See Tansill, *The Purchase of the Danish West Indies*, 78–153.

60. Three of the Dutch islands are close to Venezuela, but the other three are close to Puerto Rico.

61. The inhabitants of the Virgin Islands became US citizens as soon as the transfer took place and they were allowed to keep a small tariff on US imports, as they had almost no other source of income.

62. Rum exports had been important under Danish rule. Rum production did not cease during Prohibition, but the rum was used to make bay rum for medicinal purposes.

63. Sugar had never been very successful in the Danish West Indies, as the islands are so dry. Access to the US market might have helped were it not for the fact that Cuba and Puerto Rico were much more competitive.

64. The British readopted imperial preference after the First World War (it had been ended in 1846).
65. The Smoot-Hawley Tariff Act adopted by the US Congress in the Great Depression had led to a surge in protectionism around the world. Hull, as secretary of state under President Roosevelt, was determined to reverse this.
66. See Ryan, *Eric Williams*, 68–72.
67. The resolution of the Cuban Missile Crisis in October 1962 committed the Soviet Union not to place nuclear missiles in Cuba and the United States not to invade the island. That should have been the moment for the gradual normalization of the bilateral relationship, but it would take another fifty years before the process even began.
68. Grenada was invaded in 1983 following the violent collapse of the left-wing administration of Maurice Bishop.

5. INSTITUTIONS

1. See Maurer, *The Empire Trap*, 168–81.
2. The main additions were the islands held by Japan under a League of Nations mandate. See Chapter 3.
3. See Mearsheimer, *The Tragedy of Great Power Politics*, 363–65.
4. The Monroe Doctrine was formally buried, admittedly not for the first time, on November 18, 2013, by Secretary of State John Kerry.
5. James Monroe, quoted in Perkins, *A History of the Monroe Doctrine*, 394–96.
6. Within fifteen years Britain seized the Falkland Islands and Great Britain and France occupied the Río de la Plata region.
7. Garfield was assassinated after only four months in office.
8. Blaine took office in the middle of the War of the Pacific between Bolivia, Chile, and Peru. He was also mindful of the French intervention in Mexico during the US Civil War.
9. James Blaine, quoted in Mecham, *A Survey*, 29.
10. Benjamin Harrison, quoted in Connell-Smith, *The Inter-American System*, 40.
11. Richard Olney to Lord Salisbury, July 1895, quoted in Smith, *Talons of the Eagle*, 33.
12. When Venezuela protested, the United States agreed to add one member to the board along with the two Americans, two British, and one Russian. See Schoultz, *Beneath the United States*, Chapter 7.
13. Edward House, quoted in Mecham, *A Survey*, 73.
14. Roosevelt, "Our Foreign Policy," 584–45.
15. Sumner Welles, quoted in Mecham, *A Survey*, 78.
16. Article 4 defined the hemisphere as extending from the North to the South Poles and including Canada, Greenland, and European colonies in the Caribbean.
17. "Inter-American Treaty of Reciprocal Assistance," Avalon Project, http://avalon.law.yale.edu/20th_century/decad061.asp.
18. In theory, under the United Nations Charter, the UN was to be consulted before armed force was used by a regional body in the event of an aggression that was not an armed attack. However, Article 6 of the Rio Treaty made no reference to this.

19. In theory any state could invoke Article 5(d), but in practice it would have required US support to have any chance of succeeding.

20. Connell-Smith, *The Inter-American System*, 230.

21. Wilson's points were a mixture of broad generalities and very specific proposals for those parts of Europe that were most in dispute.

22. "President Woodrow Wilson's Fourteen Points," Avalon Project, http://avalon.law.yale .edu/20th_century/wilson14.asp.

23. See MacMillan, *Peacemakers*, 446–49.

24. Everyone in Paris knew that the Monroe Doctrine had always been a unilateral declaration and had never been a "regional understanding." Its inclusion, however absurd, was recognition of the growing authority of the United States.

25. See Egerton, "Britain and the 'Great Betrayal,'" 891.

26. The final vote on March 19, 1920, was 49–35, seven votes short of a two-thirds majority. See Fleming, *The United States and the League of Nations*, 31.

27. This was the Declaration by the United Nations signed by representatives of China, the United Kingdom, the United States, and the USSR on January 1, 1942. It was signed the next day by the other twenty-two countries that had declared war. See Russell, *A History of the United Nations Charter*, 976.

28. Argentina, under enormous US pressure, only declared war in March 1945.

29. In addition to the twenty Latin American republics, the United States could count on the support of the Philippines (still a colony), Liberia (a former protectorate), most of Europe, and China. By contrast, the USSR could only count on five votes in 1945—its own three plus Yugoslavia and Poland (the latter had not been invited by the United States to San Francisco, but did sign the charter subsequently).

30. The permanent members of the Security Council were China, France, the United Kingdom, the United States, and the USSR.

31. The Palestine mandate consisted of territory that had previously been part of the Ottoman Empire.

32. The vote was 33 in favor and 13 against, with 10 abstentions and 1 absentee.

33. The UNSC has to approve applications, giving the permanent members control over who joins.

34. See Lebe, "Diminished Hopes," 43–47. Note that it was blocked without the need for a US veto.

35. The USSR withdrew in 1950 from the UNSC in protest at this decision. This made it possible for the United States to secure UNSC support for armed action against North Korea in the same year. The Soviet Union then rejoined.

36. Taiwan was then expelled from the UNSC (and the UN) to be replaced by the PRC as the sole representative of China.

37. In addition to the five permanent members (P5), the UNSC for the first two decades had six nonpermanent members, each elected for two years. The United States could invariably count on a majority among the eleven members.

38. The United States was engaged in covert action to overthrow the elected government. See Chapter 7.

39. The General Assembly was meeting in Paris because the new building in New York was not yet complete.

40. The petition, a remarkable document by any standards, was published in the United States. See Civil Rights Congress, *We Charge Genocide*.

41. "Indian" here means "from India." See Mazower, *No Enchanted Palace*, 26.

42. The quote is from Stettinius, *Roosevelt and the Russians*, 18–19, based in part on Hull, *Memoirs*, 2:1167. Cordell Hull was US secretary of state from 1933 to 1944, when he was succeeded by Edward Stettinius. The Curzon Line had been proposed in 1919 as the border between an independent Poland and Bolshevik Russia. The border agreed on in 1921 was further east. Stalin was therefore claiming part of eastern Poland.

43. Deaths attributable to the war reached 24 million in the Soviet Union compared with 420,000 in the United States.

44. Churchill, in his memoirs, makes clear he took the lead in the percentages agreement, writing numbers on a half sheet of paper and passing it to Stalin. See Churchill, *The Second World War*, 6:226–28. On the negotiation of the final numbers, see Resis, "The Churchill-Stalin Secret 'Percentages' Agreement"; and Siracusa, "The Night Stalin and Churchill Divided Europe."

45. George Kennan to Charles Bohlen, January 1945, quoted in Siracusa, "The Night Stalin and Churchill Divided Europe," 407. Kennan at the time was based in the US embassy in Moscow, and Bohlen was a US diplomat and later ambassador to the Soviet Union.

46. "Atlantic Charter," Avalon Project, http://avalon.law.yale.edu/wwii/atlantic.asp.

47. "The Yalta Conference," February 1945, Avalon Project, http://avalon.law.yale.edu/wwii/yalta.asp, Article 2.

48. Czechoslovakia, East Germany, and Hungary, although all occupied by the Red Army, were not yet Soviet satellites.

49. Three months later, following the British elections, Churchill was replaced by Clement Attlee as prime minister. Like Truman, Attlee had little experience in foreign affairs.

50. The Long Telegram is reproduced in full in Bernstein and Matusow, *The Truman Administration*, 198–212; the quote is from 210.

51. "Truman Doctrine," Avalon Project, http://avalon.law.yale.edu/20th_century/trudoc.asp.

52. The influential Senator Tom Connally, however, had no such reservations.

53. It was labeled NSC-68, and its principal author was Paul Nitze. Although classified, the content of NSC-68 soon became widely known.

54. A *Report to the National Security Council by the Executive Secretary on United States Objectives and Programs for National Security*, NSC-68, April 14, 1950, Harry S. Truman Library and Museum, https://www.trumanlibrary.org/whistlestop/study_collections/coldwar/documents/pdf/10-1.pdf.

55. George Marshall was secretary of state from 1947 to 1949. He was succeeded by Dean Acheson.

56. Foreign Assistance Act of 1948 [The Marshall Plan], George C. Marshall Foundation, http://marshallfoundation.org/library/wp-content/uploads/sites/16/2014/06/Foreign_Assistance_Act_of_1948.pdf.

57. See Mayers, *George Kennan*, 140–41.
58. It would become in 1961 the Organisation for Economic Co-operation and Development (OECD).
59. See LaFeber, *America in the Cold War*, 57.
60. North Atlantic Treaty, April 4, 1949, North Atlantic Treaty Organization, http://www.nato.int/cps/cn/natohq/official_texts_17120.htm, Article 5.
61. The only time it has been invoked was on the day after September 11, 2001, following the terrorist attack on the United States.
62. France had tried to rebuild its Southeast Asian empire after the Second World War. It suffered a humiliating defeat at the hands of the Vietnamese in 1954.
63. CENTO was first called the Middle East Treaty Organization (METO).
64. SEATO collapsed because the United States was unable to persuade all its members to participate in the Vietnam War (it was dissolved in 1977). CENTO, which the United States never formally joined, ended in 1979 after the Iranian Revolution.
65. By contrast, the acquisition of nuclear weapons by the United Kingdom and France—both NATO members—was not seen as a threat by the United States.
66. These three countries would go on to test nuclear weapons. North Korea did the same, after first giving notice that it would leave the NPT.
67. See Skidelsky, *John Maynard Keynes*, 3:240–41.
68. As new countries joined, the US share steadily declined (it was just under 17% in 2016). However, in the first amendment of the Articles of Agreement in 1969 the majority required for key decisions was raised to 85%, so that the United States continued to enjoy a veto over key decisions even with a reduced quota share.
69. The United States had no objection to its managing director being a western European, but insisted the deputy director be a US citizen. See Kahler, "The United States and the International Monetary Fund," 94–95.
70. While the Treasury Department has been the key US agency in relation to the IMF, it is the State Department that has taken the leading role in relation to the World Bank.
71. Harry S. Truman, "Truman's Inaugural Address," Harry S. Truman Library and Museum, https://www.trumanlibrary.org/whistlestop/50yr_archive/inagural20jan 1949.htm.
72. See Woods, "United States and the International Finance Institutions," 101.
73. *Proposals for Expansion of World Trade and Employment*, November 1945, Department of State, https://fraser.stlouisfed.org/files/docs/historical/eccles/036_04 _0003.pdf.
74. "Preliminary Agreement between the United States and the United Kingdom," February 23, 1942, Avalon Project, http://avalon.law.yale.edu/20th_century/decade04 .asp, Article 7.
75. Fifty-six countries attended, but neither Argentina nor Poland signed the Havana Charter. The Soviet Union did not participate.
76. The US negotiators, however, introduced into the Havana Charter a provision that certain exceptions to trade liberalization would require approval by the IMF, where the weighted voting system gave the United States huge influence over all decisions.

77. See McIntyre, "Weighted Voting in International Organizations," 490.

78. See Aaronson, *Trade and the American Dream*, Chapter 8.

79. The participants were all fifteen countries (except the Soviet Union) to which the United States had sent invitations in 1946, plus a further eight who were subsequently invited. This gave twenty-three countries in all (including the United States itself).

80. No approval was needed, as Congress had extended the RTAA to cover the period when the negotiations were carried out.

81. Trade Agreements Extension Act of 1951, US Senate Committee on Finance, https://www.finance.senate.gov/imo/media/doc/SRpt82-299.pdf, Section 10. See also Wilcox, "Trade Policy for the Fifties," 65, who concluded that "GATT thus lives on sufferance, as welcome as a bastard child."

6. NONSTATE ACTORS

1. There are many definitions of an MNE. The least demanding is that the company has its facilities and other assets in at least one country other than its home country.

2. Hobson, *The Evolution of Modern Capitalism*, 204–5.

3. Wilkins, *The Emergence of Multinational Enterprise*, 70.

4. The Standard Oil Company and the American Tobacco Company were the most important businesses that were ordered to be broken up. Both decisions took place in 1911 (on the same day).

5. Wilkins, *The Emergence of Multinational Enterprise*, 73–74.

6. See Tugendhat, *The Multinationals*, 24.

7. See United Nations Conference on Trade and Development, *World Investment Report 2000*, 31.

8. Extraterritorial jurisdiction has a long history in the United States. It goes back to the Barbary Wars at the end of the eighteenth century, when it was not particularly controversial. It became much more so when US laws (e.g., the Trading with the Enemy Act) were used against companies based outside the United States.

9. Nye and Rubin, "The Longer Range Political Role," 130.

10. The Treaty of Rome created the European Economic Community (EEC). It would go on to become the European Community (EC) and eventually the European Union (EU).

11. See Wilkins, *The Maturing of Multinational Enterprise*, 332.

12. The amendment, which stated that foreign aid would be withdrawn if expropriation was not followed by prompt and adequate compensation, was added to the Foreign Assistance Act of that year. It was initially opposed by the State Department on the grounds that it might interfere with US strategic objectives, but by the following year the State Department had reconciled itself to the amendment and supported a revised and strengthened version.

13. The Burke-Hartke bill was sponsored by the AFL-CIO labor federation. In addition to removing tax breaks for multinational corporations, it proposed restrictions on capital exports and quotas on imports. See Judis, *The Paradox of American Democracy*, 114–15.

14. See "Lobbying Database," Center for Responsive Politics, https://www.opensecrets.org/lobby/.
15. FECA provided a means whereby corporations (and unions) could use treasury funds to establish, operate, and solicit voluntary contributions for the organization's PAC. These voluntary donations from individuals could then be used to contribute to federal campaigns.
16. See May, "Direct and Indirect Influence," 51, summarizing the work of Ravi Ramamurti on the Pfizer campaign.
17. Congress did, however, take important steps to strengthen IPRs in the 1980s by passing two trade acts, the Trade and Tariff Act (1984) and the Omnibus Trade and Competitiveness Act (1988). These threatened punishment against countries not providing "adequate" protection.
18. Ramamurti, "Global Regulatory Convergence," 350.
19. Schulzinger, *The Wise Men*, 11.
20. Edward Stettinius to Harry S. Truman, 1945, quoted in Snider, "The Influence of Transnational Peace Groups," 377. Stettinius was writing at the end of the San Francisco conference in 1945 that launched the UN.
21. See Woods, "Making the IMF," 95.
22. Abugre and Alexander, "Non-governmental Organizations," 116.
23. There is also a third sort, called grant-making public charities or public foundations. In 2010 there were 1,371 such organizations that fund internationally. They include well-known names, such as Global Health Solutions, AmeriCares, and World Vision (see Box 6.4).
24. Those NGOs concerned with religion will be considered in Section 6.4.
25. The Carnegie Corporation should not be confused with the other NGOs established by Andrew Carnegie, such as the Carnegie Foundation, the Carnegie Endowment, the Carnegie Trust, and the Carnegie Institute. See Nielsen, *The Golden Donors*, 134.
26. Carnegie Corporation of New York, *Carnegie Corporation of New York* (brochure), Carnegie Mellon University Libraries, http://shelf1.library.cmu.edu/cgi-bin/tiff2pdf.old/carnegie_jbc/box00002/fld00019/bdl0001/doc0001/carnegie.pdf, 3.
27. So anxious was Rockefeller to secure a charter from the Senate that he even agreed that the election of new trustees would be subject to disapproval within sixty days by a majority of (a) the US president, (b) the speaker of the House, and (c) the presidents of Harvard, Yale, Columbia, and Johns Hopkins Universities and the University of Chicago. See Nielsen, *The Big Foundations*, 51.
28. Like the Carnegie Corporation, the Rockefeller Foundation should not be confused with other NGOs bearing the same name and established by John D. Rockefeller Sr.
29. In 2006 Warren Buffett announced he was giving a large part of his wealth to the Gates Foundation. This has increased substantially the IGM capacity of the foundation.
30. In 2013, for example, the annual giving of the Gates Foundation ($3.3 billion) was four times larger than the next biggest.
31. Vogel, "Who's Making Global Civil Society," 643.

32. There have been numerous studies of these networks, starting with C. Wright Mills's study of US power elites in the 1950s. See Mills, *The Power Elite*; Rich, *Think Tanks*; and Parmar, *Foundations*. Some have even gone so far as to refer to these networks as a US "establishment"; see Hodgson, "The Establishment."

33. As a share of GDP, US foreign aid is typically around 0.2%. In 2000, for example, it was dwarfed by US private assistance. See Adelman, "The Privatization of Foreign Aid," 11.

34. A good illustration is provided by Isaiah Bowman, a director of the CFR for nearly thirty years and a key adviser to several US presidents. See Smith, *American Empire*, passim.

35. See Ahmad, "US Think Tanks," 4, Table 2.

36. McGann, "The Think Tank Index," 82.

37. See Abella, *Soldiers of Reason*, passim.

38. See Schulzinger, *The Wise Men*, 209–10.

39. Medvetz, *Think Tanks in America*, 7.

40. The think tank Project for the New American Century is often claimed to be the intellectual author of the second Iraq War.

41. Huntington, "Transnational Organizations," 344.

42. Tocqueville, *Democracy in America*, 224–29.

43. See Tunstall, *The Media Are American*, 27–28.

44. Madrigal, "Republic to Empire," 99.

45. Hearst did not know the explosion was accidental (that was only revealed by careful investigation much later), but it is doubtful if it would have made much difference if he had known. He had promised war and was determined to get it. On the *Maine* incident, see Schoultz, *That Infernal Little Cuban Republic*, 16–18.

46. *Time* rapidly increased in circulation and even in 1997 was selling more than four million copies per week, after which sales declined in common with almost all printed newspapers and magazines.

47. Henry R. Luce, "The American Century," *Life*, February 17, 1941, 62, 63, 65. The article was reprinted in *Diplomatic History* 23.2 (1999): 159–71.

48. See Emery, Emery, and Roberts, *The Press and America: An Interpretive History*, 272–73.

49. The FCC gave permission for the first commercial television operations to start on July 1, 1941. NBC and CBS were the first to do so.

50. Voice of America was established in 1942 by the Office of War Information.

51. Edward Jay Epstein, quoted in Tunstall, *The Media Are American*, 140.

52. This did not stop it coming to the attention of Senator McCarthy, but there is no evidence that there ever was a "red decade" in Hollywood.

53. Rosenstone, *Visions of the Past*, 44–45.

54. Wyatt, *Paper Soldiers*, 7.

55. The other international news agencies, Reuters in the United Kingdom and Agence France-Presse (AFP), were not so important, while the Soviet Union's TASS was not widely considered a "news" agency.

56. MacBride, *Many Voices, One World*, 38.
57. AT&T was one of those that had formed RCA in 1919. It went on to acquire a virtual monopoly in telephone and cable until it was broken up under the Sherman Antitrust Act in 1982.
58. The seven are Comcast, News Corporation (including 21st Century Fox until 2013), Walt Disney Company, CBS Corporation, Viacom, Time Warner, and Sony Corporation of America.
59. Halton, "International News," 500, citing a survey by the Joan Shorenstein Center at Harvard University.
60. Halton, "International News," 501.
61. This phrase, implying a divine blessing, is the title of a book on US foreign policy by Walter Russell Mead. See Mead, *Special Providence*.
62. Skillen, *With or against the World?*, 78.
63. The board was established soon after the Haystack Prayer Meeting in 1806, which was part of the Second Great Awakening. See Harvey, *The Columbia Guide to Religion*, 31–32.
64. Missionaries were also sent to US territories in North America that were not yet part of the Union.
65. See Amstutz, *Evangelicals*, 31.
66. Harold Ockenga, quoted in Amstutz, *Evangelicals*, 33; emphasis added.
67. It is safe to assume that the imperialism he was targeting was that of the Axis powers, not that of the United States.
68. Chiang Kai-shek's wife, Soong Mei-ling, was raised as a Methodist and converted her husband to Christianity before their marriage.
69. Guth, "Religion and American Public Opinion," 248.
70. Mead, "God's Country?," 40.
71. See the World Christian Database, http://www.worldchristiandatabase.org/wcd/.
72. The figure in 2015 was 126,650. See the World Christian Database, http://www.world christiandatabase.org/wcd/..
73. Following the terrorist attacks on September 11, 2001, Graham changed the name of his evangelical tours from crusades to missions.
74. Rev. Billy Graham, quoted in Stoll, *Is Latin America Turning Protestant?*, 73.
75. It is no accident that foreign governments in dispute with the United States have regularly targeted American missionaries through expulsions or restrictions.
76. See Lindsay, *Faith in the Halls of Power*, 35. Every US president after Eisenhower has attended the National Prayer Breakfast.
77. See Lindsay, *Faith in the Halls of Power*, 70–71.
78. Many US missionaries had served in China before the victory of the communists and had formed close ties with the nationalists.
79. See Chapter 7.
80. See Zinsmeister, "Is the Focus of American Evangelicals Shifting Overseas?," 1–6.
81. See Pew Research Center, "U.S. Public Becoming Less Religious," http://www.pew forum.org/2015/11/03/u-s-public-becoming-less-religious/.

82. See Smither, "The Impact of Evangelical Revivals"; and Brasil Fonseca, "Religion and Democracy in Brazil," 163–70.
83. Examples are American Samoa, Guam, the Northern Mariana Islands, and the Marshall Islands.

7. THE EMPIRE IN ACTION

1. See Gimbel, *The American Occupation of Germany: Politics and the Military*, 12–15.
2. In 1947 the United States persuaded the British to cede the ports of Bremen and Bremerhaven in their zone as they were needed by the American military for strategic purposes.
3. Neither the USSR nor the United States had envisaged a French zone, but Churchill was able to persuade Roosevelt and Stalin to add France as a fourth occupying power.
4. The Soviet Union reacted by blockading West Berlin, which had to be supplied for eleven months by air (mainly by the United States) before the USSR ended the blockade.
5. See Merritt, "American Influences," 97–98; and Hahn, *Cornerstone of Democracy*, 7–35.
6. The US military, however, retained a large number of bases in West Germany in which the US government—not West Germany—exercised sovereignty.
7. Nachmani, "Civil War," 499–500.
8. See Miller, *The United States*, 24–25.
9. See Stephanidēs, *Stirring the Greek Nation*, 239.
10. President Bill Clinton in 1999 apologized to the Greek people for this support. See Mark Lacey, "Clinton Tries to Subdue Greeks' Anger at America," *New York Times*, November 21, 1999.
11. Greece and Turkey had a long-standing territorial dispute over Cyprus, which increased in intensity after Great Britain (the colonial power) granted independence to the island in 1960.
12. By the end of 1945 membership exceeded 800,000, while affiliation with the communist-dominated Confédération Générale du Travail rose to nearly four million. See Brogi, *Confronting America*, 14.
13. Bird, *The Chairman*, 291.
14. It had 2.5 million members in 1947, making it briefly the largest in the world after the Communist Party of the Soviet Union. See Brogi, *Confronting America*, 14.
15. The expulsion by Prime Minister Alcide de Gasperi took place a few days after Sumner Welles, former undersecretary of state, had declared the Italian Communist Party to be an insurrectionary force funded by the Soviet Union. See Brogi, *Confronting America*, 1.
16. Cull, *The Cold War*, 31.
17. George Marshall to William Benton, April 1947, quoted in Cull, *The Cold War*, 35.
18. See Saunders, *Who Paid the Piper?*, 369–80.
19. The six states that formed the EEC in 1958 had been joined by six others (Denmark, Greece, Ireland, Portugal, Spain, and the United Kingdom) before the end of the

Cold War. Later, the European Union (as the EEC became) would expand to twenty-eight members.

20. It was this lack of sovereignty that persuaded France under President Charles de Gaulle to withdraw from NATO's integrated military command in 1966 and to insist on the removal of NATO assets from French soil.

21. Calleo, *The Atlantic Fantasy*, 28.

22. There were over two hundred in West Germany and over one hundred in Italy at the end of the Cold War.

23. Although the Philippines became nominally independent in 1946, it remained a US protectorate with its sovereignty restricted in many ways. See Chapter 3.

24. See Scalapino, "The United States and Japan," 44–46.

25. The Soviet Union attended the conference but refused to sign the treaty.

26. Okinawa was returned to Japan in 1972, but the United States retained its military bases on the island and the right to introduce nuclear weapons in an emergency. See Schaller, *Altered States*, 218–20.

27. Schaller, "Japan and the Cold War," 173–74.

28. Barnett, "The United States and Communist China," 149.

29. See Chapter 6.4 for the role of US missionaries in this decision. In addition, former President Herbert Hoover released a seven-point letter in January 1950 explaining why the US government should not recognize the PRC. See Ballantine, *Formosa*, 118–19.

30. Harry S. Truman, "Statement by the President on the Situation in Korea," American Presidency Project, http://www.presidency.ucsb.edu/ws/?pid=13538.

31. See Whiting, "The United States and Taiwan," 190.

32. Kissinger's secret visit to China in July 1971 was the prelude to a vote in the UN General Assembly recognizing the PRC as the sole representative of China. The ROC then left the UN, but the United States continued to grant it diplomatic recognition until January 1979. Only then did the United States recognize the PRC officially as the sole representative of China.

33. Chiang Kai-shek was not invited to Yalta, but Stalin wanted China to be part of the four-power trusteeship, along with the United Kingdom, the United States, and the USSR.

34. The 38th parallel had been proposed by two US colonels, one of whom was future secretary of state Dean Rusk, and it was accepted by the Soviet side as reasonable. It did, however, leave two-thirds of the Korean population in the south. See Buckley, *The United States in the Asia-Pacific*, 52.

35. Syngman Rhee had been educated at an American Methodist school in Korea before completing his education in the United States.

36. The Soviet Union had abandoned the Security Council in January 1950 in protest at the failure of the UN to award the China seat to the PRC government. It returned in August, after the crucial resolution on Korea had been passed.

37. Article 4 stated, "The Republic of Korea grants, and the United States of America accepts, the right to dispose United States land, air and sea forces in and about the territory of the Republic of Korea as determined by mutual agreement." "Mutual Defense

Treaty between the United States and the Republic of Korea," October 1, 1953, Avalon Project, http://avalon.law.yale.edu/20th_century/kor001.asp.

38. The United States was officially neutral before 1950, but in practice policy favored France, which was seen as a key ally in Europe. In addition, the United States was well aware that its grants to France under the Marshall Plan were being used partly in Indochina. See Thomas, "French Imperial Reconstruction," 141.

39. Australia and New Zealand, much to the annoyance of the United Kingdom, had already formed the ANZUS Alliance with the United States in 1952. See Reese, *Australia, New Zealand and the United States*, 126–49.

40. The other was Thailand, which faced a left-wing insurgency at the time and whose government welcomed US support to defeat it. In return, Thailand provided the United States with military bases all over the country that would be used subsequently to bomb North Vietnam. See Logevall, "The Indochina Wars," 138–40.

41. "Southeast Asia Collective Defense Treaty (Manila Pact)," September 8, 1954, Avalon Project, http://avalon.law.yale.edu/20th_century/usmu003.asp, Article 4, Part 1; emphasis added.

42. Five other countries sent troops, and thirty-eight provided nonmilitary assistance to the government in South Vietnam. This was less than the US government demanded, but probably more than it expected given the unpopularity of its intervention.

43. See Simpson, *Economists with Guns*, 14.

44. On the role of the Ford Foundation, see Parmar, *Foundations*, 124–48. For other actors, see Simpson, *Economists with Guns*, passim.

45. "Middle East" is defined here as the majority Arab countries together with Iran, Israel, and Turkey.

46. Spain had protectorates in northern Morocco, but the largest ended in 1956 leaving only the tiny enclaves of Ceuta and Melilla. Spain also controlled Western Sahara until 1975.

47. Lebanon and Syria, with US support, became founding members of the UN, while the United Kingdom was able to engineer the withdrawal of all French troops. See Ovendale, *Britain, the United States, and the Transfer of Power*, 1.

48. Saudi Arabia, unified in 1932 and nominally independent, was part of the British informal empire and recognized as such by the United States. See O'Sullivan, *FDR and the End of Empire*, 147–53. As late as 1941, for example, FDR had said in response to a request for American help, "Will you tell the British I hope they can take care of the King of Saudi Arabia. This is a little far afield for us!" Franklin Delano Roosevelt, quoted in Little, *American Orientalism*, 48.

49. See Ovendale, *Britain, the United States, and the Transfer of Power*, 69–74.

50. The Suez Canal was nationalized in June 1956. Britain and France then colluded with Israel to retake it by force just before the US presidential elections. Swift action by President Eisenhower soon forced a retreat by the invading forces. See Ovendale, *Britain, the United States, and the Transfer of Power*, 166–67.

51. The overthrow of King Faisal in 1958 by the Iraqi Army was seen at the time as a triumph for the USSR. See Hallock, *The Press March to War*, 55. However, a covert US

operation led to the installation of a pro-American regime in 1963. This in turn was overthrown in 1968 in the Ba'athist revolution from which Saddam Hussein soon emerged as the dominant figure. He would remain on good terms with US governments for most of the time until Iraq's invasion of Kuwait in 1990.

52. It was seen at first as an opportunity to supply the rest of the world rather than the United States itself.

53. The San Remo agreement in 1920 had excluded US companies from Iraqi oil. Britain and France only changed their minds when they become worried about US commercial retaliation.

54. Gulbenkian was an Armenian who had participated in the prewar concession controlled by Turkey.

55. This was the famous Red Line drawn by Gulbenkian and which aimed to restrict oil supplies and raise prices. The so-called Red Line Agreement was finally ended in 1946.

56. The pipeline had to pass through Iraq, Jordan, Lebanon, and Syria. Only President Shukri Quwatly of Syria objected, and he was overthrown by his army chief of staff on March 31, 1949. Six weeks later the pipeline was approved.

57. US oil companies were warmly welcomed during the long reign of King Idris. When he was overthrown by Colonel Muammar al-Gaddhafi in 1969, the relationship soured.

58. See Safran, *The United States and Israel*, 42.

59. The United States was the first country to do so (the Soviet Union was the second). Marshall could not give his support, but agreed not to oppose it. See Little, *American Orientalism*, 86.

60. After the Six-Day War in 1967, the United States sponsored UNSC Resolution 242 that called for a withdrawal of Israeli forces from territory captured in the six days of conflict. Resolution 242, however, did not call for the establishment of a Palestinian State, and US policy on a two-state solution vacillated until after the Cold War had ended.

61. It is surely no accident that by this time US oil imports—in particular, from Iran, Kuwait, Libya and Saudi Arabia—appeared to be completely secure with friendly governments in place. Unlike Truman and Eisenhower, Kennedy and Johnson were therefore less concerned about the energy security implications of leaning toward Israel.

62. See, in particular, Mearsheimer and Walt, *The Israel Lobby*, passim.

63. See Chomsky, *Fateful Triangle*, 9–32.

64. Stalin reversed his position after the United States took the dispute to the UN Security Council in 1946.

65. Dwight D. Eisenhower, "Statement by the President following the Landing of United States Marines at Beirut," American Presidency Project, http://www.presidency.ucsb.edu/ws/?pid=11133.

66. The United Arab Republic would dissolve in 1961.

67. CENTO grew out of the Baghdad Pact, which included Iraq. However, the overthrow of King Feisal in 1958 led to Iraqi withdrawal and the need for a new organization. CENTO collapsed when Iran withdrew after its own revolution in 1979.

68. Ethiopian leaders after Haile Selassie demanded the withdrawal of all US forces. US attention then switched to Somalia, Ethiopia's neighbor that guards the entrance to the Red Sea. It had previously been allied with the USSR, but supported the United States through the remainder of the Cold War. See Jackson, *Jimmy Carter*, 111–17; and Woodward, *US Foreign Policy*, 22–27.

69. See Hubbard, *The United States*, Chapter 3, where McGhee's speech to the Foreign Policy Association is summarized.

70. The imperial powers were Belgium, France, Italy, Portugal, South Africa, Spain, and the United Kingdom. Italy lost its colonies following the defeat of Benito Mussolini and would be confined to a purely administrative role in the former Italian Somaliland, while South Africa illegally retained the League of Nations mandate for South West Africa (modern Namibia).

71. The first was Sudan and the last was Namibia. After that, the African states that became independent (Eritrea and South Sudan) were the results of civil war rather than decolonization.

72. After independence in 1958, Guinea under President Sékou Touré refused to join the currency union established by France, leading to a major rift with the former colonial power and close ties with the USSR until the Soviet ambassador was expelled in 1961. See Laïdi, *The Superpowers*, 7. Ghana, under President Kwame Nkrumah, also established close relations with the Soviet Union until Nkrumah was overthrown in 1966 in a coup orchestrated by the CIA. See Blum, *Killing Hope*, 198–200.

73. See Grubbs, *Secular Missionaries*, passim, for a study of how these institutions operated in different African countries in the 1960s.

74. Three out of four US military flights across the Atlantic were still stopping in the Azores when the lease on the base came up for renewal. In return for renewal, the Kennedy administration accepted the Portuguese government condition of no US interference in its African colonies. See Rakove, *Kennedy, Johnson, and the Nonaligned World*, 121–27.

75. South Africa under apartheid feared the presence of a pro-Soviet regime in Angola on the northern border. See Gleijeses, *Conflicting Missions*, 275–76.

76. See Gleijeses, *Visions of Freedom*, 28–30.

77. Negotiations involving Angola, Cuba, South Africa, United States and the USSR concluded in 1988 with an agreement to withdraw all foreign troops from Angola immediately and grant South West Africa independence as Namibia in 1990.

78. US government cooperation with South Africa in Angola was one reason why Congress was unwilling to impose sanctions until 1986, when it passed the Comprehensive Anti-Apartheid Act. Even then it had to overcome a veto by President Reagan.

79. The British government, with US support, suspended the constitution in 1953 and imposed direct rule until 1957. See Rabe, *U.S. Intervention*, Chapter 2.

80. UFCO concentrated on banana production, but controlled other companies in Guatemala that owned the railways, ports, and telegraph facilities.

81. See Gleijeses, *Shattered Hope*, 128–29.

82. Council on Foreign Relations, quoted in Immerman, *The CIA in Guatemala*, 128. The document was written by Ambassador Adolf Berle and directed to John Cabot, assistant secretary for inter-American affairs.

83. The exile force was not expected to defeat the Guatemalan Army. However, once it was known that the exiles had US support, it was assumed that the officer class would be unwilling to confront them, and that is exactly what happened.

84. The US government had a controlling interest in the IADB, which was also headquartered in Washington, DC. It focused on long-term development loans, while USAID and ALPRO mainly distributed grants.

85. "In Office but Not Power" is the title of chapter 11 of Jagan's autobiography that describes the period from 1957 to 1961 when he had to share administrative responsibilities with the British governor. See Jagan, *The West on Trial*.

86. See Rabe, *U.S. Intervention*, passim.

87. Technically the French territories were not colonies but part of France, while the Netherlands Antilles were a part of the Kingdom of the Netherlands. However, these constitutional subtleties were of little concern to the United States, since foreign affairs and defense were in the hands of NATO allies.

88. The United States would intervene in Jamaica in the mid-1970s, however, after the administration of Prime Minister Michael Manley normalized relations with Cuba. US intervention contributed to the destabilization of the economy and the defeat of Manley in the 1980 elections. See Smith, *Michael Manley*, 214–43.

89. Trujillo had become a liability as a result of his meddling in the affairs of countries allied to the United States, such as Venezuela, while Bosch was considered sympathetic to Castro. See Gleijeses, *The Dominican Crisis*, 104–6, 303–7.

90. Allende won a plurality, but not a majority, in September 1970. Under the Chilean Constitution, the Congress had to choose a president from the two candidates with the highest number of votes, and Allende was duly elected the following month.

91. Church, *Covert Action in Chile*, 9.

92. See Church, *Covert Action in Chile*, 33.

93. The Frente Sandinista de Liberación Nacional (FSLN) had been founded in 1961 and was inspired by the Cuban Revolution. It took its name from Augusto César Sandino, who had fought the US Marines in Nicaragua between 1927 and 1933.

94. To circumvent the Boland Amendment outlawing US funding for the contras, the Reagan administration sold arms to Iran and used part of the proceeds secretly to fund the contras. See Walsh, *Firewall*, 18–22.

95. This action by the CIA was such a flagrant abuse of international law that Nicaragua was able to secure a ruling from the International Court of Justice that condemned it. However, the ruling could not be enforced, as the US government refused to participate in the case.

96. The biggest challenges to US interests were from the guerrilla movements in El Salvador and Guatemala. These would be ended by negotiations in the 1990s, leaving US interests secure.

97. Grenada, a member of the Commonwealth and a former British colony, had been ruled by the New Jewel Movement since 1979. When its leader (Maurice Bishop) was assassinated in 1983 by other members, the Reagan administration used the opportunity to intervene and establish a government more sympathetic to US interests.

8. THE UNIPOLAR MOMENT

1. Fukuyama, *The National Interest,* 3.
2. A total of 128 countries joined the WTO as founder members, but this still left around 60 outside the organization.
3. In theory other countries could do the same, but in practice the United States exercised a virtual veto since access to its market was so important for new members. Only the European Union came close to the United States in the leverage it could exercise over new members.
4. Stiglitz, "Multinational Corporations," 18.
5. The most serious was in 2008–9, when the dollar value of world trade declined sharply, but it soon recovered.
6. Taiwan joined as the Separate Customs Territory of Taiwan, Penghu, Kinmen and Matsu (Chinese Taipei) under rules that allow membership by nonsovereign entities if they have autonomy over their commercial relations.
7. Russia took nineteen years and two months to secure membership, the longest wait of any country.
8. Lawrence, *The United States and the WTO,* 15.
9. This also happened in the United States, where WTO negotiations in Seattle in 1999 were seriously disrupted by protestors.
10. It is no accident that Doha in Qatar was chosen as the site of negotiations after Seattle, as there was no danger of the local police allowing protestors anywhere near the meeting.
11. The best that could be achieved, after nearly fifteen years, was a modest agreement on trade facilitation measures. This, however, fell far short of the original ambitions for the Doha Round.
12. The one exception was the European Economic Community (EEC). Despite the very real threat of trade diversification, US governments supported the EEC enthusiastically for security reasons.
13. See Ritchie, *Wrestling with the Elephant,* for a Canadian "insider" account of how the US team negotiated CUFTA.
14. Office of the United States Trade Representative, "Fact Sheet: Investor-State Dispute Settlement (ISDS)," https://ustr.gov/about-us/policy-offices/press-office/fact-sheets/2015/march/investor-state-dispute-settlement-isds; emphasis added.
15. The most famous example is the steady erosion of the Glass-Steagall Act that placed restrictions, among other things, on dealings in securities by commercial banks.
16. See Skidmore-Hess, "The Corporate Centrism of the Obama Administration," 88–89.

17. Simon Johnson, "The Quiet Coup," *Atlantic*, May 2009, https://www.theatlantic.com /magazine/archive/2009/05/the-quiet-coup/307364/.

18. See UNCTAD, *World Investment Report 2015*, Annex, Table 2.

19. The EBRD was established in 1991 with a mandate to further progress toward market-oriented economies and the promotion of private and entrepreneurial initiative. Uniquely for a development bank, it can assist only those countries "committed to and applying the principles of multi-party democracy and pluralism."

20. Rodrik, *The Globalization Paradox*, 164.

21. See Florio, "Economists," 359–400.

22. Executive Office of the President, *National Space Policy of the United States of America*, 7–8.

23. It was originally called the Advanced Research Projects Agency (ARPA) but has been known only as DARPA since 1996. See Mazzucato, *The Entrepreneurial State*, 74–75.

24. Defense Advanced Research Projects Agency, "About DARPA," http://www.darpa.mil /about-us/about-darpa.

25. Berners-Lee, a British scientist working at the Conseil Européen pour la Recherche Nucléaire (CERN), developed Hypertext Markup Language (HTML), the uniform resource locator (URL), and uniform Hypertext Transfer Protocol (HTTP), without which the Internet would be extremely cumbersome. His inventions were not patented.

26. The largest non-US company is Samsung Electronics, based in South Korea.

27. "Annual Revenue of Global Publicly Traded Internet Companies from 2014 to 2016 (in Billion U.S. Dollars)," Statista, http://www.statista.com/statistics/276709/revenue -of-global-public-internet-companies/.

28. As recently as 1993, the share was estimated to be as little as 1%.

29. The companies are JD.com, Tencent, Alibaba, Baidu, and NetEase.

30. Its full title, published in July 1976, was *Final Report of the United States Senate Select Committee to Study Governmental Operations with Respect to Intelligence Activities*. It was named the Church Committee Report after its chairman, Senator Frank Church.

31. A US person is defined in law as a US citizen or long-term resident. A non-US person is anyone else.

32. Clarke et al., *The NSA Report*, 26.

33. Clarke et al., *The NSA Report*, 84–85.

34. See Clarke et al., *The NSA Report*.

35. The USA Freedom Act did, however, end bulk collection of all records (previously allowed under Section 215 of the Patriot Act).

36. See Harrison, "Indexing the Empire," 145. The cables themselves are available at "Public Library of Public Diplomacy," WikiLeaks, https://wikileaks.org/plusd.

37. Assange, "Introduction," in WikiLeaks, *The WikiLeaks Files*, 2.

38. The Warsaw Pact was the military alliance formed by the USSR and its European allies in opposition to NATO in 1955. It was dissolved in early 1991.

39. The White House, *A National Security Strategy of Engagement and Enlargement*, February 1995, Defense Technical Information Center, http://www.dtic.mil/doctrine /doctrine/research/nss.pdf, i.

40. Joint Chiefs of Staff, *Joint Vision 2020*, 59.
41. These efforts were generally successful. However, three states (India, Israel, and Pakistan) never signed the NPT while North Korea signed but withdrew in 2003. Israel, despite some US reservations, had acquired nuclear weapons before the end of the Cold War. The other three did so later and were subject to major US sanctions (those on India were eventually reversed; see Chapter 12).
42. Not all states of the FSU had such stockpiles, but several did including (apart from Russia) Azerbaijan, Belarus, Georgia, Kazakhstan, Ukraine, and Uzbekistan.
43. START I had been signed in 1991 by President Bush with President Mikhail Gorbachev a few months before the dissolution of the USSR.
44. The Czech Republic, Hungary, and Poland joined in 1999; Bulgaria, Estonia, Latvia, Lithuania, Romania, Slovakia, and Slovenia in 2004; and Albania and Croatia in 2009.
45. Gorbachev had been promised that NATO expansion would be limited to East Germany if German unification went ahead.
46. See MccGwire and Clarke, "NATO Expansion," 1282.
47. MccGwire and Clarke, "NATO Expansion," 1283.
48. Kristol and Kagan, "Toward a Neo-Reaganite Foreign Policy," 20.
49. Project for the New American Century, *Rebuilding America's Defenses*, iv.
50. The White House, *National Security Strategy of the United States of America*, 15.
51. The two governments, however, did agree in 2003 to the Strategic Offensive Reductions Treaty (SORT), which was superseded in 2011 by New START.
52. The Clinton administration signed the statute in 2000, but it was not subsequently ratified by the US Senate.
53. See Lutz, *Bases of Empire*, 1.
54. See Vine, *Base Nation*, 45–46.
55. Vine, *Base Nation*, 58.
56. See US Department of Defense, *The Department of Defense Cyber Strategy*, 5.
57. These special cases almost invariably involve countries in civil wars.
58. The most (in)famous is Blackwater, which is now known as Academi and is part of the Constellis Group.
59. China wanted to avoid confrontation with the United States in order to concentrate on rapid economic growth, while Russia was preoccupied with its painful transition to a market economy.
60. UN sanctions were first applied to Libya in 1992 in response to the bombing of a Pan Am flight full of US passengers (they were lifted in 2003). Those against Sudan were first applied in 2006 for alleged complicity in an assassination attempt against President Hosni Mubarak of Egypt (a key US ally). Those against Afghanistan and al-Qaeda were both adopted in 1999 to compel the Taliban to hand over Osama bin Laden.
61. It is too early to say how closely President Trump will follow this strategy, but there is no reason to assume it will not be tried.
62. Two countries (Cuba and Yemen) voted against, and China abstained. All other members of the Security Council supported UNSCR 678.

63. The best known of these incidents was the destruction of two US helicopters in Mogadishu, an episode later made into the film *Black Hawk Down* (2001). See Dawson, "New World Disorder," for an account of the event and a critique of the film.

64. Although a Chapter 7 resolution, UNSCR 1368 did not invoke Article 42 but instead referred to the right of a state (i.e., the United States) to use force in self-defense under Article 51.

65. "Regime change" was not explicitly endorsed by UNSCR 1973, although it was what the United States wanted. Whether the removal of Gaddhafi was justified in international law remains in dispute to this day.

66. The negotiations, held at an air base in Ohio, led to the Dayton Accords that ended the war in Bosnia & Herzegovina.

67. In 2005 the UN World Summit adopted the doctrine of Responsibility to Protect (R2P) in an effort to ensure that in the future humanitarian intervention would be consistent with international law. However, any action—by NATO or others—would still require a UNSC resolution under Chapter 7.

68. Russia, which has used its veto powers sparingly since the end of the Cold War, did so in the case of Syria, and some NATO members have been reluctant to become involved without explicit UN approval.

69. The coalition against IS in Iraq was broadly based, as it had the support of the Iraqi government. It was much narrower in the case of Syria, since many allies were reluctant to use force without the government's explicit approval.

70. The sanctions were first applied in 1960, but were extended after the Cold War by the Cuban Democracy Act of 1992 and the Helms-Burton Act of 1996 with extraterritorial implications (see Box 8.4). There has been a vote on sanctions against Cuba in the UN General Assembly every year since 1992. The United States always voted to keep the sanctions until 2016 when it abstained (only Israel supported the US position in that year).

71. For the full list, see US Department of the Treasury, "Sanctions Programs and Country Information," https://www.treasury.gov/resource-center/sanctions/Programs/Pages/Programs.aspx. In some cases, other countries later joined the United States in imposing sanctions.

72. The annual survey started in 1985, but had much more impact after the Cold War as allies against the USSR were never going to be punished. Unless accompanied by a waiver, decertification means a country is denied US support in various ways.

73. Report of the National Commission for the Review of the Research and Development Programs of the United States Intelligence Community, iii.

74. US Congress, Authorization for the Use of Military Force, Public Law 107-40, September 18, 2001, https://www.congress.gov/107/plaws/publ40/PLAW-107publ40.pdf.

75. The story of the killing of US citizen Anwar al-Awlaki in Yemen is told in detail in Scahill, *Dirty Wars*.

76. It is known as the Joint Unconventional Warfare Task Force executive order and exempts special forces from seeking presidential approval on each occasion. See Scahill, *Dirty Wars*, 282.

77. See Nye, "Public Diplomacy and Soft Power," 107–8.
78. US Department of State and US Agency for International Aid, *Leading through Civilian Power: The First Quadrennial Diplomacy and Development Review*, ii–iii.

9. ANTI-IMPERIALISM IN THE UNITED STATES

1. See Onuf, "Imperialism and Nationalism," 21–40.
2. On settler colonialism in America, see Hixson, *American Settler Colonialism*.
3. The obvious example is what proportion of a slave should count toward the population of a state. This led to loud protests by some opponents of the Constitution, but it could hardly be called anti-imperialist.
4. See Borden, *The Anti-Federalist Papers*.
5. "'Centinel': Number 1," October 5, 1787, Constitution Society, http://www.constitution.org/afp/centin01.htm. Centinel is generally thought to have been George Bryan from Pennsylvania.
6. See "Antifederalist Paper 14: Extent of Territory under Consolidated Government Too Large to Preserve Liberty or Protect Property," *New-York Journal*, October 25, 1787, Federalist Papers Project, http://www.thefederalistpapers.org/antifederalist-paper-14. Cato was George Clinton, the governor of New York.
7. See Brown, *The Constitutional History*, 17–29; and Lawson and Seidman, "The First 'Incorporation' Debate," 19–40.
8. Roger Griswold, quoted in Kauffman, *Ain't My America*, 15.
9. Gannon, "Escaping Mr. Jefferson's Plan of Destruction," 423.
10. Morris Miller, quoted in Hoey, "Federalist Opposition," 7.
11. Robert Toombs, quoted in Clark, *Lincoln*, 96.
12. Corwin, *Life and Speeches of Thomas Corwin*, 305.
13. Quoted in Seymour, *American Insurgents*, 32.
14. William Lloyd Garrison, quoted in DeWitt, "Crusading for Peace," 109.
15. Cadwalader Washburn, quoted in Blaine, *Twenty Years of Congress*, 1.
16. See Box 4.1.
17. A good example is provided by Frederick Douglass, who vehemently opposed the war against Mexico and yet supported the annexation of Santo Domingo.
18. The first AIL was in Boston, and it would be swiftly followed by AILs in many other cities. A national AIL was then established in 1899. See Harrington, "The Anti-imperialist Movement," 216–18.
19. See Murphy, "Women's Anti-imperialism," 244–70.
20. Carl Schurz, quoted in Harrington, "The Anti-imperialist Movement," 212. Schurz had been a leading figure in the Republican Party before the mugwump movement in the 1880s.
21. Cuba, although under US occupation, did not exercise the AIL to the same extent, as the Teller Amendment ensured that it would eventually achieve some kind of independence. See Chapter 4.
22. See Lasch, "The Anti-imperialists," 322–28.

23. See Harrington, "The Anti-imperialist Movement," 226.

24. See Lutz, *Bases of Empire*; and Vine, *Base Nation*.

25. George Washington, "Washington's Farewell Address 1796," Avalon Project, http:// avalon.law.yale.edu/18th_century/washing.asp.

26. Elbridge Gerry, quoted in Johnson, *The Peace Progressives*, 14.

27. Thomas Jefferson, "First Inaugural Address," March 4, 1801, Avalon Project, http:// avalon.law.yale.edu/19th_century/jefinau1.asp.

28. See Braumoeller, "The Myth of American Isolationism," 8.

29. See Johnson, *The Peace Progressives*, 60.

30. Hiram Johnson, quoted in Johnson, *The Peace Progressives*, 87.

31. See Johnson, *The Peace Progressives*, 135.

32. See Braumoeller, "The Myth of American Isolationism," 349–71.

33. The Senate had voted strongly in favor of joining in 1926, but a series of reservations were added that would have given the United States privileges and immunities that other countries lacked. This so unsettled other members of the Court that they proposed further negotiations. These never happened, and so the United States never joined the World Court. See Guinsburg, *The Pursuit of Isolationism*, 102–6.

34. See Langer and Gleason, *The Challenge to Isolation*, 232.

35. See Kauffman, *Ain't My America*, 80.

36. Wallace did not even win a single vote in the electoral college, yet four years before he had been the overwhelming favorite to retain his position as FDR's vice presidential nominee. How he was outmaneuvered at the convention is one of the great "what ifs?" of American history. See Stone and Kuznick, *The Untold History*, 138–40.

37. Their number included Howard Buffett, father of Warren.

38. Sterling Morton, quoted in Carpenter, "The Dissenters," 240.

39. Laqueur, *Neo-isolationism*, 19.

40. On the debate around grand strategy after the Cold War, see Posen and Ross, "Competing Visions"; see also Art, *America's Grand Strategy*.

41. See Nordlinger, *Isolationism Reconfigured*, 5.

42. See Andrew Kohut, "Americans: Disengaged, Feeling Less Respected, but Still See U.S. as World's Military Superpower," April 1, 2014, Pew Research Center, http://www .pewresearch.org/fact-tank/2014/04/01/americans-disengaged-feeling-less-respected -but-still-see-u-s-as-worlds-military-superpower. The Pew Research Center has asked the question regularly since 1991. Earlier data were taken from Gallup. Other polls, however, notably the annual survey conducted by the Chicago Council on Global Affairs, suggest a lower level of support for isolationism.

43. Trump denied in public that he was a neo-isolationist but was happy to be associated with the isolationist notion of "America first."

44. See Pew Research Center, "Faith and Skepticism about Trade, Foreign Investment," September 16, 2014, http://www.pewglobal.org/2014/09/16/faith-and-skepticism-about -trade-foreign-investment/.

45. The TPP was negotiated between twelve countries in the Asia-Pacific region, including the United States, Japan, and Canada but excluding China and India. It was signed by all states, but had not been ratified by the time of the US presidential elections in November 2016. As President Trump (2017–) has made clear his opposition to ratification, it is unlikely to go into force.

46. Thomas Jefferson, quoted in Ekirch, *The Civilian and the Military*, 46. Jefferson wrote these words in 1799, but he could just have easily done so before the Constitution was adopted.

47. Benjamin Rush, quoted in Reagan, "Book Review: *The Civilian and the Military*," 484. Reagan was reviewing Ekirch's book.

48. Henry Knox, quoted in Ekirch, *The Civilian and the Military*, 35.

49. This essay is still in print but is now called *Civil Disobedience*. See Thoreau, *Civil Disobedience and Other Essays*.

50. See Johnson, *The Peace Progressives*, 16. Taylor and Scott were the leading generals in the Mexican-American War.

51. Thomas Corwin, quoted in Ekirch, *The Civilian and the Military*, 83–84.

52. Daniel Webster, quoted in Kauffman, *Ain't My America*, 28.

53. Ekirch, *The Civilian and the Military*, 78.

54. Even so, the Civil War draft in the North provoked riots and thirty-eight officers in charge of recruitment were assassinated. See Flynn, *The Draft*, 167–68.

55. See Seymour, *American Insurgents*, 82.

56. Despite being in jail, he still managed to win 3.4% of the vote (down from 6% in 1912).

57. See Engelbrecht and Hanighen, *Merchants of Death*; and Butler, *War Is a Racket*.

58. Nye Committee, *Report of the Special Committee*, 3.

59. See Seymour, *American Insurgents*, 104.

60. See Seymour, *American Insurgents*, 105.

61. The numbers convicted of draft dodging peaked at 3,450 in 1953. See Flynn, *The Draft*, 126.

62. Quoted in Flynn, *The Draft*, 150. "P.F.C." stands for Private First Class.

63. See Brick and Phelps, *Radicals in America*, 129.

64. See Gettleman, *Vietnam and America*, 296.

65. In the Boston area, for example, one-tenth of resisters were divinity students who were exempt from the draft. See Flynn, *The Draft*, 178–79.

66. "Fragging" is the word given to the killing or attempted killing of a fellow soldier. There are thought to have been nine hundred such episodes by US soldiers during the Vietnam War. See Lepre, *Fragging*, 19–60.

67. See Think Squad, http://think-squad.com/post/13664798101/one-soldier-keith-franklin -wrote-a-letter-that.

68. Congress limited the number of military advisers the United States could send to El Salvador to fifty-five.

69. See "Peace Activists Pledge Resistance against U.S. Military Intervention in Central America, 1984–1990," Global Nonviolent Action Database, http://nvdatabase.swarth

more.edu/content/peace-activists-pledge-resistance-against-us-military-intervention
-central-america-1984-1990.

70. The School of the Americas is now known as the Western Hemisphere Institute for Security Cooperation.

71. The two organizations had a very public falling out in 2005, but this was due to tactical reasons rather than disagreement over the strategy of antimilitarism. See Seymour, *American Insurgents*, 191–93.

72. See Smeltz et al., *America Divided*, 26.

73. For Afghanistan, see http://abcnews.go.com/blogs/politics/2013/12/most-want-some -troops-in-afghanistan-despite-strong-criticism; for Iraq, see Sarah Dutton, Jennifer De Pinto, Anthony Salvanto, and Fred Backus, "Most Americans Say Iraq War Wasn't Worth the Costs: Poll," CBS News, June 23, 2014, http://www.cbsnews.com/news/most -americans-say-iraq-war-wasnt-worth-the-costs-poll/

74. Barack Obama, "Remarks by the President in Address to the Nation on Syria," September 10, 2013, Obama White House Archives, https://obamawhitehouse.archives.gov /the-press-office/2013/09/10/remarks-president-address-nation-syria. The next day, in an op-ed piece for the *New York Times*, Russian president Vladimir Putin responded, "It is extremely dangerous to encourage people to see themselves as exceptional, whatever the motivation." Vladimir V. Putin, "A Plea for Caution from Russia," *New York Times*, September 11, 2013, http://www.nytimes.com/2013/09/12/opinion/putin-plea-for -caution-from-russia-on-syria.html.

75. Barack Obama, "Remarks by the President at the United States Military Academy Commencement Ceremony," May 28, 2014, Obama White House Archives, https:// obamawhitehouse.archives.gov/the-press-office/2014/05/28/remarks-president-united -states-military-academy-commencement-ceremony.

76. Handsome Lake's vision was part of oral history until it was recorded in a document edited by Arthur C. Parker in 1912 ("The Code of Handsome Lake, the Seneca Prophet"). The quotation used here can be found in Madsen, *American Exceptionalism*, 47.

77. See Madsen, *American Exceptionalism*, 52–53. The reference to the "city upon the hill" is from John Winthrop's famous sermon of 1630.

78. See United States Census Bureau, *The American Indian and Alaska Native Population: 2010*, January 2012, https://www.census.gov/prod/cen2010/briefs/c2010br -10.pdf.

79. The book documents the story of the massacre of Native Americans at Wounded Knee in 1890. See Brown, *Bury My Heart at Wounded Knee*. On the 1973 siege, see Dunbar-Ortiz, *An Indigenous' People's History*, 192.

80. Examples are the disputes over the team name Washington Redskins in the National Football League and the Lord Jeff mascot at Amherst College (a reference to Lord Jeffery Amherst, who is alleged to have given Native Americans blankets infected with the smallpox virus in the eighteenth century).

81. See Selig, "The Revolution's Black Soldiers," 2–3.

82. Sir George Cockburn, quoted in Cassell, "Slaves of the Chesapeake Bay Area," 152.

83. The speech was delivered in Washington, DC, on April 16, 1889, at the invitation of the Bethel Literary and Historical Society. See Douglass, "The Nation's Problem," 728

84. W. E. B. Du Bois, quoted in Seymour, *American Insurgents*, 50.

85. Kelly Miller, quoted in Cullinane, *Liberty*, 71.

86. See Chapter 5.

87. See "Muhammad Ali Refuses to Fight in Vietnam (1967)," Alpha History, http://alphahistory.com/vietnamwar/muhammad-ali-refuses-to-fight-1967/.

88. See "'Beyond Vietnam,' Address Delivered to the Clergy and Laymen Concerned about Vietnam, at Riverside Church," A Call to Conscience: The Landmark Speeches of Dr. Martin Luther King, Jr., December 18, 2000, http://kingencyclopedia.stanford.edu/kingweb/publications/speeches/Beyond_Vietnam.pdf, 3.

89. Stokely Carmichael, quoted in Seymour, *American Insurgents*, 123.

90. Pastor Wright said, "And the United States of America government, when it came to treating her citizens of Indian descent fairly, she failed. She put them on reservations. When it came to treating her citizens of Japanese descent fairly, she failed. She put them in internment prison camps. When it came to treating her citizens of African descent fairly, America failed. She put them in chains, the government put them on slave quarters, put them on auction blocks, put them in cotton fields, put them in inferior schools, put them in substandard housing, put them in scientific experiments, put them in the lowest paying jobs, put outside the equal protection of the law, kept them out of their racist bastions of higher education and locked them into positions of hopelessness and helplessness. The government gives them the drugs, builds bigger prisons, passes a three-strike law and then wants us to sing 'God Bless America'. No, no, no, not God Bless America. God damn America—that's in the Bible—for killing innocent people. God damn America, for treating our citizens as less than human. God damn America, as long as she tries to act like she is God, and she is supreme. The United States government has failed the vast majority of her citizens of African descent." Rev. Jeremiah Wright, "Confusing God and Government," April 13, 2003, http://www.blackpast.org/2008-rev-jeremiah-wright-confusing-god-and-government.

91. The Pew Research Center divided respondents into (a) Steadfast Conservatives, (b) Business Conservatives, (c) Young Outsiders, (d) Hard-Pressed Skeptics, (e) Next Generation Left, (f) Faith and Family Left, and (g) Solid Liberals. See http://www.pewresearch.org/fact-tank/2014/07/02/most-americans-think-the-u-s-is-great-but-fewer-say-its-the-greatest/.

10. THE US ECONOMY

1. GDP can be measured in US dollars at current or constant prices using official exchange rates. It can also be measured in US dollars at current or constant prices using exchange rates at purchasing power parity (PPP) that reflect the actual cost of buying a basket of goods and services.

2. Official exchange rates can provide a useful point of comparison for that part of GDP consisting of "tradables" (i.e., those goods and services that enter into international trade). However, large swaths of every country's economy are "nontradable" (e.g., haircuts). In addition, official exchange rates can be subject to enormous volatility from one year to the next. PPP exchange rates are designed to eliminate both these problems.

3. The growth rate of US GDP is forecast at 2.25%, compared with 3.5% for the world as a whole. See International Monetary Fund, *World Economic Outlook*.

4. The five with a slower growth were four members of the European Union (France, Germany, Italy, and the United Kingdom) and Japan. The European Union, which is a member of the G20 despite not being a single country, also had slower growth. However, its growth is essentially the same as the four European countries already mentioned.

5. Its share of global GDP was 20.8% in the same year. See Figure 10.1.

6. By contrast, the US share of global exports of goods and services in 2000 was only 13.8%.

7. Both the import and export share fell by roughly one-third between 2000 and 2014.

8. The IMF, however, in its *World Economic Outlook* uses projections for US trade that leave its share of the global total unchanged. This seems unlikely.

9. Data on FDI flows are always given on a net basis (capital transactions credits less debits between direct investors and their foreign affiliates).

10. The value of US exports exceeded US imports on a regular basis from the mid-1870s onward. See Carter et al., *Historical Statistics*, vol. 5, 5.454–6, Table Ee1-21.

11. In 1914, on the eve of the First World War, the stock of US FDI was $2,652 million, of which $618 million was in Canada, $587 in Mexico, and $281 in Cuba and Puerto Rico. See Davis and Cull, "International Capital Movements," 787, Table 16.4.

12. Figures are not available before 1980, but in that year the United States accounted for 42% of the global FDI outward stock. See UNCTAD, *World Investment Report 2000*, 300.

13. See UNCTAD, *World Investment Report 2015*, Annex Table 2, A7–A10.

14. President Trump has even indicated his wish to *reverse* the outflow through reforms to the tax system designed to encourage firms to repatriate assets held abroad.

15. See World Bank, *World Development Indicators*.

16. None of these countries are shown in Figure 10.4, since they were not in the top twenty in 1960.

17. Net savings are the difference between federal *current* receipts and spending. The federal deficit also takes into account *capital* receipts and spending.

18. The date is either 1986 or 1988, depending on whether FDI is valued at historic cost or market values. See Landefeld and Lawson, *Valuation*, 40–49.

19. See Mann, "Perspectives on the U.S. Current Account Deficit," 135.

20. These are the famous "twin" deficits about which so much has been written. See, for example, Roubini, "The Unsustainability of the U.S. Twin Deficits," 343–56.

21. See Modigliani and Modigliani, "The Growth of the Federal Deficit," 461.

22. President Clinton introduced tax increases in his first presidency that had most of their impact in his second term. This was also the moment when the country enjoyed a brief "peace dividend" from the end of the Cold War and a boom in technology sectors that boosted receipts from capital gains tax.

23. There was a modest recovery in the personal savings rate after the Great Recession, but it remained less than half what it had been in the early 1970s. See Clinton P. McCully, *Trends in Consumer Spending and Personal Saving, 1959–2009*, June 2011, https://www.bea.gov/scb/pdf/2011/06%20June/0611_pce.pdf, 9.

24. The debt-to-GDP ratio declined briefly after the Great Recession but soon surpassed its previous peak. See Federal Reserve Bank of St. Louis, "Economic Research," https://research.stlouisfed.org/fred2/.

25. Federal debt was valued at $19.4 trillion at the end of the fiscal year 2015–16; Federal Reserve Bank of St. Louis, "Federal Debt: Total Public Debt (GFDEBTN)," https://fred.stlouisfed.org/series/GFDEBTN. Government debt, which includes state and local government, was $22.4 trillion.

26. See https://www.treasurydirect.gov/np/debt/search?startmonth=01&startday=01&startyear=2017&endmonth=&endday=&e.

27. See UNCTAD, *World Investment Report 2015*, Annex Table 2, A-7. The Bureau of Economic Analysis (BEA) has lower figures for the stock of net inward FDI, but these are valued at historic cost.

28. See, for example, numerous articles on this theme by Paul Krugman in the *New York Times*.

29. Keynes is alleged to have said, "If you owe your bank one pound, you have a problem. If you owe one million pounds, the bank has a problem."

30. See Coughlin, Pakko, and Poole, "How Dangerous Is the U.S. Current Account Deficit?" 5–9.

31. Great Britain, one of the closest US allies, was made to learn this the hard way (first in 1947, when the United States insisted that sterling be made convertible, and second in 1956, during the Suez Crisis).

32. See Zorlu, *Innovation and Empire*, Chapter 3.

33. Gordon, *Is U.S. Economic Growth Over?*, 4. Robert Gordon has developed his ideas more fully in Gordon, *The Rise and Fall of American Growth*.

34. Cardarelli and Lusinyan, "U.S. Total Factor Productivity Slowdown," 4.

35. Derived from the BEA website comparing gross private domestic investment with private consumption of fixed capital. See https://www.bea.gov/iTable/iTable.cfm?ReqID=9&step=1#reqid=9&step=3&isuri=1&903=138.

36. The fiscal stimulus, mandated by the American Recovery and Reinvestment Act of 2009, was large (about $800 billion), but 37% was in tax cuts and much of the rest was current rather than capital spending.

37. The poor state of US infrastructure became a big issue in the presidential election of 2016. A promise to massively increase spending on infrastructure was one of the factors behind President Trump's election victory in that year.

38. See World Economic Forum, *The Global Competitiveness Report*, which includes infrastructure as one of its components. The United States was in eleventh place in 2015–16.

39. American Society of Civil Engineers, 2013 *Report Card*, 8. The ASCE produces every four years a grade from A to F on the state of US infrastructure. The grades in the 2013 report varied from B– (solid waste) to D– (inland waterways and levees), for an overall average of D+. By the time of the 2017 report, the grades had hardly changed at all.

40. Council of Economic Advisers, *Economic Report of the President*, 255, 258.

41. See, for example, Blundell et al., "Human Capital Investment," 16–17.

42. See Rockland, *Sarmiento's Travels*.

43. See, for example, Denison, *Accounting for United States Economic Growth*.

44. Richard Freeman, a Harvard University economist, even used *The Overeducated American* as the title for his book on the topic. See Freeman, *The Overeducated American*.

45. See National Commission on Excellence in Education, *A Nation at Risk*, 1.

46. The National Center for Education Statistics was required by Congress to produce an annual report entitled *The Condition of Education*.

47. See Goldin and Katz, *The Race between Education and Technology*, Chapter 8.

48. The OECD periodically carries out a Programme for International Student Assessment (PISA). The 2016 scores for the United States compared to other OECD countries, based on 2015 tests, can be found in Organisation for Economic Co-operation and Development, *Country Note: Key Findings from PISA 2015 for the United States*, 2016, https://www.oecd.org/pisa/PISA-2015-United-States.pdf.

49. See Gordon, *The Rise and Fall of American Growth*, 16. Figure 1.2, which shows that between 1920 and 1970 TFP annual growth averaged 1.8% and explained most of the annual increase in output per hour worked (2.82%).

50. Labor productivity growth for the nonfarm business sector after the Great Recession fell to half what it had been before. See Bureau of Labor Statistics, "Labor Productivity and Costs," http://www.bls.gov/lpc/prodybar.htm.

51. See, for example, Cardarelli and Lusinyan, "U.S. Total Factor Productivity Slowdown," which compares TFP for each US state and finds a slowdown across the board.

52. See Grueber, 2012 *Global R&D Funding Forecast*.

53. See National Science Foundation, *Science and Engineering Indicators*, Figure 4.6.

54. See Summers, "The Age of Secular Stagnation."

55. Adams, *The Epic of America*, 415; emphasis in the original.

56. See King, *The Wealth and Income of the People*, 228, Table 44.

57. See Young, "Nearing's Income," 584–85. In fact, subsequent research showed his results to be fairly accurate.

58. See Piketty, *Capital in the Twenty-First Century*, 299, Figure 8.7. Thomas Piketty's work has been much criticized on theoretical grounds (see, for example, Jones, "Pareto and Piketty"; and Acemoglu and Robinson, *The Rise and Decline*), but there is much greater consensus around the long-term trends shown in his empirical data.

59. A good example is the Servicemen's Readjustment Act of 1944, commonly known as the GI Bill, which provided veterans of World War II with cash payments for tuition fees and living expenses to attend university, high school, or vocational training.

60. The database prepared by the team led by Emmanuel Saez and Thomas Piketty, "Table 1. Real Income Growth by Groups," http://elsa.berkeley.edu/~saez/TabFig2013prel .xls, uses market income (with or without realized capital gains). The Congressional Budget Office (CBO), on the other hand, uses a measure of income that adds government transfers to market income. And the Economic Policy Institute has carried out an analysis of income distribution shifts for each state as well as the nation as a whole. See Sommeiller, Price, and Wazeter, *Income Inequality.*

61. See Saez, "Striking It Richer," Figure 1 and Figure 2.

62. See Saez and Zucman, *Wealth Inequality in the United States,* 51, Figure 6. The authors used capitalized income to estimate wealth, which gives similar results to Surveys of Consumer Finance.

63. See Saez and Zucman, *Wealth Inequality in the United States,* Figure 1, 44.

64. See Piketty, *Capital in the Twenty-First Century,* 315–21.

65. According to the CBO, whose definition of primary income includes government transfers, the posttax share of income in 2011 received by the top quintile was 48.2% compared with 51.9% before tax. For the bottom quintile, the posttax share only went up from 5% to 6%. See https://www.cbo.gov/sites/default/files/113th-congress-2013-2014 /reports/49440-distribution-income-and-taxes-2.pdf, 5.

66. Income is defined here as market income (i.e., excluding government transfers but including realized capital gains).

67. The median is the number that separates the population into two equal halves. Thus, 50% earn above it and 50% below it.

68. See Bureau of Labor Statistics, "Economic News Release: Table 1. Median Usual Weekly Earnings of Full-Time Wage and Salary Workers by Sex, Quarterly Averages, Seasonally Adjusted," https://www.bls.gov/news.release/wkyeng.t01.htm.

69. See Federal Reserve Bank of St. Louis, "Real Median Household Income in the United States," https://fred.stlouisfed.org/series/MEHOINUSA672N. The revised series provided by the Federal Reserve Bank of St. Louis (FRED) starts in 1984.

70. See US Census Bureau, "Historical Income Tables: Households," http://www.census .gov/data/tables/time-series/demo/income-poverty/historical-income-households .html, Table H-3.

71. See Drew Desilver, "For Most Workers, Real Wages Have Barely Budged for Decades," Pew Research Center, http://www.pewresearch.org/fact-tank/2014/10/09/for -most-workers-real-wages-have-barely-budged-for-decades/.

72. See Corak, *Inequality,* 1.

73. See Conference Board of Canada, "Intergenerational Income Mobility," http://www .conferenceboard.ca/hcp/details/society/intergenerational-income-mobility.aspx.

74. See Mitnik et al., *New Estimates,* 69–72.

75. See Chetty et al., *Where Is the Land of Opportunity?*

76. See Betsy Cooper, Daniel Cox, Rachel Lienesch, and Robert P. Jones, "The Divide over America's Future: 1950 or 2050? Findings from the 2016 American Values Survey," Public Religion Research Institute, http://www.prri.org/research/divide-americas -future-1950-2050/.

11. THE DECLINE OF LEADERSHIP

1. From 2006 to 2015 there were eleven UNSC resolutions calling on Iran to suspend uranium enrichment or face sanctions.
2. The exception was just before the end of the Obama presidency, when the United States abstained on a resolution critical of Israel for building settlements in the occupied territories.
3. Heads of state and government met in September 2005 for the World Summit to discuss UN reform and produced a Summit Outcome Document that was noticeable for its emphasis on procedure and management rather than substantial reforms, although they did endorse the principle of Responsibility to Protect (R2P). See Bellamy and Dunne, *The Oxford Handbook of the Responsibility to Protect.*
4. See McDonald and Patrick, *UN Security Council Enlargement,* 13–14.
5. The George W. Bush administration voted against the establishment of the council and then refused to stand for election to it. The Obama administration reversed this decision but gave only qualified support to the council. The Trump administration regularly threatened to withdraw the United States from the council, although at the time of writing it had not yet done so.
6. When UNESCO admitted Palestine as a member in 2011, the Obama administration cut funding to the UN agency and two years later lost its vote in the UNESCO General Conference because it had not paid its dues for two consecutive years. See Blanchfield, *United Nations Reform,* 4.
7. On US influence over the IMF, see Thacker, "The High Politics of IMF Lending"; and Oatley, *International Political Economy.*
8. See Weisbrot, *Voting Share Reform,* 1–7.
9. By mid-2016 nearly 75% of the stock of IMF loans and credits was to European countries. See International Monetary Fund, *World Economic Outlook,* 6–8.
10. At the end of 2016 the largest recipients of IMF loans outside of Europe were Egypt and Pakistan, whose geopolitical ties to the United States are well known.
11. Dreher and Sturm, "Do the IMF and the World Bank Influence Voting?," 387.
12. This was the Nobel Prize laureate Joseph Stiglitz, whose trenchant criticisms of the World Bank can be found in Stiglitz, *Globalization.*
13. The US Treasury fought hard against a Japanese campaign in the 1980s and 1990s to give a higher priority to the role of the state in development economics. See Wade, "Japan, the World Bank, and the Art of Paradigm Maintenance."
14. BRICS is the acronym given to five of the most important "emerging" markets (Brazil, Russia, India, China, and South Africa).

15. The Bali Package, as it became known, covered more than trade facilitation, but the other elements soon ran into dispute. See Schnepf, *Agriculture in the WTO*, 1–15.
16. Hopewell, *Breaking the WTO*, 14–15.
17. Protests against trade agreements were a constant refrain during the US presidential election campaigns in 2016.
18. The Rio Group grew out of the Contadora Group (Colombia, Mexico, Panama, and Venezuela) that was established in 1984 to find a peaceful solution to the Central American crisis.
19. President Manuel Zelaya of Honduras was removed from office and deported from the country by the military in 2009. This action was unanimously condemned by the OAS.
20. Despite the US-supported OAS resolution, the Obama administration subsequently, and unilaterally, accepted the results of the elections organized by the Honduran military that installed a new president. See Landler, *Alter Egos*, 324–26.
21. These included a new bank, Banco del Sur, that was planned to be an alternative to the IMF. It has not yet been established.
22. See Sarotte, "Perpetuating U.S. Preeminence," 110–37.
23. NATO members are committed to spending at least 2% of GDP on their armed forces (the United States spends more than 3%), but very few of them do so. Furthermore, some of these countries only meet the threshold through extreme examples of creative accounting.
24. Sergei Karaganov, quoted in Wolff, "The Future of NATO Enlargement," 1111.
25. When Montenegro joined NATO as the twenty-ninth member in 2017, it was strongly condemned by Russia in words that implied there would be "consequences."
26. Changes to corporate taxation are expected during the Trump administration but had not been implemented at the time this book was completed.
27. When state and local taxes are added, the rate can rise to nearly 40%.
28. See Contractor, *Tax Avoidance*, 1–2.
29. The US Treasury issued a new interpretation of the tax inversion rules, but it did not block tax inversions as such. Only Congress can do that.
30. The trigger was Pfizer's plans to be purchased by Allergan, a much smaller company based in Ireland, where the corporate tax rate is one of the lowest in the world.
31. "Pfiasco: Open Warfare Breaks Out," *Economist*, April 9, 2016.
32. US Department of Defense, quoted in Paul Mozer and Jane Perlez, "U.S. Tech Giants May Blur National Security Boundaries in China Deals," *New York Times*, October 30, 2015.
33. This was the case of Uber, an aggressive, app-based independent taxi service based in San Francisco, which ran at a large loss in China for many years before selling its assets to its Chinese rival in 2016 and acquiring a minority stake.
34. Donahue, "High Technology," 3.
35. Following the San Bernardino, California, terrorist attack in December 2015, when fourteen people were killed, the FBI found an iPhone that they wanted to unlock. Apple refused to comply. See Box 11.2.

36. See Martin Maximino, "Does Media Fragmentation Contribute to Polarization? Evidence from Lab Experiments," Journalist's Resource, http://journalistsresource.org/studies/society/news-media/media-fragmentation-political-polarization-lab-experiments.

37. The extreme right media has no parallel on the left in US politics, where the most "left-wing" are identified in a 2014 Pew Research Study as *Slate* and the *New Yorker*. See Aaron Blake, "Ranking the Media from Liberal to Conservative, Based on Their Audiences," *Washington Post*, October 21, 2014, https://www.washingtonpost.com/news/the-fix/wp/2014/10/21/lets-rank-the-media-from-liberal-to-conservative-based-on-their-audiences/.

38. Steve Bannon, CEO of Breitbart, even became the campaign manager for Donald Trump in August 2016. Subsequently, he was appointed chief of strategy in the Trump administration, but left in August 2017.

39. John Ziegler, "Modern Media Has Turned the USA into the Divided States of America," http://www.mediaite.com/online/modern-media-has-turned-the-usa-into-the-divided-states-of-america-2/.

40. See "Obama Disses Think Tanks," Think Tank Watch, March 11, 2016, http://www.thinktankwatch.com/2016/03/obama-disses-think-tanks.html. See also Goldberg, "The Obama Doctrine," 70–90.

41. A social policy favored by many leading US politicians is gay marriage. This is a complete anathema to the conservative American churches that operate abroad in many countries and has led to serious friction with the US government.

42. King, *Congress and National Security*, 6.

43. Ash Carter, defense secretary, in March 2016 listed terrorism below Russia, China, North Korea, and Iran in his list of strategic challenges faced by the United States. See Lisa Ferdinando, "Carter Outlines Security Challenges, Warns against Sequestration," March 17, 2016, US Department of Defense, http://www.defense.gov/News/Article/Article/696449/carter-outlines-security-challenges-warns-against-sequestration.

44. That is not true if foreign policy is defined to include immigration, but that is usually seen as a matter for domestic policy.

45. King, *Congress and National Security*, 8.

46. See Wiktor, *Unperfected Treaties*.

47. The United States also signed in 1925 the Geneva Protocol for the Prohibition of the Use in War of Asphyxiating, Poisonous or Other Gases, and of Bacteriological Methods of Warfare, but the Senate did not pass it until 1975 (fifty years later). See Bradley, "Unratified Treaties," 309–10.

48. See Mission of the United States, "Human Rights Commitments and Pledges of the United States of America," https://geneva.usmission.gov/2016/02/24/human-rights-commitments-and-pledges-of-the-united-states-of-america/. The US government was successful and secured its seat.

49. These include the 2006 Convention against Enforced Disappearance, the 1997 Ottawa (Mine Ban) Treaty, the 2008 Convention on Cluster Munitions, and the 2002 Optional Protocol to the Convention against Torture.

50. CEDAW was even favorably voted out of the Senate Foreign Relations Committee on two separate occasions (1994 and 2002).
51. He argued that it was not a treaty and therefore could be ratified by sole executive agreement. Needless to say, this was disputed by the Senate.
52. The United States is now the only UN member not to have ratified it.
53. It required 55% of countries accounting for 55% of world emissions. Russia's ratification in 2005 was the last one needed for the Kyoto Protocol to take effect.
54. As with the Kyoto Protocol, 55% of countries accounting for 55% of emissions must ratify. This target was met before the end of 2016.
55. President Obama ratified it in September 2016 at the same time as China, whose parliament had already approved it. US ratification allowed Obama to claim joint leadership with China on the global environment, but it risked being reversed at a later date by a Republican president. Indeed, this was the promise of Donald Trump during his successful presidential campaign in 2016. President Trump then announced in June 2017 that the United States would withdraw from the agreement at the earliest possible opportunity.
56. Aspiration to global leadership was also undermined by the decision of the Supreme Court in February 2016 to suspend the implementation of the Clean Power Plan that the Obama administration needed to meet its NDCs pending a judicial ruling.
57. The Senate, for example, approved the Anti-Ballistic Missile (ABM) Treaty in 1972 and it was the executive, not the Senate, that withdrew from the treaty unilaterally in 2002.
58. All these arms control treaties received strong support from the Senate. However, START II ended prematurely in 2002 when Russia canceled it in response to the US unilateral withdrawal from the ABM Treaty.
59. The Third UN Conference on the Law of the Sea was completed in 1982, but it soon became clear it was unacceptable to the US executive as well as the Senate. The convention was then modified to meet US concerns between 1990 and 1994.
60. Jesse Helms, chairman of the Senate Foreign Relations Committee, complained that "President Clinton's decision to sign the Rome treaty establishing an International Criminal Court in his final days in office is as outrageous as it is inexplicable." Bradley, "Unratified Treaties," 311n15.
61. By then President George W. Bush had taken the highly unusual step—along with Israel and Sudan—of "unsigning" the state's signature to the statute, further isolating the United States on this issue.
62. The spending bill was so critical for the Obama administration that the president could not afford to veto it.
63. The chair, Bob Corker, was the junior senator for Tennessee and was first elected in 2006.
64. Sadly, Senator McCain was diagnosed with a rare form of brain cancer in July 2017.
65. Some scholars have called this "being asleep on the job." See Ornstein and Mann, "When Congress Checks Out," 67–82.

66. William J. Clinton, "Transcript of 'Global Challenges,'" Yale Global Online, October 31, 2003, http://yaleglobal.yale.edu/content/transcript-global-challenges.
67. See Bradley, "Unratified Treaties," 320.
68. Bill Clinton, quoted in Bradley, "Unratified Treaties," 316n39.
69. There are also congressional-executive agreements that are often used to circumvent the two-thirds majority requirement, but these still require a congressional majority in both houses. See Congressional Research Service, *Treaties*, 5.
70. The Gulf of Tonkin Resolution was passed as a joint resolution before being repealed in 1971.
71. So strongly did Congress feel about this issue that it overrode a presidential veto.
72. Quoted in Hendrickson, *The Constitution, Congress and War Powers*, 127.
73. See Chollet, *The Long Game*, Chapter 1.
74. See Landler, *Alter Egos*, 204–30.
75. Obama's actions may well have been correct, but they cannot be reconciled with his claim that America was the global leader.
76. It was called Fast Track Authority until 2002.
77. The Republicans, who held a majority in the House and Senate after 1994, refused to support a Democratic executive despite their belief in globalization.
78. The Senate was strongly in favor, but in the House it was very close (215–212).
79. The agreements were with Chile, Singapore, Australia, Morocco, Central America (including the Dominican Republic), Bahrain, Oman, Peru, Colombia, South Korea, and Panama.
80. The final two nominees in 2016, Hillary Clinton for the Democratic Party and Donald Trump for the Republican Party, both opposed TPP in their presidential campaigns.
81. This is the Regional Comprehensive Economic Partnership (RCEP) involving ten ASEAN countries together with China, Australia, New Zealand, India, Japan, and South Korea.
82. See Shaxson, *Treasure Islands*, Chapter 1.
83. See "Base Erosion and Profit Sharing," Organisation for Economic Co-operation and Development, http://www.oecd.org/tax/beps/.
84. See Deloitte, *BEPS Actions*, 2–3.
85. All signed tax treaties since 2011, for example, have remained "unperfected" in the Senate.
86. See "Loophole USA: The Vortex-Shaped Hole in Global Financial Transparency," January 26, 2015, Tax Justice Network, http://www.taxjustice.net/2015/01/26/loophole -usa-vortex-shaped-hole-global-financial-transparency-2/.

12. HEGEMONY UNDER THREAT

1. The resolution of the 1962 Cuban Missile Crisis had led President John F. Kennedy (1961–63) to promise not to invade the island. However, the collapse of

the Soviet Union brought about a hardening of congressional policy toward the government of Fidel Castro that could only be interpreted as the pursuit of regime change.

2. A few, such as Chile, had even started to do so in the 1970s.

3. The Clinton plan, launched at the Summit of the Americas in Miami, built on the Enterprise for the Americas Initiative (EAI) launched by President George H. W. Bush in 1990.

4. The model was NAFTA, and especially its Chapter 11 on investment, which provided for an investor-state dispute settlement (ISDS) mechanism that proved highly controversial.

5. See Von Bülow, *Building Transnational Networks*, 128–30.

6. ALBA initially had two members (Cuba and Venezuela) but soon expanded to eleven, with two others as associates.

7. See Cannon, *The Right in Latin America*, Chapter 5.

8. All of these were modeled on NAFTA.

9. Brazil alone (over two hundred million in 2016) has almost one-third of the LAC population. Venezuela's membership of MERCOSUR was suspended in 2016.

10. China's rapacious appetite for commodities, such as soy and iron ore, had already made it the main market for MERCOSUR exports.

11. US Department of State, "Bureau of Western Hemisphere Affairs," https://www.state.gov/p/wha/.

12. See Chapter 11.1.

13. See US Department of State, "Human Rights Reports," https://www.state.gov/j/drl/rls/hrrpt/; US Department of State, "Narcotics Control Reports," https://www.state.gov/j/inl/rls/nrcrpt/index.htm; and US Department of State, "2017 Trafficking in Persons Report," https://www.state.gov/j/tip/rls/tiprpt/ (which also has links to the *Trafficking in Persons Report* for prior years.).

14. The Clinton administration forced the military junta from office in 1994. Despite being in effect a US protectorate since then, Haiti failed to establish representative democracy. See Deibert, *Haiti Will Not Perish*, chapter 15.

15. If these countries had supported the resolution, the United States would have had the nine votes needed for the resolution to pass provided no permanent member vetoed it.

16. Shiprider agreements give US authorities the power to chase suspected drug traffickers in another country's territorial waters.

17. See US Drug Enforcement Agency, "DEA and European Authorities Uncover Massive Hizballah Drug and Money Laundering Scheme," February 1, 2016, https://www.dea.gov/divisions/hq/2016/hq020116.shtml.

18. In June 2017 President Trump announced a series of measures that partially reversed Obama's normalization of relations with Cuba, but diplomatic relations were not broken.

19. Latinobarómetro, a Chilean polling company, regularly asks the public in different Latin American countries their opinion of the United States.

20. "Guatemala Academia and Think-Tank 01," Chatham House, http://eliteperceptions
    .chathamhouse.org/essay/guatemala-academia-and-think-tank-01/.

21. The NSAg, it later transpired, had hacked into the phones of twenty-nine top Brazil-
    ian officials—not just that of President Dilma Rousseff. See "Bugging Brazil," WikiLeaks,
    https://wikileaks.org/nsa-brazil/selectors.html.

22. The island government had warned for many years that it was heading for default. Not
    being a US state, it was unable to seek protection from its creditors until Congress
    eventually passed emergency legislation in June 2016.

23. In the end, the project looked set to collapse due to the opposition of environmental-
    ists and lack of support from the Chinese government. However, the US government
    did not know that when the agreement was reached.

24. The peace agreement was signed in September 2016, in the presence of Secretary of
    State John Kerry, only to be narrowly rejected by the Colombian people in a plebiscite
    in October. A revised version was subsequently approved by the Colombian Congress.

25. See Transatlantic Declaration on EC-US Relations, 1990, http://www.comercio.gob
    .es/es-ES/comercio-exterior/politica-comercial/relaciones-bilaterales-union-europea
    /america/PDF/estados-unidos/trans_declaration_90_en.pdf. The Transatlantic Dec-
    laration was then updated in 1995 with the New Transatlantic Agenda that provided
    more detail. See The New Transatlantic Agenda, http://eeas.europa.eu/us/docs/new
    _transatlantic_agenda_en.pdf.

26. The European Community changed its name to the European Union (EU) in 1993.
    In what follows, it will be referred to as the EU only.

27. Russia shares a border with Georgia and Ukraine, while Moldova contains a *de facto*
    republic (Transnistria) that is strongly pro-Russian.

28. Russia threatened retaliation in 2013 if the Ukrainian government signed an acces-
    sion agreement with the EU. The threat worked, but Ukrainians took to the streets
    in protest leading to the imposition of a pro-US and anti-Russian government in
    2014.

29. Crimea only became part of Ukraine in 1954, when both were still part of the Soviet
    Union. It hosts an important Russian naval base on the Black Sea, and most of the
    population is ethnically Russian.

30. In the end, they did not need to worry, as the election of Donald Trump as president
    killed the TTIP.

31. Putin was president from 1999 to 2008, prime minister from 2008 to 2012, and is now
    president again since 2012. Throughout this time, he was the *de facto* leader of the
    Russian Federation.

32. The Serbian enclave, Republika Srpska, had been created in 1992.

33. South Ossetia had been a province of the Soviet Union, but after 1991 sovereignty was
    soon in dispute between the Russian Federation and Georgia. The unsuccessful
    Georgian invasion ensured that it would fall entirely under Russian influence, al-
    though it became nominally independent.

34. Kosovo had been part of Serbia until 2008, but Serbia—supported by Russia—refused
    to recognize Kosovo's independence.

35. Donald Trump, the Republican candidate, repeatedly questioned the future of NATO in view of the persistent failure of non-US allies to make a greater contribution.
36. See, for example, Kagan, *Power and Weakness*, 3–28.
37. The friction, of course, resurfaced when President Trump indicated in June 2017 that he would withdraw the United States from the Paris agreement on climate change.
38. The White House, "Remarks by President Obama, President Tusk of the European Council, and President Juncker of the European Commission after U.S.-EU Meeting," https://www.whitehouse.gov/the-press-office/2016/07/08/remarks-president-obama -president-tusk-european-council-and-president.
39. The best known example is regime change in Libya in 2011, where European states (notably France and the United Kingdom) were allowed by the United States to take the lead although they would have been incapable of doing it on their own.
40. Only Belarus turned its back on the western alliance, preferring to remain in close association with Russia.
41. Public opinion in Poland, for example, always produced the highest favorable score of the United States among all European countries and never dropped below 60%. See Pew research Center, "Opinion of the United States," http://www.pewglobal.org /database/indicator/1/group/3/.
42. In one survey, only 33% in Bosnia & Herzegovina approved of the job performance of the leadership of the United States. See Meridian International Center and Gallup, *U.S.-Global Leadership Project* (Report for 2013), 6.
43. See Office of the US Trade Representative, *Beyond AGOA*, 1.
44. US Congress, Africa Growth and Opportunity Act, May 18, 2000, https://agoa.info /images/documents/2385/AGOA_legal_text.pdf, Section 104.
45. Eligibility required that for each indicator (e.g., trade policy as ranked by the Heritage Foundation), the country in question had to exceed the median score of its peer group.
46. Those without a compact could still be "threshold" countries provided the MCC deemed they were moving in the right direction.
47. In West Africa, for example, the Chad-Cameroon Oil Pipeline was built in large part by US companies. Both countries were then deemed eligible for AGOA despite the fact that the US trade representative found widespread human rights abuse in both countries. See Office of the US Trade Representative, *2016 Biennial Report*, 19–21.
48. In FY 2016, Congress authorized $900 million, compared with some $3 billion a decade before.
49. See Office of the US Trade Representative, *Beyond AGOA*, 13, Figure 6.
50. See Office of the US Trade Representative, *2016 Biennial Report*, 22–23.
51. In addition to the "official" base in Djibouti, USAFRICOM was responsible for many other outposts across sub-Saharan Africa. See Vine, *Base Nation*, 308–14.
52. US Department of State, "Addressing Instability in Sub-Saharan Africa," http://www .state.gov/p/af/rls/rm/2016/257081.htm.

53. Power Africa was launched by the Obama administration to increase the number of people connected to the grid.

54. The countries were Burkina Faso, Ethiopia, Ghana, Kenya, Nigeria, Senegal, South Africa, Tanzania, and Uganda.

55. US Department of State, "U.S. Relations with South Sudan," October 6, 2016, https://www.state.gov/r/pa/ei/bgn/171718.htm.

56. The Middle East is defined broadly here to include Afghanistan and Pakistan.

57. Others under negotiation are Algeria, Iraq, Iran, Libya, and Syria.

58. See World Integrated Trade Solution, "Middle East & North Africa Trade Indicators 2014," http://wits.worldbank.org/CountryProfile/en/Country/MEA/Year/2014/.

59. The Oslo Accords committed Israel to recognize the Palestine Liberation Organization (PLO) as the representative of the Palestinians, while the PLO renounced terrorism and recognized Israel's right to exist in peace.

60. The US occupation of Afghanistan began in October 2001; in the Bonn Agreement later that year the Bush administration committed itself to hold parliamentary and presidential elections as soon as possible.

61. General Abdel Fattah el-Sisi seized power in 2013, but the Obama administration refused to label it as a coup as this would have required cutting off funding and losing leverage over a key ally.

62. By no means had all Sunnis supported al-Qaeda, but for many it was seen as the only bulwark against the sectarian government in Baghdad.

63. The phrase, which means "Let them hate as long as they fear," is attributed to Lucius Accius, a Roman poet.

64. Saudi intervention began as soon as its Sunni ally, President Abdrabbuh Mansur Hadi, fled the country in response to attacks by the rival Houthi government in the north of Yemen. Hadi later returned, but his government was only prevented from collapse by a Saudi aerial offensive that killed thousands of civilians.

65. The official reason given for the boycott focused on Qatar's alleged support for international terrorism, but most observers assumed it had more to do with media criticism in Qatar of the governments of the neighboring states (Al-Jazeera is based in Qatar).

66. With its only Mediterranean naval base located in Syria, Russia had a major strategic interest in the country and provided crucial support to the Assad regime throughout the civil war.

67. In 2015 over 80% of Israelis had a favorable opinion of the United States, but only 49% in the case of the US president.

68. The speech spoke of a "new beginning" to the relationship between the United States and Muslims throughout the world.

69. In 2015 the United States imported 9.4 million barrels of oil per day, of which 1.06 million (11%) came from Saudi Arabia.

70. The Turkish government was determined to crush the Kurdish rebels, who provided the United States with its most effective allies in the Syrian civil war. This led Turkey in 2016 to move away from the US position on Syria and to come closer to that held by Russia.

71. Egypt was one of only four countries to back a UN Security Council resolution for a cease-fire in Syria in October 2016 proposed by Russia. The others were China, Russia, and Venezuela.

72. During the 2016 US presidential election campaign, e-mails were leaked that revealed US intelligence on the funding of IS and al-Qaeda by Qatar and Saudi Arabia.

73. In April 2017 the United States launched a military strike against a Syrian air base in retaliation for the alleged use of chemical weapons by the Syrian regime, but it did not amount to a change of strategy by the Trump administration.

74. The Asia-Pacific region, as defined here, excludes Afghanistan, Pakistan, and the countries of Latin America with a Pacific coastline.

75. There is some double counting here, as APEC includes Canada, Chile, Mexico, Peru, and Russia that have been considered elsewhere in this chapter. However, even after stripping out these countries, bilateral trade between the United States and APEC is enormous.

76. US goods exports to China were only $116 billion in 2015. See US Census Bureau, "Trade in Goods with China," http://www.census.gov/foreign-trade/balance/c5700.html.

77. The RCEP is a proposal for a FTA between the ten members of ASEAN and the six countries with which ASEAN already has FTAs (including China). B&R involves both sea and land routes through Asia and Europe, connecting as many as sixty countries.

78. As a nonsignatory of the Nuclear Non-Proliferation Treaty that subsequently became a nuclear power, India was subject to numerous sanctions under US law. These laws had to be amended and a waiver secured from the international Nuclear Suppliers Group before the agreement with India could go into force.

79. President Obama later provided an additional reward by publicly supporting India's bid for a permanent seat on the UN Security Council.

80. See Hillary Clinton, "America's Pacific Century," *Foreign Policy*, October 11, 2011, http://foreignpolicy.com/2011/10/11/americas-pacific-century/.

81. US Department of Defense, "Joint Press Conference with Secretary Carter, Secretary Kerry, Foreign Minister Kishida and Defense Minister Nakatani in New York, New York," April 27, 2015, https://www.defense.gov/News/Transcripts/Transcript-View/Article/607045/joint-press-conference-with-secretary-carter-secretary-kerry-foreign-minister-k/.

82. This had been interrupted by the decision of the New Zealand government in 1984 not to allow visits by nuclear-powered or nuclear-armed ships.

83. US Department of State, "Democracy in Southeast Asia," November 19, 2015, http://www.state.gov/j/drl/rls/rm/2015/249788.htm.

84. The military junta permitted general elections in 2010 and by-elections in 2012, giving just enough credence to their claim to be restoring democracy. Parliamentary elections in 2015 led to the selection of a civilian as president, although the military still held 25% of all seats.

85. Born in Hawaii, President Obama lived in Indonesia for a number of years as a child.

86. President Duterte took exception to US criticism of his policy toward drug traffickers and on a visit to China in October 2016 called for "separation" from the United States.
87. See Habyarimana, *The Great Pearl of Wisdom.*

EPILOGUE

1. Mark Zuckerberg, "Building Global Community," Facebook, February 16, 2017, https://www.facebook.com/notes/mark-zuckerberg/building-global-community /10154544292806634/.

BIBLIOGRAPHY

Aaronson, Susan A. *Trade and the American Dream: A Social History of Postwar Trade Policy.* Lexington: University Press of Kentucky, 1996.

Abella, Alex. *Soldiers of Reason: The RAND Corporation and the Rise of the American Empire.* Boston: Mariner, 2009.

Abugre, Charles, and Nancy Alexander. "Non-governmental Organizations and the International Monetary and Financial System." In *International Monetary and Financial Issues for the 1990s,* vol. 9. Geneva: UNCTAD, 1998.

Acemoglu, Daron, and James A. Robinson. *The Rise and Decline of General Laws of Capitalism.* Washington, DC: National Bureau of Economic Research, 2015.

Ackerman, Bruce A. *The Decline and Fall of the American Republic.* Cambridge, MA: Belknap Press of Harvard University Press, 2010.

Adams, James T. *The Epic of America.* London: G. Routledge, 1938.

Adelman, Carol C. "The Privatization of Foreign Aid: Reassessing National Largesse." *Foreign Affairs* 82.6 (2003): 9–14.

Aguilar, Luis E. "Cuba, c. 1860–1934." In *The Cambridge History of Latin America,* vol. 5, *c. 1870 to 1930,* edited by Leslie Bethell. Cambridge: Cambridge University Press, 1986.

Ahmad, Mahmood. "US Think Tanks and the Politics of Expertise: Role, Value and Impact." *Political Quarterly* 79.4 (2008): 529–55.

Alstyne, R. W. *The Rising American Empire.* New York: Oxford University Press, 1960.

Alvandi, Roham. *Nixon, Kissinger, and the Shah: The United States and Iran in the Cold War.* Oxford: Oxford University Press, 2014.

American Society of Civil Engineers. *2013 Report Card for America's Infrastructure.* Reston, VA: American Society of Civil Engineers, 2013.

Amstutz, Mark R. *Evangelicals and American Foreign Policy.* Oxford: Oxford University Press, 2014.

Anderson, Robert E. *Liberia, America's African Friend.* Chapel Hill: University of North Carolina Press, 1952.

Art, Robert J. *America's Grand Strategy and World Politics.* London: Routledge, 2009.

Assange, Julian. "Introduction." In WikiLeaks, *The WikiLeaks Files: The World According to US Empire.* London: Verso, 2015.

Atwood, Paul L. *War and Empire: The American Way of Life.* London: Pluto, 2010.

Bacevich, Andrew J. *American Empire: The Realities and Consequences of U.S. Diplomacy.* Cambridge, MA: Harvard University Press, 2002.

Bacevich, Andrew J. *The Limits of Power: The End of American Exceptionalism.* New York: Metropolitan, 2008.

Bacevich, Andrew J. *Washington Rules: America's Path to Permanent War.* New York: Metropolitan, 2011.

Bailey, Thomas A. *A Diplomatic History of the American People.* New York: Appleton-Century-Crofts, 1964.

Ballantine, Joseph. *Formosa: A Problem for United States Foreign Policy.* Washington, DC: Brookings Institution, 1952.

Banner, Stuart. *How the Indians Lost Their Land: Law and Power on the Frontier.* Cambridge, MA: Belknap Press of Harvard University Press, 2005.

Barnett, A. D. "The United States and Communist China." In *The United States and the Far East: Background Papers Prepared for the Use of Participants and the Final Report of the Tenth American Assembly, Arden House, Harriman Campus of Columbia University, Harriman, New York, November 15–18, 1956.* New York: American Assembly, Graduate School of Business, Columbia University, 1956.

Bastert, Russell H. "A New Approach to the Origins of Blaine's Pan American Policy." *Hispanic American Historical Review* 39.3 (1959): 375–412.

Bellamy, Alex J., and Timothy Dunne. *The Oxford Handbook of the Responsibility to Protect.* Oxford: Oxford University Press, 2016.

Bello, Walden F. *Dilemmas of Domination: The Unmaking of the American Empire.* New York: Metropolitan, 2005.

Bergmann, William H. *American National State and the Early West.* New York: Cambridge University Press, 2014.

Bernstein, Barton J., and Allen J. Matusow. *The Truman Administration: A Documentary History.* New York: Harper and Row, 1966.

Bethell, Leslie, and Ian Roxborough. *Latin America between the Second World War and the Cold War, 1944–1948.* Cambridge: Cambridge University Press, 1992.

Bevans, Charles I., comp. *Treaties and Other International Agreements of the United States of America, 1776–1949,* vol. 6, *Canada-Czechoslovakia.* Washington, DC: US Department of State, 1971.

Billington, Ray A., and Martin Ridge. *Westward Expansion: A History of the American Frontier.* New York: Macmillan, 1982.

Bird, Kai. *The Chairman: John J. McCloy and the Making of the American Establishment.* New York: Simon and Schuster, 1992.

Blaine, James G. *Twenty Years of Congress: From Lincoln to Garfield.* Norwich, CT: Bill, 1884.

Blanchfield, Luisa. *United Nations Reform: Background and Issues for Congress.* Washington, DC: Congressional Research Service, 2015.

Bledsoe, A. J. *Indian Wars of the Northwest: A California Sketch.* San Francisco: Bacon, 1885.

Blount, James H. *The American Occupation of the Philippines, 1898–1912.* New York: Putnam's, 1912.

Blum, William. *Killing Hope: US Military and CIA Interventions since World War II.* London: Zed, 2004.

Blundell, Richard, Lorraine Dearden, Costas Meghir, and Barbara Sianesi. "Human Capital Investment: The Returns from Education and Training to the Individual, the Firm and the Economy." *Fiscal Studies* 20.1 (1999): 1–23.

Boot, Max. *The Savage Wars of Peace: Small Wars and the Rise of American Power.* New York: Basic Books, 2002.

Borden, Morton. *The Anti-Federalist Papers.* Chicago: University of Chicago Press, 1965.

Bradley, Curtis A. "Unratified Treaties, Domestic Politics, and the U.S. Constitution." *Harvard International Law Journal* 48.2 (2007): 307–36.

Bradley, Harold W. *The American Frontier in Hawaii: The Pioneers, 1789–1843.* Stanford, CA: Stanford University Press, 1944.

Brasil Fonseca, Alexandre. "Religion and Democracy in Brazil: A Study of the Leading Evangelical Politicians." In *Evangelical Christianity and Democracy in Latin America,* edited by Paul Freston. Oxford: Oxford University Press, 2008.

Braumoeller, Bear F. "The Myth of American Isolationism." *Foreign Policy Analysis* 6.4 (2010): 349–71.

Bremmer, Ian. *Superpower: Three Choices for America's Role in the World.* New York: Portfolio, 2015.

Brezinski, Zbigniew. *Second Chance.* New York: Basic Books, 2007.

Brick, Howard, and Christopher Phelps. *Radicals in America: The US Left since the Second World War.* Cambridge: Cambridge University Press, 2015.

Brogi, Alessandro. *Confronting America: The Cold War between the United States and the Communists in France and Italy.* Chapel Hill: University of North Carolina Press, 2011.

Brown, Dee. *Bury My Heart at Wounded Knee: An Indian History of the American West.* New York: Laurel Leaf, 1970.

Brown, Everett S. *The Constitutional History of the Louisiana Purchase, 1803–1812.* Berkeley: University of California Press, 1920.

Buckley, Roger. *The United States in the Asia-Pacific since 1945.* Cambridge: Cambridge University Press, 2002.

Bulmer-Thomas, Victor. *The Economic History of the Caribbean since the Napoleonic Wars.* New York: Cambridge University Press, 2012.

Bulmer-Thomas, Victor. *The Economic History of Latin America since Independence.* New York: Cambridge University Press, 2014.

Butler, Smedley D. *War Is a Racket.* New York: Round Table, 1935.

Calder, Bruce J. *The Impact of Intervention: The Dominican Republic during the U.S. Occupation of 1916–1924.* Austin: University of Texas Press, 1984.

Calleo, David P. *The Atlantic Fantasy: the U.S., NATO, and Europe.* Baltimore: Johns Hopkins University Press, 1970.

Cannon, Barry. *The Right in Latin America: Elite Power, Hegemony and the Struggle for the State.* New York: Routledge, 2016.

Cardarelli, Roberto, and Lusine Lusinyan. "U.S. Total Factor Productivity Slowdown: Evidence from the U.S. States." IMF Working Paper WO/16/116, International Monetary Fund, Washington, DC, 2015.

Carpenter, Ted G. "The Dissenters: American Isolationists and Foreign Policy, 1945–1954." PhD diss., University of Texas, 1980.

Carr, Raymond. *Puerto Rico: A Colonial Experiment.* New York: New York University Press, 1984.

Carter, Clarence Edwin, comp. *The Territorial Papers of the United States,* vol. 9, *The Territory of Orleans.* Washington, DC: Government Printing Office, 1934.

Carter, Susan B., Scott Sigmund Gartner, Michael R. Haines, Alan L. Olmstead, Richard Sutch, and Gavin Wright, eds. *Historical Statistics of the United States,* vol. 5, *Governance and International Relations.* New York: Cambridge University Press, 2006.

Cassell, Frank A. "Slaves of the Chesapeake Bay Area and the War of 1812." *Journal of Negro History* 57.2 (1972): 144–55.

Chalk, Frank. "The Anatomy of an Investment: Firestone's 1927 Loan to Liberia." *Canadian Journal of African Studies* 1.1 (1967): 12–32.

Chesterman, Simon, and Béatrice Pouligny. "Are Sanctions Meant to Work? The Politics of Creating and Implementing Sanctions through the United Nations." *Global Governance* 9.4 (2003): 503–18.

Chetty, Raj, Nathaniel Hendren, Patrick Kline, and Emmanuel Saez. *Where Is the Land of Opportunity? The Geography of Intergenerational Mobility in the United States.* Cambridge, MA: National Bureau of Economic Research, 2014.

Chollet, Derek H. *The Long Game: How Obama Defied Washington and Redefined America's Role in the World.* New York: Public Affairs, 2016.

Chomsky, Noam. *Fateful Triangle: The United States, Israel, and the Palestinians.* Cambridge, MA: South End, 1999.

Church, Frank. *Covert Action in Chile 1963–1973: Staff Report of the Select Committee to Study Governmental Operations with Respect to Intelligence Activities.* Washington, DC: Government Printing Office, 1975.

Church, Frank. *Final Report of the Select Committee to Study Governmental Operations with Respect to Intelligence Activities, United States Senate: Together with Additional, Supplemental, and Separate Views.* Washington, DC: Government Printing Office, 1976.

Churchill, Winston. *The Second World War,* vol. 6, *Triumph and Tragedy.* London: Cassell, 1954.

Civil Rights Congress. *We Charge Genocide.* New York: International, 1951.

Clark, Christopher M., and Derek Perkins. *The Sleepwalkers: How Europe Went to War in 1914.* London: Penguin, 2014.

Clark, Henry W. *History of Alaska.* New York: Macmillan, 1930.

Clark, L. P. *Lincoln: A Psycho-Biography.* New York: Scribner's, 1933.

Clarke, Richard A., Michael J. Morell, Geoffrey R. Stone, Cass R. Sunstein, and Peter P. Swire. *The NSA Report: Liberty and Security in a Changing World.* Princeton, NJ: Princeton University Press, 2014.

Congressional Budget Office. *The Distribution of Household Income and Federal Taxes, 2011.* Washington, DC: Government Printing Office, 2014.

Congressional Research Service. *Treaties and Other International Agreements: The Role of the United States Senate: A Study.* Washington, DC: Government Printing Office, 2001.

Connell-Smith, Gordon. *The Inter-American System.* London: Oxford University Press, 1965.

Conniff, Michael. "Panama since 1903." In *The Cambridge History of Latin America*, vol. 7, *Latin America since 1930: Mexico, Central America and the Caribbean*, edited by Leslie Bethell. Cambridge: Cambridge University Press, 1990.

Conroy-Krutz, Emily. *Christian Imperialism: Converting the World in the Early American Republic.* Ithaca, NY: Cornell University Press, 2015.

Contractor, Farok. *Tax Avoidance by Multinational Companies: Methods, Policies, and Ethics.* Newark, NJ: Rutgers Business School, 2016.

Cooper, Andrew F. *Internet Gambling Offshore: Caribbean Struggles over Casino Capitalism.* Basingstoke, England: Palgrave Macmillan, 2011.

Corak, Miles. *Inequality from Generation to Generation: The United States in Comparison.* Bonn: IZA, 2016.

Cordell, Linda, and Bruce Smith. "Indigenous Farmers." In *The Cambridge History of the Native Peoples of the Americas*, vol. 1, *North America*, part 1, edited by Bruce G. Trigger and Wilcomb E. Washburn. New York: Cambridge University Press, 2007.

Corwin, Thomas. *Life and Speeches of Thomas Corwin: Orator, Lawyer and Statesman.* Cincinnati: Anderson, 1896.

Coughlin, Cletus, Michael Pakko, and William Poole. "How Dangerous Is the U.S. Current Account Deficit?" *Regional Economist*, April 2006, 5–9.

Council of Economic Advisers. *Economic Report of the President.* Washington, DC: Government Printing Office, 2016.

Cox, Jeff, and Peter J. Tanous. *Debt, Deficits, and the Demise of the American Economy.* Hoboken, NJ: Wiley, 2013.

Cox, Michael, and Doug Stokes. *US Foreign Policy.* New York: Oxford University Press, 2012.

Crawley, Andrew. *Somoza and Roosevelt: Good Neighbour Diplomacy in Nicaragua, 1933–1945.* Oxford: Oxford University Press, 2007.

Cull, Nicholas J. *The Cold War and the United States Information Agency: American Propaganda and Public Diplomacy, 1945–1989.* Cambridge: Cambridge University Press, 2008.

Cullinane, Michael P. *Liberty and American Anti-imperialism, 1898–1909.* New York: Palgrave Macmillan, 2012.

Darwin, John. *Unfinished Empire: The Global Expansion of Britain.* New York: Bloomsbury, 2013.

Davis, Lance, and Robert Cull. "International Capital Movements, Domestic Capital
Markets, and American Economic Growth, 1820–1914." In *The Cambridge Economic
History of the United States,* vol. 2, *The Long Nineteenth Century,* edited by Stanley L. Engerman and Robert E. Gallman. Cambridge: Cambridge University Press,
2000.

Dawson, Ashley. "New World Disorder: 'Black Hawk Down' and the Eclipse of U.S. Military Humanitarianism in Africa." *African Studies Review: Journal of the African Studies Association* 54.2 (2011): 177–94.

Deas, Malcolm. "Colombia, Ecuador and Venezuela, c. 1880–1930." In *The Cambridge
History of Latin America,* vol. 5, *c. 1870 to 1930,* edited by Leslie Bethell. Cambridge:
Cambridge University Press, 1986.

Deibert, Michael. *Haiti Will Not Perish: A Recent History.* London: Zed, 2017.

Deloitte. *BEPS Actions Implementations by Country: United States.* London: Deloitte.
2016.

Denison, Edward F. *Accounting for United States Economic Growth, 1929–1969.* Washington, DC: Brookings Institution Press, 1974.

DeWitt, Charles J. "Crusading for Peace in Syracuse during the War with Mexico." *New
York History* 14.2 (1933): 100–112.

Diederich, Bernard. *Somoza and the Legacy of U.S. Involvement in Central America.* London: Junction, 1982.

Diederich, Bernard. *Trujillo: The Death of the Goat.* Boston: Little, Brown, 1978.

Dietz, James L. *Economic History of Puerto Rico: Institutional Change and Capitalist Development.* Princeton, NJ: Princeton University Press, 1986.

Donahue, Laura. "High Technology, Consumer Privacy, and U.S. National Security." Paper 1457. Georgetown Law Faculty, Washington, DC, 2015.

Donaubauer, Julian, Birgit Meyer, and Peter Nunnenkamp. *A New Global Index on Infrastructure: Construction, Rankings and Applications.* Kiel, Germany: Kiel Institute for
the World Economy, 2014.

Douglass, Frederick. "The Nation's Problem." In *Selected Speeches and Writings,* edited
by Philip S. Foner. Chicago: Chicago Review Press, 1999.

Dreher, Axel, and Jan-Egbert Sturm. "Do the IMF and the World Bank Influence Voting
in the UN General Assembly?" *Public Choice* 151 (2012): 363–97.

Dumas, J. R. P. *An Encounter with Haiti: Notes of a Special Adviser.* Port of Spain, Trinidad & Tobago: Medianet, 2008.

Dunbar-Ortiz, Roxanne D. *An Indigenous Peoples' History of the United States.* Boston:
Beacon, 2014.

Duncan, Greg J., and Richard J. Murnane. *Whither Opportunity? Rising Inequality and
the Uncertain Life Chances of Low-Income Children.* New York: Russell Sage Foundation, 2011.

"Editorial Comment: Liberia." *American Journal of International Law* 3.4 (1909):
958–63.

Egerton, George W. "Britain and the 'Great Betrayal': Anglo-American Relations and the Struggle for United States Ratification of the Treaty of Versailles, 1919–1920." *Historical Journal* 21.4 (1978): 885–911.

Ekirch, Arthur A. *The Civilian and the Military.* New York: Oxford University Press, 1956.

Ellner, Steve. "Venezuela." In *Latin America between the Second World War and the Cold War, 1944–1948,* edited by Leslie Bethell and Ian Roxborough. Cambridge: Cambridge University Press, 1992.

Emery, Edwin. *The Press and America.* Englewood Cliffs, NJ: Prentice-Hall, 1965.

Emery, Michael C., Edwin Emery, and Nancy L. Roberts. *The Press and America: An Interpretive History of the Mass Media.* 9th ed. Boston: Allyn and Bacon, 2000.

Engelbrecht, H. C., and Frank C. Hanighen. *Merchants of Death: A Study of the International Armament Industry.* New York: Dodd, Mead, 1934.

Executive Office of the President. *National Space Policy of the United States of America.* Washington DC: Executive Office of the President, 2010.

Ferguson, Niall. *Colossus: The Price of America's Empire.* New York: Penguin, 2004.

Fisher, Robin. "The Northwest from the Beginning of Trade with Europeans to 1880s." In *The Cambridge History of the Native Peoples of the Americas,* vol. 1, *North America,* part 2, edited by Bruce G. Trigger and Wilcomb E. Washburn. New York: Cambridge University Press, 2007.

Fleming, Denna F. *The United States and the League of Nations.* New York: Putnam, 1932.

Florio, Massimo. "Economists, Privatization in Russia and the Waning of the 'Washington Consensus.'" *Review of International Political Economy* 9.2 (2002): 374–415.

Flynn, George Q. *The Draft, 1940–1973.* Lawrence: University Press of Kansas, 1993.

Fojas, Camilla. *Islands of Empire: Pop Culture and U.S. Power.* Austin: University of Texas Press, 2015.

Foreman, Grant. *A Traveler in Indian Territory: Journal of Ethan Allen Hitchcock, Late Major-General in the United States Army.* Cedar Rapids, IA: Torch, 1930.

Forstall, Richard L. *Population of States and Counties of the United States: 1790 to 1990: From the Twenty-One Decennial Censuses.* Washington, DC: Department of Commerce, Bureau of the Census, Population Division, 1996.

Foundation Center. *International Grantmaking Update: A Snapshot of U.S. Foundation Trends.* New York: Foundation Center, 2012.

Fraser, Matthew. *Weapons of Mass Distraction: Soft Power and American Empire.* New York: Dunne, 2005.

Freeman, Joshua B. *American Empire: The Rise of a Global Power, the Democratic Revolution at Home, 1945–2000.* New York: Viking, 2012.

Freeman, Richard B. *The Overeducated American.* New York: Academic Press, 1976.

Fukuyama, Francis. *The National Interest.* Washington, DC: National Affairs, 1989.

Gaddis, John L. *The Cold War: A New History.* New York: Penguin, 2007.

Gannon, K. M. "'Escaping Mr. Jefferson's Plan of Destruction': New England Federalists and the Idea of a Northern Confederacy, 1803–1804." *Journal of the Early Republic* 21 (2001): 413–44.

Gardner, Lloyd C., Walter LaFeber, and Thomas J. McCormick. *Creation of the American Empire: U.S. Diplomatic History.* Chicago: Rand McNally, 1973.

Gettleman, Marvin E. *Vietnam and America: A Documented History.* New York: Grove, 1995.

Gibson, Arrell Morgan. "Indian Land Transfers." In *Handbook of North American Indians,* vol. 4, *History of Indian-White Relations,* edited by Wilcomb E. Washburn. Washington, DC: Smithsonian Institution, 1988.

Gimbel, John. *The American Occupation of Germany: Politics and the Military, 1945–1949.* Stanford, CA: Stanford University Press, 1968.

Gleijeses, Piero. *Conflicting Missions: Havana, Washington, and Africa, 1959–1976.* Chapel Hill: University of North Carolina Press, 2002.

Gleijeses, Piero. *The Dominican Crisis: The 1965 Constitutionalist Revolt and American Intervention.* Baltimore: Johns Hopkins University Press, 1978.

Gleijeses, Piero. *Shattered Hope: The Guatemalan Revolution and the United States, 1944–1954.* Princeton, NJ: Princeton University Press, 1991.

Gleijeses, Piero. *Visions of Freedom: Havana, Washington, Pretoria, and the Struggle for Southern Africa, 1976–1991.* Chapel Hill: University of North Carolina Press, 2013.

Go, Julian. *Patterns of Empire: The British and American Empires, 1688 to the Present.* New York: Cambridge University Press, 2011.

Goebel, Dorothy B. *William Henry Harrison: A Political Biography.* Indianapolis: Historical Bureau of the Indiana Library and Historical Department, 1926.

Goldberg, Jeffrey. "The Obama Doctrine." *Atlantic Monthly* 317.3 (2016): 70–90.

Goldin, Claudia D., and Lawrence F. Katz. *The Race between Education and Technology.* Cambridge, MA: Belknap Press of Harvard University Press, 2008.

Gordon, Robert J. *Is U.S. Economic Growth Over? Faltering Innovation Confronts the Six Headwinds.* Cambridge, MA: National Bureau of Economic Research, 2012.

Gordon, Robert J. *The Rise and Fall of American Growth: The U.S. Standard of Living since the Civil War.* Princeton, NJ: Princeton University Press, 2016.

Gott, Richard. *Cuba: A New History.* New Haven, CT: Yale University Press, 2005.

Grandin, Greg. *The Empire of Necessity: Slavery, Freedom, and Deception in the New World.* New York: Metropolitan, 2014.

Grandin, Greg. *Empire's Workshop: Latin America, the United States, and the Rise of the New Imperialism.* New York: Metropolitan, 2006.

Grandin, Greg. *Fordlandia: The Rise and Fall of Henry Ford's Forgotten Jungle City.* New York: Picador, 2010.

Green, Michael D. "The Expansion of European Colonization to the Mississippi Valley, 1780–1880." In *The Cambridge History of the Native Peoples of the Americas,* vol. 1, *North America,* part 1, edited by Bruce G. Trigger and Wilcomb E. Washburn. New York: Cambridge University Press, 2007.

Greenwald, Glenn. *No Place to Hide: Edward Snowden, the NSA, and the U.S. Surveillance State.* New York: Metropolitan, 2014.

Grubbs, Larry. *Secular Missionaries: Americans and African Development in the 1960s.* Amherst, MA: University of Massachusetts Press, 2009.

Grueber, Martin. 2012 *Global R&D Funding Forecast.* Columbus, OH: Battelle, 2013.

Guinsburg, Thomas N. *The Pursuit of Isolationism in the United States Senate from Versailles to Pearl Harbor.* New York: Garland, 1982.

Guth, James L. "Religion and American Public Opinion: Foreign Policy Issues." In *The Oxford Handbook of Religion and American Politics,* edited by James Guth, Lyman Kellsted, and Corwin Smidt. Oxford: Oxford University Press, 2009.

Gwynne, S. C. *Empire of the Summer Moon: Quanah Parker and the Rise and Fall of the Comanches, the Most Powerful Indian Tribe in American History.* New York: Scribner, 2011.

Habyarimana, Bangambiki. *The Great Pearl of Wisdom.* Charleston, SC: Smashwords, 2015.

Hahn, Erich J. C. *Cornerstone of Democracy: The West German Grundgesetz, 1949–1989.* Washington, DC: German Historical Institute, 1995.

Hallock, Steven M. *The Press March to War: Newspapers Set the Stage for Military Intervention in Post-World War II America.* New York: Peter Lang, 2012.

Hallward, Peter. *Damming the Flood: Haiti, Aristide, and the Politics of Containment.* London: Verso, 2007.

Haltiwanger, John, Ian Hathaway, and Javier Miranda. *Declining Business Dynamism in the U.S. High-Technology Sector.* Kansas City, MO: Kauffman Foundation, 2014.

Halton, Dan. "International News in the North American Media." *International Journal* 56.3 (2001): 499–515.

Hämäläinen, Pekka. *The Comanche Empire.* New Haven, CT: Yale University Press, 2008.

Hamilton, Richard F. *America's New Empire: The 1890s and Beyond.* New Brunswick, NJ: Transaction, 2010.

Hardt, Michael, and Antonio Negri. *Empire.* Cambridge, MA: Harvard University Press, 2000.

Harrington, Fred H. "The Anti-imperialist Movement in the United States, 1898–1900." *Mississippi Valley Historical Review* 22.2 (1935): 211–30.

Harrison, Sarah. "Indexing the Empire." In WikiLeaks, *The WikiLeaks Files: The World According to US Empire.* London: Verso, 2015.

Harvey, Paul, and Edward J. Blum. *The Columbia Guide to Religion in American History.* New York: Columbia University Press, 2012.

Haycox, Stephen W. *Alaska: An American Colony.* Seattle: University of Washington Press, 2002.

Heffer, Jean. *The United States and the Pacific: History of a Frontier.* Translated by W. Donald Wilson. Notre Dame, IN: University of Notre Dame Press, 2002.

Hendrickson, Ryan C. *The Constitution, Congress and War Powers.* Nashville, TN: Vanderbilt University Press, 2002.

Herring, George C. *America's Longest War: The United States and Vietnam, 1950–1975.* New York: Wiley, 1979.

Herring, George C. *From Colony to Superpower: U.S. Foreign Relations since 1776.* New York: Oxford University Press, 2008.

Hezel, Francis X. *The First Taint of Civilization: A History of the Caroline and Marshall Islands in Pre-colonial Days, 1521–1885.* Honolulu: University of Hawaiʻi Press, 1995.

Hitchcock, Ethan A. *Fifty Years in Camp and Field: Diary of Major-General Ethan Allen Hitchcock, U.S.A.* New York: Putnam's, 1909.

Hixson, Walter L. *American Settler Colonialism: A History.* New York: Palgrave Macmillan, 2013.

Hobson, J. A. *The Evolution of Modern Capitalism: A Study of Machine Production.* London: Allen and Unwin, 1926.

Hodgson, Geoffrey. "The Establishment." *Foreign Policy* 10 (1973): 3–40.

Hoey, John. "Federalist Opposition to the War of 1812." *Early American Review* 4.2 (2000).

Hopewell, Kristen. *Breaking the WTO: How Emerging Powers Disrupted the Neoliberal Project.* Stanford, CA: Stanford University Press, 2016.

Horie, Shigeo. *The International Monetary Fund: Retrospect and Prospect.* New York: St. Martin's, 1964.

Horne, Gerald. *Negro Comrades of the Crown: African Americans and the British Empire Fight the U.S. before Emancipation.* New York: New York University Press, 2012.

Horsefield, J. K., and M. G. de Vries. *The International Monetary Fund, 1945–1965: Twenty Years of International Monetary Cooperation.* Washington, DC: International Monetary Fund, 1969.

Horsman, Reginald. "United States Indian Policies, 1776–1815." In *Handbook of North American Indians,* vol. 4, *History of Indian-White Relations,* edited by Wilcomb E. Washburn. Washington, DC: Smithsonian Institution, 1988.

Hubbard, James P. *The United States and the End of British Colonial Rule in Africa, 1941–1968.* London: McFarland, 2010.

Hudson, Michael. *Super Imperialism: The Origin and Fundamentals of U.S. World Dominance.* London: Pluto, 2003.

Hull, Cordell. *Memoirs,* vol. 2. New York: Macmillan, 1948.

Humphreys, R. A. *Latin America and the Second World War: 1942–1945.* London: Athlone, 1982.

Hunt, Michael H. *The American Ascendancy: How the United States Gained and Wielded Global Dominance.* Chapel Hill: University of North Carolina Press, 2009.

Huntington, Samuel P. "Transnational Organizations in World Politics." *World Politics* 25.3 (1973): 333–68.

Immerman, Richard H. *The CIA in Guatemala: The Foreign Policy of Intervention.* Austin: University of Texas Press, 1982.

Immerman, Richard H. *Empire for Liberty: A History of American Imperialism from Benjamin Franklin to Paul Wolfowitz.* Princeton, NJ: Princeton University Press, 2010.

Inboden, William. *Religion and American Foreign Policy, 1945–1960: The Soul of Containment.* Cambridge: Cambridge University Press, 2008.

International Monetary Fund. *International Financial Statistics: Yearbook, 2016.* Washington, DC: International Monetary Fund, 2016.

International Monetary Fund. *World Economic Outlook, April 2016.* Washington, DC: International Monetary Fund, 2016.

Jackson, Donna R. *Jimmy Carter and the Horn of Africa: Cold War Policy in Ethiopia and Somalia*. Jefferson, NC: McFarland, 2007.

Jagan, Cheddi. *The West on Trial: My Fight for Guyana's Freedom*. New York: International, 1966.

Jefferson, Thomas. *The Life and Writings of Thomas Jefferson*. Edited by S. E. Forman Indianapolis: Bowen-Merrill, 1900.

Johnson, Chalmers. *Blowback: The Costs and Consequences of American Empire*. New York: Holt, 2001.

Johnson, Chalmers. *Dismantling the Empire: America's Last Best Hope*. New York: Metropolitan, 2010.

Johnson, Robert D. *The Peace Progressives and American Foreign Relations*. Cambridge, MA: Harvard University Press, 1995.

Johnson, Todd M., and Gina A. Zurlo. *World Christian Database*. Leiden, Netherlands: Brill, 2016.

Johnson, Walter. *River of Dark Dreams: Slavery and Empire in the Cotton Kingdom*. Cambridge, MA: Belknap Press of Harvard University Press, 2013.

Joint Chiefs of Staff. *Joint Vision 2010*. Washington, DC: Joint Chiefs of Staff, 1997.

Joint Chiefs of Staff. *Joint Vision 2020*. Washington, DC: Joint Chiefs of Staff, 2000.

Jones, Charles I. "Pareto and Piketty: The Macroeconomics of Top Income and Wealth Inequality." *Journal of Economic Perspectives* 29.1 (2015): 29–46.

Joy, Mark S. *American Expansionism, 1783–1860: A Manifest Destiny?* Harlow, England: Pearson Longman, 2010.

Judis, John B. *The Paradox of American Democracy: Elites, Special Interests, and the Betrayal of the Public Trust*. New York: Pantheon, 2000.

Kagan, Robert. *Dangerous Nation*. New York: Knopf, 2006.

Kagan, Robert. *Power and Weakness*. Stanford, CA: Hoover Institution, 2002.

Kagan, Robert. *The World America Made*. New York: Knopf, 2012.

Kahler, Miles. "The United States and the International Monetary Fund: Declining Influence or Declining Interest?" In *The United States and Multilateral Institutions: Patterns of Changing Instrumentality and Influence*, edited by Margaret P. Karns and Karen A. Mingst. New York: Routledge, 1992.

Kaplan, Amy, and Donald E. Pease, eds. *Cultures of United States Imperialism*. Durham, NC: Duke University Press, 1999.

Kauffman, Bill. *Ain't My America: The Long, Noble History of Antiwar Conservatism and Middle American Anti-imperialism*. New York: Metropolitan, 2008.

Keasbey, Lindley M. *The Nicaragua Canal and the Monroe Doctrine: A Political History of Isthmus Transit, with Special Reference to the Nicaragua Canal Project and the Attitude of the United States Government Thereto*. New York: Putnam, 1896.

Kennedy, Paul M. *The Parliament of Man: The Past, Present, and Future of the United Nations*. New York: Vintage, 2006.

Kennedy, Paul M. *The Rise and Fall of the Great Powers: Economic Change and Military Conflict from 1500 to 2000*. New York: Random House, 1987.

King, David. "The New Internationalists: World Vision and the Revival of American Evangelical Humanitarianism, 1950–2010." *Religions* 3.4 (2012): 922–49.

King, Kay. *Congress and National Security.* New York: Council on Foreign Relations, 2010.

King, Willford Isbell. *The Wealth and Income of the People of the United States.* New York: Macmillan, 1915.

Knight, Melvin M. *The Americans in Santo Domingo.* New York: Vanguard, 1928.

Kramer, Paul A. *The Blood of Government: Race, Empire, the United States, and the Philippines.* Chapel Hill: University of North Carolina Press, 2006.

Kristol, William, and Robert A. Kagan. "Toward a Neo-Reaganite Foreign Policy." *Foreign Affairs* 75.4 (1996): 18–32.

Kukla, Jon. *A Wilderness So Immense: The Louisiana Purchase and the Destiny of America.* New York: Knopf, 2003.

Kuykendall, Ralph S. *Hawaii: A History from the Polynesian Kingdom to American Commonwealth.* New York: Prentice-Hall, 1955.

Kuykendall, Ralph S. *The Hawaiian Kingdom,* vol. 3, *The Kalakaua Dynasty.* Honolulu: University of Hawai'i Press, 1967.

Kvasnicka, Robert M. "United States Indian Treaties and Agreements." In *Handbook of North American Indians,* vol. 4, *History of Indian-White Relations,* edited by Wilcomb E. Washburn. Washington, DC: Smithsonian Institution, 1988.

LaFeber, Walter. *America in the Cold War: Twenty Years of Revolutions and Response, 1947–1967.* New York: Wiley, 1969.

LaFeber, Walter. *The American Search for Opportunity, 1865–1913.* New York: Cambridge University Press, 2013.

Laïdi, Zaki. *The Superpowers and Africa: The Constraints of a Rivalry, 1960–1990.* Chicago: University of Chicago Press, 1990.

Landefeld, J. Steven, and Ann M. Lawson. *Valuation of the U.S. Net International Investment Position.* Washington, DC: Bureau of Economic Analysis, 1991.

Landers, Brian. *Empires Apart: A History of American and Russian Imperialism.* New York: Pegasus, 2014.

Landler, Mark. *Alter Egos: Hillary Clinton, Barack Obama, and the Twilight Struggle over American Power.* New York: Random House, 2016.

Langer, William L., and S. E. Gleason. *The Challenge to Isolation, 1937–1940.* New York: Harper, 1952.

Langley, Lester D. *The Banana Wars: An Inner History of American Empire, 1900–1934.* Lexington: University Press of Kentucky, 1983.

Laqueur, Walter. *Neo-isolationism and the World of the Seventies.* New York: Library Press, 1972.

Lasch, Christopher. "The Anti-imperialists, the Philippines, and the Inequality of Man." *Journal of Southern History* 24.3 (1958): 319–31.

Lawrence, Robert Z. *The United States and the WTO Dispute Settlement System.* New York: Council on Foreign Relations, 2007.

Lawson, Gary, and Guy Seidman. *The Constitution of Empire: Territorial Expansion and American Legal History.* New Haven, CT: Yale University Press, 2004.

Lawson, Gary, and Guy Seidman. "The First 'Incorporation' Debate." In *The Louisiana Purchase and American Expansion, 1803–1898,* edited by Sanford Levinson and Bartholomew H. Sparrow. Lanham, MD: Rowman and Littlefield, 2005.

Lebe, Melvin Stanton. "Diminished Hopes: The United States and the United Nations during the Truman Years." PhD diss., University of California–Los Angeles, 2012.

Lens, Sidney. *The Forging of the American Empire.* New York: Crowell, 1971.

Lepre, George. *Fragging: Why U.S. Soldiers Assaulted Their Officers in Vietnam.* Lubbock: Texas Tech University Press, 2011.

Levinson, Sanford, and Bartholomew H. Sparrow, eds. *The Louisiana Purchase and American Expansion, 1803–1898.* Lanham, MD: Rowman and Littlefield, 2005.

Lewis, Gordon K. *The Virgin Islands: A Caribbean Lilliput.* Evanston, IL: Northwestern University Press, 1972.

Lieber, Robert J. *Power and Willpower in the American Future: Why the United States Is Not Destined to Decline.* New York: Cambridge University Press, 2012.

Lindsay, D. M. *Faith in the Halls of Power: How Evangelicals Joined the American Elite.* Oxford: Oxford University Press, 2007.

Linklater, Andro. *Measuring America: How an Untamed Wilderness Shaped the United States and Fulfilled the Promise of Democracy.* New York: Walker, 2002.

Lipset, Seymour M. *American Exceptionalism: A Double-Edged Sword.* New York: Norton, 1996.

Lipsey, Robert E. "U.S. Foreign Trade and the Balance of Payments, 1800–1913." In *The Cambridge Economic History of the United States,* vol. 2, *The Long Nineteenth Century,* edited by Stanley L. Engerman and Robert E. Gallman. Cambridge: Cambridge University Press, 2000.

Little, Douglas. *American Orientalism: The United States and the Middle East since 1945.* Chapel Hill: University of North Carolina Press, 2002.

Logevall, Fredrik. "The Indochina Wars and the Cold War, 1945–1975." In *The Cambridge History of the Cold War,* vol. 2, *Crises and Détente,* edited by Melvyn P. Leffler and Odd Arne Westad. Cambridge: Cambridge University Press, 2010.

Lowrie, Samuel H. *Culture Conflict in Texas, 1821–1835.* New York: Columbia University Press, 1932.

Lutz, Catherine. *The Bases of Empire: The Global Struggle against U.S. Military Posts.* London: Pluto, 2009.

MacBride, Sean. *Many Voices, One World: Report by the International Commission for the Study of Communication Problems.* Lanham, MD: Rowman and Littlefield, 1980.

MacDonald, Paul K. "Those Who Forget Historiography Are Doomed to Republish It: Empire, Imperialism and Contemporary Debates about American Power." *Review of International Studies* 35.1 (2009): 45–68.

MacMillan, Margaret. *Peacemakers: The Paris Conference of 1919 and Its Attempt to End War.* London: Murray, 2001.

MacMillan, Margaret. *The War That Ended Peace: The Road to 1914.* New York: Random House, 2013.

Maddison, Angus. *The World Economy: A Millennial Perspective.* Paris: Development Centre of the Organisation for Economic Co-operation and Development, 2002.

Madrigal, Ea Nicole. "Republic to Empire: Anglo-American Perceptions of the Hispanic West and American Empire Building, 1800–1850." PhD diss., University of California–Riverside, 2014.

Madsen, Deborah L. *American Exceptionalism*. Edinburgh: Edinburgh University Press, 1998.

Mahan, Alfred Thayer. *The Influence of Sea Power upon History, 1660–1783*. Boston: Little, Brown, 1890.

Mahon, John K. "Indian-United States Military Situation, 1775–1848." In *Handbook of North American Indians*, vol. 4, *History of Indian-White Relations*, edited by Wilcomb E. Washburn. Washington, DC: Smithsonian Institution, 1988.

Maier, Charles S. *Among Empires: American Ascendancy and Its Predecessors*. Cambridge, MA: Harvard University Press, 2007.

Major, John. "The Panama Canal Zone, 1904–79." In *The Cambridge History of Latin America*, vol. 7, *Latin America since 1930: Mexico, Central America and the Caribbean*, edited by Leslie Bethell. Cambridge: Cambridge University Press, 1990.

Mandelbaum, Michael. *The Case for Goliath: How America Acts as the World's Government in the Twenty-First Century*. New York: Public Affairs, 2005.

Mandelbaum, Michael. *The Frugal Superpower: America's Global Leadership in a Cash-Strapped Era*. New York: Public Affairs, 2010.

Mann, Catherine L. "Perspectives on the U.S. Current Account Deficit and Sustainability." *Journal of Economic Perspectives* 16.3 (2002): 131–52.

Mann, Michael. *Incoherent Empire*. London: Verso, 2003.

Martin, Gerald. *Gabriel García Márquez: A Life*. London: Bloomsbury, 2008.

Martínez-Fernández, Luis. *Torn between Empires: Economy, Society, and Patterns of Political Thought in the Hispanic Caribbean, 1840–1878*. Athens: University of Georgia Press, 1994.

Maurer, Noel. *The Empire Trap: The Rise and Fall of the U.S. Intervention to Protect American Property Overseas, 1893–2013*. Princeton, NJ: Princeton University Press, 2013.

May, Christopher. "Direct and Indirect Influence at the World Intellectual Property Organization." In *Business and Global Governance*, edited by Morten Ougaard and Anna Leander. London: Routledge, 2010.

Mayers, David A. *George Kennan and the Dilemmas of US Foreign Policy*. New York: Oxford University Press, 1988.

Mazower, Mark. *No Enchanted Palace: The End of Empire and the Ideological Origins of the United Nations*. Princeton, NJ: Princeton University Press, 2009.

Mazzucato, Mariana. *The Entrepreneurial State: Debunking Public vs. Private Sector Myths*. London: Demos, 2011.

MccGwire, Michael, and Michael Clarke. "NATO Expansion: 'A Policy Error of Historic Importance.'" *International Affairs* 84.6 (2008): 1281–1301.

McCoy, Alfred W., and Francisco A. Scarano, eds. *Colonial Crucible: Empire in the Making of the Modern American State*. Madison: University of Wisconsin Press, 2009.

McCullough, David G. *The Path between the Seas: The Creation of the Panama Canal, 1870–1914*. New York: Simon and Schuster, 1977.

McDonald, Kara C., and Stewart M. Patrick. *UN Security Council Enlargement and U.S. Interests*. New York: Council on Foreign Relations, 2010.

McDougall, Walter A. *Promised Land, Crusader State: The American Encounter with the World since 1776.* Boston: Houghton Mifflin, 1997.

McElroy, Robert M. N. *The Winning of the Far West: A History of the Regaining of Texas, of the Mexican War, and the Oregon Question; and of the Successive Additions to the Territory of the United States, within the Continent of America: 1829–1867.* New York: Putnam's, 1914.

McGann, James. "The Think Tank Index." *Foreign Policy* 170 (2009): 82–84.

McIntyre, Elizabeth. "Weighted Voting in International Organizations." *International Organization* 8.4 (1954): 484–97.

Mead, Walter R. "God's Country?" *Foreign Affairs* 85.5 (2006): 24–43.

Mead, Walter R. *Special Providence: American Foreign Policy and How It Changed the World.* New York: Routledge, 2001.

Mearsheimer, John J. *The Tragedy of Great Power Politics.* New York: Norton, 2014.

Mearsheimer, John J., and Stephen M. Walt. *The Israel Lobby and U.S. Foreign Policy.* New York: Farrar, Straus and Giroux, 2007.

Mecham, J. L. *A Survey of United States-Latin American Relations.* Boston: Houghton Mifflin, 1965.

Medvetz, Thomas. *Think Tanks in America.* Chicago: University of Chicago Press, 2012.

Meridian International Center and Gallup, *U.S.-Global Leadership Project.* Report for 2013. Washington, DC: Gallup, 2014.

Merritt, Richard L. "American Influences in the Occupation of Germany." *Annals of the American Academy of Political and Social Science* 428 (1976): 91–103.

Merry, Robert W. *Sands of Empire: Missionary Zeal, American Foreign Policy, and the Hazards of Global Ambition.* New York: Simon and Schuster, 2005.

Middleton, Richard. *Pontiac's War: Its Causes, Course, and Consequences.* New York: Routledge, 2007.

Miller, James E. *The United States and the Making of Modern Greece: History and Power, 1950–1974.* Chapel Hill: University of North Carolina Press, 2009.

Millett, Richard. *Guardians of the Dynasty.* Maryknoll, NY: Orbis, 1977.

Mills, C. Wright. *The Power Elite.* New York: Oxford University Press, 1956.

Mires, Charlene. *Capital of the World: The Race to Host the United Nations.* New York: New York University Press, 2013.

Mississippi Department of Archives and History. *Mississippi Territorial Archives, 1798–1803.* Jackson, MS, 1905.

Mitnik, Pablo, Victoria Bryant, Michael Weber, and David Grusky. *New Estimates of Intergenerational Mobility Using Administrative Data.* Washington, DC: Pew Research Center, 2015.

Modigliani, Andre, and Franco Modigliani. "The Growth of the Federal Deficit and the Role of Public Attitudes." *Public Opinion Quarterly* 51.4 (1987): 459–80.

Montague, Ludwell L. *Haiti and the United States, 1714–1938.* New York: Russell, 1940.

Morris, Robert. *FATCA and the New Birth of American Empire.* Robert Morris, 2014.

Murphy, Cullen. *The New Rome? The Fall of an Empire and the Fate of America.* Carlton North, Australia: Scribe, 2008.

Murphy, Erin. "Women's Anti-imperialism, 'the White Man's Burden,' and the Philippine-American War." *Gender and Society* 23.2 (2009): 244–70.

Murray, Charles A. *American Exceptionalism: An Experiment in History.* Washington, DC: AEI Press, 2013.

Nachmani, Amikam. "Civil War and Foreign Intervention in Greece: 1946–49." *Journal of Contemporary History* 25.4 (1990): 489–522.

Nadeau, Kathleen M. *The History of the Philippines.* Westport, CT: Greenwood, 2008.

Nahory, Céline. *The Hidden Veto.* New York: Global Policy Forum, 2004.

Nasr, Seyyed V. R., and Stephen Hoye. *The Dispensable Nation: American Foreign Policy in Retreat.* New York: Random House, 2013.

National Center for Education Statistics. *The Condition of Education.* Washington, DC: US Department of Education, Office of Educational Research and Improvement, National Center for Education Statistics, various years.

National Commission on Excellence in Education. *A Nation at Risk: The Imperative for Educational Reform.* New York: US Department of Education, 1983.

National Science Foundation. *Science and Engineering Indicators.* Washington, DC: National Science Foundation, 2014.

Neumann, William L. *America Encounters Japan: From Perry to Macarthur.* Baltimore: Johns Hopkins University Press, 1963.

Nicholls, David. *Haiti in Caribbean Context: Ethnicity, Economy and Revolt.* Basingstoke, England: Palgrave Macmillan, 1985.

Nielsen, Waldemar A. *The Big Foundations: A Twentieth Century Fund Study.* New York: Columbia University Press, 1972.

Nielsen, Waldemar A. *The Golden Donors: A New Anatomy of the Great Foundations.* New York: Talley, 1985.

Ninkovich, Frank A. *The United States and Imperialism.* Malden, MA: Blackwell, 2007.

Nordlinger, Eric A. *Isolationism Reconfigured: American Foreign Policy for a New Century.* Princeton, NJ: Princeton University Press, 1995.

Norris, Tina, Paula L. Vines, and Elizabeth M. Hoeffel. *The American Indian and Alaska Native Population: 2010.* Washington, DC: US Census Bureau, 2012.

Nugent, Walter T. K. *Habits of Empire: A History of American Expansion.* New York: Vintage, 2010.

Nye Committee. *Report of the Special Committee on Investigation of the Munitions Industry,* US Congress, Senate, 74th Congress, 2nd sess., February 24, 1936.

Nye, Joseph S. *Is the American Century Over?* Cambridge, MA: Polity Press, 2015.

Nye, Joseph S. "Public Diplomacy and Soft Power." *Annals of the American Academy of Political and Social Science* 616.1 (2008): 94–109.

Nye, Joseph S. *Soft Power: The Means to Success in World Politics.* New York: Public Affairs, 2004.

Nye, Joseph S., and Seymour J. Rubin. "The Longer Range Political Role of the Multinational Corporation." In *Global Companies: The Political Economy of World Business,* edited by George W. Ball. Englewood Cliffs, NJ: Prentice-Hall, 1975.

Oatley, Thomas H. *International Political Economy: Interests and Institutions in the Global Economy.* New York: Pearson/Longman, 2004.

Office of the US Trade Representative. *Beyond AGOA: Looking to the Future of U.S.-Africa Trade and Investment.* Washington, DC: Office of the US Trade Representative, 2016.

Office of the US Trade Representative. *2016 Biennial Report on the Implementation of the Africa Growth and Opportunity Act.* Washington, DC: Office of the US Trade Representative, 2016.

Onuf, Peter S. "Imperialism and Nationalism in the Early American Republic." In *Empire's Twin: U.S. Anti-imperialism from the Founding Era to the Age of Terrorism,* edited by Ian R. Tyrrell, Jay Sexton, and Peter S. Onuf. Ithaca, NY: Cornell University Press, 2015.

Onuf, Peter S. *Jefferson's Empire: The Language of American Nationhood.* Charlottesville: University of Virginia Press, 2000.

Onuf, Peter S. *Statehood and Union: A History of the Northwest Ordinance.* Bloomington: Indiana University Press, 1987.

Ornstein, Norman J., and Thomas E. Mann. "When Congress Checks Out." *Foreign Affairs* 85.6 (2006): 67–82.

O'Sullivan, Christopher D. *FDR and the End of Empire: The Origins of American Power in the Middle East.* New York: Palgrave Macmillan, 2012.

Otis, Fessenden N. *Illustrated History of the Panama Railroad: Together with a Traveler's Guide and Business Man's Handbook for the Panama Railroad and Its Connections: With Europe, the United States, the North and South Atlantic and Pacific Coasts, China, Australia, and Japan, by Sail and Steam.* New York: Harper, 1861.

Ougaard, Morten, and Anna Leander, eds. *Business and Global Governance.* London: Routledge, 2010.

Ovendale, Ritchie. *Britain, the United States, and the Transfer of Power in the Middle East, 1945–1962.* London: Leicester University Press, 1996.

Panitch, Leo, and Sam Gindin. *The Making of Global Capitalism: The Political Economy of American Empire.* London: Verso, 2013.

Paolino, Ernest N. *The Foundations of the American Empire: William Henry Seward and U.S. Foreign Policy.* Ithaca, NY: Cornell University Press, 1973.

Parkinson, F. *Latin America, the Cold War and the World Powers, 1945–1973: A Study in Diplomatic History.* Beverly Hills, CA: Sage, 1974.

Parmar, Inderjeet. *Foundations of the American Century: The Ford, Carnegie, and Rockefeller Foundations in the Rise of American Power.* New York: Columbia University Press, 2012.

Pérez, Louis A. "Cuba, c. 1930–59." In *The Cambridge History of Latin America,* vol. 7, *Latin America since 1930: Mexico, Central America and the Caribbean,* edited by Leslie Bethell. Cambridge: Cambridge University Press, 1990.

Perkins, Bradford. *The Creation of a Republican Empire, 1776–1865.* Cambridge: Cambridge University Press, 1993.

Perkins, Dexter. *A History of the Monroe Doctrine.* London: Longmans, 1960.

Peterson, Edward N. *The American Occupation of Germany: Retreat to Victory.* Detroit: Wayne State University Press, 1977.

"Pfiasco: Open Warfare Breaks Out between the White House and America's Tax-Shy Multinationals." *Economist,* April 9, 2016.

Piketty, Thomas. *Capital in the Twenty-First Century.* Cambridge, MA: Harvard University Press, 2014.

Pletcher, David M. *The Diplomacy of Involvement: American Economic Expansion across the Pacific, 1784–1900.* Columbia: University of Missouri Press, 2001.

Pletcher, David M. *The Diplomacy of Trade and Investment: American Economic Expansion in the Hemisphere, 1865–1900.* Columbia: University of Missouri Press, 1998.

Pomeroy, Earl S. *The Territories and the United States, 1861–1890: Studies in Colonial Administration.* Philadelphia: University of Pennsylvania Press, 1947.

Porter, Bernard. *Empire and Superempire: Britain, America and the World.* New Haven, CT: Yale University Press, 2006.

Posen, Barry R., and Andrew L. Ross. "Competing Visions for U.S. Grand Strategy." *International Security* 213 (1996): 5–53.

Project for the New American Century. *Rebuilding America's Defenses: Strategies, Forces, and Resources for a New Century.* Washington, DC: Project for the New American Century, 2000.

Prucha, Francis Paul. "United States Indian Policies, 1815–1860." In *Handbook of North American Indians,* vol. 4, *History of Indian-White Relations,* edited by Wilcomb E. Washburn. Washington, DC: Smithsonian Institution, 1988.

Pruden, Caroline. *Conditional Partners: Eisenhower, the United Nations, and the Search for a Permanent Peace.* Baton Rouge: Louisiana State University Press, 1998.

Rabe, Stephen G. *U.S. Intervention in British Guiana: A Cold War Story.* Chapel Hill: University of North Carolina Press, 2005.

Rakove, Robert B. *Kennedy, Johnson, and the Nonaligned World.* Cambridge, MA: Cambridge University Press, 2013.

Ramamurti, Ravi. "Global Regulatory Convergence: The Case of Intellectual Property Rights." In *International Business and Government Relations in the 21st Century,* edited by Robert E. Grosse. Cambridge, MA: Cambridge University Press, 2005.

Reagan, Michael D. "Book Review: *The Civilian and the Military.*" *Public Opinion Quarterly* 20.2 (1956): 484.

Reese, Trevor R. *Australia, New Zealand and the United States: Survey of International Relations, 1941–68.* London: Oxford University Press, 1969.

Remini, Robert V. *Andrew Jackson and the Course of American Empire, 1767–1821.* New York: Harper and Row, 1977.

Report of the National Commission for the Review of the Research and Development Programs of the United States Intelligence Community, Washington, DC, 2013.

Resis, Albert. "The Churchill-Stalin Secret 'Percentages' Agreement on the Balkans, Moscow, October 1944." *American Historical Review* 83.2 (1978): 368–87.

Reynolds, David. *America, Empire of Liberty: A New History of the United States.* New York: Basic Books, 2009.

Rich, Andrew. *Think Tanks, Public Policy, and the Politics of Expertise.* Cambridge: Cambridge University Press, 2004.

Rigby, Barry. "The Origins of American Expansion in Hawaii and Samoa, 1865–1900." *International History Review* 10.2 (1988): 221–37.

Ritchie, Gordon. *Wrestling with the Elephant: The Inside Story of the Canada–US Trade Wars.* Toronto: Macfarlane Walter and Ross, 1997.

Robertson, James A. *Louisiana under the Rule of Spain, France, and the United States, 1785–1807: Social, Economic, and Political Conditions of the Territory Represented in the Louisiana Purchase, as Portrayed in Hitherto Unpublished Contemporary Accounts.* Freeport, NY: Books for Libraries, 1969.

Rockland, Michael A. *Sarmiento's Travels in the United States in 1847.* Princeton, NJ: Princeton University Press, 1970.

Rockwell, Stephen J. *Indian Affairs and the Administrative State in the Nineteenth Century.* New York: Cambridge University Press, 2010.

Rodríguez, Mario. *A Palmerstonian Diplomat in Central America: Frederick Chatfield, Esq.* Tucson: University of Arizona Press, 1964.

Rodrik, Dani. *The Globalization Paradox: Democracy and the Future of the World Economy.* New York: Norton, 2011.

Rogers, Robert F. *Destiny's Landfall: A History of Guam.* Honolulu: University of Hawai'i Press, 1995.

Roosevelt, Franklin D. "Our Foreign Policy: A Democratic View." *Foreign Affairs* 6.4 (1928): 573–86.

Root, Elihu. *The Military and Colonial Policy of the United States: Addresses and Reports by Elihu Root.* Cambridge: Harvard University Press, 1916.

Rose, Gideon. *The Clash of Civilizations? The Debate.* New York: Council on Foreign Relations, 2013.

Rosenberg, Emily S. *Spreading the American Dream: American Economic and Cultural Expansion, 1890–1945.* New York: Hill and Wang, 2007.

Rosenstone, Robert A. *Visions of the Past: The Challenge of Film to Our Idea of History.* Cambridge, MA: Harvard University Press, 1995.

Roubini, Nouriel. "The Unsustainability of the U.S. Twin Deficits." *Cato Journal* 26.2 (2006): 343–56.

Rowland, Dunbar (ed.), *Official Letter Books of W.C.C. Claiborne, 1801–16.* Jackson, Miss: State Department of Archives and History, 1917.

Ruppert, Michael C. *Crossing the Rubicon: The Decline of the American Empire at the End of the Age of Oil.* Gabriola, British Columbia, Canada: New Society, 2004.

Russell, Ruth B. *A History of the United Nations Charter: The Role of the United States, 1940–1945.* Washington, DC: Brookings Institution, 1958.

Ryan, Selwyn. *Eric Williams: The Myth and the Man.* Kingston, Jamaica: University of the West Indies Press, 2008.

Saez, Emmanuel. "Striking It Richer: The Evolution of Top Incomes in the United States." Working paper, University of California–Berkeley Department of Economics, 2015.

Saez, Emmanuel, and Gabriel Zucman. *Wealth Inequality in the United States since 1913: Evidence from Capitalized Income Tax Data.* London: Centre for Economic Policy Research, 2015.

Safran, Nadav. *The United States and Israel.* Cambridge, MA: Harvard University Press, 1963.

Salazar Torreon, Barbara. *Instances of Use of United States Armed Forces Abroad, 1798–2016.* Washington, DC: Congressional Research Service, 2016.

Salvucci, Richard J., and Linda K. Salvucci. "Las consecuencias económicas de la independencia Mexicana." In *La Independencia Americana: Consecuencias Económicas,* edited by Leandro Prados de la Escosura and Samuel Amaral. Madrid: Alianza Editorial, 1993.

Sarotte, Mary E. "Perpetuating U.S. Preeminence: The 1990 Deals to 'Bribe the Soviets Out' and Move NATO In." *International Security* 35.1 (2010): 110–37.

Saunders, Frances S. *Who Paid the Piper? The CIA and the Cultural Cold War.* London: Granta, 1999.

Scahill, Jeremy. *Dirty Wars.* London: Serpent's Tail, 2014.

Scalapino, Robert A. "The United States and Japan." In *The United States and the Far East: Background Papers Prepared for the Use of Participants and the Final Report of the Tenth American Assembly, Arden House, Harriman Campus of Columbia University, Harriman, New York, November 15–18, 1956.* New York: American Assembly, Graduate School of Business, Columbia University, 1956.

Schaller, Michael. *Altered States: The United States and Japan since the Occupation.* New York: Oxford University Press, 1997.

Schaller, Michael. "Japan and the Cold War, 1960–1991." In *The Cambridge History of the Cold War,* vol. 3, *Endings,* edited by Melvyn P. Leffler and Odd Arne Westad. Cambridge: Cambridge University Press, 2010.

Schiller, Herbert I. *Living in the Number One Country: Reflections from a Critic of American Empire.* New York: Seven Stories, 2000.

Schlesinger, Arthur M., Jr. "The American Empire? Not So Fast." *World Policy Journal* 22.1 (2005): 43–46.

Schlesinger, Arthur M., Jr. *The Imperial Presidency.* Boston: Houghton Mifflin, 1973.

Schlesinger, Arthur M., Jr. *A Thousand Days: John F. Kennedy in the White House.* New York: Fawcett Premier, 1965.

Schmidt, Hans. *The United States Occupation of Haiti, 1915–1934.* New Brunswick, NJ: Rutgers University Press, 1971.

Schnepf, Randy. *Agriculture in the WTO Bali Ministerial Agreement.* Washington, DC: Congressional Research Service, 2014.

Schoultz, Lars. *Beneath the United States: A History of U.S. Policy toward Latin America.* Cambridge, MA: Harvard University Press, 1998.

Schoultz, Lars. *That Infernal Little Cuban Republic: The United States and the Cuban Revolution.* Chapel Hill: University of North Carolina Press, 2009.

Schulzinger, Robert D. *The Wise Men of Foreign Affairs: The History of the Council on Foreign Relations.* New York: Columbia University Press, 1984.

Selig, Robert A. "The Revolution's Black Soldiers: They Fought for Both Sides in Their Quest for Freedom." *Colonial Williamsburg* 19.4 (1997): 1–19.

Senate Committee on Foreign Relations. *ITT and Chile, 1970–71: Hearings Mar. 20–Apr. 2, 1973*. Washington, DC: Government Printing Office, 1973.

Seymour, Richard. *American Insurgents: A Brief History of American Anti-imperialism.* Chicago: Haymarket, 2012.

Shaxson, Nicholas. *Treasure Islands: Tax Havens and the Men Who Stole the World.* London: Bodley Head, 2011.

Sheinin, David. *Argentina and the United States at the Sixth Pan American Conference (Havana 1928).* London: Institute of Latin American Studies, 1991.

Sherwood, Henry N. "The Formation of the American Colonization Society." *Journal of Negro History* 2.3 (1917): 209–28.

Simon, Kathleen H. *Slavery.* London: Hodder and Stoughton, 1929.

Simpson, Bradley R. *Economists with Guns: Authoritarian Development and U.S.-Indonesian Relations, 1960–1968.* Stanford, CA: Stanford University Press, 2008.

Siracusa, Joseph M. "The Night Stalin and Churchill Divided Europe: The View from Washington." *Review of Politics* 43.3 (1981): 381–409.

Skaggs, Jimmy M. *The Great Guano Rush: Entrepreneurs and American Overseas Expansion.* New York: St. Martin's, 1994.

Skidelsky, Robert. *John Maynard Keynes*, vol. 3, *Fighting for Freedom, 1937–1946*. New York: Penguin, 2002.

Skidmore-Hess, Daniel. "The Corporate Centrism of the Obama Administration." In *Corporate Power and Globalization in US Foreign Policy*, edited by Ronald W. Cox. London: Routledge, 2012.

Skillen, James W. *With or against the World? America's Role among the Nations.* Lanham, MD: Rowman and Littlefield, 2005.

Smeltz, Dina, Ivo Daalder, Karl Friedhoff, and Craig Kafura. *America Divided: Political Partisanship and US Foreign Policy: Results of the 2015 Chicago Council Survey of American Public Opinion and US Foreign Policy.* Chicago: Chicago Council on Global Affairs, 2015.

Smith, Godfrey. *Michael Manley: The Biography.* Kingston, Jamaica: Randle, 2016.

Smith, Neil. *American Empire: Roosevelt's Geographer and the Prelude to Globalization.* Berkeley: University of California Press, 2003.

Smith, Peter H. *Talons of the Eagle: Dynamics of U.S.-Latin American Relations.* New York: Oxford University Press, 1996.

Smith-Rosenberg, Carroll. *This Violent Empire: The Birth of an American National Identity.* Chapel Hill: University of North Carolina Press, 2010.

Smither, Edward L. "The Impact of Evangelical Revivals on Global Mission: The Case of North American Evangelicals in Brazil in the Nineteenth and Twentieth Centuries." *Verbum et Ecclesia* 31.1 (2010): 1–8.

Snider, Christy J. "The Influence of Transnational Peace Groups on U.S. Foreign Policy Decision-Makers during the 1930s: Incorporating NGOs into the UN." *Diplomatic History* 27.3 (2003): 377–404.

Sommeiller, Estelle, Mark Price, and Ellis Wazeter. *Income Inequality in the U.S. by State, Metropolitan Area, and County.* Washington, DC: Economic Policy Institute, 2016.

Stanley, Peter W. *A Nation in the Making: The Philippines and the United States, 1899–1921.* Cambridge, MA: Harvard University Press, 1974.

Stephanidēs, Giannēs D. *Stirring the Greek Nation: Political Culture, Irredentism and Anti-Americanism in Post-War Greece, 1945–1967.* Aldershot, England: Ashgate, 2007.

Stephens, Bret. *America in Retreat: The New Isolationism and the Coming Global Disorder.* New York: Sentinel, 2015.

Stephenson, Nathaniel W. *Texas and the Mexican War: A Chronicle of the Winning of the Southwest.* New Haven, CT: Yale University Press, 1921.

Stettinius, Edward R. *Roosevelt and the Russians: The Yalta Conference.* London: Jonathan Cape, 1950.

Stevens, Sylvester Kirby. *American Expansion in Hawaii, 1842–1898.* Harrisburg, PA: Archives Publishing Company of Pennsylvania, 1945.

Stiglitz, Joseph E. *Globalization and Its Discontents.* New York: Norton, 2003.

Stiglitz, Joseph E. *The Great Divide.* London: Allen Lane, 2015.

Stiglitz, Joseph E. "Multinational Corporations: Balancing Rights and Responsibilities." *Proceedings of the Annual Meeting (American Society of International Law)* 101 (2007): 3–60.

Stoll, David. *Is Latin America Turning Protestant? The Politics of Evangelical Growth.* Berkeley: University of California Press, 1990.

Stone, Oliver, and Peter J. Kuznick. *The Untold History of the United States.* New York: Gallery, 2013.

Storing, Herbert J., and Murray Dry. *The Complete Anti-Federalist.* Chicago: University of Chicago Press, 1981.

Sugden, John. *Tecumseh: A Life.* Bridgewater, NJ: Paw Prints, 2008.

Summers, Lawrence H. "The Age of Secular Stagnation." *Foreign Affairs* 95.2 (2016): 2–9.

Swagerty, William R. "Indian Trade in the Trans-Mississippi West to 1870." In *Handbook of North American Indians,* vol. 4, *History of Indian-White Relations,* edited by Wilcomb E. Washburn. Washington, DC: Smithsonian Institution, 1988.

Tansill, Charles C. *The Purchase of the Danish West Indies.* Baltimore: Johns Hopkins University Press, 1932.

Taylor, Paul. *The Next America: Boomers, Millennials, and the Looming Generational Showdown.* New York: Public Affairs, 2014.

Tejada, Adriano Miguel. "Estado, política y gobierno, 1795–2008." In *Historia de la República Dominicana,* edited by Frank Moya Pons. Madrid: Consejo Superior de Investigaciones Científicas, 2010.

Thacker, Strom C. "The High Politics of IMF Lending." *World Politics* 521 (1999): 38–75.

Thomas, David Y. *A History of Military Government in Newly Acquired Territory of the United States.* New York: Columbia University Press, 1904.

Thomas, Hugh. *Cuba: The Pursuit of Freedom.* New York: Harper and Row, 1971.

Thomas, Martin. "French Imperial Reconstruction and the Development of the Indochina War, 1945–1950." In *The First Vietnam War: Colonial Conflict and Cold War Crisis*, edited by Mark A. Lawrence and Fredrik Logevall. Cambridge, MA: Harvard University Press, 2007.

Thoreau, Henry David. *Civil Disobedience and Other Essays.* New York: Dover, 1993.

Thornton, Russell. "Population History of Native North Americans." In *A Population History of North America*, edited by Michael R. Haines and Richard H. Steckel. Cambridge: Cambridge University Press, 2000.

Tocqueville, Alexis de. *Democracy in America.* Translated by Henry Reeve. London: Saunders and Otley, 1835.

Todd, Emmanuel. *After the Empire: The Breakdown of the American Order.* New York: Columbia University Press, 2003.

Tugendhat, Christopher. *The Multinationals.* London: Eyre and Spottiswoode, 1971.

Tunstall, Jeremy. *The Media Are American: Anglo-American Media in the World.* London: Constable, 1994.

Turner, Frederick J. *The Significance of the Frontier in American History.* Madison: State Historical Society of Wisconsin, 1894.

Tyler-McGraw, Marie. *An African Republic: Black and White Virginians in the Making of Liberia.* Chapel Hill: University of North Carolina Press, 2007.

Tyrrell, Ian R. *Transnational Nation: United States History in Global Perspective since 1789.* Basingstoke, England: Palgrave Macmillan, 2007.

Tyrrell, Ian R., Jay Sexton, and Peter S. Onuf, eds. *Empire's Twin: U.S. Anti-imperialism from the Founding Era to the Age of Terrorism.* Ithaca, NY: Cornell University Press, 2015.

UNCTAD. *World Investment Report 2000: Cross-Border Mergers and Acquisitions and Development.* New York: United Nations, 2000.

UNCTAD. *World Investment Report 2015: Reforming International Investment Governance.* New York: United Nations, 2015.

US Bureau of Insular Affairs. *Report of the Dominican Customs Receivership.* Washington, DC: Government Printing Office, 1915.

US Congress. *Congress of the United States: At the Second Session, Begun and Held at the City of New-York, on Monday, the Fourth of January, One Thousand Seven Hundred and Ninety: An Act Providing for the Enumeration of the Inhabitants of the United States.* New York: Francis Childs and John Swaine, 1790.

US Department of Defense. *Base Structure Report: Fiscal Year 2015 Baseline: A Summary of DoD's Real Property Inventory.* Washington, DC: Government Printing Office, 2015.

US Department of Defense. *The Department of Defense Cyber Strategy.* Washington, DC: Government Printing Office, 2015.

US Department of Defense. *National Defense Budget Estimates for FY 2016.* Washington, DC: Government Printing Office, 2016.

US Department of State and US Agency for International Aid, *Leading through Civilian Power: The First Quadrennial Diplomacy and Development Review.* Washington, DC: US Department of State, 2010.

Vargas Llosa, Mario. *La Fiesta del Chivo*. Madrid: Alfaguara, 2000.

Vine, David. *Base Nation: How U.S. Military Bases Abroad Harm America and the World*. New York: Metropolitan, 2015.

Vine, David. *Island of Shame: The Secret History of the U.S. Military Base on Diego Garcia*. Princeton, NJ: Princeton University Press, 2009.

Vogel, Ann. "Who's Making Global Civil Society: Philanthropy and US Empire in World Society." *British Journal of Sociology* 57.4 (2006): 635–55.

Von Bülow, Marisa. *Building Transnational Networks: Civil Society and the Politics of Trade in the Americas*. New York: Cambridge University Press, 2010.

Vorenberg, Michael. "Abraham Lincoln and the Politics of Black Colonization." *Journal of the Abraham Lincoln Association* 14.2 (1993): 22–45.

Vorenberg, Michael. *The Emancipation Proclamation: A Brief History with Documents*. Boston: Bedford/St. Martin's, 2010.

Wade, Robert. "The Invisible Hand of the American Empire." *Global Dialogue* 5 (2003): 64–72.

Wade, Robert. "Japan, the World Bank, and the Art of Paradigm Maintenance: The East Asian Miracle in Political Perspective." *New Left Review* 217 (1996): 3–36.

Wallace, Anthony F. C. *Jefferson and the Indians: The Tragic Fate of the First Americans*. Cambridge, MA: Belknap Press of Harvard University Press, 1999.

Wallerstein, Immanuel M. *The Decline of American Power: The U.S. in a Chaotic World*. New York: New Press, 2003.

Walsh, Lawrence E. *Firewall: The Iran-Contra Conspiracy and Cover-Up*. New York: Norton, 1998.

Weeks, William E. *John Quincy Adams and American Global Empire*. Lexington: University Press of Kentucky, 1992.

Weeks, William E. *The New Cambridge History of American Foreign Relations*, vol. 1, *Dimensions of the Early American Empire, 1754–1865*. New York: Cambridge University Press, 2013.

Weisbrot, Mark. *Voting Share Reform at the IMF: Will It Make a Difference?* Washington, DC: Center for Economic and Policy Research, 2016.

Welles, Sumner. *Naboth's Vineyard: The Dominican Republic, 1844–1924*. Washington, DC: Savile, 1966.

Wells, David A. "The Truth about the 'Opium War.'" *North American Review* 162.475 (1896): 759–60.

Wells, Jeremy. *Romances of the White Man's Burden: Race, Empire, and the Plantation in American Literature 1880–1936*. Nashville, TN: Vanderbilt University Press, 2011.

West, Francis J. *Political Advancement in the South Pacific: A Comparative Study of Colonial Practice in Fiji, Tahiti, and American Samoa*. Melbourne: Oxford University Press, 1961.

The White House. *A National Security Strategy of Engagement and Enlargement*. Washington, DC: The White House, 1995.

The White House, *National Security Strategy of the United States of America*. Washington, DC: The White House, 2002.

Whitehead, Laurence. "Bolivia since 1930." In *The Cambridge History of Latin America*, vol. 8, *Latin America since 1930: Spanish South America*, edited by Leslie Bethell. Cambridge: Cambridge University Press, 1991.

Whiting, Allen. "The United States and Taiwan." In *The United States and the Far East: Background Papers Prepared for the Use of Participants and the Final Report of the Tenth American Assembly, Arden House, Harriman Campus of Columbia University, Harriman, New York, November 15–18, 1956.* New York: American Assembly, Graduate School of Business, Columbia University, 1956.

Wiktor, Christian L. *Unperfected Treaties of the United States of America, 1776–1976.* Dobbs Ferry, NY: Oceana, 1979.

Wilcox, Clair. *A Charter for World Trade.* New York: Macmillan, 1949.

Wilcox, Clair. "Trade Policy for the Fifties." *American Economic Review* 43.2 (1953): 61–70.

Wilgus, A. C. "James G. Blaine and the Pan American Movement." *Hispanic American Historical Review* 5.4 (1922): 662–708.

Wilkins, Mira. *The Emergence of Multinational Enterprise: American Business Abroad from the Colonial Era to 1914.* Cambridge, MA: Harvard University Press, 1970.

Wilkins, Mira. *The Maturing of Multinational Enterprise: American Business Abroad from 1914 to 1970.* Cambridge, MA: Harvard University Press, 1974.

Williams, William A. *The Roots of the Modern American Empire: A Study of the Growth and Shaping of Social Consciousness in a Marketplace Society.* New York: Random House, 1970.

Williams, William A. *The Tragedy of American Diplomacy.* Cleveland: World, 1959.

Williamson, John. *Latin American Adjustment: How Much Has Happened?* Washington, DC: Institute for International Economics, 1990.

Willoughby, William F. *Territories and Dependencies of the United States: Their Government and Administration.* New York: Century, 1905.

Wolff, Andrew T. "The Future of NATO Enlargement after the Ukraine Crisis." *International Affairs* 91.5 (2015): 1103–21.

Wolff, Leon. *Little Brown Brother: America's Forgotten Bid for Empire Which Cost 250,000 Lives.* London: Longmans, 1961.

Womack, Brantly. "Asymmetric Parity: US-China Relations in a Multinodal World." *International Affairs* 92.6 (2016): 1463–80.

Wood, Gordon S. *Empire of Liberty: A History of the Early Republic, 1789–1815.* Oxford: Oxford University Press, 2009.

Woods, Ngaire. "Making the IMF and the World Bank More Accountable." *International Affairs* 77.1 (2001): 83–100.

Woods, Ngaire. "United States and the International Finance Institutions: Power and Influence within the World Bank and the IMF." In *US Hegemony and International Organizations: The United States and Multilateral Institutions*, edited by Rosemary Foot, S. N. MacFarlane, and Michael Mastanduno. Oxford: Oxford University Press, 2003.

Woodward, Peter. *US Foreign Policy and the Horn of Africa.* Aldershot, England: Ashgate, 2006.

Bibliography

World Bank. *World Development Indicators*. Washington, DC: World Bank, various years.

World Economic Forum. *The Global Competitiveness Report*. Geneva: World Economic Forum, 2016.

Wyatt, Clarence R. *Paper Soldiers: The American Press and the Vietnam War*. New York: Norton, 1993.

Young, Allyn A. "Nearing's Income; King's Wealth and Income." *Quarterly Journal of Economics* 30.3 (1916): 575–87.

Zeng, Jinghan, and Shaun Breslin. "China's 'New Type of Great Power Relations': A G2 with Chinese Characteristics?" *International Affairs* 92.4 (2016): 773–94.

Zinsmeister, Karl. "Is the Focus of American Evangelicals Shifting Overseas?" *Philanthropy Roundtable*, Winter 2012, 1–6.

Zorlu, Tuncay. *Innovation and Empire in Turkey: Sultan Selim III and the Modernisation of the Ottoman Navy*. London: Tauris, 2008.

INDEX

Page numbers in italic type refer to boxes.